A BROKEN FLUTE

CONTEMPORARY NATIVE AMERICAN COMMUNITIES

Stepping Stones to the Seventh Generation

Acknowledging the strength and vibrancy of Native American peoples and Nations today, this series examines life in contemporary Native American communities from the point of view of Native concerns and values. Books in the series cover topics that are of cultural and political importance to tribal peoples and that affect their possibilities for survival, in both urban and rural communities.

Series Editors:

Troy Johnson, American Indian Studies, California State University, Long Beach, CA 90840, trj@csulb.edu

Duane Champagne, Native Nations Law and Policy Center, 292 Haines Hall, Box 951551, University of California, Los Angeles, CA 90095-1551, champagn@ucla.edu

Books in the Series

1. *Inuit, Whaling, and Sustainability*, by Milton M. R. Freeman, Ingmar Egede, Lyudmila Bogoslovskaya, Igor G. Krupnik, Richard A. Caulfield and Marc G. Stevenson (1999)
2. *Contemporary Native American Political Issues*, edited by Troy Johnson (1999)
3. *Contemporary Native American Cultural Issues*, edited by Duane Champagne (1999)
4. *Modern Tribal Development: Paths to Self Sufficiency and Cultural Integrity in Indian Country*, by Dean Howard Smith (2000)
5. *American Indians and the Urban Experience*, edited by Susan Lobo and Kurt Peters (2000)
6. *Medicine Ways: Disease, Health, and Survival among Native Americans*, edited by Clifford Trafzer and Diane Weiner (2000)
7. *Native American Studies in Higher Education: Models for Collaboration between Universities and Indigenous Nations*, edited by Duane Champagne and Jay Stauss (2002)
8. *Spider Woman Walks This Land: Traditional Cultural Properties and the Navajo Nation*, by Kelli Carmean (2002)
9. *Alaska Native Political Leadership and Higher Education: One University, Two Universes*, by Michael Jennings (2004)
10. *Indigenous Intellectual Property Rights: Legal Obstacles and Innovative Solutions*, edited by Mary Riley (2004)
11. *Healing and Mental Health for Native Americans: Speaking in Red*, edited by Ethan Nebelkopf and Mary Phillips (2004)
12. *Rachel's Children*, by Lois Beardslee (2004)
13. *Contemporary Education Issues in the Northern Cheyenne Indian Nation: The Role of Family, Community and School in Educational Performance*, by Carol Ward (2004)
14. *A Broken Flute: The Native Experience in Books for Children*, edited by Doris Seale and Beverly Slapin (2005)
15. *Indigenous Peoples and the Modern State*, edited by Duane Champagne, Karen Torjesen and Susan Steiner (2005)
16. *Reading Native American Women: Critical/Creative Representation*, edited by Inés Hernández-Ávila (2005)
17. *Native Americans in the School System: Family, Community, and Academic Achievement*, edited by Carol Ward (2005)

A BROKEN FLUTE

The Native Experience in Books for Children

Edited by

Doris Seale and Beverly Slapin

ALTAMIRA
PRESS

AltaMira Press

A Division of Rowman & Littlefield Publishers, Inc.

Lanham New York Toronto Plymouth, UK

Berkeley

A Broken Flute is co-published by AltaMira Press and Oyate. Oyate is a community-based Native organization working to see that our lives, traditional arts and literatures, and histories are portrayed honestly. Our work in the world is expressed by the suggestion of the great Lakota spiritual leader, Tatanka Iotanka (Sitting Bull) who said, "Let us put our minds together and see what life we will make for our children." We are influenced by the teachings of our elders that all children are sacred beings and that in all things we must work for the benefit of the next seven generations.

AltaMira Press

A Division of Rowman & Littlefield Publishers, Inc.
A wholly owned subsidary of The Rowman & Littlefield Publishing Group, Inc.
4501 Forbes Boulevard, Suite 200
Lanham, MD 20706
www.altamirapress.com

Estover Road
Plymouth PL6 7PY
United Kingdom

Oyate

2702 Mathews Street
Berkeley, CA 94702
510-848-6700   510-848-4815 fax
oyate@oyate.org www.oyate.org

Copyright ©2005 by Oyate
First paperback edition 2006

British Library Cataloguing in Publication Information Available

The hardback edition of this book was previously cataloged by the Library of Congress as follows:

A broken flute : the Native experience in books for children / edited by Doris Seale and Beverly Slapin.
p. cm.—(Contemporary Native American communities)
Includes bibliographical references and index.
ISBN-13: 978-0-7591-0778-6 (cloth : alk. paper)
ISBN-10: 0-7591-0778-5 (cloth : alk. paper)
ISBN-13: 978-0-7591-0779-3 (pbk. : alk. paper)
ISBN-10: 0-7591-0779-3 (pbk. : alk. paper)
1. Indians of North America—Juvenile literature. 2. Indians of North America—Juvenile literature—Book reviews.
3. American literature—Indian authors—History and criticism. 4. Children's literature, American—History and criticism.
I. Seale, Doris. II. Slapin, Beverly. III. Series.
E77.4.B76 2005
970.004'97—dc22

2005010842

Printed in the United States of America

Book design by Guillermo Prado, 8.2 design, Berkeley, California

A BROKEN FLUTE

Blown by alien breath,

The flute

Does not sing.

Held by hands unused

To touch with gentleness,

It will not sing for you.

Some harsh wild grating cry

Will come,

We do not recognize

This sound.

And then we will know,

Then it is broken.

All our days are broken

In a land turned strange.

DEDICATION

We dedicate this writing to the children of all Nations in the belief that they will continue as Indian people for generations yet to come, to those who fight for their right to do so, and to the Ancestors who guide us still.

IN MEMORY

Nilak Butler

Téveia Clarke

Paula Giese

Gogisgi

Michael Gene Lacapa

Mary TallMountain

Ingrid Washinawatok El-Issa

—D.S. and B.S.

ACKNOWLEDGMENTS

A Broken Flute owes its existence to the work, guidance, support, and good thoughts of many people. We are grateful to all of them: those who did reviews, those who wrote essays, those who shared their personal experiences. We are particularly grateful to the children who so freely gave us their stories and to their parents, who trusted us with them.

We are indebted to those who gave us encouragement, answered our many questions, and believed in the importance of what we were trying to do. Among them are Awiakta, Lois Beardslee, Sandy Berman, Naomi Caldwell, Robette Dias, John Kahionhes Fadden, Lyn Miller-Lachmann, Karen Rudolph, Dovie Thomason, and Linda Yamane. We acknowledge and thank Rudolph & Sletten Construction Company for their generous gift, which made the prepress work of this book possible.

Paula Giese left us before her work could be finished, but this book would be much less without her contribution. Deborah A. Miranda's heartfelt foreword says so clearly the price paid by Native peoples for the conquest. Barbara Landis, who has devoted her life to the families of the survivors of Carlisle Indian Industrial School, and to those who didn't survive, shared her store of knowledge with us. We thank Michael Lacapa for his gift of the beautiful cover painting, and Guillermo Prado for his artful book design—*D.S. and B.S.*

I give my thanks to: Alicia Bell, Beth Brant, Joe Bruchac, Blanche Coty, Judy Dow, Mary Egan-James, Sherry Hesch, Dan and Mary Ann Littlefield, Day Lone-Wolf, Giny McCasland, Cheryl Savageau; Barbara and Pat and T.J. for what they have given and the gift of knowing them; to mi comadre, Beverly, for all the reasons she knows and some I'll bet she never thought of; and to Keith, who held me together.—*D.S.*

I am grateful to my Heart Sisters—Barb, Cyn, Deb, Deborah, Jean, LaVera, Mar(e), and Naomi—for their love and support, generosity and good spirits. I am grateful to Doris, for walking this road with a clear vision and good heart. I thank Tom King for his seemingly endless supply of humor and irony and good wishes, just when they're needed. And Gracie and Jasper, too. I thank Michael Lacapa, wherever you are; you were a bright light that so suddenly dimmed. You are missed. I am grateful to Janeen Antoine, Judy Dow, Robette Dias, Ish, Eric Lederer, Varinthorn Nakkeow, Barbara Potter, Guillermo Prado and Jane Waite, for Being There. I dedicate this book to my Mom, who is residing with the spirits, giving them advice and making sure they eat enough. And, of course, this book is for Carlos.—*B.S.*

CREDITS

We acknowledge and thank the following authors, poets, and presses for permission to reprint the essays and poetry noted below:

American Library Association, for Cynthia Leitich Smith's "Native Now" ("Frybread- and Feather-Free"), in *Book Links: Connecting Books, Libraries, and Classrooms*, Vol. 10, No. 3.

Peter Blue Cloud, for "Waterbugs," in Simon Ortiz, ed., *Earth Power Coming: Short Fiction in Native American Literature*, Navajo Community College Press, 1983.

Joseph Bruchac, for "Bad Vision" and "The Buffalo Skull," in Joseph Bruchac, *Translator's Son* (Cross-Cultural Review, Chapbook 10), Cross-Cultural Communications, 1980.

Caitlin Press, for Heather Harris' "Moccasins to School Again," in Heather Harris, *Rainbow Dancer*, 1999.

Council Oak Books, for excerpts from Dennis McAuliffe's *Bloodland: A Family Story of Oil, Greed and Murder on the Osage Reservation*, 1994.

Curbstone Press, for Cheryl Savageau's "Summer Solstice" and "To Human Skin," in Cheryl Savageau, *Dirt Road Home*, 1995.

Nora Marks Dauenhauer, for "Village Tour, Nome Airport," in Nora Marks Dauenhauer, *The Droning Shaman*, Black Current Press, 1988.

Greenfield Review Press, for Deborah Miranda's "Stories I Tell My Daughter," in Deborah Miranda, *Indian Cartography*, 1999.

Janet McAdams, for her review of Esther G. Belin's *In the Belly of My Beauty*, in *Women's Review of Books*, Vol. 17, Issue 10-11, July 2000.

Multicultural Review, for previously publishing some of our book reviews and articles.

News from Indian Country, for Peter Cole's "Elsa Remembers," December 1997.

Jim Northrup, for "The Gift of Syrup," in *The Circle*.

Red Ink, for Reva Mariah S. Gover's "Woman Stories III" in *Red Ink*, Vol. 9, No. 1, Fall 2001.

Renegade Planets for MariJo Moore's "Old Tsa Tsi," in MariJo Moore, *red woman with backward eyes and other stories*, 2001.

Wendy Rose, for "The Well-Intentioned Question," in Wendy Rose, *Going To War With All My Relations*, Northland Publishing, 1993.

Salmon Run Press, for Kimberly Blaeser's "Living History" and Judith Mountain-Leaf Volborth's "Coyote Blue," in John E. Smelcer and D.L. Birchfield, eds., *Durable Breath*, 1994.

Margaret Sam-Cromarty's "Sphagnum Moss (Baby Moss)," in Margaret Sam-Cromarty, *James Bay Memories*, Waapoone Publishing, 1992.

Southwest Learning Centers, for Michael Lacapa's "Who Stole Oñate's Foot?" in *Native Roots & Rhythms, Journal of the Center for Indigenous Arts & Cultures*, Vol. 1, No. 1, 1999.

Theytus Books, for Drew Hayden Taylor's story, in *Furious Observations of a Blue-Eyed Ojibway: Funny, You Don't Look Like One Two Three*, 2002.

University of Arizona, for Luci Tapahonso's "How She Was Given Her Name," in Luci Tapahonso, *Sáanii Dahataal: The Women Are Singing*. © 1993 Luci Tapahonso; and Ofelia Zepeda's "Pulling Down the Clouds," in Ofelia Zepeda, *Ocean Power*. © 1995 Ofelia Zepeda.

UCLA American Indian Studies Center, for Mary TallMountain's "A Quick Brush of Wings," "She's a Hawk!" and "There Is No Word for Goodbye," in Mary TallMountain, *The Light on the Tent Wall: A Bridging*. © 1990 Regents of the University of California.

22nd California Conference on American Indian Education, for Desiree Future Goss's "A Knothead," in *Thoughts from Native Youth* (1999).

CONTENTS

FOREWORD

Dear Beverly and Doris,

This morning I sent the box of review books back to you, along with the reviews I had completed. I regret that I was not able to review many of the books, especially the "Ishi" books. I know that it is difficult for you to find reviewers, and that *A Broken Flute* is getting closer and closer to publication. But I cannot have these books in my house any longer.

Originally, I had said yes to reviewing so many books despite my grad school schedule, and despite the fact that I've been working on a second manuscript of poetry; despite the fact that this summer is my first vacation in many years, and despite the fact that my children resented the time and heart that I put into my computer already! I said yes because no one who does these reviews has "the time," and everyone you have asked has put aside major projects and their own peace of mind to get this work done. I said yes because the work needs to be done, and I can do it; and I said yes because of a dream.

Five years ago, I began to write poetry about the missions, about the histories of my Indian relatives who went into the missions. I struggled with the ugliness that revealed itself through my poetry—poems about rape, about abandonment, about deception and hatred based purely on racial terms. These things were coming out in my poems in vivid, brutal language that was deeply disturbing both to me and to those who read them. I struggled with the idea of a "poetry of witness"—telling myself, I wasn't there, I didn't see it—but knowing I am here, remembering, coping with the consequences and the connections to my people. I simply wasn't sure that I had the strength, or the right, to bear witness for my ancestors.

During that time, I was given a very important dream. I will share it with you because it is important that we acknowledge the power of dreams in our lives, and because it helps explain why I've tried so hard to finish these reviews.

I dreamt that I was part of a contemporary experiment, along with dozens of other Indian people from many California tribes. We were in a group composed of all age groups, mixed-bloods, full-bloods. Scientists in long white coats had told us that there was a way to measure racial memory, and they needed us to test this theory. We all agreed to do this, because we all longed to communicate with the ancestors we felt moving in our blood. The scientists showed us a small room. The only light was from the doorway, double doors, streaming into the darkness. We were pushed into the room. A small window above provided the scientists with a view. The people were smashed together, and suddenly we felt anxious in a way we hadn't before. I heard husbands reassuring wives, children asking questions, felt the intake of an elder's breath. Then the double doors crashed shut. The heavy wooden panels thudded into the threshold and the light was gone. There was earth beneath our feet, but we couldn't see it. There were splinters in the wooden walls and plaster beneath our fingers, but we couldn't find the door. Out of the people came an uncontrollable panic—hundreds of cries and screams. We were beyond asking for help. We simply screamed in sheer terror. People began clawing the walls, climbing on top of one another, trying to find the way out. We didn't remember who we had come with, couldn't comfort each other. I remember the sensation of opening my mouth, and a scream coming out that was so loud and harsh, my throat ached and scratched. But even in that moment of terror, even in the dream, I knew that I was opening my mouth so that someone else's scream could come out. It was my mouth, my throat, my physical pain. It was another woman's scream.

I woke up in a sweat, my throat throbbing and sore. In the dark, it took a long time for me to realize I was no longer locked in the Mission.

The dream told me that my body, my mouth, my tongue, my writing, were the vehicles for the voice of my ancestors. From that day on I tried my best to let that voice speak, whether it was through poetry, letters to the editor, or arguing with my children's teachers over school curricula such as "The Oregon Trail" unit and Columbus Day celebrations. Or doing book reviews for Oyate.

But somehow every time I picked up a book to read, or sat down to write a review, I couldn't do it. I procrastinated in part, I told myself, because I was tired, the school year had just ended, it was my first vacation in years. I went away for a week to write with wonderful women poets; when I came back, I continued to ignore the box beside my desk. Beverly called, and I lied that I had some of the books done, because in my mind, I did—well, almost. We went camping for two weeks, and I came back, and there was that damn box of books. The cats got into the packing material and spread it all over the house, reminding me with every step that I had this job to do. A month later, Beverly called again. Finally, I forced myself to actually write about the two picture books. It took me two days. Afterwards, I was surprised at the bite of my writing, at how angry I sounded. But it was the only way I could get myself to put words down on the page.

I continued in that vein. The first burst of anger produced two reviews. That felt good, in a venomous sort of way. Then I began procrastinating again, while at the same time stomping around the house muttering about colonization, idiotic white people, bones in the walls, little Indian girls as symbols for seduction and rape. I couldn't eat, and after a while even wine didn't help. I was burning up with fury all the time. My children feared to approach me. I wrote on, laboriously, slowly, sometimes taking all day to get two paragraphs down. It felt as if a dam of words was building up in me, but I didn't know how to let them out. Everything pissed me off—the news, raucous crows, dirty dishes, my son asking me to play with him. I put the books away several times, despaired that I was letting you both down. I took the books back out. I wrote, and my writing was angry; when I'm angry it feels as if I'm two years old again, without vocabulary or those lauded expository skills I teach under-graduates. I couldn't focus on the details of the books as I knew I should; the larger problems of racism and paternalism obsessed me, overwhelmed me.

The night before last, I had another dream. I was in a strange place with my children and developed a horribly painful cyst or infection in the left side of my throat. The pain was intense, constant and worsening. My voice began to fail me. I was desperate to get to a doctor but didn't know anyone to leave my children with. None of the people around me would help; they were all white, and all looked at me as if I were low-class to be sick in the first place, much less not have resources to care for my children. Finally, I convinced some people I had just met to take my children for the day while I left to find a doctor. In the dream I was stunned, saying to myself, "I never leave my children with anyone we don't know!" But it didn't matter—I had to end this pain, I had to get something to cure this pain in my throat. Hoarse and afraid, I left my children and walked away.

Again, I awoke in the dark. Again, I was shaking and bruised, touching my throat over and over to swallow away the sensation of hardness, a blockage, an infection.

That day I sat down at my desk and, driven, worked for many hours. I knew it was my last day of working on the reviews. It had been five years since the first dream about my throat, and I hadn't connected the two dreams right away. As I worked, though, I kept thinking of this second dream, and kept thinking of how hopeless I felt about ever finishing these reviews. I had long since stopped writing poetry, or even returning my friends' e-mails or letters. I didn't go anywhere, see anyone. I felt trapped between the clear need for the reviews and my own internal panic. When my children came into the room, I snapped at them. When I heard the tone of my voice, bitter and mean, that was the moment I realized that the box of books beside my desk had poisoned me, poisoned my voice. That was when I remembered my first dream, and knew that my throat was no longer open enough to convey that scream. I knew that I had done enough and that I could not do it all. That was when I decided to send the books back to you at Oyate, and write you this letter.

Indian people in this country labor under a burden of denial and racism that is overwhelming. Our suicide statistics are the highest for any group. Our economic status is the lowest for any group. We disappear ourselves, and are disappeared by others. These circumstances are not the problems; they are the symptoms that we suffer that indicate continuing and destructive colonization. But no one is listening to our voices. And that makes us crazy.

The books I've managed to review for you fall into, roughly, two categories—Invisible Indians and Construction Material. Indians are either completely denied as ever having existed, or we are used, like building materials, to construct the facade of conquest, a place to house the Doctrine of Discovery. But we are never human beings, never wronged human beings with our own honor, pride, integrity and existence who are capable of great deeds, and surviving with joy. The books I've read for these reviews deny our autonomy, our history, the simple fact that we were here first. And now I know why I couldn't finish this task. It is a task no one person can finish.

Reading all this material—which ranges from textbooks to picture books to novels to handbooks—knowing that it is widely distributed and taught, and is making publishers wealthy, understanding the totality of racism's deep and complex roots in our everyday lives, I was overwhelmed. These are not issues that I can turn on and off. I am personally affected; I am personally a target, as are my children. These are not just bad books—they are honest reflections of the society in which Indian people must live. No, say it—these books are honest reflections of the way most white people think about Indians—as invisible, or as construction material for their own historic national fantasies. Every single aspect of Indian life in this country—our schooling, the media, employment, medical care, religions, literature and arts—is governed by an invasive, cancerous, spreading racism toward Native peoples. What we see of ourselves—and what others see of us—is fragmented by false images and sorrow. In that sense, these books have been heartbreaking revelations for me. And we have to walk in that world, work in it, try to create beauty in it, raise our children in it, try to find our own ways in it. We cannot escape this reality. It will not change soon, or easily. There are days when it feels as if every day is a nightmare we wake up to, when we know there are no borders between our nightmares and reality.

I returned the books because there is only so much of that kind of emotional barrage that one person can take. If I go crazy with grief and despair, will I be able to do any good for my ancestors, my children, or myself? My dream tells me what I should have already known: No. It's time to breathe, to rest, to regroup. It's time to take in some of the beauty of being alive, being loved, being able to love. I need to remind myself that in fighting injustice, anger and bitterness must be balanced by the strength to never relinquish our right to beauty, or the healing nature of love.

Beverly and Doris, thank you for the hard, important work that you both do.

Till soon,

Deborah A. Miranda

INTRODUCTION

Since the 1980s, non-Native authors and illustrators of books for children have turned increasingly to Indian literatures, lives and histories as sources of material for their efforts. Publication of the results has become big business. Whether retellings, adaptations, or edited versions of stories; historical accounts, photographic essays or biographies, these works have been carefully produced, lavishly illustrated, and brought out with artfully orchestrated publicity. Several have become best sellers; some have won awards. They are nearly invariably well received, praised for their beauty and sensitivity, and frequently for their ecological messages, by reviewers who do not know enough to know that the works in question are inaccurate, inauthentic, patronizing, full of lies, and altogether a huge insult to the people out of whose lives so much money is being made.

On the other hand, Native writers, unless very well-known, do not find publishers in the "mainstream." This is unfortunate, not only for Indians, but for the world of letters as a whole, because some of the most original and creative work being done today is by Indian authors and artists.

A Broken Flute is not intended to be an up-to-the-moment buying guide. It is intended to bring attention to some of the gifted writers and illustrators of the past ten years or so, frequently published by Native and small presses, and also to evaluate as much as possible of the most objectionable work of the non-Native writers. Some of what is included here, essays and people's own stories, as well as the reviews, will not be comfortable reading. Nor is it meant to be. We mean it to be known what 500 years of colonized history has done to us—and that we are still very much here.

We were never meant to survive. Our histories include the publicly stated objective of our extinction. One of the more ingenious ideas to come out of this was the establishment of the Indian residential schools, where the children, forcibly removed from their parents, suffered horribly, and were forbidden to speak their own languages.

In her preface to *Writing As Witness*, Beth Brant said, "[W]ords are sacred. Not because of the person transmitting them, but because words themselves come from the place of mystery that gives meaning and existence to life." Words have great power. More than any other living beings, we are made of words. Every thing of evil ever done began with a word; also every thing of good. Words are not to be used casually, flung lightly around, without regard for their landing place. Be careful what harm you might do—or what you might call upon yourself. When we lost our words, we lost access to our past, and the stories our parents and elders might have told us. We could no longer understand each other. A people's stories carry its history, its culture, its ceremonies and spiritual practices—its identity. No language, no identity. The ones who set up the residential schools understood that very well.

Corey Harris, a young bluesman, said on the PBS series, "The Blues": "You can't know who you are until you know the past. You can't know where you're going until you know where you've been." Whole generations of our young people have grown up not knowing who they were, how to live, or how to raise their own children.

Almost without exception, those who have taken Indian stories to use for their own purposes have not understood the nature of an oral literature at all. The assumption is that, because it was not originally written, it is not really to be granted the same status as the printed word, or require the same laws for its use. Nor have they any conception of what is lost in translation.

In an essay written for the May 1997 issue of *School Library Journal*, "Preservation is Never Acid Free," Carolyn Caywood remarked on "how difficult it is to record an oral literature without altering it in the process." What happens when a story has been translated from a language as complex as, say, Navajo, into written English, and then edited, adapted or "retold," for young children? What then remains of its essential nature? Taking a story from word to paper is difficult enough, even when one knows it as well as an old shoe. Where is the gesture, the change of facial expression, the pacing, the turn of a head, the intonation, that can tell as much as the actual words? Even more so, when one is "translating" from an unknown culture. And there is this: Taking something that has not been offered to you does not make it yours. That makes it stolen. Stories are never free.

Maria Campbell is among the most gifted of storytellers. In the introduction to her *Stories of the Road Allowance People* she says,

> And although I speak my language I have had to relearn it, to decolonize it or at least begin the process of decolonization. This has not been an easy task and the journey has taken me eighteen years. I have paid for the stories by relearning and rethinking my language and by being a helper or servant to the teachers. I have paid for the stories with gifts of blankets, tobacco and even a prize Arab stallion.

Because you have conquered a People does not give you a right to their spirit. Some thought has been devoted to the "why" of this: I have concluded that it is irrelevant. We have managed to survive, some on our own ancient lands, even to have a growth in population. Our task now is to see that our children will be able to grow and live as whole human beings, and as Indian people. The dominant culture as a whole will never be able to get near to admitting that it lives on stolen land, that it has been built on stolen lives. This is not an objective statement; there is nothing objective about genocide. There will always be books; histories, biographies, social studies texts, that soften our mutual past, that call it the "inevitable result" of something or other. Our job is, as we have done here, to say "no" to that; to confront it with the truth, always.

We have managed, against all expectations and desires, to be alive. Few of us are without our scars, but we live. Good can come out of bad, but why should it have to? Those green things growing out of cracks in the sidewalk, and between railroad tracks, would grow much better somewhere else. We do this so that those coming up behind us will have a better place, and a better way to grow.

This has not been an easy thing to do. It has sometimes been appallingly hard. Those who have contributed to this book are people who have given their lives to preserving languages and the life-preserving traditional ways; to taking back some of what has been taken from us, including the bones of our relatives; and to talking to the elders before it is to late and to telling their stories. For all of us, it has been a reliving of the 500-year journey of our people. And yet. To know these people, to read their work; to work with them, has been a very great gift. I do not think there is one of us who has not been changed by the journey.—*Doris Seale*

A CULTURAL ENCOUNTER

As an indigenous storyteller and a professional storyteller, my life's work gives me the opportunity to travel many roads, to talk with many people of different cultures and perspectives. Long ago or recently, I was visiting a college or university in another city or town. It doesn't matter what college or university or what city or town, as what happened there that night or day was something that is best spoken of in general terms. I was not the guest speaker at that college or university. I had the opportunity to be a member of the listening audience come to hear a certain Noted Children's Author speak.

Remember, it doesn't matter who this Noted Children's Author was; a trickster is a trickster is a trickster. Anyway, I had had some reluctance about going, knowing that this Noted Children's Author had written seeral books which were outside of her or his own cultural identity. A couple of them had even been about my cultural identity, though not specifically my Native Nation. Now, here I prefer to tread a bit softly, for I have met non-Indian authors and storytellers who work with our stories with the consent and blessing of tribal elders. I've even met the tribal elders who have given those blessings and am not the one who will say what those grandmothers and grandfathers should or shouldn't do.

So I was discreet and downright diplomatic at the reception before the lecture. I didn't reveal my personal perspective on cultural appropriation. I didn't rant, I didn't glare. I didn't even get to ask the first question. It was asked of me. "Do you know …?" And an elder was named, a person who had passed on years back, a wonderful storyteller whom I had never met, but whose stories I had read. Then came several self-serving anecdotes that established that the Noted Children's Author had a personal knowledge of that elder. So, I had to ask, "What did that old one think of your children's book of one of his or her stories?" Now, this is the part that people don't always understand. For this Noted Children's Author was told by that elder that it was "all right." That is, all right for white kids just learning to read. I was embarrassed, thinking I had brought this shameful faint praise to everyone's attention, for those words from an elder would just about stop me dead. But the Noted Children's Author recounted that anecdote with fond pride, not understanding that the elder wouldn't have shamed or disrespected another by saying it was a bad book of a stolen story.

That same story came up in the lecture. By then, I was having trouble making eye contact, or even looking near the speaker's podium. Now, the audience learned that this story came from the Indian people not far from where the family of the Noted Children's Author (as a child) had a summer home. "We were always fascinated by Indians as kids," was the rationale for choosing this story, after failing to sell any original story ideas for the first years of the Noted Children's Author's career. "It was researched until every article of clothing or weaponry was perfectly accurate," the Noted Children's Author said, with no small measure of pride in his or her voice.

It was hard to concentrate on the Noted Children's Author's lecture, maybe because I was grinding my teeth. But there were children's books of stories from Africa, Asia, the Black South, the Caribbean Islands. It couldn't be said that this Noted Children's Author had made a career from appropriating Indian stories—it was everybody's stories that had built her or him a successful career.

By the intermission, I was puzzled. I'd visited this college or university before. I knew people in the audience. I'd seen them at festivals and shared my thoughts and feelings about cultural integrity and stories. Some of them had agreed and asked tough questions the last time we'd met; but now they sat quietly, attentively. Now, they lined up at the break to buy autographed copies of the Noted Children's Author's books.

I wasn't in line, except the coffee line. And there I saw two women I'd met on one of those earlier visits. "This is making me really angry," said one. "I mean, does research give anyone the right to take those stories and make a fortune? Are these storybooks even true to the stories they come from? I can't believe that no one's spoken up." I remembered this woman, and knew she was more likely to discuss things during the break than in the lecture discussion. "I've thought about it," she said, "and I wouldn't tell those stories. I have my own stories to tell."

Once she had walked away, the other woman spoke. "I can't believe you haven't torn into that speaker," she said. "What should I ask?" I asked her, "Why do you do that? How do you justify yourself? Shouldn't someone from here be the one to confront the issues?" "You know the answers you'd get," she replied. "The Noted Children's Author would say,

> I've loved stories since I was a child. These are stories of human conflicts, human needs, and there's only one race—the human race. I hope that the exposure I give these stories will bring them to the notice of a wider audience, making opportunities for authors of all cultures and races. I do a lot of research to make sure that everything I write is accurate and representative. I've thought about this and feel I've written nothing that misrepresented a culture. I'm sharing my love of stories and maybe opening doors for future generations of authors-of-color.

She laughed cynically; "You know the drill."

I decided I wouldn't speak up. I knew there were two women there with more than enough to say, all the right questions to ask. But there were many more audience members there clutching their recently autographed books of stolen stories. So, I waited during the question-and-answer period. I waited until time was nearly up and I could feel two sets of eyes boring into my back. Then I raised my hand.

"There's some debate" I began, "about cultural appropriation. Of using the current faddish market for 'multicultural' books to exploit the stories of other cultures, when publishers are not especially looking for 'white' stories." The Noted Children's Author was perceptibly perspiring, his or her charming smile gone wooden. "As a person of conscience, with respect for children who read your books and the cultures you've spoken about tonight, how do you deal with these issues? What is your position on the appropriateness of your writing your own version of these stories and creating your career and reputation off of them?"

Now the Noted Children's Author looked grave, looked concerned, looked thoughtful. Perhaps it was more genuine than posturing; maybe I've grown too cynical, seeing our cultural stories becoming Disney movies. "I am aware of this," the Noted Children's Author said, "and I would never, I emphasize—never—want to be accused of strip-mining the vast store of cultural stories for my personal gain." And then, well, then the song went just as my friend in the lobby had predicted:

> I love these stories, have since I was a kid. I just want to share that love, share those stories. Maybe my writing these stories will make someone aware of another culture, maybe it will open a door that creates opportunity for a young author from one of those cultures. These old stories are about the human condition and transcend race or ethnicity. My editors will tell you I write extensive author's notes, based on extensive research, to make sure that everything I write is accurate. I mean, I'll change some things to make the plot move along or make things easier to understand, but I make detailed notes.

Time was up. The women I'd talked with were the first out of the door. The autograph hounds were glaring at me like I'd belched at the table with company come to visit. "I'm glad you brought that up," the Noted Children's Author said, magnanimous and with another Disney deal on the way, "I'd hate to think people thought I'd steal to write a book."

I was unable to say another thing. Maybe that's true, to you, I thought. Maybe you still don't understand how it makes us feel at all. Maybe you think some time in the future is soon enough for a young Indian author to step through the "door of opportunity" you've so patronizingly claimed to open. Maybe you think you do it fine, you're better educated, more articulate, more meticulous in your research. Actually, I was wondering where the Noted Children's Author had first been accused of "strip-mining" our cultures. It must have been a while back, because there'd been plenty of time to rehearse all the answers. The Noted Children's Author knew the drill.—*Dovie Thomason*

OPEN LETTER TO A NON-INDIAN TEACHER

Dear Teacher,

Before you take charge of the classroom that contains my child, please ask yourself why you are going to teach Indian children. What are your expectations? What rewards do you anticipate? What ego needs will our children have to meet?

Write down and examine all the information and opinions you possess about Indians. What are the stereotypes and interested assumptions that you bring with you into the classroom? How many negative attitudes towards Indians will you put before my child?

What values, class prejudices, and moral principles do you take for granted as universal? Please remember that "different from" is not the same as "worse than" or "better than" and the yardstick you use to measure your own life satisfactorily may not be appropriate for their lives. The term "culturally deprived" was invented by well-meaning middle-class whites to describe something they could not understand.

Too many teachers seem to see their role as rescuer. My child does not need to be rescued; he does not consider being Indian a misfortune. He has a culture, probably older than yours; he has meaningful values and a rich and varied experiential background. However, strange or incomprehensible as it may seem to you, you have no right to do or say anything that implies to him that it is less than satisfactory.

Our children's experiences have been different from those of the typical white middle-class child for whom most school curricula have been designed. (I suspect that this "typical" child does not really exist except in the minds of the curriculum writers.) Nonetheless, my child's experiences have been as intense and meaningful to him as any child's. Like most Indian children his age, he is competent. He can dress himself, prepare a meal for himself, and clean up afterwards, or care for a younger child. He knows his reserve like the back of his hand.

He is not accustomed to having to ask permission to do the ordinary things that are part of normal living. He is seldom forbidden to do anything; more usually the consequences of an action are explained to him, and he is allowed to decide for himself whether or not to act.

His entire existence since he has been old enough to see and hear has been an experimental learning situation, arranged to provide him with the opportunity to develop his skills and confidence in his own capacities. Didactic teaching will be an alien experience for him.

He is not self-conscious in the way that many white children are. Nobody has ever told him his efforts at independence are "cute." He is a young human being energetically doing his job, which is to get on with the process of learning to function as an adult human being. He has been taught by precept that courtesy is an essential part of human conduct and rudeness is any action that makes another person feel stupid or foolish. Do not mistake his patient courtesy for indifference or passivity.

He does not speak standard English but he is in no way "linguistically handicapped." If you will take the time and courtesy to listen and observe carefully, you will see that he and the other Indian children communicate very well, both among themselves and with other Indians. They speak functional English, very effectively augmented by the fluency in the silent language, the subtle unspoken communication of facial expressions, gestures, body movements, and the use of personal space.

You will be well advised to remember that our children are skillful interpreters of the silent language. They will know your feelings and attitudes with unerring precision, no matter how carefully you arrange your smile or modulate your voice. They will learn in your classroom because children learn involuntarily. What they will learn will depend on you.

Will you help my child to learn to read, or will you teach him that he has a reading problem? Will you help him develop problem-solving skills or will you teach him that school is where you try to guess what answer the teacher wants? Will he learn that his sense of his own value and dignity is valid, or will he learn that he must forever be apologetic and try harder because he isn't white? Can you help him acquire the intellectual skills he needs without at the same time imposing your values on top of those he already has?

Respect my child. He is a person. He has a right to be himself.—*An Indian Mother*

(Note: This letter has circulated around Indian Country for a long time. We thank whoever wrote it.)

LIVING STORIES

A PARENT'S STORY

As part of my college coursework, I was in my daughter's classroom, correcting papers in the back of the room. The class was reading *The Courage of Sarah Noble*, and I saw my daughter squirming in her seat. So I picked up the book and saw why. As she was heading out for recess, she started to cry and told me that the kids were making fun of her and no one wanted to play with her because she was Indian. I remember she said, "Mom, the other kids won't play with me. They think what they read in the book is the way Indians are." She said they were making fun of her, saying, "Oh, she's an Indian, she's gonna scalp us and peel our skin off like the Indians in the book." All I could do was hold my daughter. I remembered reading books like this when I was her age, and I remembered my own pain.

The teacher's response was, "I can't believe you're taking this so seriously." She said, "Lighten up, it's only a book." She was acting like she was the professional and I was just a dumb parent. So I asked the principal to allow my daughter to leave the classroom while the class was reading that book. He started hollering at me, said I was implying that his staff was unprofessional, that the book would not be on the state's recommended reading list if it were not acceptable. This was the first time I had ever confronted anyone in school, and I was really intimidated. But I was doing this for my daughter. I went to the Indian parent group. We wrote a petition and gave it to the principal. We wrote a letter to the State Board of Education. But in the end, my daughter had to sit through the rest of the reading of that book in the classroom. They didn't allow her to leave. I didn't know what to do, I didn't have money to hire a lawyer. I just didn't know what else to do.

The next year, my daughter's fifth grade teacher was teaching "westward expansion." And when I went to see her, she said, "Well, I heard all about you. Why do you think you have the right to remove books from the recommended list?" And, for another year, my daughter's identity as an Indian person was attacked.

Our children don't heal from this. It hurts. It doesn't stop hurting. I noticed in her art, when she would draw pictures of herself, my daughter would draw someone with blue eyes instead of someone with brown eyes. She was trying to make herself less Indian and more white. This has scarred her. My daughter's in high school now, and she still feels insecure and "less than" because she's not white. This has hurt my children and it's hurt me. It's never-ending, it's ongoing, it's continual, it's generational. It's always.

APRIL'S STORY

One of the parents told me that there was going to be a play at school and I decided to go with her. The play was supposed to be about California history, the California Gold Rush. We had had problems with a teacher there who continued to present stereotypical plays about Indians. The whole school was there, including a lot of Indian kids. So we were watching the play, and they even said, "Eureka! I have found it!" Then they got to the part about Indians. The non-Indian kids each made a short little speech and named some of our traditional foods like deer meat and salmon. And then, at the end, everyone did a "friendship dance." Well, our kids, the Indian kids, were just sitting there—you could just see their little shoulders turn in and their heads just hung down. The mom, she had two little kids with her, and she was really upset. She looked like she was crying, and she left early.

I went and talked with some of our kids afterwards. They didn't want to talk about it; they didn't know how to express how they felt. They were shamed and embarrassed.

Later, I found the mom in the parking lot. She was still there with her kids, just standing there. We talked about what we could do to change this kind of thing. So we went to speak with the principal and this teacher. We made some really good suggestions. Talk about the sacrifices we made during the Gold Rush. How many families were here when the Gold Rush happened and how the Shasta Dam displaced a lot of families, dispersed our communities. How they flooded and destroyed our graves. The teacher just said she wasn't willing to change this play—"I'm not willing to do away with my play."

This teacher has been there a long time. She was my third-grade teacher. And she's still doing it.

—April Carmelo (Wintu/Maidu/Juaneño)

BARBARA'S STORY

They wanted to meet with me to talk about the school and see if I'd be interested in being the director. I really didn't want to go, but I fit it in between two soccer games. I walked in a little late, dressed in my coaching outfit. We introduced ourselves and Linda said, "So, Barbara, you are Native American? You don't look like what I expected. I expected the Indian princess look. I said, "No, that would be Pocahontas."*—Barbara Potter (Potawatomi)*

CORA'S STORY

One time, I was watching TV. It was a cartoon show, "Yogi Bear," and they had these little dogs and they were wearing feathers and different colors and going woo-woo-woo. It made me feel real bad. It made me feel bad because it wasn't true and it wasn't right. They had feathers in their hair that looked like they were dyed. And they were supposed to be like Indians. They were walking on two legs. And then there was another dog and he was supposed to be a white-man dog. And then a girl-dog took him into a teepee-thing and the teepee didn't look like it was made by Indians. Everybody had braids and they looked like they had wigs on. I felt bad because they were making fun of me and everything was just stereotypes. I've seen that in other cartoons. It makes me feel bad because a lot of times there are cartoons that I like and I want to watch but I don't want to watch all this stereotype-stuff.*—Cora García (Lumbee)*

CRYSTAL'S STORY

I never felt like I was part of the class, I felt invisible. When the teacher asked me what I was, I told her and she said, you can't be all that, you can only be one. I remember always feeling either kind of angry or uninterested; I was just a quiet little person in the back of the room. When the teacher talked about my culture, my voice didn't count. I was unimportant. When I was little I would say to my teacher, my grandpa said this and my grandpa said that and she would say, well that's just a story. Then my mom would get a call from the school and I'd have to hear my teacher tell my mom that I'd had another outburst and my mom would have to come to the school to hear about my behavior. And it was all because I didn't want to be there.

As I got older, I started reading books that were written by Native authors because I felt that they would have a better idea of what was going on. In high school I started speaking out and then I would be sent home and there were more parent-teacher conferences. I was never suspended or anything like that—it was always an issue of my not listening to the teacher or my having outbursts. They said I was a very smart child but I didn't know how to direct my intelligence or control my anger. What they were really saying was that I was challenging them and they didn't appreciate it. Especially in history or English—I always felt that I wasn't allowed to speak.

That's how I feel about Eurocentric education. It sets our children up for failure and they feel like I felt sitting in the back of the classroom. If you invest in pain and shame, that's what you get.

—Crystal Salas-Patten (Mescalero Apache/Lakota, Puerto Rican, Hawai'ian, Mexican)

DEBBIE'S STORY

Last year when we were home for feast, my daughter, Liz, and seven of her cousins were dancing. We were doing the Comanche. The structure, steps and movements we do for the Comanche are similar to our other Pueblo dances, like the Yellow Corn, but the clothing we wear is bright and colorful, like the clothing worn by some of the Plains tribes. Our dances are tightly structured. We gather nightly in the kiva for several days prior to the feast day. This gives us time to relearn the dance and songs. It gives the children time to learn new dances and songs. Dancers are placed in a line by the war captain, from the oldest to the youngest. I was near the front of the line. Liz was near the back. From my place in line, I couldn't see her. During practice, my mom, who wasn't dancing, said Liz was doing fine, learning the movements and moving according to the song.

On the day of the feast, we dance outside—twice in the morning and twice in the afternoon. We end the day with one dance inside the kiva. It always feels good to be home for feast. To dance. To see the kids learning the steps and songs. Making clothes for them to wear. Being with uncles and aunts. My uncle always calls Liz by her Pueblo name. He says "How's Yun Povi?"

My favorite moment is that last dance, the one inside. That's when parents can bring their children to dance beside them. The child takes a new place in line for that one dance. So Liz danced in front of me. Being near her, watching her take part… The images are vivid in my heart, in my mind. There are no words that capture that. Just feelings. Good, strong feelings.—*Debbie A. Reese (Nambé Pueblo)*

DORIS'S STORY

I am a children's librarian. I've been a children's librarian for a very long time now. So one night I'm working the night shift and these people come in—upper middle class couple with cute little girl, around four, maybe a little younger—and they're looking for books on Indians. So I take them down to the section, show them this and that, tell them why one thing is good and another is not so good, and finally they ask me how come I knew so much about it. And I'm like, well, see, I'm this Indian. And they get all excited: "Oh, Susie, come here and meet this lady—she's a real American Indian!"

Of course, I don't remember what the little girl's name was after all this time but I'll never forget what happened next. Susie comes, dragging down the floor, looking more and more unhappy, and when she gets down to the desk, she looks at me and bursts into tears. I had been sitting there, fat, dumb and happy, doing my job, and here's this little thing scared to death of me. The parents look at her—"What's the matter?"—and of course, she couldn't say. Then they turn to me and say, "Well, I guess we'll have to work on this" and I can't think of a single blessed thing to say.

Now you've gotta wonder where she got this. I don't think it was from the parents, they seemed like nice folk. So then you have to look around and see what pictures of us the world carries for little white kids. And think all the crazy stuff that white people do and say about Indians doesn't matter? Oh yes, it matters, and I will never forget.—*Doris Seale (Santee/Cree)*

DREW'S STORY

I remember a summer a long time ago when a throng of Pentecostals came to our reserve. They were there to teach the poor Indians how to play lacrosse (and some religious stuff). After two weeks in which we had mastered the lacrosse stick and ball, they packed up and left. Taking the sticks and balls with them. Leaving behind a group of Native kids who could now play lacrosse but had nothing to play with except a bible they left behind. Maybe that best explains my view of the Church.

—*Drew Hayden Taylor (Ojibwe)*

ELIZABETH'S STORY

My name is Elizabeth and, um, I have a story to tell. It's about when I was at school, and I was four and a half.

(Once when I was four) I was watching TV and Tweedy Bird was hitting Sylvester, he was hitting him on the head because Sylvester had a feather on his head because, um, he was pretending he was an Indian and, um, he was hitting him a lot of times singing "ten little, nine little Indians" and, um, every time he said a different number he would hit him.

(In school, when I was four and a half) we were sitting all around in a circle and singing "one little two little Indians" and then I came home and I wouldn't tell my mommy, because, um, I couldn't tell her, and it didn't make me feel good because, um, I was keeping it inside me, and it was really hard to keep it inside me.

And then they were singing "one little Indian, two little Indians, three little, four little, five, six, seven" again, and, um, I just said, "Stop it! Stop it right now! Stop singing that song! That's a bad song! That song is about killing Indians! I don't like it, I don't want you to sing it anymore!" I said that loud. And then the teacher stopped that song. I was scared but I just did it.

I finally said, I finally talked to my mommy about it. My mommy was proud of me, I think. And Mommy said to them, "Don't sing that song 'cause it's a *bad* song!" And that was when I was four and a half.—*Elizabeth Villiana Jeffredo Warden (Payomkawish [Luiseño]/Southern Channel Islander/Creek)*

JANE'S STORY

It is the third grade, 1972. I am a strong willed and vivacious child, popular and respected by my peers but aware that there is something about me that excludes me in some way. I am raised by white people who go to great lengths to raise me "normally." In other words it's a huge secret, my Indian self, but only from me. So I'm shamed when my teacher calls me "the smart little Indian." I cannot now recall the context, only the emotion. It was so powerful it made me cry, each and every time. This only encouraged her meanness, for as my tears began to fall she would say, "Uh-oh, class, the little Indian is going to flood the room again— better get out our canoes!" My confusion was so huge, yet at some level I totally understood I was something bad; so bad in fact that my family tried to protect me from it.—*Jane Waite*

JANE'S SON'S STORY

Anpao's in the third grade. I pick him up from school one day and in the usual "how's-your-day" conversation he tells me he's having a problem with one of his assignments. His teacher is making him write a diary like his family was on the Oregon Trail. He says, "I know we couldn't have been, plus we weren't allowed there anyway. The Oregon Constitution says only white people were allowed." Anpao's awareness and willingness to speak up makes me very proud.

When I go to speak with his teacher, she says she doesn't see the problem. She says it had never been a problem in all the many years she had been using this curriculum. I point out that she had several (brown) children in the class who would not have been allowed on the Oregon Trail.

Her response is "not to worry," that she does a unit in February on the Nez Percé "where the white people are the bad people." I tell her she's missing the point, that all children have a right to be taught honestly, that it is their world after all and they deserve to understand it. We go round and round for awhile, she maintaining her oblique defensiveness, I struggling to maintain calmness.

In the end, Anpao writes the diary; his teacher does not support him and he doesn't want to feel, ironically, excluded. I choose to allow him his security; he knows his history. He learns a lot from the experience, particularly about "mainstream" culture and how it dysfunctions.—*Jane Waite*

JUDY'S DAUGHTER JESSICA'S STORY

Last fall in my daughter's anthropology class, the professor said that all Native Americans are drunks and alcoholics. He said that there are no Abenaki in Vermont, the ones who say they are, are "wannabes" and the only history and culture they know are what the anthropologists taught them. Jessica tried to talk with the professor. She told him that the comments he was making were offensive to her and that he could learn Abenaki history from Abenaki people. His response was to swear at my daughter, and in the next class, the professor said that digging up Indian burial sites was no "big deal" and refused to listen when Jessica spoke about the laws that protect Indian remains.

Jessica filed a discrimination claim, and then, after the professor retaliated against her, she filed a retaliation claim. She finally won, and the university sanctioned the professor for intimidation, harassment and threats. I'm so proud of the way my daughter found the strength to stand up for what's right. She's a very strong young woman. But Jessica is so burnt out by this whole thing, she doesn't have the same love for education that she used to have. And that makes me sad.—*Judy Dow (Abenaki)*

LINDA'S STORY

This happened when I went to Berkeley and was returning home on the BART train with my son Robbie and he was very young at the time, maybe only four or five. I decided to stop at the Oakland Museum. I wanted to see the regalia and the other exhibits in the California History Room or whatever it's called. So Robbie and I were walking around and in walked this man with a long string of little preschool-age children in tow and they were walking about looking at the exhibits and the man announced to the children, "When the white people came, all the Indians died." At which point I looked at my son and I said, "Rob, did you hear what that man said? 'When the white people came, all the Indians died.'" And Rob said, "Well that's not true," and then I said, "I know."

And then Rob said, "Aren't you gonna tell him?" and I said something like, "Yeah, but I'm trying to think of a nice way to do it so I don't embarrass him." So I was struggling within myself how I could correct this without making the man look stupid or feel defensive and so I was just trying to think of how to delicately do that. And in the meantime, the man and the group of children were getting farther and farther away from me, and all the while Robbie kept tugging at my dress and saying, "Mom, mom." And he's tugging at me some more, "Mom, mom..." And finally he said,

"Mom do you want them to think that we're dead?"—*Linda Yamane (Rumsien Ohlone)*

LIZ'S STORY

This happened when I was in third grade. In my reading group there was this Newberry book called *Caddie Woodlawn*. I don't think the teacher had read this book, but she picked it because we were studying pioneers and someone told her it was about pioneers. And my friend at the time, pretty much my best friend Emma, was in the reading group with me. She had read *Caddie Woodlawn* when she was like six and she didn't know that it was offensive to Native Americans. And so we were reading it and when we got to the second chapter, it said, I'm not sure exactly what it said, that the Native Americans were sneaking around like dogs, and they picked up Caddie Woodlawn by her hair, and they were acting like dogs sniffing a bone. In another part it said that the Native Americans were massacring, murdering and scalping the pioneers and made belts out of their hair and skin. They made the pioneers seem like angels and the Native Americans seem like inhuman monsters. I felt hurt inside, my eyes were watering and I felt like I wanted to cry. But then I thought, there's something I can do about this.

This was the first time I ever thought about doing something about this, besides my mom's coming to school and talking about us being Native American. Usually it was like a tradition, my mom would come in every year. But nothing really happened until third grade.

When I got to this part in *Caddie Woodlawn*, I was home and I showed it to my mom and we both got uncomfortable, upset, angry. So the next day I went to school and I told my teacher, I told her I found something that's really offensive to Native Americans in this book and I would really like for us to stop reading it. So she said we would have a meeting about it that day.

I said I would prefer we stopped reading this book and pretty much everybody agreed we should stop reading it. So we stopped reading the book and my friend Emma said that she didn't want anything offensive to white people either. So me and my mom agreed to find another book and that was Birchbark House. So we read that book and we liked it so much that I did a play about it. The people in my reading group and another of my friends helped me with this play by being my actors. So that's basically what happened with me and *Caddie Woodlawn* when I was in the third grade.

—*Liz Reese (Nambé Pueblo)*

LOIS'S STORY

This happened in a school I subbed in a lot. It was a school close to the reservation district, a transition school with a very high population of Indian students. All the teachers knew me, and it was very common for them to ask me to do storytelling. I was subbing for an art teacher who had a prep period and the new principal came in. She grabbed me by the back of my collar and physically dragged me out of the room in front of the class. It soon became evident that she had mistaken me for another Native person, someone with whom she had had a confrontation. I said to her, "I'm a sub and I'm being paid to be here and I don't know who you think I am." She didn't back down. She said, "You can't just go wherever you want. If you leave the room even to go to the bathroom, I expect you to notify my secretary in writing and I want you to tell her what hall you're walking down." Then she said,

"We have Indians in this school. You scare people."—*Lois Beardslee (Ojibwe/Lacandon)*

MARIA'S MOTHER'S STORY

We were working in the kitchen, putting away the corn from our garden. My job was to bag it up after it had been cut off the cobs. We were listening to the radio, my mom and me, as we often did on these early fall weekends, when "Que Será, Será" came through our radio.

"Oh! Doris Day! I loooove Doris Day! When I was little I used to want to be just like her!" my mother said, dancing past me to the sink.

"Doris Day!?" I peered over from my task to watch her. She was filling the sink with cold water to cool the next batch of ears. She had her long brown hair fastened tightly to her head with a blue and yellow beaded barrette, one of her favorites. When she looked up at me, a strand fell on her face. She pursed her lips and blew it out of her way.

"Well, yeah. She was America's sweetheart. Everybody loved her." Another strand of hair fell near her eyes and she blinked. She retreated to the bathroom and came out with another barrette, blue and yellow like the first. She fastened it tightly to the side, making a tighter bun.

"She's not Native, you know…" I teased her. My mother is very proud of who she is, of her culture. The idea that she ever wanted to be someone else fascinated me.

"I grew up before the 1970s. It wasn't cool to be an Indian yet, she said as she took the hot corn out of the boiling water and put it into the cold water waiting in the sink. "It was hard."

"Oh…how was it hard?"

"Well, lots of things. Little things…" She sighed, and stared out our window. "Once my family had planned a vacation. We were going to travel across the country and stay at campsites as we went. But my dad had very dark skin. Too dark for some. Some of the campgrounds wouldn't let us in because he was 'colored.' We had to sleep by the railroad tracks." She smiled and shrugged.

"Really, that actually happened to you?"

"Things were different then. When I was little, I didn't really realize that we weren't like everybody else. It didn't matter. But when I started to figure it out, of course I wanted to be someone else.

Everybody does at some time in their life. Eventually they learn to accept who they are. I have."

So there you have it. My mom—artist, storyteller, wife, mother—my mom used to be a Doris Day wannabe. I leaned over and kissed her on the cheek. "Is there any more corn left to bag up?" I asked.—*Maria Beardslee (Ojibwe/Lacandon)*

MAYANA'S STORY

One day in third grade my teacher said that we were going to learn about Christopher Columbus. She said that Christopher Columbus was great, and that he had discovered America. She said all this great stuff about Columbus, but I told her that it was not right because Columbus cut off legs and enslaved the Indians whose land he was on.

The teacher said that I was not back there 500 years ago. I said, "I know, but I have proof because my stepmom has read the diary of a man who was traveling with Columbus. So she has proof and I have proof."

"Well," the teacher said, "I'm sorry, you were not there 500 years ago."

I said, "Well, neither were you!" So after that the teacher said, "Write something about Columbus that you have learned." So I went to my desk and wrote all the bad stuff Columbus had done to Indians.

When I was done I went to my teacher to show her what I had written. She said, "I'm sorry, you're going to have to rewrite this because you have to write something nice about Columbus."

So I went to my desk, and wrote that Christopher Columbus had three ships: the Niña, the Pinta, and the Santa María.—*Mayana Lea (Cherokee)*

MONICA'S STORY

I really don't like the fake cartoon and illustration in Indian books that are here in the school library. My name is Monica Spencer and my tribe is Navajo, Laguna, Kiaoni and Pueblo, all full blooded. It makes me mad when children make fun of my culture. It makes the kids think we do that when we don't. When the children grow up I don't want them to think that Indians put feathers in their hair and dance around the fire. We don't do that. And I don't think that it is right for the kids to look at the silly things they put in those silly books. One day I saw a kid running around with a feather in their hair and putting their hand to their mouths and making weird noises and I cried when that happened. So what I want you to do is put those books away and learn about our real history.

—*Monica Spencer (Laguna/Diné/Hawai'ian)*

NAOMI'S STORY

One day, I walked into Will's former elementary school and just as you go in, right next to the showcase, on the wall I saw a brown leather belt with two curly black wigs and some feathers hanging from it. A kid had done a book report and this was his visual aide.

So I walked over and read the material and they were supposed to be scalps. My heart dropped, I couldn't believe it. It made me sick, it made me want to throw up. So I said to the reading teacher, Are these supposed to be scalps? And she said, It's just a book report. Meaning that it was OK, it wasn't important enough to talk about. She didn't seem to see a thing wrong with it. I was at a loss for words because in the past I've gone in, I've talked with the kids, they know I'm Indian, they know Will's Indian. It shocked me that the teachers apparently couldn't find any better literature than *The Sign of the Beaver*. And that it was OK to illustrate it this way.

It made me sad for the children who are mostly white. And I thought, you know, these kids need good books because they don't have the privilege and opportunity to interact on a personal level with Indian kids or Latino kids who have Indian blood. So they're getting their worldview from trash.

—*Naomi Caldwell (Ramapough)*

RAVEN'S STORY

My name is Raven. When I was in the third grade, our class read *The Courage of Sarah Noble*. In this book they said Indian people were savages and murderers, they chop your head off and eat you alive and that we were not really people. When the class put on the play for the whole school, the kids started taunting me, calling me "stinky" and asking me how many people I've eaten. Nobody would play with me or even sit next to me in class. I felt so ashamed. Finally, I told my mother I didn't want to go back to school.—*Raven Hoaglen (Maidu/Konkow/Wailaki/Mono)*

ROBETTE'S STORY

I was speaking at a conference and this woman came up to me and said, "Are you sure you're a California Indian? I heard they were all extinct." I said to her, "I heard that, too."—*Robette Dias (Karuk)*

ROBIN'S STORY

My son came home one day and told me that they were studying California Indians and they were gonna be building models of missions. I asked him if he really had to do this and he said yes. So I said I would talk to the teacher because I didn't want the children to build the replicas because many, many Indian people had died building missions.

I went to school the next morning and privately asked Nick's teacher to let him pass on the actual building of the mission, that I thought it was immoral, considering how many Native people died building the original ones. I thought Nick's teacher would honor what I was saying, that it would sink in how insensitive an activity like that would be. But she just told me that Nick had to build a mission or fail that part of the fourth grade.

So Nick built his mission and brought it home. And we built a fire and we talked about it again, how Indian people were enslaved and died building missions and living in missions. Then we put it in the fire and burned it and I promised Nick that I would always stick up for him and challenge anyone who would keep opening up these scars.—*Robin Carneen (Swinomish)*

SETH'S STORY

Some people ask me how I teach the Native American culture in my classroom. I tell them that I teach the Native American culture by being Native.—*S. Sethlyn Honeycutt (Cherokee/Choctaw/Blackfoot)*

THE GIFT OF SYRUP

Ishkigamizige-giizis. I just call it the woods. It is where my maw, my grammaws, and all the grammaws before them came from. Going home I am when I go to the woods.

Spring returns to the north woods of Minnesota. Sure enough, the Shinnobs in this HUD house are excited about going to the sugar bush. We have been hearing the crows for a while now. The returning birds let us know it is time to make maple syrup.

Eagles, crows, swans, ducks, and some I don't know are flying about. I looked in the mirror and saw a brown bellied sap sucker looking back at me. The moving birds keep me looking up to see what comes next as winter fades and spring comes booming in.

Before we went into the woods we gave the three grandchildren the standard lecture.

"We are quiet in the woods because this is the deer's house and we are just visitors. See the tracks?"

At first the snow is thigh deep to adults and waist deep to the grandchildren. The snow has butt prints where someone tipped over. One day I used snowshoes to make trails. I waded from tree to tree, breaking trail for a train of grandchildren. One is carrying milk jugs, one is carrying taps, one is just watching, trying to keep up. Using a brace and bit I drill a hole at a slight upward angle into the maple tree. Using an always-handy twig I clean out the shavings. One hands me a tap and I tap-tap it into the tree. We watch to see if the sap comes through the tap. I hang the jug on the tap. With some trees, the sap pulses out of the tree, like a heartbeat almost. The kids make O shaped mouths when they see the sap coming out like that.

We got about 130 trees tapped but are bragging 150. What I like about going to the woods is I have to walk slow. That is good because it gives me a chance to appreciate what the Creator has given us.

When we went to gather the sap the kids got the standard lecture: "Spilling sap is a felony, anyone spilling sap spends a night in the box. (Oh, wait a minute, that's from Cool Hand Luke.) Just be careful with the sap. Remember, we are quiet in the woods."

The laughter of the children broke the quiet rule as they run from tree to tree, laughing, wanting to be first to empty a full jug. "Watch out for the deer poop," one little voice cautioned.

We brought the sap home and built the fire.

I like to build a base of hot coals using dry maple. Every time I go to the woods I look for dry standing maple, Cadillacs I call them. The Cadillac of firewood.

After the bed of coals is ready we add more dry wood and then stack split firewood around the kettle.

At first as it heats the wisps of steam come off in a tentative way; as the sap gets hotter, the steam comes rolling off, seemingly happy to be free.

The Shinnobs are drawn to the kettle like a magnet. As more people join the circle around the fire, each one looks around for something to do. One takes charge of the balsam branches that are used to keep the sap from boiling over. Another takes responsibility for the fire, keeping it fed and roaring. One tells stories. Once again, there is time for everyone to tell a story. At one boil we had fourteen humans and two dogs sitting there.

The fire roars on and we are reminded that we are just one of the generations that have sat around such a fire watching sap boil down. We are bathed in wood smoke.

After about seven hours of kettle time the syrup comes off the fire. We are ever so careful as we carry the hot syrup into the house for the final boil and filtering.

Now I have jars and jars of dark maple syrup.

This has been a good learning season for the grandchildren. They learned to be quiet in the woods, to respect the gifts we have been given. They also learned the way we make syrup, how to make the taps, how to drill the trees, how to collect the sap and then boil it into syrup.

Another seasonal cycle of the Anishinaabeg cycles through. We are blessed to be a part of it. We thank the Creator for the gift of syrup. Miigwech.—*Jim Northrup*

FRYBREAD- AND FEATHER-FREE

I make lousy frybread. I'm usually feather-free. I don't start conversations with phrases like "as my grandfather once said" and then burst into poignant lectures about the religious traditions related to my Native identity, let alone anybody else's.

And it's pretty stunning for me to sit down with a group of second-graders, who tell me that Indians shot arrows, went on warpaths, and lived some time before the turn of the 18th Century. From my point of view, just their use of the past tense is chilling.

That's why I create contemporary Indian characters like Cousin Elizabeth, a suit-wearing woman with a messy closet who can't go to a powwow because of her law job, and Cassidy Rain Berghoff, a fourteen-year-old fan of science fiction and Cracker Jack who often says the wrong thing and thinks her heritage is her own business.

My first picture book, *Jingle Dancer* and my first novel, *Rain Is Not My Indian Name* feature Native American characters. These books fall into the category of contemporary fiction, probably the most underrepresented type of Indian-themed book. At first, Native content was presented in historical fiction and nonfiction as well as retellings of traditional stories. However, we're beginning to see more contemporary picture books such as *Muskrat Will Be Swimming* by Cheryl Savageau, along with contemporary novels such as *Eagle Song* by Joseph Bruchac. My work is yet another voice to add to this slowly widening circle.

A challenge in writing contemporary Native American fiction is that some of my readers will be insiders, members of Native communities, and some will be outsiders, many sadly unfamiliar with Indian cultures except in the most scant and stereotypical of ways. Some would say I should therefore create an educational overlay on my fiction to help enlighten the outsider group. Yet it's important to me that none of my characters will ever be mistaken for guides on a Native American tour, and I believe it's important to both groups of readers as well.

Let me explain:

It's a small moment in my first novel, *Rain Is Not My Indian Name*. My protagonist, Cassidy Rain Berghoff, has just been informed that her ex-second-best friend, Queenie Washington, is not only a mixed-blood Indian of African ancestry, but one of Seminole heritage.

Why would Queenie's tribal affiliation be particularly noteworthy? Rain is a racially and intertribally mixed citizen of the Creek Nation, a tribe linked to the Seminoles, past and present, in history, language, tradition. Throughout the story, these two girls stand at a distance, separated by a romantic conflict over a boy in their past, linked by their grief over his death. So this added connection between them might be seen as an opportunity to educate young readers about the fascinating history linking Rain's and Queenie's tribes. Instead, the passage simply reads: "Aunt Georgia called this morning and mentioned that Queenie's great-grandfather had been a Seminole, which made Queenie a pretty close cousin after all. I was more interested in the fact that Queenie had volunteered to make Thursday's spaghetti dinner."

While young readers no doubt do learn about their own and other cultures from fiction, it's a mistake to summarily force passages of social studies in fiction. Doing so compromises the realism of the characters' perspectives and disrupts the plot structure with details unnecessary to advance the story.

Historically, children's literature has offered too many "superethnic" Native characters, focusing on what's commonly perceived as different, perhaps "exotic." In doing so, we authors have failed to portray the immense diversity of Native peoples, underestimated young readers, and, at the very least, broken the "magic" of fiction by flattening three-dimensional characters into paper dolls speaking encyclopedia-ese.

It's important to keep in mind that although some outsiders may see Native America as a mystery, to insiders it is the norm. In this case, for many young readers of the Creek and Seminole Nations, their tribes' relationship is not news.

For them, pausing the otherwise natural voice of the narrator to lecture would no doubt feel jarring and artificial. It may even send the message that this is not a book for the communities it reflects but rather one designed exclusively to teach outsiders.

But it would also be disturbing to outsider readers. By this point in the story, they know Rain. She's a wry, sensitive girl who looks up to Aunt Georgia, who's protective of her brother Fynn and his fiancée Natalie, who enjoys powwows but is not herself a dancer, and who has practically memorized every episode of *The X-Files* in her DVD collection. Though she knows of her own tribal history and traditions, she is a budding photojournalist, not a tribal historian. It would be out of character for Rain to lecture at length on the sociopolitical-historical ties between Creeks and Seminoles, especially when her mind is cheerfully preoccupied with the prospect of Queenie's cooking. Likewise, the text of my picture book, *Jingle Dancer*, includes references to powwows, regalia, frybread, Indian tacos, and the Muscogee traditional story of Bat. The realistic watercolor illustrations by Cornelius Van Wright and Ying-Hwa Hu feature a small Ojibwe dreamcatcher in Cousin Elizabeth's apartment and a large Creek basket in Grandma Wolfe's home. The thematic concepts of sharing and reciprocity as well as mixed-blood characters are integrated but never explicitly discussed. Although a few vocabulary words are defined in the author's note for adults, young readers are asked to embrace Jenna's world on its own terms.

I'm not just trying to avoid didacticism. Its fall from fashion is a mainstream cultural preference. Many authors from underrepresented communities may well draw from their own storytelling traditions in framing stories that explicitly teach. What I'm suggesting is more subtle. The personality and situational perspective of the individual character has to be considered. In my novel, for example, Rain mentions walking by a Trail of Tears painting in her hallway. But she doesn't pause to elaborate on the removal and its historical period. I can imagine a story in which this kind of reflection would be appropriate, one perhaps incorporating a journey to her ancestral lands. But that's not the story I'm telling.

Instead, the painting here is part of the backdrop. Rain is familiar with the story of the Trail of Tears, but that information is so grounded in her day-to-day worldview that she doesn't feel a need to comment on it. Native American readers will be validated by their reflection in cultural references that occur naturally, I hope, seamlessly in the story.

Meanwhile, outsiders will sometimes have to apply themselves to understand some traditions and perspectives. But even with effort, they may not catch everything. That's okay. At least they won't be patronized or cheated of a worldview that isn't all laid out for them. They'll have the opportunity to be uncomfortable now and then, and to work through it. Perhaps they'll even be inspired to learn more. Yet the story at hand dictates what is integrated and what remains unsaid. The story is where the readers' focus should be. It's my hope that all of them will be touched by the grief and humor of my characters—both Native and non-Indian—and that they'll come to care about these fictional people as individual human beings.—*Cynthia Leitich Smith*

OLD TSA TSI

Our Grandmama Toinetta could wring a chicken's neck like nobody's business. We watched, wide-eyed and scared, thinking if she could do that to a chicken, what might she do to us the next time we got into trouble?

Chicken blood would stain her dark hands, drip from her adept fingers, fall though the sticky feathers, and drop to the ground, marking a drop of death. And still we watched. We watched as the chicken became naked but not slick, little stubby places dotting its body.

We watched as Grandmama Toinetta primed the old water pump out behind her house. Primed it with rainwater that gathered in a tub just beneath the eaves of the house. The living water breathed life into that old pump until it burped and gurgled and spat out silver streams that turned red underneath Grandmama Toinetta's dark hands.

We were told that rainwater came from heaven. Grandmama Toinetta took us to the Providence Baptist Church every Sunday morning because we were too little to complain and too smart to talk back. It was there we heard a little about heaven and a lot about hell.

Hell. That was where the preacher talked about mostly. We Indian children often wondered if our ancestors who never heard this preacher's rantings and ravings had gone there, but this idea was never discussed.

The preacher said that hell was full of fire and brimstone and bad people who had spent a lot of their time here on earth drinking, cussing, and committing other mortal sins. To us, this place called hell sounded much like a place our Grandmama Toinetta's neighbors would spend a Saturday night, except for the brimstone. We had no idea what brimstone could be. Maybe it was some kind of big rock that people who were going to hell threw at chickens who refused to die from getting their necks wrung. Like our rooster, Old Tsa Tsi. He refused to die.

One early Saturday morning, our Grandmama Toinetta tried and tried to wring that old rooster's neck. We watched and waited. Waited to see his headless body flapping around the side yard, entertaining and scaring us at the same time. But Old Tsa Tsi refused to die. We figured his neck must have been made of rubber or something magical, because it sure wouldn't break in our Grandmama Toinetta's strong, dark hands. She tried and tried and finally gave up. Old Tsa Tsi then walked away proudly as if to say, "To hell with you, Old Woman! It ain't my time to go, and I sure don't want to be sitting on your table at dinner time tomorrow."

After that incident, we weren't scared of watching our Grandmama Toinetta killing chickens any more. We weren't even intrigued. We just accepted it. But we still kept our doubts about the places called heaven and hell, and no one ever explained where all of our ancestors could be.—*MariJo Moore*

WHO STOLE OÑATE'S FOOT?

A statue rests without a foot in Alcalde, New Mexico. The foot is one that belongs to Don Juan de Oñate, the so-called explorer and settler of the American Southwest.

But who stole his foot?

I stole his foot. Yes, it was me that did it because it was this foot that was placed on my neck to hold me down. It was this foot that made me feel less than human and not equal to the one who held me there. I was the man held back to feel I was of no value. Yes, I stole his foot.

My children, they stole his foot. Sure they stole it! They stole it because whenever they saw a movie with cowboys and Indians, somehow they became the bad guys. How is it that they can become less than human by fictitious characterization of their people? My children, they stole his foot.

My parents, they stole his foot. Sure they stole it! They stole his foot because they were taken from the comfort of their people's villages and subjected to a new and different culture. Our parents' songs were taken away. The words of their mothers were wiped from their mouths. They were made into a people not accepted by the conqueror or by their own families. They were a lost people. Yes, my parents stole his foot.

My grandmothers and grandfathers, they stole his foot. For it was Oñate himself who ordered hands and feet to be cut off Native Americans after defeating the Acoma Pueblo in 1599. It was our grandmas and grandpas who had to go through life without hands to touch and feel the future. Yes, my grandparents stole his foot.

It was by these deeds that we have come to take Don Juan de Oñate's foot. It is by the inhumane act that we must act. We as Americans must not lift up the deeds of cruel leaders and name institutions after them. We must bring justice to these acts rather than celebrate their existence.

We, the Native American people took his foot and ground it up into a powder and threw it into the wind. Then we took our sacred cornmeal and made four lines on the ground, so this foot will not be able to return and harm us again. We did this so we can claim our right to be as every man, a human being....

Because now you see, today Oñate, he is defeated!

Let us as a people begin to acknowledge the wrongs that happened 400 years ago and then we can begin to ask one another for forgiveness.—*Michael Lacapa*

CHARLIE'S BUNDLE

We call it "weengush," the sacred plant of the north. Sweetgrass. It is so special, so sacred, that we have no tales about its origin. No one dare approach the subject. When the children play with it as we pick it, we tell them in hushed tones not to trample it, to treat it with respect. "You are braiding the hair of our Mother Earth. It does not grow all over her body, only in a few special places." So we travel miles, even days to harvest the sturdiest and sweetest smelling of all wild grasses.

We use sweetgrass to make baskets and to trim birchbark and porcupine quillwork. It is a wrong against our people and our culture to sell it. But, as artists and basketmakers, we have a gift. We are part of a tradition of specialization essential to all cultures. We make beauty, and we share it. We are among the few who are allowed to take, transform, and utilize this sacred plant.

I have been told that, in the old days, sweetgrass baskets were used to filter drinking water. Even today, it is burned to ease the symptoms of migraine headaches. It is smudged each morning by some, to face the oncoming day's responsibilities. It is part of our kinniganik, a special tobacco mixture. We protect it. We cure and store it with the utmost care. We touch it with reverence. And we never waste a bit of it. Even the tiniest scraps are prayed over when they are burned. The locations are secret, the picking, processing, curing, and sharing of it so laden with tradition that it feels overwhelming. Now, in this heat, fighting off the bugs, the eerie calls of the watchful ravens, the overhead threats of the Thunderbirds, echoed by an awestruck three-year-old—these feelings are compounded by the fact that it is profoundly backbreaking and physically exhausting to harvest. It must be picked one blade at a time, with two hands. With each blade I stand up straight again, to clean it, to carefully remove and instantly replant any accidentally pulled roots.

I begin to make a mental list of elders and less able with whom I will share this sacred, fragrant plant. This is a tradition that carries on from the very first time I was taken here, to bring weengush to the older people, the basket makers, the ones with the knowledge and the skills, the dying language. Along with this precious secret and the mysteries that surround it come responsibilities.

My oldest child is picking quietly, tiptoeing gently. Tonight I will suggest to her that she remove from her hard-earned bundle enough sweetgrass to share. But her thoughts are already moving in the right direction, as she begins to suggest names on her own. I swell with pride. I am proud of the job I have done. I have passed on reverence to one with whom I have shared the secret of the location. I am a good mom, and she is an equally good daughter.

After I tell her that it is time to wrap and put away our own supply for the year, I nurse the baby in the tall, fragrant grass. We mutually decide that we will now pick a separate bundle for Charlie. We will not cure it, but will express mail it to him in its pure state, so as not to rob him of that pleasure, that tradition. Surely, it has been many years since he has had that opportunity. We carefully review the procedure, step by step, so that we can share it with him. It will be her job to write it down for him. I know she knows the information by heart now. She's watched and helped every year for as long as she can remember. But now I am sure, the traditional knowledge is safely bundled up inside of her.

Charlies's bundle keeps getting bigger. There is an issue of pride, making sure he isn't cheated of his heritage, his tradition, his honor. The bundle grows far larger than it would have been had we pulled it out of our own precious store. We work with a renewed energy that belies the early hour of rising, hours of driving, the heat, the strained effort of bringing children through the roughest of trails. With every blade of grass, we think of Charlie, his soft voice, his patience, his shared knowledge, his patient wife. My little girl takes off her shirt and lovingly wraps the bundle, weaving through the woods, over the deadfalls we leave in place to hide the trail. As she stares at me, exhausted, out the tailgate of the car, I sweep away our footprints. Think of me on mother's day, Charlie.—*Lois Beardslee*

DEAD PAWN

What is the price of caring for your children? This came to me when I returned home. There was Mom, sitting at the table drinking coffee with a faraway look in her eyes. It was Saturday, town day; for those on the rez the time you get up early and get on your good clothes, the sheep are fed out of the closely guarded bales of hay saved for days like this. They will be penned for the day. Grandma is dressed, long skirt and velveteen blouse, the truck is checked, all are fed. The old couple gets in the front. The rest of us crawl in the back in the bed and settle in for the ride. We see many others on the road. There is food to buy, car parts needed, twine, rope, animal medicine and goodies for the kids, a chance to eat out, maybe a movie and to see old friends.

It was a good day. We traveled on to town. There was a stop at the Navajo Shopping Center. The old folks like this place; it is like old time trading posts. My mother gets up and crawls out of the back of the pickup; she has been quiet during our ride. I follow her into the store. She looks at the many colored Pendleton shawls and stops at the counter to get a money order. We wander around and slowly there is the back of the store. Many are here; it is crowded. This is where our people pawn our hard goods—silver jewelry, turquoise, jaclo, concho belts. It is accepted as a way of life to do this. Every family has hard goods; they are hidden away like money in a bank. The family heirlooms, the treasure of each family. A question: Are you going to pawn something? It is not necessary; there is enough money for today. She walks away, looking at all the dead pawn in the cases there.

Looking, there is a bracelet made many years ago at a time when I was young. I had worked in a curio shop in Tucson. I was able to find some Morenci, a brilliant blue turquoise, hard and choice; it was good stone. I had thought for a long time about a design, using what is called No. 1 triangle wire, sterling silver. It became a large heavy bracelet favored by the old people. It was not an ordinary one for sale to tourists, but made for my children and their children. I had brought it home and showed it to my father. He put it on and wore it around the house all day. "Let me take care of it for you son; when you want it back just tell me and it will be yours." So it was left. When he passed away it remained at home.

There it was in the case. There were many there, those dead pawn. Where is the counter person? An old man comes. "That bracelet, is it really dead?" "Oh yes, it is, do you want to look at it?" My hands held it. There is the mark, my initials, the scratch from dropping it while polished, the edges softened by my father's wearing it on town day for many years. "Can this be redeemed?" The old man changed his smile.

"No, it's too late, but you can buy it back." Turning it over, there is a price, more than can be afforded. The price is too high; it goes back in the case.

When we got home that evening after a long day, I asked my mother why. She looked at me and said, "While you were away, things have been tough, your brother needed help. I gave it to him to get money. It seems that there was never enough to pay the interest, so now it is gone."

"What about him?" I asked. She told me he was having trouble with a job; the party life and drinking in Albuquerque at the Blue Spruce, Caravan East and Midnight Rodeo had taken its toll. She said, "What am I to do? If you need help, I must try." "What about the rest of the hard goods?" She wouldn't look at me. She quietly said, "They are gone too."

Somewhere they are, in some store, in some closet, in some drawer, these things that are no longer ours. They have been sold, but the value is not in the material, but the cost of a mother caring for a lost child. I wanted to get angry, to shout, to yell, but there was nothing to say. I told her it will be OK. "I am a silversmith, Mom, I can make more."

Oh, the price of caring and foolish children.—*John Rustywire*

NO, YOU CAN'T HAVE MY FIREWOOD

I first spotted her in the Humanities Council's speakers' directory. Her photo was one of the most offensive clichés of a Native American that I had seen this side of the sixties. I scanned her bio and cringed. Her "specialty" was Native American stories. The costume clichés, the stories of preference…the next step was inevitable…she would make the mental transition into being a Native American.

Within a year, she began to appear on agendas where I also appeared. Her tribal affiliation was different each time. The host administrators confessed an inability to judge the quality or veracity of her stories, but some insisted that she had used my name. She was scheduled to speak at the opening of "Sisters of the Great Lakes," an exhibition of artwork by twenty-one Native women from seven states and Canada, all of us hand-picked by our tribal elders and leaders. *Why didn't you contact one of us to do this*, I asked. She was in the directory; she was cheap, someone said. Oh yeah, they also work for less than minimum wage, her kind, because they will do anything to build up their "resumés" as Indians.

(My anger extends beyond the Wannabe Indian, to the administrator who finds it acceptable to hire a presumed Indian at such a low wage. At what point do I stop being stunned by the number of people who think that, because many Native people have lived at an economic level below that of the rest of America, that we must be used to it, that it is all right to offer us less than they themselves need to live on? When do I stop being amazed at the administrators who call me, believing that their non-profit status entitles them to offer me less than minimum wage? When do I stop being surprised that major foundations keep approving large fine arts grants for Native American projects that do not provide for paying the artists?)

If I put it to the museums and state parks that it was to be either this imposter or me, I'd lose the work. I needed the work. I needed the work at a decent wage. The volume of joint engagements built up in a few short weeks. Finally, she was scheduled to present with several of us at the Museum of Ojibwa Culture. It became a necessity for all of us that I intercede. She'd be eaten alive if she showed up to present with a dozen Indians. I left my number on her answering machine. The response was immediate.

"So, Barbara, tell me about yourself. What tribe are you?"

"I'm Ojibwe." (New tribe this week.) Yes, she knew me, and she was sucking up.

She spewed dangerous, damaging clichés with every breath.

"I am not comfortable with what you are doing," I sighed.

"OK, I'm not Indian. I'm Dutch. I have blond hair and blue eyes, too. So what?" *Spew, spew, spew.* "Do you want to know why I do this?"

"No." (I am not your friend.)

"The spirits have spoken to *me*. They chose *me* to do this, because you people have thrown your culture away!"

"Only you can know who you really are. I'm hanging up the phone now, Barbara."

"If you have a problem with what I do, go talk to *Boozhoo*."

"*Gesundheit*." I didn't tell her that it was just a suffix. I didn't want to give her that much cultural information.

Canceling her speaking engagements with a few choice quotes was pretty easy work—except for the museum that was exhibiting "Sisters of the Great Lakes." The director of one of the largest art museums in the state was afraid of being sued by Barbara if she broke the contract. It didn't matter that Barbara had misrepresented herself when she signed the contract. She didn't seem too worried about offending the Native population of the state, encouraging damaging stereotypes, or any moral obligation to hire a real Indian at a professional wage. The latter is an important issue, since Native women have the highest unemployment rate in the state. Barbara, on the other hand, has had wider options.

I did not become a Native storyteller and artist because I wanted to. (The Native part was not optional, although I secretly wanted to be like Doris Day as a child.) I did everything I was told to do. I went to college in the seventies, because I was told that that was what good Indian young people should do. There was basically something wrong with us and the way that we lived, and we should work hard and come back and educate and help our people. OK, so I got a scholarship to a high prestige private college, graduated with honors, went on to graduate school, got a 3.97 grade point average, and accumulated a pile of references big enough to choke a horse. Gee…nobody told me they weren't going to hire me, because I was colored… Seems they could have saved me considerable time and effort…

So, I fell back on skills I had learned in childhood and youth from other Indians. I began telling and illustrating traditional Woodland Indian stories and making baskets out of sweetgrass and porcupine quills. I got pretty good at it. Still, I am aware that the people at the institutions that hire me to do cultural presentations make far more in wages and benefits than I do, even though my credentials match or exceed theirs. Minority employment in educational institutions in northwest lower Michigan still tends to run pretty close to zero percent.

One summer, while on tour for the state Humanities Council (to their credit, at a very respectable wage), I noticed two middle-aged women writing down almost everything I said. Without losing too much momentum, in front of a rather large family audience, I indicated that this made me uncomfortable. One woman stopped immediately and later told me that she was from the host facility, taking notes for their newsletter and records. The other woman stopped briefly, then wrote frantically each time I looked away. I asked her to stop three times, each time interrupting the presentation and surprising the audience.

Finally, I stopped telling stories and family anecdotes about my life on the island where my grandmother used to live. I held up a large sweetgrass basket with a base of porcupine quillwork that I had made. I described the design and the technique—something she couldn't replicate. I moved about the room, leaning in, letting people look at the basket close up. It was much too valuable to pass around. When I got to the near back of the room, I leaned way, way across her picnic table, still smiling, and hissed, "If you don't stop, Barbara, I'll throw you out in front of everybody."

"I'm just trying to learn," she insisted. Hmmm…must have been expecting a pop quiz. I regret not having taken her notebook away from her.

During the same week, I spied a poster featuring three storytellers from the tour, all three of us specializing in Native American stories. There was only one Indian on the poster—me.

At the end of my tour, I approached the subject with the program supervisor. I suggested that perhaps the Humanities Council could set a precedent by encouraging the offending parties to draw from other areas of their vast repertoires, and leave the Indian storytelling to the Indians. I even provided the names of a few underemployed Native presenters. Silly me. One of the storytellers had secretly confessed to the director that she had recently discovered that she was part Native, and she had been "given" these stories to tell by several Indian "elders."

(Sigh.) Wishful new-found DNA is not the same as being followed around department stores by security guards. Any assumption that we go around "giving" our cultural material to non-Indian authors, musicians and storytellers is a stereotype. It ranks right up there with Tonto. We even have a term for the act of reinterpreting our stories and art forms for profit. It is called "cultural appropriation." It is more than amoral. It promotes stereotypes about Indians, and it causes financial damage to Native people.

Retreat! Retreat!

My island home is an inholding in the Lake Superior Provincial Park. I have no neighbors for thirty miles in either direction up and down the coast. I can bring my work there with me. I can find the solitude and inspiration to write and paint. I can find fresh spruce roots I need for my basketwork. The caribou come as close as ten feet from my window. I have no mail, no phone, no utilities. I haul in propane for the forty-year-old refrigerator. I heat with wood. I bathe and launder in the chilly northern lake. I work hard on the mainland, counting the weeks, days, and then the hours, until I am back here, in the shadow of my ancestors….It is the only place on Earth that I don't feel like an Indian. I just feel like me.

We had been on the island only a few days. Getting up to refill his cup from the percolator, my husband noticed a canoe on the beach a hundred feet from the house. He wasn't ready to talk to strangers yet. I volunteered. I politely pointed out that this particular island was not part of the park. I tend to smile through these encounters. An American couple, on vacation in Canada, they were aware that the island was not part of the park, and had been coming to it for years.

"The park really wanted it, you know," the husband insisted, indignant that it was not part of the park.

"Uncle Dick offered it to the park. They turned it down. I bought it. I get the tax bill." I defended myself for being the last Indian within twenty miles of Indian Harbor.

"I suppose you own this firewood, too!" snarled the red-headed woman, looking up for the first time from her task of loading cut and seasoned firewood into the canoe from the beach. Her face puckered with contempt.

"Well, no, I mean, I guess it washed up here." I do not think well on my feet. I watched her fill the canoe with my firewood. My birch. The only hardwood on my island. Hand cut with a bow saw, short, to fit in the wood box of my cast iron cook stove. "Borrowed" by kayakers on vacation who'd had a beach fire at my doorstep while I was on the mainland working or at the grocery store (a two-day trip). It was carelessly left on the beach unburned, to wash away in a storm, to be scattered along the coast of the big island, for me to gather by hand and haul home to dry. Now it was her firewood. Say, could I stay at her nice, warm house sometime, while on tour, save the cost and effort of finding a motel room? Did she know that I was not on vacation, that this was a way of life; and even if it was my vacation, did she expect me to spend it cutting firewood for her? Did she know that I would have to cut more wood to replace it, instead of putting in much-needed hours at my job, my work, my livelihood? Did she know that I wanted her job, her medical and dental benefits, her retirement plan, her financial security…even at the expense of leaving this paradise? Did she care?

Wherever you are, Puckerface, you can't have my firewood! That's one story Barbara will never be able to tell. Maybe I should just give away the whole experience to that woman who wants to tell Indian stories so badly for the Humanities Council.

By the way, there's a quiz at the end: What color are a caribou's eyelashes?—*Lois Beardslee*

WELCOME HOME, OUR RELATIVE

Last Friday, we laid our relative, Ishi, to rest. It was a small, private ceremony, and we conducted it in a good way. The old people had talked about opening up the ceremony to the community, because that is the way for people to pay respect, people who have feeling for him; we didn't want to deny them that. But the old people agreed, this time, to let the young people decide, and the young people felt it was best for the ceremony to be private, to prevent a disruption of the ceremony by the media

When it was discovered that the Smithsonian had Ishi's brain in a jar, worldwide media descended on us. They called our leaders at home at all hours of the day and night with no regard for their wishes or their privacy. TV, radio, print media, even authors and professors—all wanted exclusive stories, wanted a piece of us, right here, right now. I cannot find the words to describe how rude they were; the assault was overwhelming.

So the young people took on the awesome responsibility of deciding what to do. Some questions: How do we handle this? If the ceremony is private, how private? Do we ask the whole community to attend, or just some elders and community representatives? If the ceremony is public, how public? Do we invite the media? If not, how do we keep them out? If everyone knows where Ishi is buried, how do we protect him? Will grave robbers return and desecrate this sacred ground? Will Ishi's final resting place become a tourist trap?

The young people decided that, even now, we still have to protect our relative, Ishi. Even now, he can be exploited and humiliated. So the elders supported that decision, because they wanted him to have peace, and we asked a young woman and a young man from each tribe to be part of the ceremony so that they could pass it on. We told them never to forget where our relative is buried and to share his story with future generations.

My words cannot communicate to you how we felt last Friday, sending off our relative, Ishi, in this good way. We opened ourselves up to him, to the process. We cried for him and for our people. We sang for him and for our people. It was an indescribable feeling to know that we did something so right that stemmed from something so wrong.

Volumes have been written and taught about our relative, Ishi. Every fourth grader in California has been taught that he was the last "wild Indian" in California, that he was the "last Yahi." That he was rescued by anthropologists and that he became a "living specimen," housed in a museum for the rest of his life. It was obscene, dishonorable, how the white people treated our relative, Ishi, what they wrote about him, and that they never acknowledged him as a kind, generous human being. And I am astounded at what they continue to teach about him.

So when we received the ashes of our relative, Ishi, our elders determined the burial site and the process for his burial. We gathered many medicines. It was a kind of feeling, a great moment, that I wanted to share, but we shared it with nature only, and with our focus, it became complete. Our old people helped to keep us focused, to remember where our relative came from, to acknowledge the value of the mountains, to feel all of these feelings and then to let him go.

And now, a part of us can rest, to know that bringing our relative, Ishi, home is the beginning of a healing, to bring our scattered community back together. It was a tragedy that brought us together to do things in a good way.

Welcome home, our relative. You have been sung for properly, you have been cried for in a good way. Our old people said you have been taken care of and it's done. We welcome you home.—*Radley Davis*

REVIEWS: BOOKS ABOUT "ISHI"

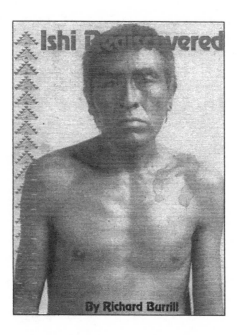

Burrill, Richard, *Ishi: America's Last Stone Age Indian.* Anthro Company (1990). 48 pages, b/w photos, grades 5-up; Yahi/Yana

Burrill, Richard, *Ishi Rediscovered.* Anthro Company (2001) 227 pages, b/w photographs, grades 5-up; Yahi/Yana

Freeman, James A., *Ishi's Journey, from the Center to the Edge of the World: A Historical Novel about the Last Wild Indian in North America.* Naturegraph (1992). 224 pages, grades 7-up; Yahi/Yana

Holcomb, L.D., *The Last Yahi: A Novel About Ishi.* Writer's Club Press, 2000. 255 pages, high school-up; Yahi/Yana

Petersen, David, *Ishi: The Last of His People.* Children's Press (1991). 31 pages, b/w photos, grades 3-4; Yahi/Yana

As every fourth grader in California knows, and as Richard Burrill writes in *Ishi Rediscovered*, "More words have been written about 'Ishi' than any other California Indian." Actually, more words have been written by white people and published by white people about Ishi than about any other California Indian. Could it be that writing about Ishi is safe? Ishi is gone. The Yahi are gone. All gone! There is nothing to be done here, no lives to save, no justice to fight for, no restitution to make, no soul-searching needed—nothing but exploring bits and pieces, traces of a life lived within the boundaries of white society.

The history of the Yana people and the experience of the man who came to be known as "Ishi" following the white invasion of California are indeed important to know and remember, and Ishi is due the respect and gratitude of any ancestor. But in remembering him, we should be mindful of the ongoing struggles of indigenous peoples worldwide, for survival, for culture and community, for the land. The encroachment of so-called "modern civilization" on traditional societies is as real today as it was for the Yana at the turn of the 20th Century.

But this is not the understanding readers will get from the books about Ishi I am reviewing here. What they will "get" is that the Yahi are quaint but extinct California Indians, that Ishi was "the last wild Indian," and that the tragedy that befell the Yana people was the inevitable result of "civilization."

These books rely heavily on Theodora Kroeber's book, *Ishi in Two Worlds: A Biography of the Last Wild Indian in North America.* And they perpetuate almost every stereotype there is about Indian peoples.

In *Ishi in Two Worlds*, Kroeber quotes her husband Alfred Kroeber in describing the five to seven individuals who comprised the last decades of the Yahi tribe, "...the smallest free nation in the world, which by an unexampled fortitude and stubbornness of character succeeded in holding out against the tide of civilization twenty-five years longer even than Geronimo's famous band of Apaches." T. Kroeber adds to this, "And for almost thirty-five years after the Sioux and their allies defeated Custer."

Neither attributed nor referenced to the Kroebers, here is how this passage appears in three of the books:

Burrill:

> They held out against civilization for forty years from 1870 until 1910. This devoted band remained completely hidden away, preserving an absolute independence. They were—without a doubt—the smallest group of free people in the world!

Freeman:

> They found a new hide-out in an abandoned grizzly bear's den…There their retreat and secret life of hiding took them twenty-five years further into the future than Geronimo's Apaches and thirty five years further than the Sioux nation that defeated Custer.

Petersen:

> Although they couldn't have known it, the workers were looking at what may have been the last Indian in North America living in the wild. Other Native Americans had long ago become part of American society. Even the famous Apache warrior Geronimo had surrendered some twenty-five years earlier.

These are prime examples of how muddled ethnocentric thinking by anthropologists such as Alfred Kroeber get diffused into the mainstream. By uncritically copying from Theodora Kroeber's text, these books perpetuate a false representation of the Yahi people in particular and of California Indians in general—and obfuscate the horror of the white invasion of California.

What could Alfred Kroeber possibly have been thinking when he described the Yahi as a "free" people? Their homeland had been stolen, their territory reduced to a strip of land fewer than two square miles in area. They no longer had the population to live their lives—exercise their culture and spirituality—in the way they had been taught. They could not even bear children. Their entire way of life changed. Where they lived, how they moved through their tiny territory, their limited options for sustenance were entirely predicated on remaining undetected by the white settlers surrounding them.

There was no self-determination in the Yahi "decision" to go into hiding, they were afraid of being murdered by white settlers just as scores of their relatives had been. We would never describe Anne Frank and her family and friends hiding from the Nazis as the will of a "free" people. They, like the Yahi, were trying to escape genocide. It is a disservice to young readers—and a lie as well—to describe the holocaust of the Yana people in such romanticized terms.

Even the title of Richard Burrill's first book is repulsive. That my ancestors continue to be described in terms of primitive, uncivilized, "Stone Age" savages irritates me to no end. At least my ancestors had the sense to recognize their instructions to live in harmony with the rest of creation and did not set out to colonize the whole world. And, someone ought to tell Burrill that the Stone Age ended some time before 1900.

Burrill trivializes the incident that led to the final destruction of the small group of Yahi. What happened is this: A group of white men, surveyors, their guides and companions, invaded a tiny village and stole all the people's material possessions—their food supplies, tools, weapons, garments and blankets—leaving only the shelters and an elderly woman behind. The invasion and theft was the direct cause of the deaths of three of the four remaining Yahi. Here is how Burrill describes this incident:

> It is sad to think that all the artifacts and materials at Grizzly Bear's Hiding Place, taken in mere curiosity, meant the difference between survival and destruction to the poor Indians. It is certain that as a group they were never heard of afterwards, and all but Ishi lost their lives as a result of fatigue, hunger, and exposure resulting from having to leave their camp. Not one gift did the white men leave to prove friendly intentions.

"It is sad." Yes, it is sad, and it is murder too. Those men knew exactly what they were doing. Some of them said they stole everything the Yahi had in retaliation for the disappearance of livestock and goods from the white ranches in the area. They didn't leave tokens of "friendly intentions" because there were none. Even Merle Apperson, who is often portrayed as a bystander to the ransacking, is pictured in Burrill's book wearing a fur blanket that was part of the loot.

Some teachers might be tempted to use Burrill's book because it contains an "Examination (25 points)" in the back. Only those who want their students regurgitating useless factoids and dangerous stereotypes rather than expanding their cultural competence or using critical thinking skills ought to do so.

Ishi Rediscovered is *Ishi: America's Last Stone Age Indian* grown to 227 pages. This version, like Burrill's earlier title, is full of archival photos, newspaper articles, maps, drawings, pictures of artifacts, and many, many photos of Ishi. In this expanded format, Burrill rambles on incoherently:

> When people do not have books to learn from, they rely on other senses. Such earth people, to introduce another name, learn more from association and participation with others, as opposed to living in separation in "upscale gated communities," for instance, which is the growing trend nowadays.

But of all the things he's done, this might well be the worst: Without attribution or acknowledgement, he's lifted from Indian writing, from Ishi's own people. On August 21, 2000, a piece written by Radley Davis appeared in the *San Francisco Chronicle*. Entitled "A Fitting Welcome Home for Our Relative, Ishi," it ended with these words:

Welcome home, our relative. You have been sung for properly. You have been cried for in a good way. Our old people said you have been taken care of and it's done. We welcome you home.

This is what appears in Burrill's book:

Ishi's brain was joined with his other remains and fully repatriated in private Indian ceremony into the Ishi Wilderness. He was sung for properly. He was cried for in a good way.

For this author to appropriate the words one of the people who were at last able to bring Ishi home is just unforgivable.

David Petersen's book attempts to put Kroeber's work into children's terms. But instead of resolving the problems with Kroeber, Petersen compounds them. Right from the beginning: "It all began on the morning of August 29, 1911, near the little town of Oroville, in northern California." No, it didn't. Why is it that white authors seem to think a story starts when white people step into the picture? Before Petersen describes Yahi life before Ishi ventured into Oroville, he tells us, "Other Native Americans had long ago become part of American society." And there, in a nutshell, is what books of this genre are really about, getting the Indians out of the "wild" and the "wild" out of the Indians and bringing us into the scope—and in many cases under the microscope—of white "civilization."

I would like to ask Petersen what part of American society he thinks Indian peoples occupied in 1900. Petersen's history is neat, uncomplicated and easy, devoid of complex realities. Unfortunately, complex realities are what our Indian children try to make sense of everyday. Here's another book and another white person who lies to them.

Freeman's book takes the error of perspective to new lows, fictionalizing Theodora Kroeber's book—one incident at a time—and making a mockery of his subject while exposing his own ethnocentric bias.

"This imaginative recreation of Ishi's life," Freeman says,

moves beyond the known facts to restore the lost background and human dimensions that the last Yahi people undoubtedly experienced. I have retold Ishi's journey using the tools of a fiction writer because Ishi's journey needs a narrative frame in the way a play needs a theater in order to come alive.

No it doesn't. Ishi's story is alive because Ishi lived, and it is arrogant to assume that Ishi and the Yana people need to have an outsider telling their story to come alive or have their human dimensions restored.

Rather than adding to our understanding of the Yahi as a people or Ishi as a Yahi, this book perpetuates the most pervasive and offensive stereotypes of Indian people. I would never give this book to my children to read. That they might wonder, even for a moment, that the perversions described here might in any way resemble their relatives or ancestors is something I don't want to risk.

In once scene, Ishi (as a boy) goes to the lookout over Yuma Canyon, which he is forbidden to do until he becomes a man. He is doing this because, "It is time to see what we are hiding from, time to know our enemy, the Saldu." By this time in the group's hiding, Ishi had witnessed and nearly died in the Massacre at Kingsley Cave, an event in which most of his family and community were murdered by white men. Wouldn't he have known by that time why they were hiding, and who the enemy was?

By throwing in a few Yahi words while disregarding Yahi speech patterns and thought processes, Freeman makes his dialogue suffer from the same stilted, pseudo-spiritual white-itis that afflicts many books written by outsiders about Native peoples. He also makes the reader suffer.

Aiku tsub, the little bearcub boy grows to be a bear like his father Tetna. It is so, we must do something, but I am the majapa and I say what we are forced to do. We will give our lives to the butterfly god Jupka and the lizard god Kalysuna and hope Coyote guides us well. It is the way.

And

Let us go to the house of women, we must not keep this dawana secret from the marimi [women], for they must know what good or bad magic Coyote may bring us. Perhaps the young cousins may not have to walk the ancestors' star path east until long after the majapa goes.

And, and, and

It is in Coyote's paws. The Coyote god will decide what is to become of us.
Coyote has no more love for the people.
Coyote hurts his own chosen people while Jupka and Kaltsuna stand beside watching. I do not understand.

Me neither, but my guess is if Coyote hears all this, he's somewhere hacking up hairballs! Not only is this dialogue stupid, it suggests that the genocide of the Yahi was not a result of white incursion, but because the Yahi gods had abandoned and betrayed the people.

Minimizing the role of whites in the Yahi demise is a common theme for Freeman:

> For twelve years, the little Yahi nation had everything it needed in the Center of the World, and the only reminder of the whites was the twice-a-day whistle blast of the black creature far down in the great Daha Valley....The people lived this good life as it had been for centuries, but with more urgency now.

Which good life is he talking about? The one where most of your community has been murdered before your eyes, where you live in the middle of a bramble patch so no one can detect your home, where you walk so that you don't leave footprints, where you have no hope to grow up, marry, bear children, and die surrounded by generations of loving relatives? Is that the "good life" Freeman is referring to? And who would need a train whistle to remind you of the white invaders? Wouldn't the reality of your daily existence be reminder enough?

Freeman seems to be fascinated with the whole Indian secret name thing, probably because Ishi did not tell the anthropologists his name. Although Freeman freely uses the name "Ishi" even before he is found by the whites, he can't seem to figure out what to call the other young man who was part of the group: "Ishi's boy cousin," "Ishi's boy cousin, now a man," "his man cousin, now a brother to him," "cousin," "cousin-brother," "cousin-as-a-brother," "my brother."

Alfred Kroeber learned from Ishi that the small group of Yahi survivors included a woman of about Ishi's age. While Ishi and the woman did not share the same parents, their relationship was that of brother and sister because of their kinship ties. Ishi could not marry her or have children with her, because such a relationship would have been incestuous. Yet Freeman manufactures a sexualized relationship between Ishi and his relative that seems also to have the support of at least some other members of the group.

> Tushi and Ishi might have married except for Yahi incest taboos....The majapa wished now that Tushi, who had blossomed into a striking woman, could have a child with Ishi....New to womanhood, she was the Yahi's only hope, yet only Ishi's boy cousin could rightfully marry Tushi.

To portray Ishi and his close relative this way negates their true relationship and deprives the reader of understanding them. Ishi was a moral and ethical person. He would not even have thought about marrying someone as close as a sister.

Later, a fire comes close to the people's tiny homeland,

threatening to destroy their material goods, sources of sustenance and concealment as well. In the midst of all this, Ishi's relative tries to seduce him. A storm arises and thunder and lighting hit around them. Ishi resists the advances of his relative and "neither of the two close ones ever spoke of their storm again."

Unfortunately, Freeman does not follow the example of his characters, bringing up this relationship over and over again.

This. Did. Not. Happen. This would not have happened. Ishi and his relative did not and would not have jeopardized their small group for a sexual dalliance. This is just disturbing and offensive.

Later "Tushi" returns to Ishi in a vision (because everyone knows we are always having visions and conversations with the spirits of our dead relatives) to tell him that his family wants him to teach the white people the ways of the Yahi (because everything is always about the white people). Which is how he comes to show up in Oroville, come under the protection of the University of California scientists and into association with the young son of Ishi's doctor. The boy, according to Freeman's story, becomes Ishi's best friend, to whom Ishi confides his most intimate thoughts.

Ishi was well over fifty years old by time he came to live in San Francisco. If he had had a relationship with young Saxton Pope, it would have been the relationship a Yahi man would have with a young boy, not that of confidante and peer. What Freeman accomplishes is to make the story of Ishi all about white people, because it is white people in the form of young Saxton Pope and the anthropologists who become the repositories for Ishi's wisdom and experience. Yet these men didn't understand him, just as Freeman doesn't understand him now.

The foreword to *The Last Yahi* sums up the attitude of the author: "On August 29, 1922, the Stone Age came to a close when the last Stone Age man surrendered at a slaughterhouse in Oroville, California." Using the term "Stone Age" six times in five pages, Holcomb posits that by learning about Ishi's "religious mythological views, one takes a large step toward understanding the evolution of ideas from the distant past to the immediate present."

His assumption that the cosmologies of indigenous California cultures "evolved" to modern Euro-American culture is not only a false idea, it is a dangerous and racist one. It implies that even if the invasion never happened, modern California life would have eventually progressed into what it is today anyway. There is no recognition that many of our so-called "primitive" precontact cultures continue to exist today, that our cultures are still alive. As any living thing, our cultures have been changed by their surrounding world, and particularly by the pressures of white supremacy, so in many ways our Native cultures today are cultures of resistance. What evolved culturally in Europe was transplanted and continued to mutate once in the United States; it is a culture with a very different worldview and way of life than ours. And yet this erroneous, racist assumption seems to be the fuel that feeds the fires of this "Ishi fascination," that California indigenous cultures—all of them—ended with Ishi, and once you've read about one primitive culture you've read about them all.

From the very beginning of this novel, the writing is so stiff and awkward, the dialogue is so contrived, the characters go about their lives in such forced, artificial ways, and the physical and cultural details are so out of sync with Native sensibilities that I just couldn't get past the first chapter. It was just too painful.

While he was alive, Ishi maintained his cultural and personal integrity. He knew who he was, what was right and wrong and what it meant to be Yahi—what it meant to be a human being. When he died, the whites committed the ultimate violation to Ishi's person. They autopsied his body and removed his brain. This is not recounted in any of the "Ishi books." To the whites, Ishi was a human specimen to be studied, not a human person to be cherished. It was not enough that Ishi was perhaps their greatest teacher, that they became famous because of their relationship with him. They also mined his body in death and inhibited his passing to the spirit world. These authors of "Ishi books" do the same thing: in turning the human specimen into a literary specimen, they mine the life of an honorable, generous man, ignoring the lessons of his experience and the wisdom of the Yana people.—*Robette Dias*

Hinton, Leanne, *Ishi's Tale of Lizard*, illustrated by Susan L. Roth. Farrar, Straus, and Giroux (1992). Unpaginated, color illustrations; grades 1-3; Yahi/Yana

The major work of Leanne Hinton, a professor of linguistics at the University of California, has been to record California Indian languages and to decrease the rate of language loss in California Indian communities. This story that Professor Hinton worked on is a teaching story told in a style typical of California Indian peoples; instructions for proper behavior are taught through narratives involving animal protagonists. In this case it is Lizard—making arrows, gathering pine nuts, killing a bear, fighting his enemies—whose actions and adventures are brought to life on the written page. The story is strong and this written "telling" maintains the lyric quality of a told story.

"This story has no real beginning or end," says Hinton in the introduction. And the story of the story would have made an interesting children's volume. In the early 1900s, the man who came to be known as "Ishi" related his people's traditional stories—in his own language—to several anthropologists, who recorded them phonetically. In 1986, linguist Victor Golla initiated and received funding for a project led by Hinton to translate and analyze the stories that Ishi told. This was a project of many minds and many hearts. Selecting parts of the very long stories Ishi generously gave to the anthropologists, Hinton put them down here, developing a sort-of "children's version."

As much as I like what Hinton has done, this book could have been a lot more. I have always been confounded by the fact that "Indian" stories are generally relegated to "children's" books. Not that the stories do not have relevance for children, they do. Rather, I think this is a way in which traditional Indian literatures are marginalized and made irrelevant. The stories passed down through our oral traditions have many purposes: some are for teaching and for remembering, some are for healing, some are ceremonial, some are for entertainment—but they are, for the most part, not exclusively for children. They are for the whole community: adults, parents, young people and children. There is something for us all in our traditional stories.

Just as a story is told for the benefit of the whole community, the story does not "belong" to any one person. I find it hard to imagine that Ishi would have claimed this story for himself. So this is really a Yahi tale of Lizard. To call this *Ishi's Tale of Lizard* is just a marketing device to capitalize on Ishi's name recognition, which is certainly better known than the name of his people. Some may see this issue as hair-splitting, but I think it's an important point to note.

Another problem that some may see as unimportant surfaces in the first line of the introduction. "Once there was a child named Ishi." This is often what happens when Indian books are geared to children's markets; in this case, euphemisms are used to tell California history. There was never a child named "Ishi." Anthropologist A.L. Kroeber referred to him as "Ishi" when the "last living Yahi" was taken—as a living specimen—to the museum of the University of California in San Francisco. His real name died with his family and community, as he told Kroeber that the Yahi never spoke their own names out loud. We will never know what "Ishi" was called as a child.

Although subtle, what this device illustrates is how our history is distorted to make it more palatable to a white market. What the white settlers did to Ishi and his people fills several chapters of horrendous barbarism buried in California history. I can't even begin to imagine Ishi's childhood. Watching most of his people shot to death in a cave when he was three or four years old. Hiding with the last handful of Yahi survivors in a remote area of northern California. Navigating the world by jumping from rock to rock or walking through streams so as to leave no trace. Desperately stealing from settlers' cabins when food was scarce, knowing that capture meant sure death. By keeping Indian stories in the children's genre, the history of California Indian peoples can be told without the nasty parts.

Clearly this book was written for non-Indian children, and that is its disappointment As an Indian parent, I can tell my children the story of Ishi and his people that is documented elsewhere, but I can't share with them the sounds, patterns and rhythm of the Yahi language, the language in which Ishi told his people's stories. Leanne Hinton could have; she knows these things.

I would like to have seen the phonetic rendition of the words Ishi used, then a literal translation of the Yahi words to English and finally the interpretation. Karuk scholar Julian Lang did this in his book of Karuk stories, *Ararapíkva: Creation Stories of the People*. Not only a book of good Karuk storytelling, *Ararapíkva* gives insight into how fluent speakers think and communicate thought. This is the importance of language preservation—not simply to keep alive the sounds and words of a people, but to transmit the ways of thinking and values and relationships embedded in a people's language.

Ararapíkva is used as a text for university courses in Native American Studies and is a resource for people learning the Karuk language. My children and I read the stories and ponder the nuances of our traditional language. While *Ararapíkva* has something for everyone and is especially a gift to our community, *Ishi's Tale of Lizard* is a childrens' story. Period. Even though Yahi is not our traditional language, I want my children to know it is important to remember it, that all California Indian languages are important and unique and precious.

In *Ishi's Tale*, Susan L. Roth reprises the colored-paper collage style she has used in her other children's books. Her illustrations are unattractive and detract from the story. In many California Indian stories, the animals are sacred beings, possessing qualities of both their own animal natures and human nature as well. The animal beings are ancestors who came to the Earth to prepare for human beings and who taught the humans everything that was necessary to live. I would like to know how an indigenous California artist would have interpreted this indigenous Yahi story, with a sensibility of California not only as a physical landscape, but a spiritual and historical landscape as well.

Although I enjoyed the story, *Ishi's Tale of Lizard* raises issues of accountability. To whom are Leanne Hinton, Susan L. Roth and the publishers who disseminate their work accountable? Ultimately when dealing with issues of culture, accountability ought to be to the people for whom the culture is a living reality. The Yahi as a people are gone, but their relatives still live in the Pit River Nation.—*Robette Dias*

REVIEWS: BOOKS ABOUT THE CALIFORNIA MISSIONS

Nelson, Libby with Kari A. Cornell, *California Missions: Projects & Layouts*. Lerner (1998). 104 pages, color photos and b/w illustrations; grades 4-up
Neuerburg, Norman, Harry Knill and Nancy Conkle, *California Missions to Cut Out: Book 1*. Bellerophon (1995). Unpaginated, b/w illustrations; grades 4-up

These books, on the surface, celebrate architecture: catenary arches, Doric orders, Espadanas, gables, incolumnations and Ionic orders. We are introduced to buttresses masonry, adobe, facades. We are told which padres were in charge of construction, how earthquakes damaged bell towers, and where the choirs sat. We are given bits of correspondence between padres, the location and decoration of sacristy and baptistery. Nelson and Cornell give precise instructions for constructing sugar cube "adobe" and how to decide between a cardboard or foam coreboard mission—clearly an important point for the many California elementary students required to build their own model missions. We are even told by Neuerburg, Knill and Conkle—apparently without conscious irony—that the Santa Barbara Mission once had three statues representing Faith, Hope, and Charity, but (in parentheses) that the originals are now in a museum "minus Faith, which was lost during the Mexican era."

I hate to break it to these publishers and authors, but Faith isn't all we lost. It is impossible for me to look through these pages without the lines of Wendy Rose's poem "Excavation at Santa Barbara Mission" pounding through my head:

> They built the mission with dead Indians.
> They built the mission with dead Indians.
> They built the mission with dead Indians.
> They built the mission with dead Indians.

This is true. Oftentimes the dead bodies of Indians, too many to bury "properly" due to raging diseases or poor nutrition, were simply added to the dirt and masonry while missions were under construction or being repaired. They were buried in walls, in floors, and at Santa Barbara, their bones were even used to make a skull and crossbones over the entrance to the cemetery. There was no respect for Native burial customs, and certainly the padres slipped up there on the Catholic interments—probably rationalizing that, well, they were only neophytes, not fully Catholics yet.

Interestingly, both books are careful to point out that *Spain* started the missions; that the missions were *Spanish settlements*, and that Spain *controlled* and *claimed* "parts of the western United States." In other words, this is

someone else's history, someone else's shame (what little we admit), and someone else's guilt. Well, why does the state of California continue to romanticize and preserve this history, then? Are we doing the Spanish ego a favor, or is there something in it for the image of the United States? And the idea that Spain controlled land called "parts of the western United States" is doublespeak at its height: Spain conquered, controlled and subjugated Native lands, which were given up to Mexico, and which the U.S. later forced Mexico to give up to American control. How easily mention of any indigenous rights of Native Californians is avoided!

These two books do not mention that not only were the Indians actually used as construction materials, but that they did the difficult construction labor, as well as the painting, artwork and mosaic work that makes these missions such emblems of "our" heritage. The books never tell their readers that there are dead Indians in the walls, that Indians were forced converts, that Indians were enslaved at the hands of the priests and soldiers, and that the wonderful "mission era" succeeded in killing almost one million Native people in a very short period of time. *Projects & Layouts* has a one-page introduction that gives a token nod to injustice:

> [T]he padres forced [Indians] to stay and work at the missions without pay. The Indians not only built the missions but also farmed the surrounding land. Many Indians died from diseases carried by the missionaries...the Indians worked long hours and led very difficult lives.

Then the book tells us to "read the six books in Lerner's California Missions series" to find out more about "mission life" (a euphemism if I ever heard one). Of course, *Projects & Layouts* is self-contained; you don't need the other books to build a mission, which is the primary focus here for both publisher and audience.

It is possible, then, for a child to build his or her mission without ever knowing the true history of genocide that is behind it. And why build such a model in the first place? What educational goal can be found in the valorization of religious and racial intolerance? To build a model mission is to build a model of genocide. Would we condone a cutout book of Auschwitz? Of Dachau? Do we have our school children construct model plantations full of enslaved African people, the whipping block, the site of human auctions? In her poem "Easter Sunday" Maidu poet Janice Gould says, "This is California with its rich, false history...the dead, I know suddenly, are buried in the walls, among the arches, and beneath this well-tamped earth." These books illustrate that rich, false history of California, where we lost Faith, not to mention Memory and Truth.

My ancestors lie in the walls of the Santa Barbara Mission, sent to their graves without prayers, gifts, or respect. And you can buy *California Missions to Cut Out* in the gift shop, take it home, and construct a model of that mission with your own hands. Your children can learn to celebrate the productive mission era in school by recreating their own small tribute to colonization. As a blurb on the back cover of *Projects & Layouts* exults,

> At last! With this new series, California librarians, teachers, and students are very close to the ideal mission source we've been seeking for years.

It's not authentic, though. Indian bones not included.

—*Deborah A. Miranda*

Lerner Publications (1996), 80 pages, color photos, paintings, line drawings, hardcover, grades 4-5:
Abbink, Emily, *Missions of the Monterey Bay Area*
Behrens, June, *Missions of the Central Coast*
Brower, Pauline, *Missions of the Inland Valleys*
Lemke, Nancy, *Missions of the Southern Coast*
MacMillan, Dianne, *Missions of the Los Angeles Area*
White, Tekla N., *Missions of the San Francisco Bay Area*

Whenever I visit fourth- and fifth-graders in their classrooms—to show children that we did and do exist—children ask me what mission I live in and if I eat acorns, and they always want me to say something in my language. When I tell them that I don't live in a mission, I eat acorns only sometimes but mostly I eat food like they do, and that my language was deliberately taken away, they are disappointed. They rush to show me the drawings they've made of the missions, and tell me what they know. They want to please me, but I can only shake my head. Again, they are disappointed; but this time they want to know what else they haven't been told.

I talk with teachers, too. Sometimes they don't like what they are hearing. They're incredulous that they don't know the history that they think they know.

This series will do nothing to dispel the many stereotypes children have been learning, and are still learning, about us and that terrible part of our history, the "Mission Era." These six books cover all twenty-one of the California missions. It is clear that the writers were given a fill-in-the-blanks outline: Early Life Along the Coast, Missions of the (X) Area, Secularization of the Missions, The Missions in Modern Times. The jacket copy, glossaries, prefaces, introductions, and afterwords are identical, as are many of the illustrations, in the same places in each book. As well, whole paragraphs and even sections are virtually interchangeable.

It is also clear that the writers don't have any particular expertise in the subject they are writing about; what we have here are ill-chosen words by ill-informed authors, and a trivialization of the holocaust perpetrated against us.

I want to quote a rather long passage to illustrate the perspective in these books.

> Using these Indians as unpaid laborers was vital to the success of the mission system. The mission economy was based on agriculture—a way of life unfamiliar to local Indians, who mostly hunted game and gathered wild plants for food. Although some Indians willingly joined the missions, the Franciscans relied on various methods to convince or force other Native Americans to become part of the mission system....Forced to abandon their villages and to give up their age-old traditions, many Native Americans didn't adjust to mission life. In fact, most Indians died soon after entering the missions—mainly from European diseases that eventually killed thousands of Indians throughout California. Because hundreds of Indian laborers worked at each mission, most of the settlements thrived. The missions produced grapes, olives, wheat, cattle hides, cloth, soap, candles, and other goods. In fact, the missions successfully introduced to Alta California a variety of crops and livestock that still benefit present-day Californians.

Here is what non-Native fourth-graders are going to get out of this: The missionaries taught the Indians how to work. Many of them died. The missions produced a lot of stuff that still benefit us today. And here is what Native fourth-graders are going to get out of this: Our lives, our cultures, our languages, our beliefs were not worth as much as cattle and oranges.

In truth, we always had a way of life based on agriculture. We still have personal harvest areas that the owners/families plant and maintain. The plants are not nor were they ever "wild" to us. Agriculture was familiar to us; slavery was not.

Another example; this one is so infuriating that I could barely tolerate reading any further:

> Many Indians in and around the Los Angeles area have kept the name Chumash or now prefer to be known as Tongva.

I am Tongva. The Chumash have their own names and their own territory. There was overlap through marital exogamy, but the Los Angeles basin is not Chumash land. We were never called by the same name. This is just insulting.

What little is said about the spiritual beliefs of Native California peoples is disturbingly shallow. Throughout the books, the authors give us some bits of truth, and then take it away by minimizing our peoples' experiences and suffering.

> European diseases began to spread to the Indian villages. The local Native Americans, who had never before been exposed to smallpox and other types of sicknesses, had no natural resistance to the illnesses. Many Tongva, especially children, became sick and died.

This is true. Then, in the very next paragraph,

> The priests, believing they needed to save the souls of the Indian children, went to the villages and baptized babies. This ritual, in which water is poured over the head, welcomed the person into the religious community. Baptized youngsters who survived their illness then were forced to live at the mission. Parents of newly baptized children began to join San Gabriel Archangel as a way to keep their families together.

Using this language—"the priests believing" and "parents... began to join"—justifies kidnapping children and enslaving their parents. Imagine how a Tongva parent might have described this: "They dumped water on our children's heads, and then took them away. When we followed, to be close to our children, the priests made us slaves."

This language continues throughout the series: The Indians "helped" build the missions. Young girls "learned" to make soap and candles. Boys "helped" to look after the fields. The Indians received food, clothing, and shelter "in exchange for" their labor. Many Indians tried to escape the "lifestyle" at the missions. Over time, many Indians "lost touch" with their age-old customs.

The Franciscan priests thought they were doing the Indians a valuable service by teaching them to become Catholic. In fact, the padres believed that this was the greatest gift they could bring to the Native community. Because of these beliefs, the padres punished Indians who refused to work hard and to learn Spanish ways.

In fewer words: Yes, there were beatings, but the priests meant well.

I could continue with countless examples of a nod toward truth in one paragraph, followed by the same old sanitized Anglo history in the next.

On page 73 of *Missions of the Los Angeles Area*, there is one sentence that is most clear: "Many Native Americans view [the missions] not as monuments but as places that caused death and suffering for thousands of Indians." Yet the books, for the most part, excuse and minimize what the missionaries did to our peoples. They prettify genocide. They don't give us a place to mourn or to grieve or to tell our stories.

The problems of these books, taken one at a time, may seem small, but it is these nibblings at our pride that undermine the future of our Indian children. I am afraid that, because these books are supposedly attractive and easy to read, they will be used in many, many California classrooms.

I showed these books to my nieces, one a fourth grader and one a fifth grader. The girls didn't like the print size, the format, the condescending attitude, and the pan-Indian graphics. Violet said, "These books make it seem that the Natives were savages and thank goodness that the white man came and saved them." Her sister, Dock, said, "Can we stop now? These books are giving me a headache." My feelings, exactly.—*L. Frank*

Faber, Gail, and Michele Lasagna, Magpie Publications; grades 4-5:
Whispers along the Mission Trail (1986). 216 pages, color and b/w photos, b/w illustrations
Whispers from the First Californians: A Story of California's First People, illustrations by Lou Ann Styles and Gail Faber, (1980, 1994). 268 pages, color and b/w photos, b/w illustrations

Whispers along the Mission Trail is a proud, exultant celebration of the Doctrine of Discovery: finders keepers, and all that. The authors' note says: "Your explorations will begin with Columbus' journey to the New World in 1492, almost 500 years ago!" so we know that 500 years is truly ancient history, as far back as anyone can possibly go. And, too, the authors assure us that

[Y]ou will sail up the coast of California with Cabrillo, Vizcaino, and other famous explorers... you will explore with daring men...journey with the Spanish padres who dedicated their lives to the beautiful missions...

Oh, and by the way, we'll also meet the California Indians "who shared this golden land with others." Not to mention their golden bodies, of course.

I have never been a proponent of brainwashing, but this book illustrates the ideal way to convince young children in need of role models that to "explore" and "discover"—read *invade* and *steal*—is good, *even if the place you "explore" or "discover" has already been explored or discovered by its own indigenous peoples.* This book erases Native history or any idea that Native peoples lived prior to 1492 except as mindless creatures wandering the land, waiting for direction. The book also erases any notion that Indians still live in California, that many tribes are still struggling for federal recognition, or that "Indian" is a concept that exists outside of the missions. Many Indians in Northern California, for example, were *never* missionized; *their* hell was known as the Gold Rush. But that is not as easy to romanticize—no "beautiful" missions left behind.

Worst of all, this book actually valorizes theft by saying it wasn't theft at all—it was *sharing*! (So why is modern California so reluctant to *share* its golden land with Mexico? What's this border thing about?) Children are set up to identify with Columbus, Cabrillo, even astronauts Sally Ride and Kathryn Sullivan, as "explorers," and are told that *everyone* is an explorer. (Woe be to the child who is thinking, "But I don't want to take someone else's home; something must be wrong with me!") Children are assured, and almost threatened, "It is in everyone's heart to *search and find and know*!" (my italics) What child can deny she wants to know more about the world? Unfortunately, "search and find and know" are translated into greed and theft and appropriation when we use North American history as our prime example.

The visual construction of the book itself reinforces the message of the text. The (generic) Indians portrayed here do not look as if they deserve a whole continent of their own. The line drawings of Indians are unattractive, crude and lend themselves to multiple misinterpretations by children (for example, my son thought a drawing of an Indian rubbing medicine onto Father Serra's leg was a form of punishment, despite the fact that he could easily read the caption). Indians portrayed in this way have few, if any, facial expressions, and the body language conveys dullness and lack of intellect. The use of more skilled drawings by European artists at the time of colonization are concerned with emphasizing the most exotic and savage images of Indians—for example, a famous drawing on page 133 depicts tattoos, body paint and near nudity. The caption adds, "During the dance the Indians would take glowing coals from a fire and put them in their mouths." What is a young child to make of this except that Indians were from a primitive culture and insensitive to pain? The physical, mental and psychological preparation for such a ceremony is not necessarily something everyone should have access to, but knowing that there was such a system of preparation, and that it was too sacred to be shared, is information that would help children to place this picture into some kind of context. Using these pictures and information without providing any other contextual or cultural cues is irresponsible at best and racist at worst.

The use of models and dioramas to portray "typical" Indian houses, villages, or other scenes of daily life is yet another instance of European-created "others," doing what Europeans think they should be doing. Reminiscent of the ways museums display dinosaurs and "cavemen," the overall tone indicates that there are no real Indians left, and it is perfectly fine to manipulate their images and bodies into whatever positions and cultural oddities the museum curators desire. There exist, however, numerous photographs and Native-created depictions of such scenes that could have added reality to this book. Why were such materials not sought after?

Finally, there is the absence of contemporary California Indians, as well as no information about their current lifeways, accomplishments and legal battles. This amount of "traditional" material, reinforced so many times within the authority of a classroom setting, speaks "dead civilization" to the children absorbing the lesson.

It is only a matter of time before some Native parent or educator sues a California school district, citing the hundreds if not thousands of offensive references to Indians and descriptions of the missions as symbols of progress rather than of genocide. Public schools discuss slavery, the European Holocaust, and sexually transmitted diseases. But addressing the reality of racism in the history of California seems more difficult. As a California Indian, as a mother, as a writer, let me advise potential buyers or teachers: there is no excuse for such a textbook in the hands of children.

Here I go again: If *Whispers from the First Californians* is a revised edition, why do the authors still not have the correct population statistics? They give the familiar but outdated figure of 310,000 Indians yet again; this time, footnotes cite Sherburne F. Cook's article in *The Handbook of North American Indians, California*, 1978. This is a good time for Deborah's Lecture #101: *Sometimes what's written in books about Indians, especially California Indians is (gasp) wrong*. No! Even in such anthropological bibles as the *Handbook*? Yes. Even the *Handbook* can be flawed. This is why taking all one's data from a single source, or a small set of sources, can lead one's final product astray.

So let this figure serve as my example. As I have stated elsewhere, the current "official" number of Native peoples living in what is now called California was, pre-invasion, about one million. I found this out through two separate avenues: first, I asked myself, only 310,000? And I trusted my instincts: doesn't sound like enough, and it's an old figure that I'd seen everywhere; everyone citing from the same older sources. Then I *asked*, sending out queries to both Native folks and the academics who study Native population statistics. And I was given the most current figures, with new sources. This took me a total of two days, including the day I spent getting to a library to confirm the information myself. While I use this new figure here, I wouldn't be surprised to see it revised in the near future, and in fact will be watching for that; it's a responsibility that goes with the territory of information.

There are many, many pieces of information in the revision of *Whispers* that are outdated and incorrect. The authors showed inordinate dependence on a few non-Native, older materials, and books with titles like "THE Cahuilla," "THE Northern Maidu," "THE Pomo." The pretense that there is some way of *knowing* everything, every last detail, of Indian lives, souls, and histories, is a kind of disease that textbooks spread. This desire to see everything, to define, make sense of it, and organize it into units of food, crafts, hunting, dances, is nothing less than a desire to control and conquer. Perhaps the best thing that children can be taught about anything is the concept of *not knowing*, not needing to know, accepting change, and being comfortable with that level of discomfort. There are "facts" that change when more studying has been done; there are mysteries in the world that we cannot explain, and one of the simpler ones is the mystery of community or family. What makes the Pomo "THE Pomo"? What makes an Indian doctor real and not someone's fearful caricature? It's nothing that we can *know*, or fully understand. It may not be something we are able to write about, comment on, in definitive, contained ways.

That said, let me add that this revised edition has obviously been the target of great efforts on the part of the authors. There are far fewer offensive line drawings, many more current photos of Native people (identified by tribal affiliation rather than the generic "Indian" so frequent in the previous version), and a revised and longer section discussing the realities of Native life in the missions (though this often seems to slam the Spaniards, and much less effort is spent on the post-American rule injustices). What I don't see, other than a few short bios with

photos, is the real inclusion of Native Californians into this curriculum. Individual citizens of different tribes are brought in only to illustrate points about basketry, ecology, storytelling—a tokenizing that reduces their voices to, in fact, "whispers." Nowhere do I find the actual voices of Native scholars, anthropologists, poets, musicians, parents, grandparents or other leaders directing the scope of this text, or giving reasons why some areas may not be discussed without giving offense, or telling us why statistics are so hard to find for Native Californians, or discussing issues of federal recognition and the repatriation of Native belongings being held in museums. These are the issues that Native peoples are concerned with, are working toward, and which would most benefit the interaction between non-Indian schoolchildren and Indians. Does a non-Native child who "knows" how to make a tule skirt or acorn soup really gain a better idea of the difficulties involved in getting tribal land returned?

This continued emphasis on concrete, practical aspects of Indian lives—how to hunt, cook, weave, use plants and animals—has not changed in the newer edition. I'm not sure what the fascination is with these particular aspects. Is this how Americans would choose to have their own lives written about and studied? Let's see....

"Americans shop very carefully for their **groceries**. Using very sharp **scissors**, the female of the household first searches through **newspapers** and flyers for the **coupons** she knows her family needs. She keeps these coupons—printed on colorful pieces of **shiny paper**—in a special pouch called a **wallet** or **coupon file**, which sits on the upper handle of her **shopping cart**. The shopping cart, usually constructed of **stainless steel** with four black composite **wheels**, has a clever seat and **strap** installed, so that the female can carry her young children with her...."

My point is this: Would most people define their daily lives by these minute details? Are our souls and hearts, our families and hopes, confined to the obsessive reconstruction of anthropological data?

No, of course not. Most of us take care of the details of our lives—sometimes carefully, sometimes not—while we are thinking, loving, fearing, changing, hoping, hurting, learning, creating. Certainly, Native life was much different in many ways, pre-invasion, than it is now, and different still again from European-American lives. But the essentials of being human are very similar; and change and movement are and always have been a natural part of Native life. This book presents Indians as being frozen in time, doing the same grinding routines (pardon the pun) for thousands of years. To perpetuate the stereotype of "how Indians lived" as if that *is the most important information to be learned*, is wrong.

My recommendation: Look for Native-authored materials and speakers to construct a curriculum; don't use *Whispers*, no matter how convenient it may seem.

—Deborah A. Miranda

Faber, Gail, and Michele Lasagna, *Pasquala: The Story of a California Indian Girl*, illustrations by Gail Faber. Magpie Publications (1990). 95 pages, b/w illustrations; grades 4-5; Yokuts

The difficulty of reading *Pasquala*—part of the *Whispers* curriculum for California fourth-graders—makes me aware, once again, of the ways language can be manipulated to serve its master. In this case, the language used is what I call "colon-ese," the tongue of the colonizer. Below, I have provided quotes in colon-ese, and my own Native translations.

Colon-ese: "The story of Pasquala is considered a legend. Although there is no proof that this legend is true, a girl like Pasquala may have lived and the events that happened to her in this story could have actually taken place." (from the introduction)

Translation: Writers have the authority to make up anything they like, including a person of a completely different, but actual, culture in which the writers have never lived. They then have permission to manipulate the character's action to depict historical facts about that actual culture in ways that are outright lies. These lies include the idea that indigenous resistance to colonization was wrong, that resistance was based not on injustice and the violation of human rights, but on primitive emotions and inflexible beliefs, and that the best thing an indigenous girl—symbol of her people's fertility and future—could do was become a martyr in the best Christian tradition (preferably while in the process of saving the colonizer's skin, simultaneously sacrificing the lives of her closest living relatives).

Colon-ese: "Before the coming of Europeans, California was the home of 150,000 Indians!"

Translation: (1) Colonization wasn't violent, wasn't theft, wasn't bad—Europeans just sort of "came." The passive nature of this statement denies the violent invasion of a homeland, and the painful deaths of thousands of human beings at the hands of Europeans as a direct consequence of that invasion. (2) Population, when it comes to pre-invasion Indians, is really unimportant. The authors of this book, published in 1990 and bearing the stamp of a California State Approved Textbook, *did not bother to research the most basic, and first, fact in the book.* I did. A Native pre-invasion population of over one million human beings is now accepted as a more realistic figure, and was indeed available as early as 1979, when Jack Norton (Hupa, Yurok, and Cherokee) used the figure, with proper citations, in his book, *Genocide in Northwestern California*. This same figure is accepted in academic circles, given in such reliable texts as *Ethnology of the Alta California Indians*, edited by Lowell Bean and Sylvia Brakke Vane. But why insist on correct figures? One answer: respect. The unjust deaths of almost one million people should not be so conveniently forgotten or ignored, particularly by those who assert to be telling the truth to children. (3) Let's not talk about the population of California Indians after the "coming of the Europeans"! Bean and Vane estimate between 10,000 and 20,000 Indians—total—survived the missions, secularization, and the Gold Rush. A one- to two-percent survival rate, at best. (4) "California *was* the home…"? California is *still* the home of thousands of Native Californians and mixed-blood people, as well as many thousands more from other parts of the United States. Look around closely. There could be one nearby.

Colon-ese: "Each tribe spoke…" "Can you imagine 50 different dialects spoken in an area 350 miles long and 75 miles wide?" "Many Yokuts tribes lived…" "With their tule boats, the Southern Valley Yokuts used the rivers…" "…a way of life that will always be a part of the whispers of California…"

Translation: Indian languages are dead. (Indians are dead.) (Indians aren't important factors in this country's history/politics/future.) Anyway, they were a Tower of Babel disaster, what do you expect? Tribes no longer live in California. Indians "used" the land, i.e., had a purely functional relationship, not a spiritual connection, with the land. Indians will always be a part of our wonderful California heritage, kind of like the dinosaurs in La Brea Tar Pits. Not anything you should worry about or have any moral attitudes about now.

Colon-ese: The Plot. A young Yokuts Indian girl lives a *traditional* life with her people. Her days consist of gathering and preparing food, interspersed with legends (pity her, poor thing: no religious training, no deeper moral life, no literacy, no *real* music, no *culture*!) After a trip to the ocean, Pasquala eats something that disagrees with her (those Indians didn't know about Red Tide) and becomes ill. Her parents take her to a nearby mission where the padre there "cures" her. In time, the family accepts baptism, Spanish names, and roles as neophytes (new Catholics-in-training). Their new names are José, María, and Pasquala. The father becomes ill and dies, but first tells his wife and daughter they should go home, which they do. The tribe shuns the two survivors, for reasons that are never defined other than the "shame" of having been at the mission. The girl and her mother are worked "like stones in a basket" and then put aside; in other words, they are no longer true citizens of the tribe. The uncle is cruel and unforgiving toward his sister-in-law and niece. There is no going back. Pasquala is hurt by the tribe's coldness; when she overhears plans to attack the mission where she once lived, she decides to run away back to the mission to warn the padre. When she has accomplished this task, the padre tells her that she has earned her name. Knowing that the mission has had time to defend itself, Pasquala dies because the trip was "too much" for her. Her spirit passes on to the "here-after" complete with owl hoots (everybody knows that when Indians die, an owl hoots).

Translation: The Plot. Indians were naturally cruel and simplistic in their relationships with one another. Almost all Indian men are weak in some way (the father is a coward, ashamed of living at the mission, eventually dies miserably; the uncle at home is misogynistic, unforgiving and cruel), and the complex supportive familial connections among women tribal citizens—grandmothers, aunties, sisters, cousins—is non-existent. Gentle padres know best how to handle the easily/eagerly-conquered Indians, and how to run their lives. The transition from a free lifestyle to a missionized lifestyle was easy; there was no shortage of food, no rapes, no beatings, no enforcement of the Spanish language, no European-spread diseases, no coerced baptism. Right. There is no such thing as an Indian religion: "legends" are told in simplistic Tonto-speak style, are not connected to a deeply spiritual and complex religion, but to superstition and hearsay (and are derived from highly edited and stylized non-Indian anthropological sources). There were no prohibitions on sharing sacred knowledge (implication: not a real belief system, but primitive behaviors easily explained). The "Rattlesnake Doctor" is an ethnological specimen, completely disconnected from his religious role, and the tribe participates in almost zombie-like fashion in the doctor's ceremony (mindless animals without an individual soul or mind). Through the Mission Experience, Pasquala is given the gifts of medicine, music, religion, cultivated food, the knowledge to weave civilized wool instead of pagan baskets, and, in the grand finale, thanks to her new moral training, Pasquala is given a *soul*—because she is willing to give it up for the good of the missions.

Colon-ese: "[The padre] chose the name José for my father and the name María for my mother. He gave me the name of Pasquala, and told me it meant 'one who loves and helps others.'"

Translation: Indians, like animals, may be named by their masters. José and María are symbolic names for Joseph and Mary, Christ's earthly parents. For a better translation of "Pasquala," let's look at the source of her name. Pasquala is a derivation of "paschal," as in "paschal lamb." My dictionary defines paschal lamb as "1. Among the ancient Hebrews, the lamb slain and eaten at the Passover. 2. Any of the symbolic representations of Jesus." Pasquala, then, is a painfully obvious symbolic "Jesus," a sacrificial lamb who dies for the sins of her people. In this case, the sin is being Indian.

This is a book that should not be allowed into classrooms except for adults, as an example of the insidious nature of colonization—*Deborah A. Miranda*

(I am grateful to Phil Zastrow and Buffy Mitchell at Humboldt State University's Indian Teacher and Educational Personnel Program, and Alan Levanthal of San Jose State University, for verifying that the pre-invasion population information was available at the time *Pasquala* was published.)

REVIEWS: BOOKS ABOUT THE NAVAJO LONG WALK

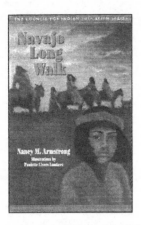

Armstrong, Nancy M., *Navajo Long Walk*, illustrated by Paulette Livers Lambert. Roberts Rinehart/Council for Indian Education (1994). 120 pages, b/w illustrations; grades 4-6; Diné (Navajo)

In 1863-64, to end Diné resistance to white intrusion, the U.S. Cavalry launched a scorched-earth offensive against Dinétah. From the Continental Divide to the Colorado River, they destroyed fields, orchards, hogans, and livestock. The six-month sweep, which thoroughly disrupted the Diné way of life, resulted in the capture of some 8,000 Diné, who were marched to a barren concentration camp called Bosque Redondo. The survivors of this "Long Walk" were confined there for about four years. Thousands fled further west. In 1868, the imprisoned Diné were finally allowed to go back to a portion of their ancestral lands, and given two sheep per person with which to support themselves and reconstruct their nation's economic base.

Here is Armstrong's take on all this, from the introduction:

> In the early 1860's, the United States government was under pressure from ranchers, farmers and other Indian tribes in Arizona and New Mexico to put a stop to raiding by the Navajos.... The army decided they must be moved to a reservation and assimilated into the American way of life.

Navajo Long Walk, a story of this forced march and imprisonment, is said to be "told through the eyes of Kee, a Navajo boy, and his family." But it is really told through the eyes of the author, who infuses it with her cultural outsider's worldview.

The story: Young boy and his family thrown into crisis, boy hates white soldiers, boy helps his family survive in a harsh land, boy finds out that soldiers are really kind, boy learns English and makes friends with soldier's son and learns that white people aren't so bad after all, boy's family returns to land and is reunited, boy and family are happy

once more. "Ultimately," according to the book jacket,

> Kee realizes the frailty of his people in the presence of the white soldiers and that to survive, they must find a way to get along with the white man.

Besides Kee and Hasba, the names of the characters—Wise One (grandma), Gentle Woman (mom), and Strong One (dad)—are merely a convention to help young readers remember who is who. Also, the people's self-name is Diné, not Navajo, and their ancestral land is Dinétah, not Navajoland. In English, the characters would probably have just referred to themselves as "the people."

In a matriarchal society such as the Diné, Grandma would be the head of the family, and as such, she would call the shots. She would probably tell stories to keep courage alive. But here, as Kee is constantly referred to a "the man of the family," Grandma's only role seems to be to preach and nag and philosophize about giving peace a chance:

> Hate can do nothing but hurt the one who hates.... For many moons I have been saying this stealing of animals and people from other tribes and from white people must come to an end. There can be no happiness until people learn to live in peace with one another.

And mom chimes in, too:

> My son, such a feeling can bring only unhappiness. We must keep songs of beauty and bravery in our hearts. Even though the time seems so very long, we must believe our misery will come to an end.

Throughout the book, Kee and his little sister mouth off at Mom and Grandma, grumble, complain, and are just plain disagreeable. In traditional Diné society, this kind of behavior would not be tolerated, especially in times of crisis. At the end, Kee is so happy that he begins to sing the Blessingway "chant." This is ridiculous. The Blessingway is a ceremony, conducted by a medicine man—and children do not sing it.

Armstrong has done what many non-Native authors of children's literature about Indians do: taken a very painful part of history, a story that is still told today by elders to their grandchildren, and said, "oh, well, *that* happened, and it was really terrible, but the soldiers weren't all bad, and it was really the Indians' fault anyway, and now everything is fine."

In truth, the Long Walk to Bosque Redondo was a death march, and the soldiers were not good people. They raped, they murdered, they laid waste to the land, they considered the people less than garbage, and tried to starve them into submission. And, in many cases, did. But, regarding the "frailty" of the Diné, Armstrong might have done well to visit the Four Corners area where, between the sacred mountains, the Diné Nation, led by their elders, continues to resist the U.S. government and Peabody Coal and anybody else who dares tell them that the land isn't theirs.—*Beverly Slapin*

Bruchac, Joseph (Abenaki) and Shonto Begay (Diné), *Navajo Long Walk*, illustrated by Shonto Begay. National Geographic Society (2002). 47 pages, color paintings; grades 4-up; Diné (Navajo)

By the 19th Century the Europeans who came to this land had already claimed it for their own without regard for the original inhabitants. They saw its richness—the agricultural bounty, the great forests for their timber, the mineral wealth—and they wanted it all for themselves. Already they had caused great dislocation for the Indian Nations. By the 1800s the watchword for dealing with the Native population was "Indian Removal." Thus, the uprooting of whole peoples and their relocation to some of the most inhospitable places that could be found.

In this book, Bruchac and Begay have given us the Diné story. Shonto Begay's paintings come out of the deep pain of his own history. His words about them, although brief, convey the tragedy of the near-destruction of a way of life, a way of being in the world, "in the holy space within the four sacred mountains," that is older than we can know. Bruchac's text begins with the winter day in 1864 when Kit Carson arrived in Canyon de Chelly with a contingent of soldiers and Ute Indians to drive the people out. They were forced to flee, leaving their flocks of sheep and goats behind them. Their hogans with stores for the winter were burned. Their carefully cultivated peach trees were chopped down.

From there, Bruchac goes back to a history leading up to the time of Removal, to the Spanish who attacked for slaves, to the Americans with their soldiers, their "treaties" with promises that they had no intention of keeping, general chicanery, treachery, and outright murder. In the 1860s, one General James H. Carleton was appointed military commander of the New Mexico Territory. His decision to remove all the Diné from their land led to one of the worst tragedies of Native-white relations: the Navajo Long Walk to Bosque Redondo, a distance of close to 500 miles. Bruchac chronicles this nightmare journey, the events preceding it and its aftermath in a straightforward fashion, letting the facts speak for themselves.

Nobody knows for sure how many people died, "[p]erhaps

one in every ten of the people who sent out on that trip died along the way, their frozen bodies marking the trail."

The place that they went to was unfit for human habitation. General Carleton must surely have been insane, because he was able to say, of the Bosque Redondo, that it was "the best pastoral region between the oceans. Within ten years, the Navajos would be the happiest and most delightfully located pueblo of Indians in New Mexico, perhaps in the United States."

The last chapters tell how, due to the rising tide of public indignation and their own determination, the people got to go home. And "on June 18, 1868, a column of Navajos ten miles long set out"—for home.

The combination of Bruchac's text and Begay's beautiful and terrible paintings are a chronicle for young people of a shameful episode in United States history. The last painting of the people celebrating their impending freedom is an epiphany; a joyful contrast to the nearly unbearable beauty of those that came before.—*Doris Seale*

O'Dell, Scott, *Sing Down the Moon*. Houghton Mifflin (1970). 137 pages; grades 5-7; Diné (Navajo)

Scott O'Dell made a career out of writing young adult historical novels about "minorities." He received both popular and critical acclaim: the Newbery Honor in this case, Jugendbuchpreis, twice, and the Hans Christian Anderson Author Medal, among others. His work has been praised for its sensitivity and meticulous accuracy.[1] He is said to have given "voice to the oppressed, to those who lost their lands and their cultures."[2]

There are few writers able to put themselves, believably, into the heart and mind of a culture not their own. Scott O'Dell was not one of them; yet this book, continuously in print for thirty-four years, can be found in virtually every fifth-grade classroom, every elementary school library.

In *Sing Down the Moon*, O'Dell tells the story of the 1864 Navajo forced march—the Navajo Long Walk—to Bosque Redondo. Like most well-written first-person narratives, this book is exciting. I have seen children really love it. However, O'Dell infuses the story with his own European values as "universal" and Diné values as "other." In other words, he portrays Diné people as weird. Young readers who are not Native will readily identify with the protagonist; Diné readers will not.

It is morning, after a long-awaited rain. Bright Morning, the young protagonist, says:

> I felt like singing. I wanted to leap and dance with joy, yet I stood quietly and watched the river running between the greening cottonwood

trees, for I knew that it is bad luck to be so happy. The gods do not like anyone to show happiness in this way and they punish those who do not obey them. They punished my brother. They let the lightning strike him when he was coming home from a hunt. My brother had shot a six-pronged deer and was singing because it was the first deer with six prongs that anyone had shot that summer. The lightning struck him and he died.

Diné do not generally "leap and dance with joy" after a rain. More likely, a prayer of thanksgiving is said. This thing about "it is bad luck to be so happy" is pure bunk. And Diné who hunt do so for food, not for trophies—a sterile doe might be shot, not a six-pronged buck. And why hunt when you have sheep in the corral?

This book is rife with errors, big and small.

• Bright Morning refers to herself and her people as "Navahos" ("In the tribe I belong to, the Navahos,..."). "Navaho" is a corruption of an enemy word. The people did and do refer to themselves as Diné.

• Bright Morning constantly "explains" her culture—erroneously—to the reader. "In the tribe I belong to, the Navahos, sheep are mostly owned by the women." Women own and take care of the sheep, not "mostly."

• The names of the characters are not Diné names: Bright Morning, Tall Boy, Running Bird, Little Beaver, Old Bear, Shining Tree, Little Rainbow, Meadow Flower. And Diné don't name themselves, they are given names.

• The Spanish slavers are depicted as nice guys, or at least inoffensive, as is the woman who buys Bright Morning. The enslaved people are fairly happy, and their accommodations are luxurious. Rosita, for instance,

> came from a poor tribe and a poor family and she liked all the food she got to eat, the clothes the Señora bought for her, the soft bed, and the big room.

• The cultural content is all wrong. In one scene, an old Apache woman is cooking dog stew, and tries to steal Bright Morning's dog. Apaches didn't eat dog meat as daily fare, only for special ceremonies or if they were starving, and they certainly didn't steal other people's animals unless they were on a raid. And when Bright Morning goes to sleep in the slave quarters,

> An owl flew into a tree outside the window. He was silent for a long time and then he began to make churring sounds, the same sounds that owls made at home. It was a good omen.

Diné do not regard the sound of an owl as a "good omen."

• Ceremony is made trivial, prayers are called "chants," and the people's complex spirituality is described as

superstition. In preparation for a raid, the warriors "dance and sing and beat on drums." The medicine man's "bag of curing things" consist of "two round blue stones, a small object with an oval knot in it that looked like an eye, one eagle feather and a groaning stick, a piece of wood from a lightning-struck tree." It is hinted at that the Spanish slavers capture Bright Morning because she "jumped up and began to dance" (expressing happiness again, supposedly a taboo). And finally, O'Dell's interpretation of kinaaldá, the womanhood ceremony, is dead wrong. In four days, the kid is treated like a drudge: she is supposed to grind the corn, milk the goats, chop the wood, weave a blanket (!), and plant the pinto beans. All to make her "industrious, obedient, and comely." In truth, the kinaaldá is exhausting, but it is a time of great honor for a young woman. She helps grind corn and makes the huge corn cake for all her relatives. Her female relatives massage her to mold her into beauty. She runs to the rising sun, to the east, because the farther she runs, the longer she will live.

• White depredations are minimized, and intertribal battles are exaggerated:

The soldiers, erroneously called "Long Knives," threaten to burn the people's village, and finally do, because the people are not "keeping the peace" with the Utes:

> If he [a Long Knife] learned that they were on a raid somewhere, he would come back and burn the houses and kill everyone in the village. Even the women and children he would kill, even the sheep and the dogs.

And in the description of the Long Walk, which was in reality a death march, the soldiers are not so bad:

> "Cast your eyes around," (the father) said. "You will see many people sitting beside their fires. They are hungry but not starving. They are cold but they do not freeze. They are unhappy. Yet they are alive."

However, it is her own people who are most frightening to Bright Morning. Tall Boy and Mando

> gave a piercing war cry. I had heard this cry before, many times since my childhood. It always froze my blood to hear it, and it did now. It sounded to me as if some evil spirit had leapt out from the far depths of the earth. The cry was not a human sound nor the sound that any animal makes whether in pain or fright.

• Bright Morning's mother is portrayed as mean and hard-hearted. When Bright Morning leaves the sheep in a storm, the mother refuses to talk to her daughter or to let her herd the sheep again until the following year. In truth, a trusted child would not leave the sheep alone, *especially* in a storm. And the family would come get them and bring them home. Also, children are not nagged and rarely if ever scolded; teaching is done by story and example. That is different from the icy "silent treatment" Bright Morning's mother gives her. In another episode, Bright Morning's mother tells her, "You have thirty sheep and they all need shearing. But before they are shorn there are beans and squash to plant." Besides the fact that this is not how Diné parents talk to their children, shearing sheep and planting are communal activities, not chores done by individual children.

• When Tall Boy is wounded in battle, he is seen as useless, a "cripple." Bright Morning's mother tells her:

> "Your sister has told me that he has an arm that will never again pull a bowstring or throw a lance. That is bad fortune. He will no longer be a warrior nor a hunter. He will have to sit with the women. Perhaps he will learn to weave and cut wood and shear sheep."

The fact that someone has been wounded in battle does not make him useless; on the contrary, Tall Boy would be regarded a hero. There would be a ceremony, probably an Enemy Way. Besides, need it be said that weaving, cutting wood and shearing sheep are activities that take both hands (and arms)?

• The narrator, in several places, describes her own people in animal similes: "We were like animals who hear the hunter approach but from terror cannot flee" and "Like sheep before the shepherd, we went without a sound." (By the way, has anyone out there ever heard a flock of sheep? They are pretty noisy. You know, baaa, baaaa.)

• Finally, there is no such thing as a "Navaho wind" or a "Navaho rain." Rains are described as being male or female, but the elements of creation do not belong to the people, and are not described this way.

In the postscript, O'Dell similarly watered down history. "Before this time (1863-65)," he said, "many treaties were made between the Navahos and the United States. Most of them were broken, some by the whites, some by the Indians." This is just not true. Every single treaty between the U.S. and the Indians was broken by the whites. This is documented fact, not hyperbole. Later on, he said, "The Navahos were held prisoners at Fort Sumner until 1868. Late in that year, they were set free, each with a *gift* of a sheep and a goat." (Italics mine.) And still later, "Some 1500 Navahos died at Fort Sumner from smallpox and other diseases. But the group who survived has grown to more than 100,000." In truth, people were beaten, raped, starved, and shot, and many also died of disease. The fact that the Diné have managed to survive and even thrive is testament to their great strength, not an implication that the Long Walk was not so bad after all.

Fifth-grade teachers stuck with class sets of *Sing Down the Moon* might have students compare O'Dell's version of kinaaldá with *Kinaaldá: A Navajo Girl Grows Up*, the beautiful photoessay by Monty Roessel (Lerner Publications, 1993). They can also compare the first chapter, where Bright Morning abandons the sheep, with the first chapter of *Black Mountain Boy: A Story of the Boyhood of John Honie* by Vada Carleson and Gary Witherspoon (Rough Rock Press, 1993). Then read the rest of the book, and have the class discuss why they think elderly white guys win awards for writing this kind of crap.

O'Dell completely failed—if he ever tried—to understand the Diné way of being in the world. *Sing Down the Moon* is not a book that can be fixed.—*Beverly Slapin*

NOTES

1 Stott, Jon C., *Native Americans in Children's Literature*. Oryx Press, 1995.

2 Maher, Susan Naramore, "Encountering Others: The Meeting of Cultures in Scott O'Dell's *Island of the Blue Dolphins* and *Sing Down the Moon*." Children's Literature in Education 23, 1992.

Turner, Ann, *The Girl Who Chased Away Sorrow: The Diary of Sarah Nita, a Navajo Girl, New Mexico, 1864.* **Scholastic (1999). 194 pages, b/w photos; grades 4-7 Diné (Navajo)**

The Navajo removal—the Long Walk from Fort Defiance to Fort Sumner in 1864—was an atrocity. It was a campaign of extermination; it was a death march for the Diné families forced out of their territories by the U.S. government.

As Tiana Bighorse describes it:

> The Long Walk is a tragic journey over frozen snow and rough rocks. There are a few wagons to haul some food and some things that belong to the white soldiers. The trip is on foot. People are shot down on the spot if they say they are tired or sick or if they stop to help someone. If a woman is in labor with a baby, she is killed. There is absolutely no mercy. Many get sick and get diarrhea because of the food. They are heartbroken because their families die on the way. Right outside Fort Defiance when the trip just starts, they sleep there and leave lots of bodies there. That's the way it is for the rest of the trip. There are bodies here and there and everywhere along the trail. About four thousand Navajos make the walk from Fort Defiance to Fort Sumner.[1]

Ann Turner, the author of *The Girl Who Chased Away Sorrow*, knows (or has been told) that a Diné child in 1864 would not have had a written language or access to pencil and paper, not to mention a diary to carry around on a death march. But in order to fit her version of the story of the Long Walk into the "Dear America" template, the author has a Diné grandmother, a survivor of the Long Walk, dictating the story to her granddaughter, who transcribes it in journal format. In addition, because this is a "children's book," Turner whitewashes the gruesome historical events, and distorts cultural practices and lifeways to fit her story.

As an outsider, Turner has the presumption to step inside a community to tell its story, while ignoring the community's identity and the notion of how history is traditionally recorded and passed on. Instead, she takes a modern European technique for passing on history and pastes it onto this traditional culture.

> "My granddaughter, this summer I want to tell you all that happened during the Long Walk so you can write it down in the book that white teacher gave to you." ...My pencil flies over the page as I write down everything Shimasani says. I only hope that this book is big enough for all the things she will tell me.

A BRIEF DIGRESSION

A brief digression and math activity here. Grandma is thirteen years old in 1864, when the Long Walk begins. When she dictates this "diary" to her granddaughter, she is described as "old," so if we guess she's between seventy and one hundred, the date of this telling would be somewhere between 1921 and 1951. In any event, white teachers in residential schools did not hand out blank books to Diné children, nor would it be likely that a twelve-year-old child would have the skills to accomplish such a task. Rather, white anthropologists often descended upon reservations to "collect" stories from elders. They took notes and often used tape recorders.

DINÉ STORYTELLING

A Diné child being told a story by an elder would be honored, she would just sit quietly and listen. She would not take notes—that would be rude, and Grandma would just walk away. The elder would tell a story to be learned, not written down—oral tradition is alive and well in Dinétah. But here we have a child, frantically trying to get every single word down on paper, because her grandmother wants her to—as a transparent device to fit Scholastic's "diary" format.

"It's unreal," Gloria Grant told me, "that a Diné grandmother would demand that her granddaughter write. Because it's an honor to be told a story; you just sit there and not do one thing, that's how you take in a story and learn." And Evelyn Lamenti told me, "I can't imagine a Diné child whipping out a paper and pencil; she just wouldn't have the need. It would only be a stranger who would do that."

This book doesn't work, on any level. Turner clearly knows nothing about Diné ways of being.

- She gets the belief system backwards:

> I can almost hear the land breathing—a deep, silent sigh. I think it says, You are the people I want to live on me—you Diné. You will care for me, like a mother for her child.

Hasn't Turner ever heard the phrase Mother Earth? As Danny Blackgoat says, "I am a Navajo and I belong to the earth. The earth is my mother, my provider, and my caretaker. I am her child. She nourishes me from her body and her soul."[2]

- Her attempts at "Indian humor" are pathetic: "Grandfather jokes, 'That dog of yours is from the Pouring Water clan, and he's pouring water all over my knees!'" While joking is often self-directed, clan names are not ridiculed.

- Her metaphors are just more of those romantic-sounding imaginary Indian speech patterns that white writers seem to like so well: "I will weave the story into you, like a spun thread, to make you strong, for when we remember, we are strong." Grandma would have said, "I want to tell you a story" or just "Come, sit down." Or she'd just start talking.

NAMES

If a traditional Diné elder were telling a story in a formal manner, she would begin by stating her name, then her mother's clan, then her father's clan. She would say where she was from, and add any other identifying information. Then she would begin her story. This is not done in *The Girl Who Chased Away Sorrow*.

Sarah Nita is not a traditional Diné name, and would not have been a name given to the grandmother in 1851, the year she was born. She would have been given a name by which she was known and recognized, an indirect or relationship name by which she would be addressed by a family member, and a nickname, by which she would be referred to as a child. Later on, she might also be given a ceremonial name. And they would all be in Diné. It was only after 1868, when Diné children were grabbed up and forced to go to residential school, that their traditional names were taken away and replaced with anglicized names.

It is quite possible that Sarah Nita might have been the name of a Diné child at the time the "writing down" is taking place, sometime between 1931 and 1951. But in this book, the child has the same name as her grand-mother. This does not make any sense.

THE NARRATIVE

The story as written here is not how a Diné elder speaks or tells a story. It does not have a Diné rhythm, it does not have a Diné speech pattern, it is clunky and linear. The elder would be speaking in Diné, and would not translate Diné words into English. The granddaughter would be totally versed in the nuances of Diné language, and—especially if she had gone to "white man's school"—she would be bilingual.

"There is no way for some of the words in our storytelling to be translated into English," Gloria Grant told me. "Translating into English just dilutes it, it loses a lot of meaning; it loses much of the sense of purpose. So this is unreal, that a grandmother would tell these stories in English."

And Grandma would not call herself "Navajo," she would call herself "Diné," people.

Evelyn Lamenti told me:

> Storytelling would take place in the hogan, and with all family members present. There would be food, they would talk about things that have gone on, and it comes up informally. If a grandmother is passing something on to one of her grand-daughters, it's a special quiet time. But if it's really negative, if it's really scary, it's just not told to the child alone. If there are a lot of bad thoughts that are plaguing the person, if she needs to talk in a way to relieve herself of a concern or worry, then that's handled by a medicine man. A grandmother would just not unburden herself to a child. If a child is in the hogan when the grandmother or grand-father is talking, that story becomes part of her, but it just wouldn't be done, something as unpleasant as this, just with the child. It just wouldn't be done.

In truth, some elders will not speak of every detail about the tragedy that came to be known as the Long Walk because the pain is too great. Others will not speak of it to spare their grandchildren the pain that they have experienced in the remembering of these stories. But— "Grandmother says she will not tell everything that happened, because it would take too long and my book would have no more pages left"—is just plain ridiculous!

KEEPING UP COURAGE

During this time of incredible hardship and sorrow, it was the elders and leaders who kept the people going. This from Tiana Bighorse:

> Barboncito is glad he is with the people, and some warriors that are with him are really a great help to the people. Barboncito doesn't get tired, and he just helps everyone on their feet so they don't get shot. Barboncito...gets the captain to agree to let the kids take turns riding on the wagon when they get tired...Some old men and old ladies, they have a hard time. Barboncito doesn't know how long it is going to take. He just has to keep the people going. He just has to keep giving them courage to keep on their feet.... Barboncito is glad when they get there so the people can rest, even if it is a terrible place to be. He is glad not to lose everybody.[3]

Some elders may have told stories when they got the chance—ancient stories, powerful stories, stories from the beginning of time, stories about coming up from the other worlds, stories of mothers and fathers and hero children, stories to keep up courage and hope.

Yet our young protagonist, who seems to be modeled more on Shirley Temple than a traditional Diné child, takes on the task of cheering everybody up with a bunch of silly little "Don't-Worry-Be-Happy" stories that she makes up on the spot to "chase away sorrow." In one of them, "Worried Girl" learns from "Grandfather Owl" (who, trust this, is not a teacher in the Diné belief system)

> that singing could push sorrow away, that telling stories could keep sadness outside the hogan. She earned a new name—The Girl Who Chased Away Sorrow.

Singing could push sorrow away? On a death march? In the face of starvation? With friends and relatives getting shot all around? What an outrageous trivialization this is!

RAIDING

"Raiding happened," Gloria Grant told me,

> in order for us to survive. You know, they burned our fields, they killed our animals, they ran our sheep and horses off the cliffs. People to this day have never recovered. It's a very emotional topic for us. People starved, children starved, babies starved because they took away our sources of food. They burned our peaches right here in the canyon where we lived. It was filled with orchards that have still never been restored. Raiding was not our way of life. We were forced to somehow feed our families.

But this isn't what the Long Walk was about. It wasn't about the itty-bitty raiding parties that went on. That was the façade they presented about us. It's all about natural resources; it always has been and continues to be. We've got the land, they want it, and they'll do anything to get it.

But Turner uses this occasional raiding—the rationale the U.S. government used for the mass destruction of Diné lands and livestock, and for the removal of the people—as historical fact. In her historical note, she says: "For many years, Navajo peoples had raided the white settlers in New Mexico," and one of the captions says, "In the 1860s, many white Americans feared the Navajo because of their nomadic and raiding lifestyle." In this story, raiding is an everyday thing, an occupation of sorts. Our young protagonist says, early on, "The only thing I can do is pretend to be brave, like my father going off on a raid."

THE "KINDNESS" OF SOLDIERS

The soldiers during this time period were vicious characters who joined the military because it allowed them to raise hell on the frontier. Throughout the Long Walk, they shot, they beat, they raped, they committed acts of unheard-of cruelty and barbarism. There may have been isolated instances of humanity during this death march, but it's a disingenuous thing to focus on this, as Turner does, without taking a hard look at the brutality, without looking at the underlying issue, the theft of land.

Yet, while the protagonist in this book makes vague references to "mean" soldiers, and even rape ("some of the soldiers are cruel to our women"—a reference children are not likely to understand), I counted seventeen instances of the kindness of soldiers—and of one soldier in particular with whom a young woman falls in love—in this little book. There are shots heard in the background, and one shooting of an unnamed pregnant woman. It is only when we get to the historical note that we find that "the sick, the old, and women giving birth were sometimes shot along the way, for they could not keep up." Even here, it is implied that it was the people's fault that they were shot.[4] And using the word "sometimes" disingenuously implies that shooting people was an out-of-the-ordinary occurrence and a practical necessity.

"When they talk about white soldiers being nice," Gloria Grant says,

> they're trivializing our experience. They're trivializing our history, and romanticizing it. They were real successful at hurting us, at removing us, at exterminating us. That's what the Long Walk was about, and they're just trying to pretty it up.

A CONTINUING WHITEWASH

Some would argue that, however this book has been cleaned up, at least children will learn something about the tragedy called the Long Walk. The notion seems to be that translating Native experiences into a European worldview and form—while pretending to be an indigenous worldview and form—is a good thing.

But in the guise of trying to educate, what Scholastic is actually doing—in both *My Heart Is On the Ground* and

The Girl Who Chased Away Sorrow—is continuing to whitewash the Native experience and continuing the historic campaign of extermination, only this time in books for children.

"*The Girl Who Chased Away Sorrow*—this whole story—is about white America's guilt trip," Gloria Grant told me.

> They're always going to trivialize our history. To us, there are oral accounts of the Long Walk. They are things that happened, they are our stories. We still have to live with it today. White America just doesn't want to account for the atrocities that they committed against us. They don't want to understand—or teach their children—that we put our umbilical cords in this earth. This is our land, this is where we're from. And this is where we're staying.

I hope this book does not fall into the hands of non-Native children who think that reading it will teach them anything about Indian history. I sincerely hope that well-meaning white teachers will not give Diné children this book, but I fear that the opposite will be true.—*Beverly Slapin*

(I thank Gloria Grant and Evelyn Lamenti for sharing with me their family and historical memories.)

NOTES

1 Bighorse, Tiana, *Bighorse the Warrior*. University of Arizona, 1990.

2 Hooker, Kathy Eckles, *Time Among the Navajo: Traditional Lifeways on the Reservation*. Foreword by Danny K. Blackgoat. Museum of New Mexico, 1991.

3 Johnson, Broderick H., ed., *Navajo Stories of the Long Walk Period*. Navajo Community College, 1970.

4 On pages 127-128, a soldier shoots a pregnant woman who is about to give birth. Turner apparently got this story from *Navajo Stories of the Long Walk Period*. Navajo Community College, 1973. On pages 30-31, the young woman "was shot when she no longer could keep up with the others." What's interesting, besides the fact that there is no attribution to this or any other resource material, is that Turner changes the wording slightly in her historical notes, from "when" to "for," thereby taking the blame off the soldiers and putting it onto the people who were shot.

LITTLE HOUSE ON THE OSAGE PRAIRIE

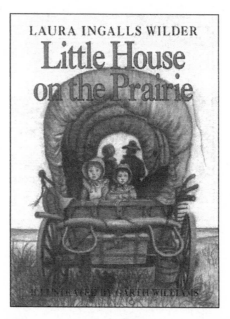

Wilder, Laura Ingalls, *Little House on the Prairie,* **illustrated by Garth Williams. HarperCollins (1935, 1953, 1981). 335 pages, b/w illustrations; grades 4-up; Osage**

The tens of millions of adoring fans of Laura Ingalls Wilder's books and of the television series based on them should be grateful that the Osages didn't dismember her when they had the chance. One day, I was staring at a map of the Osages' rectangle of reservation in Kansas and my eyes stuck on a red dot in the middle of it, signifying a "Point of Interest." The words "Little House on the Prairie" came into focus.

Little Laura Ingalls, her sisters and their beloved Ma and Pa were illegal squatters on Osage land. She left that detail out of her 1935 children's book, *Little House on the Prairie,* as well as any mention of ongoing outrages—including killings, burnings, beatings, horse thefts and grave robberies—committed by white settlers, such as Charles Ingalls, against Osages living in villages not more than a mile or two away from the Ingalls' little house.

Mrs. Wilder's unwitting association with the Osages would last a lifetime. She started writing the "Little House" children's books—there were nine—in the 1930s, in her sixties, while living in a big house located on former Osage land in the Missouri Ozarks. The "Little House" books—especially the one that took place "on the Prairie" of the Osage reservation in Kansas—would be much read, broadcast and beloved. Shortly after World War II, the State Department ordered Mrs. Wilder's books translated into German and Japanese, the languages of the United States' most recently defeated enemies, who had just joined the list of America's other Vanquished, including American Indians. The "Little House" books were "positive representations of America," the U.S. government decreed, a good way to show other peoples of the world the American Way. Obviously someone in government forgot to consult the Osages.

After the Civil War, caravans of white settlers started overrunning the Osage reservation, and the Ingalls family joined them in 1869. They were drawn there by the U.S. government's giveaway of 160-acre plots of free land to each adult settler under the Homestead Act of 1862, signed by Abraham Lincoln early in the Civil War as a way to keep the hearts and minds of poor northern people planted firmly in the Union, and maybe win some from the South. The subliminal message of the law was "Stick with us, and we'll reward you—if you win this war. Trade in your slums for the wide-open spaces of the West, where you can be your own boss, on your own land. All you have to do is kill a couple of Confederates." Railroads passed the good news to Europe—or at least to northern

Europeans, such as the hard-working Swedes, Norwegians and Germans. The railroads' flyers, however, never made it to the Italians or Slavs. A song was even written to give settlers something to sing while traveling west, either to America or to their new homesteads west of the Mississippi:

> Oh, come to this country
> And don't you feel alarm
> For Uncle Sam is rich enough
> To give us all a farm!

Osage writer John Joseph Mathews could have been staring at a family portrait of the Ingallses when he described the covered wagons filling up Osage land as being full of "dirty-faced children peering out from the curtains, and weary, hard-faced women lolling in the seat beside evil-eyed, bearded men." The actor Michael Landon was horribly miscast as Pa in the television series "Little House on the Prairie." Landon was too sweet-faced, clean-shaven—and focused. The real Charles Ingalls wore a two-foot long vinery of beard. His dark, narrow, hard, glassy, chilly, creepy eyes would, a century later, stare out of photos of Charles Manson, the Hollywood murderer. Pa's résumé reads like that of a surfer bum in search of the perfect amber wave of grain. He couldn't stay in one place or hold down a homestead. He moved from Wisconsin, professing overcrowdedness, to the Osage reservation, back to Wisconsin a year later, then to Minnesota, where he was eaten out by grasshoppers, then to Iowa, where he worked in a hotel, then to South Dakota, where he finally settled in De Smet.

In *Little House on the Prairie*, Mrs. Wilder described one encounter with an Indian she identified as Osage by his scalp lock and leather leggings. A tall Indian, she said, suddenly materialized in the doorway, without anyone hearing him, then walked in the house and squatted by the fireplace, without saying a word. Pa joined him, and Ma served them dinner. They ate in silence. They smoked pipes in silence, using Pa's tobacco. That done, the Osage spoke.

Pa shook his head to signal that he did not understand the Indian's language. The Osage got up and walked out—in silence. Pa may not have understood what the Osage was saying, but he did recognize the language—French.

Sitting on the beach and reading *Little House on the Prairie* for the first time—I did not do so as a boy because it was a *girl's* book—I find myself growing dismayed at its popularity. It took several trips to my local library to find a copy (about a half-dozen were listed in the card catalog—all checked out—and I could not bring myself, at age forty-one, to tell the librarian I wanted to reserve one).

Why are children still reading a book so unsuitable for children? I keep asking myself.

If Pa Ingalls had built his little house on the periphery of an antebellum southern mansion and Mrs. Wilder had described its Black slaves in the same terms she depicted the Osage Indians, her book long ago would have been barred from children's eyes, or at least sanitized like some editions of Mark Twain's *The Adventures of Huckleberry Finn*. Mrs. Wilder's book even contains the popular variation of General Sheridan's racist remark about what constitutes a good Indian. I find to my amazement that I take personally her denigration of the Osages, and it bothers me that no one has ever noticed her portrayal of Indians, or objected to it. What commentary does it make on the status of Native Americans in our society that in 1991 you can't find a library copy of a fifty-six-year-old book replete with anti-Indian ethnic slurs, not because it is out of print or circulation, as it should be, but because it is in such demand by impressionable children?

I would not want my child to read *Little House on the Prairie*. I would shield him from the slights she slings upon his ancestors. They appear in her book only as beggars and thieves, and she adds injury to insult by comparing the Osages—who turned Thomas Jefferson's head with their dignity and grace— to reptiles, to garbage or scum (depending on the definition of the word she actually uses). Mrs. Wilder assigns them descriptive adjectives that connote barbarism, brutality, and bloodthirstiness, and makes much ado about their odor. But she makes light of their obvious plight: In one passage, she describes almost mockingly the skeletal figures of two Osages who are fed cornbread by Ma, the eating noises they make and the pitiful sight of them stooping to eat specks of food they spot on the floor.

The Osages were hungry because white men such as her father were burning their fields, forcing them at gunpoint from their homes and threatening them with death if they returned, stealing their food and horses, even robbing their graves—all to force them to abandon their land. There is no proof, of course, that Charles Ingalls took part in these crimes, but I assume that he did, since he was sleazy enough to willfully steal their land, their most valuable possession. He did disappear for four days—according to the book, it took that long to get to Independence and back, all of ten miles away—and returned with food and other supplies. He unabashedly told little Laura, trying to explain why he had moved the family to the Osage reservation, that because they and other whites were there, the Army would drive the Indians away.

In the words of the Osages' U.S. agent in 1870, even being "kind and generous to the Indians....[does] not relieve these men from the reproach of being trespassers, intruders, and violators of the nation's law."

The annual reports of the Osages' U.S. agent to his superiors in Washington, the commissioners of Indian affairs, provide the chapter of *Little House on the Prairie* that Laura Ingalls Wilder failed to write:

The Ingallses moved onto Osage land in 1869, about ten miles southwest of Independence, and only about five miles from the Kansas border with Indian Territory. The Ingallses were not alone. That year, more than 500 families trespassed on the reservation and "built their cabins near the [main] Indian camps"—in the Ingallses' case, only a mile or so away. The 1870 U.S. census listed the Little House—and the Ingallses as its occupants—as the "89th residence of Rutland Township," although "a claim was not filed because the land was part of the Osage...Reserve."

Squatters had "taken possession of [the Osages'] cornfields, and forbidden them cutting firewood on 'their claims,'" wrote agent G. C. Snow. The Osages "have had, to my certain knowledge, over 100 of their best horses stolen [in the past month]. I learn that scarcely a day passes that they do not lose from five to twenty horses....Not one of [the horse thieves has] as yet been brought to justice, or one in a hundred of the Indians' horses returned to them."

The settlers "threaten me with Crawford's militia, and say they will hang me if I interfere with them," the Indian agent complained, referring to the Kansas governor. Samuel J. Crawford was so opposed to Indians in general and Osages in particular that he once told a white constituent, Theodore Reynolds, complaining about problems over filing a claim because of a mixed-blood Osage, Augustus Captain: "Shoot the half-breed renegade and I will pardon you before the smoke gets away from your gun."

U.S. agent Isaac T. Gibson wrote in his annual report for 1870 that settlers had grown bolder, forming vigilante groups

> pledged to defend each other in the occupation of claims, without regard to the improvements, possession, or rights of the Indians. Many of the latter were turned out of their homes, and threatened with death if they persisted in claiming them. Others were made homeless by cunning and fraud.

> While absent on their winter hunt, [the Osages'] cribs of corn and other provisions, so hardly earned by their women's toil, were robbed. Their principal village was pillaged of a large amount of [casks], and wagon-loads of matting hauled away and used by the settlers in building and finishing houses for themselves. Even new-made graves were plundered with the view of finding treasures, which the Indians often bury with their dead....

> The question will suggest itself, which of these peoples are the savages?

The outrages of 1870 were a turning point for the Osages. At that spring's payment in provisions of promised treaty annuities, the government again pressed the Osages to sell their Kansas lands. In 1865, the Osages ceded under pressure nearly four million acres on the northern and eastern perimeters of their reservation, and in 1868 were forced to agree to sell their eight-million-acre "diminished reserve," as the government called the remainder of their land, to a railroad corporation for nineteen cents an acre. But President Ulysses S. Grant withdrew the treaty in 1870 when it became obvious that the Senate would not ratify it amid an explosion of outrage from settlers that the sale would put the Osage lands in the hands of the railroads and not in theirs. Gibson noted the weariness of the Osages at the 1870 spring annuity payment, quoting "one of their headmen" as complaining, "Why is it that our Great Father can never even send us our annuities, without asking us to sell and move once more?" The Indian added, "We are tired of all this." Gibson described the Osage as having "the look and tone of a man without hope."

It was in this spirit that the Osages agreed to sell, and luckily for them, their decision to wave the white flag coincided with a radical change in the government's Indian policy. President Grant had just relieved the Army from administrative responsibility for Indian affairs, and turned the whole problem over to Quakers, such as Gibson. They saw in the Osages the chance to inject a missing ingredient—fairness, or at least their conception of it—into official treatment of Indians. The Quaker commissioners of Indian affairs—"true friends of the Indians," they regarded themselves—persuaded Grant to up the ante: $1.25 per acre, and the opportunity for the Osages to use their money to purchase a new reservation in Indian Territory. Grant had no choice but to agree. The president had announced his "peace policy" with much flourish and fanfare in his inaugural address on March 4, 1869, and would have suffered a humiliating embarrassment if he had rejected his new Quaker commissioners' counsel.

When the Osages signed the treaty on September 10, 1870, they became the richest Indians in America with nearly $9 million in the U.S. Treasury—although their signatures on the Kansas removal treaty actually put them between reservations, having given up one and having only the historically questionable word of the U.S. government that they would get another.

The Quaker commissioners hailed their treaty as "so just that in itself it marks an era in the history of our government in its legislation on Indian affairs," and as proof "of the overruling goodness of God." But the Osages did not share the Quakers' joy. The morning after they signed the treaty, "the air was filled with the cries of the old people, especially the women, who lamented over the graves of their children, which they were about to leave forever," a Kansas newspaper reported.

Most of the Osages left Kansas in late fall for their annual winter buffalo hunt on the plains, and did not return, staying instead in Indian Territory. Laura Ingalls—and her readers—did not know it, but she witnessed a watershed moment in the history of the Osages—their removal from Kansas—when one morning she looked out the window of the little house and saw a traffic jam of Indians riding past. They came from the creek bottoms to the east and rode west, past the house, on an old Indian trail that later was paved and became U.S. Route 75.

One of the Osage warriors who rode past the little house that day was my great-great-grandfather, and one of the Osage women Laura saw was my great-great-grandmother.

The Ingalls family left Kansas a few weeks later. Mrs. Wilder claimed that a cavalry troop rode in one day and warned Pa to vacate or be evicted, since the house was located just inside the Osages' diminished reservation. But that could not have been the reason the Ingallses left Kansas and moved back to Wisconsin. The U.S. Army had not moved one squatter off the Osages' land when it was their reservation, so why would that happen when there no longer was an Osage reservation in Kansas?

The Ingallses' neighbors were not through with the Osages yet. Nearly twenty mixed-blood Osages had decided to remain on farms they had developed and improved over the years, and to formally enter the white man's world by becoming U.S. citizens. They secured a special treaty with the good citizens of Independence to allow them to stay. But in the weeks after the main body of Osages left Kansas, the mixed-bloods' farmhouses, one after another, were burned down.

One night, the white neighbors of Joseph Mosher broke into his house—a mile or two from the Little House on the Prairie—dragged him, his wife and children out of their beds and into the yard, where they beat them and torched the house.

Then they took the Osage man to the nearby woods, and pistol-whipped him to death.—*Dennis McAuliffe, Jr.*

(Note: For those who missed the award-winning TV series broadcast from 1974-1983, ABC planned to launch a six-hour *Little House* miniseries on ABC in the fall of 2004. HarperCollins planned to publish a special tie-in edition of Mrs. Wilder's book, *Little House on the Prairie*, at the same time. And finally, *Little House* was named by the American Library Association and the National Endowment of the Arts as a choice for their "Bookshelf on Courage" promotion to libraries.—Editors.)

ELSA REMEMBERS

Elsie was in one of her remembering-the-old-days moods. We were sitting around a fire outside with snow all around. The kids were skating on the rink their parents had flooded. It was early, but the sun had gone down a long time ago. That's how it always seems up north. Winter means dark. And cold.

"Yup. When I was a girl, there was lots of giving." Long pause.

You knew better than to talk during those pauses. "But there was none of this fancy wrapping paper and ribbons and plastic stuff." The light from the crackling fire danced in her eyes. As she spoke, I thought about how beautiful she was. What was she now—eighty five? She knew I was daydreaming and stopped talking. I came back. And she went on.

"Back before those residential schools. Before it was against the law to speak Indian. Before people got greedy and in a big rush." Another pause as she let the reel of her memory unwind. "We didn't need a special time of the year to give. Back then, we were in touch with the Creator—not just one by one, but everybody." Another pause.

"We didn't go to those shopping centres. Didn't go to the store except for flour and sugar and tea. And bullets." She smiled. I could tell she was a little girl again in her mind. At a trading post. Probably with one of her uncles or older brothers. Her parents didn't go into town much. But she liked the things that sparkled. And those ribbony candies with red and yellow and green stripes. She told me about how she looked forward to going in to get supplies in the spring.

"The gifts we got usually had to do with reaching a certain age—or with somebody getting married or going through a special ceremony. At about fourteen, my brothers got rifles. That was always a big sacrifice. My parents never had any money. They just traded for what they needed. It was just the odd times they got cash. I remember the first time I saw real money. It was on the table and I asked my mom what it was." She sipped her tea as though it held her memories in it. Smiling and rocking gently on the log she was sitting on, she continued.

"We never went in for all this Christian stuff. Christmas and Lent and Easter and the rest of it. The missionaries didn't get up to where we were until I was about ten. Sure, we celebrated the days getting longer and the changing moon and the seasons. But we didn't cut down a tree and put it in the living room. Or put up notices and invite people to talk who were just big-shots with nothing to say." She laughed quietly and chewed on her biscuit. No one spoke or hardly breathed.

"Then the priests and government people and the mounties came and said I had to go to school. We didn't know what they were talking about. But I went." I knew she'd eventually get around to talking about giving gifts. I'd learned over the years you didn't rush Elsa. You waited until she got around to whatever it was she wanted to talk about.

"Residential school. I had to leave my parents and my brothers and sisters. The younger ones. I had to leave my village, my forest—leave the only thing I knew." Her voice wavered a little. "I had to go to school to learn how to read and write and figure. We tried to talk to those people in suits and uniforms but they said there was no arguing. So I went. Everybody figured it was just for a while—a month or two. Then I'd be back. We'd all be back. That's not how it happened."

The sound of the children skating—the little ones, unsteady newborn deer, older ones gaining confidence in their bodies, learning balance. Laughter and whoops of excitement. The odd whimper or cry from childhood woes and accidents. Whipping around, throwing snow, pulling and being pulled in toboggans, sliding on their backs or stomachs. Sounds of young life full of itself, full of that good spirit. A sharp contrast to the deep shame and loneliness that I knew Elsa felt seventy-five years ago at the residential school. Bunkbeds, uniforms, cold, empty buildings. Like the hollow insides of dead insects. Praying to powers and beings that had nothing to do with her own life. "You weren't allowed to talk about rocks and trees having spirits. They whipped you if you sang your own songs, prayed your own prayers. In your own language."

Somewhere under that joy was an indwelling sorrow connecting this old woman to the young girl—

and the nuns and priests. I think about the stripping away of her family and culture. What a brave child she must have been. She had to be or they'd have broken her. It made me mad to think of them grinding her pride into the ground and filling in the empty space with shame. A shame so deep and lingering that she still unconsciously lowered her voice and eyes when there were priests around.

"When I was a girl we didn't have electricity or running water. Candles and pails—that was good enough. We made things from what we found in the forest—from skins or wool or wood or bone. Stones. Whatever there was. My mother always said it was good to do things with your hands. She was a great one for everybody, always doing something."

As she spoke, Elsa was beading a brooch for one of her great-grandchildren. Her hands moved as if they didn't need her eyes to guide them.

"Lots of times we just gave things to people because they needed them or because we felt like it. We listened to those voices inside. Giving didn't have anything to do with calendars or how many shopping days were left."

As Elsa spoke, the other people around the fire paid close attention to her. They all respected her for who she was—her words. And her actions. But they still did other things—like beading, knitting, sewing, making their kids or somebody else's behave, putting wood on the fire. Some chewed on pieces of straw or grass. Some stared into the fire—silent. I refilled her mug. For me, the slightest smile that brushed across her lips was worth a thousand spoken thank-you's. Elsa pulled her scarf tighter, moved closer to the fire, threw in some tobacco, then came back and sat down on her log. Then she closed her eyes and sipped her tea.

What a lot of pain I thought—and joy! What a beautiful universe of a woman in this small old body. What a blessing! Thank you, Creator.

"In that school—they made you wear these white man's clothes. Everybody dressed the same. We must have looked like a bunch of mushrooms." Pause. "None of us spoke English. We just had our own language." Another pause. "'Stop speaking that heathen language,' they'd say. Yeah. We learned all about sin. About how bad it is to be Indian. About praying in a dead language at the same time our own was dying. Talk about prison. I'm surprised they didn't lock us up and make us break rocks with hammers." She laughed hoarsely and coughed. I patted her back. Oh, her eyes when she laughed—like creek pebbles. How close, I thought, joy and pain become. Elsa, I thought, you are a gift. And I love you.

"The way I learned back home was when you picked plants or stones or bark, you gave thanks for them. Whether you were making medicine or just something pretty. You purified yourself. Your thoughts. You didn't just go around and collect whatever you wanted and put it in a bag and give it to somebody. You put yourself into your gift. Like you put yourself into prayer. That's how we did it back in those days." The fire flared up. We knew there were spirits around. There always were when there was good talk. The wind whipped up the fire and the children behaved better. They knew, too—that something was happening.

"Sometimes I feel like an old nag—going on about the old days, the old ways." Silence again. "But if we don't talk about it, nobody does anything—about anything." Pause. "It's not just talk. You know I'm no big talker." We all knew she had long periods of silence, but she also liked to talk. "It's the beginning of change. Like a spark waiting for the wind. Like the first raindrop." She dozed for a while, her mug held steadily in her lap. Her fingers like willow branches, wrapped around the cup like a basket. Her breath silent and steady, slow. When she woke up a few minutes later, no one had spoken—as though her silence were sacred. As though talk wasn't an option.

"This Christmas stuff, putting oranges in socks and decorating. There's parts of it that are okay. But you got to remember that when you give something, you give thanks first to the Creator. You don't just pat yourself on the back and forget where your breath comes from. There's spirit in what you give when it comes from your heart. And the spirit stays there. It connects you. It's sharing yourself." Another sip. I could tell she was getting tired.

"I'm pretty well done my ranting—for tonight. But you know." Long pause. "I like giving things to those kids. And sometimes I wrap them up. Just to see them open them. And sometimes we put a tree up in the house. That was fun." Pause. "It's not that we were Christian. We knew all about that. From experience. It was something nice to do when the nights were long and the days were short. If you have to stay inside, you might as well celebrate." I felt like applauding. But it wouldn't have been appropriate. For me.

As I was leaving Elsa after walking her home, she slipped something into my hand—smiling and not saying anything, just smiling. When I opened it a few days later, after the days started to get longer, I found the brooch I'd been admiring her bead as we sat by the fire that night. The one I thought she was making for her great-great granddaughter. There was also a tobacco tie. Usually it's the young ones who give it to the elders. Next time we have a sacred fire, I'll offer it to the Creator for my friend Elsa.

Hiy hiy!—*Peter Cole*

MY HEART IS ON THE GROUND
AND THE INDIAN RESIDENTIAL SCHOOL EXPERIENCE

Rinaldi, Ann, *My Heart Is On the Ground: The Diary of Nannie Little Rose, A Sioux Girl, Carlisle Indian School, Pennsylvania, 1880* (Dear America Series). Scholastic (1999). **203 pages, b/w photos; grades 4-7; Lakota**

INTRODUCTION

There is a story about how this essay came to be. In March of 1999, Debbie A. Reese, a doctoral student at the University of Illinois, saw *My Heart Is On the Ground* in a local bookstore. Reading through the book, she was outraged and called Beverly Slapin, who had already ordered a review copy from Scholastic and had not been looking forward to reading it. A day later and equally outraged, Beverly called it the "worst book she had ever read." Both women began talking about this book to colleagues.

Debbie contacted Barb Landis, a research specialist on the Carlisle Indian Industrial School. Barb had also read the book and felt it was a terrible depiction of a tragic period in Native American history. A series of internet and telephone discussions followed, and the circle came to include Marlene R. Atleo, Naomi Caldwell, Jean Paine Mendoza, Deborah A. Miranda, LaVera Rose, and Cynthia Smith. We quickly drew up a first draft of what came to be this review with each of us contributing particular areas of knowledge about Carlisle Indian School, Lakota culture and history, and critical evaluation of children's books; and a few days later, Debbie raised the issues it contained at a children's literature conference at the University of Wisconsin in Madison.

As individuals, we write and speak in many voices, but we feel that our collective authorship of this piece adds to its strength. This piece represents a first-time collaboration among nine women. Some of us are Indian and some of us are not. Some of us are parents and grandparents and some of us are not. We all call ourselves teachers in some way; as well, we are learners. For purposes of practicality, we are listing our names alphabetically.

We do this for our children and grandchildren—Elizabeth, Carlos, Will, Michael, Michele, Stephanie, Miranda, Danny, Robert, Aimee, William, Thomas, Terri, Jamal, Kiana, Rose, Brittany, Shelena, Noah, Kevin, Tyson, Tara, Alexandria—and for their children and the next seven generations.

A BRIEF DIGRESSION ABOUT PRATT, CARLISLE,
AND THE RESIDENTIAL SCHOOL EXPERIENCE

Because Captain Richard Henry Pratt figures so prominently in this book, it might be good to look at who he was and what his relationship was to Carlisle Indian Industrial School. Born in 1840, Pratt began his military career by enlisting in the Union army in 1861. As a young cavalry officer, he commanded a regiment of Buffalo Soldiers—a Black regiment, that, along with hired Indian scouts, were used as mercenaries, Indian-fighters, for the benefit of white expansionism during the post-Civil War period. In 1875, Pratt was assigned the command of Fort Marion, the notorious prisoner-of-war camp in Saint Augustine, Florida, where Kiowa, Comanche, and Cheyenne prisoners were taken as hostages to ensure the subjugation of their people.

A decade later, Chiricahua Apache men, women, and children were also sent to Fort Marion, where the children were separated from their parents and sent on to Carlisle. It was at Fort Marion that Pratt began to formulate his early ideas about "civilizing" the Indians: he cut off their hair, replaced their traditional clothing with military uniforms, organized them into hierarchical-structured regiments, and taught them English. After enrolling several of the Fort Marion prisoners at the Hampton School for Negro Children in Virginia, Pratt recruited young children from the Standing Rock Agency and his ideas about Indian "education" began to take shape.

In 1879, Pratt founded the Carlisle Indian Industrial School, which he ruled with an iron hand, his stated philosophy being "kill the Indian and save the man." Carlisle, and the Indian residential schools that followed, were set up to break spirits, to destroy traditional extended families and cultures, to obliterate memories and languages, and especially to make the children deny their Indianness, inside and out.

Sun Elk, from Taos Pueblo, told of his experiences at Carlisle in 1890:

> They told us that Indian ways were bad. They said we must get civilized. I remember that word, too. It means "be like the white man." I am willing to be like the white man, but I did not believe Indian ways were wrong. But they kept teaching us for seven years. And the books told how bad the Indians had been to the white men—burning their towns and killing their women and children. But I had seen white men do that to Indians. We all wore white man's clothes and ate white man's food and went to white man's churches and spoke white man's talk. And so after a while we also began to say Indians were bad. We laughed at our own people and their blankets and cooking pots and sacred societies and dances. I tried to learn the lessons—and after seven years I came home..[1]

During the period in which *My Heart Is On the Ground* takes place, Native people were confined to reservations and not allowed to leave without permission of the government-appointed Indian agent assigned to their reservations.

Alvin Josephy writes:

> By the mid 1870s, reservations had become virtual prisons, ruled like empires by authoritarian agents who were given almost total power over the Indians. Shut inside the reservations, where outside eyes could not see them, the Indian peoples were subjected to unspeakable abuses. Housing monies were stolen, food rations were inadequate or spoiled, people were left to die without medical treatment or medicines, others were forcibly separated from their families to be punished without trial for real or trumped-up offenses, and individual Indians were frequently murdered.

The Indians were at the mercy of a system of corrupt government officials and private suppliers and speculators, known collectively as the Indian Ring, who, taking advantage of public indifference, cheated the powerless tribes. Trapped on the reservations, without freedom and the ability to provide for themselves in time-tested fashion or make their complaints known, the Indian families lived in poverty and misery.[2]

Many parents were coerced into sending their children to these early schools. Many times, children were kidnapped and sent far away to schools where they were kept for years on end. Commissioner of Indian Affairs Thomas Jefferson Morgan described his procedure for taking the children from their families. He said:

I would...use the Indian police if necessary. I would withhold from [the Indian adults] rations and supplies... and when every other means was exhausted...I would send a troop of United States soldiers, not to seize them, but simply to be present as an expression of the power of the government. Then I would say to these people, "Put your children in school"; and they would do it.[3]

Still, some parents found ways to avoid sending their children to the schools. In her autobiography, Helen Sekaquaptewa (Hopi) remembers that parents taught their children to play a game similar to hide-and-seek to avoid being taken away to residential school. Brenda J. Child (Ojibwe) reports:

The most painful story of resistance to assimilation programs and compulsory school attendance laws involved the Hopis in Arizona, who surrendered a group of men to the military rather than voluntarily relinquish their children. The Hopi men served time in federal prison at Alcatraz.[4]

Many children died at Carlisle, and they died running away from the institution. Child, in her study of residential schools, found that running away was a universal thread that ran across residential schools and across generations. Physical and emotional abuse, including sexual abuse, is well documented in the stories of survivors of the residential schools in the United States and Canada. Children were beaten and worse for not understanding English, for speaking their languages, for minor infractions of military rule, for running away, even for grieving. Many died of illnesses, many died of abuse, and many died of broken hearts.

It must be remembered also, that at this time, the Indian residential schools were a cross-cultural experience for children who were taken from their parents and families, who were abruptly thrust into a foreign world, who were harshly punished for not knowing what was expected of them.

Lone Wolf (Blackfoot), tells this story:

It was very cold that day when we were loaded into the wagons. None of us wanted to go and our parents didn't want to let us go. Oh, we cried for this was the first time we were to be separated from our parents. I remember looking back at Na-tah-ki and she was crying too. Nobody waved as the wagons, escorted by the soldiers, took us toward the school at Fort Shaw. Once there our belongings were taken from us, even the little medicine bags our mothers had given to us to protect us from harm. Everything was placed in a heap and set afire.

Next was the long hair, the pride of all the Indians. The boys, one by one, would break down and cry when they saw their braids thrown on the floor. All of the buckskin clothes had to go and we had to put on the clothes of the White Man.

If we thought that the days were bad, the nights were much worse. This was the time when real loneliness set in, for it was when we knew that we were all alone. Many boys ran away from the school because the treatment was so bad but most of them were caught and brought back by the police. We were told never to talk Indian and if we were caught, we got a strapping with a leather belt.

I remember one evening when we were all lined up in a room and one of the boys said something in Indian to another boy. The man in charge of us pounced on the boy, caught him by the shirt, and threw him across the room. Later we found out that his collar-bone was broken. The boy's father, an old warrior, came to the school. He told the instructor that among his people, children were never punished by striking them. That was no way to teach children; kind words and good examples were much better. Then he added, 'Had I been there when that fellow hit my son, I would have killed him.' Before the instructor could stop the old warrior he took his boy and left. The family then beat it to Canada and never came back.[5]

Part of the education students received at residential schools included distorted instruction about who Indian People were. Chippewa student Merta Bercier wrote:

Did I want to be an Indian? After looking at the pictures of the Indians on the warpath—fighting, scalping women and children, and Oh! such ugly faces. No! Indians are mean people—I'm glad I'm not an Indian, I thought.[6]

Many of those who survived Carlisle came out thoroughly brainwashed, and suffering from what we now call "post-traumatic stress syndrome."

"The point of brainwashing," Paula Gunn Allen (Laguna/Sioux) says,

> is to take away all sense of self, of community, of value, of worth, even of orientation, to be replaced by habits of mind and behavior that the captor finds acceptable. The boys and girls at Carlisle Indian School were trained to be cannon fodder in American wars, to serve as domestics and farm hands, and to leave off all ideas or beliefs that came to them from their Native communities, including and particularly their belief that they were entitled to land, life, liberty, and dignity.

> In a short time, the child comes to love and admire his captor,...a not uncommon adjustment made by those taken hostage; separated by all that is familiar; stripped, shorn, robbed of their very self; renamed.

> By and large the procedure was successful, although the legacy of damaged minds and crippled souls it left in its wake is as yet untold. Psychic numbing, Post Traumatic Stress Syndrome, battered wife syndrome, suicide, alcoholism, ennui—are there any names for psychecide? A century after..., the great-great grandchildren of decultured Indians struggle to find the world that was ripped away...by a deliberate, planned method euphemistically called education.[7]

A BRIEF DIGRESSION ABOUT NAMING

When the administrators at Carlisle took the Indian children's names away, they knew what they were doing in the long, painstaking process of "killing the Indian." In taking away the linguistic Indian name—which had been a source of strength, cultural pride and psychic identity—and making the "new" names very common, written everywhere, used again and again, they in effect erased all spiritual aspects of the children's identities.

Traditionally, Indian children did not have their names spoken often. When someone was referred to, it was usually either by relationship or by a nickname. But the children knew who they were: they belonged to the name, and the name belonged to them, and to no other. Naming and self-naming was a fluid, ongoing process that changed throughout a person's life according to circumstance, personal experience, loss, triumph, foolishness, or social commentary. So a person could have (at least) a birth name, a baby name, several nicknames, a child name, a "young adult" name, an adult name, and an elder name. In addition, there might be a "secret" or ceremonial name, known only by the individual and the holy person who gave that name.

Compare all this, if you will, to the act of "renaming" at Carlisle, as related by Ota K'te, Plenty Kill, who became known as Luther Standing Bear:

> One day when we came to school there was a lot of writing on the blackboards. We did not know what it meant.... None of the names were read or explained to us, so of course we did not know the sound or meaning of any of them.

> The teacher had a long pointed stick in her hand, and the interpreter told the boy in the front seat to come up. The teacher handed the stick to him, and the interpreter told him to pick out any name he wanted.... When the long stick was handed to him, he turned to us as much to say, "Shall I— or will you help me—to take one of these names?" He did not know what to do for a time....

> Finally, he pointed out one of the names written on the blackboard. Then the teacher took a piece of white tape and wrote the name on it. Then she cut off a length of the tape and sewed it on the back of the boy's shirt. Then that name was erased from the board.... Soon we all had names of white men sewed on our backs.[8]

Once the children's naming in this random way became enforced, they were denied the ability to express their life stories in name, an act of independent, autonomous identity central to Native ways of being in the world. It was a small, but important, step in "killing the Indian."

With this history in mind, let us now turn to the children's book, *My Heart Is On the Ground* by Ann Rinaldi.

ABOUT THE DEAR AMERICA SERIES AND *MY HEART IS ON THE GROUND*

The Library of Congress Cataloging-in-Publication Data summary of *My Heart Is On the Ground* states, "In the diary account of her life at a government-run Pennsylvania residential school in 1880, a twelve-year-old Sioux Indian girl reveals a great need to find a way to help her people."

In this account, Nannie Little Rose, who refers to herself as "Sioux," describes her life at Carlisle Indian Industrial School, where she has been sent to be educated in the English language, and "American" customs and lifeways. Although determined to make her people proud, she finds this new world overwhelming—from its inside buildings and cumbersome dress, to the requirements that she take an English name, submit to having her hair cut, and adapt to a foreign culture. With the arrival of Nannie's friend, Lucy Pretty Eagle, the tenor of the story shifts. Lucy's propensity to lapse into self-induced trances causes her to be buried alive by the white people who mistakenly think she has died; and Nannie, who was not there to save her, suffers from not only grief but overwhelming guilt. But Nannie overcomes all of this, and adapt she does. Resolute in learning all she can in order to share her knowledge with her people, Nannie Little Rose meets every challenge and overcomes every obstacle, finally deciding to become a teacher "to help other blanket Indian children to learn."

All of the books in the "Dear America" series are identical in format. Each book begins with a title page, followed by "the diary." An epilogue tells us what happened to the protagonist and her descendants afterwards. A "Historical Note" and a section of photographs followed by a section called "About the Author" gives a biographical sketch and then quotes directly from the author about her research. The fictional aspect is played down, with the dedication, acknowledgments, and CIP pages in the back.

The authors of the books are not identified on the book covers or on the spine. Each cover carries the "Dear America" logo, a small image of the protagonist, the book title, and a place/time note that indicates setting. Each book looks like a genuine diary. The books are attractive to look at and comfortable to hold. Special features include a sewn-in satin ribbon bookmark and cream-colored pages cut with a deckled edge that give them the look of quality diaries.

The portrait of the child on the cover of *My Heart Is On the Ground*, originally entitled "Cree Indian Girl, Little Star," is listed on the permissions page as "Indian Girl, Little Star." It was done by James Bama, a painter of romantic western and Indian subjects. The child in the portrait has her long hair parted and loose. She is wearing a headband, with two eagle feathers hanging straight down near her left temple. Her head is tilted forward, and her eyes are lowered. Behind her portrait is an underlay of an 1892 photograph of the Carlisle students, their hair cut short, in front of the school.

Discussions with child readers, teachers, and librarians reveal initial confusion about the fictive nature of this series. The epilogue, especially, continues to confound both professionals and young readers. Are these real diaries? Are these fictional diaries of real people? Are the epilogues, at least, real? Given the format of this series, it's hard to tell, unless one is an expert, a detective, or just naturally suspicious.

"Launched in September 1996, and with over five million books in print," according to Scholastic, "Dear America has become one of the most popular book series in America, charting regularly in the Top 5 on Publisher Weekly bestseller lists." The "Dear America" series clearly has mass appeal, and Scholastic aggressively markets these books to nine- to twelve-year-old girls. Marketing strategies and tie-ins include the "Dear America Desk Collection," a "new line of desk accessories for fans of the best-selling book series," and a series of six hour-long "Dear America" movies on HBO.

The "Dear America" website, also playing down the fact that this series is fiction, states:

> Dear America invites you into the personal experience of girls from different times in American History. The books and television show are inspired by real letters and diaries from girls who lived in extraordinary circumstances. You will experience firsthand what it was like to grow up and live in another time and place.

and

Open Their Diaries.... Make History Your Own! Today's most distinguished authors lend their voices and talents to these moving narratives—presented in an intimate diary format—with each book extensively researched and inspired by real letters and diaries of the time.

My Heart Is On the Ground is described simply as, "A Sioux girl is sent to the Carlisle Indian School to help save her people."

The "Dear America" series continues to receive overwhelming critical acclaim. *The Chicago Tribune* notes that the "Dear America diaries represent the best of historical fiction for any age," and *School Library Journal* cites the books as "engaging and accessible."

Like the series, *My Heart Is On the Ground* has received extremely favorable reviews. *School Library Journal* says, "Rinaldi depicts widely divergent cultures with clarity and compassion.... The period, the setting, and Nannie herself all come to life. An excellent addition to a popular series."

And *Booklist* states,

> The entries are a poignant mix of past and present—Nannie's life with her family, encounters with other students, the horrific death of a friend, the efforts of both well-meaning and misguided adults. They burst with details of about culture and custom, adding wonderful texture to this thought-provoking book, which raises numerous questions as it depicts the frustration, the joy, and the confusion of one of yesterday's children growing up in two cultures.

THE REVIEW

> There I found the Indian burial ground, with dozens of white headstones bearing the names of the Native American children from all tribes who died while at the school. The names, with the tribes inscribed underneath, were so lyrical that they leapt out at me and took on instant personalities. Although many of these children attended Carlisle at dates later than that of my story, I used some of their names for classmates of Nannie Little Rose. (p. 195)

> Like Lucy Pretty Eagle, not all the children in the book were at Carlisle that first year. But like Lucy Pretty Eagle, their personalities came through to me with such force and inspiration, I had to use them. I am sure that in whatever Happy Hunting Ground they now reside, they will forgive this artistic license, and even smile upon it. (p. 196)

Individuals in the field of children's literature may dismiss our concerns and ask, "But is it a good book?" We think not. From a literary perspective, it lacks consistency and logic. As a work of historical fiction, it is rife with glaring factual errors. As a work of "multicultural" literature, it lacks authenticity.

Appropriation

Appropriation of our lives and literatures is nothing new. Our bodies and bones continue to be displayed in museums all over the U.S. and Canada. For the last hundred years, many of our traditional stories have been turned into books for children without permission and with little if any respect given to their origins or sacred content. Now, Rinaldi has taken this appropriation of Native lives and stories one step further. That she would take the names of real Native children from gravestones and make up experiences to go with them is the coldest kind of appropriation. These were children who died lonely and alone, without their parents to comfort them. They were buried without proper ceremony in this lonely and sad place. Native people who visit the cemetery today express a profound sense of sadness.

Rinaldi chose to name this book by appropriating a Cheyenne proverb that goes, "A Nation is not conquered until the hearts of its women are on the ground. Then it is done, no matter how brave its warriors nor how strong their weapons." In its original form, this statement is about the strength and courage of Indian women. In its original form, the phrase suggests total defeat, the conquering of a Nation, the death of a way of life. Throughout this book, the child protagonist, Nannie Little Rose, uses the phrase "my heart is on the ground" whenever she happens to feel sad or upset. This is a trivialization of the belief system of a people.

Lack of Historical Accuracy

A basic criterion of historical fiction is that facts about people who actually lived and events that actually happened must be accurate, or, at least, any deviations clearly spelled out. This is especially important in books for young readers. Factual errors abound here; they are on nearly every page.

- There was no such person as "Chief Sitting Bull of Cheyenne nation." (p. 14) His name was Tatanka Iotanka, whom the whites called Sitting Bull. He was a spiritual leader, not a chief; and he was Hunkpapa Lakota, not Cheyenne.

- American Horse was not a "chief of the Red Cloud Sioux." (p. 20) He was a cousin to Red Cloud.

- Spotted Tail did not take his band west to "be free." (p. 12) He left Whetstone Agency to get away from the alcohol that ran heavily there.

- The Cheyenne and Oglala "Sioux" were not the only ones to fight Custer. (p. 50) Hunkpapa and Arapaho were also part of the battle.

- The whites did not "give" the Lakota the Black Hills in a treaty (p. 12); by treaty, the people were able to retain a portion of what had been theirs for millennia. They are still fighting to keep it.

- In a diary entry, composed only six months after her arrival at Carlisle, Nannie Little Rose writes in perfect English, but transcribes Red Cloud's speech into her diary, using stilted language instead of Red Cloud's own flowing and eloquent words (pp. 103-104).

- Spotted Tail sent his sons to Carlisle because he knew it was going to be important for them to learn to speak, read and write English. He did not instruct his daughter, Red Road, to recruit children or to convince them to go. Yet in this book Red Road says, "You must learn the white people's ways. To help our people. You will see great trees with red apples. You will ride on the iron horse. You will wear a school dress." (p. 27) As George Hyde notes:

    [B]efore he openly supported the plan and offered his sons as pupils, [he] stipulated that his daughter Red Road and her husband Charles Tackett should go with the children...and be paid a salary to act as their guardians.... [He] had the mentality to realize that these children, in faraway Pennsylvania, would be terribly frightened and unhappy if some adults of their own tribe were not there to protect and advise them.[9]

- When Spotted Tail visited Carlisle in 1880 and found his children, unhappy, in military uniform, drilling with rifles, he insisted that they return with him to Rosebud. In Rinaldi's rendition of this episode, Nannie writes:

    We all knew Max and his three brothers did not wish to go, not even Paul. There was much screaming and crying. Red Road tried to calm her little brothers. Spotted Tail made them take off their citizens' clothing and put on their blanket clothing. He had to drag Max into the wagon. (p. 121)

But according to historical accounts, the scene was just the opposite:

    Spotted Tail [talked] in private with his sons and the other boys from Rosebud and found that most of them were miserable and homesick.... None of them had learned English or to read or write.[10]

    [He] took all his children, apparently four sons, a grandson, a granddaughter, and another small boy he claimed as a close relative. He carried them off under guard of Sioux chiefs and headmen, daring Pratt to try and stop him. Pratt was too overwhelmed to attempt that. He had to guard the rest of his school, as there were indications that a general stampede for the train might take place. As it was, some of the heartbroken children who were being left at the school managed to steal away and hide themselves on the train.... At Harrisburg the train was searched again and a little Oglala girl (Red Dog's granddaughter) was found and dragged screaming back to captivity.[11]

- Rinaldi paints Pratt as a model of sweet reason, kind to the children, counseling them, talking with them about their futures: "Mr. Captain Pratt has been having private talks with every student in our class. He is making sure we are doing the right lessons for what we want to become." (p. 167) Again, written accounts paint a different picture:

> It seems curious that church people, humanitarians, and idealists should fall so much in love with
> Pratt. He was a quite ordinary army officer who had developed a marked ability for knocking the
> spirit out of the Indians and turning them into docile students who would obey all orders. Pratt
> was a domineering man who knew only one method for dealing with anyone who opposed his
> will. He bullied them into submission.[12]

- All of the references to loaning money or having access to money are inaccurate. (p. 122)
  Money was not available to the children, no matter how much they had earned. It would have
  been highly unlikely for Nannie to have given her brother money without the approval of the
  administration.

- Contrary to Rinaldi's statement in the historical note that "most of the graduates were able to
  earn a living away from the reservation," and "others went on to higher education," evidence
  points to the opposite. Earning a living "away from the reservation" meant going into Indian
  service and working on a reservation or agency—or in one of the dozens of off-reservation
  boarding schools modeled after Carlisle. And very few children graduated. Of the total population of 10,000, only 758 students—or fewer than 10%—graduated. More students ran away
  than graduated—1,758 runaways are documented.

Lack of Cultural Authenticity

The events in *My Heart Is On the Ground* are not plausible. In 1880, a Lakota child of the protagonist's
age would have been well educated by her aunties and grandmothers in Lakota tradition and lore,
and ways of seeing the world and behaving in right relation to it. She would probably have had
younger children to care for, as well as older sisters in her extended family, her tiospaye, to emulate.

- A Lakota child in 1880 would not have referred to herself as "Sioux." (beginning at p. 6) It is
  a French corruption of an enemy-name used by the Ojibwe. She would have referred to herself by her band (Sicangu) or location (Spotted Tail Agency) or by her familial group, her
  tiospaye. And she would certainly not have referred to Indian men as "braves."

- A Lakota child would not have been misinformed about her own people: "I come from a place
  called Dakota. My people belong to the Great Plains tribe." (p. 12) Nor would she have voiced
  stereotypes such as "Our men are very brave and honorable. Our women are noble." (p. 12)
  Nor would a Lakota child have used phrases such as "our men" and "our women"; she would
  probably have referred to people by their relationships, e.g., "our mothers" or "our grandfathers." Nor would she have used the French word "travois"—she would have used the Lakota
  word, or its English equivalent, pony-drag (p. 33).

- If this Lakota child had in fact been given a diary (which is highly unlikely at Carlisle in 1880),
  she would probably have been much more circumspect in her writing, because she would have
  known that words have power, even written words. And she would have known that she could
  be severely punished for speaking her thoughts.

- She would probably not have written about the wholesale slaughter of the buffalo, broken
  treaties, land theft, and "ann-u-itees" (p. 5 and throughout), nor would she have written dis-
  paragingly about the white people—including the teachers who would read this diary—who
  held the power of life and death over the children.

- And a Lakota child certainly would not indict her own people for the theft of the land—"our
  chiefs have made large mistake in giving over our lands." (p. 5 and throughout)

- Children who knew some English were used at Carlisle and other residential schools to help
  control the other children. The respect they were taught at home for their elders was used
  against them in residential school. They were not taught to be simple interpreters, or "Friends-
  To-Go-Between-Us" (p. 3 and throughout)—they were taught to be informants, and used as
  such.

- Children were severely punished for speaking their own languages. They were beaten, confined, forced to eat lye soap, and worse. Although they often would speak their own languages in secret, perhaps whispering after lights-out, they would not have engaged in such risky behavior in the dining room or in front of Pratt. (p. 69)

- Children might certainly have made fun of their teachers in secret, giving them names like "Miss Chipmunk," but again, they would not write negatively about white adults (in a place where there was no privacy of any kind): "She is bad to the eye. Fat and ugly." (p. 13)

- On page 7, Nannie says, "The white people are very powerful. They know almost everything on the earth's surface and in the heavens also. So much to learn!" Here, the young reader is set up to believe that Lakota people had/have no scientific knowledge, no education system. By the age of twelve, Nannie would have been educated by her elders in Lakota history, ways of the Earth, Stars, Thunders, Spirits, and healing plants. Although the wisdom of these things was passed down through the oral tradition, it does not diminish the wisdom of the people. To assume that, one week after arriving at Carlisle, Nannie would have negated all of her traditional teachings is unbelievable.

- After a week at Carlisle, Nannie says, "I think Missus Camp Bell (a teacher) would make a good Sioux woman." (p. 11) Does "Missus Camp Bell" know about traditional ways of being? How could she know how to care for a traditional Lakota family if she is not connected to the culture? Could she do quillwork, find food, skin animals, cure skins, prepare meat, make traditional clothing?

- Lakota children were taught to be deferential, cooperative, and respectful to their elders. A Lakota child would not have written about her mother, "My mother is jealous of Red Road because she is so young and pretty." (p. 11) Most plural marriages included sisters or cousins so that there was harmony in the family. Young girls learned quillwork from their mothers or aunties. Nannie would not have gone to Red Road's tipi to learn quillwork.

- On page 4, Nannie says, "I have been on no battles or hunts. Of what worth am I, a girl of twelve winters?" A young Lakota girl feeling worthless? One of the seven sacred ceremonies involves a girl's passage. At 12, she would have certainly known her importance to her own family and community as both a cherished child (*wakanyela*, sacred being) and a new young woman.

- Brothers and sisters have a special bond in Lakota society that was even more pronounced in this time period. They were taught to honor each other above all others, including spouses. That way, if there was a divorce, they could turn to their siblings for help. Given this bond, a Lakota girl would not criticize her brother this way: "He much time acts like a fool.... On the way here he made much trouble.... Whiteshield is always trouble." (pp. 9-10)

- Moreover, Nannie would not have been shamed by her brother's doing a war dance in the yard: "You are no warrior.... A warrior does not shame his people." (p. 39) More than likely, she would have supported everything he did because he was being extremely brave in rebelling.

- Nannie would not have considered her brother "spoiled" for having been honored for counting coup on a dead enemy at age twelve. "Spoiled" is not a Lakota concept; the honoring of children is; and counting coup is counting coup, whether the enemy is dead or alive.

- And, of course, Whiteshield would not have referred to his sister, or any girl, in a derogatory way, such as: "Only a stupid girl would say such a thing." (p. 39)

- When Whiteshield, in an act of open rebellion, does a war dance, this is how Nannie describes it:

    There was a strange figure carrying a torch and doing a dance. He was wearing only a breechclout and moccasins. In his belt he had a knife. Around and around he danced while he chanted a war song. (p. 37)

This "strange figure" is her brother. He would be known to her and not be considered strange. If he were dancing a particular dance, she would name it and understand its significance. If he were singing, she would know the words and what the words meant. If all of their traditional clothing had been taken to be sold or destroyed as was the case at Carlisle, where did he get a breechcloth and moccasins? And where did he get a knife?

- "He hates baths," Nannie says of her brother. (p. 16) Traditionally, Indian people bathed every day. This has been documented. Whiteshield may have disliked bathing at the school, in tubs, which would have been far less sanitary than bathing in a lake or stream; but this suggests that Indians didn't like bathing when in fact they bathed much more regularly than the newcomers.

- However, the rebellious Whiteshield finally does a brave deed, according to Nannie: He catches, and brings to the guardhouse, a "tramp" who crawled over the school wall, entered the grounds, and stole some wood. (p. 82) For children who are raised to be generous above all things, it is highly unlikely that they would participate in capturing a poor homeless person. And in any event, it would certainly not be seen as an act of bravery.

- Nannie's father would not have asked her to do an act that would have been her brother's responsibility:

Then he says I must study and work and obey, and do one act of bravery.... I must bring him honor with this act. I ask him if he would also ask one act of bravery from my brother.... [H]e shakes his head and says...my brother is older, but I am wiser. (p. 30)

It just would not have happened that way. Men and women have different roles in Lakota society; they are not subordinate, they are just different.

- Nor would her father have ever suggested that she take on a vision quest. (p. 30) This was and is a male activity. Women experience moontime (menstruation) and special ceremonies and practices to acknowledge them.

- Nannie says, "My grandmother...has powerful medicine. She has visions. She tells them to the shaman, our holy man, who explains it to our people." (p. 31) If a child's grandmother indeed had visions, she might or might not share them with a spiritual leader. But visions are a private thing; they wouldn't be "explained" to anyone. And "shaman" is not an Indian term.

- Nannie would not have said, written, or thought: "I think sometimes that Pretty Eagle is going to be a shaman, even though she is a girl." (p. 33) Pretty Eagle is a child, and only post-menopausal women can attain the status of spiritual leader.

- Later, Rinaldi has Nannie's grandma teaching Pretty Eagle to go into trances, which she practices, and sending her on a vision quest, where her "spirit helper" tells her to come to Carlisle and "show the children it is not wrong to be here..." (pp. 75-76) This passage suggests a Native spiritual affirmation of the mistreatment of Indian children at Carlisle.

- Nannie says, "We learned about the Devil in Sunday school. I think he is like some of our medicine men. He can change his shape if he wishes." (p. 40) To compare a respected and loved spiritual leader to the foreign Christian concept of "devil" is not something a Lakota child, steeped in Lakota cosmology, would do. More likely, she would compare the "devil" to an evil spirit.

- Nannie's mother asks, "What will you learn? To be more silly than you are?" (p. 32) Lakota children were and are treated with more respect than that. The Lakota did not and do not talk down to their children.

- Nannie says to Pretty Eagle, "We will gather all the wildflowers on the plains and put them in front of every tipi." (p. 33) This is not something that Lakota children would do. This would be considered wasteful and overlays a European perspective on Lakota daily life.

- Nannie fasts "to find her spirit helper," something she, as a young woman, would not have done. When the doctor orders her to eat, she does, with gusto, then feels guilty: "I had two pieces [of chocolate cake]. How can I ever be pure enough to find my spirit helper when I love choc-o-late cake so?" (p. 58) This reflects an overlay of European-style guilt upon Lakota belief and ritual. Lakota children would have preferred a big bowl of soup, some frybread and for "dessert," a bowl of wojapi instead of chocolate.

- Nannie describes Sun Dance, the most sacred ceremony of the Lakota people, this way:

> Part of me is missing. I feel like a young warrior in our Sun Dance, who has had the skin near his breasts cut and sticks put in the openings. The sticks are fastened to two ropes and I am left hanging, to show my bravery. (p. 29)

This description reflects a lack of understanding of Sun Dance, a thank-offering for the good of the community. In Sun Dance,

> participants offer Wakantanka the greatest gift they have, their flesh and blood.... The dancers move in a circle around and around and around. The circle represents our universe.... As the participants dance, they pray hard for their personal prayers and the prayers of the entire Lakota nation. Family members and friends stay nearby to offer their support and send their own prayers to Wakantanka.[13]

Moreover, a Lakota child in 1880 would not likely think about talking to strangers about (or writing about) Sun Dance in any way, nor would she obsess over it or dream about it (pp. 123, 127, 131).

- And a young woman in art class would not be drawing pictures of Sun Dance, as Red Road does (p. 60). She just wouldn't.

- Later in the diary, Nannie says,

> Today we buried Horace Watchful Fox. The ground was hard and cold. I know some of the boys and girls wanted to tear their garments, cut their hair, cover themselves with mud, and slash at their arms because the Death Angel took Horace. But we were made to stand in citizens' clothing, clean and quiet. (p. 44)

This is more a description of Rinaldi's fantasy than it is of a Lakota grieving ceremony. Moreover, it is unlikely that children of other Nations would participate in a Lakota ritual, nor would children of that time period have engaged in the same kind of grieving ceremony as adults.

- And Indian children would not be gathering evergreen and berries to make funeral wreaths (p. 43) unless they had been forced to by school officials.

- The passage where Nannie describes her father shows a lack of understanding of the clothing traditional people wore:

> He is wearing his chief's garments. A shirt with fringe and beaded bands on the shoulders and sleeves. Also his chief's leggings with beads, his bear claw necklace, and his braids are wrapped in otter tails. On his head is a stick headdress. I know he wears it to show the white people who we are. But no other men on the reservation wear their chief's clothing. I think my father wishes to be what he once was, maybe so. (pp. 29-30)

Tribal leaders did not dress in headdress and regalia every day and every moment. And none of us can even guess as to what a "stick headdress" might be.

- A Lakota child would not have been able to give away the possessions of a friend who has just died. (p. 147) At home, it would have been the parents' responsibility; and here, at Carlisle, everything would have been taken away from the children anyway.

- The characterization of Belle Rain Water is also confusing. Hopi children were and are taught to be quiet, respectful people. Hopi children in the foreign culture of a residential school would be even more likely to keep to themselves or to try to seek out their relatives, rather than openly engage in conversation, not to mention arguments, with people outside their culture. For a Hopi child to be so belligerent and aggressive just does not fit with how her society would have raised her.

- Later, Belle Rain Water, in apology, gives Nannie a prayer stick. A Hopi child would not have given a "prayer stick" to a Lakota child. (p. 145) First of all, sacred objects like these are not things children have or share, especially intertribally. Second (see above comment), all the children's things were taken away from them; they were not permitted to own anything of a cultural or spiritual nature. And finally, where would Belle Rain Water have gotten an eagle feather?

- Wealth is not, and never has been, measured by the number of poles in a tipi! (p. 41) Wealth was measured by how much one gave away, not by how much one collected.

- Among the Plains peoples, kinnikinnic ("kin-ni-kin-nic") is not tobacco. It is willowbark shavings often mixed with tobacco (p. 15).

- Lakota people did not grow corn and wheat in 1880. (p. 62)

Stereotypes

A basic criterion of good children's literature is that it is free of stereotypes, but stereotypes abound in children's books about American Indian peoples. They are usually found in descriptive passages about Native characters. A few authors like Rinaldi take this one step further, by placing stereotypical language and images in an Indian child protagonist's narrative.

Stereotypical Language

Throughout, Rinaldi uses stereotyped language to express Lakota (or "Indian") speech and thought patterns. These include over-emphasis on compound words (e.g., "Friend-To-Go-Between-Us," "Time-That-Was-Before," "night-middle-made") to "sound Indian," when there is no basis for such use. For instance, Rinaldi makes up the term "Friend-To-Go-Between-Us" as Nannie's word for "interpreter." Yet there is a Lakota word for "interpreter": *iyeska*, literally, one who speaks well. The original term meant "translator," since most translators at the time were the mixed-blood children of Indian women and white traders. Hanco'kan is the Lakota word for midnight.

Rinaldi also uses romantic-sounding metaphors throughout the book: "the path between my mother and me is filled with rocks," (p. 27) "the council fire burns bright," (p. 21) "his spring is poisoned with anger," (p. 49) and of course, the ever-present "my heart is on the ground." A favorite among us is this multi-metaphor: "And her words are not empty gourds, with nothing inside to quench our need, but full of meaning, from which I drink hope." (p. 29)

Throughout, Nannie romantically obsesses over the concepts "bravery," "honor," and "nobleness." Nannie also repeatedly uses the term "blanket Indians" as descriptive, rather than as a derogatory term used by whites at the time, to refer to traditional people.

As well, Nannie Little Rose speaks and writes in the stilted speech pattern we call "early jawbreaker" at the beginning of the book ("My teacher, Missus Camp Bell, say I must write in this book each day. She calls it die-eerie. It is the white man's talking leaves. But they talk not yet.... Teacher tells it that I know some English, that she is much proud of me, but wants be more proud."). (p. 3) Yet, in only ten months, Nannie is speaking and writing perfect if not eloquent English, except for when she "lapses" back into "Indian" thought-patterns.

Stereotypical Nobility

Throughout, Nannie "explains" Lakota belief and ritual to the child reader, a transparent literary device we find annoying. As well, these "beliefs" are wrong. Besides the Sun Dance and mourning ritual, discussed above, there are many examples of this.

- "With my people we believe that all things have a spirit. A war club has a spirit. A prairie dog has two spirits." (p. 81) This is a gross oversimplification of the belief that everything has life and purpose.

- "In order to be brave I must have a spirit helper." (pp. 30-31) This obsession with bravery and "spirit helpers" runs throughout the book, and again is a gross oversimplification of the value of courage.

Nannie is obsessed with doing "a brave deed to bring honor to my people." This is practically the only thing she thinks about. At the end of the book, young readers are left to believe that her "brave deed" is to play the part of a pilgrim in the school's Thanksgiving play. In the scene that is supposed to show her victory, this little girl has successfully made the transition from Indian to white—she has become a clear victim of colonialism.

Stereotypical Treatment of Girls and Women

Derogatory references to girls and women abound in this book. Besides coming from Nannie herself (e.g., "Of what worth am I, a girl of twelve winters?"—p. 4), most of these references are mouthed by her brother, Charles Whiteshield ("only a stupid girl would say such a thing—p. 39, "women's dreams are worth nothing"—p. 67, "he says I am not a warrior, just a girl"—p. 105). This is not, and never has been, a Lakota way of expression; and is the opposite of honored brother-sister relationships (see above).

As well, traditional Lakota girls and women were not obsessed with appearance. That is not meant to say that they did not dress well. But concepts such as "fat and ugly" (p. 13) and "young and pretty" (p. 11) are not Lakota concepts.

Long hair had and has great significance for Lakota people. Traditionally, hair was and is cut only at a time of mourning. At Carlisle, children's braids were lopped off to frighten and subdue them, to "cut them off" from their people. When Pretty Eagle gets her hair cut, Nannie says,

> Pretty Eagle is very frightened. I held her hand while they cut her hair. When it was cropped short, Pretty Eagle shook her head and only she laughed. "It feels so light," she said. "I think I will like it." (p. 71)

This is not how Lakota children experienced this awful first assault. Often, they screamed and cried, and would be beaten for it.

In describing the practice of Lakota courtship, Nannie says,

> If I came of age to wed before our ways were done, the man, he puts on his best robe and walk by our tipi. Then he come closer and grab of me. I would struggle, but he would win. If I like him I bring him water and ask him to come another time. (pp. 5-6)

This description is a mixture of TV-caveman ritual and fantasy. In any event, it is nothing like traditional Lakota courtship. By the age of twelve, Nannie would probably have received traditional womanhood instruction from her elders in addition to having witnessed the courting process (and perhaps giggled about it many times with her girlfriends).

A BRIEF DIGRESSION ABOUT LUCY PRETTY EAGLE AND COLONIALISM

We don't know very much about Lucy Pretty Eagle. We know that her Lakota name was Take the Tail, that she was the daughter of Pretty Eagle, that she came to Carlisle from the Rosebud Agency at age ten on March 9, 1884, and that she died four months later. Hers is the first gravestone in the Carlisle cemetery.

According to the author's note,

> Some research indicates that Lucy may not have been dead when she was buried. She could have been in a self-induced trance, to try to appeal to spiritual powers for any number of reasons. (p. 180)

So Rinaldi has taken a well-known ghost story that has been circulating around Carlisle for several decades, embellished it further with her own interpretation of Lakota cosmology, and crafted a children's book around this "event."

Whether Rinaldi did this unconsciously or not, an Indian girl being buried alive is a gruesome metaphor for colonization and the spiritual, cultural and psychic suffocation and trauma Indian children suffered at Carlisle and other residential schools.

But this is much more than a metaphor: Nannie Little Rose, Lucy's friend, knew about the trance-like states and blames herself for not being able to tell the white people in charge that Lucy wasn't really dead. Here we have Indian children responsible for the death of Indian children—after all, the white people had just made an "honest mistake." And the story, crafted this way, allows both Rinaldi and the non-Native reader to avoid the issues and erase the real reasons that many, many children died at the residential schools: malnutrition, tuberculosis, pneumonia, smallpox, physical abuse (including sexual abuse), and—no less importantly—broken hearts and spirits, and loneliness.

Moreover, the "trance-mistaken-for-death" scenario that Rinaldi uses here again perpetuates the stereotype that Indians died or were decimated because they were Indians: unable to adapt, unwilling to change and—worst of all—physically and emotionally different from white people. A possible translation of this scene: Lucy is killed, not by the tragic residential school experience, not by the loss of parents and homeland, not by inadequate diet or disease—but by her own "Indianness." In other words, Indian people have only themselves to blame for their own demise. They just couldn't become civilized—it was inherently, genetically impossible.

It is entirely possible that Rinaldi may not even be conscious of what she's done. Such stereotypical colonialist attitudes as expressed in this book may be so embedded in the American psyche that we often miss it even at its most blatant. We call this to the non-Native reader's attention because it is easy to miss otherwise, this attitude that colonization is "meant to be" or "inevitable." It is neither.

A BRIEF DIGRESSION ABOUT PERSPECTIVE

In many ways, *My Heart Is On the Ground* reflects what can go wrong when a non-Native author writes about Native cultures. One of the more controversial questions in literature is who should be writing books that include characters or themes related to members of a particular ethnic, racial, or religious group. Those who prefer that such books be written from within communities perhaps justifiably fear exploitation, misrepresentation, or having their voices preempted. However, some non-Indians have written quality books about Native peoples, histories, and cultures, so it won't be argued here that only Native authors can write Native-themed stories.

While many fine books are written by authors outside of a community who do their homework, the voice of an insider still offers a unique perspective that is in many ways a rare gift to young readers. We sometimes see stories from those who have married Native people, borne Native children, been adopted into Native families, or known Native people who called them "friend." Even more directly, we sometimes see stories by Native people, stories that have been passed down or reshaped to reflect family and personal histories.

Indeed, books written by Native authors do not usually contain conventions that are typically used to signal the book as being about a Native character. For example, characters in books written by Native authors don't speak in guttural English. They don't act like savages and they don't seem like mystical creatures. Rather, they are often eloquent speakers. But this eloquence may not fit the non-Native reader's (or publisher's) expectations of how Natives speak, so they may reject the book as not being "authentic enough."

But on more subtle grounds, Indian writers have to do their research as well. A story from one's great uncle may actually be more authentic than anything written by someone with a Ph.D. in anthropology. A childhood experience may lend itself to a scene, even a whole story. Not everything crafted by Native writers will necessarily present the most popular or desirable or comfortable picture, even within their communities, certainly to the mainstream. Although each story will have the individual storyteller's own vision and voice, they are all taking care to fulfill their responsibility.

An outside researcher, however careful, who goes on to write a story based entirely on written words—especially the words of another outsider—rather than experiences may craft a book that few would hesitate to share with children. However, these authors may unknowingly mimic misconceptions or stereotypes inherent in the research material, and still others may "whitewash" history to make the non-Native audience more comfortable with issues like stolen land and forced assimilation.

Indian voices are grossly underrepresented in books with Native characters and themes. It is common that African-American literature classes or book lists feature a number of books by African-American authors and illustrators. It is common that Asian-American and Latino literature classes and book lists feature a number of books by Asian Americans and Latinos. It is also common that Native-American literature classes and book lists often fail to feature a single title by any person with any sort of tie to a Native community. The proportional disparity is staggering. A child could read literally hundreds of books with Native characters and not one by anyone who had ever so much as shaken hands with a real live Indian.

FINAL COMMENTS

Despite all the documented horrors of the "noble experiment" that was Carlisle, *My Heart Is On the Ground* casts the Carlisle Indian Industrial School in a positive light as though it were a good thing. Rinaldi even says in her author's notes, "Those first Sioux children who came to Carlisle could not have been happy there. But it was their only chance for a future." (p. 177)

The legacy of Carlisle and the other Indian residential schools—this "future"—is a legacy of hopelessness and despair, of alcoholism and other substance abuse, suicide, dysfunctional parenting; an open, gaping century-long wound that will take many more years for the Indian communities all over the U.S. and Canada to heal.

Yet, the only "bad" characters in this book are Indian people—Belle Rain Water, a jealous, spiteful Hopi child, who eventually comes around to seeing the error of her ways; Charles Whiteshield (Nannie's brother), a "renegade" who "acts like a fool" and makes "much trouble," and whose behavior "shames" Nannie, until he eventually comes around to seeing the error of his ways; Goodbird (Nannie's mother), who is jealous and spiteful; White Thunder (Nannie's father), who ignorantly tries to maintain the old ways; and Spotted Tail, who takes his children back, even though they don't want to go home.

Nowhere in this book is to be found the screaming children, thrown onto horse-drawn wagons, being taken away from their homes. Nowhere is to be found the desperately lonely children, heartbroken, sobbing into the night. Nowhere is to be found the terrified children, stripped naked and beaten, for trying to communicate with each other and not understanding what was expected of them. Nowhere is to be found the unrelenting daily humiliation, in word and deed, from the teachers, matrons and staff. Nowhere is to be found the desperate runaways, lost, frozen in the snow. Nowhere to be found is the spirit of resistance. Nowhere.

Resistance among the Indian students was deep, subtle, long-lasting and valiantly carried on for as long as residential schools existed. Besides running away, this resistance took many forms—physical, spiritual, intellectual. Children destroyed property and set fires. They refused to speak English. They subverted teachers' and matrons' orders whenever they could. But except for Charles Whiteshield's "war dance," which is presented as a shameful thing, that resistance—and the courage it represents—receives no attention in this book. As in Francis LaFlesche's *The Middle Five* and Basil H. Johnston's *Indian School Days*, an Indian author would have made this resistance a central part of such as story.

To those who would argue that "it is possible" that a Native child might have had Nannie Little Rose's experiences, the overwhelming body of evidence—written and oral—suggests otherwise. The premise of this book—that a Native child would come in and, within a period of ten months, move from someone who reads and writes limited English and has a totally Indian world view to someone who is totally fluent in a language that is foreign to her and totally assimilated to a foreign culture—and be better for the experience—is highly unlikely. Brainwashing did not come readily. Brainwashing took time.

Given the marketing and distribution forces behind *My Heart Is On the Ground*, we know that it will probably be more widely read than any other book about the residential school experience. The book adds to the great body of misinformation about Native life and struggle in the United States and Canada. This one book epitomizes the utter lack of sensitivity and respect that has come to characterize the vast majority of children's books about Native Americans. Non-Native readers of *My Heart Is On the Ground* will continue to be validated in whatever feelings of superiority they may have; Native children will continue to be humiliated.

Rinaldi goes on to say in the author's note that "I am sure that in whatever Happy Hunting Ground they now reside, they will forgive this artistic license, and even smile upon it." (p. 196) This is the epitome of white fantasy: that Indian people will forgive and even smile upon white people, no matter the atrocities—past and present.

—Marlene R. Atleo/ʔeh ʔeh naa tuu kwiss, Naomi Caldwell, Barb Landis, Jean Paine Mendoza, Deborah A. Miranda, Debbie A. Reese, LaVera Rose, Beverly Slapin and *Cynthia L. Smith*

NOTES

1 Nabokov, Peter, *Native American Testimony*. Viking (1978, revised 1991), p. 222.

2 Josephy, Alvin M., Jr., *500 Nations*. Knopf, 1994.

3 Josephy, *ibid.*, p. 432.

4 Child, Brenda J., *Boarding School Seasons: American Indian Families, 1900-1940*. University of Nebraska, 1998, p. 14.

5 Nabokov, *op. cit.*, p. 220.

6 Josephy, *op. cit.*, p. 434.

7 Allen, Paula Gunn, ed., *Voice of the Turtle: American Indian Literature 1900-1970*. Random House, 1994, pp. 111-112.

8 Standing Bear, Luther, *My People, the Sioux* (1928, University of Nebraska, 1975), in Allen, *ibid.*, pp. 116-117.

9 Hyde, George E., *Spotted Tail's Folk: A History of the Brulé Sioux*. University of Oklahoma, 1979, p. 278.

10 Hyde, *ibid.*, p. 290.

11 Hyde, *ibid.*, pp. 292-293.

12 Hyde, *ibid.*, p. 289.

13 Rose, LaVera, *Grandchildren of the Lakota*. Lerner, 1999.

REVIEWS: BOOKS ABOUT THE INDIAN RESIDENTIAL SCHOOLS

Archuleta, Margaret L. (Pueblo), Brenda J. Child (Ojibwe), and K. Tsianina Lomawaima (Hopi), editors, *Away from Home: American Indian Boarding School Experiences, 1879-2000.* **Heard Museum (2000). 143 pages, b/w and color photos, color illustrations; high school-up**

Away from Home was produced as a companion volume to a multimedia exhibition called *Remembering Our Indian School Days: The Boarding School Experience*, which opened in 2000 at the Heard Museum in Phoenix and will be on view through 2005. It's a collection of photographs, paintings, collages, poems, stories and reminiscences of people who survived—or didn't—the attempt to wipe them out. The Indian residential schools were by their very nature places of violence, abuse and neglect. Assimilation—read "cultural genocide"—did not come quickly or easily or well. "Beginning in 1879," says the dedication,

> tens of thousands of Native [children] left or were taken from their tribal homes to attend Indian boarding schools, often long distances away. Some struggled bitterly. Some suffered in silence. Some succumbed to tuberculosis or influenza and lost their lives. Others flourished and built a new sense of self within a wider world, while preserving Indianness in their hearts. This book is dedicated to them all.

Look carefully at each picture. You will see isolation and loneliness. You will see photographs of terrified, homesick children, trying to look brave. You will see a collage of photos of young people doing domestic and farm labor, captioned "We Learn to Work and Earn Money." You will see a student report that describes a young woman as "rather thickset" with an "even" temperament. There is a painting of a little girl who ran away and was found frozen to death. There is a photo of Indian children dressed as Pilgrims and a child wrapped in an American flag. Look at the photo of courageous Hopi parents, imprisoned at Alcatraz for refusing to let their children be taken away. Look at the picture of the graves of children who died lost and alone at the Carlisle Indian Industrial School.

The final photographs are of a group of Sherman Indian High School cheerleaders, posing with their pom-poms, laughing and having the time of their lives. Taken at a reunion and open house in Riverside in 1999, these photos may very well remind us, as Frank H. Goodyear says in his foreword, "that in the end, the goal of cultural genocide failed." Maybe. Maybe the worst is over. Maybe there's hope yet.

This beautiful and awful book—a gathering of many voices—ought to be required reading for all teachers of American history, and for all students whose textbooks fail to discuss this shameful part of the U.S. war against the Indian peoples.—*Beverly Slapin*

Bunting, Eve, *Cheyenne Again,* **illustrated by Irving Toddy (Diné). Clarion (1995). 32 pages, color illustrations; grades 2-3; Cheyenne**

In *Cheyenne Again*, Bunting tells the story of a ten-year-old Cheyenne boy who, in the late 1880s, is taken far from his family and sent to Carlisle Indian Industrial School, more than 1,000 miles away, to "learn the White Man's ways." "The corn is drying out," his father says. "There will be food in this place they call school. Young Bull must go."

Toddy's acrylic and oil paintings are perfect for a residential school story, especially when he contrasts the open, light expanse of the Great Plains with the depressingly dark confines of the school. The child's pain also, as Young Bull's hair is forcibly cut while others, with short hair, look on. And his running away, with only a thin blanket for cover, into a blizzard. Toddy has been there. As a former student at Intermountain Indian School in Utah, he holds the stories in his heart.

In Bunting's telling, on the other hand, conditions appear far better than they were. "Kill the Indian, save the man"—Captain Richard Henry Pratt's harsh motto—was much more indicative of the treatment meted out to the lonely, miserable children than Bunting cares to reveal. Children whose parents voluntarily sent them to Carlisle went there, not to "learn the White Man's ways," but to learn English. Bunting does not mention the many deaths— from malnutrition, from diseases, from beatings, from broken hearts. Nor does she mention the jail cells and the arbitrary punishment such as having lye rubbed into young mouths for the sin of not knowing what was expected. She whitewashes the abject wretchedness of the children's lives.

There would have been no kindly teacher to offer "salve to sooth the place the chain has rubbed," to console a child by telling him, "Never forget that you are Indian inside. Don't let us take your memories." Pratt's "teaching" methodology was designed to force the children to deny— and later, forget—their Indianness, inside and out. Any teacher encouraging a child to remember who he was would have been fired on the spot.

On the last page, Young Bull, having drawn pictures in a ledger book of warriors riding on painted ponies, breaks through "the lines across the page" and rides once again with his relatives "across the golden plain." He has again become, as Bunting so facilely makes possible, "Cheyenne again."

By ending the story here, Bunting is able to sidestep, not only the misery of the boarding schools, but also their legacy. It's ongoing, and many people still bear the scars.—*Beverly Slapin*

Cooper, Michael L., *Indian School: Teaching the White Man's Way*. Clarion (1999). 104 pages, b/w photographs; grades 4-6

The Indian residential school era encompassed one of the most blatant expressions of cultural, even physical destruction in the history of North America—the wholesale taking of Indian children away from their large extended families and tribal nations and thrusting them into a foreign world, where they were abruptly, systematically and totally deprived of their Indianness. In the residential schools, children's names, languages and clothing were taken away and their sacred objects destroyed. Their hair was cut to cut them off from their people. They were beaten and worse—even jailed within the schools—for minor infractions of rules they didn't understand. They were made to eat lye soap for trying to communicate with each other in their own languages. Many children died in the residential schools, of disease, malnutrition, and broken hearts. For those who survived, brainwashing did not come easily, but when it did come, it was total. For the most part, the adults who came back to their tribal Nations looked and behaved like white people. They were no longer able to communicate with their families, they were rude to their elders, they did not know their place in the world. Neither brown nor white, they could not fit in anywhere, and many succumbed to alcohol or suicide. This legacy of hopelessness and despair still persists today, as whole Indian communities struggle to come to terms with—to heal from—the devastation of the Indian boarding school era.

The rationale for the residential schools was, as Carlisle founder Richard Henry Pratt often said, to "kill the Indian and save the man." But the actual reason was economic: By taking away the children, the U.S. government was able to take away and maintain control of the Indian land base.

None of this is explained in Michael L. Cooper's *Indian School: Teaching the White Man's Way*, a poorly written, shallow and superficial treatment of the boarding school era for fourth- to sixth-graders.

Here, Cooper defends the indefensible by making sweeping generalizations about Native peoples ("When they were teenagers, Native Americans married, had children, and went on the warpath"), patronizing statements ("The chiefs were still angry about losing the sacred land"), simplistic historical analyses ("White people wanted Indians to replace their teepees [sic] with houses and their bows and arrows with plows"), rationalizations ("Not only were Indian names difficult to pronounce, but names such as Ota Kte, which translated as Plenty Kill, evoked a savage past"), and euphemistic language to soft-pedal daily atrocities ("Punishment was not always fair").

Cooper's sloppy research is apparent throughout, especially in his use of photos. Here, he unquestioningly parrots the disinformation put out by Pratt's publicity campaign. For instance, there is a full-page photo of a George Catlin drawing of a man participating in a Mandan ritual, in which he personifies O-kee-pa, the Mandan spirit of evil (Lonna M. Malmsheimer, "'Imitation White Man': Images of Transformation at the Carlisle Indian School," *Studies in Visual Communication*, vol. 11, no. 4, fall 1985). Pratt circulated this photo of a white-made drawing of a Mandan ritual as a representation of tribal life in general, and disingenuously called it "First Boy Recruited." Cooper's caption: "This drawing depicts how one boy, who had been participating in a tribal ceremony, looked when Captain Pratt first talked to him about attending boarding school."

Indeed, the cover of *Indian School* shows the famous "before-and-after" photos of Tom Torlino (Diné), as he appeared upon entering Carlisle and three years later. In the first photo, the young man is dressed traditionally and his hair is long. In the second, he is dressed like a white man of the time and his hair is cut short. As in the other "before-and-after" photos, there is a marked contrast in skin color, apparently to show that acculturation had the effect of lightening one's complexion. Again, Cooper comments only that "Here is a Navajo student when he arrived, and the same young man three years later."

There is another photo, of a little boy in full military dress. How this child came to be at Carlisle is a story of great pain, and this story was available to Cooper. I cannot tell it here; it is sufficient to say that this child was not a student. Cooper's caption: "The boarding schools accepted very young students. This boy was only four years old."

The other photos—and Cooper's captions—are equally offensive. A photo captioned "A Shoshone family in their teepee (sic)" shows a woman, a man and five children sitting on the ground under what appears to be a small lean-to, definitely not a spacious, enclosed tipi. Another photo depicts a young man in a loincloth, holding a drawn bow, posing in front of fake scenery. Cooper's caption: "An Indian boy before being introduced to the white man's way." Yet another posed photo shows a young man, maybe in his twenties, standing in a canoe. Cooper's caption: "Indian students, like this boy in a canoe, learned to spend their free time like other American young people." When photos are not mismatched (some of the "before-and-afters" are actually of different people!), they are generalized. In most, Cooper does not name the people or their tribes; they are just "Indians." In many, the reader is left to guess which boarding schools the photos are from. Even the two-page map of "Indian boarding schools" is confusing in that it fails to indicate the dates in which these schools existed, and which ones exist today.

Children today—all children—need to be given the opportunity to understand history, even the parts that illustrate one people's inhumanity to another people. In order for this understanding to occur, children need to be able to make a connection between the history being taught and their own lives. By dehumanizing Indian peoples in text and picture, by justifying the atrocities committed in the name of "civilization," by presenting Pratt's disingenuous propaganda as fact, Cooper makes this connection impossible, and adds to the vast body of disinformation being taught about Indian peoples.

Indian School: Teaching the White Man's Way could have been written fifty years ago, just this way. Containing no analysis, no insight, no critical thinking, it is an offensive mishmash of bad writing and sloppy research. It is unfortunate that teachers will probably use this book as the "factual" companion to Ann Rinaldi's atrocious *My Heart Is On the Ground* (Scholastic, 1999).—*Beverly Slapin*

(I thank Naomi Caldwell, Janeen Antoine and Barb Landis for assistance. And I thank Lonna M. Malmsheimer for her important work.)

Grutman, Jewel H., and Gay Matthaei, illustrated by Adam Cvijanovic. Unpaginated, color illustrations; grades 5-up; Lakota:
The Ledgerbook of Thomas Blue Eagle. **Thomasson-Grant (1994).**
The Journal of Julia Singing Bear. **Thomasson-Grant (1995).**
The Sketchbook of Thomas Blue Eagle. **Chronicle Books (2001).**

Jewel H. Grutman, her twin sister, Gay Matthaei, and Adam Cvijanovic have created "fictional historical autobiographies" based on the work of Lakota people in the late 19th Century. The *Ledgerbook* and *Journal* are based on Lakota children's experiences at the Carlisle Indian Industrial School, and the *Sketchbook* is based on Sitting Bull's experiences with Buffalo Bill's Wild West Show.

The Ledgerbook of Thomas Blue Eagle looks just like an old ledgerbook, with stamp-framed dark green cloth covers, stitched pages, marbled endpapers and hand-calligraphied text superimposed on a background of brown-washed lined pages. The illustrations are supposedly modeled on the existing pictographic drawings done by the students at Carlisle.

It's not until page 68 that young readers will find out—if they squint—that:

> Thomas Blue Eagle is a fictional character. Neither he nor any of the other persons depicted in his ledgerbook actually existed. Thomas Blue Eagle's ledgerbook supposes that the artist was able to tell his story in narrative form using both the white man's words and the Indians' picture stories. While no such ledgerbook has come to light, some may have been produced.

This is bunk. For a number of reasons, there are no pictographs from Carlisle showing life at Carlisle. First, it is highly unlikely that Lakota children would have written or drawn about that which was breaking their hearts, especially at Carlisle. Second, they would not have been encouraged to draw scenes of contemporary life in a traditional—"primitive"—style. What was encouraged was the production of Plains-style drawings—horses and tipis—that had income potential. And finally, even if the children wanted to produce a journal like this, and even if they were given the materials and encouraged to do so, the cognitive dissonance resulting from the attempt to illustrate writing in precise florid English with traditional artwork would have made such a thing highly improbable. Not to mention: Children were taught to write on the lines of lined paper, not across them; and children learning to write in calligraphic style would have been publicly ridiculed for drawing all over their writing.

Everything about the children—their whole way of looking at everything, their whole way of thinking, their whole way of relating to each other and being in the world—were so alien to Victorian American values that they had to be destroyed. Everything vital to their lives had to be taken away, as quickly as possible. The ledger drawings here—and these books—are bizarre because they set up an unreal depiction of what these children's lives were like. Had they been encouraged to tell or depict their real stories, a different picture would have emerged.

But that was not so. Anything the children produced that was unfavorable to the school was hidden away. There are letters that the children wrote that were never mailed and there were letters that parents sent that were never given to the children. These currently reside in the Carlisle Indian School student folders at the National Archives in Washington, D.C., and were available to the authors.

The original drawings in the Carlisle collection[1] are graceful and stylized, subtly colored, with muted tones. Most of them are delicately outlined and not everything is colored in. The horses are beautiful. In one drawing, for example, two riders—one Cheyenne and the other a cavalry officer—meet. The drawing, rendered in black ink and colored pencil, is beautifully detailed: the Cheyenne rider wears a ribbon shirt of calico with a bone breastplate and choker. His moccasins, leggings, headdress and blanket are fully colored in, as is his horse's tail wrap. The colors are black and white, with muted shades of red and yellow, together comprising the four sacred colors. There is also a touch of blue. The cavalry officer's uniform is also detailed, as is his saddle, in black, blue and yellow. Both horses are very lightly penciled in with a hint of color to differentiate them. In the Carlisle originals, a variety of media is used to suggest color and design—ink, chalk, pencil and sometimes watercolor or crayon. The outlining is done in lead pencil or pen and ink and the paper is unlined.

Cvijanovic's pictures for the *Ledgerbook* and its sequel, the *Sketchbook*, do not even come close to resembling the originals. In the "ledgerbook," all of the space is filled in with garishly bright colors, the designs and colors are wrong, and the technique—using black outlines heavily colored in with markers and crayons—seems intended to show this type of art as "primitive," rather than detailed stylized drawings done by skilled artists. Even sky, grass and trees are colored in, something not found in the existing originals. On the last page of the "ledgerbook" is a picture of a young man surrounded by horses and buffalo on a grassy field, with squiggly "dream lines" coming out of a rising sun and tied to some kind of birds. He is facing the dawn and he is wearing a Ghost Dance shirt. Not only had the Ghost Dance and the Wounded Knee Massacre not happened yet, but not one of the original Carlisle drawings depicts this sacred garment. I can't imagine why Cvijanovic would do this.

In the "sketchbook," the drawings are toned down somewhat, and Thomas Blue Eagle's painting technique has been transformed from a pictographic style to one with varied dimensionality, probably an indication that he is learning "real art" from being exposed to the Europeans. But there are some howlers here: While the text describes the "light of the sunset on the dirty water" in Venice as making "the water look like the rust papers inside the covers of this sketchbook," the water is depicted as pristine, blue with green highlights. The artwork in the *Album* consists of gray paintings based on the late 19th-Century photographs taken by William F. Illingworth and John N. Choate, and color illustrations that do not look like the beautiful quillwork designs they are supposed to represent.

Anyone familiar with the autobiographies and work of Luther Standing Bear, Sitting Bull, Rosebud Yellow Robe and Ella Cara Deloria[2]—all Lakota—will surely recognize episodes, placed here without attribution but with, in many cases, mutation or mutilation. And the story about being saved by the eagles is actually a Lakota story from mythic times,[3] oddly placed as a "real time" event in the "ledgerbook."

The authors and illustrator are on shaky ground interpreting the Carlisle drawings at all; they'd have to know all about Lakota culture and history and obviously they don't. The text reveals the same inattention to verisimilitude.

Crying for a vision is a serious matter. One does not receive a vision while hiding in a tree (*Ledgerbook*). The Lakota leaders who sent their children to Carlisle did not do so in order for them to "understand the strange rules and power of the white man," but to learn English (*Ledgerbook*). The contents of medicine pouches are not likely to heal stab wounds, nor would there be room in one for a pipe, nor were young people at Carlisle permitted to keep such things (*Ledgerbook* and *Album*). A bear cub would make an unlikely pet, cute while he's little, and a major problem when he got big, into everything. (*Album*). One doesn't usually get a "dream vision" in the middle of a circus performance, nor would one refer to herself as a "relative of White Buffalo Calf Woman"

(*Album*). Lakota children did not engage in adult mourning rituals (*Album*). A child would not casually tell a white guy the story of White Buffalo Calf Woman, nor would she be likely to know the whole story (*Album*). Custer's attack at the Washita was a massacre, not a battle (*Album*), and the Allotment Act was not a good thing (*Sketchbook*).

What's so insidious about these books is that the authors and illustrator have portrayed what was a nightmare for the Indian children as something that was good for them. At the end of their six-year stays at Carlisle, Thomas Blue Eagle and Julia Singing Bear emerge none the worse for wear. Thomas has "learned the white man's ways...learned his numbers and tools...learned to tell my stories with the white man's words," and Julia finds herself "not all Indian and not all white but true to what I had become."

How awful. This is very different from the experience of a great many of Carlisle students, who suffered from what we now call post-traumatic stress syndrome. Pratt's "noble experiment" was in fact a cruel anomaly that created an entire generation of people who couldn't function in this world.

The Ledgerbook of Thomas Blue Eagle, The Sketchbook of Thomas Blue Eagle, and *The Journal of Julia Singing Bear* rival Ann Rinaldi's *My Heart Is on the Ground* as a model for purposeful ignorance and white entitlement.

—*Beverly Slapin*

(This review is for Doris. I thank LaVera Rose, Barb Landis and Joyce Szabo for their assistance.)

NOTES

1 See, for example, the image on the cover of Linda F. Witmer's *The Indian Industrial School, Carlisle, Pensylvania, 1879-1918.* Cumberland County Historical Society (1993).

2 See Ella Cara Deloria's *Waterlily* (University of Nebraska, 1988); Sitting Bull's accounts related in Dee Brown's *Bury My Heart at Wounded Knee: An Indian History of the American West* (Holt, 1970); Luther Standing Bear's *My People, the Sioux* (Houghton Mifflin, 1928; University of Nebraska 1975); and Rosebud Yellow Robe's *Tonweya and the Eagles and Other Lakota Tales* (Dial, 1979).

3 This story was set down by Rosebud Yellow Robe, *ibid.*, but it's quite possible the authors may have gotten it via Paul Goble's less authentic *Adopted by the Eagles* (Bradbury, 1994) or the version by Emery and Durga Bernhard, *Spotted Eagle & Black Crow: A Lakota Legend* (Holiday House, 1993).

Harper, Maddie (Ojibwe), *"Mush-hole": Memories of a Residential School,* **illustrated by Carlos Freire. Sister Vision (1993). Unpaginated, color illustrations; grades 4-up; Ojibwe**

When Maddie Harper was seven years old, she found herself "in an institution with about 200 other little girls like myself." That institution was the Brantford School in Ontario—the children called it "mush-hole" because mush was their daily fare. Here, Harper tells of her childhood experiences, escape at age fifteen and eventual recovery from the negative values and cultural degradation she was forced to endure at "Mush-hole."

> We were told what time to get up, what time to eat, when to pray and when to go to the bathroom. Everything was time; everything was regulated, and I realize that during the process they had stolen my will...my will to do anything and my freedom of choice in all matters. If we didn't do what we were told they'd take you to the principal's office and they'd pull down your pants and give it to you on your bare ass.

In the accompanying picture, there are two little girls in short hair and pink dresses. There is a large clock, and gears, and a hand holding a whip. One child is crying, terrified, and the other is trying to get to her. The other pictures are equally as evocative: Harper's eight years at the school, her alienation from her community, her descent into alcoholism and finally, her return to traditional ways and recovery.

I met a young woman a while ago from the same reserve as Harper, who hadn't known that "Auntie Maddie" had written a book. "Auntie Maddie," she said, "was always there for us. Whenever any of us got into it with our parents, we knew we could just go over to Auntie Maddie's. She always had room for us and she was always there for us." *"Mush-hole"* is the story of how Auntie Maddie's life came full circle.—*Beverly Slapin*

Jack, Agness (Shuswap), ed., *Behind Closed Doors: Stories from the Kamloops Indian Residential School.* **Secwepemc Cultural Education Society and Theytus (2000). 206 pages, b/w photos; high school-up; Shuswap**

This is a very difficult book to read. So much pain on every page. It would be a hard heart that doesn't feel it. It was "behind the closed doors" of the Kamloops Indian Residential School in Kamloops, British Columbia, that the children—the ones who survived—suffered the "mental, spiritual, emotional and physical abuse and trauma" that was to haunt them their entire lives. Many of those who physically recovered from that place never recovered their spirits.

"There are many survivors out there," the dedication reads,

> and many more have lost their lives as a direct or indirect result of this school. While attending residential school, the children felt a hunger, not only for food but also for love and comfort from their mothers and fathers, grandparents, aunts and uncles and even from their brothers and sisters.

Thirty-two people who attended Kamloops tell their stories here, "so their families and communities (and all Canadians) could learn and understand what happened… so that history is never repeated."

This project was funded by the Aboriginal Healing Foundation, established by the Canadian government after it acknowledged and apologized for its role in the development and administration of the residential schools. Those who told their stories here did so with the support of their families and medicine people at their side.

"I remember some girls who had run away from school," one elder recalls.

> They were caught and we were all down in the recreation hall. Benches were lined up, with the girls laying on them with faces down and with just panties on. I believe it was Father Kennedy who strapped the girls one after the other.

Another elder says,

> The teachers called us savages. I remember that, called us "dirty savage, you'll learn," stuff like that. I felt bad, I felt real dirty….I felt like I was singled out to get the straps all the time….Sometimes they just told me it was because I lost one side of my sock. They were trying to teach us the ways of God and they called us savages and dirty Indians.

"As we read these stories," the editors write, "we can only begin to understand the loneliness and despair those individuals lived with every day of their lives."

Behind Closed Doors needed to be written. May the telling and sharing of these stories bring peace and healing to wounded spirits.—*Beverly Slapin*

Littlefield, Holly, *Children of the Indian Boarding Schools, 1879 to Present.* Carolrhoda Books, 2001. 48 pages, b/w photos; grades 4-7

It is a fact that Carlisle and the other Indian residential schools that followed were set up to break spirits, to destroy traditional extended families and cultures, to obliterate memories and languages, and especially to make the children deny their Indianness, inside and out.

The reasons for the Indian residential schools were economic. By turning Indian youngsters into "brown white people"—farmers, tradespeople and servants living individually on farms and in cities instead of tribal citizens living collectively on the land—it became easier to complete the land grab that had begun more than 300 years earlier. The residential school experiment in assimilation, begun in 1879, was only moderately successful. In "killing the Indian and saving the man," the Indian residential schools were a source of multigenerational grief and sorrow that continues today for Indian families in the U.S. and Canada.

Littlefield's book is far better than Michael L. Cooper's *Indian School: Teaching the White Man's Way* (Clarion, 1999). That having been said, *Children of the Indian Boarding Schools* cannot be recommended. And that is a shame, because it is apparent that Littlefield really tried to do a good job. But she doesn't name the demons; she doesn't acknowledge what colonization does to people. Her constant use of heavy modifiers such as "sometimes," "may have," "most," "usually," combined with her tentative writing style, essentially robs this book of any power.

It would be have been more historically accurate to say, for example, "It was U.S. governmental policy to remove Indian children from their families and nations to speed up the process of assimilation." (See David Wallace Adams, *Education for Extinction: American Indians and the Boarding School Experience, 1875-1928*; University Press of Kansas, 1995). Rather, Littlefield says, "An army officer named Richard Henry Pratt believed that Indian children should be taken away from their families." To ascribe official U.S. policy to one man or to the "beliefs" of "European Americans" is soft pedaling the language and trivializing the history; it is retelling a convenient fairy tale that perpetuates the denial of the Indian Holocaust. Such language is not used to describe the horrors of the European Holocaust. It is not used to describe the horrors of slavery in this country.

In another place, Littlefield says, "Many of these adults believed they were helping Indian children. They tried to be kind. Others were cruel. Almost all the teachers taught the children that Indian ways were foolish and wrong." In "About the Author," Littlefield says that the system "was meant to destroy [the children]," but in the body of the book, because she apparently does not want to step on toes, she does not commit to this and therefore does not inform. In fact, the intent *may* have been benevolent, but the effect was poisonous.

The last chapter, "Understanding Historical Photographs," has merit in that it encourages children to think critically.

But even here, the watered-down text makes the section unreliable. Saying, for instance, that "photographers who visited the Indian boarding schools were usually invited or hired by school leaders," belies the fact that the precisely posed and doctored photographs were a propaganda tool to raise funds for the schools.

Good writing comes from passion, not from fear. Colonization of the mind and spirit—as well as the land—is not something that ought to be glossed over. Our children are perfectly capable, with good guidance and the proper material, of understanding the realities of violence and colonization. Only with this understanding will come the will and ability to fight it. Our children deserve better.
—*Beverly Slapin*

Loyie, Larry (Cree), with Constance Brissenden, *As Long as the Rivers Flow*, illustrated by Heather D. Holmlund. Douglas & McIntyre (2002). Unpaginated, color illustrations; grades 3-6; Cree

In 1944, ten-year-old Cree youngster Lawrence Loyie was taken to St. Bernard's Mission residential school in northern Alberta. The purpose of the now-infamous Indian residential schools in Canada and the U.S. was to strip Indian children of their dress, languages, cultures and ways of seeing the world so that they would become "brown white people." In almost all cases, children were taken by force or the parents were arrested or threatened with arrest for refusal to surrender their children.

As Long as the Rivers Flow is the story of Lawrence's last summer before entering this alien world from which he would emerge a different person. This brief and important time in his life was a summer of memories that would have to last him for several years. Lawrence helped care for an abandoned baby owl and traveled with his extended family to their summer camp in the bush. While the men hunted, the women and children picked and dried sacks of saskatoon berries, smoked meat for the winter, gathered wild mint and medicine plants, fished; and "for the last time, Lawrence and his cousins swam in the cool, clear river." After Lawrence and his grandma face off a huge grizzly and Grandma plugs it with one shot, Grandpa gives him a new name: Oskiniko, Young Man.

In a few places, the writing is contrived because cultural information for the reader is placed into a family dialogue. When the children find a baby owl, for instance, they try to think of an appropriate name.

"Let's call him Ooh-Hoo," Lawrence said.

"Ooh-Hooh means owl in our language," said Papa. "That makes it a good name."

Stating the obvious for informational purposes interrupts the flow of the story. But this is just a minor quibble, because this story is so important; for the most part, the writing is good and the book reads well.

Holmlund's detailed watercolors are perfect. These are real people. Some are obviously copied from snapshots, but you know what Grandma looked like, you know what Grampa looked like. The land is there, you see the sunlight coming through the trees, the boys jumping into the river, Grandma shooting the bear; you see what the parents are feeling, you feel the children's terror.

At the end of the story, the day the children had been dreading

> finally arrived. After breakfast, the children dressed in their best clothes. They stood close to Mama and Grandma. Grandpa put his arm around Grandma's shoulders.
>
> A big brown truck with high sides pulled up. Two men got out. They both wore black and looked like giant crows.
>
> "Hurry up," one of them said to the other children loudly in English. "It's time to get on the truck."
>
> The children pulled back, terrified of the strangers. Maruk clung to Mama's skirt.
>
> Papa spoke to Lawrence in their own language.
>
> "Be brave, Oskiniko. Take care of your younger sister and brothers."
>
> The strange men lifted the crying children one by one onto the truck. Papa watched, his face angry, his fists clenched.
>
> As the men closed up the back of the truck, Lawrence began to cry, too.
>
> The sides of the truck were high. He couldn't see his family. He couldn't see Ooh-Hoo sitting in a tree.
>
> As the truck pulled away, all Lawrence could see was the sky.

On the facing page, four young children sit in a corner of the truck, huddled together, crying, scared to death, not knowing what's going to happen to them. This was the real lived experience, for countless Indian kids, of that "noble experiment" Pratt envisioned.

Larry Loyie, now an elder, is to be honored for his courage in telling his story; may this bring him healing. Constance Brissenden and Heather D. Holmlund are to be thanked for their understanding and compassion. May all children grow up knowing what happened then, and may this never happen again.—*Beverly Slapin*

Olsen, Sylvia, with Rita Morris (Tsartlip) and Ann Sam (Tsartlip), *No Time to Say Goodbye: Children's Stories of Kuper Island Residential School*, illustrations by Connie Paul (Tsartlip). Sono Nis Press (2001). 175 pages, b/w illustrations; grades 4-up; Tsartlip

Based on the told stories of a number of Tsartlip people, *No Time to Say Goodbye* is a fictional account of five children taken by government agents from Tsartlip Day School and brought to Kuper Island Residential School in the 1950s. There, as with the other Indian residential schools, the children are isolated and their lives become regimented by chores, bells, line-ups, arbitrary rules, corporal punishment and public humiliation. Homesick and confused, they cope as best they can. Sometimes the older children pretend to be brave for the sake of the younger kids:

> Thomas' legs wobbled as he made his way towards the school. The group was so tightly stuck together that they tripped over each other's feet....Joey began to cry. Thomas put his arm around his little brother and whispered, "Don't worry, Joey, it'll be okay." He wished he could believe his own words.

> At five years old, Joey thinks only of escaping. He worked on one escape plan after another. But with each plan came another problem he couldn't quite figure out. Weeks passed and he still didn't have a plan that would work. Then months passed....Then years.

Children who read *No Time to Say Goodbye* will know, as much as anyone can who has not been there, what it was like.

In her preface, Olsen acknowledges the six former students from Kuper Island Residential School whose stories are the basis for this book, and who were its editors. Now elders, they "hope that young people for many generations will learn about this neglected but important part of history." All royalties from the sale of this book support Tsartlip First Nation youth programs.

—Beverly Slapin

Rice, Bebe Faas, *The Place at the Edge of the Earth*. Clarion (2002). 192 pages; grades 5-9; Lakota

Bebe Faas Rice, author of numerous young adult mystery/ghost/horror stories including *Music from the Dead* and the six-title "Doomsday Mall Series," has chosen for her latest project an Indian ghost story set at the site of the Carlisle Indian Industrial School (1879-1918) in Carlisle, Pennsylvania. Whether her intention was to show middle-school readers the horrors of the Indian residential schools or to publish yet another pulp fiction ghost story, she has created an obscene appropriation of one of the most tragic episodes in the history of the U.S. government's attempts to "assimilate" Native children into the white mainstream.

The plot centers around two thirteen-year-old protagonists: a white girl dealing with teenage angst, a new stepfather, and moving with her family to historic "Fort Sayers"; and the ghost of a Lakota boy who died in the late 1800s when Fort Sayers was an Indian boarding school. The two meet in a time warp; each appears to the other as a ghost. Jonah Flying Cloud, trapped between worlds, appeals to Jennie Muldoon to help him reach the land of his ancestors. In order to send Jonah on his journey, Jenny must dig into the unsavory past of the residential school and its surrounding town, and bring out the truth about the "place at the edge of the earth."

The story is told in alternating first-person narratives. This is Rice's first mistake. Here are the rest:

People do not sing their death song unless they're dying; to send a child away to an unknown place with a death song is the last thing a parent would do; and children do not sing "death chants," not to show grief or for any other reason. Those few people who in the early days voluntarily sent their children to Carlisle did not do so in order for them to "learn the ways of the white man"— but to learn English. This was so that the people would have some protection against the white man's lies and chicanery. By far, the greatest number of children who ended up there were taken by force, against their parents' will. The names that Rice has chosen for her Native characters are ridiculous. She apparently thinks they "sound Indian." Children at that time did not refer to themselves as "Indians." Children in residential school did not wash their own mouths out with lye soap. Children did not cut their own hair and mutilate themselves as a sign of rebellion. Lakota people did not kick and beat their dogs. Lakota people do not look each other in the eye as a sign of telling the truth. Crazy Horse was not a chief, nor did he get his name in the way Jonah describes. Eagle feathers do not make people strong and set them free. Placing an embroidered 101st Airborne patch—the "Screaming Eagles"—on a Indian grave is not the same, nor is it better than the eagle feather that Jonah's ghost had requested. And since an eagle feather is just a feather until it is blessed, who was supposed to have done the blessing? *Akicita* are not "spirit guides," and eagles are not *akicita*.

Rice has lifted ideas and phrases from Red Cloud, Sitting Bull, Standing Bear, Ohiyesa (Charles Eastman) and even Black Elk—without attribution. On the other hand, she uses cockamamie "Indian" metaphors such as "already his hatred of the Wasichus had set his feet on the snake-path of bitterness and violence."

The author has her Indian characters describing Lakota ceremony and customs, some of which she made up. A thirteen-year-old Lakota almost-man would not be likely to know enough about the women's moontime rituals to be able to explain them in detail in English in the 1800s. And even if he did, he certainly would not talk about them to a white person.

Part of this story is the lynching of Jonah's friend, Swift Running River, who had killed "the chief of the school." After a mob of townspeople string him up, Jonah hastens his death so that he can "die quickly and with honor." The lynching is the scandal that Jenny and a friend uncover. There is no documentation that a student at Carlisle ever killed a staff member. There is no documentation that an Indian student was ever killed in this way. It would have been extremely unlikely that a Lakota youngster, for any reason, would ever hasten the death of a friend, even to ease his suffering. He would instead have stood by his friend until the end.

If Rice actually believed in a Spirit World, if she actually understood what it might be like to be trapped between worlds, she would not have been able to write so casually about this boy's spirit seeking help in this way. The plot device of an Indian ghost seeking help from a young white person is not new in children's literature. In this case, it becomes a misuse of tragic circumstances that would be totally beyond the powers of this teenage girl to remedy.

The effects of the damage done by Carlisle and other such institutions are being felt to this day. Rice has written this book from a point of near total ignorance of Native lifeways and cosmologies, and has even gone so far as to do so in the first person. This is unacceptable. *The Place at the Edge of the Earth* should never have seen publication.—*Beverly Slapin* and *Doris Seale*

(Thank-you to LaVera Rose and Barb Landis.)

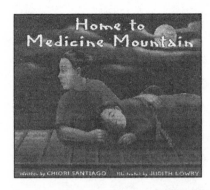

Santiago, Chiori. *Home to Medicine Mountain*, illustrated by Judith Lowry (Maidu/Hamawi). Children's Book Press (1998). Unpaginated, color illustrations; grades 2-4; Maidu

Judith Lowry is one of the great Native artists. This is her story, and I am a little puzzled as to why the publishers decided to have someone else write it down. A family story, it is about her father and uncle who as little boys were taken away to boarding school. They were miserable. Everything was different; everything was strange. Uniforms and stiff new shoes. March from dorm to breakfast to school. Speak only English. Peculiar food. And clocks, always ticking away the time. At night, the littlest boys cried, in their loneliness and sadness.

Benny Len dreams of home, of all the good things there: Grandmother's house, where time didn't march, the Bear Dance in the spring. The worst thing: they couldn't go home. The school paid for the ticket to get them there, not to get them back. They would spend the summer at the school. But Stanley watches out for his little brother, and knows his heart is breaking. And one night....The rest of the story tells how Stanley gets Benny Len up and out and onto a freight train, and home.

The pictures are wonderful. They show all the unhappiness of these regimented kids, all the longing for home, the courage of Stanley and Benny Len's journey, and their joy at getting there. I particularly love the cover illustration, of the boys on top of the train, Benny Len wrapped in the blanket, while Stanley holds him firmly in place, and faces into the wind.

The back page tells a little bit about Judith Lowry, and has a picture of her father and uncle, as they are now—standing on the railroad track. It's them, all right.

For those of us who never made it home, the best part of the book is that Stanley and Benny Len did. From those of us who never made it home: Thank you, Judith Lowry. —*Doris Seale*

Sterling, Shirley (Nlakapamux), *My Name Is Seepeetza.* **Douglas & McIntyre (1992). 126 pages; grades 5-up; Nlakapamux (Interior Salish)**

At the age of six, Seepeetza—aka "Martha Stone"—encounters the residential school system for the first time. At Kalamak Indian Residential School—K.I.R.S. for "curse"—she gets "smocks, bloomers, and undershirts," all exactly like everyone else's, head doused with coal oil to kill non-existent nits and lice, hair chopped off.

> We had to put all our own clothes and things in our suitcases which she locked in a storage room.... she kept yelling at us to hurry up or Sister Superior would strap us. Sister Superior carries the strap in her sleeve all the time. It looks like a short thick leather belt with a shiny tip....After that Sister Maura asked me what my name was. I said, my name is Seepeetza. Then she got really mad like I did something terrible. She said never to say that word again...

Based on the author's own experiences and written in journal form, *My Name is Seepeetza* is dedicated

> [t]o those who went to residential schools, and those who tried to help, may you weep and be made free....May you recover the treasure that has been lost, the name that gives your life meaning, the mythology by which you can pick up and rebuild the shattered pieces of the past, your own ancient language...

Part of the power of the story is its simple, straightforward, childlike telling. Those who endured this will know that there is no exaggeration, no overstatement here. Probably at least some of these people thought they were doing A Good Thing. In the popular words of a somewhat earlier phase of "Indian education," "Kill the Indian and save the man"—or was it the other way around? Sort of like degerminated corn meal, which is all you can get in the supermarkets: it will last forever, but what the hell good is it?

By the late 1950s—the time here—some of the worst abuses were beginning to be corrected. In Sterling's story, the kids get to go *home* (for Christmas and summer); no one is maimed for life (at least not physically); and no one gets killed (except by accident). Yet, the constant attrition of the spirit, the constant humiliation and cruelty—not because the kids are bad, just because they are Indians—take their inevitable toll. The contrast with Seepeetza's loving family, and home life on her father's big ranch, is especially bitter. No reason at all why she should ever have been taken away from here, except it was "the law."

Who should read this book? Our own children, so they know: yes, it really was this bad. Those who keep saying, "but you're all so *angry*," so they can know some of why. But most of all, put this book beside *The Diary of Anne Frank*, *Sadako and the Thousand Paper Cranes*, *The Upstairs Room*, and *Hiroshima No Pika*, in case you should be wanting to talk to children about what we do to each other, and how we survive it, or not.—*Doris Seale*

Tohe, Laura (Diné), *No Parole Today.* **West End Press (1999). 47 pages; grades 7-up**

The first words in Laura Tohe's book are those of Richard Henry Pratt, the founder of the Indian boarding school system that devastated Indian lives throughout North America. Addressing the World Baptist Convention in 1883, Pratt said:

> In Indian civilization I am a Baptist, because I believe in immersing the Indians in our civilization, and when we get them under holding them there until they are thoroughly soaked.

Tohe's great-grandfather was one of the first Diné students to attend Pratt's Carlisle Indian Industrial School, and she likens her own Indian school experience to serving a prison sentence. *No Parole Today* is Tohe's poetry and personal narrative about this time in her life and the challenges of maintaining her identity in a system whose aim is to destroy it.

In an opening piece, a response to Pratt, Tohe writes,

> A hundred years after you made your statement to the Baptists, we are still here. We have not vanished, gone away quietly into the sunset, or assimilated into the mainstream culture the way you envisioned....[W]e continue to survive with the strength of the spirit of our ancestors. Our grandmothers and grandfathers taught us to hold to our beliefs, religions, and languages. That is the way of survival for us....I voice this letter to you now because I speak for me, no longer invisible, and no longer relegated to the quiet margins of American culture, my tongue silenced.... To write is

powerful and even dangerous. To have no stories is to be an empty person. Writing is a way for me to claim my voice, my heritage, my stories, my culture, my people, and my history.

In first grade, the children received their first "Dick and Jane" books, in which they were introduced to white society in the form of Father, Mother, Dick and Jane and Sally, who drove around in cars and said "oh, oh, oh" a lot. In "Dick and Jane Subdue the Diné," Tohe describes how the schools made the taking away of language a priority:

> See Father.
> See Mother.
> See Dick run.
> See Jane and Sally laugh.
> oh, oh, oh
> See Spot jump.
> oh, oh, oh
> See Eugene speak Diné.
> See Juanita answer him.
> oh, oh, oh
> See teacher frown.
> uh oh, uh oh
> See Eugene with red hands, shape of ruler.
> oh, oh, oh
> See Eugene cry.
> oh, oh, oh
> See Juanita stand in corner, see tears fall down face.
> oh, oh, oh
> Oh see us draw pictures
> of brown horses under blue clouds.
> We color eyes black, hair black.
> We draw ears and leave out mouth.
> Oh see, see, see.

While most of Tohe's writing focuses on her coming of age in this hostile alien environment, her later pieces are written from her perspective as an adult, and her final poem, "At Mexican Springs," is a thing of beauty and hope:

> It is here among the sunset in
>> every plant
>> every rock
>> every shadow
>> every movement
>> every thing
>
> I relive visions of ancient stories
> First Woman and First Man
> their children stretched across
> these eternal sandstones
> a deep breath
> she brings me sustenance
> life
> and I will live to tell my children these things.

For everyone who has survived the Indian residential schools, and for everyone who never knew of their existence, *No Parole Today* is a gift. Laura Tohe's writing is spare and honest, with no polemic; proof of the government's utter failure to take away Indian voice.

—*Beverly Slapin*

Whelan, Gloria, *The Indian School*, illustrated by Gabriella Dellosso. HarperCollins (1996). 89 pages, b/w illustrations; grades 3-5

Following the death of her parents in 1839, eleven-year-old Lucy is sent to live with her aunt and uncle who run a mission school for Indian children in northern Michigan. There, she meets Raven, a girl her own age, and Raven's little brother, Star Face. After their village was decimated by a smallpox epidemic, both had been brought to the school by their father, Lost Owl, so that he can go off to Canada to hunt. Lucy questions the harsh rules and restrictions placed on the Indian children, Lucy establishes a friendship with Raven, and when Raven escapes and a crisis develops, Lucy stands up to her aunt and resolves the problem.

Indian School was named a 1996 "Pick of the Lists" by the American Booksellers Association. Despite its being described as "gripping, accessible, historically accurate fiction," it is not. The whole premise is absurd.

There were no Indian residential schools in Michigan in 1839; there weren't even Indian day schools. The first Indian day schools—which the government contracted with the churches to administer—were established in the Indian communities in Michigan during the 1860s. Boarding schools were a later phenomenon, closer to the 1900s. Indian children who were sent to residential schools were sent out of state, at the earliest to Carlisle in Pennsylvania, which opened its doors in 1879.

In the time period in which this story takes place, from 1835-1840, there was a series of smallpox epidemics of varying intensity throughout the area. There was a huge epidemic in the Saginaw Valley; Indian communities were decimated as two out of three people there died. But *Indian School* doesn't reflect the nature of how Native people moved and interacted and utilized resources at that time. There would have been relatives, if not in this immediate family's village, in a neighboring village. Families intermarried, and there was a lot of travel back and forth, covering hundreds of miles of territory. Children could be transported by canoe across one end of Lake Superior to the other, all the way to Minnesota to relocate, or they could go north or go inland. Even in the midst of a smallpox epidemic, there were always relatives to go to. It's unheard of that an Indian parent would dump his kids with white strangers rather than leave them with family, even in times of epidemic. We did everything we could to keep our kids with us.

By the 1830s people were more likely to trap from their home areas. You'd have a certain area to trap in and, for a number of reasons, you'd check the traps at least once a day. The big game was equally as depleted on the Ontario side as it was on the Michigan side, and you wouldn't go hundreds of miles—into someone else's territory—to run a trapline for beaver, much less take off and leave your kids with white strangers while you did so. And there were always fish to depend on.

Despite the assumptions of many writers from outside the culture, there are no such things as "Indian" names; rather, they are specific to the languages and cultures of specific Nations. Lost Owl, Star Face and Raven are not Ojibwe names. Ojibwe names are rarely based on nouns. As Indian people, we make certain choices in how we name our children; it is demeaning to assume that we'd throw together any old names.

Indian School encompasses sweeping assumptions—the author's fantasies, maybe—of Indians confined to small enclosed reservation areas, of disease coming in and wiping out whole populations, of the necessity of traveling up to Canada where the game is more plentiful, and, perhaps most terrible, that we would leave our kids at the drop of a hat with white people who abused them, just so we could go hunting. And why does the author see as necessary for an Indian boarding school experience to be seen through the eyes of a white protagonist, who also does all the problem solving? And what could possibly have been the author's motivation for inserting this—"Raven said dog was very tasty cooked in maple syrup, but we did not think of trying that"—if not to further distance the non-Native child reader from the Indian family? The circumstances under which a dog might be eaten would have been so profound that a child wouldn't blurt out something like that as if it were an everyday occurrence.

The subtext—unspoken assumption—of this book is that we make poor choices, and childish choices, and are incapable of raising our children to be full human beings without the supervision and authority of non-Native people. It's a concept as old as Manifest Destiny.
—*Lois Beardslee,* with *Beverly Slapin*

POEMS

Sphagnum Moss (Baby Moss)

By my door she stood
an old bag in her hand.
The bag she held
was full of moss from the land.

She asked me: Do you need
fresh moss for baby?
Yes, I said,
it keeps the baby dry.

She smiled, If you want
I will get more for you.
Knowing her skill,
I nod my head.

She goes early
to the wet swamps
to find and pick moss
for a little baby.

She never wears gloves,
her hands red from cold.
She loves
gathering the soft moss.

She chooses a spot
where the sun shines a lot.
The wet cold moss has to dry
before she brings some to me.

Over the years I never used
anything so soft and fine
for a baby's behind
as the moss she brought with a smile.

—*Margaret Sam-Cromarty* (Cree)

She's a Hawk!

But she's a hawk! Tatiana said,
      roundbutton eyes flaring.
      I heard her grumble,
      How come Gisakk so dumb?

The young man picked it up.
      The body was a little fist,
      head revolving with a
      fierce yellow stare.
      It's an owl, he said.

Gisakk! What's matter you?
      Already he full grown.
      I tell you it mouse hawk.
      She's a hawk!
Grabbing the bird
      she hurried along the boardwalk,
      shaking her head
      frowning all the way
      out of sight.

—*Mary TallMountain* (Koyukon)

gisakk: white man

How She Was Given Her Name

One cold winter afternoon,
the baby ran outside when no one was looking.
She ran, laughing, and waving her arms around.

"The baby!" someone yelled and we ran out after her.
She heard us and ran even faster,
down the sloping hill to the orchard.
We could hear her laughing and squealing.
The dogs were bounding alongside her in the snow.

Finally, she was caught, and when they brought her inside,
she was still laughing, her cheeks and arms red.
She was just happy, breathing hard, and eyes sparkling.
She hadn't been outside all winter.

"She escaped," my brother said.

After that time, she tried to run outside when she thought
no one was watching, and she ran for the road each time.

So her name became "Beep-beep"
because she liked to be a roadrunner
and she liked having people try to catch her.

—*Luci Tapahonso* (Diné)

Moccasins to School Again

Thirty years ago I learned the hard way
not to wear moccasins to school.

Times have changed.
Multiculturalism
is official government policy.

People don't read the policy manuals.

Today a friend told me.
Her little boy in kindergarten
was so excited about
the moccasins his granny made him.

Home-tanned moosehide,
beaded moccasins.
Full of love, pride, sweat.

That little boy wore them everywhere,

proudly,

"Mommy, can I wear my moccasins
to school
to show my class?"

Same mistake I made
thirty years ago.

He came home from school.
Hid his moccasins.
"Where are your moccasins?"

"Teacher said they stink.
Shouldn't bring things like that to school."

Like my teacher thirty years ago.

Thinks she has the right

to wound a child
and his entire culture.

—*Heather Harris* (Cree/Métis)

My Precious Little Nephew

My precious little nephew
was born one fall,
with long black hair
and big black eyes.

My precious little nephew
knew more than his years,
before he could walk
he wanted to dance.

When he hears the drum
he cannot play
for fear he will miss a beat,
my precious little nephew.

My precious little nephew
is to be a traditional dancer,
practicing for hours
in his room by himself.

My precious little nephew
wakes up to his treasured belongings
over his bed...his beadwork,
his moccasins, his regalia.

My precious little nephew
learned early to be
respectful of others,
for that is the Indian way.

My precious little nephew
entered school this fall
at the age of four,
so eager to learn and share with others.

Today, my precious little nephew
came home form school...

He was told to memorize a song with "war whoops."
He was told to bring a hanger to school for a bow.
He was told to bring a nylon to wear over his face,
so he can be an "Indian."

Today, I saw a change in
my precious little nephew...
Confusion, shame, and self-doubt
were some of the questions on his face.

All he knew about life
so far
is that he is
proud to be Indian.

My precious little nephew,
who just turned five...
What honor
has been taken from you?

What harm will come to you
as a young Indian student
in the years to come?

My precious little nephew.

—*Cindy La Marr* (Paiute/Pit River)

Bad Vision

When he fasted three days
(the way the old men
in the books told him to)

he sat on a rock
two miles from the highway
where he'd left his Thunderbird

sat there singing the songs
he'd learned from a tape
bought from the museum

waited for Coyote
or Deer or Eagle
to give him words
he could take back
to tell the others
he's had his vision

but when the dream came
on the morning
of the fourth day
it ate him.

—*Joseph Bruchac* (Abenaki)

Indian Teeth

After drilling and shaping and prepping the tooth,
he gives me a temporary, tells me to come back in two weeks
but when I do
guess what
someone wrote down the wrong shade of tooth color
and the crown is
too white
so he sends me home to wait some more
and in another two weeks I come back
get into the chair, open my mouth
and while my lips are distended with rolls of cotton
and my poor little tooth is bare to the world
Dr. Doug asks in a cheerful tone, *So!*
are you a whale-lover too?

I tell him that was a loaded question
thinking you don't know how loaded, buddy
thinking—he doesn't know I'm Indian?!—
Having a moment of abrupt identity dysfunction
do I *look that* white?!
surreptitiously examining my skin, thinking of my hair, my eyes,
the silver and turquoise turtle at my throat—
and my teeth, my grandmother's beautiful teeth—
guess I forgot my headdress today left the papoose
outside with the pony hitched up at the door
and my Indian I.D. is home in a drawer—
and he asks after a puzzled pause So what do you think of what those Makah
are doing up there?

and I say I thought my own tribe had done much the same in the past
and that the Makah had made me proud
to be related even distantly to their fierceness, devotion
and those sleek cedar canoes

and he is speechless until he thinks to ask
which tribe I come from
and I tell him
Chumash, Esselen, Ohlone, Costanoan
the Chumash being the only ocean-going California tribe
who occasionally took a whale out there in the swells
but more often traveled hundreds or thousands of miles
to trade with artisans of other tribes
for jewelry, furs, feathered baskets, inlaid bowls, and all the fine arts
of living in beauty
of working in beauty
of worshipping beauty in all the details of existence

oh yes they *used to* do that he says then bites his own tongue
so it won't say "but they shouldn't be so primitive NOW"
and I lie there thinking of all the photos of trophy salmon on his walls here
and the boat he sails to Gig Harbor to get home when the Narrows Bridge is closed
and his children at a private Academy
and I see that his money can't buy him
the same fishing rights of the lowliest Indian in Washington State

I see how many times he's caught his limit
and had to quit the fun before he wanted to go home
and how angry it made him
that a bunch of sloppy uncouth Indians have more rights than he did
I see how a whale had become all the fish he can never take
all the waters his yacht will never sail as intimately as the Hummingbird
all the lands he can't be at home in as I am when walking the Salinas Valley
or the dry Tehachapi mountains of my childhood
and I don't answer when he jokes to his assistant
that a really good Jerry Springer Show would be the Makah Tribal Chairman
up against some guy from Greenpeace
that would really be a sight!
Just fix the fucking tooth, I say
but the rolls of cotton steal my thunder

On my way home, I laugh
surprised
that my anger gives up so easy
that I'm not viciously swearing up a storm
but the fury won't come

I'm tired of worrying about white men who offend me:
I keep seeing her, that whale, turning toward the canoe,
paddle strokes and arms flying in unison
arc of a harpoon
a moment when living is not separate from the bloody moments of death
when people dance in the fine rain
on the wet beach
hunters bringing home the whale who has answered their songs
proving that work is not separate from prayers
beauty is not separate from function
I keep seeing

a tribe tasting the tissue of a being who presented herself to the harpoon
with a grace she still remembered after generations of absence
I believe they could taste that grace in her flesh,
in creamy layers of fat
a taste like power—sudden, pungent, strange—
an old flavor strong on the tongue—

and I realize what he knows, this dentist:
that no matter how much money he makes off my poor Indian teeth
he can't buy
what he saw happen at Neah Bay:
colonization is a disease
that prevents the victim from understanding anything that's not for sale
and can't be stolen

like ancestors
who are magic,
    like whales
        who are grace incarnate
and give up that gift
for a song.

—*Deborah A. Miranda* (Ohlone-Costanoan Esselen/Chumash)

Village Tour, Nome Airport

I

The tour guide
slides her glossy smile
toward the native seamstress.
"May I touch your coat?"
She does, without an answer.
"They make them by hand."
As if frozen, the seamstress sat.

II

Already freezing,
a youth sits in handcuffs,
on his way to isolation
in California,
becomes part of the tour.
"They all go to jail," she says.

—*Nora Marks Dauenhauer* (Tlingit)

The Well-Intentioned Question

Here you are
asking me again
what is my Indian name

and this was the time
I promised myself
I would tell the truth

and stand hard
and smooth
as madrone

tight as mesquite
answering you.
my Indian name

soars in pinyon-wood flutes,
stopped at one end
by asphalt; my Indian name

catapults like condors
gliding inland to die
on the power of prayer;

my Indian name bumps
on the backs
of obsidian-hard women

sighting me with eyes
Coyote gave them;
My Indian name

howls around the black hats
of Indian men
on Friday night search

for fairness of failing that
for fullness; my Indian name
listens

for footsteps
stopping short of my door
then leaving forever.

—*Wendy Rose* (Hopi/Miwuk)

To Human Skin

My father's eyes were blue
like his grandfather's
but if I trace the line
of nose and chin
it is his grandmother's face
I see. Abenaki woman.

His heart was green and growing,
as if he'd lived for centuries,
an old forest tree man
rooted in the rocky soil
now called new england,
as if Gluscabe's arrow
had just pierced the bark
and turned it to human skin.

Ndakinna, I want to tell him now.
Ndakinna. There is a name
for this place you call in English
the home country.

Over the last meal
we'll ever eat together
he tells me, I'm going up north,
up to the old home country,
Abenaki country. He smiles
in anticipation, his feet
already feeling the forest floor,
while my stomach tightens
with the knowledge that he
is going home. I push
the feeling away. But when spirit
talks to spirit, there is no denying.

Through the long days of mourning,
I see my father's spirit
walk into the bright autumn woods.
Red, gold, and evergreen,
they welcome him back,
his relatives, green of heart
and rooted, like him,
in the soil of this land
called Ndakinna.

—*Cheryl Savageau* (Abenaki)

A Quick Brush of Wings

Olivia tells:
"One time just before breakup
K'ilmoya, little Beaver
In Mukluk Slough, stick up her head.
Look around, say 'How are you?'
Kids run home scared.
We go down, she's gone."

"Last winter," Tatiana says,
"Albert's getting water.
He yell, 'Yoona-oo! Yoona-oo!'
It's Christmas tree, sure enough,
Shining on river ice.
It's like a bush on fire.
In the morning it's gone."

Lidwynne nods, "Same night,
My dog Grumpy start howling
In woman's voice. I go out.
She's staring like Owl at nothing.
I don't know what it is.
A few days later
That poor Grumpy go crazy!

Marie snips a tail of sinew.
"When Nicky is in hospital down Tanana
I'm on death watch.
Cold fingers touch my neck.
Feels just like icicle dripping.
I hear feet walk away.
Right then the old man die."

Something cold feathers my arms—
A quick brush of wings. I tell them
Across an ocean I had dreamed
Dotson, the Raven, flying
Upside down.
His eyes were like red coals.

"Ahh!" The sewing women
Suck in their breaths.
"Lots of spirits all over, this year,"
They whisper.

—*Mary TallMountain* (Koyukon)

Summer Solstice

For seven days I heard the cat
as she padded full-pawed
up the driveway,
crying steadily as she walked,
as if she were calling kittens
or a mate.

She stopped beneath the Japanese maple,
the place she'd chosen
to drop the tiny mouse
I hadn't seen she was carrying.

The mouse crouched in front of her
stunned or hypnotized,
and the cat looked around,
and began to sing.

Her voice rose and fell
in all the inflections known to cats.
The rolling tones that start deep in the throat
then open to invitation, the inquisitive hum
she'd used when nuzzling kittens, the demanding wail
I'd gotten used to hearing outside the kitchen door.

The mouse,
delicate-boned, velvet-furred,
never moved, never twitched
an ear or hair.

This went on for some time.
It was a very small mouse,
maybe born this spring
before the grasses bloomed.

I don't know how long exactly I watched,
but long enough for me to think
she doesn't really want the mouse,
long enough that in a fit
of human understanding
I thought to save the mouse,
and walking toward them,
spoke the cat's name.

She looked up,
her eyes intent and distant,
then calmly picked up
the waiting mouse
and with one sure bite,
bit off its head and ate
bones and fur and all,
until there was nothing left
but a drop of blood
on her whiskey brow.

For seven days she did this
an hour or two before sunset
and after that first day I watched
from wherever the cry caught me,
surprised each time
by ceremony.

There is a love between hunter and prey
that I am just beginning to understand.

On the threshold of summer,
beneath the red-leafed tree,
she sang the terrible song
that turns the seasons.
And the earth, having its fill of light,
turned again toward darkness.

—*Cheryl Savageau* (Abenaki)

Living History

Walked into Pinehurst, sunburned, smelling of fish,
Big Indian Man paying for some gas and a six pack,
Looking at me hard.
Dreamer, I think, too old for me.
Heads right toward me.
"Jeez," he says, "You look just like your mom—
You must be Marlene's girl."
Pinches my arm, but I guess it's yours
he touches.
Hell, wasn't even looking at me.
Wonder if I'm what they call living history?

—*Kimberly Blaeser* (Anishinaabe)

Stories I Tell My Daughter

1.

Once when I was eight we came home in the dark
up our winding dirt road through a tunnel
of thick spring leaves, and our headlights
turned maple and salal into a green
glowing vein leading us sleepily to our beds.

Suddenly the headlights caught an owl,
wingspan as wide as the windshield,
every creamy feather etched in perfection,
round eyes huge and yellow
with pupils black enough
to swallow me up. His curved beak
opened in surprise
at being face to face
with this steel creature whose own eyes
shown unblinking and wild.

       The owl didn't cry out but I did,
lunging forward into the dash,
hands beating against what was invisible
between us. I shouted, No!
Don't—The owl spread every pinion,
drummed hard against the skin of air
between life and death,
lifted upwards—up—over

and we drove on home, giddy with fear.
All summer I lay awake on cool sheets, window open,
waiting for a low urgent call.

2.

At thirteen, I played the drums, first chair,
ahead of boys who called me squaw.
I stopped wearing braids,
stood with my back to them,
my hair thick down my back
like a cloak no looks could pierce.
Their dirty jokes and snickering
made my strokes tighter, sharper,
hands curved around the wooden sticks
in an easy grip, as if they were tools
I had always used.

       Then there was heat
against my back, a low warning breaking
through the rhythm,
stench of singed human hair.
When I whirled around, it was Damon,
the one who always called to me in the halls,
I'll give you a little papoose, squaw!
holding a butane lighter, flame high,
orange and blue. In his hand
he held a chunk of black hair,

my hair,
burned off, smoking
in the still bandroom air.

                              That day

I took bloody sticks home to my mother,
who said she expected nothing less
from a girl
        who spoke
                to owls.

—*Deborah A. Miranda* (Ohlone-Costanoan Esselen/Chumash)

Pulling Down the Clouds

Ñ-ku'ibadkaj 'ant 'an ols g cewagi.
With my harvesting stick I will hook the clouds.
'Ant o 'i-wañ'io k o i'-hudiñ g cewagi.
With my harvesting stick I will pull down the clouds.
Ñ-ku'ibadkaj 'ant o 'i-siho g cewagi.
With my harvesting stick I will stir the clouds.

With dreams of distant noise disturbing his sleep,
the smell of dirt, wet, for the first time in what seems like months.
The change in the molecules is sudden,
they enter the nasal cavity.

He contemplates that smell.
What is that smell?
It is rain.
Rain somewhere out in the desert.
Comforted in this knowledge he turns over
and continues his sleep,
dreams of women with harvesting sticks
raised toward the sky.

—*Ofelia Zepeda* (Tohono O'odham)

Woman Stories

III

"Excuse Me,"
you say, "but could you shake
her hand? She's never seen a real
Indian before." We're in Oklahoma.
Green Country, or Red, depending
upon who you ask. A delicate child
takes two steps and leans into me
clamoring for warmth; shy and relieved
at once. The mother in me pats,
squeezes, and ignores the terry-cloth
Pocahontas dress. I lied, suppressed
my distaste. I said nothing. I should
have told that pretty little girl the truth.
I should have whispered it so I wouldn't
scar her sweet cream skin. "Real Indians
don't always hear the wolf cry to the blue
corn moon."

—*Reva Mariah S. Gover* (Skidi-Pawnee/Tohono O'odham)

REVIEWS: BOOKS OF POETRY

I am thinking about poetry. How far back it goes. And those we now refer to as "hominids." I don't believe they were so different from us. In one way or another, they were our ancestors. "Animals," maybe. Animals love their young and care for them, grieve when they die; grieve when they have lost a mate. Feel. They may possibly not think in the same ways we do—although sometimes I wonder—but they feel. All the same emotions. And communicate.

Poetry is the third sound. After music, after sound itself. What sounds we had or did not; some think at first we spoke only mind to mind. A hollow log, a stick. Breath blown through a hollow reed. A voice sent back, to all that is. Back and back.

Poetry is a connection to that time before time. Except for music, pure sound, it is our closest connection to the Beginning. It makes us remember what we were supposed to be. It makes us look at what we have become. The job of the poet is akin to that of the shaman; to go out and bring us back truth. To look ourselves in the face is the hardest thing.

For young people, poetry is very important; to know that all those feelings are not unique to them—to know that *feeling* is not unique to them. Show them how to do it themselves, and they will have a way to say how they feel; maybe to begin to understand what they might be. For Indian kids, Native poetry is a validation of who they are.—*Doris Seale*

Alexie, Sherman (Spokane/Coeur d'Alene), *First Indian on the Moon.* **Hanging Loose Press (1993). 116 pages; high school-up**

Alexie's first book, *The Business of Fancydancing*, was named a *New York Times Book Review* Notable Book of the Year. The *Times* called him "one of the major lyric voices of our time," and the *American Book Review* compared him to Crazy Horse: "The high spirit of Crazy Horse....is alive in this book, and dances powerfully throughout." These words don't seem to have very much to do with what Alexie is saying about being an Indian at the end of the 20th Century. The poems in this book deal, either precisely or peripherally, with that issue. His writing is both plainer and so much more than all the things that have been said about it. The near-impossibility of loving across color lines:

> Sometimes when an Indian boy loves
> a white girl and vice versa
> it's like waking up
> with half of the world
> on fire. You don't know
> if you should throw water
> onto those predictable flames
> or let the whole goddamn thing burn.

Which brings me to another point. One reviewer, trying, maybe, to prove something about his own perceptiveness, said that Alexie uses fire as a metaphor; based, apparently, on such poems as "Genetics" and "Fire Storm." Alexie writes,

> On January 13, 1981, my sister Mary and her husband Steve died in a trailer fire. After a long night of drinking, a curtain drifted on wind from an open window, touched the hot plate left burning, and created the ash I gather now.

That is tragedy, not "metaphor." To think otherwise, one would have to be either remarkably obtuse or remarkably insensitive—or both. (Maybe it was the "drunken Indian" bit that makes it a metaphor?) Alexie's writing comes from a place between "I was a fisherman for 15,000 years/before you stumbled onto my shore..." and the "Great American Western" that began in 1492. A place where it is hard to find any balance.

Alexie's writing never promises a happy ending, only that there will be times when it is possible to hope that there might be one:

> and although the whites say
> you can't hear anything in space
> I say we'll hear each other breathe
> I say we'll hear each other move
> I say we'll hear each other whisper
> I love you
> and I will say it in my own language
> I'll say it in the little piece
> of my own language that I know
> and I'll say it like it's the last thing I'll ever say:
> *quye han-xm=enc, quye han-xm=enc, quye han-xm=enc.*

—*Doris Seale*

Awiakta, Marilou (Cherokee), *Abiding Appalachia: Where Mountain and Atom Meet.* **St. Luke's Press (1978, 1986). 94 pages; grades 7-up**

Awiakta's work has appeared in many anthologies and periodicals. She is the author of *Selu: Seeking the Corn Mother's Wisdom* (Fulcrum, 1993) and is a contributor to *Speak to Me Words: Essays on Contemporary American Indian Poetry* (University of Arizona, 2003), to mention but a couple of her accomplishments.

The poems in *Abiding Appalachia* make a story, from The Beginning, through the Cherokee Removal, Tsali's sacrifice for his people, and the Prophet's foretelling of the coming of the atom, to Awiakta's childhood being inside fences and locked gates, but with the freedom of the woods and creeks.

The poem, "Test Cow" is an uneasy foreshadowing; as an adult, she says, "The atom was poetry in my childhood—images, rhythms—a presence beautiful, mysterious and dangerous....Then the atom went awry...."

Awiakta speaks, has always spoken, for the balance, for life against abuse and destruction; against the users, the takers. Her warnings are subtle.

> Beauty is no threat to the wary
> who treat the mountain in its way,
> the copperhead in its way,
> and the deer in its way,
> knowing that nature is the human heart
> made tangible.

But watch out. Awiakta is a country woman, a mountain woman, an Indian woman. None of these comes puny. With such gentleness, with such beauty, she tells us, you are dancing on the edge of the volcano. Take heed.

—Doris Seale

Belin, Esther G. (Diné), *From the Belly of My Beauty.* **University of Arizona (1999). 85 pages; high school-up**

Esther G. Belin's first collection tells the story of the "city cousin," one of the many "URIs, urban raised Indians." Hers is a postmodern landscape littered with Similac, Mickey D's cheeseburgers, empty Bud cans, Virginia Slims, sno-cones and Coors. This is not poetry of what Geary Hobson calls the "My-heart-soars-like-an-eagle" variety. Belin writes very much in the tradition of the early "bad ass" poetry of Nila Northsun. The voice is a tough one, whether it's her character Ruby asking "What the fuck are you looking at/fuckin' A. I hate white people" or the speaker of the autobiographical poem "From the Stench of My Belly" who shouts: "ONE DAY I REALIZED THERE IS NO PAIN IN KICKING ASS."

While rife with references to popular culture, Belin's work never loses sight of history. In "Euro-American Womanhood Ceremony," a poem about the generation of children sent to Indian residential schools, she writes about what happened to the girls:

> Instead of fasting and sweating and praying and
> running
> They set the table and vacuumed and ironed and
> nursed and fed
> and gave birth and birth and birth to a new nation of
> mixedbloods
> and urban Indians.

It is this new nation that Belin emerges from and seeks to document. In a concluding essay she notes that her voice and the voices of other Natives are not theirs alone but are a "voice collective [that is] mixedblood, crossblood, fullblood, urban, rez, relocated, terminated, non-status, tribally enrolled, federally recognized, non-federally recognized..." In the same essay she writes,

> Sometimes there are experiences too delicate to
> re-live through memory, which often happens
> when re-retold by the constructed yet sinuous
> voice of nonfiction. Sometimes the whimsical yet
> sinuous voice of poetry will suffice.

Whimsey is one of Belin's most effective tools; her poems defy predictability, often taking unexpected turns away from sentimentality, from too much earnestness, as in "Ruthie Rae, My Kid":

> I first knew you in the womb
> echoing my heartbeat
> twisting your life cord
> Churning Thai green curry #17.

The middle section of the book comprises a group of poems about a character named "Ruby," a name that clearly signifies a kind of ultimate redness. "Ruby" is an Indian Everywoman; in these poems, she is the narrator's friend or relative, twin or double. Sometimes Ruby and the narrator travel side by side, as in "Falling Stars":

> With Ruby at my side
> I hitchhike in moonless night
> twelve-pack in my jacket
> cans cold
> weigh down my sleeves
> clink clink
> chilling my tits

These whimsical gestures suggest the poet-narrator's unwillingness to take herself too seriously, yet what lies beneath them is both substantial and edgy. Several poems have fill-in-the-blank sections. "How Art Opens

Ruby's Eye" forces the reader to conjure up a suitable epithet to conclude the phrase:

> Invited to see art through native
> hands more than image
> of you drunk
> -en
> greasy _____

In "Jenny Holzer Inspiration," Belin writes, "I will remember/ White _____/makes me nervous…" suggesting that anything white will do to fill in this particular blank, that all things white are suspect and unsettling.

With a relentless attention to numbers and numbering, Belin questions what happens when the unquantifiable, that is, human beings, are quantified. "Ruby in Me #1" begins with birth order and segues into blood quantum, invoking, along the way, the ghost of alcohol:

> middle child
> smart child
> 1/4 Navajo
>   1/4 Navajo
>   1/4 Navajo
>   1/4 Navajo
> four parts equal my whole
> #311,990
> enrolled=proof
> 50
> 80
> 100 if you can stand
> it…

She is, through these various innovative strategies, calling attention to the language's instabilities and inadequacies, participating fully in the "reinvention of the enemy's language," which Joy Harjo and Gloria Bird have called one of the chief concerns of Native women writers.—*Janet McAdams*

Bruchac, Joseph (Abenaki), *No Borders*. Holy Cow! (1999). 101 pages; grades 7-up

It would be no exaggeration to say that Joe Bruchac is a most prolific writer. Fiction, non-fiction books for children and young adults, little kids picture books—name it, he's done it. But he is first and foremost a poet.

The poems in *No Borders* are Joe's voice; a voice I know, from occasional conversations over the years, meetings here and there, and a tape of his reading of the poems from *Translator's Son*, solace for many a dark night. There is a peacefulness to his poetry, even when he is writing about things that are far from peaceful. There is a sense of a man come to terms with himself; a knowing that

things are as they are—and that doesn't necessarily make them right. And hope:

> So we listened
> to the sound of rocks
> & water reflecting
> a land made of legends,
> waiting further directions
> from sun, wind & season

The pain of things that cannot be changed is not absent, either. In "Men of the Forest," on meeting an orangutan, prisoner in a German zoo:

> Its eyes
>   hold questions
> an elder might ask
> of a child.
> So my old people,
> men of the forest,
> were brought to this Europe
> put on exhibit,
> seen as less
> than human.
> We hold our hands up
> palm to palm
> feeling the warmth
> of ancestry
> pass
> through the centuries
> and the vanished glass.

Read these slowly, let them sink in, like the Female Rains, into new-turned Earth.—*Doris Seale*

Dauenhauer, Nora Marks (Tlingit), *Life Woven With Song*. University of Arizona (2000). 135 pages, b/w photographs; grades 7-up

This collection of poetry, prose and plays is a selection of the writing of one of the foremost of Native writers. Her life's work has been to preserve Tlingit language and oral literature and thus, the culture of her people.

In this case, the title truly describes the book. Dauenhauer grew up in as close to a traditional way as is possible for any of us now, in a loving and artistic family. They were boat-builders, wood-carvers, bead-workers and musicians.

This is not to say that life was without difficulties. But, she says,

> Most of the memories recalled here are happy ones. Where the images are neutral, negative, or discouraging, I like to think that they reflect our ability to continue as individuals, as a family, as a community, as a people.

The writing here reflects that. It is a portrait of a life lived in harmony, of a functional society that manages to exist into the 21st Century. It is a song flung into the face of all the stereotypes, all the "Indian experts" who speak of us only in the past tense, who continue to insist that Native peoples no longer exist as viable cultures. It is also very enjoyable reading. A favorite story: "Egg Boat." The book is illustrated with family photographs, some from productions of the plays, and an exquisite jacket painting by JoAnn George.

Life Woven With Song is a wise and lovely work.

—*Doris Seale*

Dubin, Margaret, ed., *The Dirt Is Red Here: Art and Poetry from Native California*. Heyday (2002). 82 pages, color photos, color illustrations; high school-up

In the time before the white men, there were at least one hundred distinct and separate Indian tribes in California; more, some say. Out of an original 300,000, the estimated death toll of conquest is 200,000. What does the average person know about California Indians? "*Were* there any?" "I thought you guys were all dead!" This collection gives the lie to both comments. It includes an editor's introduction, giving brief, necessary historical information, and the work of thirty poets and artists. Dubin notes that the experiences of Native Californians have been "diverse and profound." The contents of this book definitely reflect that.

If there is an underlying theme other than the common experience of devastation, it is that of reclamation. Reclamation of cultures, of traditional knowledge, of languages, of homelands: reclamation of self. The poems speak of the ways in which these things have been taken. Not all the poets believe with equal assurance in the possibility of return. And yet, hope seems to spring up, as irrepressible as a weed growing between railroad tracks. From Shaunna Oteka McCovey's "The Brush Dance Boy Lives in Phoenix, Arizona":

Sing me dreams
of smoke and root
feel the sun rise in my heart
after the morning dance.
Jump center into my soul.

The companion painting, Frank Tuttle's "In the House," is perfect. And humor: Greg Sarris' "When My Great-Great Grandfather Tom Smith Caused the 1906 Earthquake." The art work also runs the gamut, from Fritz Scholder's bronze, "Painted Man #1," for whom healing does not seem likely, to Kathleen Smith's light-filled "My People's Home: Upper Dry Creek." Some paintings

seem best observed from an oblique angle, and with a respectful eye: Rick Bartow's "Nickwitch" and "Questions of Beliefs" among them. His "Fox Spirit" seems so clearly something terribly damaged but still living that it makes the stomach clench. Judith Lowry's paintings, "The Obedient Wives" and "The Rescue" are breath-taking and terrifying.

There are beautiful objects: George Blake's elk antler, leather and silver "Dude Boot," Bradley Marshall's regalia pieces and carved and inlaid "Elkhorn purse 2000," and Linda Aguilar's and Linda Yamane's exquisite baskets.

Coyote, appropriately enough making an appearance in L. Frank's "Coyote On the Road to Wisdom Sans Map" walking through a fire field, and Bartow's "Coyote and the Dust Devil," looking as though his brain feels a little scrambled, might say something about the dilemmas of colonized peoples—keeping in mind that Coyote is indestructible. He's already been killed at least a thousand times.

The Dirt is Red Here is a treasure trove. The last word goes to Deborah A. Miranda, "The Language of Prophets":

Out of grey clouds
right to left
one hawk
eight herons/over dark water.
One fierce year—
eight years of stillness.
Green pines take
what fog lets go.

—*Doris Seale*

Dumont, Marilyn (Cree/Métis), *A Really Good Brown Girl*. Brick Books (1996). 78 pages; high school-up

A Really Good Brown Girl is a collection of poetry and memories about land, family, and the multiple boundaries imposed by the continuing colonization of the Métis people. The book is divided into four sections: "Squaw Poems," "What More Than Dance," "White Noise," and "Made of Water."

Dumont's first pieces talk about white people's judgments and the internalized shame that results:

You are not good enough, not good enough, obviously not good enough. The chorus is never loud or conspicuous, just there.

As a child in school, Dumont learns how to watch and remember, how to become invisible, how to deny being Indian, how to follow and how to be a really good brown girl, looking "poised, settled, like I belong." She also learns to resist, and as an adult, challenges her professor who tries to correct her spoken English.

> I say, "really good." He says, "You mean really
> well, don't you?" I glare at him and say emphati-
> cally, "No, I mean, really good."

The first section is also about family, "polish[ing] the linoleum with our dancing," about parenting in difficult circumstances, about the violence meted out to Native women. The poems in "What More Than Dance" and "White Noise" are about Dumont's continued encounters with the white establishment and also with her identity as a Native woman. Her strong voice is tempered with a good sense of irony about images of Indians—and not a little humor as well. In "Circle the Wagons," Dumont writes:

> There it is again, the circle, that goddamned
> circle, as if we thought in circles, judged things
> on the merit of their circularity, as if all we ate
> was bologna and bannock, drank Tetley tea, so
> many times "we are" the circle, the medicine
> wheel, the moon, the womb, and sacred hoops,
> you'd think we were one big tribe....Are my
> eyes circles yet?

In the final section, "Made of Water," Dumont returns to her family, searching for answers and healing torn relationships. With a mature voice, she speaks to her father, now gone:

> I have carried your pain   in metal buckets and
> I still go for water   every so often
> and that water   is so cold and hard
> that it stings my hands,   its weight makes me feel
> my arms will break at the shoulders and yet
> I go to that well   and drink from it because
> I am, as you,   made of water.

Dumont's direct and bold, powerful and poignant writing is all about survival: resisting the effects of colonization, challenging the white definitions of "Indian," telling the realities of Native lives, and encouraging other Native women to find their voice.—*Beverly Slapin*

Dunn, Carolyn (Creek/Cherokee/Seminole), *Outfoxing Coyote.* **Painted Horse Press (2002). 95 pages; high school-up**

Coyote is considered by many Indian Nations to be the trickster, the master magician who uses his/her powers to teach us something. But sometimes when we fail to see our own humanness in these teachings, we become the target of Coyote's backward medicine. We con ourselves. It takes strong, ancient, feminine power to outfox Coyote.

Realizing the mysterious importance of shape shifting, Dunn takes us into the worlds of Coyotesse, Turquoise Woman, Deer Woman, Warrior Woman, and Eagle Woman. Through this shifting we realize the importance of finding answers to essential questions: How can we know our people unless we know as they knew? See as they saw? Become as they were? Simply put, we can't. But Dunn's writings give us clues how to do so, how to outfox the trickster in ourselves, how to see with our eyes closed.

In the poem "Deer Hunter," she reveals candidly the mystical mixture of confusion, love, desire, shame and awakenings:

> She was trying to warn me—
> and I looked into her eyes
> perhaps now I can save myself.
> ...I look to the ground
> and see my feet
> hooves covered with dust
> and stained with blood
> pours from the open wound
> of my breasts
> to the earth
> where it dries
> and forms red stones
> shining
> and I shape them into a necklace
> of deep crimson
> nearly black.

The most powerful poem for me is "Tahlon of the Bird Clan," which Dunn wrote for her son. The words sing softly from the page to my mind and settle in my heart, reminding us that we Cherokee are children of the stars, just as we know stars are birds.

Outfoxing Coyote is a treasure.—*MariJo Moore*

Hogan, Linda (Chickasaw), *The Book of Medicines.* **Coffee House Press (1993). 87 pages; high school-up**

Linda Hogan may be better known for her fiction, nonfiction and autobiography than for her poetry, but she is a poet, and a fine one, with several titles to her credit. Much of Hogan's poetry comes from that edge where there is always a presence, something other. It is a place where one could meet anything, where reality—as we have come to define it—becomes slippery and unsure; a place where "we are walking another way/than time."

Hogan's poetry has been called "elemental," and that is true, in the old and original sense of that word. And she calls to something in us that is also "other." This is very fine work. One does not necessarily think of a collection of poetry as something that cannot be put aside, but *The Book of Medicines* is just that. Haunting, maybe. Surely, it stays with you.—*Doris Seale*

Keeshig-Tobias, Lenore (Ojibwe), ed., _Into the Moon: Heart, Mind, Body, Soul_, illustrations by Darla Fisher-Odjig (Ojibwe/Potawatomi). Sister Vision (1996). 113 pages, b/w illustrations; high school-up

In the early 1990s, Beth Brant was asked to facilitate a Native women's writing workshop in Toronto. This book is one result. It cannot be said to be comfortable reading, but keep in mind that these women are all here, and writing, because they have managed to stay alive. For far too many Indian women, this is not a foregone conclusion.

The poems and stories speak of the ways in which their lives have been threatened and distorted; of their concern for the Earth, "Before it really is too late": "I see my mother/lying there raped"; "What grows has life purpose... to cleanse the air, provide shelter and give warmth."

Banakonda K.K Bell writes of a day spent with a young client, "seventeen years old, violent, dangerous, and very hungry for love, love she is afraid to have and afraid to do without. Hungry to learn, but afraid to know—hungry and outright raw with her need."

There is writing as refuge: "A place to be alone and safe in," and as safety valve: "At these times, pen and paper save me/Until the next time," and a clear sense that a life warped can only be "fixed" so far.

Beauty, too; a mother's proud and loving poem about her son, and the title poem that tells of the essential balance of relationship between woman and moon: "She tells us when to plant a seed, when to give birth, when to die."

And survival, what it comes down to, in the end, for us: "I am reminded that life is to be lived. This is what I have done—lived with love, pain, fear...but I have kept my face toward the light."

The illustrations, simple pen-and-ink drawings, extraordinarily powerful, express, embellish and enhance the text. Essential.—_Doris Seale_

McAdams, Janet (Creek), _The Island of Lost Luggage_. University of Arizona (2000). 74 pages; high school-up

A fish-shaped milagro placed into a bullet hole, a piece of chrome from an exploded car, the severed hands of Taino waving in pink-tinted water, orange popsicles and green mangoes, and the Island of Lost Luggage, where "the disappeared, the lost children and the Earharts of modern life" line up—McAdams' stunning poems connect all of these, seamlessly weaving together individual and community, personal and political, then and now.

The connection is the struggle to remain human—on the land, in the body, in right relation to all; to remember

the beginning of the great catastrophe:

> At Guanahani, they swam to the caravel
> bearing parrots and balls of cotton thread,
> these people so unlike him they could not
> not be saved.

—and to acknowledge the resistance that continues:

> Six young men knot kerchiefs over their faces
> and hoist the coffin onto their shoulders,
> kicking up small clouds of dust
> down the Boulevard of Heroes

Amid references to revolution in Mexico and El Salvador, "Saturday Night Live" and "The Twilight Zone," the story of "Stone Soup" and the childhood games of "Scissors, Rock & Paper" and "Red Rover," there is advice to travelers after the thousand-year war, the environmental holocaust:

> Be suspicious of the songs of sparrows
> for there are no sparrows.

There are words of caution and advice: to refuse to look around us—

> We know about selfishness, but not greed,
> know about hunger, but not starvation.

—to deny that we are all related, that we each have a particular place in a collective consciousness, is to suffer the consequences of that denial. There is great wisdom here, if you pay attention, and words of incomparable beauty and reflection:

> ...There are days
> when we can forget all but this color,
> this leaf, or the appearance
> of small stones under water.

The Island of Lost Luggage is an awesome work.

—_Beverly Slapin_

Midge, Tiffany (Hunkpapa), _Outlaws, Renegades and Saints: Diary of a Mixed-Up Halfbreed_. Greenfield Review (1996). 104 pages; high school-up

Being a mixed-blood is no easy road: Tiffany Midge makes her art from the collision of irreconcilables. These are no "pretty poems." The writing is sometimes funny—if Indians couldn't laugh, we'd all be dead—heart-stopping, as in "July 1972":

> It is my birthday. I ask my mother, "when I grow
> up will I be a full-blooded Indian?"

There is beauty here, and irony not always short of bitterness, pain—all the things that make us human—and ultimate survival. Midge's poetry is informed by an in-your-face refusal either to romanticize her life, or to accept the place that has been "assigned" to us: to accept extinction.

> listen,
> can you hear the dead talking?
> They are saving and resurrecting us all

At the Custer monument, it says,

> Warning: Beware of rattlesnakes.

And beyond those signs there are others. Spoken in the softest and most ancient of whispers. Carried by the furious wind that blows forever across the wide sea of prairie, the big sky of endless horizon. Whispers carried along the eternity of flowing waters—

> Warning: Beware of ghosts.

—*Doris Seale*

Miranda, Deborah A. (Ohlone-Costanoan Esselen/Chumash), *Indian Cartography*. Greeenfield Review (1999). 99 pages; high school-up

The Indians in California were never meant to survive, much less experience a resurgence of culture and literature heading into the 21st Century. Our demise was legally and officially planned, executed, and very nearly carried out....I want to tell the story of things intrinsically evil and hateful that happened to us.... of flogging, rape, kidnapping, European-carried diseases like syphilis and smallpox, torture, enslavement and starvation which....were also parts of the Missionized Indian's day....My life has been an embodiment of separation, division, reconciliation, and loss. I am Indian: I am mixed-blood: I am Indian.

It is important to know these things, because Miranda's poetry is born out of this. It is all the more astonishing to know that, and see how much of beauty has come out of tragedy. There is anger here, and grief: "Certain Scars," "Sorrow as a Woman," "Lost Language," "Without History" are some titles, but also "Going On," and ""Heartwood":

> Heartwood remembers, gathers itself for the next leap. I
>   close my eyes just as the whole world takes wing.
> And ultimately,
> This
> is how a
> path changes

> ....And
> there you are. Saved. You didn't go
> through, under, over, or around.
> You didn't move at all. This
> is the trick at the heart
> of impossibility:
> hang on past all
> endurance, and
> then, let
> go.

Indian Cartography is an extraordinary validation of the endurance, strength of a People, and of the woman who has made the journey delineated here.—*Doris Seale*

Montejo, Victor (Maya), *Sculpted Stones/Piedras Labradas*, translated by Victor Perera. Curbstone (1995). 107 pages; grades 7-up; Maya

> If our ancestors came to life
> they'd surely give us, their descendants
> thirteen lashes for being
> sleepwalkers and conformists.
> They always advised us
> to struggle, build and forge ahead
> so that no one's left behind,
> and no one's forgotten by his brothers.
> Yet today we Maya
> remain hushed up
> and have even forgotten the message
> that might inspire us to break the silence.
> That's why if our ancestors came back to life
> they'd give us thirteen lashes
> to cure the amnesia of centuries
> which has made us forget our names.

Victor Montejo is a poet, a human rights activist and an anthropologist, studying in depth his own people. After the massacre of his village in 1981, in which Guatemalan soldiers killed his brother, Montejo's name appeared on a death squad list and he was forced to flee to the U.S. Since then, his life's work has been to make known, in a variety of ways, the continuing human rights violations confronting the Mayan peoples.

After *Testimony: Death of a Guatemalan Village*, after *The Bird Who Cleans the World and Other Mayan Fables*, after a spectacular children's version of the Mayan sacred book, the *Popul Vuh*, comes this book of poetry, *Sculpted Stones*. Here, in Spanish and English, Montejo's poems express the resilience of the Mayan peoples, expose the Guatemalan army's attempt to destroy the indigenous population, and give lie to textbook anthrobabble about "history" and "culture."

In the first poem, "Interrogation by the Ancestors," Montejo asks,

> Just think:
> what can we say
> to the ancients
> when they return
> with thunder and lightning
> and ask about the fire
> they left with us
> in the cone of the great volcano?

And for the poor, betrayed, sad, humiliated, plundered, frightened people, there is this advice (beginning, of course, with an anthropological discourse):

> Among the Maya
> to cure a fright
> you put a fresh-laid egg
> in the armpit
> of the frightened person
> and in that way
> the self-worth and health
> that the phantom has stolen
> will return to the afflicted.
> But, how can we cure
> the pain and fear
> built up over the many centuries
> of plunder and negation
> of our Mayan identity?
> Someone said
> the egg is a great idea,
> but in our day it's better
> to confront
> and do battle
> with those causing the fright,
> then endure the centuries
> warming turkey eggs
> in your armpits.

This is really good advice; *Sculpted Stones* is testament to a people's tenacious determination to survive in the face of centuries of colonization.—*Beverly Slapin*

Moore Marijo (Cherokee), *Spirit Voices of Bones.* Renegade Planets (1997). 95 pages; high school-up

Vine Deloria compares Moore's poetry to "a long cool drink of water on a hellishly hot day." That's a good description. There is a clarity to this writing, a pristine quality that reflects the title—spare, pared down, a voice that says, this is reality, look at it. Quit fooling around. Look at the "invisible connectedness of all things/past, present, and future." "To Celebrate Not Explain the Mystery":

> and in this celebration I would find
> the explanation that requires no explaining
> the knowledge that requires no knowing
> the answer that requires no questioning
> and then I would understand
> and then I would not understand
> and then it would not matter.

Moore invites us to a new way of seeing, not through the constructs we have created, but behind them, to a reality we have not imagined.

It's interesting that Deloria should mention water; there is a Cherokee tradition of going to the water for healing, and these poems offer healing; healing for our blindness, our pig-headedness, our stubborn refusal to admit where these things are leading us. And healing for those who have been held under a hellishly hot sun for far too long.

The last poem—"Solidarity in the Night"—is a spectacular finale, with interpretations in Athabascan, Eastern Cherokee, Saponi/Yesah, Ojibwe, Lakota, Chickasaw, Choctaw, Muscogee, Abenaki, Yup'ik, Hawai'ian and Diné.

There are notes on the poems, and the cover art is by the author. *Spirit Voices of Bones*: pure and simple, a true gift.

—*Doris Seale*

Ochoa, Annette Piña (Yaqui), Betsy Franco, and Traci L. Gourdine, eds., *Night Is Gone, Day Is Still Coming: Stories and Poems by American Indian Teens and Young Adults.* Candlewick (2003). 145 pages; grades 7-up

There are eighty poems and stories in this volume, by young people ages eleven to twenty-two, and from a variety of Native Nations. Some are about what we would expect from early efforts: some are spectacular; all are moving. I was struck by the themes that show up consistently, themes shared with older writers by not always in such an "out-there" way; identity and land, over and over, identity, over and over, the land. For anyone who thinks things have changed substantially for Native youth, read this. It is true that they are no longer jammed into residential schools against their will. It is true that one way or another quite a few are making it to higher education. But these kids are still wondering who they are, what they can make of their lives, whether the Earth will continue to be destroyed. I am reluctant to quote from any specific poem or story because while some may be more polished than others, all do one of the things any good writing is supposed to: whop you upside the head. The title, whether intentional or not, says it all: night is gone, day is coming. Maybe. Essential.—*Doris Seale*

Ortiz, Simon (Acoma), *After and Before the Lightning.* **University of Arizona (1994). 135 pages; high school-up**

This is but one of Simon Ortiz's many works of poetry, fiction, non-fiction, collections. It came out of a winter that he spent in South Dakota, teaching at Sinte Gleska College on Rosebud. The poems are full of the bitter cold, the winter darkness:

> On a daily basis and in a moment-to-moment way, I found this poetry reconnecting my life to all Existence....Every line and word, every image and thought, every sensation and emotion was an explicit item and notation about what was happening in my life that winter on the South Dakota prairie.

The land possesses this book, the people, what it has done to them, what it promises, what has been done to them by others.

> This land is barren, poor.
> The people just as poor.
> I ask a foolish question,
> halting on the possibility.
> "How...can? Can they...?
> the people get back...
> their lives?"
> Answers falter.

Simon Ortiz is from Acoma, one of the most beautiful places on Earth. He is a writer of such stature that the only honorable way to speak about him seems to be in his own words. In *A Good Journey* (Turtle Island, 1977), he quotes from an interview. Asked, "Why do you write? Who do you write for?" he says:

> Because Indians always tell a story. The only way to continue is to tell a story and that's what Coyote says. The only way to continue is to tell a story and there is no other way. Your children will not survive unless you tell something about them—how they were born, how they came to this certain place, how they continued.

The belief in story, the importance of telling, informs all of Ortiz's writing. It tells us something very important about ourselves as human creatures, and ourselves in relationship to all else that exists.—*Doris Seale*

Sam-Cromarty, Margaret (Cree), *James Bay Memories.* **Waapoone (1992). Unpaginated; grades 7-up**

Cree territory in Quebec has been, and remains, under threat from the James Bay Hydroelectric Project. "Phase I of James Bay, built in 1975" has caused "massive physical destruction, disrupted the migration, feeding and reproductive patterns of wildlife, and released quantities of natural mercury from the soil that have contaminated the rivers and the fish, and poisoned the people for whom fish is a dietary staple." In the resulting dislocation, "alcoholism, drug abuse, violence and suicide have become major problems."

This is the background of Sam-Cromarty's poetry. She writes with utter simplicity about a good way of life, one they had endured for thousands of years. She does not say that it was perfect—or easy—just that it was good.

> The green forests
> Tree-ringed lakes
> It was home to me
> and the wild things.

The destruction of that way of life is reinforced with photographs: two, of First Rapids, show a "before"— wide, strong river, rocks, white-water—and "after," a scene of desolation; steel, concrete, as far as the eye can see. "In this time/of steel/and of speed," the River Chisasibi, "the happy river was lost/It weeps now/It seeks/golden sands."

The last photograph in the book is of the back view of a young man and the t-shirt he is wearing. It says, "The land is, and has been for thousands of years, the economic base of my people. Left alone for another thousand years we would still survive." Just so.—*Doris Seale*

Rose, Wendy (Hopi/Miwuk), University of Arizona, high school-up:
Bone Dance: New and Selected Poems, 1965-1993. **(1994). 108 pages**
Itch Like Crazy. **(2002). 124 pages, b/w photographs**

Wendy Rose has been writing for a very long time and her poems have been widely anthologized; finally, here is *Bone Dance*, an anthology of her own work. Showing no mercy for wannabes who "turn holy in a temporary tourism of our souls"—or anthropologists—"skullmongers (who) whisper among themselves and plot," Rose gives voice to a woman, murdered at Wounded Knee Creek; to Truganinny, the last of the Tasmanians, her body stuffed and put on display; and Julia Pastrana, similarly humiliated; to the skeletons stored in a museum and the human bones in the adobe walls of the Santa Barbara Mission; to the whirling Earth, singing a throat song; and to the old woman Loo-Wit, pseudonymously called "Mount St. Helens," spitting her black tobacco skyward:

> she finds her weapons
> and raises them high;
> clearing the twigs
> from her throat
> she sings, she sings,

shaking the sky
like a blanket about her
Loo-Wit sings and sings and sings!

In *Itch Like Crazy*, Rose's poems are more songs of conquest and genocide, "Clan mothers, granddaughters, all those the missionaries erased," prayers for a rattlesnake on the road and the buffalo at Yellowstone, and itching like crazy for "being born into a family that could not keep its secrets straight."

In three sections—"These Bones," "This Heart," and "Listen Here for the Voices"—Rose paints vignettes through the eyes of the generations. With a word-vision of Taino "gathering shellfish, unafraid, splashing the little ones, laughing"—and welcoming the newcomers, Rose begins a chronology that continues with her own family stories. Here, amid old photographs of family members—actual and possible—she describes herself as "the family karma kickback," the mixed-blood historian who finds that "the people from whom I come were the perpetrators of those very acts that ignited my rage."

Writing with incomparable beauty and clarity and imagery one can't help but see, Wendy Rose has been called "angry." She has been called a "protest poet." She has been called a lot of things by people who would rather not deal with the issues she raises. Issues of genocide, of dislocation, of what it is to be an urban Indian, of what it is to be a "halfbreed" woman in this society. Wendy Rose's words can rip your heart out, and it's about time she got that Pulitzer Prize.—*Beverly Slapin*

Savageau, Cheryl (Abenaki), *Dirt Road Home*. Curbstone Press (1995). 92 pages; high school-up

Cheryl Savageau is a storyteller, has been writer-in-residence in Massachusetts schools, and is the recipient of National Endowment for the Arts and Massachusetts Artists Foundation fellowships. *Dirt Road Home* contains poems from the previously published *Home Country* as well new poems and stories.

New England Indians have a history of being written off as not being "real Indians," a bunch of half-breeds at best, who have completely lost their traditions. For a long time, Abenaki people were not "Indians," they were "French-Canadian." Growing up in Vermont, I knew vaguely about this—those "Saint Francis Indians," said with a curl of the lip. "Survival this way"; hiding in plain sight. Savageau's poetry speaks to this, and to what extent lives have still managed to be lived in the old way.

You taught me the land so well
that all through my childhood

I never saw the highway,
the truckstops, lumberyards,
the asphalt works,
but instead saw the hills,
the trees, the ponds on the south end
of Quinsigamond...
Driving down the dirt road home,
it was the trees you saw first,
All New England a forest.

Home. That's what this book is about. Coming home to place, coming home to self. For any of us who grew up in this way. For others: maybe an understanding of how it is that we have survived as Native people. And for some, most accomplished and beautiful poetry.—*Doris Seale*

Scofield, Gregory (Cree/Métis), Polestar, high school-up: *The Gathering: Stones for the Medicine Wheel.* (1993). 91 pages
I Knew Two Métis Women. (1999). 143 pages

The Gathering is Scofield's first book of poetry. It begins with the beautiful "Black Bear's Grandson," translated into Cree by Freda Ahenakew. Each section is an arm of the Medicine Wheel, poems for the four directions: "West/Arrival," "North/Searching," "East/Dreams," "South/Healing." The best word to describe this writing is "powerful." Power walks around and through the poems on four, long-clawed, dark-furred feet. What they are "about": the harsh reality of city living—"So easy to fall through a crack/On the street"—being a mixed-blood, trying to find home, and the dreams that haunt us until we can find a way to know who we are—*Katipamsoochick*; "The people who own themselves."

Behind the words, ice, snow, stars that blaze in the sky on bitter winter nights, the carcajou, the bone-chill of wolf-song to lift your spirit out of your body—home. In 1993, I had never read anything like this: I haven't still. I don't think I ever will.

Subtitled "The lives of Dorothy Scofield and Georgina Houle Young" and dedicated to "those two most incredible women. And for Aunty Donna, Aunty Shirley, Mom Maria, Michelle, Virgie and the generations to come," *I Knew Two Métis Women* is an act of love in poetry. This was no conventional family arrangement—I can hear the social workers grinding their teeth—but, as with so many Indian arrangements, it worked.

Not all halfbreed mothers
wear cowboy shirts or hats,
flowers behind their ears
or moccasins
sent from up north.

...read The Star, The Enquirer,
The Tibetan Book of the Dead
...know how to saddle
and ride a horse,
how to hot-wire a car
or siphon gas.

Scofield's love and admiration for these women shines through every word.

my patch-quilt mother
with a hat so beat up
only a miracle
kept it on her head.
Running to meet her,
I saw her eyes charm up a smile.
"Look!" she said
glowing in her new sweatshirt:
METIS & AND PROUD OF IT.

And their love for him. Lucky boy, to have been so loved. Wise man, to know it. *I Knew Two Métis Women* received the 2000 British Columbia Book Award. Easy to see why.—*Doris Seale*

Seale, Doris (Santee/Cree), *Ghost Dance.* Oyate (2000). 96 pages; high school-up

Doris Seale's collection sends me in the direction of thorns and tenderness. Her poem, "Civilized" gives early warning to readers that her voice is neither predictable nor legendary; listing the commands coming to her from the dominant anti-Indian culture, she writes:

Not so loud,
Not so sad,
Not so happy,
Not so mad.

Rising in indignation and pride, the poem continues the irrational and inhumane "rules" she's being asked to live by:

Not so flamboyant
—good—
—bad—

until finally, the poem makes the real message clear in a final line that Seale spits out with all the venom and sadness of a woman who has heard these words too many times in her lifetime:

Not so goddammed Indian.

This is what I mean by "thorny" writing—writing that is a thorn in the side of non-Indian readers, folks who never question the parameters of "Indian" as taught to them by history and North American Manifest Destiny. The title of this poem, "Civilized," works to pull in the reader with what is considered a compliment, a praise-worthy state—and then zaps us with what that state really means for Native peoples. Not "so" loud, Not "so" sad—in other words, Indian proportions of loudness, of sadness, in fact of any kind of human expression, are unacceptable, and must be trimmed here, cut off there, tweaked elsewhere, so that Indians "fit" into something defined as "civilized" or non-threatening. Doris Seale's anger is sharp in this poem, and she accomplishes this admirably with terse, choice words that create and re-flect 500 years of forced assimilation in a mere eight lines. I like to think these words are spare enough to slice through many layers of restraints.

Yet Seale also includes in this stinging collection one of the hallmarks of Native women's survivance and resis-tance writing: love poems. These are sensual, erotic, frightening and seductive, the way good love poems should be; each one using the same lean and wiry con-struction that works like rebar or a skeleton to craft bare essence. Poems for lovers, for children, for friends are all included; but most importantly, the book ends with what I consider a love poem for Seale's self, for her identity as a Native woman. In "They Will Be Beautiful," Seale chants all the ways that the bones of her body will someday enter back into the source from which they emerged—the earth—and thus achieve a standard by which indigenous aesthetics can be seen: part of, in connection with, and centered around, the elements of homeland. She writes,

The long bones of my body
Will be polished
By the wind
By the rain
By the sand
By the sun...

In this way, Seale imagines the elements of the world acting upon her bones, rather than the other way around (as in human beings instigating massive upheavals of soil, habitats, ecosystems, tribal communities). The world will change her; the elements will "polish" her, bring out inner light, have their way with her—and not inci-dentally, help her complete a transformation:

They will be made to glow,
Like old ivory.
Then they will be
Truly beautiful.

The tenderness toward old bones here goes beyond the

poet's personal desire to be judged beautiful, and alludes to the thousands and thousands of indigenous remains that are captive, artificially preserved, withheld from their final journey within the confines of museums, laboratories and private collections. To be "truly beautiful," we must reenter the cycle of the elements; this is not personal ambition or culturally trained belief, but an honest acknowledgement of the power that such a cycle has to maintain a working balance.

That balance, Seale tells us, is true beauty; not the violence of forced and false assimilation or oppression, but the letting go, the willingness to take part in a transformation as part of a mystery larger than ourselves, and yet part of each one of us. I recommend this book for many reasons, but primarily because it is the combination of thorniness and tenderness that gives us Seale's gift of clarity.

In thinking about books by Native women that are overlooked and under-appreciated, I realized Seale has way too much company. Three other books sitting on my shelves epitomize the diversity and strengths of "non-canonical" indigenous literature. All three books—*No Parole Today* (West End Press, 1999) by Laura Tohe (Diné), *From the Belly of My Beauty* (University of Arizona, 1999) by Esther Belin (Diné), and *The Island of Lost Luggage* (University of Arizona, 2000) by Janet McAdams (Creek)— are the first collection of each poet's work, but that is where obvious similarities end. Each book takes the reader in a different and visceral direction, and all are necessary to the task of mapping Native women's journeys through the late 20th Century. In this review, I have given you a taste of one direction; I urge you to seek out and bring these writers into your classrooms, scholarly discussions, and lives.—*Deborah A. Miranda*

Smelcer, John E. (Ahtna), and D.L. Birchfield (Choctaw/Chickasaw), editors, *Durable Breath*. Salmon Run (1994). 169 pages; high school-up

Even though it is out of print, this anthology is worth mentioning because it is such an excellent introduction to the work of Native poets. Forty-four are represented here, some well known—Joy Harjo, Joe Bruchac, Linda Hogan, Sherman Alexie, Simon Ortiz. Others will be less familiar to the non-Native reader, but no less important.

Durable Breath would be good to use with high school students, and well worth tracking down for this purpose. For anyone who loves poetry, reading it will be a pleasure.

Duane Niatum's introduction is a bonus:

> [I]f one reads and listens closely to these contemporary authors...he or she will recognize certain fundamental beliefs and attitudes on the nature and spirit of language and the native North American's continued reverence for the sacred power of words.

There are many wonderful poems in this book; I like this one, "Loon Shares with Kayak" by Glen Simpson (Tahltan), because it says so much about the relationship between humans and the rest of life on Earth.

> In the timeless light of Arctic night
> we cycled where the rivers met,
> fishing in a rush of shouldering waters.
> For us there was no other place,
> no coming dawn,
> no yesterday.
> Sharing was, despite those yellow eyes,
> a sign of kinship;
> a promise made;
> all weapons laid to rest.
> Somehow our gifts were multiplied:
> we left with vision clearer than we brought.

—*Doris Seale*

TallMountain, Mary (Koyukon/Athabascan): *Continuum*. Blue Cloud Quarterly (1988). Unpaginated; grades 7-up
The Light on the Tent Wall, illustrations by Claire Fejes. American Indian Studies, University of California (1990). 96 pages, b/w illustrations; grades 4-up
A Quick Brush of Wings. Freedom Voices (1991). 54 pages; grades 7-up
Listen to the Night: Poems for the Animal Spirits of Mother Earth. Freedom Voices (1995). 54 pages; grades 7-up

Mary TallMountain is probably not terribly well known outside the Native community, except in the San Francisco Bay Area—although she was interviewed by Bill Moyers for his PBS poetry series. She was never a "personality." Her output was comparatively small; from the *Blue Cloud Quarterly* chapbook of fourteen poems, through her last book, *Listen to the Night*, plus the things published in collections. There are those who would say that, of Native women poets, she was the best; that she never put a word down wrong. This is not because of any of the things that generally make people famous, but because she lived, and wrote, at the center.

Listen to the Night was not published until after her death, and I have not been able to read it until now, although I have had it for a long time. This book embodies all the things for which she, and her work, are held in honor. There are the things in her writing that we don't know we remember, until she says it for us; the words on the page, and what is not said, but nevertheless there; the surprise, the shock of recognition.

Long ready for the journey, she spoke of her wolf, "going west/going home."

> I must go to the Cliff house
> to damp and drip and spiderwebs
> Wolf is howling closer
> I shall wait there.

Beyond this, Mary TallMountain's last word to us—maybe is the last lovely poem in the book: "I Am All These."

In *Continuum* she said,

> It is wonderful to have passed through the main changes and emerged mellow and wiser, able to pass some wisdom on to other women younger or elder, to help them write for themselves happy and creative aspects.

She did that, all right. She was our elder. She is very greatly missed.—*Doris Seale*

Tapahonso, Luci (Diné), *Saanii Dahataal: The Women Are Singing*. University of Arizona (1993). 95 pages; high school-up

Tapahonso's poems and stories carry a strong sense of place, relationship and the need for balance in all things,

> ...because it has always been this way.
> It has worked well for centuries.
> You are here.
> Your parents are here.
> Your relatives are here.
> We are all here together.

To know where your feet are, to carry with you who you are, no matter where you are, is a theme that is a constant. And the importance of story, because if you don't know your story, how can you know anything else?

The unexplained lives here, too, and the sometimes down-right spookiness of life lived outside the reach of city lights. There is humor and delight in the poem about a runaway baby:

> So her name became "Beep-beep"
> because she liked to be a roadrunner
> and she liked having people try to catch her.

And in the story of a little dog who had an unexpected adventure. And, of course, just plain beautiful writing. The teaching is: "Remember the Things They Told Us." Always.—*Doris Seale*

Whirlwind Soldier, Lydia (Sicangu Lakota), *Memory Songs*, illustrated by Keli Shangreaux (Lakota). Center for Western Studies (1999). 60 pages, b/w illustrations; high school-up

> This Lakota poet (?) don't know
> form
> free verse,
> prose
> oxymoron
> or rhyme creation....

Maybe, but she writes with beauty and grace of un-bearable things, while always seeing the purpose, the balance, the intent—relationship—of existence. One comment about her work, "I truly enjoyed these poems," puzzles me. "Enjoyed" wouldn't be the word of choice, one would think:

> Times she wished to leave behind
> memories that fill her hollow breast
> times she wanted to sing her death song
> weeping for what she could
> not have, times she wanted to
> throw those relentless sorrows
> to the spirit wind....

Poems to the loss of a child; exquisite, heart-rending, yes. Unforgettable, yes. Enjoyable? Try to read *Memory Songs* without tears. Whirlwind Soldier ends with the story, written with tenderness and humor, of the birth of her grandson, Khayo Wakinyan Ahi, during a violent thunderstorm—thus accounting for part of his name—who "felt the power of Wakinyan for many years after. He was seven years old before he stopped predicting thunderstorms." Her writing is living embodiment of the idea that a People is truly preserved by the courage and refusal to be defeated of its women.—*Doris Seale*

Woody, Elizabeth (Warm Springs), *Luminaries of the Humble.* **University of Arizona (1994). 128 pages; high school-up**

With complex and exquisite precision, Woody tells how it is now for Native people, and out of what past that came to be, for us and the Earth with whom we still try to live in the proper way. Her writing can be, although not always, dense with imagery and layered with meaning, so you have to pay attention. Those meanings may not be what you had first supposed.

In many ways, *Luminaries* is a sorrow song, for loss, the death of a river; loss of life, of land—even our very words—our languages; for the "stress and grief over the irreversible change on the surface of the land." Identity, how we have been written off. "[C]ancer collects in the downwinders of the Hanford Nuclear Reservation. The difficult colloquies of a people who are marked as expendables."

At the same time, Woody gives us ways of seeing ordinary things—the "humble"—that we may never have imagined: "Rolling sand fizzles...." That is, in fact, exactly the sound made when the surf rolls in and then pulls back. It fizzles. In the moment of reading those three words, you can hear that sound, although you may be a thousand miles from the nearest ocean. Or, "hipbones that are lilies of carnal acceptance."

The very beauty of the writing intensifies the pain of the lesson, of understanding the story that Woody is telling here. But it is always amazing how much of Native poetry carries a sound of hope:

> The Earth is a shield, the drum of love
> the first murmur, the terror
> a powerful woman so whispers
> into his ears at night.
> Vision is not dream, but the absolute mind viewing
> continuity, itself, straight in the clear circle.

This is not a book to read quickly, or only once. The more you read, the more you will know. And, "[i]t is all right to cry, because you have a heart, and the tears stop it from having the pressure build from forgetting to care." —*Doris Seale*

Zepeda, Ofelia (Tohono O'odham), *Ocean Power: Poems from the Desert.* **University of Arizona (1995). 89 pages; grades 7-up**

These poems celebrate life lived, not just "close to the Earth" but inseparable from it. One comes away from Ocean Power with the thought that any other way of living is irrelevant. This is how we were meant to be. There are people in the world who still live this way.

> With dreams of distant noise disturbing his sleep,
> the smell of dirt, wet, for the first time in what seems
>   like months.
> The change in the molecules is sudden,
> they enter the nasal cavity.
> He contemplates that smell.
> What is that smell?
> It is rain.
> Rain somewhere out in the desert.
> Comforted in this knowledge he turns over
> and continues his sleep,
> dreams of women with harvesting sticks
> raised toward the sky.

My daughter once said to me, "When you sit on the ground, you sink into the Earth." This how to read this book. Sink into it.—*Doris Seale*

REVIEWS: SLIAMMON STORIES

Our traditional stories are a challenge to the thinking skills of children and adults alike. That is their purpose. Even stories that appear to be simple are quite deep and sophisticated. Non-Native children and their teachers, who may not be used to stories that do not tell them what to think, may turn the last pages, looking for the "morals." But if they look carefully enough, they will find that our teachings are inside the stories, not appended to them. These excellent stories, produced by the Sliammon Band and School District No. 47 in Powell River, B.C., come from the tradition of the Sliammon, Klahoose and Homalco people of the "Sunshine Coast" of British Columbia.

—*Marlene R. Atleo/ʔeh ʔeh naa tuu kwiss*

Adams, E. Tlesla (Sliammon) and Sue Pielle (Sliammon), *Mink and Granny*, illustrated by B. Dick (Sliammon). (n.d.). 15 pages, color illustrations; grades 1-up

Evan Tlesla Adams and Sue Pielle/Thap Wut combine their efforts as performance artists to present the teaching-learning dynamics between the little boy, Mink, and his Chi chia (granny). The story is a lively demonstration of how children are traditionally steered away from harm, but if willful, allowed to come face-to-face with the outcome, to learn their lesson publicly. The interaction between child and grandparent is set in a journey instigated by Mink, who longs to visit his grandfather, Kook pah in the north. The indulgent caregiver Chi chia reluctantly allows Mink to talk her into the long journey, and Mink soon becomes bored. When they finally reach Kook pah's, Mink—like all children, ever curious—immediately demands to have what is in the biggest and most beautiful of the treasure boxes that lines Kook pah's walls. Chi chia, resigned to Mink's determination, and Kook pah, ever indulgent and helpless to deny his grandson, warn him. But Mink throws the box open, releasing the power and fury of the West Wind, which blows him and his Chi chia down the straits back to their homeland. Mink is ultimately embarrassed as the whole village witnesses the shameful end of his journey. The color illustrations are expressive and lively.

MacKenzie, Hugh, *Pah*, illustrated by Butch Dick (Sliammon). (n.d.). 18 pages, color illustrations; grades 1-up

Grandfather tells this story of a great *No'Hom* (feast) at the Beginning of Time, given by the fish so that they can receive names in order for fishers to know what they catch. Raven—Pah hah kee lah, or "Pah" for short—is invited to witness the naming, even if he is only there for a free meal. After being instructed in feast etiquette by his grandfather, Pah witnesses as the many curious-looking fish file into the feast: Rat fish, Tyee Salmon, Herring, Minnow, Eulachon, Perch, Rock Cod, Flounder—each fish displaying the unique characteristics which give it its name (in the Sliammon language, which unfortunately isn't revealed in this story). As a snide remark escapes his lips, Pah cannot suppress his own character and "splits" into a double of himself. The appearance of Red Snapper, with soup bowl eyes and a puffy stomach and Coho, with a long hooked snout makes Pah gasp, disturbing the solemnity of the occasion. Pah proves to be an unsuitable witness, not eligible for the feast food. This story illustrates the protocols of the witnessing of solemn cultural practices. Public rudeness requires public restitution with a bigger feast than the one spoiled by the initial rudeness. Feast food is not "free." The expressive color illustrations convey the balance between the illustrations of the story being told and the frame of the story, fishes of identifiable species swimming in a blue kelp bed border on each page.

Sliammon Indian Band, *Mink and Cloud*, illustrated by J. Bradley Hunt (Heiltsuk). (1983). 23 pages, color illustrations; grades 1-up

J. Bradley Hunt's stylized illustrations situate this story of Mink and his pursuit of Cloud as a wife in the depths of mythic time. Although Mink had had many wives over his lifetime and Cloud warns him that she changes with the wind, he is not deterred and insists on marrying her. The couple has good times—floating in the warm blue skies and in the cool starry nights—while Cloud is large and fluffy and has substance. But when she becomes gray and thin and ragged in a storm, Mink can no longer hang on to her. When he crashes to the ground, all the children pity his lifelessness. As Mink revives, Cloud, in her alluring full and fluffy form, sails overhead. It is then that they both know their relationship cannot work, and Mink set off to find a more suitable partner. This little story is an important commentary on the necessity of a good fit between marriage partners if they are going to support each other in good times and bad.

Sliammon Indian Band, *Mink and Grey Bird,* **illustrated by Scott Galligos (Sliammon). (n.d.). 23 pages, color illustrations; preschool-up**

Scott Galligo's sophisticated traditional artwork places this Sliammon/Klahoose story about Mink deep in mythic time and place. The story is about two young men in the fullness of youth. After his grandmother agrees to pour ashes on Grey Bird when Mink pins him to the ground, Mink, feeling full of himself, challenges Grey Bird to a wrestling match. The match begins, and when the dust settles, grandmother finds that she has poured the ashes on her own grandson. Mink disingenuously comes up with all sorts of excuses but knows he is really lying to himself. This simple little story teaches that we need to be able to recognize when we are lying to ourselves.

Walz, R.E. (Sliammon), *Mink and Whale,* **illustrated by Krist Peters (Sliammon). (1994). 23 pages, color illustrations; grades 1-up**

This story warns both Sliammon children and adults about how the obvious isn't so obvious after all. Mink is the rascal who disturbs reality this way and that. A cranky Mink, skunked in fishing, becomes belligerent with a killer whale successfully fishing nearby. The killer whale taunts Mink and they become embroiled in a duel of cunning until Mink and his brother end up in the whale's belly. In the whale, the Mink brothers battle for their lives. Finally, at his wit's end, Mink attacks Whale's heart with his knife until Whale agrees to beach himself to deliver the Mink boys home. But the folks at home have seen the whole affair and are waiting—with ropes and spears—to get the Mink boys who never tire of playing tricks on them. So Mink and his brother hide themselves in the shadow of the dorsal fin of the killer whale and elude the villagers once again. With Mink providing the object lessons, this story teaches about the many ways we can be tricked and taken advantage of.

REVIEWS: CARVING A DREAM

Of Northwest Coast carvers, probably Bill Reid and Robert Davidson are known outside the Native community, to museum and gallery visitors and "collectors." But there is more to the story.

After the Native holocaust, after the destruction wrought by war, disease, the theft of children, and the outlawing of spiritual and cultural practices, there began to be, somewhere in the middle of the 20th Century, a rebirth. It began here and there, slowly but surely, and continues to grow. And there was almost always, someone, somewhere, who against all odds, still knew how to do it, whatever it might be. The three books reviewed below are about part of that renewal.—*Doris Seale*

Jensen, Vicki, *Totem Pole Carving: Bringing a Log to Life*, photographed by the author. Douglas & McIntyre (1992). 175 pages, b/w photos; high school-up; Nisga'a

In the early 1990s, Nisga'a artist Norman Tait received a commission to carve a forty-two-foot ceremonial doorway pole for the Native Education Centre that was then under construction in Vancouver. This book is the story, written down in minute, painstaking detail by Vicki Jensen, of how Tait, with a five-man crew, carved that pole. Tait:

> [M]ost poles have only sporadic pictures taken of them and occasional interviews with the artist. Next thing you know, the pole is raised and only the carvers are aware of how it really happened.

After initial reluctance—"I immediately imagined a camera and a tape recorder distracting me from teaching and carving"—Tait found that

> [T]he documentation project turned out to be fun. It was a real morale booster for the crew....I think the project helped to settle the crew down. They talked about what the book might say and wanted it to succeed....Being interviewed helped them put words to the experience of carving and helped them to understand who they were. They didn't realize they had it in them. But when the carvers heard themselves talking, they heard their own power.

Jensen "learned when it was important to stay out of the way, when questions could be asked and when to be quiet." Thus, a sort of partnership evolved, resulting in this remarkable document.

Sometimes Tait would use the photos to check out the work, and Jensen came to realize that "what the crew was learning"—the youngest being Tait's nineteen-year-old son—"was as important as what they were doing."

This is a book about which anything the reviewer can say seems superfluous. At 175 closely-written, large-format pages, it is certainly not a children's book, maybe not even for young adults unless they have an interest,

but it is intensely absorbing reading. Leaving it so much in the words of the carvers, Jensen shuns the "Indian expert's" irresistible need to "interpret" everything. The word that comes to mind is "transformation," for *Totem Pole Carving* was a transformation, for the men carving the pole, for the author living it with them, and cannot help but be for the reader coming to it with an open heart.

The name of the pole is "Wil Sayt Bakwhlgat": "The Place Where the People Gather."

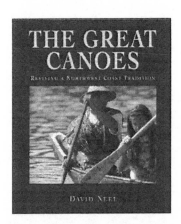

Neel, David (Kwagiutl), *The Great Canoes: Reviving a Northwest Coast Tradition*, photographs by the author. Douglas and McIntyre (1995). 135 pages, color photos; high school-up

Maybe the one object associated with Northwest Coast Nations in the mind of non-Native America is the totem pole. But certainly nothing was of more importance to the people than the canoe. Don't think birchbark here. We're talking about something carved from a 500-year-old tree, fifty feet long and six feet high at the prow. Not all were, or are, this big, but

> The canoe is today, as it has always been, much more than just a boat....Today, in its renaissance, the canoe carries the knowledge of a millennia-old culture as well as the dreams and aspirations of a younger generation. It is a vessel of knowledge,

symbolizing the cultural regeneration of many nations...deeply affecting all those who come into contact with it.

This quote is from David Neel's introduction, in which he tells of the 1989 Paddle to Seattle, of other events in the rebirth of the great canoes and of his decision to carve his own canoe; of the extraordinary effort that that entailed.

The body of the book is formed from accounts by people who participated in these events, illustrated with excellent photographs; and the concluding essay, "The Canoe Way of Knowledge," is a summation. In the words of Joe Washington, Lummi elder, "It is the cedar canoe that connects to the old ways." Or this, from a mother:

> Drinking means nothing to my son now. All he wants to do is get in that canoe. He's out in the water, paddling. He wants to carve. He wants to know the cedar.

And one last quote, from David Neel again:

> The canoe retains a spirit once encased in a living body hundreds of years old....[W]e...are people of the cedar. Along with the salmon, the cedar is the basis for our traditional culture. It is as though this sacred vessel has been sent by our ancestors to guide us into an uncertain future.

This is a deeply moving book, one in which the people say, again and again, what it means to them to be part of the renewal of their lifeways, to be among the Nations that, against all expectations, have refused to die.

Vickers, Roy Henry (Tsimshian/Kwakwaka'wakw /Haida), *Spirit Transformed: A Journey from Tree to Totem*, photographs by Bob Herger. Rain Coast Books (1996). 82 pages, color photos; high school-up

> What is a totem? Well, I am not sure....The word comes from Europe somewhere. It seems the establishment has chosen to call the society of aboriginal people who have lived on the West Coast of North America for thousands of years a "totemic society," whatever that means. We know that the art form is more than 2000 years old. In the Tsimshian language our word for a totem is ptsan, and that word is older than the knowledge of what it means.

There are many different types of poles, for many different purposes: family crests, house poles and mortuary poles, to name but a few. And there were hundreds of them, all over the Northwest Coast, which were hauled away by the carload by the "collectors" of the 19th- and early 20th Centuries. So this art form too, is a kind of rebirth.

More personal and individual, *Spirit Transformed* is the artist's account of the carving of the Salmon Totem for Saamich Commonwealth Place in Victoria, for the 1994 Commonwealth Games. Vickers tells us that this pole is carved in the style that is traditional for the Salish people. Text and large, full-page photographs cover the work, from commission through choosing the tree, the carving, and the raising of the pole. The photographs also include reproductions of four of Vickers' paintings: "The Salmon," "The Watchman," "Kitkatla Winter," and "The Salmon Legend." They are exquisite. Throughout the book, Vickers pays tribute to the people who helped him in many and varied ways. Do not be put off by the "coffee table" look to the book, nor the posed quality of some of the photos. The word "journey" in the subtitle is well chosen. For Vickers, this was as clearly a journey to insight and self-knowledge as it was to the Salmon Totem, a return, a reconnecting, to a past that is not, after all, beyond recall.

Simply written, this should easily be used with high school students, and even with the upper elementary grades.

REVIEWS: INDIAN CHILDREN'S ART

The quality of life for Native children varies, as it does for everyone, depending on where they were born, family circumstances, and the luck of the draw. Bruce Hucko works with children who have at least the advantage of living on ancestral land, where ancient ways remain, to one degree or another, viable. Not all are so fortunate. The titles reviewed here show the astonishing capability of children when allowed to express themselves on their own terms, perhaps with a nudge here, or a bit of technical advice there.—*Doris Seale*

Hucko, Bruce, *Where There Is No Name for Art: The Art of Tewa Pueblo Children,* **photography by the author. School of American Research (1996). 118 pages, color and b/w photos, color paintings; grades 6-up**

Bruce Hucko is that rare individual, one who can look across a cultural canyon without preconceptions, and with respect for what he sees. An art teacher—"art coach," he says, Hucko spent several years working with the children of the Pueblo schools of San Juan, Santa Clara, San Ildefonso, Pojoaque and Nambé. This collection of children's art and words is one result.

In the introductory material, Hucko notes, "The record of publications about the Pueblos is a dismal one that includes repeated instances of betrayal, exploitation, and miscommunication."

How is this book different? It is not presented as a case study. There is no "interpretation." There is no psychological or anthropological jargon. It is not about Bruce Hucko. It is about the children and their art, and as much of their lives as they were willing to share. Their lives are not presented as part of a "living museum," and the book was done with the full participation and consent of community, parents and children.

The art is discussed without condescension, as art. Is there a budding Picasso here? A Helen Hardin? A Lucy Lewis? A T.C. Cannon? Probably. Who knows? Who cares?

The children are themselves. Like a stone, a tree, a flower. They have a pretty good idea of who they are and how they fit into a world that is both modern and very old. They speak for themselves, articulately, about their work, and with a degree of self-understanding that will no doubt come as a surprise to adults used to a system of child-rearing that rewards the child most who is most capable of feeding back what is expected of her.

Is some of the art "better"? That will be in the eye of the beholder, and age has nothing to do with it. Two that absolutely knocked my socks off were done by six-year-olds.

Hucko, Bruce. *A Rainbow at Night: The World in Words and Pictures by Navajo Children.* **Chronicle Books (1996). 44 pages, b/w photos, color paintings; all grades; Diné (Navajo)**

A Rainbow at Night was put together with a young audience in mind. Hucko has taken the work of twenty-three children and positioned each painting with a paragraph of his own text about Diné life, a photograph of the young artist, and a paragraph of the child's own words about what she or he has created. A slimmed-down format is certainly appropriate for young readers, but of necessity does not give *Rainbow* quite the depth of *Where There Is No Name for Art.* Hucko's text here seems to be more interpretive. Perhaps that also was necessary for the shorter format: forty-four pages as opposed to 118, but it does give the impression that this title was designed more specifically for the non-Native reader.

The art and the children's comments about it reflect their own Diné world, and are equally compelling. For anyone who has seen that land, some of the paintings, such as "Cultural Mountain," "Navajo Scarecrow," and "Sunset Culture," give a strong sense of place. And Steward Sam's "My Chindi," and what he says about it, are enough to make the hair stand up on the back of your neck.

The comments addressed to the reader for each painting, in an apparent effort to be "interactive," are superfluous, intrusive, sometimes irrelevant and take up space that had better been devoted to expanded comments from the young artists. This seems so unlike Hucko's style that one wonders if it was something wished on him by the publisher. Or maybe it's just the teacher in him.

In any case, it is the artwork and what the kids say about it that count. Twelve-year-old Delphine Tanner, quoted in the introduction, says, "In these paintings you'll find many symbols, designs and ideas that you may not understand, but if you look closely, read our comments, and just think about it, you might understand." That was probably enough.

Where There Is No Name for Art and *A Rainbow at Night* are both beautiful books, and go a long way towards dispelling some of the bizarre ideas held in the dominant culture about what life is like for Native children, right here, right now.

Children and Teachers of Ibapah Elementary School (Goshute), *Pia Toya: A Goshute Indian Legend.* **University of Utah (2000). Unpaginated, color paintings; preschool-up**

> In the time before the people, the land we know as Ibapah Valley was a large mountain region. Isapai-ppeh, the coyote, lived there on one lonely mountain.

Ah-ha, it's Coyote again.

Kinniih-Pia, Mother Hawk, lived there too, and on that day she caught a mouse for her breakfast. Now, Coyote was hungry and saw the mouse. He distracted her just long enough to grab it. Big mistake. "Coyote saw Mother Hawk coming. He saw her sharp claws. With a 'yip, yip, yip'," he just managed to escape. This made her *really* angry. "Coyote knew he was in trouble." On the third pass, "The dust of a thousand storms whirled in the air.... Boulders crashed down the mountain. Trees swayed in the mighty wind storm." Coyote ran for his life. Mother Hawk calmed down. When the dust settled, there was a huge mountain, and a deep valley. Coyote left. The story says he was ashamed, but I bet it wasn't for long. And that's how the mountain Pia Toya, and the Deep Creek Range came to be.

This is a really beautiful book; beautifully put together. The illustrations, some done by students, some by teachers, with a variety of techniques, are lovely. The combination of pen, watercolor, cut paper and markers give them a living, almost translucent quality that is perfect for the story. The one of Mother Hawk at the height of her rage is spectacular. She is coal black and stuff is flying all over the place.

The nice thing about *Pia Toya* is that it is based on a traditional Goshute creation myth the children have heard from their elders and storytellers, such as Maude Moon, whose picture is included in the "About the Legend" section, giving it the feel of real story, told and retold, honed through time. There is also some information about the Goshute, their history and their culture.

Students at Oscar Blackburn School, South Indian Lake, Manitoba (Cree), *How Eagle Got His Good Eyes* **(written by fifth-grade students and illustrated by seventh-grade students). Willowisp Press (1995). Unpaginated, color illustrations; preschool-up**

Winner of a "Kids Are Authors" award, this story has very much the flavor Native animal tales. A long time ago, in Canada, there was an eagle who had no eyes. As you might guess, he didn't catch much food. One time, Nanabush had the thought that he could be chief of all his people. He also thought a headdress would help, so he decided to shoot Eagle—for the feathers. When that didn't work, he tried trickery, that being his natural bent, anyway.

The story tells how Eagle got his eyes, and Nanabush learned a lesson, maybe. Until next time. There is a translation into Cree, by Margaret Moose and Shirley Ducharme, and the pictures are large, full of color, and a perfect fit. The one of an angry Eagle is a winner. "Nanabush was afraid to go near Eagle." Why am I not surprised?

Students of G.T. Cunningham Elementary School, *We Are All Related: A Celebration of Our Cultural Heritage.* **G.T. Cunningham Elementary School (1996). 56 pages, color illustrations; preschool-up**

This book is the work of twenty-eight children from a variety of backgrounds, and is the result of an "Artist-in Residence" program at G.T. Cunningham school. There is a forward by Cree artist George Littlechild, who was a substantial influence on the project, with its "emphasis on First Nations culture through exposure to stories, legends, beliefs and ideas as revealed by First Nations teachers and elders."

Each double-page spread has, at the top of the left page, "I Am," a child's words, introducing herself, family, artwork, and opinion of the project. At the bottom, "The Elders Speak." On the right is a collage of the child's artwork, family photographs, surrounding the child's photo. And below it, the child's statement, "To me, 'we are all related' means_____," with a translation into his original language.

This is more structured than the other collections, and Littlechild's style is a clear influence (his own work, "Ancestors," follows his foreword), but each young person's work carries its own individual stamp. Alice Walkus (Kwakwaka'wakw) draws an eagle and ancestor pole, Kevin J.B. Li draws a dragon, and Eric Peter Cho, a tiger, and so on. And their words show a clear understanding of the phrase, "We are all related." Ian Hien Gia Tuti Pham: "We are all in the circle of life." Richie Yurevich Mihailo Curtis Marshall: "Purpose, passion, service, with these you will have a more balanced life." Roderick Karl Lee: "Everything on Earth has a purpose."

These children's families come from all over the world, and yet they are here, working together; understanding, perhaps better than most adults, what biologists call the web of life. Perhaps there is hope for us, after all.

REVIEWS: INDIAN CHILDREN'S WRITING

These are all Indian voices, from adults about what it was like to live an Indian childhood, and from children about their lives, here, now. They are all written from the heart, to share with other Indian children, and also with the world. All of these titles are highly recommended.

Doris Seale contributed the review of *Dancing With the Wind.—Beverly Slapin*

Dancing With the Wind: The ArtsReach Literary Magazine.
ArtsReach (1989-2004)

This publication is an annual anthology of stories and poems by students from the ArtsReach Imaginative Writing Program. This work is from young people in second grade and up, probably making these anthologies the most comprehensive collections of Indian children's writing. Most of the volumes have been edited and introduced by well-known Native writers.

In his introduction to v. III, N. Scott Momaday says something very important:

> [C]hildren speak and write a language of their own. Here is much that is original, for children have a more natural and immediate hold on originality than have most of us....Directly behind these writings is an oral tradition that is extremely rich and highly developed. The stories rest upon a continuity of storytelling that is thousands of years old. The poems...are descended from truly ancient songs and prayers and spells and charms. Their context is magic, a profound belief in the efficacy of language....Children know better than we that words are among the most powerful and beautiful entities on earth.

In a time when so many of our children are cut to fit the box, few things could be of more vital importance than giving them a forum for this expression. Before we have lost it all. One poem: it is by fifth-grader José Moreno. The title is "Like a Bullet."

One day I am
at a desert and
I see a coyote
howling at the moon
while it's raining
blue and black
feathers and I
look up at the
big black sky
and I see a
falling star and while
I'm wishing, I
see a pascola
dancing to the
music like a
bullet in the sky.

Hirschfelder, Arlene, and Beverly R. Singer (Santa Clara Pueblo), editors, *Rising Voices: Writings of Young Native Americans.* Scribner's (1992). 115 pages; grades 6-up

"What is writing, after all?" asks Beverly Singer in her foreword.

> Indians write in much the same way and for similar reasons as anyone, but the content of our writing springs from memory, designs, songs, dances, dreams, and life evolving from a Native American past, present, and future.

In this collection of more than sixty poems, songs, stories and short essays gathered from sources spanning over one hundred years, young people speak about family, culture and community, and their vision of the future. Divided into six sections—"Identity," "Family," "Homelands," "Ritual and Ceremony," "Education," and "Harsh Realities," the writings are, for the most part, about hope and courage. But far and away the most chilling of these pieces, written during the early years of the Indian residential schools, are reflections of the effects of forced assimilation and what would later come to be called "brainwashing." And there are poems of resistance, resistance that leads to freedom, if not of the body, of the spirit: A group of Diné students wrote in 1933:

If I were a pony,
A spotted pinto pony,
A racing, running pony,
I would run away from school.
And I'd gallop on the mesa,
And I'd eat on the mesa,
And I'd sleep on the mesa,
And I'd never think of school.

Ferris, Sean, ed., *Children of the Great Muskeg.* Black Moss (1985). 84 pages, b/w and color illustrations; grades 2-5

The Cree and Métis children, mostly middle schoolers, of Moose Factory and Moosonee in Northern Ontario are the poets, writers, artists and visionaries of this collection of drawings, paintings and writing about life in the Great Muskeg, as Sean Ferris says,

> that awesome haunted expanse of stunted spruce, tamarack, bogs and ferns that is their people's physical and spiritual homeland. The bush hovers at the edges of these rough-and-tumble subarctic settlements on the Moose River and is an elemental force in the children's imaginative lives.

Using a variety of media and techniques—watercolors, marking pens and colored pencils, pen and ink, crayons—the children here draw their lives. There are moose (of course), bears, fish, helicopters over breaking ice floes, pitched tents, ski-doos, and many, many, geese in flight. And very scary imaginations of what the dreaded Windigo might look like. The pictures are simply done in terms of line and color but all together they form a vivid picture of how the children see themselves as part of the land, community and culture.

Unless they're taught to be "polite," to "behave," children tend to be blunt and honest. In subjects such as "Me," "My Struggles," "It Would Be Better If," and "Friends," expressions of hopelessness and despair mingle with insight and hope. Alcoholism and violence and intense hardship are undeniably here, but so are the land, the animals, the weather—all that makes the Great Muskeg home.

MY STRUGGLES/Christie Ann Fletcher

I struggle to clean up the house.
To help with the dishes.
I struggle to help me and my friends.
I struggle to start the ski-doo.
I struggle to get along with my brother.
But most of all I struggle to live.

Sean Ferris and the children have put together a beautiful little book of "images of a world where the people and the earth are of one mind…where ravens and dogs scavenge muddy roads and winter winds cut to kill," and where "children of the Great Muskeg hunt down their visions and voices and make art that lives." This book isn't art for art's sake, but art for life's sake.

Anglesey, Zoe (Chicana), ed., ¡*Word Up! Hope for Youth Poetry.* El Centro de la Raza (1992). 123 pages, grades 4-up

"I think that everyone, being human, is a poet, like all birds sing," says Father Ernesto Cardinal, the great Nicaraguan poet and teacher and the inspiration for this book. The children of the Hope for Youth Poetry Workshop demonstrate that poetry is also a way of building community and generating power.

Here, as Anglesey says in her introduction, "are poems about family members, dangers children face, the things children enjoy in particular, and about those abstractions that all poets attempt to write about, like love, terms of justice and death." Encouraged to write about anything they wanted in any vernacular that was their own without someone chastising them for "bad grammar," youngsters saw "their poems fly from notebooks to the copy machine and word processor." In English, Spanish, and "Spanglish," that collage of two street-bonded vocabularies, the children express their humor and intelligence, their fears and concerns, what is important to them, and their need for society to change.

BILINGUAL IN A CARDBOARD BOX/Javier Piña

Soy Mexicano/I'm an American
Puedo cantar canciones del corazón/I am mute
Puedo ver los colores de la puesta del sol/I am blind
Puedo escuchar las voces de los pajaritos cantando/I
    am deaf
Soy indígena bailando al cielo que llora/I'm forever
    seated in a chair with wheels
Todos me respetan/I'm labeled by pointing fingers
Tengo mucho dinero/I live in a cardboard box
Estoy riéndome con el mundo alegre/I am sad
Salgo con mis amigos/I am alone
Estoy soñando/and I don't want to wake up!

¡*Word Up!* is for all of us, and our children.

raúlrsalinas and Jennifer Shen, editors, *Seeds of Struggle, Songs of Hope: Poetry of Emerging Youth y Sus Maestros del Movimiento.* El Centro de la Raza (1997). 78 pages, b/w illustrations; grades 4-up

It is never too early to expose children to good poetry. This excellent volume, done by the young people and their teachers who participated in El Centro de la Raza's summer youth leadership conference's writing project in 1997, is a companion to ¡*Word Up! Hope for Youth Poetry* from El Centro de la Raza (1992). In Spanish, English and Spanglish, the poems and artwork in *Seeds of Struggle* are an example of what our youngsters are capable of, when they are acknowledged as our most valuable resource.

In their introduction, Hap Bockelie and raúlrsalinas write: "When oppression becomes so unbearable to a people, poetry, among other forms of expression, flows and gushes forth, as part of the human spirit's rebel scream against injustice." It is the nurturing of this scream in a safe environment that has produced, for the past three years, pieces such as this group poem:

> Hay que poner atención
> la historia de nuestra gente
> Quieren robar de repente
> Don't you know this is our home
> El Centro es nuestro cantón
> Para seguir la nación
> De conquistas y traiciones
> We have truth in our canciones
> You can't buy us out with fear
> People shed tears for what is here
> They gave us their corazones.

Riley, Patricia (Cherokee), ed., *Growing Up Native American*, foreword by Inés Hernández (Nimíipu/Chicana). Morrow (1993). 333 pages; grades 7-up

"What does it mean to grow up Native American?" Riley asks in her introduction.

> There are as many answers to that question as there are Native American people. Certainly, there are as many stories. Stories of oppression and survival, of people who grew up surrounded by tradition, and people who did not. Stories of the pressures of forced assimilation and stories of resistance, of heritage denied and of heritage reclaimed. A multiplicity of stories.

This multiplicity of stories, in all their permutations, is about land and language, indoctrination and rebellion, but most of all, about two things: decolonization of the land, and decolonization of the mind. In choosing stories that resist defining who is and who is not Indian, Riley has contributed to this decolonization effort.

These stories, most of which have previously been published, are from the great writers and storytellers: Simon Ortiz, N. Scott Momaday, Louise Erdrich, Leslie Marmon Silko, Luther Standing Bear, Geary Hobson, Anna Lee Walters, Ella Cara Deloria, Ignatia Broker, Joseph Bruchac, Sara Winnemucca Hopkins, Linda Hogan, Francis LaFlesche, Basil Johnston, and others.

From an eight-year-old's first participation in a buffalo hunt, to the resistance of a group of boys in residential school, to a fourteen-year-old locked in battle with a nun, to a child's conjuring an ancestor with words on a drawing, to a strange kid with no social graces struggling to find out who he is, to a little girl's first encounter with poverty and injustice, the twenty-two stories here tell the lives of Indian young people. And give them strength.

It is a good thing that Riley has dedicated this collection "to the Native American children of the past, present, and future." After all, as the young people earnestly set about the task of becoming adults, this is what their lives are about.

Francis, Lee (Laguna), ed., *When the Rain Sings: Poems by Young Native Americans*. National Museum of the American Indian in association with Simon & Schuster (1999). 76 pages, b/w and color photos; grades 4-up

A collaboration between Wordcraft Circle of Native Writers and Storytellers, the National Museum of the American Indian, and ArtsReach, *When the Rain Sings* is a unique collection of thirty-seven poems from Indian young people ranging in age from seven to seventeen. Most of the poems are in response to, and accompanied by, photographs of people or objects from the children's cultures; and are clearly marked by their varied life experiences. "*When the Rain Sings*," writes Francis in a short descriptive piece, "presents the heart-songs of the youth of Native America."

This project grew out of Wordcraft Circle's mentoring program for new Native writers. The program originated with the first Returning the Gift Festival in 1992, and is a modern manifestation of the time-honored tradition of giving back. In her introduction, Elizabeth Woody (Warm Springs) calls the young students "a bridge connecting the past to the present." "So full of knowledge, health, and expressive designs of their own making," she writes, "these young people and their poems articulate the future of our communities."

In a poem entitled "I Always Begin with I Remember," sixteen-year-old Vena A-dae Romero (Cochiti/Kiowa) writes (in part):

> I remember the day history almost disappeared.
> The day Indian children's mouths were stuffed with
>   English words,
> and almost suffocated out of existence,
> but they lay hidden in memory until it was safe, almost
>   too late.
> I can remember the stories of a thousand generations,
> growing tall and green, bearing sweet yellow fruit,
> eaten at the dinner table with Da-oo and Ba-ba
> watching the black leak out of their hair with each
>   story.
> I can remember the day my spirit began to rattle.
> When memories encased in teardrops fell onto paper.
> When the stories became waves, the silent words
>   became medicine.
> I can remember the day memory became my hero.

Lee Francis recently traveled to the other side. This book is his legacy.

Dolan, Marlene (Cree/Dakota), ed., _"Just Talking About Ourselves": Voices of Our Youth._ Theytus Books. Color illustrations; grades 4-up. Volume 1 (1994), 113 pages; volume 2 (1994), 96 pages; volume 3 (1996), 110 pages.

There are few hearts that will not be moved by the young people whose poems, short stories and visual art are held in these pages. There is raw pain and grief, and the drawings are achingly beautiful. Some charcoal, some acrylics on canvas, some watercolor and ink, some outlined in pencil and carefully traced over with color. I have seen non-Indian teachers flip through these books and put them down. Maybe that is a good thing. Maybe these poems and stories are meant for Indian children only, so they can see that the demons can be faced head-on and healing is possible. Maybe other children and adults need to know what has been done, what real pain feels like and what it looks like on a page, what havoc has been wreaked on a community and how children suffer still. I don't know. I suspect that Marlene Dolan and her youth editing teams didn't have an easy time of it. In Volume 3 she writes, "To the First Nations youth of British Columbia, I dedicate this publication. May their dreams become reality and their spirits grow with each day of their lives." To this, Roy Henry Vickers adds, "My prayer is that you walk in the goodness, truth and beauty that is you." To this I would add, what you have produced is a blessing, important beyond knowing. I wish you all well.

I give you this from Andrew Jones (Diné), eleven years old, 1985, in _Rising Voices_:

> Canyons, Echoing
> going away—coming back
> repeating my voice

REVIEWS: ARTS AND CRAFTS BOOKS

"Dress-up" and "masking" activities that seem inexplicably popular in arts and crafts books and curricula promote the idea that "Indian" is some kind of game or fantasy role, made of "costumes" and "artifacts" pieced together from trash. They promote disrespect for a past in which what are now called artifacts were then genuine parts of our daily life and survival, ingenious inventions with which we made use of local materials and conditions. And these ways become neither beautiful nor meaningful to children who make tin-can drums, cardboard-box totem poles, masks, rattles, sand paintings and "costumes."

The following are reviews of some arts and crafts and activity books "about" Indians.—*Paula Giese*

Kalmenoff, Matthew, *Plains Indians Diorama to Cut and Assemble.* **Dover (1985). 32 pages, color plates; grades 5-6**

The book consists mainly of color cutouts printed on stiff paper. Some are to be cut, glued to oak tag board, folded and glued together to make a little box, with a proscenium-arch stage formed by a rectangular opening in the front, a floor, back and interior sides painted to resemble the Great Plains of the 19th Century, and a backdrop showing a Plains village. A second backdrop —a distant buffalo herd—can be slid in, at least if you shave its sides down a bit and hold it on with tape. The box's top is open, for putting in the, ah, Indians. Cutouts, I mean—they tend to fall over.

In Kalmenoff's artistic rendition of the dozens of people represented in the cutouts and backdrop village, no one is smiling. No faces look relaxed. Square, lumpy, with pushed-in, flattened wide noses, they are a mean-looking, glowering lot. Even kids appear zombie-like with peculiar, recessive chins.

Accompanying the text, Kalmenoff tells us "The Plains chieftains…are imprinted on our memory, as are the tragic debacles at Little Bighorn ('Custer's Last Stand') and Wounded Knee…." Wounded Knee was actually a massacre of a band who had surrendered and were being brought in to imprisonment on the Pine Ridge reservation. Many of us consider the Greasy Grass (Little Bighorn) a brief moment of triumph, caused by the arrogance of an officer notorious for the massacre of the survivors of Black Kettle's band of Cheyenne.

"Their very names—the Cheyenne, the Blackfeet, the Comanche, the Crow, the Arapaho, and, best known, the Sioux (or as they called themselves, the Dakota)…" Um, yeah. The Dakota as they call themselves are Eastern Woodland people, not out there on the Plains. *They* call themselves Lakota. We also get a sprinkling of random Indian words, such as "calumet" (from the Eastern Seaboard) to describe the "peace pipe." According to Kalmenoff, "Inhaling its smoke was supposed to clarify one's thoughts and impart divine power." Actually, the pipe is an altar, the smoke a connection between the people and the spiritual.

Kalmenoff's mini-history ends with this:

> As the buffalo itself has been rescued from near-extinction, there is reason to believe—it certainly is to be hoped—that the remarkable culture of the Indians of the Great Plains of North America will not be permitted altogether to vanish.

Hey, thanks, guy.

Kavasch, E. Barrie, *Earth Maker's Lodge: Native American Folklore, Activities and Foods,* **illustrated by Chris Wold Dyrud, Tim Foley, and Joyce Audy Zarins. Cobblestone (1994). 159 pages, b/w illustrations; grades 4-6**

In the late 1970s, I had a book by Kavasch that dealt with Native American uses of wild plants for medicines, and especially foods. I remember it as being quite impressive, and thus expected more of the present book than was delivered.

This book is organized into five thematic sections: Stories, Dreams and Spiritual Objects; People, Places and Legends; Projects and Crafts; Puzzles and Games; and Recipes.

The food section is sort-of OK, but except for the occasional "camping out" activities, traditional (precontact) Native methods of food preparation cannot be done in today's homes and city apartments. Kavasch has a "fish baked in clay" campout procedure that is do-able (but you should put some herbs inside the fish first). For the rest, the recipes use various Native-introduced foods such as corn, beans, and chocolate to make "today" foods, using stoves and refrigerators. There's a strange "pemmican" that contains no meat. There's no frybread, bannock, or posole.

The biggest problem is that much of this book is a mishmash. Citations or credits are rarely given in full, and most of the originals couldn't be found anyway. But where I was able to find some of the source-credited stories from ready-to-hand sources such as Erdos and

Ortiz's collection, I found that the already brief and smoothed-down stories there had been subjected to a meaningless copyediting, further shortening them and dumbing down the vocabularies. Some stories are not by Native writers. Editorial judgment about both editing and story selection is unreliable at best.

Some of the craft activities are presented with inadequate diagrams, if any, so that making them becomes trial and error. Other activities just plain won't work, and weren't tried by Kavasch or anyone else, such as a bullroarer made from a tongue depressor. Certain "activities" are straight-up New Age in Indian guise. Example: Seneca Stone Reading ("Color—Sparkles—This is called a star rock. It means you have lofty ideals, charm, and charisma. Black—You are seeking the light (understanding)...").

My heart just fell when I came across "Story Beads." I first encountered and tried this activity when I was nine or so; it was in the Sunday newspaper kiddie feature. You cut and glue-coat a long triangular strip of paper and roll it around a pencil, so the point ends up on the outside center of a long "bead" whose rolls bulge slightly in the center. You paint or shellac them, but you cannot "sand them when they are completely dry," because if you do, they most likely will fall apart. These things are unspeakably ugly. This is an ancient (as these things go) example of Trash Craft, and is like all too many of the recycled activities in this book.

Story beads are small carvings, usually animals, usually of various shells and stones and sometimes turquoise. They are separated on a long (sometimes multi-stranded) necklace by small chunky turquoises, but decent-looking beads can be used since turquoise is expensive. Little packets of story beads can be bought at most bead shops. The "story" of the resulting necklace is made up by the necklace-wearer for her kids, with episodes relating to the little figures, as she goes around the necklace. These necklaces are called "fetish" by traders, but they were actually made by Indian women, modeled on rosaries. Story bead necklaces are fun to make and use (to tell stories to little kids with, and encourage them to tell you stories about), and the materials to do it right don't cost all that much. And now, back to Kavasch-crafts.

Kavasch suggests kids tie knots in *magazine* pages and take them camping to use as "firestarters." Clay-coated magazine pages are singularly useless as kindling, and require a brisk fire to burn entirely just for trash disposal. At least *some* part of the camping experience is to learn to live a day or two in the woods without lugging in a lot of crap, such as a big bag of paper "knots" to use as "fire-starters." Not only is the idea fundamentally wrong-headed, but you have to bring this big bag of trash *back out* of the woods when you find it doesn't work.

A piece on "Navajo Code Talkers" perpetuates the misinformation that the World War II Marine code talkers simply spoke Diné to each other, thus frustrating Japanese crypto-analysts. Not so. The Diné expert recruits made up a usable code based in part on the Diné language, and using Diné words to replace "Able, Baker, Charlie, Dog..." (but without the alphabetic correspondences) used by radio operators when spelling for exact clarity was required. Other codes represented numbers, place-names, and the like. It was a lot more complex and intellectually demanding than "talking Navajo to each other." After the codes had been devised, all the code talker recruits had to learn them. Because they weren't speaking Navajo; they were speaking *a code that Diné had devised based on their own language.* Ot-nay ust-jay ome-say ig-pay atin-lay, either.

Kavasch's is the best of a bad lot of imitation art-crafts books, but only because the sheer volume in comparison to the size of most of them gives her a few good hits. So it's a question of whether you care to pay for a mixed bag of some interesting, workable (with a little trial and error) stuff buried in a large amount of trash.

Me, I'd rather spend the money on some good beads.

Maher, Jan and Doug Selwyn, *Native Americans*, illustrated by Marcia Pomeroy and Sue Durban. Turman Publishing (1991). 38 pages, b/w illustrations; grades 3-4

There are two positive things to be said about this book: (1) There are none of those stupid puzzles or idiotic games and they don't make any sacred masks out of paper bags. (2) At the end, there are miniature bios—very, very miniature—of three well-known Native writers and two other professionals, so non-Native students will learn that at least five Native people exist and have names.

Now for the bad news: Just about everything else.

Kids will learn that "Clans are large family groups... named after animals, plants or objects." No, not always. Anishinaabeg (Odawa, Ojibwe) will be disconcerted to learn that "[c]hildren are in the same clan as their mother" since this is a very large tribal group with patrilineal clans. Clans is it for "Native American families," ignoring all the tribes—such as Dakota, Lakota, and most others of the Plains—who never had clans. Clans are rather complicated to explain, even just the clans of any tribe that still has them (most tribal clan structures are not in good shape today because of white interference with traditional life) and except for Native children who need to learn them, clans are best bypassed by non-Indian kids. Clans make little sense without the language for proper kinship terms.

A mini-environmental section reduces the numerous and complex different Native worldviews to a single simplistic ecological belief, praying to spirits, and not hurting anything ("All things were part of the web of life."). The phony version of Chief Seeathl's speech (see review of Susan Jeffers' *Brother Eagle, Sister Sky*) is used as source material for this lesson, although no sources, references, or reading lists are given for anything.

Balancing the good news against the bad news, don't buy this thing.

Meiczinger, John, Watermill, 32 pages, b/w illustrations; kindergarten-grade 3:
Indian Crafts and Activity Book **(1989)**
How to Draw Indian Arts and Crafts **(1990)**

In the activity book, you get scattered bits of tribal mis-information. Make a headdress (cutting feathers out of paper) and "pretend you are a brave Indian warrior." Make "teepees" by rolling a paper cone. Did you know that "the Indians of the Great Plains built teepees to live in while they hunted buffalo"? Other times they must of lived in condos or igloos, eh?

An "Iroquois mask" is made from a sheet of red construction paper. ("A mask colored red was thought to be very powerful.") This particular "craft" has come to be presented so many times in so many "let's be Indians" books that the Grand Council of the Haudenosaunee Confederation (Iroquois traditional government) had to issue a long policy statement about not exhibiting or photographing or replicating their sacred masks at all.

Other activities: making "pottery" out of flour and salt dough, a "Chippewa serpentine dance" with a "toe-heel step" and somebody beating "a 1-2 beat on the tom-tom." There are a few picture stories, including one about the "First Thanksgiving," and totem poles made by sticking cutout eyes on champagne corks (champagne corks? from the school cafeteria?).

This book is completely worthless for learning anything real about the variety and beauty of our cultures, the ingenious ways in which we conducted the everyday business of food and shelter—nor is there any suggestion that we no longer live in those ways any more than white people, descendants of the invaders, live in log cabins or underground sod huts.

How to Draw gives instructions on how to turn simple geometric shapes into simplistic renditions of "teepees", arrowheads, tomahawks, wampum, Northwest Coast masks, a "Kachina" doll. (The actual purpose of Katsina dolls is to teach Native kids to recognize the regalia of the hundreds of Katsina dancers who appear at their own Pueblo communities.) These books were prepared by a person who is himself entirely without artistic talent, who knows nothing of any actual Native Nation's life, history, arts or crafts. Sheer ugliness in a book purportedly having something to do with some kind of art.

Rubens, Dale Teitel, *Native Americans: Projects, Games and Activities for Grades K-3*, illustrated by Barry Koch.
Adams, Barbara, *Native Americans: Projects, Games and Activities for Grades 4-6*, illustrated by Keith Neely.
Troll (1994). 96 pages, b/w illustrations

These two books have exactly the same format (except that the one for older children includes a couple of "legends" and some lessons). The content is similar for beginning and upper elementary grades; there's no distinction in difficulty levels (so the "Tlingit" section—grades 4-6—is a rehash for those unfortunate children who met it in grades K-3.) Although there are different authors, both books have bad writing and amateurish illustrations.

There's a common format to each lesson: "Meet the (Tribename)" is followed for the younger kids by "A Day in the Life of a (Tribename) Child," followed by little word puzzles, dumbly easy mazes, and "activities," including some that were obviously never tried and don't work. For older children, "A Day in the Life" is sometimes replaced by a "Read Aloud Tale," a dumbed-down version of a legend, taken from secondary sources that had already simplified and condensed it. Other than the tribal designation, no credits are given for the legends' sources. Very heavy on rewrite (simplifying, removing color and life) from tales told by Joseph Bruchac, mainly from the *Keepers of the Earth, Keepers of the Animals, Keepers of Life* series by Bruchac and Michael Caduto, although a few seem to have been cribbed from other Bruchac collections.

These books—like many others of the type—present "tribes" as they supposedly existed before first contact with whites, in a mishmash of summary stereotypes. The presentation is always boring, with only slight variations: They lived in (X) type of housing, they wore (X) type of clothing. The men hunted/fished/were warriors. The women took care of kids/prepared food/did some kind of minor agriculture. The kids played, the girls helping the mommies, the boys imitating the daddies. Everybody loved everybody and everything. The tribes wandered around a lot (usually). This is all told in the past tense; we don't exist anymore, ya know.

Rarely, a bit of actual history is mentioned. For instance, "Hundreds and hundreds of Mandan and people from other tribes died during several [smallpox] epidemics," but that happens only when whatever canned source these people once read so emphasized disasters caused by whites that they couldn't avoid saying something. Generally, history stops in the middle of the simplistic and repetitive primitive.

Both books have craft activities that include making travesties of sacred masks. "Kachina" masks (from paper bags) in "Meet the Hopis" and Mohawk False Face masks (called "frightening false faces") in *K-3*. In *4-6*, "Meet the Seneca" takes another whack at False Faces, and students can make buffalo masks and invent some kind of hopping around for the Mandan buffalo-calling dances, vanished now except for the paintings of Bodmer and Catlin.

In the *K-3* book, there's the worst map of North America I've ever seen. Hudson's Bay opens to the east, and Greenland is right on top of this opening, abutting the Maine, Nova Scotia, and Labrador Atlantic shores. The map purports to show "approximate areas where most members of the ten Native American tribes discussed in this book live today." This is done by placing little drawings of the purported housing in precontact days very roughly where there are now reservations—often off by a state or so (though the map is so distorted you actually couldn't lay on state boundaries).

This puts a Cherokee longhouse in what might be Oklahoma and so on, suggesting that tribes, when moved to reservations, continued to live in the precontact ways that in fact had long been changed. The Cherokee, for instance, were dispossessed because they had developed the land, with white-style housing, community halls, boat landings, warehouses, a printing facility, schools, and, of course, farms—and their white neighbors couldn't stand not to have what they saw that the Cherokee had accomplished.

Also featured in the *K-3* book is a picture alleged to be famed Nez Percé Chief Joseph, wearing a headdress and resembling a twenty-five-year-old white guy.

In the *4-6* book, there's a vision quest—"You're praying for a vision of an animal so you can capture its spirit and acquire its strength. Close your eyes. What do you see?" Write or draw whatever. In actuality, the prayers and self-sacrifice of fasting and thirst are for a helping vision; "capturing the spirit" of an animal is not a Native concept.

For "Making a Drum" (out of a coffee can), teachers are told to use pieces of old inner tubes for the heads—never mind that tires have been tubeless for at least decades. For making a rattle, the teacher is supposed to cut a hole in a gourd and scrape out the seeds. Presumably, the gourds are already dried, because they're supposed to be soaked "in water for several hours" first. Actually, you clean out the seeds and meat from a fresh gourd, dry it (for months), then insert the stones in that rattle. Sometimes special stones, a prescribed number.

Then with their tin-can drum and non-rattling gourds, the kids can "perform the Friendship Dance." Here, students "do a slow, shuffling step around a circle," with boys pulling girls in, then vice-versa. While a muffled whumping is coming from the tin can and no sound from the unprepared gourd. There are friendship dances; the Menominee traditional one (taught them by visiting Lakota) involves an intricate dance pattern where dancers from each of two groups wind up shaking hands with each other. The story of this dance involves peacemaking efforts in order to present a united front to the white invaders.

REVIEWS: PHOTOGRAPHY, "SHOOTING BACK"

From the beginning, drawing, painting, and later photographing Indians have been hugely popular. These likenesses have been taken, without the subjects' consent, with reluctant acquiescence, distorted out of all reality. More frequently than the photographers could have desired, their work reveals the subjects' reactions of resignation, distress, or anger. The "superstition" of "the-camera-steals-your-spirit" arises in connection with Native peoples' great reluctance to be photographed. In that regard, Gerald Vizenor's essay, "Ishi Bares His Chest: Tribal Simulations and Survivance," in Partial Recall quotes Susan Sontag:

> [T]he camera is the ideal arm of consciousness in its acquisitive mood....[T]here is something predatory in the act of taking a picture. To photograph people is to violate them, by seeing them as they never see themselves, by having knowledge of them they can never have; it turns people into objects that can be symbolically possessed.

I submit that this comes a lot closer to what Native people felt, and still do, about having their pictures taken by outsiders. Those two words say it, don't they? Picture: taken.—*Doris Seale*

Lippard, Lucy R., ed., *Partial Recall: Photographs of Native North Americans*. New Press (1992). 199 pages, b/w photographs; high school-up

Partial Recall looks at the way Native peoples have been portrayed through photography, with responses to specific photographs from twelve mostly well-known Indian artists and writers. The foreword by Leslie Marmon Silko (Laguna) is followed by Lucy Lippard's leading essay, giving historical background and setting the framework for what follows.

Lippard speaks of "a kind of cultural cannibalism that is still played out in our popular culture," and a "distorted memory of primeval contentment," the skin overlaying "[t]he indigenous tragedy of a people surviving genocide.... [that] is *the* tragedy of this country, affecting everyone far more than most of us realize. It lies buried, invisible beneath the histories....It is the bump under the carpet of colonialism, the nightmare at the edge of communal sleep."

So the "natural" world becomes backdrop for "nature's children"; pictures are used to demean as well as romanticize. "Frontier photographers gleefully photographed Native women in various stages of undress, especially bare-breasted. If this was not their natural custom, they were often disrobed in the aid of prurient commercialism." These images, says Christopher Lyman, "did not strike the white public as pornography only because their Indian subjects were generally thought to be less than human."[1]

In "Rosebuds of the Plateau: Frank Matsura and the Fainting Couch Aesthetic," Rayna Green (Cherokee) looks at Matsura's "Two Girls on Couch." She contrasts it with the "noble savage" image, and sees something out of the ordinary. These two young women in their Victorian dress are not "being taken advantage of." They look right out at you: "The direct, unflinching gaze could turn you into a pillar of salt." The girl on the left might be smiling, just a little.

Jimmie Durham (Cherokee) writes about the famous photograph of Geronimo in his Cadillac—was it a Cadillac, or is that just Bill Miller's song? "Geronimo," Durham says, "as an Indian 'photographic subject' blew out the windows" because it doesn't fit the myth, that must constantly be reinvented, of "the most bloodthirsty Indian warrior of all time."[2] His name was Goyathlay, and he loved children, all of his dying before him. In not one of his photographs does he look "conquered," at all.

Joy Harjo (Muscogee), Suzanne Benally (Diné), and Jolene Rickard (Tuscarora) talk about family pictures and what they mean. This is something familiar to us, Indian women. What were their lives like? In what ways am I who I am, because of them?

Gerald Vizenor (Ojibwe) writes about a photograph of Ishi—that was not his name—for which the man was asked to strip down to the waist to appear "primitive." "He is not the last man of stone. He is not the obscure other," Vizenor writes, "the mortal evidence of savagism, or the last crude measure of uncivilization in the dead voices of racial photographs."

Gerald McMaster (Cree) writes about the residential schools, and what the photos taken there say about them. Paul Chaat Smith (Comanche) does a wildly, sadly, bitterly funny, "Every Picture Tells a Story." Hard to describe, but essential reading. Ramona Sakiestewa (Hopi) is a renowned weaver. She talks about two photographs by Jo Mora, of Hopi dancers, of the significance of the fabrics they wear, and the ways in which Mora's work was vastly different from the work of other photographers of the time.

Partial Recall is a big book with a lot to say, presenting its material in ways that will have occurred to few non-Native people.

The only odd note is David Seals' essay on "Wounded

Knee, 1989" by Sarah Penman. David Seals, or Seal, or Davydd ap Saille, "descendant of the Huron prophet, Deganawidah," and author of one of the worst books to be made into a pretty good movie, who "lives in the Black Hills"[3] chooses to attack the subjects of the photograph, and their lives rather than to deal with the idea of pictures taken by outsiders.

His particular target is the central figure, of whom he says,

> His is a macho expression, that of a man like those Mary [Crow Dog] described as wife-beaters and rapists....[H]is is the typical grimace of too much pride....[T]he image of this man is an allegory of the machismo, the alcoholic chauvinism, the rural narrow-mindedness that has always weakened the Lakotas. Sitting Bull was murdered by his own drunken relatives, but today his descendants rant and rave endlessly about needing new leaders like Sitting Bull. Why? So they can kill such a man or woman too?

Life is not easy for most Native people, anywhere. Some places are worse than others. South Dakota probably falls in the "worse" category. People still live there though, and make a life. In order to live what the more fortunate consider a decent life, you first need to have something to do it *with*. There are places where there is very little of that something. That has been written about, and there are ways to do it. This is as bad as anything I have read, and after it all, Seals says: "Indians are damn tough and I love them." Somehow I don't think *they* love *him*.

I am at a loss to understand why Seals' diatribe was considered worth putting in this book, especially when compared to Gail Tremblay's (Onondaga/Mi'kmaq) beautifully crafted essay on Hulleah Tsinhnahjinnie's (Diné/Muscogee/Seminole) "Mattie Looks for Steve Biko" that immediately precedes it.

The last third of the book is a gallery of photographs from various times and places, reproduced without commentary, apart from the original captions. All by themselves, they reinforce the words of both editor and contributors to this volume.

NOTES

1 Lyman, Christopher M., *The Vanishing Race and Other Illusions: Photographs of Indians by Edward S. Curtis.* Smithsonian Institution, 1982.

2 This was the original caption on this photograph.

3 From information about the author, *Partial Recall*.

Aperture, *Strong Hearts: Native American Visions and Voices*. Aperture (1995). 119 pages, b/w and color photographs; high school-up

As might be expected from Aperture, *Strong Hearts* is glossier than the other books in this group. Don't be fooled. Except for the technical quality, this is not a coffee-table-Indians-book. The work of twenty-nine Native photographers is purely "anti-Curtis" and all those others responsible for the noble savage/vanishing redman images. Of the photographers included, only one, John C.H. Grabill (late 19th Century) is not Native.

In "Ghost in the Machine," Paul Chaat Smith talks about his Comanche relatives, and the Comanche encounter with technology. They "frantically tried to acquire the new guns," the Walker Colt .44 caliber repeater, without much success: "[I]magine a member of the Crips trying to buy a dozen Stinger rocket-launchers in the midst of the 1992 riots in L.A.: not impossible, but really, really difficult." And cameras: "[T]hose books and the photographers behind them are like big-game hunters on safari, and their big game is the real Indian....They search for ghosts, for elders trapped in amber."

N. Scott Momaday (Kiowa) introduces the work of Horace Poolaw (Pohd-lok, "Old Wolf"). Lee Marmon's (Laguna) work, and photographs of Indians in general, are discussed at length by Theresa Harlan (Laguna/Santo Domingo/ Jemez). A few photos are reprinted from *Shooting Back From the Reservation*, some from Zig Jackson's (Mandan/Hidatsa/Arikara) "Indian Man in San Francisco" series, James Luna's (Luiseño) "I've Always Wanted to be an American Indian," and much more.

Given the poverty-stricken/drunken Indian stereotype that is the backside of the "noble savage" coin, I think it took courage for Richard Ray Whitman (Euchee/Creek) to do his 1985 "Street Chiefs" series. The title of his section is "Plea to Those Who Matter." This is not a plea for pity. These old men matter too much for that. Jeffrey Thomas (Onondaga/Mohawk) has "attempted to show a tradition-based reality by confronting one of the most stereotyped images of Indians: the male powwow dancer." All the photos are in black and white.

The volume closes with two double-page spreads of Monty Roessel's (Diné) color photographs, and Ken Blackbird's (Assiniboine) lovely "Eagle Staff," backlighted by the setting sun. The front and back end papers are from the "Kiowa Ledger Book," ca. 1880.

This is a truly beautiful book, in heart and spirit, also.

Bia, Fred (Diné), and T.L. McCarty, *Of Mother Earth and Father Sky: A Photographic Study of Navajo Culture,* **photographs by Fred Bia. Rough Rock Press (1983). 69 pages, b/w photographs; grades 7-up; Diné (Navajo)**
Heisey, Adriel, and Kenji Kawano, *In the Fifth World: Portrait of the Navajo Nation,* **with a foreword by Peterson Zah (Diné). Rio Nuevo (2001). 88 pages, b/w and color photographs; grades 7-up; Diné (Navajo)**

Two from Dinétah, one old, one new, both important.

In her forword to *Mother Earth,* McCarty notes that she is not Navajo, and that her text must, of necessity, be an outsider's view, but she does a pretty good job. Her section headings, for a brief summary of the history, are: "The Emergence," "In Dinétah," "Expansion, Conflict and Defeat," "Return and Resettlement." and "A New Balance." Obviously this is not up-to-the-minute, but it gives a good overview.

The photographs are by a Navajo, of Navajo land and people, and I wish the publishers had been able to afford a better grade of paper to print them.

Technically, they are grayed out; in composition, they are spectacular. Some of them are as good as anything Ansel Adams ever did. They speak to the concept of balance, *hozho.* Interspersed among pictures of the land, cattle, sheep, dwellings, are portraits of children, adults, elders. This is how it is: not separate, all one.

Fifth World is the work of two men: one, an Anglo pilot and photographer who also writes; the other, a Japanese-American photographer and writer married to a Diné woman. It is pretty interesting to see how Heisey and Kawano ended up doing this. Neither one of them is pretending to be anything he isn't, and they have put together a pretty good book. Heisey does fly-over pictures of the land; Kawano does people. The faces of his subjects are of those who are looking at someone they trust, a friend. A couple of them, you just have to laugh: one, two little girls, LeAnn and Rochelle Holiday, twins, all dressed up, squinting at the photographer, with identically skeptical, gap-toothed expressions. Any kids, anywhere: what is this guy up to, anyway? The aerial photographs reveal the breath-taking beauty of the land in a way that I have not felt since looking out over the

New Mexico Earth from Acoma Pueblo. *Fifth World* seems like a family album—well, in a way it is. No "living history," just people, going about their lives.

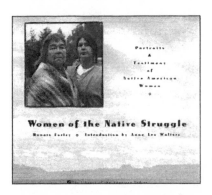

Farley, Ronnie, ed., *Women of the Native Struggle: Portraits & Testimony of Native American Women,* **photographs by the editor, introduction by Anna Lee Walters (Pawnee/Otoe). Orion (1993). 158 pages, b/w photographs; high school-up**

One of the unfortunate aspects of the publishing industry is that nearly all of the best writing by or about Native people goes out of print almost as soon as it comes into it. The junk stays around forever. *Women of the Native Struggle* came out of a program of the Learning Alliance focusing on the "contributions of women in Native politics, arts, medicine, and so on." Farley was approached about turning it into a book, and this collection of photographs and writings is the result.

Many women speak here. The chapter headings are "Remembering," "Life Givers," "The Light Within," "The Earth as Our Mother," "The View From the Shore," and "The Children: Our Future." Some of the women are well known throughout the Native community, and outside; all deal with issues of vital importance to us. Some have stood in the forefront of resistance to things that threaten our survival and the survival of our children as Native people. For others the struggle is quieter, but no less intense. "In the last 500 years," Anna Lee Walters writes,

> Native people have been tested on endless levels.... [T]hey nevertheless know who they are and what their continuing presence has meant over millennia. Tested beyond human understanding and endurance... they have consistently returned to the most ancient reference points to guide them to the present day.

There is so much wisdom here, such clear-sighted understanding of what faces us, such determination. This is a very important book. It is a pity and a shame that it is no longer available.

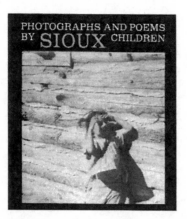

Hubbard, Jim, *Shooting Back From the Reservation: A Photographic View of Life by Native American Youth*, with a foreword by Dennis Banks (Anishinaabe). New Press (1994). 96 pages, b/w photographs; grades 5-up

From the introduction:

> Young people all over the United States are desperate for recognition and affirmation. For many kids, such as those who are homeless, who live in inner cities, where dreams are shattered with drugs and violence, or those who are on reservations, the desperation is even more profound. They often lack even the most basic opportunities.

The intent of the Shooting Back project is to "provide a window of opportunity by teaching them photography so they can interpret *their* visions of the world."

The premise is that life on reservations must be negative, and both some pictures, and some of the children's comments do show that aspect. Perhaps the folks at Shooting Back, and the editor, may have been a little surprised at how many of these young people have chosen to photograph moments of goodness and laughter. Their comments often reveal that their feelings about the reservation are that it is a good place to be. Summer Clarke (Hualapai), age nine, says,

> We live in houses. We go to school. There are twelve-hundred people living in Peach Springs. We go to the river....We have dogs and cats. We have horses. Peach Springs is good. Peach Springs is pretty....We love Peach Springs.

Pictures and writing by the young always reveal so much more perception and understanding than the adult world tends to expect of them. This book is no exception.

Libhart, Myles, and Arthur Amiotte (Lakota), editors, *Photographs and Poems by Sioux Children*, with an essay by Arthur Amiotte. Tipi Shop (1971). 80 pages, b/w photographs; grades 4-up; Lakota

The poems and photos in this book are from an exhibition arranged by the Indian Arts and Crafts Board of the U.S. Department of the Interior. It comes with a long and scholarly introduction by Arthur Amiotte, who was at that time instructor of the cultural visual arts program at the Porcupine Day School, which all of these young people attended. This is an old book. Much of what he says may seem dated now, and of course all the contributors are long grown. Given the history, some may no longer be with us.

Nevertheless, the poems and photographs, and what they say, are too powerful to pass up. The stark beauty of the Plains land, and what the children see, and feel, and say, are overwhelming. Just one, from Delores Pourier, grade seven, age twelve:

> An open window means:
> freedom
> to let in or let out
> to let light in
> to let air out
> to climb in to escape
> or out for freedom
> for hot days to open
> for cold days to shut.

There may still be stray copies of this book floating around. If you ever find one, grab it. You won't be sorry.

REVIEWS: PHOTOESSAYS OF INDIAN CHILDREN

All of the following books are photoessays about Indian children whose lives include, to some extent, modern and traditional ways of being in and seeing the world. For the most part, they are written by and photographed by outsiders, and their intended audience is non-Native children—to show "us" how "they" live. This is done with varying degrees of success. On the other hand, some of the books are written and photographed by people from within the cultures, and here, the results are generally better. Where known, the author's tribal affiliation is indicated in parentheses next to the name.

The individual reviews are organized alphabetically by author and photographer, with longer discussions when authors have created more than one work. The reviews of series are organized alphabetically by series title. Because individual titles in a series can vary widely in quality, the series entries contain discussions of multiple titles, organized alphabetically by author and photographer.

I thank Doris Seale, Naomi Caldwell, Judy Zalazar Drummond, and Debbie A. Reese for their invaluable assistance on this piece. Doris and Judy contributed several of the reviews, which bear their names at the end.—*Beverly Slapin*

Ancona, George (Maya/Chicano), color photographs by the author:
Earth Daughter: Alicia of Acoma Pueblo. **Simon & Schuster (1995).**
Mayeros: A Yucatec Maya Family. **Lothrop (1997).**
Pablo Remembers: The Fiesta of the Day of the Dead. **Lothrop (1993)**
Powwow. **Harcourt Brace (1993)**

"When I grow up, I want to be a potter and also go to college to become a lawyer," says Alicia Histia, who is a daughter of Acoma potters Jackie Shutiva Histia and Greg Histia. The beautifully photographed book called *Earth Daughter* is a visit with the Histia family as Jackie teaches Alicia the fine art of making pottery: "Working with the clay is a slow process," says Ancona. "It cannot be rushed; clay doesn't want you to be angry with it." Ancona, who is an accomplished photographer, also writes well, without polemic, without romanticism: "Dancing behind her mother and in front of her older sister, Alicia follows her mother's steps. Dust rises from the earth as the dancers' feet move to the rhythm of the drums. And so Alicia continues her pueblo's traditions, growing into her place among her people, her clan, and her family." *Earth Daughter* is one of my favorite books of this type.

The family in *Mayeros* is related to George Ancona through

his mother. Here, he writes with love of family, knowledge of history, and accuracy that can only come from a personal relationship.

Ancona's photographs are stunning, clear and natural and respectful of their subjects. He transmits a sense of history and continuation of a strong and vibrant culture in a very interesting way: inserted into a photo of his Yucatán relatives in front of their house is a photo of a carving of an almost identical house over the entrance to a temple at Uxmal; right next to a drawing on an old Mayan dish of a woman making tortillas on a metate is Doña Satulina grinding spices on a stone metate; an ancient Mayan drawing of a god using a planting stick to plant maize is next to a photo of Don Elias planting in the exact same way; and next to a photo of Armando carrying firewood using a tumpline is a reproduction of an ancient Mayan calendar figure using a tumpline.

Ancona ends his book by showing his nephews back at school after working on the milpa and spending a week at festival, studying hard, not only for their future, but because their people have always valued education. This he demonstrates with an illustration of a Mayan scribe drawing on a codex, from a painting on an ancient vase. Ancona makes sure the reader knows the Maya had a complete and rich library—thousands of years of history, science, and legend—which the Spanish burned in an attempt to destroy their books and language and thus destroy their culture. As Ancona shows, their attempt failed.—*Judy Zalazar Drummond*

All elementary and middle school teachers in America should have *Pablo Remembers* on their shelves, ever at the ready to pull out the end of September. That would give them a full month to prepare their students to understand and participate in El Día de Los Muertos, beautifully defined in George Ancona's photojournalistic essay.

The photographs of a healthy, happy, confident Mexican family show a solidarity with the past I have seldom seen. Ancona does not poke fun at the idea of dead relatives coming to visit, rather, he puts it in perspective: "For Pablo, this year's celebration is especially important. His *abuelita*, his grandmother, died two years ago and he misses her very much. But through the loving intimacy of the fiesta, he knows he will celebrate her memory again and again throughout his life."

Ancona also gives historical background, tracing this festival, or fiesta, back to ancient Egyptian times, then to Rome and Spain, and to this hemisphere, where "the celebration of the Day of the Dead grew from the blending of Aztec beliefs about death with Catholic beliefs that the Spanish conquistadors brought to the people of Mexico."—*Judy Zalazar Drummond*

In *Powwow*, Ancona takes the reader to Crow Agency, Montana, to the Crow Fair, the largest powwow held in the U.S. Ancona's photographs are a brilliant kaleidoscope of color and movement, and his text simply describes the "modern tradition" of regalia, drums, dance styles, contests, giveaways, honoring—the parts of the intertribal coming-together that is called "powwow."

Brown, Tricia, *Children of the Midnight Sun: Young Native Voices of Alaska*, color photographs by Roy Corral. Alaska Northwest Books (1998)

There is a lot of good in this book. The photographs are luminous, as the children and their families invite the reader into their homes and neighborhoods. The interviews allow the children to speak for themselves. Here, Robert Nageak, a twelve-year-old Iñupiaq, says about his favorite place along Avuk Creek: "It's real pretty.... The calves roam around the creek, and the bulls...man! When you see the bulls, their antlers are huge—they're like four feet across." This is how kids talk. There is no pretension. It is clear that the author has affection for them.

But a major problem here is Brown's treatment of the history of the area and its people. She glosses over the destructive role of the missionaries in practically eradicating language and traditions, saying that they "discouraged" people from conducting potlaches and practicing traditional arts. Similarly, she cites U.S. concerns with "safety" as the reason for removing the Aleuts to an abandoned cannery in Southeast Alaska during World War II, when in fact the U.S. removed the people in order to use the land as a military base. Few of the elders returned because most had died of broken hearts. And, several times, she speaks of the Bering Land Bridge theory as fact, ignoring both the people's origin stories and current theories about the migration of the people from south to north.

In the hands of a skilled teacher or librarian, used with more accurate historical material, this book has value.

Garcia, Guy, *Spirit of the Maya: A Boy Explores His People's Mysterious Past.* Color photographs by Ted Wood. Walker (1995)

Palenque is one of the most beautiful places I've ever seen; the small valley is green and lush and the buildings look like they were designed to fit each into its own space. There is a great sense of history here, calm and tranquil and one imagines that it would be a lovely place to live. It is this place that Guy Garcia chose for a contrived, illogical photo-story of a Mayan boy, "exploring" "his people's mysterious past."

Kin lives traditionally with his family, yet whines about helping his mother, wants to speak Spanish instead of the Mayan language, and wants to cut his hair short "but his father won't let him because it's traditional for the Lacando'n to wear their hair long."

Inspired by a book, Kin goes off to the temples, by himself, a tourist in his own people's traditional lands and sacred places. He wonders what each thing he sees represents— "Those large carved heads over there—are they pictures of Maya priests or of the Sun Gods?"—and then answers himself like a scholar. To illustrate Garcia's travelogue, Kin jumps over a gap in a wall, climbs a narrow stairway, lies on what he thinks could be Pacal's tomb, and generally acts more like a white kid in an MTV video than a Mayan child in his own territory. Kin is depicted as so ignorant that it takes a tourist to direct him to Pacal's tomb.

This tour makes him feel lonely and Kin tells his father "he never wants to come back." But after seeing his own likeness in a huge head sculpture of Pacal, Kin can "for the first time in his life, know how it feels to be a king."

A traditional Mayan child would not think or behave in such a culturally ignorant way. A traditional Mayan father would not send a child to "explore" the temples by himself. And no traditional Mayans worth their salt would neglect to pass on their history and culture to their children. This book is insulting.—*Judy Zalazar Drummond*

Gravelle, Karen, *Growing Up: Where the Partridge Drums Its Wings,* **color photographs by Stephen R. Poole. Franklin Watts (1997)**

Akwesasne is Mohawk for "where the partridge drums its wings," and here, young readers meet ten-year-old cousins Chantelle and David Francis and their families, who live on the Akwesasne Reservation. The full-color photos show Chantelle and David—kids who are both modern and traditional—at school, at home, at play, and most of the photos do not seem to be posed. Gravelle does a good job of explaining the efforts to relearn the language, the concept of sovereignty, the confrontation between the Mohawks and the provincial government at Oka, and internal conflicts as well. But the text is not without fault. Some is unnecessarily written in the past tense. The term "reservation" is defined as "land set aside" rather than land retained. The description of women's leadership roles in the Haudenosaunee Confederacy is very weak. Gravelle hints at, but does not actually say, that the Great Law of Peace was the forerunner of the U.S. Constitution. There is a full-page ramble about dreamcatchers. And there is no mention of the terrible industrial pollution of Akwesasne air and water, which has made subsistence hunting and fishing impossible. Still, there is a lot that is good here, and parts of this book can be used together with good historical (Joe Bruchac's *Children of the Longhouse*) and traditional (Tehanetorens' *Legends of the Iroquois*) material.

Hazen-Hammond, Suzan, *Thunder Bear and Ko: The Buffalo Nation and Nambe Pueblo,* **color photographs by the author. Dutton Children's Books (1999)**

This is a perfect example of what can happen when an outsider tries to interpret another people's culture through her own romanticized framework. Here, Hazen-Hammond travels to Nambé Pueblo to document a significant event for the people—the return of the buffalo. While the information itself is accurate, a friend from Nambé told me that the author here reveals sacred events and knowledge that elders ask not be shared. Moreover, the text is contrived: "Thunder Bear could almost feel what it was like to be a buffalo," and elsewhere, "He knew he wasn't wise now, but someday he would be—wise like his father, wise like his grandfather, wise like his ancestors." I don't understand why outsiders like to think that Indians have cornered the market on wisdom. The photos of the people are posed, and the author

seems to go out of her way to highlight the "exotic" about them. There is even a red tinge to the photos of the people, making them appear, well, red. Even the ugly design of the book shouts "ethnic" (uh, multicultural). And I don't know why the author thought it was a good thing to place herself and her car—with the buffalo—on two pages, reminiscent of those boring "how-I-spent-my-summer-vacation" themes.

Hoyt-Goldsmith, Diane, color photographs by Lawrence Migdale. Holiday House.
Apache Rodeo, **1995**
Arctic Hunter, **1992 (Iñupiaq)**
Buffalo Days, **1997 (Crow)**
Cherokee Summer, **1993**
Day of the Dead: A Mexican-American Celebration, **1994 (Aztec)**
Lacrosse: The National Game of the Iroquois, **1998**
Potlatch: A Tsimshian Celebration, **1997**
Pueblo Storyteller, **1991 (Cochiti)**
Totem Pole, **1990 (Tsimshian)**

Writing a children's book entirely from a child's perspective is a formidable task. The book should read well, carry the young narrator's perceptions and feelings, and the vocabulary should be believably authentic. And if the author comes from a people with a different way of looking at the world than does her subject, she must be prepared to set her own values aside. I know few people who do this well.

In all of her earlier books (*Apache Rodeo, Arctic Hunter, Cherokee Summer, Day of the Dead, Potlach, Pueblo Storyteller, Totem Pole*) Hoyt-Goldsmith's perspective is clearly that of an outsider pretending to be a child from inside a particular Native Nation. The results are, for the most part, predictably awful.

The photos by Lawrence Migdale range from good to excellent—my favorites are from the *Potlach* book, especially the ones showing the pole raising.

Most of the information in these earlier books is either dead wrong or so watered down as to be unreliable. Conquistadores are "explorers," stolen land is "land exchanged," and reservations are areas of land "set aside by the U.S. government as a place for Indian people to live." In addition, the writing is belabored, with things explained several times. For instance, in *Arctic Hunter*:

> [W]e send fish along for the elders who are too old to go out to camp anymore. We are taught to share what we catch. Sharing is one of our most important Iñupiaq values.

Often, the author lets the reader know that she has found some *really interesting stuff* by ending the sentence with an exclamation mark: "A totem pole is like a library for a tribe!" (No! It's not! Totem poles are story-markers, and tribes have libraries! With books!)

Finally, these books end with a summing-up paragraph in romanticized language that comes straight out of a white author's fantasy: "I am proud of my (X) heritage. I am proud of my (X) people. Every day I am learning to live in harmony with the world." They are practically interchangeable and very boring and besides, I don't know anyone—child or adult—who talks like this.

In *Buffalo Days*, the author has ditched the first-person narrative, but the wooden, dumbed-down style of writing remains. In a sentence referring to the tribal herd, for instance, she uses twenty-two one-syllable words before coming to one with two syllables: "They are so big and strong that they can run right through the kind of fence that would hold a herd of cattle." As in her earlier titles, the author here lapses into sweeping generalizations that make no sense (e.g., "People who come to the fair are able to experience a way of life that existed during the Buffalo Days"). White depredation of the buffalo (whom the author refers to as "wild") is smoothed over, residential schools are mentioned but not spoken about honestly, reservations are still "land set aside" for Indians, and Hoyt-Goldsmith seems to think that all powwow regalia is traditional clothing and all powwow dances are traditional. But more perplexing is why she refers to Clarence Three Irons, Jr., by his nickname, "Indian," thirty-four times (e.g., "Indian and his friends eat Indian tacos."). Nicknames are used by family and friends, not by teachers, casual acquaintances or unfamiliar adults. It is disrespectful for an outsider to refer to a child by his nickname. And finally, I don't know why the author has chosen to highlight an Indian child with short hair who wears a wig as part of his powwow regalia.

All of this having been said, I really like Hoyt-Goldsmith's newest book, *Lacrosse: The National Game of the Iroquois*. This is a photoessay about Monty Lyons, a thirteen-year-old lacrosse player, grandson of Onandoga Faith-keeper Oren Lyons. But it is more about this most sacred of games itself, called the "Creator's Game." Hoyt-Goldsmith gives a brief history of the Haudenosaunee Confederacy including the Great Law of Peace, an overview of the history and rules of lacrosse, a comparison between traditional and modern lacrosse, and a description of how the traditional lacrosse stick is constructed, and the importance the game still holds for the people who are called "Iroquois." The information is accurate, the writing is good and clear, and Migdale's engaging color photos draw the reader into the action.

I don't know if Hoyt-Goldsmith has matured, or is listening more to the families whose stories she is telling, or

if the Lyons family insisted on—and got—editorial control. Whatever the reasons, *Lacrosse* is a way better book than any of the others.

Jenness, Aylette, and Alice Rivers (Yup'ik), *In Two Worlds: A Yup'ik Eskimo Family*, b/w photographs by Aylette Jenness. Houghton Mifflin (1989)

The first photo here is of a teenage Alice Rivers with one of Aylette Jenness's babies; the second photo is of Aylette with two of Alice's grandbabies. This book, which grew out of a friendship that spans more than twenty-five years, is a collaboration between two women of vastly different backgrounds. That they truly like and respect each other is evident in both text and photos. While Jenness, a photojournalist, did most of the writing, the voices of Rivers and her family are very much here.

In Two Worlds is a photo-documentary of the enormous changes—some positive, some negative—that have come about in the small Yup'ik town of Scammon Bay, Alaska, over the course of four generations. Except for a few portraits, none of the photos seems posed—here is a large extended family and their community, working at fish camp and berry picking, seal hunting and butchering, cooking and baking, going to school and shopping, passing on dance and ceremony, and just being together.

Jenness is an accomplished photographer, and she has resisted the temptation (if she ever had it) to romanticize the family and community. Rivers and her family, not the least of whom is great-grandma Mary Ann, have a lot to say. This is a lovely, honorable book. (I would also like to have seen how Jenness's family has changed over the past four generations, but that may be another book.)

Keegan, Marcia, color photographs by the author:
Pueblo Boy: Growing Up in Two Worlds. Cobblehill/Dutton (1991)
Pueblo Girls: Growing Up in Two Worlds. Clear Light (1999)

Keegan has lived in this part of the country for a long time. Both books are practically identical, and are about children in the Roybal family, with whom she has a relationship. Her photos here, although mostly posed, are well crafted and do not seem to be contrived. But Keegan's writing clearly reflects her own outsider belief system, and as such, it is unsatisfactory.

On the very first page of both books is the obligatory "just-like-you-but-follows-traditions-too" sentence: "Timmy Roybal is a ten-year-old Pueblo Indian boy. Besides doing the things that any other ten-year-old boy would do, Timmy follows the traditions of his Native American heritage./Sonja Roybal is a ten-year-old Pueblo Indian girl, and her sister Desiree is eight years old. These sisters, besides doing the things any other girls would do, follow the traditions of their Native American heritage." Next comes the paragraph about Spanish "explorers," followed by the constant use of the word "belief" to describe Native cosmology. This is not just something that Keegan does; it is done in most books written by outsiders. Stated flatly, like this: "The people of San Idelfonso believe that spirits live in the earth, the sky, the waters, and in special sacred places," the "beliefs" seem like make-believe, not a sophisticated cosmology rich with symbolic meaning. Both books end with a paragraph about the pride of being Indian and living in two worlds: "Timmy likes to belong to two cultures. He feels he has the best of both worlds./Sonja and Desiree are proud of their Indian heritage…. Sonja and Desiree belong to two cultures, the traditional Pueblo Indian world and the twenty-first century world of computers. They feel they have the best of both worlds." While many Indian children are secure in the knowing of who they are and what they have come from, the constant use of this "pride" stuff is patronizing.

Kendall, Ross, *Eskimo Boy: Life in an Iñupiaq Eskimo Village*, color photographs by the author. Scholastic (1992)

This is a portrait of seven-year-old Norman Kokeok who, with his family, lives in an Iñupiaq village called Shishmaref, in Alaska. The photos, mostly portraits, are very good. Here is Norman at school, not liking it very much; riding in a plane to the dentist, liking it even less; ice fishing with the other villagers, liking it better; and hunting birds with his friends, liking it best of all. Fortunately, the text is free of romanticism; these are people going about their lives, which in this case, revolve around obtaining and preparing food.

Unfortunately, the text is also free of humor. And the afterword, about "modern-day Eskimos," is unacceptable in its portrayal of the people as helpless victims: "A gentle, trusting people, they proved easy prey…" Despite its merits, this book is depressing.

LaDuke, Winona (Anishinaabe) and Waseyabin Kapashesit (Anishinaabe), *The Sugar Bush*, photographs by John Ratzloff. Rigby (1999)

Here, Wasey and her mom Winona take young readers on a trip to the sugar bush, where the sacred maple trees give the people sap to make maple syrup, sugar and candy. There is history here, too, and an unspoken story of how we are all related. With luminous photos and easy-to-read text—and without polemic—Wasey and her mom show how the Anishinaabe people are tied to the land. Inserted into a color photo of a healthy green forest is an archival black-and-white picture of how the barren land looked one hundred years ago after loggers cut down the forest for lumber. "My mother taught me," Wasey says, "that you can only cut down a forest once. But if you leave it standing, you can walk through it and taste its sweetness year after year." This is a beautiful book.—*Doris Seale*

McMillan, Bruce, *Salmon Summer*, color photographs by the author. Houghton Mifflin (1998)

Each summer, the salmon return to spawn in the streams of Kodiak Island, Alaska. Here, nine-year-old Alex Shugak, Jr., and his father work together at subsistence fishing, the salmon harvest, and *Salmon Summer* is a photographic journal of their time together. "There's an abundance of salmon for all," says McMillan, and his full-color photographs of the land and the people—and this most sacred of fishes—are stunning. Here are eagles, bears, magpies, gulls, and a momma fox, all getting their share. Here is Alex giving a salmon to an elder. Here is Alex's little brother, Larry, chewing on smoked salmon— yum! Here are side-by-side photos of salmon eggs and salmonberries, and they really do look alike. Unlike a lot of photoessayists, McMillan has scrupulously avoided the temptation to "teach" about the Aleut—he puts down what he sees, and he is very good at it.

Mott, Evelyn Clarke, *Dancing Rainbows,* **color photographs by the author. Cobblehill/Dutton (1996)**

It's Feast Day at San Juan Pueblo. Andy Garcia and his grandson Curt spend the day together, Andy teaching, Curt learning, both participating in this major community event. The photos are well crafted; many are posed, some are not. Two children dance, with a look of intense concentration on their faces. A line of elders drums and sings. Andy and his grandson share a joke. Two dogs sit attentively, waiting by the horno for a piece of freshly baked bread to fall out. Some of the text is well done, with subtle unstated lessons: "Andy wakes up early on Feast Day. He prays in the hills. He asks for a good mind, a good heart, and a good life. He sprinkles some cornmeal as a gift to the earth."

But the book is flawed in serious ways, perhaps fatally. A friend as told me that there are a lot of inaccuracies here. Besides these, there is too much emphasis on the Comanche Dance, which is a dance given to the Tewa people, not a traditional dance. There is the use of the inappropriate word "costume" instead of "regalia," and there is the use, many times, of the word "believe" to oversimplify the complex Tewa cosmology. And two more things stand out. One is the explanation of Indian-white relations in a way that sanitizes history, and the other is the careless use of language: "The men yelp loudly for the Comanche Dance. They wear fancy costumes." Non-Indian children reading this are going to put their hands to their mouths and—you know—yelp loudly.

Rendon, Marcie R. (Anishinaabe), *Powwow Summer: A Family Celebrates the Circle of Life,* **color photographs by Cheryl Walsh Bellville. Carolrhoda/Lerner (1996)**

> Can you find the beginning of a circle? Or the end of a circle? Once a circle is made, it has no beginning or end. It continues on and on. According to Native tradition, the circle of life is endless. It has no beginning. There is no end. In the original teachings of my people, the Anishinabe, the spirit of the human being travels from the spirit world to this world at birth. And at death, the spirit travels back to the spirit world. So it is that the human spirit completes a full cycle, or circle, of life.

This book is so beautifully made, in words and pictures, it is hard to stop quoting from it. *Powwow Summer* is not so much "about" powwows—although there is good information here—as about life, death, parenting, tradition, and love of the community's children. Here, readers join Sharyl and Windy Downwind and their large extended family, including five foster children, as they give honor to, and are honored by, their community.

In one year's time, Shian was crowned princess and passed on the title with a giveaway. A child was born, and a grandmother died.... In the circle of a family, in the circle of a community and tribe, a family is loved and cared for, and grows.

Reynolds, Jan, *Frozen Land: Vanishing Cultures,* **color photographs by the author. Harcourt Brace (1993)**

Reynolds' perspective, stated in her introduction—"Perhaps we can learn from the relationship the Inuit have with their natural surroundings before their way of life vanishes forever"—is clear. This "let's-photograph-the-snowflake-before-it-melts" contrivance says far more about the author than the book does about the Inuit family she photographs. The photos are stiff; most of them are posed. The writing is boring and didactic. And finally, on the last page, an indigenous child is "proud to learn the ways...." Not recommended.

Solá, Michéle, *Angela Weaves a Dream: The Story of a Young Maya Artist,* **color photographs by Jeffrey Jay Foxx. Hyperion (1996)**

Here, a Mayan child in one of the villages in the Chiapas mountains of southern Mexico learns from her *abuelita* (grandma) and community how to card and spin cotton and wool, prepare dye, and, finally, to weave her first sampler on a hand-made loom. There is a lot of useful information here. Young readers will learn of the traditional artistry of a materially impoverished but culturally rich people, and illustrations and explanations accompany full-color photographs of the seven sacred designs of this particular village (ancestors, butterfly, flowering corn, scorpion, snake, toad, and universe). But the photos of the people seem staged to provide visuals for the story, whose plot seems contrived. There is no attribution for the snippets of legends interspersed throughout the text; I assume from the bibliography (which is limited to two sources that are more than ten years old) that they came from Dennis Tedlock's translation of the *Popol Vuh.* I wish the author had at least used Mayan sources for a Mayan story. I also wish she had made mention of the heroic struggle for the land of the Mayan people going on, now, in Chiapas.

Thompson, Sheila (Carrier), *Cheryl Bibalhats/Cheryl's Potlach,* **color photographs by Tim Swanky (Carrier), Carrier text by Dorothy Patrick (Carrier). Yinka Dene Language Institute (1991)**

Cheryl, who looks to be about eleven, is a citizen of the Caribou Clan of the Lake Babine Band, Carrier Nation. In the summer of 1988, the Caribou Clan in Burns Lake,

British Columbia, gave her a naming potlach. Here, in simple Dene and English text, Cheryl describes the potlach her family and clan are giving so that everyone will know her new name, Deele:

> Mrs. Louie is at my side. She leads me into the hall. She tells everyone my Indian name. I am now Deele. I am now an important part of the potlach system. Mom and Dad stand beside me. They ask all the people to watch over me as I grow up…. This is a day I will always remember. I am now a girl with two names. My friends at school will call me Cheryl. The people in the town will know me as Cheryl. But, the next time there is a potlach, the Dineeze' will stamp the talking stick—one, two, three. He will say, "Welcome, Deele. Let me show you to your potlach chair."

The photos are very good, and this is an excellent response to the way potlaches are described in textbooks.

Wolf, Bernard, *Beneath the Stone: A Mexican Zapotec Tale*, color photographs by the author. Orchard (1994)

Wolf's photographs here are absolutely wonderful. I know these people. There is a real feeling of the family, at home, at work, and in the marketplaces of Oaxaca.

A few things particularly bother me, however. When Leo and his father have kept poverty at bay by selling their tapetes—I do this myself at the local flea market—they visit Monte Albán, the Zapotec city that was a thriving metropolis and trading center about 2,500 years ago. His father tells Leo "that the Zapotecs leveled the entire top of this mountain to build this city. How did they do that? he wonders. No one knows." This disbelief comes more from the author than from Leo's father, who would have known that the Zapotecs had very sophisticated technology and were incredibly talented builders. And, Wolf states that from the mountaintop of Teotitlán, "It is believed that, either by signal fire or reflected light, the ancestors 'spoke' to the Place Beneath the Stone." Here, Wolf's use of quotation marks around the word "spoke" tells the child reader, "but it really wasn't so," which trivializes the complex belief system of a people.

In the marketplace, the reader is treated to photos of all kinds of delicious food, and then we see that even "fried grasshoppers!" are sold here. It is a fact that insects are eaten all over the world; they are an important and cheap source of protein. But here, Wolf's use of an exclamation point signals otherness, weirdness to young readers, who will invariably think that it is "yucky" for people to eat grasshoppers.

Finally, Wolf's section on Zapotec history is fairly accurate until the end, where he says that life for Mexico's "diverse Indian cultures has vastly improved. In spite of lingering racial prejudice, these people are treated with some respect now. Most importantly, they are left to pursue their own life-styles and traditions." The Zapatista Revolution in Chiapas belies this; one need only read the newspaper to see that indigenous rights have been negated for many years and are being fought for on a daily and continuous basis. —*Judy Zalazar Drummond*

Wood, Ted, with Wanbli Numpa Afraid of Hawk (Lakota), *A Boy Becomes a Man at Wounded Knee*, color photographs by the author. Walker (1992)

In December 1990, some 300 Lakota men, women and children rode their horses 250 miles, in bitter sub-zero weather, to bring their people out of a hundred-year mourning for those relatives killed in the Wounded Knee Massacre. Braving weather that dropped to fifty degrees below zero, this courageous, committed group rode from Bigfoot's camp to Wounded Knee to end the mourning through a traditional ceremony known as Washigila, "Wiping the Tears." The Bigfoot Memorial Ride was that ceremony, and one of the riders was eight-year-old Wanbli Numpa Afraid of Hawk.

In his introduction to *A Boy Becomes a Man at Wounded Knee*, author Ted Wood says "[A]n eight-year-old Lakota boy rode too, on a trip that would teach him his past and make him a man from then on. This is his story." But this is not Wanbli's story; it is Wood's interpretation, from an outsider's perspective that he is unable or unwilling to put aside, of Wanbli's story. Wood has taken a people's journey into healing and turned it into one boy's journey into manhood. An eight-year-old child, even if he does something brave, is still a child. He is still *wakanyeja*, a sacred being, a child.

This ride was a phenomenal event. Lots of children went, lots of teenagers went. They went because, even though their parents were afraid for them, they had committed themselves to endure this tremendous hardship—with the adults—to remember the courage of their ancestors and to heal their people. They didn't do it because they wanted to be adults.

I don't know what Wanbli really told to Wood. Almost more than any of the other books of this kind, this is clearly not in a child's words. To turn this event—a community's healing itself after a hundred years of mourning—into an child's quest for adulthood, is unforgivable.

PHOTOESSAY SERIES

"Library of Intergenerational Learning: Native Americans" series, PowerKids/Rosen (1999)

Kavasch, E. Barrie, author,
Apache Children and Elders Talk Together
Blackfoot Children and Elders Talk Together
Crow Children and Elders Talk Together
Lakota Sioux Children and Elders Talk Together
Seminole Children and Elders Talk Together
Zuni Children and Elders Talk Together

These books, released together for younger elementary students, take a cookie-cutter approach to the subject. Each cover shows a photo of an elder and a child from a specific Indian Nation. Except for the Zuni book, whose cover depicts a child wearing a plain t-shirt, everyone else is dressed in full regalia. The elders and children are not together as the titles suggest, but rather there are separate photos cut out and pasted next to each other. Behind them is an underlay of people, all in full regalia, dancing. Each book has information about a specific Nation, with an overemphasis on food, dance, ritual, and—pride. Most of the photos are adequate; some, especially the family portraits and portraits of the elders, are excellent. I would like to have seen, as the titles suggest, "children and elders talking together." Instead, the books just contain, separately, quotes from the children and quotes from the elders. And again, as in so many of this type of series, I suspect that many of the children did not actually utter what they are quoted as saying.

There is a careless, thrown-together feel to these books, which suggests that they were quickly assembled in-house. Some of the photos and captions are, well, goofy. There is one, for instance, of a guy wearing a headdress accompanied by a young woman in full regalia. He is driving a customized bright red three-wheel motorcycle with a sidecar. The caption says, in all seriousness, "The Crow may have adopted some modern things from the world around them. But their history will always be a part of their lives." There is another photo, of a family, on a porch, with their dogs. One of the younger children is

holding a puppy. The caption says, "The Aragon family members support and help each other." I'm also wondering how it was decided which words were deemed to require pronunciation assistance—"rite (RYT)," "clan (KLAN)," "tribe (TRYB)," and which were not—St. Xavier, Chiricahua, Sioux. Young children deserve better than this.

"My World: Young Native Americans Today" series, Beyond Words (in association with National Museum of the American Indian)

Belarde-Lewis, Miranda (Tlingit/Zuni/Cherokee), *Meet Lydia: A Native Girl from Southeast Alaska*, photographs by John Harrington (Siletz). 2004 (Tlingit)
Secakuku, Susan (Hopi), *Meet Mindy: A Native Girl from the Southwest*, photographs by John Harrington (Siletz). 2003 (Hopi/Tewa)
Tayac, Gabrielle (Piscataway), *Meet Naiche: A Native Boy from the Chesapeake Bay Area*, photographs by John Harrington (Siletz). 2002 (Piscataway/Apache)

Meet Naiche is dedicated to Roberta Blackgoat, a Diné elder, one of the leaders in the struggle to hold on to Navajo lands at Big Mountain. There is a photo of her participating in a Piscataway ceremony, where "participants say their thanks for the renewal of Mother Earth. She has followed her original instructions, to wake up. Now we have followed our original instructions, to take care of her." *Meet Mindy* is dedicated to the author's nieces and nephews, "who continuously remind me of how much there is still to learn and pass on." And *Meet Lydia* is "for my grandparents, for the kids of the present, and those yet to come." Together, these three titles view life from inside the culture; they are about Indian children living their lives as integral members of their families, cultures, and communities.

Naiche Woosah Tayac, the author's cousin, lives in a rural Maryland community; Mindy Secakuku, the author's niece, lives with her family near Phoenix; and Lydia Mills, the author's cousin, lives with her mom in Juneau during the school year and travels to Hoonah and Excursion Inlet to spend summers and school holidays with her dad. On the first pages of each volume, next to a color photo of them, the authors introduce themselves and their people. The books have a nice look to them, with color photos of the youngsters and their extended families engaged in work, play and ceremony. There's a picture of Naiche holding up a framed photo of the Apache leader whose name he carries. In the photo of Mindy's father carving a katsina doll, with a finished doll beside him, you can see the smoothness and softness of the cottonwood. The Yah-ne-wah Dance photos are luminous, and I also like the picture of Mindy after the dance is over, a big grin on her face. And the photos of Lydia's dad teaching her to fish with a gaff hook, of Lydia reading to the Tlingit language enhancement class, and of Lydia's aunt rehearsing a Tlingit song with Lydia and her brother, are excellent.

There are also archival photos and pictures of objects from the museum's collection, and of historical, cultural and language information about each particular Native nation set off from the narratives. The first-person narratives, written by the adult authors who worked closely with the children, read well and for the most part do not seem contrived. "When I was really little," Lydia says,

> I used to sit on my dad's shoulders and watch the dances, but during the past two Celebrations, my brother and I took part in the dances with our culture club. At the last Celebration we performed our dances about twice a day on each of the three days. Our practicing paid off, because everyone told us we did a really good job. Dancing so much made me feel exhausted but proud.

But these books are not without problems. In some places, ordinary events are overemphasized. Why, for instance, was it seen as necessary to show Mindy in the bathroom, brushing her teeth? There is also, in places, a self-conscious use of the word "special"—special foods, special ceremonies, special dances. This kind of thing distances children from each other, rather than bringing them together. And it's too bad that the jacket copy, identical in all three books, shouts, in very large type:

> If I were Native American, would I live on a reservation? In a tipi? Would I go to a regular school? Wear moccasins? How would I be different from other kids? If I were a Native American today, what would my life be like?

Considering the loving, caring way that these books were created and how they affirm the lives of Indian children, the jacket copy does just the opposite—it sends a subtle message to Indian children that these books are not for them. Anyone who purchases these otherwise exceptional books would do well to throw away the jackets.

"We Are Still Here" series, Lerner

Braine, Susan, (Assiniboine), *Drumbeat, Heartbeat: A Celebration of the Powwow*, color photographs by the author, 1995

Braine is a citizen of the Assiniboine Nation, but it's the Northern Cheyenne reservation in Lame Deer, Montana, that she calls home, and where she returns each summer for the Fourth of July powwow. Like the other volumes in this series, *Drumbeat, Heartbeat* gets up close and personal,

as Braine talks about what the powwow means to her:

> There are many, many Indians like me who choose to live and work away from the place where our families and hearts are. Many of us make it a priority to go back home to visit and replenish the soul.

With good clear language and many good photos, Braine tells about the various parts of the powwow—from powwow etiquette to grand entry to drums to round dances, contest dancing, and honor songs, to giveaways—and explains how that replenishment happens. It is fitting that Braine's focus at the end of this book is on the giveaway, for it is "giving away" that is a core value, still practiced today.

Hunter, Sally M. (Anishinaabe), *Four Seasons of Corn: A Winnebago Tradition*, color photographs by Joe Allen (Lakota), 1997

Hunter is grandma to twelve-year-old Russell, and here, Russell and his large mixed-blood extended family learn the traditions of corn from his Ho-Chunk grandfather. In each of the four seasons of corn, there is something to do, from planting, harvesting, and drying the corn, to making corn soup, and, of course, to giving thanks. As the author says in her personal note, "We are blessed by the earth when we pick a beautiful crop of Ho-chunk corn. And we are blessed with a beautiful family of Ho-chunk children."

As with the other volumes in this series, there are a cursory few sentences of the history of the particular Indian Nation. Here, the sentence, "In the 1830s, the Win-nebagos had to give up their land to the United States government," is a lost opportunity to explain to young readers the concept of Manifest Destiny. This is important and ought not to be minimized.

King, Sandra (Ojibwe), *Shannon: An Ojibway Dancer*, color photographs by Catherine Whipple (Lakota), 1993

At thirteen, Shannon Anderson lives in Minneapolis with her grandma, sisters and cousins. She attends Four Winds School, which has an Ojibwe language immersion pro-

her friends. And, when she's done with her homework, Shannon works on her fancy shawl dance outfit with her grandma. Although some of the photos here are very good, others are disappointingly dark. Still, this book speaks volumes to Indian kids who live in the city, who cannot, for some reason or other, go home:

> A young person like Shannon, who was born in a city, also belongs. She holds a place in her tribe, and in a certain part of the Earth. This place belongs only to her and cannot be taken or given away. This is what Shannon's grandma meant when she told Shannon that wherever she goes, all that she is goes with her.

Mercredi, Morningstar (Chipewyan/Cree/Métis), *Fort Chipewyan Homecoming: A Journey to Native Canada*, color photographs by Darren McNally, 1997

Mercredi is the mother of twelve-year-old Matthew Dunn, whose visit with his Indian relatives in his mother's childhood home is the subject of this book. His parents are divorced, and Matthew spends alternating years with each of them. Having been raised a city kid, this is Matthew's first experience with subsistence hunting and fishing, and being with the land. "Going home allows my heart and spirit to rest," says Mercredi.

> Fort Chipewyan is a place where my people have lived for thousands of years, a place where I can breathe clean air and drink fresh water.... My grandpa used to lay spruce branches on the floor of our tent to use as a mattress. The smell of spruce trees takes me back to the safe place I knew as home.

The photos of the land are luminous, and those of Matthew attempting to catch a fish and cook bannock are excellent. And I liked the book even more when I realized that Matthew is the young actor in "Moccasin Flats." Although I highly recommend this book, the discussion of treaties is weak. Treaties are agreements between sovereign Nations. The treaties between the sovereign First Nations peoples and Canada did not "give" Indian people "the right to continue traditional activities such as fishing and hunting" or "give" Indian people "areas of land called reserves." Rather, by agreement, the Indian people *retained* their traditional activities and *retained* some of their traditional lands. This wording may seem insignificant, but it is important for all young readers—Indian and non-Indian—to understand the history of Indian-white relations on this hemisphere.

Nichols, Richard (Tewa), *A Story to Tell: Traditions of a Tlingit Community*, color photographs by D. Bambi Kraus (Tlingit), 1998

"Let's go for a walk," Fran tells her granddaughter, Marissa, "I have a story to tell you." Here, at a family reunion, Marissa visits the Tlingit community of Kake for the first time, meets her many relatives, and learns some of the stories and traditions of the Eagle and Raven clans. For Grandma, this is a time of remembering; for Marissa, it's a time of learning. Frances Nannauck Kraus is the photographer's mother, and this story was inspired by a paper she wrote as a teenager in a boarding school.

Bambi Kraus, who is Marissa's auntie, is a wonderful photographer. This is a very personal story, and it makes all the difference.

Peters, Russell M. (Wampanoag), *Clambake: A Wampanoag Tradition*, color photographs by John Madama, 1992

Here, we meet twelve-year-old Steven Peters, who lives in Plymouth, Massachusetts, near the traditional Wampanoag home, Mashpee. It is at Mashpee that he learns from his grandfather, Fast Turtle (Russell Peters), how to prepare for and put on an appanaug, a traditional clambake, the first feast of summer. This one is being put on in honor of an elder, Hazel Oakley, in appreciation of her many years of service to the community; and Steven also is honored with the gift of an eagle feather. The photos of the land, people, animals, and—yum!—food, are lovely, but I have a problem with one picture. It is totally impossible for a twelve-year-old's room to be that clean unless it's being set up for a photograph!

Regguinti, Gordon (Ojibwe), *The Sacred Harvest: Ojibway Wild Rice Gathering*, color photographs by Dale Kakkak (Menominee), 1992

> For 11-year-old Glen Jackson, Jr., this warm summer day was important. It was a day he had waited for all year. It was the first time his father would take him out to gather *mahnomin*, the sacred food of the Ojibway people. This is the day he would become a wild ricer.

Here, Regguinti describes, in the kind of loving detail that speaks of experience, an important part of life and community on the Leech Lake Reservation. The photographs, especially of the land and of the rice beds on the water, are beautiful. This book might be especially instructive for kids who think that rice comes out of an Uncle Ben's box.

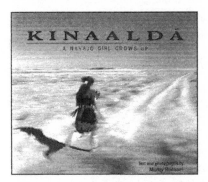

Roessel, Monty (Diné), color photographs by the author:
Kinaaldá: A Navajo Girl Grows Up, 1993
Songs from the Loom: A Navajo Girl Learns to Weave, 1995
Songs from the Loom is an account of the author's daughter, Jaclyn, as she learns to weave from her grandma, Roessel's mother. Roessel begins by telling the story of how, when he came home from school one day, he heard his mother singing and saw her weaving. She told him then that, as long as she had her loom, she was home: "This is who we are.... The loom connects me with the sacred mountains, and the song connects me with my mother." Now it is time for Grandma to teach the songs, the stories, the prayers to Jaclyn. It is also time to teach her to shear the family sheep, to spin wool into yarn, to make natural dyes, to weave, and perhaps most importantly, to take care of her weaving tools. The photos are excellent: Here, Grandma and granddaughter are silhouetted against the dawn as they sprinkle pollen toward the sun. Here, you can see the sheep being sheared, probably complaining. Here, you can feel the frustration as Jaclyn learns that weaving isn't as easy as it looks. But my favorite photos (and, I am told, the publisher saw these as a problem) are in the progression, over the two years of the making of this book, of Jaclyn from little girl to young woman.

Kinaaldá is about the coming-of-age ceremony of another young woman, thirteen-year-old Celinda McKelvey, which takes place at her grandma's home in Sheep Springs, New Mexico. Roessel's photos are gorgeous, especially the ones of the land, and the cover photo is exquisite. Here is Celinda, soon to be welcomed into the circle of women, doing what Diné women have done for millennia, running east, toward the rising sun. With her female relatives assisting her, and with the ceremony only two days instead of the traditional four, Celinda initially thinks this whole thing will be a snap. But that is before she finds out just how grueling the ceremony is: grinding pile after pile of corn meal, staying awake all night, running long distances, and following exacting instructions from her grandma, mom, and aunties. There is humor here, and a closeness of family and Nation that comes from knowing who you are forever. The only weakness in this book is probably due to the heavy hand of the editor. Some of the writing, in what I call "third-person instructive" ("the Navajo believe," "The Navajos, or the Diné, as they call themselves") is unnecessary in a book of this sort, and is notably absent from Roessel's later work.

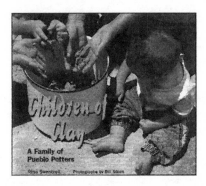

Swentzell, Rina (Tewa), *Children of Clay: A Family of Pueblo Potters*, color photographs by Bill Steen, 1992

It is morning, the sun is not very high in the sky, and Gia (grandma) Rose sets out with some of her children, grandchildren, and great-grandchildren to the clay pit to dig the brown-orange clay they will need for their work as potters. After saying a prayer of thanksgiving to Clay-Old-Woman, the digging begins. Later, there will be food, stories, and plenty of time to splash and jump in the cool stream. Into the next days and weeks, the family prepares the clay, and then grownups and children get together and "laugh and talk while they coil, pinch, press, and smooth the clay to bowls and figures of animals and people." And still later, they gather again, this time to fire the pieces. The photos here are very good; you can clearly see the beauty of the land as well as the details of the pottery. The only thing I dislike here is the "history page," where the predation of the Spanish conquistadores is minimized. And, as in some of the other early volumes, a "legend" is shortened to fit neatly onto a two-page spread. My feeling is that Rina Swentzell may have argued against both of these.

Wittstock, Laura Waterman (Seneca), *Ininatig's Gift of Sugar: Traditional Native Sugarmaking*, color photographs by Dale Kakkak (Menominee), 1993

The story of Ininatig, the sugar maple, reminds people of the importance of the lifesaving maple sugar. Here, for two or three weeks each spring, an Anishinaabe elder named Gahgoonse, or Little Porcupine ("Porky" for short) holds his sugarbush camp by Lake Independence, Minnesota, where he teaches students from the city the serious business of collecting sap, and making maple syrup, candy, and sugar—and, of course, the giving of thanks for providing this most sacred of trees. The photos are very good; I especially like the expressions on the faces of the children tasting the syrup.

Yamane, Linda (Rumsien Ohlone), *Weaving a California Tradition: A Native American Basketweaver,* **color photographs by Dugan Aguilar (Maidu/Pit River/Northern Paiute), 1997**

This is my favorite of the series, in part because Linda is a friend, but mostly because she is an accomplished writer, artist and basketweaver, and she cares about every word and every stitch. Here, with Dugan Aguilar's well-composed and naturally lit photos, Linda clearly and interestingly conveys the plant gathering, preparation and weaving that eleven-year-old Carly Tex (Mono) learns from her family. Carly's interests include riding her bike, working with computers at school, hanging out with her friends, and playing flute and piano. But the heart of the book is in the details about traditional basketweaving, a demanding art that takes a lot of time and a lot of patience if it is to be done right. Here, Carly and her mother and aunties enjoy the good times of the gathering and the delicate precision of the work. It is clear that there is a comfortable relationship here among writer, photographer, and subjects: the writer is not following people around, taking notes; the photographer does not busy himself shooting fake scenarios.

"The World's Children" series, Carolrhoda/Lerner

This series contains twenty-two volumes, six of which are reviewed here. They are fairly similar in form and design. In each, the photos are well crafted, showing real children, real families, real communities and the land. But the content of most of these books is heavy on picture-postcard travelogue, especially around sacred sites the authors call "ruins," and weak on issues facing the peoples of the regions. Of this series, only *Grandchildren of the Lakota* is enthusiastically recommended.

Hermes, Jules, *Children of Guatemala,* **color photographs by the author, 1997**

This is an interestingly uneven book. It is not blatantly patronizing or ignorant; the author is really working at being

an observer, even though he constantly shows his frame of reference—downtown Minneapolis. For example, he says that "[t]he market offers a break from everyday work and gives friends a chance to catch up on the latest news." Jules! No, wait! The market is the goal! The object of the week's labors! The place to sell what you produce, to trade for essentials, to buy what you need to feed your family! Then, it is a place to hear the news, to catch up on important events, and, always, a place to socialize. It's not the mall!

On the other hand, Hermes is not afraid to discuss political situations, from the horrible 1990 massacre by the government in Santiago Atitlán, to the 80,000 Maya who have been brutally murdered by their own government since 1978, the longest "civil war" ever. He also talks about the lack of government support for public education and shows teachers and students picketing for quality education.

Hermes ought to have mentioned Rigoberta Menchú, the Mayan hero who won the Nobel Peace Prize for her unflagging quest to educate the world about Guatemala's genocide against its indigenous peoples. That would be the most logical extension for study from this beautifully photographed book.—*Judy Zalazar Drummond*

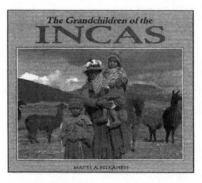

Pitkanen, Matti A., *The Grandchildren of the Incas,* **color photographs by the author, 1991**

The photographs here are stunning; they are of people being themselves, looking into the camera more with pride than with fear. They are a gritty look at how the Quechua and Aymara have been able to survive Spanish conquest. Many continue traditional ways, living in the mountains, herding sheep, llamas and alpacas, and of course, farming the rugged slopes of the Andes Mountains.

The text is, for the most part, clear and accurate, especially about farming and herding. I found it curious, though, that the author tells us that almost every man, woman, and child wears a hat, but doesn't mention the extreme cold and the need to protect the head from hypothermia, even though everyone wears sandals. He also mentions people leaving their mountain villages to work as servants in the cities to "make more opportunity for" themselves, but does not say that they are trying to help their families survive.

What bothers me most is the glossing over of the Spanish conquest. When Pitkanen says that "[n]ow the treasures are gone and so are many of the Inca's buildings," the brutal manner in which the Inca Empire was destroyed and the people forced into slavery, with the survivors thrust into abject poverty, comes off as trivial. To his credit, the author mentions that the Inca fought back and that, "[d]uring the last half of the 20th Century, the Quechua have begun to work together to make some changes. They have regained some of the land that was taken from them, and they are starting to demand that the people in government pay attention to their needs."

Overall, I would use the book, mainly for its realistic photos: an unromantic look at a people struggling for survival. But I would direct students to look up Tupac Amaru and read about indigenous resistance movements. They might learn a lot about what was done in the name of Christianity and the people who are still fighting for their lives.—*Judy Zalazar Drummond*

Rose, LaVera (Lakota), *Grandchildren of the Lakota*, color photographs by Cheryl Walsh Bellville, 1999

This is a beautiful photoessay by a Lakota writer and grandmother about the lives of the children in her own *tiospaye*—her extended family—and community and their place and importance in a particular Native society.

The history of the Lakota people—in two well-written pages—adequately touches on the issues of land theft, treaty abrogation, and residential schools. On another two-page spread, there is discussion of reservation life, tribal law, oral tradition and tribal schools. There is discussion of what is important to the people—traditional adoptions, generosity, honoring, and most of all, the children:

> The Lakota word for children is *wakanyeja*, or sacred being. Children were the most important gift from *Wakantanka*, the Great Spirit, to Lakota people. Children are the future of the Lakota Nation, so it is important to treat children with respect and kindness.

The luminous photos of land, family, and community, the faces of the children and the elders, are lovingly rendered. Throughout, this *unci's*—grandma's—words are just as much for her own children and grandchildren as for the children of strangers:

> When I look at my granddaughter Brittany I see the future of the Lakota people. My grandmother told me her story just as I have told my story to Brittany. One day, Brittany will pass her story on to her own grandchildren.

Grandchildren of the Lakota is the best portrayal I know of Lakota people today for younger children.

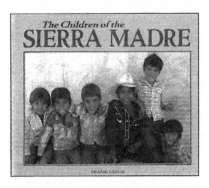

Staub, Frank, color photographs by the author:
***Children of the Sierra Madre*, 1996**
***Children of the Tlingit*, 1999**
***Children of Yucatán*, 1996**

In *Children of the Sierra Madre*, Staub highlights the U.S. influence on Latin America, using as an example the Tarahumara who live in the Sierra Madre region of Mexico near Chihuahua. He describes a strong class system in this region, ruled by the "white" Mexicans with the "mestizos" doing all the work, even though many of his photos show "white" Mexicans and mestizos doing just about same thing. I don't know, as a Chicana, I think we're all pretty much a mixture of whoever landed on our shores or stormed up our creeks.

Staub obscures the issues of the theft of Tarahumara land and impoverishment of the people by presenting fact as opinion: "[M]any Tarahumara want to live apart from Mexicans, whom they think of as intruders in their land." He describes the Tarahumara, rather than as the freedom fighters they have always been, regarded by most Mexicans with awe because of their steadfast opposition to colonialism, as merely "wanting to stick to the old ways."

In Staub's discussion of Tarahumara religion, he says, "Many Tarahumara have combined Catholicism with their traditional religious beliefs. They believe the Christian god is the same as their god, called Onoruame (Great Father) or Repa Beteame (He Who Lives Above)." Way wrong. Part of the Tarahumara's self-imposed isolation is to worship the gods they choose. The Catholic Church reluctantly had to let the mestizos as well as the indigenous population maintain their own gods, as long as they took the form of the Catholic ones. For example, the Virgin of Guadalupe, with her dark skin and close ties with the people, is not the Virgin Mary; she is the people's representation of Tonatzín, the goddess of home and hearth, and is only one of the aspects of Cuatlique, the Mother of the Gods. The church let that one slip by because forcing Guadalupe out would have caused mass revolt; it was easier to "say" she was the Virgin Mary. Every church in Mexico has at least one statue of the Virgin of Guadalupe, usually where Jesus should be; in small churches there often is no statue of Jesus at all. This book is terrible.—*Judy Zalazar Drummond*

Children of the Yucatán is more of the same—a travel guide rather than a children's book, highlighting the exotic in dress, food, marketplaces, and of course, "ruins." To the Maya, these "ruins" are temples, holy places that, despite the best efforts of the conquistadores and the Catholic Church, have endured.

Deeply embedded throughout the text is an attitude of paternalistic superiority and colonialist arrogance. Here is but one example out of many insulting passages:

> One reason the people of Yucatán treat their ancestors with such respect is that they have provided their grandchildren with an important source of income. People come from all over the world to see the wonderful stone structures the ancient Maya left behind. And when visitors come, they spend money on food, hotels, and souvenirs.

This is one of the worst racist, elitist, patronizing, and paternalistic attitudes toward another culture I have seen in my thirty-five years of teaching.—*Judy Zalazar Drummond*

In *Children of the Tlingit*, Staub justifies the cultural degradation and near annihilation brought about by the missionaries beginning in the late 1800s, after the U.S. took possession of Alaska:

> The missionaries saw that the Tlingit way of life was very different from their own. The Tlingit wore different clothes, ate different food, spoke a different language, performed different ceremonies, and held different spiritual beliefs. All of these differences led the missionaries to think that much of the Tlingit culture was evil.

These are not books I would give to any child—Indian or non-Indian—or any caring adult, except to use as bad examples.

A GUIDE FOR EVALUATING PHOTOESSAYS

Are the children described as "just like you" in spite of the ways that they are connected to their own cultures and traditions? Is there a comparison, stated or unstated, with white society as norm?

OR

Are the children described as living within their own cultural norms, with traditions and lifeways both old and new?

Are the children's everyday activities—school, play, home life—described as somehow inconsistent with what the author believes to be "traditional" life?

OR

Are the children's everyday activities seen as part of a continuum between old and new?

Are the children seen as functioning in a cultural vacuum? Do they participate in "ceremony" without cultural roots or context? Are the children and their families selected and exploited for their looks, for the way that they live, for their participation in their cultures? Is what is seen to be "exotic" about the children's lives emphasized, while their day-to-day lives are de-emphasized?

OR

Do the children have a real cultural connection with their elders, with their community? Are they seen as living their lives in a delicate balance of old and new?

Is the text contrived? Is there an overemphasis on "wisdom" and cultural "pride"? Are children always seen as being "proud" of their cultures and "happy" to be living "in two worlds"?

OR

Are children seen as bicultural, maybe bilingual, naturally going back and forth between the old and the new?

Are the children seen only with their nuclear families?

OR

Are they seen as an integral part of a large extended family, clan, community?

Where extended families are shown, is the emphasis on men and boys, while elders, women and girls are relegated to the background?

OR

Are all family members, especially elders, shown as living and working together in culturally appropriate roles?

Are children seen as "children of nature," instinctively hugging trees and talking to rocks?

OR

Are children seen as having been taught by their elders the sacred responsibility we all have toward all forms of life?

Is material poverty over-emphasized?

OR

Is material poverty placed in an honest cultural and historical context?

Is history distorted to de-emphasize the depredation of Native lands or desecration of sacred sites? Is colonialism described as "exploration"? Are reservations described as land "given" to Indian people "in exchange for" land surrendered?

OR

Is history put in the proper perspective? Are the issues of land theft, treaty abrogation, residential schools, discussed honestly?

Are Native peoples discussed in the past tense, even in the context of a contemporary photoessay? Is the past unconnected to the present?

OR

Is the continuity of cultures represented, with values, matters of the spirit, ways of seeing the world, as an outgrowth of the past and connected to the present and future?

Are sacred traditions and ways of seeing the world described as a flat, simple set of "beliefs," out of context and without background? Are they made to appear exotic? Are they trivialized?

OR

Are sacred traditions described as part of a sophisticated cosmology, rich in symbolism?

Are sacred aspects of a culture photographed or described in detail even when there are cultural prohibitions against doing this?

OR

Does the author stay within culturally proscribed limits?

Are the photos contrived? Is there a visual emphasis on regalia, sacred sites, ceremony? Are people dressed in regalia while doing ordinary things?

OR

Do the photos reflect real people living real lives?

Is the dialogue contrived? Is this a "first-person" account written by an outsider, pretending to be the child?

OR

Is the child actually speaking?

Is the perspective from outside the culture? Is the author just visiting for long enough to write a book?

OR

Is the perspective from inside the culture? Is the author of the Nation being portrayed? If not, is the author intimately familiar with the children, family, Nation being portrayed?

If the author is from outside the culture, is the author's own worldview superimposed upon that of the children and families? Are the author's own judgments apparent?

OR

Does the author have the capacity to look at a culture without making visual or textual judgments?

Is the vocabulary judgmental? Are there blatant or subtle overtones in the language? Are regalia called "costumes"? Are sacred sites called "ruins"? Are prayers called "chants"? Are the words "primitive" or "prehistoric" used anywhere in the book?

OR

Is the language respectful? Are appropriate terms used in naming and describing people, places, events and objects?

Is the art a mishmash of "generic Indian" designs to lure the potential customer to an "ethnic" or "multicultural" book?

OR

Is attention paid to accurate, appropriate, tribally specific design and color?

—*Naomi Caldwell, Debbie A. Reese, Beverly Slapin*

REVIEWS: BOOKS ABOUT DREAMCATCHERS

Dreamcatchers have become the ubiquitous "symbol" of Native culture in non-Indian schools and homes. They are often imported from many parts of Asia as well as Mexico and sold through catalogs and at "ethnic art" stores. They are even sold at powwows by Indian people forced to usurp traditional items from one another simply to survive.

Traditionally, dreamcatchers were pretty things hung over cradleboards for babies to look at and play with. The making of dreamcatchers, and the finding and processing of materials to do so, were used to teach young people practical skills such as building wigwams, fishing weirs and snowshoes. It was only in the late 1800s, when white encroachment forced Indian peoples into impossible situations, that dreamcatchers started to take on heavier significance.

Children's books about dreamcatchers have become practically an industry of its own, running the gamut from crystal-woogly spirituality to stories demonstrating how-to-feel-good-about-appropriating-Indian-arts.

Lois Beardslee contributed the review for *The Dreamcatcher: Keep your happy dreams—forever!* and Barbara Potter contributed the review for *Dreamcatcher* by Audrey Osofsky.—*Beverly Slapin*

Brook, Jasmine, and McCabe, Lianne, *The Dreamcatcher: Keep your happy dreams—forever!* **Illustrated by Helen Cann. Smithmark (1999). 29 pages, color illustrations; grades 2-4**

This book's creators try to give the impression that these are actual Native American stories and that the removable dreamcatcher that comes in the cover of this book is authentic as well. The images and text have about the same kind of authenticity that *Little Black Sambo* has to African-American culture.

The stories are preceded by a jumbled explanation about dreamcatchers that implies that Indians are just one giant ethnic group with one language. The stories themselves are basically fantasies that anyone can somehow become Indian by grabbing onto a bunch of "power" baubles and clichés.

The choices of topic and language are offensive: "Sam was River Creek's living legend, the last of the Native Americans in these parts…" "[B]eside her was a boy, his hair as jet black as his horse." "[The shaman] carried a staff and his face was as lined and cracked as the sunscorched earth…" Native people in America today are not relics, we do not all have hair like a horse, and we don't fall back on a bunch of wrinkled old hippie-trippie shamans to make day-to-day decisions in our lives.

The book's imagery is clichéd and damaging. The repetitive use of headbands, buckskin fringe and the cross-legged sitting style in the depiction of Native people sends the message to young readers that we can't possibly be real Indians without them. The dreamcatchers themselves are boorish and ugly. We most certainly do not hang lockets, pinecones, peacock feathers, candy, photos, pacifiers, plastic flowers, and other miscellany from them. One illustration shows an ancient Egyptian-style frieze-like mishmash of geometric designs, arrows, thunderclouds, unidentifiable mammals with large canine teeth, a Southeast Asian cobra in a Boddhisatva sheltering pose, and a liquor bottle! A liquor bottle? How could anyone possibly think that alluding to socioeconomic and cultural dysfunction is an acceptable form of cultural presentation? What place could this possibly have in a children's book—except to promote the insidious images of Indians as alcoholics? Who could even remotely benefit from such slander? This is a horrid little book.

Farmer, Bonnie, *Isaac's Dreamcatcher,* **illustrated by Anouk Pérusse-Bell. Lobster Press (2001). Unpaginated, color illustrations; preschool-grade 2**

Five-year-old Isaac is saddened by a bad dream he had the night before, so his kindergarten teacher, Miss Louise, tries to dispel his fears. When her initial effort fails, she shows him how to fashion a dreamcatcher from pipe-cleaners, string, colored beads and feathers. While they work, Miss Louise (who is Native American) tells Isaac (and by extension, the young reader) all about dream-catchers. Isaac takes the dreamcatcher home, and it works its magic. No more bad dreams. The author, according to the jacket copy, "has been enchanted by dreamcatchers and their mystique for many years," and makes and sells them at crafts fairs. An inaccurate "historical note" and instructions for making dream-catchers using simple craft materials complete this book. This contrived little story, a vehicle for the author to showcase her fascinating avocation, is worsened by the stylized art that exaggerates the supposed physical characteristics of people of color. Not recommended.

"Finder," *A Story of the Dreamcatcher*, illustrated by Mona Woodard. Mother Bird Books (1996). Unpaginated, b/w illustrations; preschool-grade 2

This is supposedly how the dreamcatcher came to be. A long time ago, the children started having bad dreams. The parents didn't know what to do, so they consulted a shaman, who went to counsel with the spirits. He did this by sitting down cross-legged (you know, "Indian style") and falling asleep, whereupon the spirits, also called elements—earth, air, fire and water—couldn't figure out how to help, either. Fortunately, Grandmother Spider was listening, and she wove—a dreamcatcher! So everyone started making dreamcatchers "and so, at last, Great Spirit looked into the dreams of the children and smiled!" This preposterous little story is helped neither by the ugly black-and-white drawings nor by the ridiculous poems that follow.

McCain, Becky, *Grandmother's Dreamcatcher*, illustrated by Stacey Schuett. Albert Whitman (1998). Unpaginated, color illustrations; grades 2-up; Ojibwe

Told in the first person, this is about a child, ten or eleven maybe, who goes to stay with her grandma for a week while her parents look for a home near dad's new job. Grandma lives "way out in the woods by a lake," and Kim is afraid to be without her parents. She has nightmares. So Grandma makes her a dreamcatcher and tells her the dreamcatcher story. It works. Grams and Kim go fishing, make dreamcatchers, parents come back, all is well again.

Why does the author think that an Ojibwe child would be afraid to spend a week at her grandma's house? And doesn't she think that an Ojibwe child, with two Ojibwe parents and an Ojibwe grandma, would already know what a dreamcatcher is?

The directions for making a dreamcatcher at the end of the book turn Ojibwe tradition into simple arts-and-crafts activities for non-Native youngsters who then think they are doing something "Indian."

The author's probable good intentions aside, this book fails because it is an outsider's perspective pretending to be an Indian one.

Maynard, Meredy, *Dreamcatcher*. Polestar (1995). 137 pages, grades 5-up; Mohawk

This young-adult-coming-of-age-novel-with-an-Indian-theme-featuring-dreamcatchers (a sub-sub-sub-sub genre, I suppose) has a mixed-blood Mohawk girl in search of her cultural identity enthusiastically teaching a white boy all things Indian (including False Faces, vision quests,

Chief Seattle's speech, and dreamcatchers), so that he can come to terms with the death of his father. The superficial and usually incorrect "facts" interspersed throughout (e.g., the Ojibwe used dreamcatchers to catch bad dreams, and a matrilineal society means that each clan was ruled by a matron) combine with terrible writing to produce a book to be seriously avoided.

Osofsky, Audrey, *Dreamcatcher*, illustrated by Ed Young. Orchard (1992). Unpaginated, color illustrations; grades 1-3; Ojibwe

This is a saccharine bedtime story set in the author's romanticized version of the long ago "land of the Ojibway." The story is yet another version of how Indian families use dreamcatchers to protect their babies from bad dreams. A baby naps in its cradleboard, while all around family members go about their daily activities. Then "the sun goes home to sleep" and the dreamcatcher is hung on the cradleboard. Of course, the dreamcatcher, made by big sister, works as it is supposed to and the baby sleeps peacefully, entertained by good dreams.

The illustrations portray an idealized if not downright stereotypical "Indian life"—you know, farming, weaving, fishing and playing. One illustration shows big sister carefully making the dreamcatcher. She holds it in her left hand, a hand that has six fingers! (Why did Young do that?) Of course, the father wears fringed buckskin and the women wear their hair in two braids accessorized with a headband.

Cultural stereotypes aside, this story might set a quiet bedtime mood for a child if it weren't for the horrific sequence of nightmares to illustrate how "dark dreams" are "caught like flies" in the dreamcatcher. I cannot imagine what would possibly cause a baby, an Indian baby, to dream of a raggedy man thumping through the dark with a glowing birchbark mask, or a bony, long ghost leg with a moccasin stuffed with straw sneaking into the wigwam. This impossible dream sequence comes straight out of a white author's—rather than an Indian baby's—fantasy. Not recommended.

REVIEWS: BOOKS ABOUT KOKOPELLI

Bryant, Kathleen, *Kokopelli's Gift*, illustrated by Michelle Tsosie Sisneros (Santa Clara, Navajo, Mission). Kiva Publishing (2003). 32 pages, color illustrations; grades 3-6; Pueblo

Haley, Gail E., *Kokopelli, Drum in Belly*, illustrated by the author. Filter Press (2003). 32 pages, color illustrations; grades 2-up; Diné (Navajo)

Sterns, Michael, *Kokopelli & the Butterfly*, illustrated by Gayle Deal and Joseph V. Cioffi. Kichita Productions (2000). 64 pages, color illustrations; grades 1-3

These three children's books about Kokopelli, all written by cultural outsiders, will undoubtedly appeal to people who collect Kokopelli lamps, Kokopelli coasters, Kokopelli napkin rings, Kokopelli-printed toilet paper, and the like.

Kokopelli & the Butterfly, according to the jacket copy, is "a love story that takes place in tribal times." Now, which "tribal times" are these? Kokopelli is portrayed as a stud of a human being, like Disney's Tarzan maybe, only darker and with a slightly larger loincloth. Kokopelli travels all over the world, teaching the "tribes" all about "environmentalism, appreciation of nature's beauty, kindness to animals, tolerance of diversity, and peaceful conflict resolution." When he finds a beautiful butterfly imprisoned in a cage, Kokopelli defies the "tribe" and frees it. Beautiful butterfly transforms into beautiful woman. Surrounded by beautiful animals, "Samsara" and Kokopelli go off into beautiful sunset and live beautifully ever after. Sigh.

In *Kokopelli's Gift*, the people are suffering from drought. Along comes Kokopelli, whom the villagers distrust. He plays on his flute a song that sounds like a canyon wren, and a child offers him a gift of some small stones. Soon the villagers are also offering gifts along with their request for return of the rain. So Kokopelli produces a singing toad and a singing locust, plays "the song of rain," and tells the villagers to sing and dance along: "Make your footsteps pound the earth like raindrops!" They do. "Their footsteps pattered over the ground.... The flute howled like a fierce breeze." (How does a flute howl and what is a fierce breeze?) Then comes "crackling thunder and howling wind" and—rain! Kokopelli then disappears, and "as the wind gusted toward them, they could hear the faint notes of a flute." According to the art, the story is set in an "ancient" time when people had horses and wore ribbon shirts and highly decorated cotton print fabrics.

Kokopelli, Drum in Belly is another "ancient" Native American tale, this time ascribed to a Diné creation story. Here, Kokopelli's mesmerizing flute music accompanied by the drumbeats emanating from his belly convince the Ant People to follow him out of the Dark World, up through four other worlds, until they reach the "Green World," where their bodies shrivel up and they become the First People. On the way, Kokopelli teaches them about growing food and being nice to each other. I'm not sure what is supposed to be represented by Haley's bold acrylic paintings: "ant people" wearing minidresses and feather-like antennae stuck into headbands become "human people" with antennae-like feathers held in place by burden baskets. And, despite the author's "wishes to express her deep admiration to the Navajo people for preserving Kokopelli's story," Kokopelli is not part of the Diné pantheon.

The cosmology of the peoples called "Pueblo" is complex. All of the Katsinam are spirits on differing levels; there's a whole network of where each one stands in the hierarchy. Traditional people who practice the rituals know this; it's generally kept secret. Lois Beardslee, whose Masters thesis focused on Kokopelli, said that "the Kokopelli that appears in the popular icons was manufactured by Elsie Clews Parsons and Florence Hawley in the 1930s and has been misappropriated ever since; in terms of Native American iconography, it's one of the biggest hoaxes of the 20th Century."

A Hopi storyteller whose name one might recognize right away if I said it and has asked me not to say it, told me this: "In our traditional beliefs, Kokopelli is a Katsina of fertility, he is a deity. He does not go around playing a flute; he's carrying a cane or rod. And he's not a 'humpback,' he's carrying a burden. Whenever he appears in our rituals, he is copulating. When the Katsinam come out, he goes around trying to hump people. Grown men run from him! It would be more appropriate to put his image on a bottle of Viagra or on a condom vending machine than in a children's book."

If one could choose a mini-genre of children's books with the most abysmally, stupefyingly offensive stereotypes, this would be it.—*Beverly Slapin*

(Thank-you to Lois Beardslee.)

WHEN I LOOK IN YOUR EYES OF DARKNESS

Highwater, Jamake, *Eyes of Darkness*. Lothrop, Lee & Shepherd (1985). 191 pages; grades 7-up; Dakota

"Tell me what I see when I look in your eyes.
Is it you, baby, or just a brilliant disguise?"
(Bruce Springsteen)

"If imitation is the sincerest form of flattery,
plagiarism must be the sincerest form of imitation."
(Anonymous)

In *Indian Boyhood* (1902), Charles Eastman/Ohiyesa tells some traditional stories he heard in childhood from a Santee elder. He writes,

> I will try to repeat some of [Smoky Day's] favorite narratives as I heard them from his own lips. I went to him one day with a piece of tobacco and an eagle-feather,... hoping for the privilege of hearing him tell some of the brave deeds of our people in remote times.

Then, having given credit where credit is due, he recounts the stories. Eastman himself is the subject of a note in the front matter of Jamake Highwater's young adult novel, *Eyes of Darkness*:

> *Eyes of Darkness* is a work of fiction, but its historical perspective is derived from the life and works of Charles Alexander Eastman. To all such sources I offer my acknowledgements.

This is a remarkable piece of understatement. It would be hard to find a work of fiction more deeply indebted to Eastman's life, work and "historical perspective." Every chapter of *Eyes of Darkness* contains elements of either *Indian Boyhood* or *From the Deep Woods to Civilization* (1916), autobiographical works about Eastman's childhood and early career as a doctor. By "elements" I mean not only events, but phrases, sentences, even whole paragraphs, some at best only minimally paraphrased—without once mentioning either source. A parallel reading of the three books reveals the full extent of Highwater's "debt" to Eastman.

Eastman (1858-1939) grew up in a traditional Santee environment, which he describes in his first book, *Indian Boyhood*. Called Hakadah at birth, he was given the name Ohiyesa, Winner, after playing a key role in an important lacrosse victory. *Indian Boyhood* ends with the return of his father, who had been presumed dead for many years but was actually serving time in prison, where he had converted to Christianity. Eastman's eighth book, *From the Deep Woods to Civilization*, begins with Ohiyesa's departure from traditional life to join his father in the "civilized" world. Renamed Charles Alexander Eastman, he attended Dartmouth, became a medical doctor, and moved to Pine Ridge, South Dakota, to begin his practice. There he met and married Elaine Goodale, a white woman who was supervisor of Indian Schools in the Dakotas and Nebraska. Eastman spent much of his life serving as a "translater" for Native people to whites, writing a number of informational and autobiographical books about Native life. *Indian Boyhood* and *Deep Woods* are among the few written first-hand accounts of Indian life in the late 1800s.

When Jamake Highwater's *Eyes of Darkness* was published in 1985, it received positive reviews from the book critics, and was a 1985 Children's Notable Book in the Social Studies. Though out of print, it is still found on young adult multicultural booklists.

While Smoky Day's contributions to *Indian Boyhood* are set off with quotation marks, showing respect for both source and reader, readers of *Eyes of Darkness* are clearly meant to get the impression that the prose is Highwater's own—in fact, the front flap of the dust jacket calls *Eyes of Darkness* a "brilliant, original novel."

Eyes of Darkness may be a novel, but it is hardly original. If anything about it is "brilliant," it's the writer's slick job of appropriating Eastman's material. It's not that Highwater is skillful at disguising the fact that most of the effort is not his own. He sometimes paraphrases so closely that few words differ from Eastman's account, but his paraphrasing is often clumsy, and he makes a number of puzzling changes and omissions. His great triumph seems to have been correctly judging and capitalizing on the public's lack of awareness of Charles Eastman.

The beginning and end of *Eyes of Darkness* owe much to *Deep Woods*, in which Eastman recounts his experiences of 1890-91 on and near the Pine Ridge Reservation. These chapters frame the rest of the novel, which tells of the protagonist's childhood and adolescence, taking heavily from *Indian Boyhood* and to a lesser extent, *Deep Woods*. Chapter 2 of *Eyes of Darkness* is titled, "Hakadah, the Pitiful Last"—as is Eastman's first chapter—and the similarities do not end there. Highwater's methods of disguise are also apparent in his chapter "First Offering," which parallels Chapter 4 of *Indian Boyhood*, "Hakadah's First Offering."

Though most of *Indian Boyhood* is narrated in the first person, Eastman wrote "Hakadah's First Offering" in the third person. He recalls when Uncheedah, his grandmother, announced that he must give up "one of your belongings—whichever is dearest to you" for his first offering to the Great Mystery. The boy was not sure how to proceed, Eastman relates, but with growing awareness of the gravity of the situation, suggested sacrificing such important possessions as his paints, or even his pony. But his grandmother felt she knew the most appropriate offering to the Great Mystery: "his friend and companion," his "splendid black dog," Ohitika. Since Hakadah did not catch on, Uncheedah eventually had to tell him, "You will be pleased to give up the dearest thing you have for your first offering. You must give up Ohitika. He is brave; and you, too, are brave. He will not fear death; you will bear his loss bravely."

Eastman says Hakadah was at first unable to speak, but remembering how a man was expected to act, "[h]e swallowed two or three big mouthfuls of heartache and the little warrior was master of the situation." Gaining permission to prepare the dog in private, the boy hugged Ohitika tightly and sang his death song, drawing consciously upon what he had learned about how a man should feel and behave. After carefully applying red paint to Ohitika, the boy blackened his own face in mourning. Then, Eastman writes:

> Hakadah came out of the teepee with his face looking like an eclipsed moon, leading his beautiful dog, who was even handsomer than ever with the red touches on his specks of white. It was now Uncheedah's turn to struggle with the storm and burden in her soul. But the boy was emboldened by the people's admiration of his bravery, and did not shed a tear. As soon as she was able to speak, the loving grandmother said, "Not so, my young brave, not so! You must not mourn for your first offering. Wash your face and then we will go." The boy obeyed, submitted Ohitika to Wacoota, and walked off with his grandmother and Wahchewin.

In rewriting this event, Highwater makes liberal use of Eastman's text, but instead of the "little warrior," the protagonist is now sixteen. As in *Indian Boyhood*, Uncheedah tells the boy he must sacrifice what is dearest to him. In dialogue much like Eastman's, Yesa gradually comes to understand that he must sacrifice his beloved friend, the dog (in this case the yellow dog), Wabeda. Yesa says he will paint his dog for the offering. While his beautiful younger cousin Oesedah looks on, Yesa sings his dog's death song, hugging the dog and trying not to weep. When he finishes painting Wabeda, he paints his own face. Next:

> Yesa now came out of the lodge with his black face looking like an eclipsed moon, leading his beautiful dog, who was handsomer than ever with the red designs painted upon his yellow body. It was Uncheedah's turn to struggle with the storm of tears that burdened her. But the young man was encouraged by the people's admiration for his bravery as he and his dog walked through the encampment, surrounded by whispering men and women.

> As soon as Uncheedah was able to speak, the loving grandmother murmured, "No, my young brave, it is not permitted for you to mourn for your first offering. Go to the creek and wash the charcoal off your face, and then we will go." Yesa silently obeyed. He left his precious dog with Mysterious Medicine and walked off with his grandmother and Wahchewin.

Hakadah's first offering is a significant step toward becoming a man with a particular place among the people. Eastman's account of this event has considerable emotional impact in Hakadah's gradual movement toward full understanding of what is expected of him; in Uncheedah's inner struggle to stand firm in her sympathy for the child; and in the boy's at-first reluctant acceptance of what he must do.

While Highwater relies on Eastman's plotting and phrasing, he turns up the emotional decibel level. The beautiful and innocent Oesedah weeps openly several times as the sacrifice proceeds, eventually running off to cry by herself. Complicating the mix is Yesa's deep attraction to the girl, who is the daughter of the woman who assists Uncheedah. In Highwater's book, the lodge is very crowded. (Oesedah, an imaginative and playful younger cousin, is mentioned in *Indian Boyhood*, but not in connection with the sacrifice of Ohitika, and never with amorous undertones.) Where Eastman says Hakadah "was emboldened by the people's admiration of his bravery," Highwater adds the image of Yesa's walking through a crowd of whispering villagers. But nowhere is the substitution of the operatic for the understated more apparent than in the contrast between the final scenes from the two "First Offering" stories.

In Eastman's account, when Wahchewin brings Ohikita's body back to the cave where the boy and his grandmother wait, Uncheedah scatters paints and tobacco, and they stand a few moments.

> Then she drew a deep breath and began her prayer to the Great Mystery: "O, Great Mystery, we hear thy voice in the rushing waters below us! We hear thy whisper in the great oaks above! Our spirits are refreshed with thy breath from within this cave. Oh, hear our prayer! Behold this little boy and bless him! Make him a warrior and hunter as great as thou didst make his father and grandfather." And with this prayer the little warrior had completed his first offering.

There the episode ends. No so in Highwater's version:

> The old woman drew a deep breath and began to intone in an echoing whisper her prayer to the Great Mystery. "O, Great Mystery, we hear your voice in the rushing water below us! We hear your whisper in the great oaks of these mountains! Our spirits are refreshed with your life-giving breathing that fills this cave. O, hear our prayer! Behold this young man and bless his life! Make him strong and wise as you also made his father and his grandfather before him!" With this prayer the tears finally leaped into the grandmother's eyes, and she knelt on the earth, gazing at the body of Wabeda, while Yesa opened his mouth and shouted out a long, desperate cry of victory. For a moment he saw the Moon hanging massive and heavy in the darkness of the cave, but then it vanished, and with it died the last fragile innocence of his childhood. In some strange and inexplicable way he had been transformed by the greatness of his sacrifice. And now something new and powerful filled his heart.

As he does so often throughout *Eyes of Darkness*, Highwater makes the emotional drama explicit and belabored—the echoing whisper, the leaping tears, the victory cry, the lovely cousin who has run off weeping. Some may feel this increases the impact of the story. Others may find Eastman's account sufficiently dramatic, if quieter. Either way, the story is still not Highwater's.

Eyes of Darkness is a disguise—flimsy, but somehow successful. As Forrest (Asa) Carter with *The Education of Little Tree*, Highwater seems to have had a joke at the expense of the reading public. It could be argued that any work of fiction is an attempt to trick the audience, at least temporarily, into believing that a story could be real. Still, there is a difference between creating a story and plundering another writer's work.

Why did he do it and how did he get away with this sincerest of imitations? Those two questions hung in the air throughout my parallel reading experience.

If Highwater had indeed created a "brilliant, original novel," why does his publicity now state that the book is "based on the life of Charles Eastman"? There is a great difference between acknowledging the source of one's "historical perspective" and saying that the book is based on someone's life story.

If, on the other hand, *Eyes of Darkness* is based on the life of Charles Eastman/Ohiyesa, why did Highwater change the names of key characters, including the protagonist (!)—while Hakadah remains Hakadah, Ohiyesa becomes Yesa, Dr. Charles Alexander Eastman becomes Dr. Alexander East and Elaine Goodale becomes Elaina Goode—and insert imagined events, motives and emotions while eliminating others? Why didn't Highwater write a biography of Charles Eastman using Eastman's own words—in quotes?

Perhaps more troubling than why he did it is the fact that the disguise went undetected for so many years. How could one man's Indian boyhood become another man's acclaimed novel? If he thought no one would recognize his stripmining of Eastman's autobiographies—he was pretty much right. *Eyes of Darkness* is on a number of "multicultural" reading lists that feature nothing by Eastman. And that is a shame, because Eastman's accounts of his own life are much better reading.—*Jean Paine Mendoza*

PAUL GOBLE

There goes that white guy
Paul Goble, telling another
story about me...
My attorney will Sioux.

Paul Goble has written and illustrated nearly thirty titles, all but one based on the lives and stories of the Plains peoples, and has received praise and awards for them, even a Caldecott. Some of his graphics have been reproduced in Native publications.

In the beginning at least, there seemed to be some understanding, and some humility about the fact that he was venturing into a world that he could never more than partially comprehend. In his first book, *Red Hawk's Account of Custer's Last Battle* (1969), Goble said "thank you" to "Lakota Isnala" for help with the book and stated that "what is wrong in this book is due to my lack of understanding." In *Death of the Iron Horse* (1986), he said,

> Like everything else to do with war, the derailment [of the train] had sad and unpleasant aspects.
> But from this distance in time, we can see that the Cheyennes were simply fighting for their lives.

Whether Goble has reacted to an increasing insistence in the Native community that it is time for us to tell our own stories, or at the very least that they should be retold accurately, or to criticism of himself specifically is unclear, but as a young friend put it, "Man, something happened to him!" His work has come with increasingly longer lists of references, mostly to ethnographic texts from the late 19th- and early 20th Centuries, as a sort of justification. Lately, Goble has been specializing in Iktomi stories—Iktomi, for those who may not know, being the Lakota "trickster" figure. The introductory material in these books, "About Iktomi," gives the impression that Goble has come to believe in his entitlement to do pretty much what he wants to with any of our stories, and that the result should be beyond criticism. In *Iktomi Loses His Eyes*, a "Note to the Reader" tells us that "there is no 'authentic' version of these stories. The only rule in telling them is to include certain basic themes."

Iktomi is, of course, much more than the fool he appears to be in these particular stories. Goble does acknowledge this in his introductions, but he also says—in *Iktomi and the Coyote* (1998)—"nowadays he [Iktomi] has been relegated mostly to his Trickster role, his other aspects having been forgotten amid modern world pressures." Whatever that may mean. In *Iktomi and the Berries* (1989), Goble gives Iktomi these words: "I don't like it—that white guy, Paul Goble, is telling stories about me again...." In *Iktomi and the Ducks* (1990), it's "There goes that white guy, Paul Goble, telling another story about me....My attorney will Sioux." By *Iktomi and the Buzzard* (1994), it's a diatribe:

> Hi, kids! I'm Iktomi—and proud of it! Don't read this book. That white guy, Paul Goble, is stealing
> my stories and making money off of them. This book is ethnically insensitive material about me;
> its racial epithets just bring me into contempt, ridicule, and disrepute....

From *Iktomi and the Coyote* (1998): "[O]nly Native Americans can tell Native American stories. So, let's not have anything to do with them. Huh?" And finally, in *Iktomi Loses His Eyes* (1999):

> This is more lies about me by that white guy....I've warned you about him before. And he doesn't give me a penny of his royalties. So tell your librarians to ban the book. Huh? You're cool kids! I love yer!

"Cool," as opposed to those Indians, who may have begun to think their stories might be their own to tell—or not—as they choose? The words I have quoted so far all come from introductory material—out of Iktomi's mouth, of course. In the stories themselves, there are little asides in smaller print meant, according to the author, to reveal Iktomi's thoughts:

> I won't take the car today. I look like a real chief. I AM a real chief! My warbonnet and trailer (Eagle-friendly feathers made of dyed domestic goose)...My otter fur (imitation) necklace with mirrors... (*Iktomi and the Coyote*)

> I'm an elder, so I must be wise. (*Iktomi and the Coyote*)

> I'm a great hunter—it's in my ancestral blood. I wish I had brought my AK-47. (*Iktomi and the Coyote*)

> Today I'm getting in touch with my subconscious....My eagle feathers...My roach...My face paint.... (*Iktomi Loses His Eyes*)

A final illustration from *Iktomi and the Buzzard* shows Iktomi, rather the worse for wear, spotting an eagle feather lying on the ground and thinking: "An eagle feather! I should make another dance outfit."

We are supposed to believe that all this is meant to be funny. Maybe you have to be Indian to understand just how offensive, insulting and mean-spirited it is—or maybe it is possible to see that it is not just Iktomi that Paul Goble is making fun of anymore. And I might mention in passing that if you have eagle feathers on your dance regalia, they are meant never to touch the ground. If they do, there is a specific procedure for retrieving them.

It is not about the money. Although Native people might be forgiven a certain amount of resentment toward the people who are making such a tidy living off other people's lives, that is not the point. How many other ways are there to say it? Non-Indian people have no more "right" to take our stories and make of them what they will than they did to take our land, our sacred objects, our children, and the bones of our beloved dead. In a self-serving autobiography written for children, *Hau Kola—Hello Friend*, Goble tells us that as a child in England, "Always my greatest interest was in everything related to Indian people," and that "An Indian lady [unnamed] once wrote to me: 'I've always thought the *wanagi* (spirits) are close to you. Some of your illustrations reveal that the ancestors come to visit you in your dreams.'" Paul Goble, so he says, has been befriended by Native people. He should be ashamed. His work has come to be a mockery of the "everything related to Indian people" that he professes to so admire.

It is neither possible—nor desirable—in this space, to comment on every work by this author, but there is one further thing that needs to be mentioned. The story of White Buffalo Calf Woman, Pte San Win, is one of the central mysteries of the people commonly known as the "Sioux"—Dakota, Lakota, Nakota. Among Her gifts was the Calf Pipe, a gift that has become an essential part of the ceremonies of many more Nations than one. This is the story that Goble has attempted, in an act of supreme arrogance, to "retell" in *The Legend of the White Buffalo Woman* (1998). He has taken as his source the first chapter of Joseph Epes Brown's *The Sacred Pipe: Black Elk's Account of the Seven Rites of the Oglala Sioux*[1], and "framed it with other related myths" [sic]. The author's note attempts to "explain" "this most important of all Lakota sacred legends" by saying that the "Great Spirit....caused a white buffalo cow calf to be changed into a woman, who gave the pipe" so that the "people could pray and commune with him." That is his version. Goble speculates as to the time frame during which this may have happened, suggesting the late 1600s, "but this may be a too recent date"—hedging his bets, one presumes—and tells us that the Pipe was given to the Sans Arcs. Well, it is true that they are part of the Lakota Nation, but the Sans Arcs are not Oglalas. Goble says that he has "not illustrated the Sacred Calf Pipe, of which no likeness should be made," thus leaving the reader free to conclude that he has seen it, while never actually having said so. Very slick, if I do say.

The story, as set down in the first chapter of Brown's book, is simple enough to be entirely comprehensible to children, with very little editing. Certainly there was no need to "frame" it with any "other related myths." "End of the Old World," "The Nation is Born Again," "Sadness of War," and Goble's tacked-on, and entirely spurious, ending to the sacred Woman's visit, have nothing whatsoever, *at all*, to do with the story. Goble concludes with this whole riff about why She is called White Buffalo Woman, and how "her Buffalo People gave the red stone [pipestone] so everyone could make pipes." Apart from all other considerations, I do believe that in most spiritual practices it is understood that not "everyone" can make a sacred object.

The song that White Buffalo Calf Woman sang as She approached the camp of the people is this, as written down in Brown:

> With visible breath
> I am walking
> this nation
> I walk toward
> And
> my voice is heard
> I am walking
> with visible breath
> I am walking
> this scarlet relic
> I am walking.[2]

Goble's version reads:

> With visible breath, I am walking,
> Toward this Nation, I walk,
> And my voice is heard as I walk.
> With visible breath, I am walking,
> With this red pipe, I walk.

How is this better? If Goble wanted to do something useful, he could have explained the significance of "breath" in Lakota belief.

A starred review in *Publishers Weekly* called this book "a fluid retelling....Ever sensitive to his audience, Goble handles difficult subjects with finesse...his message is one of hope for reconciliation among people...."

In the author's note to the Bison edition of *Brave Eagle's Account of the Fetterman Fight* (1992), Goble said this:

> I wrote the book for Indian children because I wanted them to know about and to feel proud of the courage of their ancestors. I have written all of my books primarily with Indian children in mind....

Assuming, apparently, along with many anthropologists, that we have so lost our traditions, cultures and histories that we must be taught them by a white person.

There is no reconciliation for us to the things that have been done to us, to the things that are believed about us, to the fact that, even now, there is nothing of ours that is not fair game. If some white person wants it, there is nothing precious or sacred enough not to be touched.

Is it necessary to say, in the 21st Century, that this is not right?—*Doris Seale*

NOTES

1   University of Oklahoma Press, reissued in 1989.

2   From the foreword by Arthur Amiotte in *The Gift of the Sacred Pipe: Based on Black Elk's Account of the Seven Rites of the Oglala Sioux, as originally recorded and edited by Joseph Epes Brown*, edited and illustrated by Vera Louise Drysdale. University of Oklahoma Press, reissued in 1995.

The Buffalo Skull

You've been walking for hours
when you first see it.
It glows beside a rutted road
where Red River wagons
filled with the slaughter
of the northern herd
passed creaking, carrying
hides and then rasping
of Slota fiddles.

You thought your eyes
had mapped these hills,
that even the falcon
in the cottonwood's crest
was a landmark.
But the rocks beneath
your feet remember
Lakota and Shyleh
Absaroke and Arapaho,
and those whose names
are now unknown
with mammoth and ground sloth
and giant lion.
Reaching out both hands
you grasp the horns.
Your palms freeze to them,
the way a finger
cleaves to an ax blade
at 40 below.

Sun paints bone red,
wind whips your hair,
the prairie dives into your skin.

And there is time
for one deep breath
before Thunder parts your eyelids.

—*Joseph Bruchac* (Abenaki)

REVIEWS: BOOKS ABOUT BUFFALO

The buffalo were very important to Native peoples, especially those of the Plains. Deliberate slaughter of the buffalo, a government tactic to defeat the Indians, was very successful: Not only was the livelihood taken away but something that had been of deep spiritual significance was destroyed. To this day, a special relationship remains between Native peoples and the Buffalo Nation. Because of the hard work and commitment of several tribal organizations, some buffalo herds have returned to Indian Country. The misunderstanding of our relationship with the buffalo is the basis for most of the books reviewed here.

Beverly Slapin contributed the reviews for *Buffalo Before Breakfast* and *Buffalo Days.—Doris Seale*

Brodsky, Beverly, *Buffalo: with Selections from Native American Song-Poems illustrated with original paintings*, illustrated by the author. Marshall Cavendish (2003). 37 pages, color paintings

Brodsky tells us that the "roots" of this book lie in her visits to museums, "where I gazed at ancient paintings of buffalo by Shoshone, Sioux, and Cheyenne artists."

The resultant art is reminiscent of the work of Leonard Baskin, and Fritz Scholder, with maybe a touch of Picasso, and some of her paintings are clearly based on Catlin, Bodmer, and Alfred Jacob Miller. Brodsky does not make clear whether the two pages of Native objects—parfleche, buffalo robe, shield—are copies of the actual objects or products of her imagination. I am inclined to the latter. Her "Crow Parfleche Made from Buffalo Rawhide" is a rectangular box and her "Sioux Spoon Made from a Buffalo Horn" would be impossible either to use as a dipper or to eat from. The inclusion of "Cheyenne Ghost Dance Moccasins" is at the least insensitive, since the only way something like that could have been acquired was from a dead person—"souvenirs" collected by the soldiers after the Wounded Knee Massacre. And the "Sioux Buffalo Hide Tipi Cover" must surely be a work of fantasy, with its top-to-bottom, side-to-side, whirling— sunflower? supernova? or what?

There are some serious problems with Brodsky's attributions of the "song-poems."

"Clear the way/In a sacred manner I come" is referenced to Diane Hoyt-Goldsmith's *Buffalo Days*. It is not there. Brodsky cites "Bear Eagle, contemporary Teton Sioux Lakota" as the author, but a friend believes that it comes from the White Buffalo Calf Woman cycle, which had been my first thought. Whatever it is, it is *not* about "the return of a rich culture from the past," Brodsky's interpretation.

"He! They have come back racing./Why, they say there is to be/a Buffalo Hunt over here,/Make arrows! Make arrows!/says the Father, says the Father." Brodsky's gloss on this:

A scouting party on a journey to find the buffalo might have sung this song as they raced back to camp. Perhaps a shaman also sang this song during a New Moon ceremony. The lines explain that the Creator, or Great Spirit, wants arrows to be made. The Sioux formed arrows from the buffalo's hind leg. The dried the heavy sinews and cut them up into arrow points.

This is not any of those things. This is a Ghost Dance song. Brodsky got it from James Mooney's *The Ghost Dance Religion and the Sioux Outbreak of 1890*. That is her reference. Look at the Ghost Dance song on page 27. It is the same thing, it is exactly the same thing. It scans the same way. The feeling is the same. This is what the Ghost Dance was about. The Peoples of the Plains had lost everything. The buffalo had been deliberately slaughtered as an avowed part of U.S. government policy, so that the People would have nothing to live on. The prophet Wovoka told that if the people would dance and sing in this way, the buffalo would come back. And so they did. Sang these songs. And it gained them nothing. It all ended in the thunder of the Hotchkiss guns at Wounded Knee. It is absolutely heartless for Brodsky to say, "The dance became part of a movement in the 1880s to preserve Native American Plains culture," that the "Ghost Dance ceremonies celebrated the peace the Indians enjoyed before the Europeans invaded their land. Their rituals expressed the hope that all people would again live in peace." It wasn't a celebration of anything. It was a last-ditch desperate attempt to ward off the end of all things.

Whatever else it may be, *Buffalo* is not a children's book. Most of the pictures will scare the living daylights out of them. And the subtitle is a complete misrepresentation. This is not "song-poems illustrated with original paintings." Brodsky went looking for some words so she could make a book to showcase her paintings, and she has understood none of them.

Sadly, when the Indian population declined along with buffalo and whole tribes were wiped out...many of the sacred objects were either lost or destroyed. I am grateful, therefore, for all the material I was able to find in museums and library collections....I too feel my paintings have gained strength from the images of the past, deepening my understanding and spirituality as I move into the future.

This is so far beyond entitlement that I have no words for it. This woman has understood nothing.

Clark, Ann Nolan, *There Still Are Buffalo*, illustrated by Stephen Tongier. Ancient City Press (1992). 44 pages, b/w illustrations; grades 2-4

Ann Nolan Clark was a prolific children's author, with most of her output focusing on aspects of Native life. In the 1940s, she wrote a series of books for the BIA. Five of these have been reissued; this story of the life of a buffalo bull is one of them.

The framework seems to be the attempt of "the Sioux People" to preserve the remnant of the once-great herd. The story begins with the birth of a "baby" bull, who is fated to become "Chief of the Thundering Herd," and ends with the day he "chooses the lonely trail" and "goes away/to end his days/as a proud buffalo should end them."

There Still Are Buffalo is written in an overwrought, semi-poetical style that can hardly have appealed to children at any time. Nothing in it gives any evidence that Clark knew very much about either buffalo or Indians. In one scene she writes:

> Once
> the range riders,
> the Indian cowboys,
> tried to drive the buffalo into new pasture.
> They ran the herd hard.
> They confused and frightened them.
> They circled and turned them
> using their strongest and fastest,
> their best-trained curring ponies.
> The great beasts ran/in terror, in panic.
> ...A young calf fell forward,
> went down to the ground
> under the death-pounding hooves
> of the running herd,
> ....The yelling cowboys,
> the pursuing cowboys
> closed in upon the herd...

Odd behavior for people concentrated on saving something. And imagining the ideas about Indians young children will get from reading this passage is no stretch.

What was the motivation for resurrecting this thing? Was "first published by the BIA" supposed to be a recommendation? *There Still Are Buffalo* is a product of its time. And that's where it should have stayed: unpublished and forgotten.

Culleton, Beatrice (Ojibwe/Métis), *Spirit of the White Bison*, illustrated by Robert Kakaygeesick, Jr. (Ojibwe). Book Publishing (1985). 62 pages, b/w illustrations; grades 4-up

Little White Buffalo is "born under a rainbow," but close to the end of the time of the great herds. Her young years are spent doing little buffalo things, in the innocence of childhood. She is a well-drawn and real character, but there is nothing here that is inconsistent with animal behavior.

As with all innocence, hers comes to an end. Hunters come, and she is temporarily separated from her family and the herd. During this time, she is saved from a cougar attack by a would-be mountain man: "Holy cow, I heard that there were white buffalo around, but I ain't never seen one before." This is her first face-to-face encounter with a human creature. Later, she meets another, "a dark-skinned man," and they become friends of a sort. But this is after a new kind of hunter has come, one who does not hunt for food, but only for the slaughter. For both White Buffalo and Lone Wolf, the time is now short.

In the end, after a battle with four soldiers out for the fun of it, the two friends make the journey to the Great Spirit world together: "My spirit would return again in the future to walk with those who were gentle but strong. I would be seen by few, perhaps in visions, perhaps in dreams."

Spirit of the White Bison is a heart-breaking but beautifully written short novel. Culleton says of her work,

> In this story, a White Bison tells about the decimation of the buffalo. It was not a quiet, accidental extermination. The horror was that the killings were deliberate, planned, military actions. Destroy the livelihood of the Indians and win a war.

With the exception of *Pte Oyate*, this is the only one of these books that does not slide over what happened, or excuse it as the inevitable result of something-or-other.

Doner, Kim (Cherokee), *Buffalo Dreams*, illustrated by the author. WestWinds (1999). Unpaginated, color illustrations; grades 3-up

On August 24, 1994, a white buffalo calf was born on the Heider family farm in Wisconsin. For Native people, this was an extraordinary thing; the fulfillment of prophecy.

Since that time, thousands have made the journey to see Miracle and bring her gifts. This is the background of Doner's story of a young family—Mom, Dad, Sarah and her little brother, Joe—who take that trip.

Dramatic tension is created when little Joe climbs into the barnyard because he wants to "touch magic"—a friend having told him that the white buffalo calf is "magic"—and Sarah faces down an angry Mama buffalo to rescue him. At that point, the baby comes out of the barn, and puts her nose in Sarah's hand: "In a moment of forever, Sarah held magic."

It is a little hard to see where Doner was going with this. The power of that moment becomes diffused because of the dreamcatcher subplot and elements of the story that require more explication than they receive.

Who are these people? The family name is Bearpaw, but no Nation is given. Do we assume that they are Lakota because Sarah is familiar with the story of White Buffalo Calf Woman? What do dreamcatchers have to do with that Lakota story—except as something for Sarah to leave for Miracle? The dreamcatcher is present throughout the book, as a small gray drawing at the bottom of the page, progressing from frame and binding to completed object; and as instructions for how to make one on the last two pages of the book. Granted that dreamcatchers have become more ubiquitous than Kokopelli, they are an Ojibwe innovation—not just "Native American"—their original use being to hang on babies' cradleboards. The one that Sarah has been making and gives to the little buffalo has all kinds of stuff on it, beside the usual fluff-feathers and beads: a tiny stuffed buffalo, what looks like a beaded bracelet, some photographs, what might be tickets of some sort, and other, less identifiable objects.

In one rather disconcerting scene, Sarah's father gives her an eagle feather for her dreamcatcher, "from Grandpa's old headdress....The bird that flies closest to heaven will give your dreams strength." What is this about? An eagle feather is a great honor, given for accomplishments, particularly for those benefiting the people in some way, not just to give a child better dreams. And Grandpa's "old" headdress? Is this some old thing to take apart, and not the treasure that anyone I have ever known would consider it?

After the story, the author gives the reader her own, rather different, version of the story of White Buffalo Calf Woman. Some might take issue with her use of the word "braves" for the two young men who first see her, and the Pipe that the holy Woman gave to the people, being called "peacemaker." Although in common non-Native use it is described as a "peace pipe," it is not. It is the Calf Pipe.

In her author's note, Doner says that she began this book after being "inspired by remembered legends, a stirring news story, and the charming face of a white buffalo calf." Perhaps if she had just stuck to that, her story would have left a less amorphous impression.

The illustrations tend to leap out at us, often seeming too big for the page, but the baby is undeniably adorable, as indeed she was.

Esbensen, Barbara Juster, *The Great Buffalo Race*, illustrated by Helen K. Davie. Little Brown (1994). Unpaginated, color illustrations; grades 3-5; Seneca

This is a "retelling" of Arthur C. Parker's story, "The Buffalo's Hump and the Brown Birds," from his book, *Skunny Wundy and other Indian Tales*, originally published in 1926. In it, the buffalo, who have been waiting for the great race to new fields, smell rain to the west. Young buffalo wants to go immediately, Old Buffalo counsels patience, and they come to blows. Young Buffalo wins, and he and his followers tear off. So do Old Buffalo and his group, by a different route. At the end of their journey, both find only more dry grass, and no rain. The Masterful One, manifesting from the darkening clouds, punishes Young Buffalo for his deliberate cruelty to the ground-dwelling creatures on his mad dash—"I thought it only sport"—and Old Buffalo, because he should have known better, giving them humps and down-facing heads, so they'll see what is beneath them from now on. Young Buffalo becomes the Red Buffalo of the underground, and Old Buffalo the White Buffalo of the clouds, who will warn in times of danger.

Esbensen closely follows the framework of Parker's story, sometimes nearly his exact wording.

Parker: "You are a destroyer of birds, and henceforth the brown birds shall depend upon buffalos for food and protection."

Esbensen: "You are a destroyer of birds. So from this day forward, those small brown birds shall depend upon buffalo for food and protection."

But mostly, Esbensen unnecessarily elaborates Parker's telling, to the story's detriment. "The great day was coming for the race to new fields" (Parker) becomes:

> Every year in those far-off times we only dream about now, the Tribe of Buffalo would gather together to choose a day for the race to new fields. Every year the buffalo would chew the juicy green grasses until only the shortest stems remained. When this happened, they would

prepare themselves to race to the tall, lush grasses that grew in their other fields over the far horizon.

Parker's story is a good one. It deals with a number things: what the buffalo look like and their relationship with those birds, but also how we are required to behave in the world, and the relationship of all to each. Nothing that Esbensen has done to it does anything except detract from it.

Esbensen's illustrations are quite attractive, except maybe for the buffalo's facial expressions. The "patterns and costumes were inspired by" examples of traditional dress from books and museums, but the appearance of the Masterful One—here called by Esbensen "Haweniyo, the Great Spirit"—begs description. He is wearing a sort of fringed, white buckskin mini-dress, with thigh-high lace-up leggings, tied at the knees, and he has a white buffalo head. His spear has become a lightning bolt, which he wields in a kind of martial arts, "karate" leap-and-chop fashion.

In her "Note to the Reader," Esbensen tells us, not that Parker wrote the story, but that it was "taken down" by him, and that "[t]his old tale, like all Seneca legends, was told during the long winter nights by Seneca storytellers," thus implying that it is free for the taking. It is not clear though how she would justify so much use of his actual written words. If Esbensen liked the story, it seems to me that the honorable thing to do would have been to have it illustrated, as Parker told it. Of course, then she couldn't have been listed as author, could she?

Freedman, Russell, *Buffalo Hunt.* Holiday House (1988). 52 pages, color illustrations, grades 5-up

Buffalo Hunt is a curious mix of information, factoids, dubious statements and ambiguity; and there is little to be learned here about the Plains peoples. They are always "the Indians," as in "the Indians thought," "the Indians would hunt," "the Indian village." The names Mandan, Comanche, Sioux, Northern Cheyenne, are men-tioned in passing, but there is no tribal differentiation, no indication that any of these Nations might be in any ways different from each other. Plains ecology of the time is not touched upon.

> To the Plains Indians, the buffalo...was the most important animal on earth....The buffalo kept their bellies full and their bodies warm. It sup-plied raw materials for their weapons, tools, ornaments and toys. The rhythm of their daily lives was ruled by the comings and goings of the great buffalo herds.

This, in substance, is true. The book as a whole does not give much room for the child reader to form any impression other than that "the Indians" spent *all* their time chasing buffaloes.

"It is little wonder that the Indians worshipped the buffalo," Freedman says. To hold a creature sacred, to honor it for what it is and the ways it makes a par-ticular way of life possible, is not the same thing as worship. We "worship," if you will, *Wakan Tanka*, the Giver of all life. The Nations of the Plains were pro-foundly grateful for buffalo, one of that Being's best gifts. In our way, the whole Earth is sacred, *Makoce Wakan*, and any animal who gives up its life so that we may live is thanked, because its life is as sacred as ours.

Of statements that are at least open to question, there are many. A few of the many:

- Does anybody still really think that Native people expected "to go to a happy hunting ground in the sky" when they died?

- "Sometimes an arrow would strike with such force that it would be completely buried. It might pass all the way through the animal, come out the other side, and drop to the ground." Picture the size of a buffalo....

Were arrows ever made of cane? Not the ones to shoot buffalo, I'll bet. *Could* a bow be made from "elk or moun-tain-sheep horn"? If so, how? How does Freedman know that "about 250,000 Indians were living in the region," in the early 1800s? Did Lewis and Clark conduct a cen-sus? And finally, I'm having a real lot of trouble trying to get my mind around this:

> If a herd was small enough, the Indians some-times surrounded the buffalo on foot...and formed a tight ring. Then they ran in circles around the herd, whooping and yelling and waving their arms as the terrified animals milled about in confusion. Slowly the Indians closed the circle until they were close enough to let go with their arrows and spears.

I'm sorry, given the temperament of your average buffalo, all I can see is a bunch of dead Indians.

There isn't a footnote in the book, no citations, and no bibliography. Possibly, some of the quotes from Catlin, somebody named Tom LeForge, and "a famous Sioux shaman"—and other things—might be true, but how are we to know where Freedman got them? It is almost impossible to escape the conclusion that this omission was deliberate.

Sometimes it seems as though Freedman is "telling the pictures." For instance, there is a George Catlin painting, "Buffalo Dance of the Mandan Indians." The text reads: "Indian dancers imitated the movements of the buffalo—pawing, milling, stampeding—in hopes of encouraging a herd to approach." Another Catlin, of buffalo mired in very deep snow, and some hunters around them. The text: "When snow covered the plains... the Indians could kill them easily with spears, arrows, or guns." And, of yet another Catlin, "Buffalo Hunt under the Wolfskin Mask," Freedman says, "In winter, when the grass offered little cover, a hunter might sneak up on a herd disguised in a buffalo robe. Or he could drape himself in the skin of a white wolf." Why does he assume this is a winter painting? Winter on the plains means snow, and lots of it. And "white" wolf? Well, in Catlin's painting, the wolf hides do look sort of white, but with the exception of the occasional, and very rare, albino, white wolves live in the arctic lands.

Some things probably go without saying, such as, "Without horses, the Indians had to travel on foot…" or "Sometimes on a long journey the dogs would grow tired…" None of this is too earth shaking, maybe, but as a whole, it doesn't say much for Freedman's scholarship, and the last chapter truly calls his intentions into question.

> By the early 1800s, trading posts were springing up all over the West. White traders wanted buffalo robes and tongues for profitable markets in the East. In exchange, they offered guns, tools, tobacco, whiskey, and trinkets. The Indians had always hunted for their own needs. Now, by killing a few more buffalo, they could obtain the white man's goods. Soon the Indians were killing for their hides and tongues alone.

> During the 1830s and 1840s, hundreds of thousands of robes were shipped east. By then, white hunters were beginning to kill more buffalo than the Indians.

> By the 1860s, Indian tribes found that buffalo were disappearing from their traditional hunting grounds.

> There were still about eight million buffalo left on the plains in 1870, when a newly invented tanning process sealed the fate of the remaining herds.

Indian war parties attacked the hide hunters wherever they found them, but the hunters could not be stopped.

> At one time, perhaps sixty or seventy million buffalo had roamed the plains. By the early 1880s, the endless herds had been wiped out…. With the buffalo gone, the proud and independent Plains Indians became a conquered people….Swept by starvation and disease, the great hunting tribes were confined to reservations, where they depended on government food rations. Their children were sent to boarding schools to learn the language and customs of the white man.

Here, Freedman implies that the Plains people themselves started the slaughter so that they could get stuff, while suggesting a certain empathy with the "proud and independent Plains Indians" who were "swept by starvation and disease" and "confined to reservations." He demonstrates "objectivity" by saying that, "white hunters were beginning to kill more buffalo than the Indians." Then he leads the reader to assume that by the time "the Indians" figured out what was going on it was far too late. This is simply, provably, not true. The people of the plains had been fighting back for a long time.

Freedman says that it was a chemical process that "sealed the fate" of the buffalo, but not a word about the U.S. government's mandate to exterminate them. "Sixty or seventy million buffalo," but not a word about the numbers of Plains people dead of that same "starvation and disease," or killed outright by hunters and the army. Their children were "sent to boarding schools to learn the language and customs of the white man"—where they were beaten and abused, and many of them died. With rare exceptions, what they learned was how to be laborers and household help. No words about this.

It could be said that *Buffalo Hunt* is not as bad as many early titles—no bloodthirsty savages scalping innocent settlers. I say long time gone for the lies and the half-truths, way past time for the whole truth. Freedman has a certain reputation as a children's author, and that's what he should have done—told the truth, and no shading.

Hoyt-Goldsmith, Diane, *Buffalo Days*, photographed by Lawrence Migdale. Holiday House (1997). 32 pages, color photographs; grades 3-5; Crow

Buffalo Days is a photo essay about Clarence Three Irons, Jr., who lives with his family in the land of the Bighorn Mountains of Montana. Here, in Crow Country, they raise cattle and horses, and Clarence's father helps to manage the tribal buffalo herd. The term "buffalo days" refers to the old days, when this most sacred of animals roamed North America, providing sustenance for his relatives, the humans. "Buffalo Days" also refers to the Crow Fair and Rodeo that the people celebrate each summer. Rather than focusing on the struggle to bring back the buffalo from near-extinction as the Crow and other Indian Nations have done, Hoyt-Goldsmith places emphasis on the more "colorful" aspect of Crow life.

In this book, she ditches the clunky first-person narrative technique that characterized her earlier work, but the wooden, dumbed-down style of writing remains. In a sentence referring to the tribal herd, for instance, she uses twenty-two one-syllable words before coming to one with two syllables: "They are so big and strong that they can run right through the kind of fence that would hold a herd of cattle." As in her earlier titles, the author lapses into sweeping generalizations that make no sense (e.g., "People who come to the fair are able to experience a way of life that existed during the Buffalo Days"). White depredation of the buffalo (whom the author refers to as "wild") is smoothed over, residential schools are mentioned but not spoken about honestly, reservations are still "land set aside" for Indians, and Hoyt-Goldsmith seems to think that all powwow regalia is traditional clothing and all powwow dances are traditional.

But more perplexing is why she refers to Clarence by his nickname, "Indian," thirty-four times (e.g., "Indian and his friends eat Indian tacos."). Nicknames are used by family and friends, not by teachers, casual acquaintances or unfamiliar adults. It is disrespectful for an outsider to refer to a child by his nickname. And finally, I don't know why the author has chosen to highlight an Indian child with short hair who wears a wig as part of his powwow regalia.

Lawrence Migdale's full-color pictures are sharp and evocative, especially the aerial photos of the land, and the herd of buffalo, kicking up dust.

Kershen, L. Michael, *Why Buffalo Roam*, illustrated by Monica Hansen (Cherokee). Stemmer House (1993). 31 pages, color illustrations; grades 2-4

The people are hungry. "Whitewolf went and prayed for many moons." Spirit asks for his most precious thing. Whitewolf tries everything. Only when he brings his baby son are his prayers answered. Spirit allows him to keep everything, and gives buffalo, as a reward for Whitewolf's loyalty.

L. Michael (Mike) Kershen was ten years old when he was inspired to write this by a two-week unit on Indians, after which "the students wrote creative stories about what they had learned..." "By living in Oklahoma, Mike effortlessly experiences the richness of Native American cultures. He has classmates and family friends who are Native American." He has attended powwows and his parents own "original" art by (unnamed) "well-known" Indian artists. All this seems a little too uncomfortably similar to "Some of my best friends are...."

That Mike's story was strongly influenced by the Biblical tale of Abraham and Isaac is obvious, as his father notes in a lengthy afterword explaining how his connections made possible the publication of his son's story. These connections also made possible the use of Hansen's art work; lovely despite the disconcerting transparent hand of Spirit, reaching out of the sky, a la Michelangelo, in a couple of the illustrations.

It would seem that the young author's heart was touched by something he learned. It is hard not to be moved by his wanting to write this; it is always a hope that out of the hearts of children will come a better world. However, it is hardly possible for a child—or anyone else—to understand very much about rich, complex, and previously unknown cultures after a mere two-week study. It is a bad idea to encourage children to write "creative stories" about these cultures and let them think that what they are creating is Indian. There are many Native stories about the coming of the buffalo; this bears no resemblance to any of them. And one oddity: despite the title, we are told how the buffalo came, but never why they roam.

LaDuke, Winona (Anishinaabe), *Pte Oyate: Buffalo Nations, Buffalo People*, illustrated by Julie Brown Wolf (Lakota), Joe Lafferty, (Lakota), Don Montileaux (Lakota), and Ernest Whiteman (Arapaho). Honor the Earth (1998). 26 pages, b/w illustrations; grades 7-up

Pte Oyate is very different from nearly all that is written about the relationship of Native people and buffalo. In twenty-six pages, LaDuke discusses the plains/buffalo ecosystem, the history of the destruction of "the largest migratory herd in the history of the world," what the people are doing to bring back the buffalo, and what that, in turn, would do for the people and the land. And it's full of information, including a list of organizations working with buffalo restoration.

One might be surprised to learn that, prior to 1998, the state of Montana shot down more than 2,500 buffalo from the Yellowstone National Park herd, when they passed that "invisible border from National Park to state land." That number made up a third of the Yellowstone herd. "It was that deja vu feeling....the snow was red with blood," Rosalie Little Thunder said of the 1996-97 slaughter. "What has changed from 1855 to 1997?" Little Thunder was one of those who protested that shooting, and was arrested and charged with criminal trespass for her efforts.

LaDuke gives the backstory—the historical buffalo killing—succinctly, in one and a half pages. That, and the photo on the facing page of, literally, a hill of buffalo skulls, give a very clear picture of the magnitude of the disaster and its continuing legacy for the peoples of the plains. LaDuke is speaking of Pine Ridge, but this could apply equally to any of the buffalo peoples—or just about any other Indian Nation:

> [L]ike the Yellowstone herd, they have been besieged and shot down, but they are still alive. A large part of their lives, however, takes place within a cycle of immense grief and despair that remains unresolved.

One of the remarkable things about this book is that it looks as much forward as back. Nearly half of it is devoted to the work of reestablishing the buffalo and restoring the land. Birgil Kills Straight, the Iron Cloud family, Alex and Debbie White Plume, Richard Sherman and Marvin Kammerer, a South Dakota rancher, spoke with LaDuke about this. Sherman talked about a "culturally appropriate system based on the values and philosophy of the Lakota....It doesn't seem to take too long...to heal the land once it starts....it's happening right here on our buffalo pasture."

Faith Spotted Eagle, coordinator of the Brave Heart Project Learning Circle (*Inhanktunwan Winyan*) talks about women and buffalo:

> When women had the relationship with buffalo, we were able to learn from that, and pass that on to younger women. The underlying teaching is that primacy of the relationship with buffalo.

LaDuke speaks of change.

> This spring, more calves will be born, and some new grass will grow...In that spring grass will be a promise for the future.

Pte Oyate is an honest, intelligently written book; a book written by someone who knows what she is talking about, a book full of promise; promise and hope. The past does not leave us, but we are not condemned to repeat it endlessly. We also have a future: "And so the healing process begins."

Osborne, Mary Pope, *Buffalo Before Breakfast*, illustrated by Sal Murdocca. Random House "Stepping Stone" (1999). 76 pages, b/w illustrations, grades 1-3; Lakota

This title is part of the popular easy-to-read "Magic Tree House" series. The magic tree house belongs to a magical librarian from the time of King Arthur. She magically travels through space and time collecting books, and, having met eight-year-old Jack and seven-year-old Annie, shows them how to transport themselves—magically. In each title, the two children and Teddy, an enchanted dog, travel back or forward in time, meet interesting people and events, encounter a crisis, figure out a solution, and return home. This formulaic series is neither particularly well written nor particularly well researched, yet young readers love these books, and apparently, their teachers do, too.

In *Buffalo Before Breakfast*, Jack and Annie, looking for "a gift from the prairie blue," one of four magical gifts that will free Teddy from his spell, are transported to a Lakota encampment in the early 1800s—where everyone speaks English so they can teach our two intrepid protagonists (and, by extension, the young reader) all about Lakota life.

With eleven-year-old Black Hawk as their guide, they go off by themselves to look at a herd of buffalo. Black Hawk, a self-proclaimed experienced hunter, somehow messes up and the buffalo threaten to stampede. Jack rescues Black Hawk, and Annie, "surrounded by buffalo—*calm* buffalo—"pats them and talks to them, and the rest of the herd calms down, too.

Eleven-year-old Lakota children were *children*, not experienced buffalo hunters. Children did not go off by themselves to encounter herds of buffalo. And *no one*—not even a little white girl from the 20th Century—would be naïve enough to stand in the middle of a herd of buffalo and try to pat them. She wouldn't be standing there very long. But Annie was not trampled, we later find out, because she saw "the spirit of White Buffalo Woman" who stopped the buffalo.

When the three return to camp, Grandmother lectures Black Hawk about his behavior and refers to Annie as "Buffalo Girl" and and Jack as "Rides-Like-Wind." There is a "pipe ceremony," during which Grandmother teaches the kids, in four very short sentences, all about "White Buffalo Woman" and then presents them with an eagle feather "for (their) courage."

Having obtained their "gift from the prairie blue," Jack and Annie prepare to return home. The people break camp "to follow the buffalo" (even though the buffalo are right there). The people walk off and Jack and Annie run back to the tree house.

> *By now, the Lakota are walking west*, Jack thought. "Soon everything will change," he said sadly. "The buffalo will vanish. The old way of life for the Lakota will vanish, too." "But the Great

Spirit won't ever vanish," said Annie. "It will *always* take care of Black Hawk's people." Jack smiled. Annie's words made him feel better.

Back home, Annie figures out that perhaps little Teddy "had something to do with White Buffalo Woman" because

> "One second Teddy disappeared in the grass. Then White Buffalo Woman appeared," said Annie. "When White Buffalo Woman disappeared, Teddy appeared." "Hmm…" said Jack. He stared at the little dog. Teddy tilted his head and gave Jack a wise look. "Well…" said Jack, "maybe Teddy has good medicine." "*Now* you understand," said Annie, smiling.

The "White Buffalo Woman" mentioned here is actually White Buffalo Calf Woman, a sacred being of the Lakota. She does *not* appear at the behest of little enchanted dogs to rescue little white kids who get themselves into ridiculous situations.

On one level, this is just another volume in an innocuous young children's series. On another, Osborne has set her story in a time period that is part of quite recent American history. She is writing about people who were and are real people. And she has distorted that reality out of all recognition. It is one thing to set a fantasy in a prehistoric world in which little is actually known. It is quite another to set it in a world and time of tragic dimensions from which the Lakota people suffer still. Some things just should not be grist for the hack writer's mill.

Roop, Peter, *The Buffalo Jump*, illustrated by Bill Farnsworth. Northland (1996). Unpaginated, color illustrations; grades 2-3

A young boy, having a temper tantrum because he has not been chosen to run in front of the buffalo,

> notched an arrow and aimed at a raven….He would bring bad luck upon his family if he harmed the bird. Still, Little Blaze wanted to strike out against something, anything, to make him feel better.

Running in front of the buffalo would mean that he would be the one to stampede them over the jump. He wants to do this so he can get a new name. But on this day his older brother, who has been chosen, stumbles and falls, and is saved by Little Blaze. So they jump off together, into "a small cup of rock jutting out from the cliff," and Little Blaze is a hero.

Buffalo are not easy to kill. It was always dangerous. In the days before horses, one of the ways in which the Plains peoples were able to kill the buffalo and make their meat for the winter was to stampede them over a cliff. If the need was great enough, a warrior might be chosen—choose himself, actually—to run ahead of the

herd, and lead it onto the rocks. Sometimes, maybe once in a lifetime, once in a hundred years, the *Wicasa Wakan*. Not a boy. Some of the largest of the buffalo bulls can weigh up to 3,000 pounds, with a top speed of close to forty miles an hour. Out-running a stampeding herd is an unlikely option, especially for a child, one who appears from the illustrations to be not more than ten years old.

If there was a rock ledge below the lip of the jump, if it was wide enough, it might at least theoretically be possible for a jumper to land on it safely and survive. But not onto "a small cup of rock." Running at top speed, one's trajectory would be *out* and over, not straight down.

The Indian names in this book, as typically chosen by non-Native writers, are referenced to animals: Morning Eagle, Curly Bear, and the name given to Little Blaze after he saves his brother—Charging Bull. The father has no name, and there are no other characters except for figures in the background of the illustrations, sort of "extras." Especially notable is the absence of women and girls. In the bustle of an encampment getting ready for the hunt, their presence would be very evident—as it would be, anyway. Is Roop unaware that the women were the ones who butchered the buffalo after they were killed?

Nobody ever talked like this: "Come, my sons. The sun has shone on our tribe. Let us celebrate this good jump. And let us celebrate the brave deeds of both my sons."

The reader will not know the tribal affiliation of the characters until the last sentence of the last page. Apart from this, there is nothing in the text to distinguish these folk from any other Plains people—nor is there in the illustrations, which are uniformly dark. Even in the scenes that should be sun-filled, there is a darkness on the land, on the people; a standard technique for delineating "primitive" peoples. And—just idle curiosity—why are the boys shown wearing full pants under their breechclouts?

The story owes more to Roop's imagination than to any understanding of the people about whom he is writing. His author's note tells us:

> The site that inspired this story is the Madison Buffalo Jump in Montana. Standing on the cliff, looking down at the ledge where the ahwa waki landed as a thundering herd of buffalo plunged over the cliff, made me wonder what would happen if…?

Roop also thanks various organizations for, among other things, "first publishing 'Little Blaze and the Buffalo Jump' so that Native American children could learn about their ancestors." As though we were incapable of telling our children these things ourselves.

Taylor, C.J., *The Secret of the White Buffalo*, illustrated by the author. Tundra. (1993). Unpaginated, color illustrations; grades 2-4; Lakota

The account of the coming of White Buffalo Calf Woman and the gift of the Sacred Pipe is the central mystery of Lakota belief and ritual. Taylor's version of this story is junk from start to finish. She says that she adapted it from "stories" in *Black Elk Speaks*, and *Myths and Legends of the Sioux* by Marie McLaughlin. Marie McLaughlin was wife to that Major McLaughlin who was Indian agent on Standing Rock when Sitting Bull was assassinated, and she is probably the last person any rational human being would go to for authentic information on anything to do with the Lakota.

And that is probably irrelevant, since Taylor pretty much makes things up to suit herself. She gives names and characters to those who are called only "scouts" by Black Elk: "Black Knife" and "Blue Cloud." She makes up whole conversations: between these two, for the chief, even for White Buffalo Calf Woman Herself. She twists the whole meaning and focus by creating a setting of strife among the people, thus implying that this was the reason for the holy Woman's appearance: "Arguments broke out over who should do the work of the village. Children paid no attention to their parents. Parents lost patience with their children." When the chief is told who is coming, this is what he says:

> You have not listened to us when we tried to make peace among you. Black Knife did not listen, and he is gone. If we do not listen, we may perish. Are you ready to listen now?

In fact, the coming of White Buffalo Calf Woman had *nothing* to do with any such conflict. She came to bring a gift for the good of the people and to teach them certain rites. She taught them how to keep the Pipe. The first Pipe Holder was High Hollow Horn. He was a real person. There have been Pipe carriers since that time. There is no such thing in our story as

> When [the people] were tempted to quarrel among themselves, they remembered that only through peace could they solve problems and prosper.

White Buffalo Calf Woman is always described as beautiful, yet the illustrations are among the ugliest I have seen. The holy Woman Herself looks as though She is turning up Her nose at a bad smell. And the "secret" of the white buffalo? What secret? C.J. Taylor has created a completely bogus version of a sacred event, for purposes only she knows.

Wilkinson, Todd, *Bison for Kids*, photography by Michael H. Francis, illustrated by John F. McGee. NorthWord Press (1994). 48 pages, color photographs, color illustrations; grades 4-6

"Recommended and Approved by Ranger Rick," the National Wildlife Federation's kiddie logo, a little raccoon wearing a cowboy hat and holding the Earth in one hand, Bison for Kids gives new meaning to the term "dumbing down."

> Although bison look familiar, most people know them by another name: American b-u-f-f-a-l-o.

> Bison also have close ties with people....In fact, the Sioux Indians have their own special name for bison, "Tatanka" (TAH-TONG-KUH).

> In 1913, the U.S. government made a "buffalo nickel" with the picture of a bison on one side and the face of an Indian on the other.

> The rarest bison of all is the white buffalo, which is worshipped by Native Americans.

> A bison has shapes as no other animal.

> Bison maintain their body heat because they are nomads, travelers on the move in search for their next meal.

> [B]uffalo chips [dung] have been called "decorations" of bison country. It's fun to toss them through the air like frisbees.

> Native Americans...still celebrate the bison at festivals called pow wows.

There are some rather nice photographs of buffalo here, but the cartoony little illustrations do not exactly add an aura of authenticity. There probably are "more bison alive now than there were 100 years ago"—that wouldn't be hard—but all "150,000" of them are hardly "roaming across the prairies and open pastures." Actually, if they have the misfortune to wander off their designated territory, they get shot.

A Knothead

To come out
And call you a knothead
Would not be a nice thing to do.
However,
I can not help
But notice
That woodpecker
Landing on you.

—*Desiree Future Goss* (Chukchansi)

THIS IS ABOUT COYOTE

Of all the stories taken by non-Native authors and illustrators, the most are about Coyote. I've given a lot of thought as to why. Probably nobody has had a more intense campaign of extermination waged against him—except maybe Indians. Maybe now he is considered tamed, controlled, safe—like us. Now he can be romanticized, claimed, an icon to be added to the spoils of victory—like a buffalo in a cage.

Anthropologists and ethnologists seem always to have been particularly fascinated by the trickster figures of "primitive" peoples. Anansi, Rabbit, Raven, Iktomi, Crow, Gluskabi—also called "culture hero," although neither term suits him exactly—and, of course, Coyote. More than any other, he has become ubiquitous in white culture, from "Southwest-style" motif, to the Wile E. Coyote of Saturday morning cartoons.

For Native people, Coyote is many things: one of them is not cute. As with all trickster figures, he is both more, and less, than human. Besides being such a fool, he is also a supernatural being. This does not necessarily have to appear in every story, but that knowledge informs the stories. We can laugh our heads off at some of the messes he gets himself into, but we also know who he is, and what he is capable of. In some ways, he is us, frequently in some of our worst aspects. For us, Coyote is not just more than we care to say, he is more than we can say. We are not supposed to tell Coyote stories before the first frost, or after the first Thunder. There are storytellers, people who will not tell Coyote stories at all. So with some of the stories reviewed here. Coyote is essentially untranslatable. For him, "good" and "evil" are not opposites, but a continuum.

"Coyote.... has consistently evaded academic capture and definition and has tricked nearly every commentator into at least one laughable generalization," says Barre Toelken.[1] Shonto Begay tells a story of a coyote crossing in front of the pickup. His aunt pulls off the road, and his uncle gets out to sprinkle pollen. After, he says:

> Coyote crossing...is neither a good nor bad omen. It is just how you react to it. Coyote learned all our lessons in mythic times. He carries with him wisdom and strength as well as the dark side of us. So here, My Nephew, I give you this pollen bag. Use it often.[2]

Coyote is not the innocent animal buffoon that he is portrayed as in so many stories here. Coyote is still slipping sideways, just this side of vision, on our backtrail, and, as always, evading definition.

Be careful how you say his name.—*Doris Seale*

WiisAgiMYiiNgunH = Coyote
Lois Beardslee

NOTES

1 Barre Toelken, in Lopez, Barry, *Giving Birth to Thunder, Sleeping With His Daughter: Coyote Builds North America*. Avon (1977), p. xi.

2 Begay, Shonto, *Navajo: Voices and Visions Across the Mesa*. Scholastic (1995), p. 39.

REVIEWS: BOOKS ABOUT COYOTE

Begay, Shonto (Diné), *Ma'ii and Cousin Horned Toad: A Traditional Navajo Story,* **illustrated by the author. Scholastic (1992). Unpaginated, color illustrations; preschool-grade 2; Diné (Navajo)**

Ma'ii, being hungry—as well as lazy—not only eats up all hard-working Cousin Horned Toad's corn, but schemes of a way to trick Horned Toad out of his farm. When Ma'ii swallows Horned Toad, he gets, maybe not more than he bargained for, but surely something different.

This is a really good Coyote story, with pictures that manage to be both beautiful and very funny. An afterword says a little about Coyote and the Horned Toad in Diné stories, and includes a glossary of Diné words. Highly recommended.—*Doris Seale*

Bierhorst, John, *The People With Five Fingers: A Native California Creation Tale,* **illustrated by Robert Andrew Parker. Marshall Cavandish (2000). Unpaginated, color illustrations; grades 1-3**

Here, Coyote as Creator decides to make people, because "[t]his earth cannot stay naked." So he enlists the aid of the animals, who help him make mountains and valleys, rivers and creeks, willows and bushes and plants, roots, berries and all kinds of food. Then Coyote dreams and places the sun, moon and stars. And when he finally creates people, all the animals, terrified of the noise, leave. But the people are here, and they are all different except that they all have five fingers.

There are parts of this story that I have heard before: of Coyote placing the stars, of animals planning together for the coming of the humans, of lizard's paw becoming the prototype for people's hands. But *The People with Five Fingers* seems to have been put together as a generic "How Diversity Came to Be" or "How Multiculturalism Came to Be" story with elements of California Indian stories thrown in. Bierhorst's introduction says,

> The story...predicts a day when the land would be filled with many different kinds of people, whose ancestors would come not only from America but from Europe, Africa, and Asia.

And in the story, Coyote says, "They will speak different languages...and they will be different in color." In fact, the concept that all the people are different but they all had five fingers is a post-contact construction, because the whole idea of "different kinds of people" didn't exist until after contact. In creation stories, there is no diversity because there is no need for diversity. In California creation stories, there is no diversity; there are just people.

Most troubling is that there are no source notes, no attribution for this story. Indian stories from what is now known as California belong to Nations, clans, bands, families and individuals. Stories are sometimes traded, stories are sometimes sold. In these cases, the stories no longer belong to their original owners; they are given up to their new owners. So there is no such thing as—nor has there ever been—a "Native Californian creation tale."

Also troubling is this from Bierhorst: "The people came together to trade. They learned each other's languages. And they shared stories." This creates the illusion that all California Indian peoples got along; it also rationalizes Bierhorst's taking elements of different stories and throwing them together. This reminds me of something that Métis storyteller Maria Campbell has said about Native stories, and I paraphrase: "Just because we offer you a cup of tea doesn't mean we're giving you the teapot."

Even where Coyote is given some creative tasks or roles, Creator is still above Coyote. In some cases, Coyote is Creator's administrative assistant, in some cases he's just a silly dog. Even if Coyote is given the role of making something, even if his name has a capital "C," he's not Creator.

"All of our stories have a variety of characters," Buffy McQuillan (Yokayo/Nomlaki) told me. "Coyote is one of them but he represents different things to different people. To imply that we're all similar shows that Bierhorst doesn't understand us or our storytelling. It's rude." Not recommended.—*Beverly Slapin*

(Thank-you to Buffy McQuillan.)

Blue Cloud, Peter/Aroniawenrate (Mohawk), *Elderberry Flute Song: Contemporary Coyote Tales,* **illustrated by the author. White Pine Press (1982, 1992). 138 pages, high school-up**

In these fifty-six poems and stories, Coyote the comedian, Coyote the amoral, Coyote the obscene—well, you know, Coyote—creates daylight and chases the moon, goes on a trip to England and exposes anthropologists, discusses relativity and does some things with a certain part of his body (the part he is famous for) that some might think impossible. The black-and-white pen-and-ink drawings—practically each one shows Coyote with a full-toothed grin (or is it a sneer?)—are perfect. *Elderberry Flute Song* and Blue Cloud's *The Other Side of Nowhere: Contemporary Coyote Tales* (White Pine, 1990) are classics; each story is to be savored.—*Beverly Slapin*

Carpelan, Mary J. (Shasta/Cahuilla), *Coyote Fights the Sun: A Shasta Indian Tale*, illustrated by the author. Heyday Books (2002). Unpaginated, color illusrations; preschool-up; Shasta

In this traditional Shasta story filled with geographical references, Coyote decides to shoot the sun for misleading him about the coming of spring. As usual his plans backfire; as he goes one place to wait for the sun, it comes up somewhere else. "The three days that Coyote tries to shoot the sun," Carpelan writes, "are the three days of the spring equinox. Quartz Hill, Duzel Rock, and Mount Shasta line up at the southern icknish patch. And if you look closely at that rock pile, you can still see Coyote waiting." Carpelan's watercolor pictures leave enough for a young child's imagination. Highly recommended.—*Beverly Slapin*

Children's Press, Adventures in Storytelling, Unpaginated, color illustrations; preschool-grade 1:
The Naughty Little Rabbit and Old Man Coyote, illustrated by Rick Regan (Cherokee). 1992; Tewa
The Coyote Rings the Wrong Bell, illustrated by Francisco X. Mora. 1991

These two stories are from a series prepared to "encourage development of oral and written language skills in the classroom and acquaint students with the traditional literature of other countries." Each consists of a story audiotape accompanied by a wordless book of pictures and a resource guide. Each book has an introduction, instructions for use of book and cassette and information on the storyteller and illustrator. The text for each story is found in the back of the books.

The resource guides cover such things as basic storytelling techniques, "theme or moral," type of tale, origin, interpreting the story, "Native American storytelling," activities—making a piñata, making a storyteller figure, making a pueblo ("Extending Multicultural Understanding")—etc. It is hard to see how building a "pueblo" out of cardboard boxes can do anything to "broaden multicultural awareness."

The tapes might not have been bad if they were not accompanied by instructions on how to listen, turn the page—Coyote howls when it's *time* to turn the page.

These are two pretty simple little stories with fourteen pages of resource-guide overkill. None of the material suggests any discussion of the actual cultures from which the stories come, focusing rather on such things as "Discussing the story/thinking critically."

Although a Native storyteller is cited for each of the books, attribution for these stories remains unclear. The author listed for *Coyote Rings the Wrong Bell* in the CIP box is actually the illustrator; the story is told on the tape by someone else. The advice given to children about how to tell the story by the "author" of *Naughty Little Rabbit*—"Take the story that I have told you and tell it again, even though it means changing the location or adding something extra to juice it up a little"—is advice that I find hard to believe would come from any Native storyteller, much less an elder. This is all very suspect. It seems very much like another case of using a Native person to validate something that, in the end, may be edited out of all recognition or even completely rewritten by the editors of a series to suit their own purposes.

No doubt all the material that comes with these books will make the series attractive to teachers, but these two books are very graphic examples of the worst kind of cultural theft.—*Doris Seale*

Cole, Judith, *The Moon, the Sun, and the Coyote*, illustrated by Cecile Schoberle. Simon & Schuster (1990). Unpaginated, color illustrations; grades 1-3

This is called an "original folktale," which seems to be a bit of an oxymoron. "The Sun (who "ruled over the day") was by nature hot tempered, and the Moon (who "ruled over the night") loved a good argument; so when they saw each other at dawn and dusk, they usually quarreled." When the argument turns to whose creatures are prettier, Coyote gets involved. Gets wishes, gets vain, gets punished.

Maybe the author and illustrator had a mind to create an amusing story for children. Maybe they had a mind to tap into the multicultural marketplace. But whatever their motives, making up a "coyote story" out of their culture and illustrating it with ugly "representations... based on southwest indian (sic) kachinas (sic)," is not only cultural appropriation, but a manipulation of the child reader as well.—*Beverly Slapin*

Dominic, Gloria, *Coyote and the Grasshoppers: A Pomo Legend*, illustrated by Charles Reasoner. Rourke (1996). 48 pages, color illustrations, color photos; grades 2-3; Pomo

Dominic gives no credit for the source of this story and I was unable to find a version from or about Clear Lake to check it further. Perhaps my reluctance to do other than suggest interpretations and flaws in this story can serve as a valuable lesson. I have over twenty years of learning and studying stories of a few Nations (my own and near-dear friends and extended family), and that does not qualify me to interpret the stories of another people and their culture. This book lacks that awareness or restraint.

My friend folklorist Barre Toelken spent some forty years living and working with Diné friends and family and Coyote stories before making the decision to return those important stories, and no longer being an accomplice in their misunderstanding and abuse. He wrote in his introduction to Barry Lopez' *Giving Birth to Thunder, Sleeping With His Daughter* (Avon, 1977),

> [T]o get beyond Coyote's fascinating façade we do in fact need to know his local, specific tribal manifestations. And to know these, we need to know the tribal language, the tribal lore about storytelling events, and the local taboos concerning when a story may be told, by whom, to whom, and under what circumstances.

Coyote and the Grasshoppers does not meet any of these criteria. Although the story explains a feature of the land in the Pomo homelands, it lacks a feeling of place, a connection to the land that is vital to the stories of a people and a culture with strong ties to specific locales. The illustrations give lie to the text of the story. There is a drought, lakes have dried up, people, animals and plants are dying from lack of water—and yet page after page of Reasoner's illustrations have grassy, green rolling hills! We never know what act or imbalance created this disharmony and lack of water. We do not know why the people's prayers and songs—not "chants"—fail to call the rain. Instead, Coyote, in a selfless and self-sacrificing manner that is somewhat atypical of him, thinks only of the children and endures great hardship and effort to bring back the lake—with no ulterior motive!

In truth, Coyote is more than the one-dimensional "naughty boy" he has been oversimplified and trivialized into being in many characterizations. But this characterization is just as limited and senseless as the others. Here we have a more sentimental Coyote who is strong and unselfish. This is not a bad lesson for children; but choosing and reshaping a story to make the author's point is not a culturally sensitive thing, or even a wise thing, to do with Coyote stories that are taken out of context, out of season and out of culture.

In the simplistic section at the back of the book called "The Pomo," one old photograph particularly stands out: a Pomo woman who seems to be trying not to look at the camera holds a baby's hand while a little boy looks on. The mother and her children are wearing ill-fitting western-style clothing, and she holds a load of sticks and kindling in one arm. The caption says "A Pomo family dressed in their Sunday best." Why "Sunday best"? This comment makes a mockery of the obvious poverty of this little family, and by extension, of all Pomo people.—*Dovie Thomason*

Dwyer, Mindy, *Coyote in Love*, illustrated by the author. Alaska Northwest Books (1997). Unpaginated, color illustrations; preschool-grade 2; Coquille

Coyote's in love, this time with a star. Actually, his deep abiding love borders on harassment, and the star, who is really a "sky being," pulls him into the sky, "higher and higher through the clouds," and then drops him, crash! into the top of a mountain "so hard that the mountain exploded, leaving only a HUGE GAPING HOLE," which of course soon becomes filled with his lovesick tears. And that's how according to Dwyer, Oregon's Crater Lake was formed. It's another overdone, rhythmless vehicle to showcase an alleged artist's "bright, whimsical renditions of Coyote," who, right now, may be cooking up a way to get back at her.

Dwyer says her version is "based on a story by Coquelle (sic) Indian storyteller Susan Walgamott," who, I have a feeling, is embarrassed that her name is mentioned here. And Dwyer's statement that she hopes "the retelling of this story keeps it alive and encourages children to explore the rich traditions of Native American cultures" is arrogant.—*Beverly Slapin*

L. Frank (Tongva/Ajachmem), *Acorn Soup*, illustrated by the author. Heyday (1999). 64 pages, b/w line drawings; high school-up

I've near busted a gut over L. Frank's cartoons for years, so when I heard she was going to put them together in a book, I could hardly wait. This book, like a really good piece of chocolate, was worth waiting for.

For those who have never seen L. Frank's cartoons about Coyote, well, they're hard to describe. Of course, the captions are almost always written backwards. This is Coyote, remember, always has to make things more difficult. One may be tempted to use a mirror, but the captions slow the reader down enough to take in the full meaning. Maybe. Coyote is a tease, remember, and he teases us into understanding—or not.

Like Coyote, L. Frank is a smart aleck. She can't help herself, even admits it in the introduction. She's also politically astute, so you see, for instance, Coyote "along the parade route" selling balloons—on one is Isabella, on another is Ferdinand, on another those three ships, and on the fourth, a California mission. As in most of the cartoons, Coyote sports a stupefyingly wicked grin. In another drawing, there's a two-headed Coyote in missionary garb, with that grin again, saying "Trust me."

At these renditions of Coyote's revisionist history, and those of "Coyote as simple man," some readers will laugh out loud, and some will just say "huh?" For those who don't "get" it, there's an appendix (with Coyote using a pointer on a diagram of a human torso) with brief explanations of the cartoons.

On the cover is Coyote of course, fully clothed, floating on a lake with his mouth open. There are four fish, three in the water, and one jumping right over his mouth. The caption says, "Coyote fishing. Fish laughing."

I was sorry to miss L. Frank's exhibit at the American Indian Contemporary Arts Gallery in San Francisco, but I can see in my mind's eye some of the patrons commenting on the genius of her minimalist art, while L. Frank, with Coyote behind her, tries not to laugh out loud.

The title, L. Frank says, is from the Marx Brothers movie, "Duck Soup." I knew that.—*Beverly Slapin*

French, Fiona, *Lord of the Animals: A Miwok Indian Creation Myth*, illustrated by the author. Millbrook (1997). Unpaginated, color illustrations; grades 2-4; Miwuk
Sage, James, *Coyote Makes Man*, illustrated by Britta Teckentrup. Simon & Schuster (1994). Unpaginated, color illustrations; grades 1-2; Crow and other Nations

In *Lord of the Animals*, French, drawing on extremely dated anthropological sources has written a creation "myth": Coyote, after having made the world and all the creatures in it, decides to create a "Lord of the Animals"—"If he is to rule over us, he has to be a very superior creature." So the animals argue about how this superior creature should look and behave—"the fur and feathers fly!"—and Coyote finally creates someone who's supposed to look like an Indian, arms crossed on chest, headband with feather.

This book is an offensive mishmash. Perhaps most importantly, no indigenous cosmology on the face of this continent sees humans as "Lord of the Animals." That is a Christian concept, not an Indian one. The southwest-style designs have nothing to do with Miwuk culture. (And Miwuk people don't—and never did—live in tipis.) French states: "This tale is one of the surviving vestiges of an elaborate culture of hunter-gatherers which has virtually vanished." This is simply not true, and reveals the depth of her ignorance.

In *Coyote Makes Man*, Sage has combined a number of stories from various sources. Unlike French's book, Sage's interpretation leaves out the non-Indian concept of humans as superior to the other animals, and Techentrup's collage artwork makes no attempt to look "Indian." But the story, like *Lord of the Animals*, is clunky and humorless and the pictures are ugly. And his statement that "I hope that this tale will inspire young readers to explore the richness of Native American mythology and culture" is insulting.—*Beverly Slapin*

Goldin, Barbara Diamond, *Coyote and the Fire Stick: A Pacific Northwest Indian Tale*, illustrated by Will Hillenbrand. Gulliver/Harcourt Brace (1996). Unpaginated, color illustrations; grades 1-3

Coyote and the Fire Stick is loosely based on a Karuk story, as well as the fire-bringing stories of other peoples of the Northwest Coast. As with *Fire Race*, the dialogue is belabored, and carries a "cultural lesson":

> "Coyote, you have taught us so many things: how to make fish traps and how to spear salmon, how to dry the fish and store it for the winter," they said. "Now we need Fire. We are tired of the cold and the dark. You are so wise, Coyote. Can you help us get Fire? We cannot do it without your help."

Here, "evil spirits" keep the fire. In Mary Ike's Karuk telling,[1] fire is held by the *pishpish* (Yellow Jackets). In Barry Lopez's version,[2] the *skookums* have it. And in Erdoes and Ortiz's Klamath telling,[3] fire is held by Thunder. In none of the fire-bringing stories I have heard have the fire-keepers been described as "evil." Powerful, yes. Selfish, yes. But not "evil." Whether this is only a simplification, or a value judgment, it is disturbing. So much of Native belief was—and is—considered "evil"; this is at least an unfortunate choice of words.

Goldin also cleans up the story, to its detriment. In Lopez's version, Coyote decides "to ask his three sisters, who always lived in the form of huckleberries in his stomach, to help him.... He defecated." Goldin has Coyote's sisters remaining in his stomach.

The illustrations attempt to keep the details right: the houses are OK, there are boats and racks of salmon drying. But the faces don't work, the people are wearing generic Northwest cedar-bark outfits, and the "evil spirits" look more like Trolls than anything else. Not recommended.—*Beverly Slapin*

NOTES

1 Kroeber, A. L., and E.W. Gifford, *Karok Myths*. University of California, 1980, pp. 11-12.

2 Lopez, Barry, *Giving Birth to Thunder, Sleeping With His Daughter: Coyote Builds North America*. Avon, 1977, pp. 11-13.

3 Erdoes, Richard, and Alfonso Ortiz, eds., *American Indian Trickster Tales*. Viking, 1998), pp. 18-19.

Hayes, Joe, *Coyote &: Native American Folktales*, illustrated by Lucy Jelinek. Mariposa Publishing (1983, 1993). 75 pages, b/w illustrations; grades 3-6

In this collection of Coyote stories, Hayes retells stories he has found in old anthropological collections; so they are actually retellings of retellings. He assures readers that these are not "sacred" tales, but stories "told for entertainment," that they "do not belong to any single tribe," and that they are a "combination of the inspiration of the old stories and the imagination of the storyteller." Bunk. Stories belong to individuals, families, clans, Nations. To take a little of this and a little of that and mix them together, call them "Native American Folktales" and put your name to them is to steal and to lie. Neither Joe Hayes nor Lucy Jelinek truly understands this Being called Coyote. If they had, they probably wouldn't have produced this book. —*Beverly Slapin*

Johnston, Tony, *The Tale of Rabbit and Coyote,* **illustrated by Tomie dePaola. Putnam (1994). Unpaginated, color illustrations; preschool-grade 1; Zapotec**

"One full moon night, Rabbit found a field of chiles. He was so pleased to see them, all glossy and green, that he jumped right in and ate the biggest ones." Needless to say, the farmer is not pleased. So he makes a wax doll....

When Coyote comes along and finds Rabbit hanging in a bag waiting to be lunch, Rabbit talks him into trading places, and the chase is on. Rabbit outsmarts Coyote at every turn, until at last he climbs a ladder to the moon. But Coyote has never been able to find that ladder, and that is why "to this very day, Coyote sits gazing at the moon. And now and then, he howls at it, for he is still very furious with Rabbit."

An author's note tells us that the story is from the town of Juchitán, in Mexico. Johnston's version is done with wit and a light touch. The illustrations add in no small measure to the humor, but I'd be willing to bet that when Coyote got stung by the wasps, he did say something besides "conejo malvado."

One small caveat: One could wish that the farmer had been drawn a little less as a caricature. Otherwise, I really like it.—*Doris Seale*

King, Thomas (Cherokee), *A Coyote Columbus Story,* **illustrated by William Kent Monkman (Cree). Douglas & McIntyre (1992, 2002). Unpaginated, color illustrations; all grades**

A Coyote Columbus Story was originally published Canada in 1992 because nobody in this country would touch it with a ten-foot pole. Ten years later, it remains the only children's book about the Columbus "encounter" written from a Native perspective.

You see, it all started because what Coyote loved to do better than anything else in the world was play ball.

It was Coyote who fixed up this world, you know. She is the one who did it. She made rainbows and flowers and clouds and rivers. And she made prune juice and afternoon naps and toe-nail polish and television commercials. Some of these things were pretty good, and some of these things were foolish. But what she loved to do best was to play ball.

The problem is that when Coyote is bored, she sings her song and dances her dance and in the process of calling up someone to play ball with, she gets beavers, moose, turtles, and finally, humans. And that would have been OK, except that she kept changing the rules, so finally the people wouldn't play with her anymore. So the next time she sings her song and dances her dance, she's also thinking about changing the rules and doesn't pay attention to what she's doing. What she gets is this: "three ships and some people in funny-looking clothes carrying flags and boxes of junk." And the rest, as they say, is history.

This is a very funny book. Probably a full appreciation of it depends on a certain knowledge of history—and not necessarily the kind we learned in school. It is also a very good illustration of the way in which Coyote continues to live in Native storytelling, and is worlds away from most of the "retellings" to be found in the field of children's literature. The illustrations are zany and satirical—where not actually crazed—and suit the text perfectly.

For those who have said about this book that genocide is not funny, there is this: Humor has been our salvation. If we couldn't laugh, sometimes at really awful stuff, there wouldn't be *any* of us here.—*Doris Seale*

King, Thomas (Cherokee), *Coyote Sings to the Moon,* **illustrated by Johnny Wales. Key Porter Books (1998). Unpaginated, color illustrations; grades 2-up**

It was long ago, before the animals stopped talking to the humans. Coyote wants to join Old Woman and the animals in singing to the moon. But, insulted by the animals (something about his atrocious singing voice), he in turn insults Moon, who packs her bags, slides out of the sky, dives down into the pond and plays chess with the sunfish—leaving everyone in the dark. So Old Woman and the animals try to get her back up to the sky. So of course Coyote—who keeps crashing into trees and rocks and wet moss and has an unpleasant encounter with a skunk he didn't see because, well, it was too dark—wants to help again. So Old Woman hatches a plan, which includes Coyote in a starring role. In case anyone thinks this is one of those "how-it-came-to-be legends," it's not. Not even close. Tom King made it up.

This is a hilarious story by a brilliant writer who knows

and understands Coyote. Unfortunately, the same cannot be said of the illustrator. The drawings are too dark, and Coyote looks like a buffoon, which is, of course, only part of who he is.—*Beverly Slapin*

Kootenai Culture Committee, Confederated Salish and Kootenai Tribes, *Coyote Stories of the Montana Salish Indians,* **told by Pete Beaverhead and Eneas Pierre (both Salish), illustrated by Tony Sandoval, Alameda Addison, and Andy Woodcock (all Salish). Salish Kootenai College and Montana Historical Society (1981, 1991). 62 pages, b/w illustrations; grades 1-up; Ktunaxa (Salish)**

In "Coyote Gets Lovesick," told by Pete Beaverhead, Coyote is so struck by the beauty of the chief's daughter—"'Hay, yo! Beautiful! That's the way it is. She is beautiful! Beautiful! Beautiful! Beautiful!' Coyote couldn't stop saying how beautiful she was. 'Beautiful! Beautiful! Beautiful!'"—that he forgets to eat and drink, and of course, dies of starvation. He comes back to life of course, and that's why people no longer die of lovesickness. In "Coyote and Raven," told by Eneas Pierre, hungry Coyote tricks Raven into dropping the grease he is carrying. And in "Coyote's Dry Meat Turns Into Live Deer," Pete Beaverhead tells how sharing is never enough for Coyote, whose greed gets the best of him. The black-and-white drawings are excellent. Highly recommended.—*Beverly Slapin*

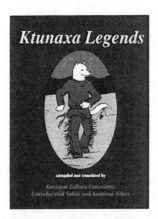

Kootenai Culture Committee, Confederated Salish and Kootenai Tribes, *Ktunaxa Legends,* **illustrated by Francis Auld, Debbie Joseph Finley, Verna Lefthand, and Frannie Burke (all Salish). Salish Kootenai College (1997). 380 pages, b/w line drawings; grades 2-up; Ktunaxa (Salish)**

The stories here are told by Native elders in the way in which the people actually say them—without apology, explanation, adaptation, retelling, editing, or anthropological gobbledygook. If you "get" them, good; if not, that's OK too. Most of them are about Coyote, and they run the gamut of his behaviors: good, whether by accident

or design; bad; and just plain foolish. Sometimes he gets his comeuppance, but good. But he always comes back, because he is a supernatural being.

He is *never* portrayed as "cute."

There are stories here that will seem familiar, from the versions told by people of the other Native Nations, but many of these have not seen print before this, or at least not in any form that would make anyone want to read them. The illustrations are by a variety of artists; all are line drawings that very well fit the spirit of the stories. Some are so funny that they make you smile even before you have read the text.

A map showing the locations of Ktunaxa communities is included, and it's good to have the photographs of the storytellers. Valuable as source material, of course, without question, but the book is a delight, and children will love the stories. The introduction gives some history, and the reason for doing the collection:

> Preservation, protection, perpetuation and enhancement of the culture and language have been a continuous goal of the Committee, but it has been an everlasting goal of the people.

Clearly written with no mind to please white audiences, this book is almost as though to say, you want to take our stories, you want to retell them? Now, see how they are *supposed* to be. In the face of the enormous takeover of Native literatures by those who apparently think they can do it better, this stands as the real thing.—*Doris Seale*

Kreipe de Montaño, Marty (Prairie Band Potawatomi), *Coyote in Love with a Star,* **illustrated by Tom Coffin (Prairie Band Potawatomi/Creek). Abbeville (1998). Unpaginated, color illustrations; all grades; Potawatomi**

This is a well-done modern adaptation of a traditional Potawatomi tale, this time with Coyote leaving the reservation and heading for New York City, where he gets a job as rodent control officer at the World Trade Center. Lonely for home and looking for escape from the noise of the city, he goes up to the observation deck for some solitude, and there is smitten by a star in the night sky. At first, star ignores Coyote; but after awhile they begin to dance together. Soon, they figure out that they are just not a match, and the star drops Coyote into Central Park, where his landing creates the reservoir. And ever since, coyotes have been scolding that night star, for dropping their grandfather.

The drawings go well with the story; clearly the author and illustrator worked together. The Potawatomi reservation is depicted as a vast, green expanse; sharply contrasted with New York City, painted as crowded and noisy. I especially like the details such as a moving van with the sign "Navajo Freight Line" and the bus with a Calvin Klein ad, the Cuban-Chinese restaurant next to Ray's Pizza, Java Joint, Kabobs, and Sushi Bar, and the trash can with trash on the sidewalk next to it.

There are many versions of this story; this one is especially fun.—*Beverly Slapin*

London, Jonathan, *Fire Race: A Karuk Coyote Tale*, illustrated by Sylvia Long. Chronicle Books (1993). Unpaginated, color illustrations; grades k-3; Karuk

There are probably as many stories about how animals got fire as there are Native Nations on Turtle Island. London has based this one on "various versions of the Karuk myth." One that is written down was told to and recorded by A .L. Kroeber and E. W. Gifford by Mary Ike.[1] Compare openings.

Ike's:

> Coyote grew at Panamenik: that was his place: he lived there long. Now others grew elsewhere. Then Coyote said, "Let us get fire."

London's:

> Long ago, the animal people had no fire. Day and night, they huddled in their houses in the dark, and ate their food uncooked. In the winter, they were so cold, icicles hung from their fur. Oh, they were miserable!

Then one day, Wise Old Coyote gathered everybody together. "We have heard about fire," he said. "But the only fire is far upriver, at the world's end. It's guarded by the Yellow Jacket sisters high atop a snowy mountain. They are wicked, and will not share it. But listen, if we all cooperate and work together, we can steal the fire." There was much fearful murmuring about the Yellow Jacket sisters, but all grew quiet as Coyote told them his plan. Then he went on his way. (I've heard Coyote called a lot of things. Wise wasn't one of them.)

Ike concludes her story in this way:

> There are only two trees that make fire well, willow at the river and cedar on the mountain. Cedar grew at the same time; it was Buzzard who made fire on the hill....he had made it with cedar bark made fine. He blew hard on the tinder, it blazed up, and he burned his face and head and looked as he does now.

In London's version, Buzzard does not appear at all.

> Frog burst out of the water, and spat the hot coal into the roots of a willow growing along the river. The tree swallowed the fire, and the animal people didn't know what to do. Then once again Coyote

came along, and the animal people said, "Grandfather, you must show us how to get the fire from the willow." So Old Man Coyote, who is very wise and knows these things, said, "Hah!" And he showed them how to rub two willow sticks together over dry moss to make fire. From that time on the people have known how to make fire. From that day on the people have known how to coax fire from the wood in order to keep warm and to cook their food. And at night in the seasons of cold, they have sat in a circle around their fires and listened as the elders told the old stories....

It is not so much that London changes things—it seems to be almost a natural impulse with so many retellers of Native stories. Or even that his verbosity becomes just plain boring. It's that you don't change the nature of the story. For Native peoples, Coyote is a trickster—like Anansi, like Rabbit, like Mantis. He is a liar, a sneak, a cheat, and a thief (all helpful traits for stealing fire, no?). He gets up to some very nasty things from time to time. It is true that he sometimes accomplishes things. It is also true that, more times, he just manages to outsmart himself, and most of the things he accomplishes are done by accident—a sort of byproduct of whatever scam he was trying to work at the moment. London treats his Coyote with a whole lot too much respect. Coyote is not really a person we honor, in that way— more like, you better have a healthy respect for his ability to make trouble, and keep out of his way—even if you laugh at him. And that's how it is, "even to this day."

The illustrations don't make it either. The things that Sylvia Long (of *Ten Little Rabbits* fame[2]) has put on the animals—such as dentilium and abalone shell necklaces—don't make the book look any more "Indian"; they just look silly. And isn't that a woman's hat that Coyote is wearing?

Mary Ike's story, even as written down by anthropologists, is good. This one is terrible.—*Doris Seale*

NOTES

1 Kroeber, A. L., and E.W. Gifford, *Karok Myths*. University of California, 1980, pp. 11-12.

2 Grossman, Virginia, and Sylvia Long, *Ten Little Rabbits*. Chronicle Books, 1991.

Lopez, Barry, *Giving Birth to Thunder, Sleeping With His Daughter: Coyote Builds North America.* **Avon (1977). 169 pages; high school-up**

This is a book that many people are using as a resource. There are sixty-eight stories from forty-three Nations, a foreword by Barre Toelkin, an introduction and bibliographic notes. Here, Lopez lists his sources, largely scholarly publications. He also cites George Bird Grinnell, Joseph Epes Brown, Walter Capps, J. Frank Dobie, Mourning Dove, Zitkala Sa—"Gertrude Bonin"—among others. Although not all his sources are those I would have used—Gary Snyder is one who comes to mind—and there is little indication that Lopez has consulted any living Native storytellers, he does seem to have made an effort to do an honorable job and not to trivialize the material.

This is not a children's book. Lopez' work would be considered inappropriate for them, because he has retained the sexual and scatological references. He says, in the Introduction:

> A number of things make this collection unique.... First, it includes Coyote's erotic adventures. Sexual references, as well as stories of cannibalism and bodily functions were almost invariably expurgated.... the deletion of such offensive material projected an unfaithful version of Coyote...

One difficulty in preparing such a collection is that there are many versions of nearly every Coyote story. So there can hardly be one "right" version. This is a fact of which many who use Native material have made much. However, there is an obligation to make every effort to adhere to the heart and spirit of the stories. This, I believe, Lopez has tried to do. One could pick at his work, particularly his sense of being the only person who had really gotten it right, but when compared to some of the other titles reviewed here, this begins to look pretty good.—*Doris Seale*

Mayo, Gretchen Will, illustrated by the author. Walker (1993). 36 pages, color illustrations; preschool-grade 2:
Meet Tricky Coyote!
That Tricky Coyote!

The press release for these two books mentions 1993 as the Year of Native Peoples, "making this a perfect time to explore Native American folklore with young readers." Each contains six stories, the same acknowledgments, and the same afterword—"Who is Coyote?"—by Jay Miller of the Newberry Library.

These books are perfect examples of the phrase "dumbing down." Each story is idiotically simplified. Also cleaned up. In the *real* version of the story Mayo calls "Burrrrrrrrup!" (I hope I got the right number of r's here), that isn't burping that Coyote's doing after eating too much cheese.

The illustrations are of like quality. Of them, Mayo says, "People imagine Coyote in many ways. Some say Coyote shimmers. This is the vision that grew in the artist's mind as she got to know Coyote..." So in every one of them, he's outlined in gold.

Although she notes the story "Tricky Coyote" as a Comanche version, Mayo has chosen to illustrate the story with a very blond, very Anglo, cowboy: "Like many American Indian stories, this one has grown and changed as it was passed from group to group." Not that much.

It's odd how Coyote is spoken of outside his own environment, sometimes "wise, strong and powerful," sometimes "endearing," because of his "similarities to human nature" (publisher's flyer):

> Meet Tricky Coyote!
> He thinks he can do anything.
> It's true, Coyote did some good things.
> He gave us fire. He made the mountains.
> He put the stars in the sky.
> Such important work!
> You would think Coyote could behave.
> But he doesn't.
> He is greedy.
> He is silly.
> He cheats.
> He brags.
> What a mischief-maker!
> When will you learn, Coyote?

This is not cute. Whatever he is, Coyote is not cute. "Retell" our stories, if you must—you will anyway, whether we want you to or not—but *don't* make them stupid.
—*Doris Seale*

McDermott, Gerald, *Coyote: A Trickster Tale from the American Southwest*, illustrated by the author. Harcourt Brace (1994). Unpaginated, color illustrations; preschool-grade 3

McDermott's fiery colors, sharp lines, and a trickster character who looks and acts like Wile E. Coyote (except not as funny) combine to make this title a favorite for children and reviewers. Here, the vainglorious Coyote (who is bright blue) wants to fly like the crows and be "the greatest coyote in all the world." Actually (and unbeknownst to McDermott), he's the *only* Coyote in all the world. So he convinces a flock of crows to lend him some feathers. Whereupon Coyote becomes so annoying, the crows take their feathers back— midflight. And Coyote, like old Wile E., falls a long way, gets up none the worse for wear (except now he's the color of dust), and goes on to find more trouble.

The author, one of several popular strip-miners of Native stories, tends to have his stories fall flat as well. The people in whose territory these stories reside know that Coyote is a supernatural Being, and as Doris Seale says, "that knowledge informs the stories." McDermott's vaguely Zuni designs—including crows wearing headbands, the leader wearing a turquoise necklace and a pendant inlaid with turquoise, coral, jet and abalone—a blue Coyote, and CIP data identifying this as a legend of "Indians of North America" do not make it so.

—*Beverly Slapin*

Morgan, William (Diné), collector, *Navajo Coyote Tales*, adapted in English by Hildegard Thompson, illustrated by Jenny Lind. Ancient City Press, (1949, 1988). 49 pages, b/w illustrations; grades 1-3; Diné (Navajo)
Roessel, Robert, and Dillon Platero (Diné), *Coyote Stories of the Navajo People*, illustrated by George Mitchell. Rough Rock Press (1991, 2003). 100 pages, color illustrations; grades 4-6 (younger for read-aloud); Diné (Navajo)

Coyote Stories of the Navajo People is one of a series of books developed by the Navajo Curriculum Center of the Rough Rock Demonstration School for use with Diné children, as an alternative to the books illustrating "blond-haired, blue-eyed children, running to meet their father when he comes home from work." There are fourteen stories here, some of which will be familiar from other sources. "Coyote Loses His Eyes," for example, is one written down in many different places.

This is an interesting collection. Some of the stories do end with "and that is why, such-and-such, even today," but because they are being told for Native children by Native people, there has been no compulsion to "explain" or elaborate on tales that have been honed in the telling, over and over again, for who-knows-how-many centuries. And the introduction says some very important things: that these are winter-telling stories, and therefore, "those who contributed these stories have requested they be used only during the winter months," and that "these tales are part of the enormous mythological treasures of the Navajo people. They are not meaningless or merely colorful cartoons...They have great significance to the Navajos... They are considered actual occurrences and are not the results of artistic imaginations."

Navajo Coyote Tales begins with a singularly inept introduction:

> During the last decade or so many of the customs which formerly characterized the Navajo people have tended to disappear. Among these apparently dying customs is story-telling....To shorten the hours of darkness, people wanted to remain awake as long as possible....The myths and legends of the Navajo have close analogy to the multitude of stories and fables which are inherited from our Greek, Roman, Celtic and Germanic ancestors...

There are six stories, with language adapted for beginning readers for the purpose of providing "Navajo children, who are learning to read, with materials familiar to them." The book was first published by the BIA in 1949, and the foreword is by Robert W. Young, "Specialist in Indian Languages," whatever that may mean. The story "Coyote and Horned Toad" does not compare favorably with either the version in *Coyote Stories of the Navajo People* or with Shonto Begay's *Ma'ii and Cousin Horned Toad*. It seems to me that children would be better off hearing these stories from their elders rather than trying to read these watered-down adapted versions.—*Doris Seale*

Mourning Dove (Okanagan), *Coyote Stories*, edited and illustrated by Heister Dean Guie. University of Nebraska (1933, 1990). 246 pages, b/w illustrations; grades 5-up; Okanagan

Coyote Stories, first published in 1933, has been reissued with an introduction by Jay Miller, telling something of Mourning Dove's life and the ways in which her material was modified to suit the temper of the times.

> Though concerned with the decorum of these stories, Mourning Dove did include some carry-overs and hints from the traditional contexts, but she carefully avoided calling attention to them. Her treatment of Coyote is particularly cursory, requiring further explication....Despite claims of traditional authenticity [the] legends are not true to Salishan recitations.

Miller takes the opportunity to go on at some length about "recitation"; how audiences were expected to respond, which sound was to be made in order to encourage the storyteller, depending on whether the people came from the "ay" chain or the "ii" chain, etc. All this may be of some anthropological interest. It seems an odd kind of introduction to write for a book you might want someone to read. Whatever Miller may mean by a "particularly cursory" treatment of Coyote, whatever may have been edited out of Mourning Dove's work, the fact remains that the stories in this collection, more than many, retain the flavor of the spoken word and traditional story form. The difference made by having grown up with the stories, as against "retelling" them from other printed collections, is evident. Rhythm, pacing, circularity—all here.

The stories are set down with charm and humor. Coyote's essential character comes through quite clearly, from his first beginnings as a being of power, on "Naming Day," through his journey to the sky world along the "Arrow Trail."

It would behoove us to remember what life was like, those times, and that no Native writer's work saw print without some sort of white imprimatur. Enjoy the stories. Be glad that you have them, in this human way, and remember that Mourning Dove and others like her made a road that made it a little easier for the rest of us to follow.—*Doris Seale*

Oughton, Jerrie, *How the Stars Fell Into the Sky: A Navajo Legend,* **illustrated by Lisa Desimini. Houghton Mifflin (1992). Unpaginated, color illustrations; grades preschool-2; Diné (Navajo)**
Taylor, Harriet Peck, *Coyote Places the Stars,* **illustrated by the author. Bradbury (1993). Unpaginated, color illustrations; preschool-grade 2; Wasco**

There are many different versions of this story. Taylor cites two sources for hers: "Coyote Scatters the Stars" in *They Dance in the Sky: Native American Star Myths* by Jean Guard Monroe and Ray A. Williamson (Houghton Mifflin, 1987), and "Coyote Places the Stars" in Barry Lopez' *Giving Birth to Thunder, Sleeping With His Daughter: Coyote Builds North America.* Taylor's retelling does not very much resemble either of them, beyond the fact that all of them contain a coyote, some arrows, and the stars. She also seems to have missed the point that Coyote acts out of his usual

inability to keep his paws out of anything and not from out of any desire to be creative. (The book is dedicated "to stargazers everywhere, and to their dreams.")

In every version of the story that I know, someone— First Woman, Our Mother, Black God—about which more later—is carefully placing the stars in the sky, in a pattern, for a purpose. Short version: Along comes Coyote and grabs them, and sploosh! Up they go. And that was that. Sometimes the stories say that's why the stars have so little pattern, or the patterns have so few names. Taylor chooses to make Coyote a hero, being the one who got the whole idea in the first place. After he got through making all this beauty, he called all the animals, who gave a great feast for him, and "decreed that Coyote was the most clever and crafty of all the animals." This made Coyote so happy that he said, "I will always be your friend and the friend of your children's children." So, if you happen to hear "the magical howl of Coyote [he] is calling you to go to your window, to gaze at the star pictures, and to dream."

The illustrations are pretty, but they and the story seem to have more to do with the southwest-style coyotes that you see all over the place than anything else.

Oughton says that her version is a

> retelling of a legend told to the Navajo Indians by Hosteen Klah, their great medicine man, at the turn of the twentieth century. It is part of the mythology that details the mysteries of Earth in the beginning.

The jacket copy says, "She was inspired to write how the stars fell into the sky after coming across a brief reference to the legend in a National Geographic article." By offering no further information, Oughton has made it difficult, but not impossible, to compare her work with the original.

By one of those odd chances that are not chance, a copy of an old book happened to fall into my hands. It is called *Navajo Creation Myth: The Story of the Emergence* by Hasteen Klah. In an introduction, Mary C. Wheelwright says that he was a Medicine Man, and the grandson of Narbona, who was killed under a flag of truce in 1847. This book chronicles the Diné emergence, from the first through the fourth worlds, and all the things that happened to make the world we live in, through the "Journey of the Two Children to Estan-ah-ah-Hehay."[1]

Whether Oughton had access to this book or only saw a mention of it in her "National Geographic article," one can't say. In any case, her story bears almost no relation to the one set down here, which is told as part of the "Beginning of the World Song." In her book, First Woman is worried about how they are going to "write the laws for all to see," in order to help the people. First Man gets aggravated and says, "Take your jewels and write them in the sky." So she's doing that, when Coyote comes along. She lets him help, but he doesn't like how long it takes, so he flings them out. First Woman screams at Coyote and weeps, because "There was no ending what Coyote had done." And that is why "The people rose and went about their lives...never knowing the reason for the confusion that would always dwell among them."

The story in the Klah book that is told as part of the "Beginning of the World Song" is simply that the spirits are placing the stars, and Begochiddy invites Etsay-Hasteen, First Man, and Etsa-Assun, First Woman, to help. Coyote wants to help, but when they wouldn't give him more than three stars, he grabbed two pawsful and flung them all over the sky. The end.

The business about the "laws" apparently comes from Monroe and Williamson, where Black God says, "Look at all the beautiful patterns I have created. These patterns will provide humans with rules to live by on earth." In any case, what Oughton says is true: "She was inspired to write *How the Stars Fell Into the Sky*." and it is her story. She has basically made it up to suit herself. Take the story, rearrange it, make it "make sense," pad it, so that it's long enough to be a book, "explain" everything, add a moral, and you have something that is a shell with no substance—sort of like white rice or "degerminated" corn meal.—*Doris Seale*

NOTE

1 All spellings of Navajo words are from the book.

Ramirez, Alex O. (Rumsien Ohlone), *Tjatjakiymatchan (Coyote): A Legend from Carmel Valley*, illustrated by the author. Oyate (1995). Unpaginated, b/w illustrations; preschool-up; Rumsien Ohlone

"Fox was truly a proud fur person, and reasonably so. There was also Coyote, and one of his favorite pastimes was playing tricks on Fox." But to be tricked by Coyote twice in one day! Here, Ramirez tells how that happened. It's evening in the Carmel Valley, and Ramirez's grandfather, after hearing Coyote howl, would say, "Sta solo" (He's lonely). And then he'd tell this story.

The writing is a lovely thing, round, and with many levels of meaning, both in the prologue and in the story itself; past and present, coming together. And,

> Today, I wonder if those were tears I saw as (Grandfather) lifted his eyes to the darkened ceiling. I wonder if he was remembering times he had heard about—when Mother Earth was

very young and beautiful and our people would gather in their warm lodges and listen as the Elders told their stories.

The soft pencil illustrations complement the mood of the story. This is how it should be done.—*Doris Seale*

Root, Phyllis, *Coyote and the Magic Words*, illustrated by Sandra Speidel. Lothrop, Lee & Shepard (1993). Unpaginated, color illustrations; grades 1-3

> Once, my children, when the world was new, all words were magic words. For that is how the Maker-of-all-things spoke the world into being. "Earth," she said. And the earth hung in space green and blue and shining.

And so on, until,

> Us, too, she made, my children. Last of all.... Then, because she was tired from all her work, the Maker-of-all-things closed her eyes and slept.

Everyone was happy and content except Coyote, who was bored. So he set about making mischief with the magic words, until he had created so much commotion that it woke up the Maker-of-all-things. And she said, OK, no more magic words. But Coyote pleaded for magic, because what would the world be without it? So she relented and said magic could still exist in stories.

> And so it is, my children, that there are still magic words in the world, and I have just told you some of them. So it is, too, that Coyote goes around making up stories. He is trying to bring magic into the world.

Root's disclaimer is that this is an original story:

> It is not a legend or a myth. It came out of my life, as all stories must. This story was given to me by a trip to the desert, a brilliant autumn day, and a wily four-legged trickster named Coyote. It was given to me to tell. I give it to you.

This is because back home in Minnesota, "Coyote offered to tell me that storytellers are creators." Right. And, although *Coyote and the Magic Words* "shares many things with many Southwestern stories," it is "not a story of any group or tribe of people." So I guess we have here a generic Indian—oops, Coyote—story. The illustrations, soft pastels, are rather pretty, I guess. The Maker-of-all-things is definitely a Native woman, and so are all the people portrayed, Native people. And there's the loom and the pueblos and the pottery. It would be hard for most not to see this as a Native story. It would be hard not to see this story as an attempt to cash in on the current fashionableness of things Indian and the current fashionableness of things multicultural. But whoever would have thought Coyote would be "in"?

—Doris Seale

Sekaquaptewa, Eugene (Hopi), teller, *Coyote & the Winnowing Birds*. 96 pages
Talashoema, Herschel (Hopi), teller, *Coyote & Little Turtle*. 91 pages translated and edited by Emory Sekaquaptewa (Hopi) and Barbara Pepper, illustrated by Hopi children. Clear Light (1994). color illustrations; preschool–grade 3; Hopi

These two stories, based on Hopi stories told by Herschel Talashoema and Eugene Sekaquaptewa, are Hopi-English stories done at the Hotevilla-Bacavi Community School. They are accompanied by sections on Hopi grammar, Hopi-English/English-Hopi glossaries and pages of information on the Hopi alphabet, language structure and pronunciation. The stories are told in a beautifully simple, straightforward way, with illustrations by Hopi children.

In *Coyote & Little Turtle*, the turtles are looking for food. Little Turtle gets tired, so he goes off under a bush to sleep. When he wakes up, everybody is gone, and he begins to cry. Coyote, who was also out hunting, hears him and thinks he is singing. Coyote threatens to do a couple of unpleasant things to Little Turtle unless he sings again, to which Little Turtle says, OK fine, but when Coyote says he's going to throw him into the spring, Little Turtle says, "Oh, noooo!...." Well, you know how it goes.

In *Coyote & the Winnowing Birds*, Coyote sees the birds winnowing their grass seed, and, feeling hungry, schemes of a way to catch them. So he tells the birds that he wants to fly with them, and they fix him up with some feathers. Once they get him up there, though, not being stupid, they pull out his feathers, and down goes Coyote, splat. And that's the end of that.

"This is the way you'll have to be," the birds said to Coyote. "It's your own fault, since you wanted to hurt us by lying to us."

Those who are put off by the way this story ends should keep in mind that any Native audience would know that this is far from the end of Coyote, who always comes back to life and will be getting into some new kind of devilment tomorrow.

These stories could easily serve as a genuine window on another world for non-Native children. It's hard to imagine any child not enjoying the stories and pictures. However, they were designed primarily for use with Hopi children, and this is most important, because "we must now begin to record and preserve the language for our future and for the children whom we love and cherish."

No language, no identity.*—Doris Seale*

Stevens, Janet, illustrated by the author. Holiday House. Unpaginated, color illustrations; kindergarten–grade 3
***Coyote Steals the Blanket: A Ute Tale*. 1993**
***Old Bag of Bones: A Coyote Tale*. 1996; Shoshone**

Coyote Steals the Blanket is the one about how Coyote stole a blanket from an ancient rock, and nearly got creamed for doing it. The story is retold from Gail Robinson's and Douglas Hill's collection, *Coyote the Trickster*,[1] and is so attributed. Although the Robinson/Hill version is too long and literary to tell aloud easily, Steven's attempts to punch it up are not an improvement. One example: the simple:

> "I am just wandering," said Coyote, "today I will go farther along this canyon and see what is at its end. Tomorrow, who knows?"

becomes:

> Coyote darted in and out, back and forth among the rocks. "I go where I want, I do what I want, and take what I want," he bragged. "I should be crowned king of the desert."

As usual, there are many versions of this story, including one in which Coyote had originally given his blanket to the rock and then tales it back, and another one, in which Coyote gives the rock something we won't men-tion. So it is not possible to say that Steven's story is not "right." What is wrong with it is that it clunks. The pictures are somewhat amusing, in a slapstick Wile E. Coyote kind of way, but the words have no rhythm, no pacing, no flow. They carry no feel at all of the human voice. There doesn't seem to be any point to the way she has changed the ending—except maybe to show the little listeners that Coyote doesn't gain anything from his bad behavior? I do think most people would get that...

Old Bag of Bones is more of the same. "Loosely based" on "Old Man Coyote and Buffalo Power" in Alice Mariott and Carol K. Rachlin's *Plains Indian Mythology*,[2] this alleged Shoshone story has decrepit old Coyote complaining again, this time about his lack of youth, strength, power. So he goes to Young Buffalo, whom he knows will help him, since "he provides food, shelter, and clothing for the people..." So Young Buffalo changes him into a Buffote (buff-OH-tee), which is young, strong Coyote without the power. So Coyo—uh, we mean Buffote—meets other old animals and wants to share his recaptured youth with them ('cuz Coyote's such a sharing kinda guy), but they're not interested because they have wisdom, respect, and experience...

We rarely come across a story that is so boring and relentlessly didactic. It is hard sometimes not to say, "This book is stupid. It is really, really, stupid." —*Doris Seale* and *Beverly Slapin*

NOTES

1 Robinson, Gail, and Douglas Hill, *Coyote the Trickster*. Crane Russak, 1976.

2 Marriott, Alice, and Carol K. Rachlin, *Plains Indian Mythology*. Crowell, 1975.

Strauss, Susan, *Coyote Stories for Children*, illustrated by Gary Lund. Beyond Words (1991). Unpaginated, color illustrations; grades 1-3

This is part of a series called "Tales from Native America." Jacket copy says that "author and storyteller Susan Strauss is well known across the United States for her performances in conjunction with organizations such as the National Park and Forest Service, the Smithsonian Museum of Natural History, and the Roger Tory Peterson Institute." That qualifies her to write about Coyote, I guess. Her stories come framed in all kinds of dedications, thank-yous, acknowledgments and quotes, from all kinds of Native people: Brave Buffalo; "a Pueblo man"; Agnes Vanderburg, "Flathead Indian Elder"; Ed Edmo, Sr., "Shoshone-Bannock elder"; "a Modoc friend of mine"; and Black Elk, "a very famous Sioux Medicine Man."

Strauss speaks of the "inspiration" that was provided for her stories. It is good that she used that word, because her versions certainly take off on their own. An example of her style:

> Now, long ago... and I mean LONG ago...in the days before the coming of the human beings... there were only animal people. There were the four-leggeds...the deer people, the raccoon people, and the great big bear people. There were the snake people, the frog people, and the

insect people. In those days there were even plant people and rock people. The rock people are the oldest people in the world. They were here before anyone else...and for that, they deserve a lot of respect.

Egad.

The stories in this little book fail if for no other reason on a question of style. Too many words, too many cute little interpolations, too much trying to make them "child-like," probably too much trying to change them enough so that she could call them hers, and get a book out of it—and all the Native name-dropping doesn't mean a thing. Not recommended.—*Doris Seale*

Strete, Craig Kee (Cherokee), *Little Coyote Runs Away*, illustrated by Harvey Stevenson. Putnam (1997). Unpaginated, color illustrations; preschool-grade 2

I have never heard a Coyote story in which Coyote is "Little"; he usually gets into messes because he's characteristically greedy or lazy or horny or some combination of these attributes. Maybe this one is not *that* Coyote, maybe he's just a kid coyote named "Little Coyote."

Little Coyote doesn't like to listen to his mom, and when she tells him to wash his fur before eating, well, that's just the last straw, and he decides to run away. Mom, not terribly worried, reminds him to take his medicine bag to protect himself from danger, and off Little Coyote trots. After encountering a "green grass-eating giant goat," a "black-billed big-winged buzzard," and a "brown-backed, big-toothed bear," he's used up all his medicine, and there's a "horde of honking cars" to contend with. All this is just too much for a little coyote, "so he turned around and unran away" home, where he receives a welcome-back hug from his mom, happily cleans his fur, and settles down in his snug, warm den, where "home is the magic."

Anyone who has ever seen a coyote up close knows that they, like wolves, have eyebrows. And this little guy's expressions—ranging from mad to determined to hesitant to worried to *really* worried to content—are priceless. Stevenson's pictures, in pastels of golds, browns, and blues, are perfect.

Since *that* Coyote has never been known to learn a lesson, let it be assumed that *this* coyote will probably not grow up to be him.—*Beverly Slapin*

Taylor, Harriet Peck, *Coyote and the Laughing Butterflies,* **illustrated by the author. Macmillan (1995). Unpaginated, color illustrations; preschool-grade 2; Tewa**

This woman somehow manages to take a very funny story about how the butterflies trick the ever-oblivious Coyote over and over again, and turn it into a Lesson for Us All About Friendship And Sharing. The pictures are pretty, though.—*Beverly Slapin*

Ude, Wayne, *Maybe I Will Do Something: Seven Coyote Tales,* **illustrated by Abigail Rorer. Houghton Mifflin (1993). 75 pages, b/w illustrations; grades 4-6**

Ude's

> basic conception of Coyote is based on traditional American Indian tales, and many of the incidents in these stories also come from traditional tales. At the same time, I've tried to give Coyote more personality than he's usually given. For that, I've had to draw on my own imagination: what would a character like Coyote

really be like? Thus, these stories are a combination of traditional and newly imagined material.

Well, that's OK, I guess, but it really is unsettling when a story you know all of a sudden takes off on a flight of fancy. As for Coyote's "personality," I always thought he had more than enough for most people....

Ude says that "[t]here seem to be few Indian tales of a 'very beginning,'" and that's just plain not so. Just one from my own people is that at first there was nothing, except Inyan, Rock, until he got lonely and split himself, to begin everything that is. And there are many, many more.

So Ude does this thing:

> Since these stories begin in the very early days of the world, Coyote and the others have to learn how things work. Certainly, they don't know very much to start with. In fact, they aren't even sure where they are or how they got there, much less what powers they have, or how to use them. They're a little confused at first—but then, Coyote is always a little confused, even today.

Ude is a good writer; he doesn't make Coyote cute, and the illustrations are a knockout, but the book is just plain weird. And aside from paying tribute to Paul Radin, Franz Boas, and George Bird Grinnell, it would have been nice if he had mentioned that the people at Fork Belknap—where he "first knew American Indians as playmates"—are Assiniboine and Gros Ventre, not just "Indians."—*Doris Seale*

Coyote Blue

Coyote had a bad case
of the blues one day.
His paws, deep in his pockets,
he padded about
pretending that he was invisible.

Lone-Hare, in passing with great haste,
accidentally bumped into Coyote
who, very upset and shaken,
snapped at Lone-Hare, "How dare you
bump into me. Can't you see
that I'm invisible!"

—*Judith Mountain-Leaf Volborth* (Blackfoot/Comanche)

WATERBUGS

Fox Young Man was sitting by a mountain pool watching waterbugs circling one another, first one way, then another. He thought they resembled half-shells of small black nuts. They moved so swiftly that it was hard to keep focused on them. The edge of the pool was shallow and the shadows of the waterbugs went faster than their owners, having to climb stones and plants.

Coyote was passing by and came over to sit by Fox Young Man. He looked at the pool to see what was so interesting. All he could see were waterbugs and water. "Uh, what are you looking at, Fox Young Man?"

"I'm watching those waterbugs. They sure move fast. I wonder how they do it? Do you suppose they paddle around with legs? If they do, their legs must really move. Or maybe they have under-belly fins and a tail so think we can't see it, huh?"

Coyote sat awhile watching. The waterbugs really were kind of fascinating. He motioned across the pool to where a stream entered. "See that grass over there? Well, it's a kind of salt grass that's covered with tiny bugs that live on the salt warts that grow around the roots. That's all those little bugs eat, of course, and that's why they live underwater, 'cause if they ever surfaced they'd probably turn into salt crystals.

"If you went over there, you would see little bubbles always popping from those bugs burping. Yes, those bugs are so small that we can't see them. They're called Carbonated Buggers 'cause there's so many of them.

"And those waterbugs, that's all they eat, those little Carbonated Buggers. So they're always full of gas. And that's how they swim so fast. They just fart themselves in circles all day long. You can actually hear them farting if you stick one ear underwater, plug the other and close your eyes."

Fox Young Man looked at Coyote. "Coyote, I think you're making it up," he said.

"No, I wouldn't do that. It's an old, old story. Coyote Old Man himself told it to me. It was back when World-Maker was creating everything. He was working so fast one time, without resting, that he got what's called 'verbatim' which is when you get suddenly real dizzy and start talking to yourself. He got spots in front of his eyes swimming around.

"Now, because he was World-Maker, he figured that he'd created those spots for a reason. He was at a pool at the time, just making the first frog. So he took some of the spots swimming before his eyes and put them on Frog Person. But they weren't circling around on frog's skin, of course. They were just sitting there, but they looked okay so he left some on Frog Person.

"But he took the rest and turned them into waterbugs. And that's why so many pools of water look like eyeballs reflecting the sky and having waterbug spots swimming around in them. Yes, that's probably how it all happened."

Coyote got up then and walked away, saying over his shoulder, "Well, I gotta be going home for some mush. I guess I'll see you again if I ever run into you." So Coyote went over a hill, then circled back and looked at the pool from behind some brush. Sure enough, there was Fox Young Man with his head underwater, eyes closed and a paw covering one ear.

Coyote walked over the hill again and met Flicker. "You ever want to know about waterbugs," he told Flicker, "just go ask Fox Young Man. He'll tell you all about them."

"What?" said Flicker. "Coyote, what are you talking about?"

"Me?" answered Coyote. "Oh, I'm just letting you know how stories are born. That's all."

—Peter Blue Cloud

THIS IS ABOUT RAVEN

Fascination with what is called in English, the "Tricksters" of mythical traditions from all over the world is in truth a fascination with ourselves, our weaknesses, frailties and imperfections. The humanity of "Trickster" provides a window on ourselves, an opportunity for self-reflection in the safe and non-threatening frame of a story. In such stories the natural, supernatural and social worlds come together in ways that provide a cultural model of the universe, a model that is challenged, and twisted and tried by the antics of the "Trickster," a model that, however it is transformed, remembers itself. Consequently, telling and retelling myths is serious cultural work probably best pursued by those who are part of the cultural tapestry, woven into the very design, understanding the rules of transformation, the raveling and unraveling of cultural Beings. Myths help us to get a sense of the purpose of life.

Traditional storytellers in the Northwest tradition know their listeners and their listeners know them. Built into the language of the Northwest Coast are terms of address that place the teller and the listener in a sacred, structured relationship with moral obligations. Thus stories are told and retold in a mutual worldview, referencing common ancestral Beings in landscapes of territorial memory in which cultural meanings are worked out. "Tricksters" can be especially valuable teachers today in an era where Gaia, Mother Earth and Uranus, Father Sky, have been confounded through the technology of contemporary life. Their common ancestor, the androgynous "Chaos," seems to be once again ascendant. Particularly, in an era where Science is ascendant to deal with this Chaos, Myth seems to be eclipsed. And while Science answers questions about causes or "how," the "Tricksters" can help to challenge us to purposeful thinking.

Of the "tricksters" of North American traditions, Coyote and Raven are possibly the most renowned. "Raven" abounds in children's literature, seemingly the "trickster" of choice. Possibly Raven looks like an easy "trickster" to retell a story about. After all, Raven is "just" a bird. But "Raven the trickster," while having all the attributes of natural "birdness," also has the attributes of the supernatural in time and knowledge as well as the psycho-social understanding of the common culture of the story being told. Thus, "Raven" can mirror us holistically from the dawn of time into the haze of the future and all points in between. Consequently, in these reviews, we will look at a series of Raven stories set mainly in the Pacific Northwest in which Raven is a central figure of creation, a figure that helps us understand the moral universe of the diverse cultures of the Northwest Coast.

Beverly Slapin contributed the review of *Sika and the Raven.—Marlene R. Atleo/ʔeh ʔeh naa tuu kwiss*

REVIEWS: BOOKS ABOUT RAVEN

Cameron, Anne, Harbour Publishing, b/w illustrations; grades 2-up:
How Raven Freed the Moon (1985), illustrated by Tara Miller. 30 pages
Raven Goes Berrypicking (1991), illustrated by Gaye Hammond. 30 pages
Raven & Snipe (1991), illustrated by Gaye Hammond. 28 pages
Raven Returns the Water (1987), illustrated by Nellie Olsen. 28 pages

Nanaimo-born Anne Cameron is a non-Native woman who has made a career of taking traditional Northwest Coast First Nations stories out of their cultural context and adapting them for non-Native audiences. In many of these stories, Raven is recast as female, while the Raven of myth is by convention male, but is actually both male and female. Because Raven makes every rule, Raven breaks every rule. For some reason known only to Cameron, she makes the other characters female, too. In almost all of these stories, Raven gets "her" comeuppance in a way that is not usually characteristic of First Nations traditional tellings.

The black Raven sits starkly on the front cover of *Raven Goes Berrypicking*. This smallish, shiny, bright yellow book with the red title is attractive. Gaye Hammond's illustrations are naturalistic, black-and-white line drawings of birds, vegetation and coastline. The canoe, berries, and collection of birds suggest a Northwest Coast setting for this story.

Gull, Cormorant and Puffin are introduced as "girlfriends" whom a female Raven suggests go berrypicking with her. The theme is Raven's greed on a berrypicking excursion in which Raven systematically exploits her friends. There is nothing playful about her—she is a cold, calculating, opportunistic, glutton preying on her friends. While suspicious, they are loath to believe the worst until it becomes obvious. Then they become vio-

lent and vengeful: one blinds Raven with the sun, another wraps her in a blanket and another ties her up. Her beak is wrapped tightly so she cannot devour any more of their hard-won food. They beat her up "[b]ecause you are a glutton…[b]ecause you are a cheat…[b]ecause you are always up to something." After being allowed to choose her punishment, Raven spends four days gathering food to replace what she had gobbled up. When she is finished she tells them how sorry she is but they do not forgive her; Raven is in the end alone and lonely.

There is no "compassionate mind" at work here; only the heavy hand of the Avenger. This story is the antithesis of the search for peace, harmony, and friendship that our traditional stories convey. This retelling comes across as petty and mean. Yes, food is important but relationships are more important.

Misunderstandings and mistakes are errors but reconciliation is necessary for community living and friendship. Raven and the others are left debased, not only as mythical beings but even as creatures. This story could leave First Nations children feeling devalued if they identify with culture heroes who are portrayed this way.

Because this story is supposed to provide social lessons, the background needs to be consistent with actual happenings, so, for instance, that the ripening of the berries is out of sync is antithetical to traditional knowledge. And this is a collection of birds who never, in nature, hang out together. And at the end of our traditional stories there should always be hope.

The shiny, bright red cover of *Raven & Snipe* features a stylized Raven and Snipe in a circle, back-to-back as if in a standoff, each with a salmon egg in its beak. This retelling of the story of the deception of Raven by Snipe takes a nasty turn compared to the Clutesi telling and to other traditional versions. Snipe is not content to let Raven merely fail to reproduce the salmon eggs in the same sleight-of-hand Snipe uses; she coerces Raven into first burning herself and then causing herself to hit her leg so hard that she, in great pain, gives up trying. The dappler snipes are portrayed atypically as not only gathering but also storing and preserving food. The moral of the story, that Raven does not bother Snipe on the beach, is not an intuitive First Nations teaching. Raven and Snipe in nature occupy two different niches on the beach. Raven tracks up the sand when the tide is out and he doesn't have to get his feet too wet. Snipe is a dabbler who breezes along in the water up to his knees to sift for his preference in food. A respectful retelling would at least get the "facts" of the legend right.

In *Raven Returns the Water*, a water shortage on the Northwest Coast where rainfall is among the highest in the world is an unlikely theme for one of our traditional stories. But this is just another example of Cameron's style of setting up oppositions. Here, the showdown is between Raven and Frog. Raven has found that Frog has sucked up all the water, and means to teach her a lesson about Respect, Sharing and Living in Harmony. So Raven pierces the unsuspecting frog, gathers up the gushing water, and rearranges it over the parched land. Of course, in Cameron's catholic interpretation, Raven is forever taunting Frog, and Frog is forever doing penance by croaking "sor-ry, sor-ry." In her retelling, Cameron recasts poor Raven as a moralist because Raven certainly isn't a role model! In our stories, Raven embodies the whole spectrum of morality by teaching us how not to behave, but he himself is not a moralizer because he can't tell people how to behave.

In our traditional story about Raven stealing the light, Raven causes himself to be born into a noble family who has access to the light, steals the sun from the Sky Chief, and flies off with it. As told, it is a complex story, full of metaphor and "light."

But in Cameron's rendition, which she calls *How Raven Freed the Moon*, the Sky Chief and his daughter become a naïve old fisherwoman and her daughter, the sun becomes the moon, and somehow the daughter's magical pregnancy turns into a baby appearing at the door. Worse, Cameron keeps young readers "un-spellbound" by reminding them *seven times* that this baby is Raven before the characters have an inkling of their seduction. It's as if she thinks that children cannot follow a story that has Raven changing his shape. And in the end, when they have been stolen from and thoroughly duped, the women conclude that the end was worth the means because "Moon looks much better in the sky than it ever looked in that box." Culturally, this story makes no sense, and this moral is not one I would want my grandchildren to come away with.

Clutesi, George (Tse-shaht), *Son of Raven, Son of Deer: Fables of the Tse-Shaht People,* **illustrated by the author. Clutesi Agencies (1967, 1994). 125 pages, b/w illustrations; grades 5-up; Tse-shaht**

Chief George Clutesi's stories of Ko-ishin-mit come from the Tse-shaht people, citizens of the fourteen-Nation Nuu-chah-nulth peoples who live along windward side of the West Coast of Vancouver Island. Clutesi was a Tse-shaht speaker, and these are stories that *Nan-is* (grandparent) Clutesi would tell to his *Ka-oots* (grandchildren) to socialize and shape them in the moral universe of Tse-shaht. Seven of the thirteen stories are about *Ko-ishin-mit*, son of Raven. In each, Raven becomes the object of the lesson. This Raven is culturally embedded and specifically demonstrates particular teachings with clarity and humor. Raven becomes entangled in Nuu-chah-nulth norms so that the children who listen need not become entangled.

Most of Ko-ishin-mit's encounters are associated with a preoccupation about food getting. The stories of Raven's encounter with Herring Rake, Eagle, Bear and Snipe are all lessons about a fundamental Nuu-chah-nulth value: it is not good to mimic others (in how you try to get your food). The owner of the herring rake does not instruct Raven on the fine points of its use because Raven pretends he knows how. But Raven gets caught in the backlash as the herring rake comes up out of the water and hits him in the nose. Raven copies Eagle's fishing technique, but since he does not have the keen eye and swiftness of wing, he fails to bring salmon home for supper. Bear pours highly prized oil from his paws to anoint the salmon meal, but when Raven tries to do the same nothing comes out of his appendages. When Snipe uses sleight of hand to produce choice salmon eggs from his spindly legs Raven is impressed, but when Raven copies the maneuver he comes up not only empty-handed but hurt. The not-so-hidden lesson here is that there is always more to what is going on than meets the eye, that each individual being has a particular integrity, and that copying others violates that principle.

The story of Raven and the Shadow people is about materialism. Raven sets out with his wife to an island that abounds with wonderful objects that he immediately begins to load in his canoe. Pash-hook sits by the fire warming herself while he loads until the canoe can hold no more. He finds her rooted beside the fire. Only when he returns everything to its place is she freed. She reports that there are Shadow people who own the objects that held her down. Raven learns that material objects have rightful owners even if they are invisible.

Finally, Skate uses his physical attributes to evade Raven's spear in a spear-throwing contest and pins Raven's feet to the dirt. Ultimately, Skate graciously frees Raven who acknowledges his defeat and the good sportsmanship of Skate. Using one's physical attributes is clever but nothing to hold over another with attributes that are less advantageous. Clutesi tells these traditional stories in a time-honored way, through the eyes of a cultural person who makes clear teachings in a compassionate manner, to encourage a child's compassionate mind.

Enrico, John, *Raven and the Moon and The Oystercatcher: Two Haida Legends,* **illustrated by Maureen Yeltatzie. Pacific Educational Press: (1984). 24 pages, b/w illustrations; grades 2-4; Haida**

The two stories in this slim volume are "adapted and retold" from a translation of early stories told in Haida Gwaii in 1908 to J. R. Swanton, who was a fairly major ethnographer of Haida traditional stories. Yeltatsie's illustrations are stylized and relatively crude black-and-white drawings. The motifs, the architecture of the long-house, the robes and style of dress and hair treatment, the house posts and the outside provide an air of authenticity to the visually gloomy book.

"Raven and the Moon" explains the Haida origins of the moon, sun and stars. It "stars" Raven who typically transforms himself into an object that will allow him to be where no one suspects. When, as Raven-the-child, he absconds with the Moon-Light, he trades some for the desire of his heart: food, fish. And then just as typically, Raven fumbles the precious, hard won Moon-Light, breaking it into pieces. He throws the pieces into the sky: the Moon, to give light at night, the Sun, to give light by day and the leftover bits and pieces, stars to light the night.

Part of the conundrum here has to do with the moon and the light. Traditionally, all social activity was regulated through Moon cycles, so the light was also about social control and social order. In some ways, this story is really about Raven's bestowing social order on the people. In return, people gave Raven food. By helping to "illuminate" the people and providing them order in their "darkness," Raven's physical needs are provided for. So these stories always have a social-cultural dimension. But the story in this book leaves all this out. What is this story about? You can't tell; it's "just" a children's story, bereft of all cultural dimension. This is not about Raven the provider, Raven the bringer of culture, Raven the maker of rules; it shows only the part of Raven—the thief, the glutton, the "trickster"—that is thought to be appealing to children.

The companion story is about how the "Oystercatcher" came to be. Yaan Jaad, the daughter of the Southeast Wind moves to an alien land when she marries the son of the North Wind. She is so ignorant in her new home that when she breaks off icicles that hang in the house she does not know that they are her husband's father's fingernails until he groans in pain. When she and her husband gather shellfish, the North Wind starts blowing but she wants to keep picking. She then spends two days, immobilized, frozen in the sea before remembering to call her father, the Southeast Wind, to come and get her. In the meantime she turns into Oystercatcher with her face and beak red from the cold and her legs frozen

white. The Oystercatcher becomes the embodiment of the woman's failings.

Traditionally, women moving to an alien environment needed special stories like this to help sensitize them to their new living conditions. In these stories, there are usual several levels of interpretation. This is a story about Oystercatcher, but this is really a story about a woman who marries a totally different being, and is unable to adapt to a new environment. When you're in another's territory, it becomes important to learn the rules, and this is what, I think, the story's trying to teach. As the problem becomes articulated, we are reminded of the problem.

In our tradition, there are no special stories "just" for children. If a child hears this story at an early age, it would probably be the story of oystercatcher, and when the child becomes developmentally ready, that child "hears"—or understands—the rest of it.

This is a typical "retelling for children," in that it's without context; it bypasses the social dimensions of the story. Stories are supposed to say something, and when you take it out of the culture, it's merely about how a bird gets to be the way it is.

These two stories had the potential to be very engaging and culturally illuminating since they are based on authenticated texts. Unfortunately, the poor illustrations and the lack of clarity of the text, which probably reflects the lack of active participants of Haida "knowers," make this volume of questionable value.

Hammerschlag, Dr. Carl A., *Sika and the Raven,* **illustrated by Baje Whitethorne, Sr. (Diné). Turtle Island Press (1999). Unpaginated, color illustrations; grades 1-3**

A young girl named Sika mentions to her Uncle Eli that she would like to have a baby of her own, so, of course, he tells her a story. In the story, a young girl asks "Grandfather Turtle" for a baby of her own, and she is told that she must pass the test of keeping Raven caged for a year. Not "a raven" but Raven himself. Of course, Raven talks the child into letting him out, and Grandfather Turtle tells her she is not yet ready for a child: "For now, Earth Mother's creatures are your family. Reach out and touch them, and let them find a home in your heart." Then he turns Raven black and makes him caw instead of sing.

I don't know why non-Native people seem to like to think that all Indian children's questions are answered with stories. I also don't know what keeping Raven in a cage has to do with having a baby. And I especially don't know what the point of this whole thing is supposed to be.

We're told that *Sika and the Raven* is "based on a Native American legend," but we're not told which one, or which Nation owns it. There's a cornfield, a jungle, some Spanish words, and Raven, so we don't know where this thing is supposed to take place. Baje Whitethorne's lovely paintings are wasted on this piece of junk.

Kuharski, Janice, *Raven's Gift*, illustrated by Jo-Anne E. Kitchel. Richard C. Owen (1999). 16 pages, color illustrations; preschool-grade 2

Summary: "Clever Raven tricks the Chief of the Sky into sharing light with all the creatures of the earth." According to the inside back cover, Kuharski writes poems and plays, and Kitchel's artistic style is influenced by her stint in the Peace Corps in the West Indies. There is a note that explains that this "retelling" is nonfiction: "A legend is a story that comes down from the past. The story of how Raven brought light to a dark world is a legend told by many tribes of Native American people."

Although "legend status" is evoked here, there is no cultural or contextual connection to the past from which this story supposedly springs. This retelling, as is typical in children's literature, breaks the thread of the past when the author and illustrator have not had the cultural experience to maintain that thread. The legend is neither situated nor socially embedded anywhere, as if there is no coherent cultural past from which it sprang. "The Chief of the Sky" is a generic Indian depicted by culturally chaotic clothing, housing, hairstyle, and background design. How Raven becomes the child is a critical part of the "trickery," but that part is completely omitted. The illustrator and author clearly do not believe the legend because when Raven becomes a boy, he is still wearing a skirt of black feathers suggesting that he cannot be truly "Raven" and truly a "little boy" without some overlap. The attributes of Raven during his transformations are key principles of the legend that don't make it across this "retelling" barrier. Native people have always known that you can't tell what something is by how it looks, but it is a lesson not yet learned by some authors of "children's books about Raven."

This book is inflated in its claims and pathetic in its delivery. While the words are at a primary level, the claim of any relationship between this book and the legend of Raven constitutes a deceit unsuitable especially for a primary classroom.

MacKenzie, Hugh, *Pah*, illustrated by Butch Dick (Sliammon). Sliammon Board and School District No. 47.(n.d.). 18 pages, color illustrations; grades 1-up; Sliammon

Grandfather tells this story of a great *No'Hom* (feast) at the Beginning of Time, given by the fish so that they can receive names in order for fishers to know what they catch. Raven—*Pah hah kee lah*, or "Pah" for short—is invited to witness the naming, even if he is only there for a free meal. After being instructed in feast etiquette by his grandfather, Pah witnesses as the many curious-looking fish file into the feast: Rat fish, Tyee Salmon, Herring, Minnow, Eulachon, Perch, Rock Cod, Flounder— each fish displaying the unique characteristics which give it its name (in the Sliammon language, which unfortunately isn't revealed in this story). As a snide remark escapes his lips, Pah cannot suppress his own character and "splits" into a double of himself. The appearance of Red Snapper, with soup bowl eyes and a puffy stomach and Coho, with a long hooked snout makes Pah gasp, disturbing the solemnity of the occasion. Pah proves to be an unsuitable witness, not eligible for the feast food. This story illustrates the protocols of the witnessing of solemn cultural practices. Public rudeness requires public restitution with a bigger feast than the one spoiled by the initial rudeness. Feast food is not "free." The expressive color illustrations convey the balance between the illustrations of the story being told and the frame of the story, fishes of identifiable species swimming in a blue kelp bed border on each page.

McDermott, Gerald, *Raven: A Trickster Tale from the Pacific Northwest*, illustrated by the author. Harcourt Brace (1993). Unpaginated, color illustrations; grades 2-5

In this brightly illustrated volume, a highly stylized Raven looks like he is in coastal Alaska stealing the Sun. But that is only a guess, because the stereotypical illustrations of totem poles, Chilkat-type dress, house styles and wooden boxes are the only cultural clues to suggest the Pacific Northwest as a place of origin. The author's introduction indicates the highly generalized feeling he has for Raven and the cultures of which Raven is a central character. The story consists of the bare essentials of the classic thread of how Raven pities the People who live in darkness, journeys to bring back Light for them from the House of the Sky Chief and that they feed Him in return.

First Nations myth is typically anchored in real places, sacred places and minimally, each First Nations culture has its own particular details that may be obscure to non-Native sensibilities. Retellings such as this take out of cultural context the sacred stories that are about survival principles of First Nations peoples. The anthropological designation "Pacific Northwest" is the home of many diverse First Nations cultures, complete with their own unique Raven myths. Universalizing and generalizing retellings such as this degrade sacred cultural teachings into mere tales.

The narrator breaks into the story in three places, prompting the reader with questions to emphasize what he perceives to be the critical features: "Who do you think the child was?" "What do you think the ball was?" "And why do the people always feed Raven?" The sacred reciprocal relationship established between Raven and the People to whom he brought light is obscured in this object lesson. While bright and visually inviting, the generalizing nature of the story underscores its lack of authenticity and tendencies to stereotype. It's not a book that I would buy my grandchildren to contribute to their cultural self-esteem as First Nations children.

Oliviero, Jamie, *The Day Sun Was Stolen*, illustrated by Sharon Hitchcock (Haida). Hyperion (1995). Unpaginated, color illustrations; grades 3-up; Haida

This book is ostensibly about Bear's stealing the Sun as a consequence of Raven's flawed creation. Haida artist Hitchcock's stylized figures clearly indicate the mythological nature of the story's characters set against a naturalistic landscape background. Each page is framed with the bear motif because the story is about how Bear, uncomfortable in the thick fur that Raven had gifted him with, steals the Sun from the sky and hides it in a cave. With the Sun out of the sky, it takes a strategy of heroic proportions to return things to order. A young boy, *Ts'ina dahju* (small fish), has a vision for such a solution. He knows Bear's habits intimately and transforms himself to get into the cave. Not only does *Ts'ina dahju's* strategy work brilliantly, it causes Bear to fling the Sun back into the sky. The story reveals why the amount of fur the animals have increases and decreases with the seasons and why Bear hibernates.

The Day Sun Was Stolen confounds the mythological and the natural. In traditional stories about how things came

to be, the mythology makes sense of the natural or social order. Here, the natural order needs to be interfered with in order to be set right. This is not an unusual thing, but it is a complex story, and this telling is just too flat and boring. There is no excitement, no affectivity, to anchor the message. In addition, the rich Haida red is missing from the illustrations, conveying a general feeling of "flatness" and again, lack of excitement about the story itself. Because traditional oral stories rely so much upon the affectivity of the storyteller, this "flatness" is an important shortcoming in what could have been an engaging little volume.

Reid, Bill (Haida), and Robert Bringhurst, *The Raven Steals the Light*, illustrated by Bill Reid. Douglas & McIntyre (1984, 1996). 109 pages, b/w illustrations; grades 7-up; Haida

Five of the ten Haida stories penned in this volume are sacred in a most particular manner, as Raven the Trickster provides a mirror on the self. Bill Reid, the son of a Haida mother, knew nothing of his cultural heritage until he was called home through his work. Through artistic expression—jewelry, drawings, monumental sculptures—he reproduced the cultural forms of his homeland. For the written parts of these stories, Reid, who in the latter part of his life found fine motor movement difficult, collaborated with Robert Bringhurst. At the beginning of each story, Reid's meticulous illustrations bring the signs and the symbols together in a way that is so important to the peoples of the Northwest Coast. But what makes this book so special is the intimacy between the visual and textual mirroring of the stories.

In true First Nations tradition, Reid begins by citing the lineage of his stories, which is of critical importance to us. Then, Bringhurst's introduction explains the perspective of the stories: that they predate "historical" time but are told in real time; history and the present come together in the telling in a place where the Haida people live today.

These hilarious stories are no watered-down, sanitized "children's" versions. They contain, as Reid says, "a good selection of bestiality, adultery, violence, thievery and assault, for those who like that sort of thing."

Raven as the Great Trickster makes his grand entrance as the One Who Brings the Light to the People. But to bring the Light he first must steal it from the Sky Chief who keeps it in a box. First, Raven takes advantage of Haida social dynamics by causing himself to be born into the noble family that has access to the light. Then by playing on the empathy that elders have for children, he gets his hands on the ball of light, transforms again into his true state, and flies off with it.

Next, Raven takes a jaunt from the Islands of Haida Gwaii to the Mainland of the West Coast, visiting the Beaver people who invite him to feasts of salmon. But suddenly, when the Beaver people are at home, relax and take their fur off, the salmon turn into beaver food, hard sticks. After figuring out how to get to the salmon, Raven rolls up the landscape full of salmon so he can easily carry it in his beak. As he flies back to Haida Gwaii, he drops his roll, scattering the many little lakes and rivers with an abundance of salmon all over the islands.

In the time after the Flood, Raven is alone and lonely on Haida Gwaii. There is light, but there is no one to share it with. So after a few tries, Raven causes new people to emerge, and between the land and the sea in the tidal flats men and women as stormy as the headlands begin to flourish on Haida Gwaii.

Now that the Islands are populated, Raven roams the beaches always looking for food. Catching sight of a fisherman magically producing an endless supply of fish, Raven waits until the fisherman leaves and then makes his move. Embodied as the fisherman, Raven returns to the man's wife who is fooled—and thrilled—by the amorous attention she receives. But the real fisherman returns, beats Raven to a pulp and drops him into the latrine. Here he, um, finds the wife again, after which he is killed by husband and friends.

After being dumped into the ocean, Raven turns himself into a fat spring salmon, swims upward to the light of home—and suddenly finds himself in the belly of a killer whale. Changing back to his Raven form…

While the Raven fittingly dominates the pages of this volume, "The Bear Mother and her Husband," "Nanasimgit and His Wife," "The Wasgo (Seawolf) and the Three Killer Whales," "The Eagle and the Frog," and "The Dogfish Woman" round out the collection of Haida stories that Reid and Bringhurst, Raven-like, charm us with. The transformations abound in the territory of Haida Gwaii and bring the time "before history" into the present together for us to see.

Shetterly, Susan Hand, *Raven's Light: A Myth from the People of the Northwest Coast*, illustrated by Robert Shetterly. Atheneum (1991). Unpaginated, color illustrations; grades 1-3

Inspired by a raven they raised and released, the author and illustrator here decided to "recreate" a story about "Raven." The dust jacket copy says this story is a lively "recreation of the myths of the Tlingit, Haida, Kwaklutl (sic), and Tsimshian Peoples of the Pacific Northwest," a story in which these diverse cultures are generalized into one cultural expression. Typical of these "retellings," the authors have come up with a story that reflects the values and interests of non-Native wildlife conservationists rather than the cosmology from which the story originates.

This story does not unfold in traditional order, nor does it contain the traditional elements that connect it to our culture. The Shetterlys' version of Raven bears little resemblance to the agent of transformation who makes and breaks social orders. Rather, their Raven exists in darkness and accidentally participates in a flawed creation. Where the story sounds more recognizable, Raven is born to the daughter of the chief who owns the Light. But then, they supposedly have a party at which the "shaman" recognizes bird attributes in the child, and publicly exposes him. This is not part of our story and just would not happen publicly at a feast. Plus, a major celebration of a birth would be unlikely; people would wait until they were reasonably sure that the child would survive. A child born out of suspicious circumstances could be seen as a social problem and would not likely be the focus of a public feast. While in our traditional story, Raven plays with our value of permissive child rearing to get what he wants, here the Shetterlys make it the daughter's fault that Raven steals the light. And then, to make matters worse, they have a small girl trading a salmon to unwittingly get "that something in the basket" from Raven.

While the illustrations are colorful, they are crude and caricature cultural paraphernalia and practices, in particular the willy-nilly use of masks as well as the aggression and confrontation depicted between people in what is supposed to be a sacred ritual. The depiction of a figure planted upside down in the house, an illustration of punishment of the worst order, is totally inappropriate in this context.

From a cultural perspective, the text and illustrations in *Raven's Light* create a certain dissonance that could be conflictual for our children and reinforce stereotypical thinking about us in non-Native children.

GOODBYE, COLUMBUS: TAKE TWO

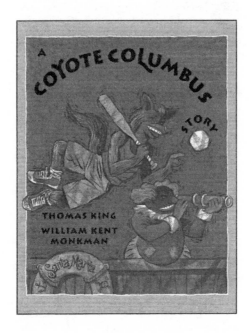
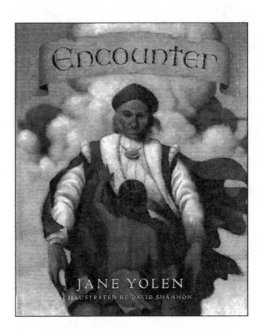

King, Thomas (Cherokee), *A Coyote Columbus Story*, illustrated by William Kent Monkman (Cree). Douglas & McIntyre, 1992. Unpaginated, color illustrations, all grades; Taino
Yolen, Jane, *Encounter*, illustrated by David Shannon. Harcourt Brace Jovanovich, 1992. Unpaginated, color illustrations, grades 1-3; Taino

How do you explain Christopher Columbus? Without having your lesson rated R for extreme violence, how do you tell children honestly about this cultural "hero" whose own writings offer a clear picture of what he wanted to do—and did—about the people whose home he "claimed" for Spain? How, especially, do you explain him to children whose sense of time makes last month "long ago"?

In 1992, the Quincentennial of Columbus' failed voyage to Asia, two children's books were published that offer unusual explanations—unusual in that neither of them makes Columbus a hero. Both are meant for young readers who may already know a little about Columbus. There the resemblance ends. The books, *Encounter* and *A Coyote Columbus Story*, take very different approaches to the Columbus problem.

Encounter, a work of historical fiction, is written by well-known European-American author Jane Yolen and illustrated by David Shannon, also European-American. Twelve years after its publication by U.S. giant Harcourt Brace Jovanovich, *Encounter* enjoys great popularity with librarians and teachers, who can even purchase a curriculum guide to go with it. Schoolchildren are most likely to encounter it in early October.

On the other hand, Thomas King, who is Cherokee and Greek, tried for years to find a U.S. publisher for *A Coyote Columbus Story*. Eventually it found a home with Canadian publishing house Douglas and McIntyre. William Kent Monkman (Cree) illustrated the book. There is no curriculum guide for *A Coyote Columbus Story*. Schoolchildren in the U.S. are far less likely to encounter it than to encounter *Encounter*.

The author's note at the end of *Encounter* states,

> I thought it would interest readers to hear a Taino boy speak. We don't have an actual record of that, so I have recreated what he might have said—using historical records and the storyteller's imagination.

We'll get back to the storyteller's imagination in a minute. The story opens when the narrator, who is nameless throughout, dreams of three great-winged, toothed birds that arrive on the sea, bringing destruction. He wakes, walks to the shore and finds three ships anchored not far away: his nightmare birds. He knows they hold great danger, but the adults around him repeatedly dismiss his warnings—he is "but a child." He is thus helpless as his people welcome and try to please the pale, outlandish strangers who issue forth from the ships—whom young readers will recognize as Columbus and his crew. The strangers kidnap several villagers including the boy. Terrified, he makes a desperate dive from the ship and swims to an island, where he continues his fruitless efforts to warn the people of what he learned about the strangers in his dream.

At the book's end, the narrator, now an old man, slumps against a bright Caribbean shoreline, lamenting what has come to pass:

> But even those who saw the great canoes did not listen, for I was a child. So it was we lost our lands to the strangers from the sky. We gave our souls to their gods. We took their speech into our mouths, forgetting our own. Our sons and daughters became their sons and daughters, no longer true humans, no longer ours.

"So it was." But was it so? In a book with a Taino perspective on Columbus, the author's note would have been a perfect place to cite sources and back up the "storyteller's imagination" with bits of the historical record. For instance, a reader might wonder where the author got the idea that Taino elders would find a child's dream unimportant. Of course, in fiction the storyteller's imagination can have free reign. It's not impossible that an indigenous culture like the Taino would have disdained dreams, or would have taken the W.C Fields approach to children's concerns: "Go away, kid, you bother me!" But it seems just as likely, considering the value of dreams in other Native societies, that the boy's horrific vision would grab his elders' attention. (It probably would get his peers' attention, too, if this boy had any friends his own age. But he seems to be the only child in the community.)

To be sure, European cultures give children a lesser place in society. Western children's literature even has a somewhat subversive tradition for dealing with adults who dismiss or disrespect children—they often get some sort of comeuppance. This book embodies that tradition, with a vengeance: Taino adults rebuff the prescient child, and their whole culture (to hear the narrator tell it) disappears. Teachers and students who read *Encounter* will probably believe they are privy to the authentic Taino belief system, though it actually appears to be speculation with a distinctly Western flavor.

There is a more pressing reason for readers to know in what ways the book is based on authoritative sources such as contemporary Taino scholars or leaders. The author has affixed blame for the events lamented by the narrator: not only on Columbus, the man with the swords and guns and gold-hunger, but also on the Taino people themselves. They fail to heed the boy's warning, but also they become greedy for the swords, mirrors and guns and somehow do not notice for themselves how the strangers' faces change when they encounter gold. Especially given the genocide that followed, it seems unlikely that a Taino explanation of Columbus would be: "We brought it on ourselves."

If only my people had listened, young readers are told over and over: "May it be a warning to all the children and all the people in every land." They could have been saved if they had—what? At no point does this story suggest how the Taino people might have stopped the "pale strangers," only that they *should* have. One wonders what would have stopped Columbus or those who came after. Now *there's* a cogent question, but it's not in the *Encounter* curriculum guide.

Not only did the Taino ignore the narrator's warnings. To hear the Taino narrator tell it from his seat by the sea, they also actively surrendered their culture without much compelling cause. They "lost" their lands, "gave" their souls, "took" the foreign speech and "forgot" their own, "became" something other than true human beings.

Now, when someone mugs you at knifepoint and takes your billfold, you don't tell people, "I lost my wallet." You don't say you "gave the keys" to a carjacker with an Uzi. If the punishment for speaking your own language is having your tongue cut out, you don't say, "Oops, I forgot the old way to talk. De nada."

By the end of *Encounter*, the narrator must have witnessed and survived the horror that overtook his people and compelled the changes he describes. It seems unlikely—un-Taino—that he would say they brought it on themselves. Maybe that's the Taino point of view but more likely it is Imperialism 101, Lesson One: Blame the Victim.

First-hand descriptions of that horror are available today, in the translated writings of onetime priest Bartolomeo de las Casas, who (flawed though he may have been) decried the brutal treatment the Taino suffered at the hands of the Spanish. If Yolen has read any such accounts, it is not apparent in either the text or the author's notes.

The narrator recalls that the strangers "took five of our young men and many parrots with them. They took me." The author's note states:

> Columbus carried away ten young Taino men and women (or six, according to different sources) from the various islands they visited, carting them back to Spain as slaves. Later when the islands were colonized by the Spanish, the native religions, languages and lifestyles were changed forever.

"Took," "carried away" and "carted back" are not the words I would choose if it had happened to me, and it seems safe to say they do not represent the young Tainos' perspective on being ripped from their families and everything they knew. As is so often the case when European Americans write about Native-white relations, word choice matters, particularly when one purports to present a Native viewpoint.

"Visited" is another clue that *Encounter* has no actual Taino perspective. When someone comes into your home, claims it for his own, and makes off with your possessions and your children, that is not (and never was) a "visit." Even if they leave a coffee cake.

Finally, both author and illustrator use passive voice to describe the years after the events in *Encounter*. Islands *were* colonized; religions, languages and lifestyles *were* changed, artifacts (David Shannon notes) *were* melted and burned. As if there were no agents of the destruction. As if those things just kind of—happened.

The narrator, a survivor of those terrible times, would know better than that. Taino children today know better. Colonization meant conquest, and conquest meant home invasion, rape, torture, kidnapping, enslavement, destruction of religious artifacts, murder, even mass murder in the name of the (supposedly) Christian god. Passive voice creates an aura of blamelessness, but someone melted and burned those artifacts. Someone forced the new gods, the new language, the alien lifestyles upon the Native peoples of the Caribbean and beyond. Someone maimed or killed those who didn't accept or escape. No laws protected the Taino from the Spanish, who possessed not only gold-lust, but greater firepower and no moral compunction about inflicting harm on brown-skinned human beings.

But nowhere in the narrator's reflection are the words "conquer" or "kill," nor is there evidence of resistance to colonization. Though the book makes it seem as if the Taino readily acquiesced, sheeplike, the record shows otherwise. Against enormous odds, they founded the tradition of Native resistance and survival in the Americas—the 500-year struggle to retain indigenous homelands, languages and cultures.

To be sure, *Encounter* critiques the Columbus myth of courage, adventure, and glory. It emphasizes the gold-lust that drove this cultural hero and his followers, and it even pokes fun at some of their egocentric interpretations of Native behavior. He is presented as a bad guy, but he's a bad guy who couldn't have done what he did without the compliance of none-too-admirable Native people. The "storyteller's imagination" in *Encounter* remains essentially European-American.

It is hard to imagine a picture book that successfully brings humor to the first contact between Europeans and the indigenous peoples, but Thomas King and Kent Monkman manage it with *A Coyote Columbus Story*. Laughing at outrageous situations is, after all, part of the indigenous tradition of survival.

This is a "very original creation story" of sorts. Like many tales from the indigenous oral traditions on which it is based, it is for an intergenerational audience. Anachronism and human-like animals abound. Its messages and lessons are multilayered, and it travels in a circle. The storyteller's cadence and the grammatical shifts and slips that characterize some oral traditions make it a fun story to read aloud.

A Coyote Columbus Story is not set in a Taino world, but in an "American" world. Its grasslands and hardwood forests are inhabited by that mysterious sometimes-hero and Big Deal of continental story-telling traditions, Coyote. Coyote is a girl this time around, a girl who loves baseball and wants someone to play with her. But she is no ordinary girl. Tired of throwing, hitting and catching the ball all by herself, "she sang a song and she danced a dance and she thought hard, and pretty soon along came some beavers." The beavers didn't just "come along," of course, but they are only the first of Coyote's creations to refuse a ball game. Finally, she sings, dances, and thinks so hard her nose falls off, and "right away, along come some human beings." Pleased to join her at first, they soon realize that Coyote makes up the rules and she always wins. They stop playing ball with her. Coyote gets bored. "When Coyote gets bored," says the storyteller, "anything can happen. Stick around. Big trouble is going to come. I can tell you that." Readers can guess what sort of "big trouble" this means: "three ships and some people in funny-looking clothes carrying flags and boxes of junk."

Monkman's illustrations manage to make the Europeans menacing and ridiculous at the same time. Their skin tones are blue, green and purple, in contrast to Coyote's human beings, who are shades of brown. Columbus and crew dress in ensembles that include gym shoes, fishnet stockings, berets, neckties, pince-nez glasses, as well as thoroughly patched 15th-Century court attire. There's even an Elvis impersonator in pink high-heel pumps, while Columbus, with orange hair and purple face, looks like a really nasty clown.

Right away Columbus and his men poke around in the homes of Coyote's friends, and throw fits when they don't find what they want. They are looking for India and "things we can sell." Gold. Chocolate cake. Computer games. Music videos. Eventually they decide to sell the human beings. While Coyote laughs her nose off at this "bad idea full of bad manners," those Columbus men kidnap a bunch of her friends at gunpoint (take a close look at those guns) and she ends up swimming after the ships.

> Wait a minute, says Coyote. What about my friends you have locked up in your ships? You got to let them go. Tra-la-la-la-la, says Columbus, and that one goes back to Spain and sells the human beings to rich people like baseball players and dentists and babysitters and parents.

In this story, Native people have a rich and dynamic culture well before the Europeans show up. They have good times. They make choices—skydiving, wrestling, other bits of anachronism—that get the point across to the contemporary young reader: Significant things happened in the Americas before 1492. It's easy then to see the Europeans as intruders. Native people in that time and place viewed their own dress as the norm, not as exotic. By drawing the Native characters in contemporary casual dress, Monkman invites the reader to think, "These are just like people I know. They wear blue jeans and baseball caps." When Columbus and his crew arrive, we immediately distinguish them from the first people by their bizarre skin and hair colorings and their outlandish outfits. We see them more-or-less through the eyes of the people who saw them come ashore. The presence of Coyote, and the way this character is presented, also reflect a Native view of the world. Note: I don't say "the" Native view, because Coyote operates differently from culture to culture. In this case, Coyote is the one who is supposed to fix up the world, but instead gets it bent out of shape.

> You're supposed to fix up this world, cry those beavers and moose and turtles. You're supposed to make it right. But you keep messing it up, too. Yes, says those human beings, you better watch out or this world is going to get bent. Everything is okay, says Coyote. I made a mistake but I'll take it back. I'll take Christopher Columbus back. You'll see, everything will be balanced again.

It's not fair to overanalyze comedy; it takes the fun out. Even so, the reader should note the skillful juxtaposition of humor and pathos here. The genuinely (if briefly) remorseful Coyote sings, dances, and thinks really hard—but of course she cannot call back Columbus.

Someone could argue that if I'm taking *Encounter* to task for giving the aftermath of 1492 a passive voice, I can't give *Coyote Columbus* a pass. After all, Thomas King doesn't mention conquest or killing either. But he's still telling the story from a Native perspective. By making this a Coyote story, King provides a context (familiar in many Native traditions) in which all manner of things might happen. Coyote seems to be without ill will, but somehow things just go from bad to worse once she gets an idea. Everything changes, goes out of balance, for the animals and the humans who had been having a pretty good time before those ill-favored strangers showed up. King does not make Columbus the *only* bad guy, which is historically accurate. When that one is gone, along comes that Jacques Cartier, and he is going to be trouble, too, just in a different part of the continent.

It is hard for the very young to make sense of history. For a young child who imagines that Grandma was born when dinosaurs still walked the earth, the history lessons that must accompany any discussion of the October 12 U.S. "holiday" can be puzzling indeed. Maybe it is time we dropped it altogether. If there were no October 12 commemorative day, we could undoubtedly find another Italian or Italian American whose past is not so checkered to honor with a day away from work and school. Then teachers would not be in the untenable position of having to explain Columbus to children who are not ready to read what he (or de las Casas) actually wrote. There would be no need for children's books to remake colonization and genocide as bloodless events that occurred in the passive voice. No doubt the debate would continue over whether or not the Taino share blame for what happened, but the people debating it would be (we hope) less impressionable and better informed by primary sources (or translations thereof) than are the six-year-olds who are today treated to the myth of courageous, heroic Columbus.

Do we want the *whole* truth in a book for young children? Maybe not. But how useful to their understanding of history is a story that ultimately blames the Taino for what happened to them at the hands of the Europeans? It may take courage to mess with the Columbus myth at all. But by making him a greedy, scary figure, and then making the Taino complicit in their own destruction, *Encounter* ultimately undoes whatever good it purports to do.

The storytelling and illustrations in *A Coyote Columbus Story* clearly hail from an alternative reality. Children are not likely to come away believing in tipis at the seashore, any more than they believe that moose wore swim trunks or Columbus was purple. But more significantly, no child is going to set this book down with the idea in mind that Native people's greed and indifference caused their own downfall. Nor are they likely to imagine that Native people just let themselves be overrun, or that they have ceased to be true human beings. *A Coyote Columbus Story* is no finger-pointing lament. None of its characters slouches in defeat with body parts morphing into thin air, as does the narrator at the end of *Encounter*. The reader sees indignation, not stoicism, on the faces of the people being kidnapped. When the people disguise themselves as animals, and when they head for Penticton, there is the Native refusal to be colonized. The People may have put a good distance between themselves and that baseball-loving, singing-and-dancing Coyote, but they have not ceased to exist. They are not tragic. Look at them shaking their fists and scowling at Coyote. (And look at that moose shinnying down a tree.)

In most Native traditions, Coyote is an ambiguous figure, present from the beginning. What he—or she—accomplishes for good seems to be mostly by accident, although not always. Coyote is also self-absorbed, greedy, foolish, destructive, and perfectly capable of provoking a Columbus-size disaster. Coyote will do as Coyote does, but in King's story, they, the Native people, are not set up to take the blame for Columbus and what came after. "Those Columbus people" are responsible for their own bad manners.

None of the Taino are willing participants, as in fact they were not.—*Jean Paine Mendoza*

DECONSTRUCTING THE MYTHS OF "THE FIRST THANKSGIVING"

What is it about the story of "The First Thanksgiving" that makes it essential to be taught in virtually every grade from preschool through high school? What is it about the story that is so seductive? Why has it become an annual elementary school tradition to hold Thanksgiving pageants, with young children dressing up in paper-bag costumes and feather-duster headdresses and marching around the schoolyard? Why is it seen as necessary for fake "pilgrims" and fake "Indians" (portrayed by real children, many of whom are Indian) to sit down every year to a fake feast, acting out fake scenarios and reciting fake dialogue about friendship? And why do teachers all over the country continue (for the most part, unknowingly) to perpetuate this myth year after year after year?

Is it because as Americans we have a deep need to believe that the soil we live on and the country on which it is based were founded on integrity and cooperation? This belief would help contradict any feelings of guilt that could haunt us when we look at our role in more recent history in dealing with other indigenous peoples in other countries. If we dare to give up the "myth" we may have to take responsibility for our actions both concerning indigenous peoples of this land as well as those brought to this land in violation of everything that makes us human. The realization of these truths untold might crumble the foundation of what many believe is a true democracy. As good people, can we be strong enough to learn the truths of our collective past? Can we learn from our mistakes? This would be our hope.

We offer these myths and facts to assist students, parents and teachers in thinking critically about this holiday, and deconstructing what we have been taught about the history of this continent and the world.—*Judy Dow and Beverly Slapin*

(Note: We thank Margaret M. Bruchac, Doris Seale, Lakota Harden, and the Wampanoag Indian Program at Plimoth Plantation.)

Myth #1: "The First Thanksgiving" occurred in 1621.

The Pilgrims decided to have a three-day celebration feast to give thanks for a good harvest. Thus began the first Thanksgiving.[1]

The first Thanksgiving was a celebration of the Pilgrims' very first harvest.[2]

The feast at Plymouth in 1621 is often called The First Thanksgiving.[3]

The pilgrims wanted to give thanks for all the good food. That was the first Thanksgiving.[4]

Fact: No one knows when the "first" thanksgiving occurred. People have been giving thanks for as long as people have existed. Indigenous Nations all over the world have celebrations of the harvest that come from very old traditions; for Native peoples, thanksgiving comes not once a year, but every day, for all the gifts of life. To refer to the harvest feast of 1621 as "The First Thanksgiving" disappears Indian peoples in the eyes of non-Native children.

Myth #2: The people who came across the ocean on the Mayflower were called Pilgrims.

Once upon a time in the land of England, there lived a small group of people called Pilgrims. The Pilgrims were unhappy, because...[5]

The people were called Pilgrims.[6]

These are the Pilgrims, who farmed the new land,...[7]

1 little, 2 little, 3 little Pilgrims, 4 little, 5 little, 6 little Pilgrims,...[8]

Fact: The Plimoth settlers did not refer to themselves as "Pilgrims." Pilgrims are people who travel for religious reasons, such as Muslims who make a pilgrimage to Mecca. Most of those who arrived here from England were religious dissidents who had broken away from the Church of England. They called themselves "Saints"; others called them "Separatists." Some of the settlers were "Puritans," dissidents but not separatists who wanted to "purify" the Church.[9]

Myth #3: The colonists came seeking freedom of religion in a new land.

The Pilgrims wanted their own religion....So the Pilgrims decided to leave England.[10]

The Pilgrims had left England because King James did not want them to practice their own religion. They were in search of a new home.[11]

They left their old country because they could not pray the way they wanted.[12]

The Pilgrims wanted to worship God in their own way...[13]

Fact: The colonists were not just innocent refugees from religious persecution. By 1620, hundreds of Native people had already been to England and back, most as captives; so the Plimoth colonists knew full well that the land they were settling on was inhabited. Nevertheless, their belief system taught them that any land that was "unimproved" was "wild" and theirs for the taking; that the people who lived there were roving heathens with no right to the land. Both the Separatists and Puritans were rigid fundamentalists who came here fully intending to take the land away from its Native inhabitants and establish a new nation, their "Holy Kingdom." The Plimoth colonists were never concerned with "freedom of religion" for anyone but themselves. It wasn't until around the time of the American Revolution that the name "Pilgrims" came to be associated with the Plimoth settlers, and the "Pilgrims" became the symbol of American morality and Christian faith, fortitude, and family.[14]

Myth #4: When the "Pilgrims" landed, they first stepped foot on "Plymouth Rock."

The Pilgrims landed at Plymouth Rock.[15]

This is the harbor, marked by a huge stone where first steps were taken to chart the unknown,...[16]

The Pilgrims came/To Plymouth Rock/One snowy, cold December...[17]

On top of the gravel the glacier deposited huge boulders it had carried from distant places. One settled in Plymouth Harbor....A wandering pilgrim, it left its home in Africa two hundred million years ago....Eons later, battered by glaciers, all 200 tons of it came to rest in lonely splendor, on a sandy beach in a cove. This boulder is Plymouth Rock....Yet to Americans, Plymouth Rock is a symbol. It is larger than the mountains, wider than the prairies and stronger than all our rivers. It is the rock on which our nation began.[18]

Fact: When the colonists landed, they sought out a sandy inlet in which to beach the little shallop that carried them from the Mayflower to the mainland. This shallop would have been smashed to smithereens had they docked at a rock, especially a Rock. Although the Plimoth settlers built their homes just up the hill from the Rock, William Bradford in *Mourt's Relation: A Journal of the Pilgrims at Plymouth*, does not even mention the Rock; writing only that they "unshipped our shallop and drew her on land."[19] The actual "rock" is a slab of Dedham granodiorite placed there by a receding glacier some 20,000 years ago. It was first referred to in a town surveying record in 1715, almost one hundred years after the landing. Since then, the Rock has been moved, cracked in two, pasted together, carved up, chipped apart by tourists, cracked again, and now rests as a memorial to something that never happened.[20]

It's quite possible that the myth about the "Pilgrims" landing on a "Rock" originated as a reference to the New Testament of the Christian bible, in which Jesus says to Peter, "And I say also unto thee, Thou art Peter, and upon this rock I will build my Church and the Gates of Hell shall not prevail against it." (Matthew 16:18) The appeal to these scriptures gives credence to the sanctity of colonization and the divine destiny of the dominant culture. Although the colonists were not dominant then, they behaved as though they were.

Myth #5: The Pilgrims found corn.

> During their first hard year in America, the Pilgrims found corn buried in the sand of Cape Cod. ....This important find gave the Pilgrims seeds to plant—and these became the seeds for survival.[21]

> On their way back they found Indian graves and some Indian corn.[22]

> The men dug down into [a hill of sand] and—there was a little old basket filled with corn! Now they had corn to plant. They found other baskets. These were big baskets, and it took two men to carry one. They filled their pockets with corn.[23]

> The men keep exploring. They find wonderful things—corn, baskets, a spring.[24]

Fact: Just a few days after landing, a party of about sixteen settlers led by Captain Myles Standish followed a Nauset trail and came upon an iron kettle and a cache of Indian corn buried in the sand. They made off with the corn and returned a few days later with reinforcements. This larger group "found" a larger store of corn, about ten bushels, and took it. They also "found" several graves, and, according to *Mourt's Relation*, "brought sundry of the prettiest things away" from a child's grave and then covered up the corpse. They also "found" two Indian dwellings and "some of the best things we took away with us."[25] There is no record that restitution was ever made for the stolen corn, and the Wampanoag did not soon forget the colonists' ransacking of Indian graves.[26]

Myth #6: Samoset appeared out of nowhere, and along with Squanto became friends with the Pilgrims. Squanto helped the Pilgrims survive and joined them at "The First Thanksgiving."

> When Spring came, two men named Squanto and Samoset appeared and made friends with the surviving Pilgrims.[27]

> Squanto was the Pilgrims' teacher and friend. He helped save their lives and made sure their little settlement survived in the rocky New England soil. By saving the Pilgrims, Squanto became one of our first American heroes.[28]

> Squanto spoke really good English. He had even been to England. Squanto had no family, so he acted as though the Pilgrims were his family. He liked them so much he came to live at Plymouth.[29]

> One day, a kind Indian came to the Pilgrims' village. He like the Pilgrims and wanted to help them. Soon, more Indians came. They were nice and showed the Pilgrims how to....[30]

Fact: Samoset, an eastern Abenaki chief, was the first to contact the Plimoth colonists. He was investigating the settlement to gather information and report to Massasoit, the head sachem in the Wampanoag territory. In his hand, Samoset carried two arrows: one blunt and one pointed. The question to the settlers was: are you friend or foe? Samoset brought Tisquantum (Squanto), one of the few survivors of the original Wampanoag village of Pawtuxet, to meet the English and keep an eye on them. Tisquantum had been taken captive by English captains several years earlier, and both he and Samoset spoke English. Tisquantum agreed to live among the colonists and serve as a translator. Massasoit also sent Hobbamock and his family to live near the colony to keep an eye on the settlement and also to watch Tisquantum, whom Massasoit did not trust. The Wampanoag oral tradition says that Massasoit ordered Tisquantum killed after he tried to stir up the English against the Wampanoag. Massasoit himself lost face after his years of dealing with the English only led to warfare and land grabs. Tisquantum is viewed by Wampanoag people as a traitor, for his scheming against other Native people for his own gain. Massasoit is viewed as a wise and generous leader whose affection for the English may have led him to be too tolerant of their ways.[31]

Myth #7: The Pilgrims invited the Indians to celebrate the First Thanksgiving.

> The Pilgrims invited their Native American friends to a great feast.[32]

> "Join us," they said to the Indians. "Join us in a big feast of Thanksgiving. It will be a very special holiday."[33]

> The harvest was/So plentiful/The Pilgrims were delighted—/They prepared to have/A giant feast,/And the Indians were invited.[34]

> To celebrate, the Pilgrims decided to have a big party—a harvest festival. And they invited their new Indian friends to join them.[35]

Fact: According to oral accounts from the Wampanoag people, when the Native people nearby first heard the gunshots of the hunting colonists, they thought that the colonists were preparing for war and that Massasoit needed to be informed. When Massasoit showed up with ninety men and no women or children, it can be assumed that he was being cautious. When he saw there was a party going on, his men then went out and brought back five deer and lots of turkeys.[36]

In addition, both the Wampanoag and the English settlers were long familiar with harvest celebrations. Long before the Europeans set foot on these shores, Native peoples gave thanks every day for all the gifts of life, and held thanksgiving celebrations and giveaways at certain times of the year. The Europeans also had days of thanksgiving, marked by religious services. So the coming together of two peoples to share food and company was not entirely a foreign thing for either. But the visit that by all accounts lasted three days was most likely one of a series of political meetings to discuss and secure a military alliance. Neither side totally trusted the other: The Europeans considered the Wampanoag soulless heathens and instruments of the devil, and the Wampanoag had seen the Europeans steal their seed corn and rob their graves. In any event, neither the Wampanoag nor the Europeans referred to this feast/meeting as "Thanksgiving."[37]

Myth #8: The Pilgrims provided the food for their Indian friends.

> The Wampanoag smoked their pipes, tasted English cooking, and presented a dance to the Pilgrims.[38]

> The pilgrims hunted wild turkeys. They picked fruits and berries. When there was enough food, they all had a feast.[39]

> They knew they could never have survived without the Indians, so the Pilgrims invited the Indians to join them in a feast.[40]

> The twelve women of New Plymouth began great preparations. From the kitchens came the savory smell of roasting geese and turkey. An abundance of corn bread and hasty pudding was being prepared. Stewed eels, boiled lobsters, and juicy clam stews simmered over the fires. Before the feast, Squanto was sent with an invitation to Massasoit and his chiefs....The Indians were in no hurry to go home as long as the food held out, and the holiday-making carried on for three days.[41]

Fact: It is known that when Massasoit showed up with ninety men and saw there was a party going on, they then went out and brought back five deer and lots of turkeys. Though the details of this event have become clouded in secular mythology, judging by the inability of the settlers to provide for themselves at this time and Edward Winslow's letter of 1622,[42] it is most likely that Massasoit and his people provided most of the food for this "historic" meal.[43]

Myth #9: The Pilgrims and Indians feasted on turkey, potatoes, berries, cranberry sauce, pumpkin pie, and popcorn.

> There were meat pies, wheat breads, and corn puddings. There were berries, grapes, dried plums, and nuts.[44]

Many tables are filled with the same foods the Pilgrims and Indians shared. There is cranberry sauce and a big turkey stuffed with breadcrumbs, herbs, and nuts. Also there are sweet potatoes, beans, squash, and cornbread. Sometimes there is a tasty pumpkin pie for dessert.[45]

Corn was cooked in many ways. There was popcorn, too![46]

There was eel and cod and lobster and quahogs and mussels and wild turkey and cranberries and succotash and berry pies.[47]

Fact: Both written and oral evidence show that what was actually consumed at the harvest festival in 1621 included venison (since Massasoit and his people brought five deer), wild fowl, and quite possibly nasaump—dried corn pounded and boiled into a thick porridge, and pompion—cooked, mashed pumpkin. Among the other food that would have been available, fresh fruits such as plums, grapes, berries and melons would have been out of season. It would have been too cold to dig for clams or fish for eels or small fish. There were no boats to fish for lobsters in rough water that was about sixty fathoms deep. There was not enough of the barley crop to make a batch of beer, nor was there a wheat crop. Potatoes and sweet potatoes didn't get from the south up to New England until the 18th Century, nor did sweet corn. Cranberries would have been too tart to eat without sugar to sweeten them, and that's probably why they wouldn't have had pumpkin pie, either. Since the corn of the time could not be successfully popped, there was no popcorn.[48]

Myth #10: The Pilgrims and Indians became great friends.

The Pilgrims lived in peace with their Indian neighbors.[49]

They had food and houses and warm fires. The Indians were their friends. They were free in this new land.[50]

All of the Pilgrims took part. So did their Indian friends.[51]

Together the Pilgrims and Indians lived in peace and grew in friendship.[52]

Fact: A mere generation later, the balance of power had shifted so enormously and the theft of land by the European settlers had become so egregious that the Wampanoag were forced into battle. In 1637, English soldiers massacred some 700 Pequot men, women and children at Mystic Fort, burning many of them alive in their homes and shooting those who fled. The colony of Connecticut and Massachusetts Bay Colony observed a day of thanksgiving commemorating the massacre. By 1675, there were some 50,000 colonists in the place they had named "New England." That year, Metacom, a son of Massasoit, one of the first whose generosity had saved the lives of the starving settlers, led a rebellion against them. By the end of the conflict known as "King Philip's War," most of the Indian peoples of the Northeast region had been either completely wiped out, sold into slavery, or had fled for safety into Canada. Shortly after Metacom's death, Plimoth Colony declared a day of thanksgiving for the English victory over the Indians.[53]

Myth #11: Thanksgiving is a happy time.

Today, Thanksgiving is a happy time when families gather together.[54]

It's a time to remember the Pilgrims and their first Thanksgiving.[55]

Thanksgiving reminds us of the little band of people who founded the Plymouth Colony in Massachusetts. Each November it reopens a favorite chapter in our nation's history.[56]

All over the country, people gather their families together and have a feast. They thank God for the good things of the past year. They eat turkey. They remember the brave Pilgrims and the first Thanksgiving Day.[57]

That was the first Thanksgiving! It's a story we'll never forget. It's something we celebrate every year.[58]

Fact: For many Indian people, "Thanksgiving" is a time of mourning, of remembering how a gift of generosity was rewarded by theft of land and seed corn, extermination of many from disease and gun, and near total destruction of many more from forced assimilation. As currently celebrated in this country, "Thanksgiving" is a bitter reminder of 500 years of betrayal returned for friendship.

REFERENCES/RECOMMENDED BOOKS

Grace, Catherine O'Neill, and Margaret M. Bruchac (Abenaki), *1621: A New Look at Thanksgiving.* National Geographic, 2001, grades 4-up

Hunter, Sally M. (Ojibwe), *Four Seasons of Corn: A Winnebago Tradition.* Lerner, 1997, grades 4-6.

Peters, Russell M. (Wampanoag), *Clambake: A Wampanoag Tradition.* Lerner, 1992, grades 4-6.

Regguinti, Gordon (Ojibwe), *The Sacred Harvest: Ojibway Wild Rice Gathering.* Lerner, 1992, grades 4-6.

Seale, Doris (Santee/Cree), Beverly Slapin, and Carolyn Silverman (Cherokee), eds., *Thanksgiving: A Native Perspective.* Oyate, 1998, teacher resource.

Swamp, Jake (Mohawk), *Giving Thanks: A Native American Good Morning Message.* Lee & Low, 1995, all grades.

Wittstock, Laura Waterman (Seneca), *Ininatig's Gift of Sugar: Traditional Native Sugarmaking.* Lerner, 1993, grades 4-6.

REFERENCES/PRIMARY SOURCES

Bradford, William, *Of Plymouth Plantation, 1620-1647,* originally published in 1856 under the title History of Plymouth Plantation. Introduction by Francis Murphy. Random House, 1981.

Bradford, William, *Mourt's Relation: A Journal of the Pilgrims at Plymouth,* first published in 1622. Introduction by Dwight B. Heath. Applewood Books, 1963.

Council on Interracial Books for Children, *Chronicles of American Indian Protest.* CIBC, 1971.

Winslow, Edward, *Good Newes from New England: A True Relation of Things Very Remarkable at the Plantation of Plimoth in New England,* first published in 1624. Applewood Books, n.d.

NOTES

1 Stamper, Judith, *Thanksgiving Fun Activity Book*. Troll, 1993.

2 Kinnealy, Janice, *Let's Celebrate Thanksgiving*. Watermill, 1988.

3 Bartlett, Robert Merrill, *The Story of Thanksgiving*. HarperCollins, 2001.

4 Ruelle, Karen Gray, *The Thanksgiving Beast Feast*. Holiday House, 1999.

5 Ross, Katherine, *The Story of the Pilgrims*. Random House, 1995.

6 McGovern, Ann, *The Pilgrims' First Thanksgiving*. Scholastic, 1973.

7 Greene, Rhonda Gowler, *The Very First Thanksgiving Day*. Atheneum, 2002.

8 Hennessy, B.G., *One Little, Two Little, Three Little Pilgrims*. Viking, 1999.

9 Correspondence with Abenaki scholar Margaret M. Bruchac. See also Plimoth Plantation, "A Key to Historical and Museum Terms," www.plimoth.org/education/field_trips/ft-terms.htm; "Who Were the Pilgrims?" www.plimoth.org/library/whowere.htm; and Chuck Larsen, "There Are Many Thanksgiving Stories to Tell," in *Thanksgiving: A Native Perspective*, p. 50. Also see Council on Interracial Books for Children, *Chronicles of American Indian Protest*, pp. 6-10.

10 Hayward, Linda, *The First Thanksgiving*. Random House, 1990.

11 Jackson, Garnett, *The First Thanksgiving*. Scholastic, 2000.

12 McGovern, Ann, *op. cit.*

13 Gibbons, Gail, *Thanksgiving Day*. Holiday House, 1985.

14 See Note 9.

15 Ross, Kathy, *Crafts for Thanksgiving*. Millbrook, 1995.

16 Greene, Rhonda Gowler, *op. cit.*

17 Roloff, Nan, *The First American Thanksgiving*. Current, 1980.

18 George, Jean Craighead, *The First Thanksgiving*. Puffin, 1993.

19 See William Bradford's *Mourt's Relation: A Journal of the Pilgrims at Plymouth*, p. 19.

20 Conversation with Douglas Frink, Archaeology Consulting Team, Inc. See also Plimoth Plantation, "The Adventures of Plimoth Rock," www.plimoth.org/library/plymrock.htm.

21 Stamper, Judith, *op. cit.*

22 Barth, Edna, *Turkeys, Pilgrims, and Indian Corn: The Story of the Thanksgiving Symbols*. Clarion, 1975.

23 Dalgliesh, Alice, *The Thanksgiving Story*. Scholastic, 1954.

24 Hayward, Linda, *op. cit.*

25 See Bradford, William, *op. cit.*, p. 28.

26 See "The Saints Come Sailing In," in Dorothy W. Davids and Ruth A. Gudinas, "Thanksgiving: A New Perspective (and its Implications in the Classroom)" in *Thanksgiving: A Native Perspective*, pp. 70-71.

27 Bartlett, Robert Merrill, *op. cit.*

28 Fink, Deborah, *It's a Family Thanksgiving!* Harmony Hearth, 2000.

29 Donnelly, Judith, *The Pilgrims and Me*. Grossett & Dunlap, 2002.

30 Whitehead, Pat, *Best Thanksgiving Book: ABC Adventures*. Troll, 1985.

31 Correspondence with Margaret M. Bruchac about the relationship between Samoset, Tisquantum, Hobbamock, and Massasoit. See also Grace, Catherine O'Neill, and Margaret M. Bruchac, *1621: A New Look at Thanksgiving*.

32 Skarmeas, Nancy J., *The Story of Thanksgiving*. Ideals Publications, 1999.

33 Whitehead, Pat, *op. cit.*

34 Roloff, Nan, *op. cit.*

35 Kamma, Anne, *If You Were At...The First Thanksgiving*. Scholastic, 2001.

36 See Grace, Catherine O'Neill, and Margaret M. Bruchac, *op. cit.*

37 For a description of how the European settlers regarded the Wampanoag, as well as evidence of their theft of seed corn and funerary objects, see *Mourt's Relation*. See also Grace, Catherine O'Neill, and Margaret M. Bruchac, *ibid.*

38 Stamper, Judith, *op. cit.*

39 Ruelle, Karen Gray, *op. cit.*

40 Ross, Katherine, *op. cit.*

41 Daugherty, James, *The Landing of the Pilgrims*. Random House, 1987.

42 See Winslow, Edward, *Good Newes from New England: A True Relation of Things Very Remarkable at the Plantation of Plimoth in New England*.

43 See Champagne, Duane, *Native America: Portrait of the Peoples*. Visible Ink (1994), pp. 81-82; and Larsen, Chuck, *op. cit.*, p. 51.

44 Jackson, Garnet, *op. cit.*

45 Gibbons, Gail, *op. cit.*

46 McGovern, Ann, *op. cit.*

47 Metaxas, Eric, *Squanto and the First Thanksgiving*. Rabbit Ears, 1996.

48 See Plimoth Plantation, "No Popcorn!" www.plimoth.org/library/thanksgiving/nopopc.htm, and "A First Thanksgiving Dinner for Today," www.plimoth.org/library/thanksgiving/afirst.htm. See also Grace, Catherine O'Neill, and Margaret M. Bruchac, *op. cit.*

49 Kinnealy, Janice, *op. cit.*

50 Dalgliesh, Alice, *op. cit.*

51 McGovern, Ann, *op. cit.*

52 Raphael, Elaine, and Don Bolognese, *The Story of the First Thanksgiving*. Scholastic, 1991.

53 See "King Philip Cries Out for Revenge," pp. 43-45; and "There Are Many Thanksgiving Stories to Tell," pp. 49-52, in *Thanksgiving: A Native Perspective*. See also Grace, Catherine O'Neill, and Margaret M. Bruchac, *op. cit.*

54 Bartlett, Robert Merrill, *op. cit.*

55 Kinnealy, Janice, *op. cit.*

56 Barth, Edna, *op. cit.*

57 Rogers, Lou, *The First Thanksgiving*. Modern Curriculum Press, 1962.

58 Rockwell, Anne, *Thanksgiving Day*. HarperCollins, 1999.

TAKE TWO COYOTE STORIES AND CALL ME
IN YOUR NEXT LIFETIME
(some thoughts on storytelling, healing and appropriation)

It was a beautiful day at the Bay Area Storytelling Festival in Tilden Regional Park just outside of San Francisco. There were birds singing and the wind carried both its own music and the scent of the tall eucalyptus trees that arched over the field where I had just finished telling a traditional Abenaki story. But the young Anglo woman who was standing in front of me was not hearing the birds or feeling the cooling breath of the wind at that moment. She was too angry for that. Too angry and too busy accusing me of stealing the story I had just told (and the song that I sang as part of the story) from her.

"I wrote you a letter telling you about that song two years ago," she said. "You never answered my letter. Then a few months later I read an article you wrote in which you talked about that song and you never acknowledged me!"

I listened, waiting for a moment in which I could say a word. But such moments can be few and far between when you are being confronted by angry property owners who think they have caught you crawling out their window with their best silver in your bag. So I waited longer. I looked over her shoulder at the tent where I was supposed to perform again in five minutes and I waited a little longer. I waited while she told me how she had researched Indian cradleboards and even carried one around with her now when she told the story. Finally she paused.

"I never got that letter," I said. "Could I ask you to sing the song to me as you learned it?"

"Way-away dzidzis," she sang.

"Ohnh-honh," I said, "those are the vocables that I used to use in the song before I started using the words 'kaa-wi dzidzis,' meaning 'sleep thou, baby.' How did you happen to learn it that way?" I asked, seeing that the light was still not seeping in to clear away her anger.

"I sang it just as I learned it from the Native American storyteller who taught it to me four years ago," she said emphatically.

"Was her name Dovie Thomason?" (Ironically, I later learned that Dovie had never taught her the story, that the woman had merely heard Dovie tell it.)

"Yes," she said, surprised for the first time, "how did you know?"

"Because she asked my permission to tell it eight years ago."

Possession, it is said, is nine-tenths of the law. I wonder if the ones who first made up that maxim had any other sort of possession in mind as well, such as being so convinced that you know someone else's culture that you feel you possess it more than they do, or feel as if you have been (shades of psychic channel-surfers) possessed by the spirit of Indians of the past who are more real then those of today. (Ever hear of a book called *Return of the Bird Tribes* in which an Anglo named Carey told the world that he was in direct contact with the spirits of such departed American Indians as the founders of the Iroquois League and thus he knew much more about Iroquois people than did contemporary Iroquois? My Tuscarora friend Rick Hill reviewed this book as "bird droppings.")

Ownership. Who owns a story after it has been told? I was taught that many of our stories are meant to entertain, to teach, even to heal. Because of that, they must be heard and shared. But, these days, at a risk. A risk of the stories being, shall we say, misappropriated—a risk that was as unlikely in the old days as it would be today for a modern M.D. to have a patient in for a diagnosis, prescribe the medicine to cure his illness or perform the necessary operation and then, a week later, to discover that former patient out doing the same diagnosing, prescribing and operating. I think of another Native storyteller from the west who no longer performs at storytelling festivals because so many of the people who came to them were taping his stories as he told them and then adding them to their own repertoires without his permission, without acknowledging where the stories came from, even changing and reshaping them. Possession. Possessiveness. Dispossession.

I find myself for a moment flashing back to an old episode of the British TV show "Monty Python's Flying Circus" in which John Cleese, as the highway "Davy Moore" who "robs from the rich, gives to the poor," suddenly realizes that the rich, when robbed, become poor and thus he must give them back their belongings. "This redistribution of capital is trickier than I thought," he says.

A few years ago I got a phone call from a professional storyteller—a non-Indian. This storyteller had heard a summary of another of the traditional Abenaki stories I tell from someone else who had heard me tell it. The message of this story was so wonderful the storyteller said—who had never met me before—that he had written a rhymed poem retelling the story. He read it to me over the phone. I listened until the poem was finished.

"That's nice," I said. I was being polite.

"Isn't that wonderful?" the other storyteller said. "And I already have a contract to have it published as a book by a major children's publisher."

That was when I stopped being polite.

It would take more space that I have in this brief essay to say all that I said then. I talked about the way stories reflect not just the material aspects of our cultures, but also something deeper, which can only be described as spiritual. I talked about the specific knowledge about specific tribal traditions that is needed to tell such stories as they should be told. I explained that I had spent seven years learning that story before I ever wrote it down or told it in public. And I also said that I would give neither my blessing nor my permission for the story to be published in the version I had just heard over the phone, well meaning though it had been. Some things I said more than once, more than twice. It was hard to explain perhaps, because there is this long American tradition of taking things from Native American people without even thinking about it. But the other person listened—just as that storyteller at the Bay Area Storytelling Festival eventually listened. The rhymed version of the story was not published and that Anglo storyteller—whom I now consider a friend—has in recent years made some very sensitive public comments about not appropriating Native American stories.

There is a great hunger in American culture for meaningful stories. We need new stories. Many of the old ones that were imported from Europe (like influenza, measles and smallpox) have taught us all the wrong things. Defeat your enemies, defend your property, slay all the monsters, make lots of wealth, marry the princess or the prince (or both?) and live happily ever after. Those are very scary messages to me, especially when we realize just how few of us survive to live happily ever after when we are trapped at the edge of such tales.

Those of us who are Native American writers and storytellers will continue to find that the stories we tell touch the hearts and the spirits of the people who hear them. They do need to hear those stories and we need to tell them. A Navajo acquaintance of mine who is a traditional healer told me that once he realized he had that gift he knew that he had to become a healer or he would become sick himself. Still, he tried to fight it. He had a career already in law enforcement. But he ended up being a healer. It was what he had been given to give. So the option of just stopping or just not telling our stories to any except a few, may not be the option that is best to choose.

Our problem, though, is when that hunger for the healing in stories becomes blind possessiveness, acquisitiveness. At that same festival in California, a friend from a Native organization called Oyate had a book table. This conversation between her and a woman who happened by is typical of that day and many others:

—Do you have any books of coyote stories?—*Yes, we have a book of Okanagan Coyote stories and a book of Navajo Coyote stories.*—What's the difference?—*Well, this book is Okanagan Coyote stories and this book is Navajo Coyote stories.*—Don't you just have a book of plain coyote stories?—*This book is Okanagan Coyote stories and this book is Navajo Coyote stories.* At which point the woman left in a huff.

So we need to tell our stories and make it very clear what stories we are telling and where they came from. We need to defend them in the way, perhaps, that the Iroquois defended the Great Law of Peace. Instead of defeating our "enemies" we need to clear the cobwebs from their eyes and comb the snakes from their hair. As Oren Lyons, a contemporary Onondaga Faithkeeper, explained it to me, the Peacekeeper and Hiawatha placed an eagle on top of the tall white pine tree that they planted to symbolize the League. That eagle would always be watchful for danger approaching. But the tree had four white roots that stretched to all the directions. Anyone who was willing and patient enough to trade those roots, to follow all the rules of the League, could stand beneath the great tree's peaceful shade.—*Joseph Bruchac*

REVIEWS: AUTHORS "A" TO "Z"

Author Unknown, "Created by" Warner, Gertrude C., *The Boxcar Children: The Mystery of the Lost Village*, illustrated by Charles Tang. Albert Whitman (1993). 121 pages, b/w line drawings; grades 3-up; Diné (Navajo)

Henry, Jessie, Violet and Benny used to live alone in a boxcar. Now they have a home with their grandfather, who, every week or so, takes or sends them on an adventure. In this one, according to the blurb on the back cover, "[t]he Boxcar children learn lots of interesting things about the Navajos."

It is believed that there are the remains of a "lost village" in a forest right outside the Navajo reservation. No one has been able to find this "lost village," so the kids, with the permission of their Navajo hosts, go out, dig, and find artifacts. They also solve the mystery; go to the powwow and dance, and save the forest from real estate developers.

None of the "interesting things" the children learn have anything to do with reality. There is no forest within one hundred miles of the Diné reservation. Lightfeather, Running Deer, and Kinowok are not Diné names. The "Lightfeather" home, a two-story ranch house with a basement and a lawn, is not what Diné live in on the reservation. The Diné reservation covers hundreds of thousands of acres, and the idea of fencing it is ridiculous. Fried chicken and stuffing, mashed potatoes, bacon and eggs, and chocolate layer cake are not daily Navajo fare. There is no such thing as a "reservation stable"; animals live in corrals near the homes of their owners. One cannot get from place to place by walking; that's why Navajos have pickups. Navajo rugs do not generally have animal patterns; they have geometric ones. Diné spirituality is rich and complex; their deeply held beliefs are not superstitions.

In a subplot, Amy Lightfeather teaches Jessie how to make an authentic Navajo buckskin dress. Traditional dress for Diné women is generally pleated skirts and velveteen blouses or a blanket dress. In any case, it takes more than a half hour to complete regalia; it can take years. "With some jewelry and a pouch," Amy gushes to Jessie, "you'll look just like a Navajo girl." Somehow I doubt it.

There is only one Diné Nation, not a bunch of "Navajo tribes." Diné have, to say the least, great respect for owls, and do not take the call of an owl lightly. People may have a healthy respect for Coyote, but it is not for his "wisdom." The "peace pipe"—so-called—is a sacred object of the Plains peoples. The Snake Dance is a ceremony of the Pueblo people; Diné are not generally fond of snakes. Cornbread is square; frybread is generally round. Everyone does not join hands "in a closing song, watching as the huge bonfire turn[s] to embers." For the last song of a powwow, dancers and spectators may gather around the drum, after which the drum is generally danced out. Dreamcatchers are not toys.

There is nothing redeemable here. The author seems to have learned about Diné life and history from a scout handbook. Diné are maligned; the book gives the impression that going out and digging up artifacts is "fun." It is, in fact, not only a desecration of burial grounds, it is against federal law.

The creator of this series, Gertrude Chandler Warner, died in 1979. The books are still being written. I attempted to find out the name of the author of this book. The publisher's representative said that "it's not our policy to divulge the names of the authors of this series." I can see why.—*Beverly Slapin*

Ahenakew, Freda (Cree), *Wisahkecahk Flies to the Moon*, illustrated by Sherry Farrell Racette (Timiskaming). Pemmican (1999). Unpaginated, color illustrations; grades 1-2; Cree

Looking at the moon, Wisahkecahk gets the idea that it would be wonderful to ride it, "[a]nd why couldn't that happen?" Walking wasn't getting him too far, so he asked a crane to take him up. Holding onto the crane's legs, he "felt as though his arms were being pulled out of their sockets, and of course the cran was also exhausted," but they both make it. Wisahkecahk finds that he has "pulled the crane's legs to an abnormal length," but that's OK. "'He will be able to walk around the earth with good speed,' said Wisahkecahk." That's true: he does.

Crane goes back to earth and Wisahkecahk has a good time admiring everything, until the moon begins to shrink. The problem of how to get down is solved when the moon shrinks to nothingness. Coming in for a landing, he asks earth to make him a soft landing spot. Covered with mud, can't see, Wisahkecahk is not happy: "[S]uch spots as this will be waste land and will be of no use whatsoever to anyone. They will be called 'muskegs.' These exist today and are of no apparent value to man."

Wisahkecahk is what the anthropologists call a "culture hero," such as Gluscabi and other demi-god figures. He definitely has creative powers, but not always a lot of forethought. This is but one of his many stories.

Ahenakew is a writer well known in the Native community, and a Cree speaker. One of her concerns is the preservation of the language; her story is told in both Cree and English. Racette's pictures are both beautiful and funny. She perfectly captures the gawky beauty of Crane, and Wisahkecahk's delight at all the beauty he sees around him.—*Doris Seale*

Alexie, Sherman (Spokane/Coeur d'Alene), *The Lone Ranger and Tonto Fistfight in Heaven.* **Atlantic Monthly (1999). 223 pages; high school-up**

Alexie's writing is complex. It can range from the absolute brutality of "Independence Day" in *The Business of Fancydancing* to the tenderness of "A Good Story" in this volume. He tends to bring white readers face-to-face with things most of them would prefer not to have thrust in their faces; some of the rest of us would rather not have to look at them every day.

The usual suspects appear in this book: Victor, Thomas Builds-the-Fire, Big Mom, Lester FallsApart, and a Junior here and there. The stories can have a nearly apocalyptic vision, an ironic humor, writing that Kafka would be proud of. Some of them might lead one to believe that all Indians are dysfunctional. There is a poignancy that underlies this. Alexie's characters come straight out of life as it is for far too many Indian people—poverty, alcoholism, despair and defeat—but they never become clichés. And "Humor was an antiseptic that cleaned the deepest of

personal wounds." That is from "The Approximate Size of My Favorite Tumor," one of the most touching things I have ever read. Jimmy Many Horses is dying of cancer, and his wife leaves him because he will not stop making jokes about it. When she comes back and he asks her why, Norma says, "Because someone needs to help you die the right way....And we both know that dying ain't something you ever done before." Alexie can be facile, with his off-the-cuff throwaway lines. And then again, there are times when he says something in a way that that opens up a window in the mind:

> People can do things completely against their nature, completely. It's like some tiny earthquake comes roaring through your body and soul, and it's the only earthquake you'll ever feel. But it damages so much, cracks the foundations of your life forever.

And moments of pure beauty:

> And finally this, when the sun was falling down so beautiful we didn't have time to give it a name, she held the child born of white mother and red father and said, "Both sides of this baby are beautiful."

In a story called "A Drug Called Tradition," Victor relates how Big Mom gave him a "little drum [that] looked like it was about a hundred years old, maybe older. It was so small that it could fit in the palm of my hand." She called it her pager: "Just give it a tap and I'll be right over," she said. He never used it:

> But I keep it real close to me, like Big Mom said, just in case. I guess you could call it the only religion I have, one drum that can fit in my hand, but I think if I played it a little, it might fill up the whole world.

That's as good a place to stop as any. When he puts his heart into it, the man can write like an angel.—*Doris Seale*

Allen, Elsie (Pomo), *Pomo Basketmaking: a supreme art for the weaver.* **Naturegraph (1972, 1992). 67 pages, b/w photos, line drawings; grades 7-up**

Pomo Basketmaking weaves together a real story with real art, clearly written with numerous photographs and drawings, and will be accessible to younger readers as well as adults. Elsie's book is a Native woman's personal history woven into a life of an art that is more in harmony with nature, more environmentally-centered—because of its use of living plants—than any other.

Publisher Vincent Brown, in the introduction, wrote that the basketmaker

> worked constantly with sky and earth and living plants, with great patience and devotion, to create

something of superlative beauty. She watched the sky and also felt the sky; its changing moods and signs of what was coming, so that she knew by the literal feel of the air, something reaching her inner being, that now was the time to make a trip to the eastern mountains to collect the inner bark of the Redbud tree...

Later parts of Elsie Allen's life *after* the seventy-two years of it she chronicles here concern water more than sky—the drowning of a Pomo valley that had been the major source of basketry plants, especially sedge, whose roots are the sewing or weft, by the dam that now forms Lake Sonoma.

Pomo women led the opposition to the drowning. Elsie Allen, then in her eighties, was the principal Indian consultant employed in a court-mandated Warm Springs Dam Cultural Resources Study. Though there was concern at the drowning of burial grounds and Pomo village sites, Elsie's main concern was to try to save the plants, so necessary for continuation of the millennia-old art of Pomo basketry. That's not touched on in this book, which was completed in 1972.

Elsie Allen (1899-1990) was a tribal scholar, and renowned basketmaker whose family had long practiced this art. According to Kathleen Smith (Bodega Miwok/Dry Creek Pomo), herself a scholar of a younger generation,

> Elsie felt this urge that if she didn't share what she knew, it would die. She didn't want it to die, so she broke with the real strong tradition of not teaching it to those outside your family. She got a lot of flack, but the time was right for people to listen to her.

Elsie was apparently the first weaver to teach Pomo basketry outside her immediate family. This book, written with the help of her granddaughter and considerable help from the publisher in photography and drawings, is a part of what and how she shared—her life, as well as the demanding art and environmental knowledge.

Elsie's early life was hard, as it was for most California Indians of the early 20th Century. Subjected to the U.S. Army massacre at Bloody Island in 1850, imprisoned at Round Valley and Fort Bragg, the Pomo had pooled money from labors—and basket sales—to buy back some small patches of their land. But by the early 20th Century this land had been lost to extreme racism, to swindles and to the inability to keep up mortgage and tax payments.

Elsie was raised by her grandmother in the Cloverdale area, where nature was her teacher. There were no other children for her to play with, and the little girl made dolls for herself of cattail grass. She gave names to her playmates—the bushes, trees, willows. She describes an early near-fatal illness that was cured by her grandfather, an Indian singing doctor, which she felt gave her some health protection in later life. When her mother remarried after her father's death, Elsie lived with her great-uncle and grandfather who worked for local ranchers. In summers, they lived in a traditional house made of willow, "and my grandmother built me a bed that was high off the ground, on cross-pieces of willow resting on four large stakes driven into the ground," and a mattress of corn husks. The high bed "was to keep it out of range of snakes."

Elsie's life became harder when she was taken away from her family and sent to one of the government residential schools, whose intent was to destroy Indian language and culture. Through the years of raising her children, when she worked as a domestic, did field labor for white farmers, and—in her softest job, washing clothes—she had little time to make baskets. Those she did make were buried with relatives, which saddened and discouraged her.

Elsie's mother, Annie Burke, and other older relatives, were accomplished weavers. Annie Burke had a large basket collection she showed at state fairs. She wanted Elsie to continue this tradition, and not to bury her baskets with her, as was Pomo tradition. She wanted Elsie to have all those baskets, to learn from and to teach with—to teach that "Pomo people aren't dumb," by showing these beautiful products of art, knowledge, skill and work. Elsie promised to do this, and upon her mother's death, when Elsie herself was sixty-two and her children and grandchildren no longer needed her full-time support, became a full-time basketmaker.

> This means gathering and properly preparing the plants used—willow, sedge roots, bulrush roots and redbud. Elsie discusses gathering the plants, and the relation of the weaver to the earth, water, sky, and seasons. It is a life wholly integrated with both processes and products of the natural world. Gathering roots and shoots became increasingly difficult because the traditional plant-gathering sites were being built upon and fenced, sprayed with poisonous pesticides that killed birds and small animals as well as plants considered weeds.

A note from the publisher appears in the section where Elsie discusses each of the four traditional plants:

> People who have land where sedge roots grow can allow basketweavers to gather roots.... Please let local Indians or the publishers know if you have land that might be used for root gathering.

(I called the publisher to find out if anyone had volunteered to let Indian women gather roots on their land in the quarter-century this book has been in print. The publisher's widow—who with the aid of her children runs the press and was actively involved with Elsie Allen's book—said no, in twenty-five years, no one has ever contacted her to say Indian women may gather roots on their land.)

After a discussion about the gathering and preparing of plants, Elsie gives step-by-step instructions on weaving different kinds of baskets. This practical and beautiful introduction to the weaver's art is interspersed with family pictures of other generations of weavers.

Usually, the life story of a person who interests you must end with the book written about it. Elsie lived 20 years longer. Her plant and basketry experience gave her a central role in two big environmental issues led by Pomo women: the Warm Springs Dam (which created Lake Sonoma, flooded and filled in 1985) and the Inter-tribal Sinkyone Wilderness Park.

In the late 1970s, the U.S. Army Corps of Engineers decided to build a dam at Warm Springs in Lake County, in traditional Pomo homeland. This would flood the valley where most of the Pomo basketmakers of Mendocino and Lake counties got almost all their basket plants. It would also drown old burial grounds and old village sites. There was no fighting it; one Pomo reservation (Coyote Valley) had been entirely drowned already; all the people living there had had to leave. The Pomo—especially older women—wanted to save as much as they could.

Elsie Allen became a primary consultant in a group of mostly Pomo women, a few archaeologists, and some supporters attempting to inventory all that would be lost when the reservoir filled behind the Warm Springs Dam, and to try to compel the government to save as much as they could. Elsie's expertise was the plants and their sites. In 1985, the dam was finished, and Lake Sonoma flooded the entire valley—one of the few remaining places in California where sedge, willow and bulrush roots could be freely gathered. The women arranged to transplant some of these plants, partly onto some volunteered private land, and part to be maintained under the supervision of Ya-Ka-Ama, the native plant nursery that was gained by Pomo occupation of an abandoned CIA spy base in 1970.

The determined efforts of these older Indian women established that plants needed to continue activities central to the continuing *life* of an Indian culture may require legal protection under environmental laws, though ultimately they didn't get it in the now-flooded valley. They did stop the dam and get some funding for the investigation and salvage projects. This is a different

principle—and to tribes with still-living traditions of use-gathering perhaps as interesting—as claims that some vast project will destroy sites that are sacred, claims the courts have ignored from the Tennessee Valley Authority's Tellico Dam boondoggle to Badger Two-Medicine Mountain and many other places.

—*Paula Giese*

Arlee, Johnny (Salish), *Mali Npnaqs: The Story of a Mean Little Old Lady,* **illustrated by T.J. Sandoval (Salish). Salish Kootenai College (2003). 60 pages, b/w illustrations; all grades; Salish**

This here Mary Bent Nose is a real mean old lady. She just grumbles all the time. She complains about everything. She slams the cup down on the table. She slams the door. She walks around with a mean expression on her face. When people say hello to her, she doesn't answer them. She never looks around. She never smells the flowers. She never listens to the birds singing. She is just mean.

Well one day, the things in her house decide they have just had enough. After talking the situation over with each other, the door decides to stick, the chair decides to fall over, the chimney decides to smoke and the pot decides to boil over. They'll show her, that mean little old lady.

They do, and then they tell the old lady that that's what she's going to get unless she changes her attitude: "Mary, nothing will be good for you if always you are grumbling." So, from that day on,

> Never again did she grumble, that little mean lady. Never again it sticks, the Door. Never again it plugs up, the Chimney. Never again it boils and will spill all over, the Pot. And never again it falls over on the floor, the Chair. And from then on, always and good they lived together. That is all.

Sandoval's pen-and-ink line drawings, showing the mean

little old lady and her pretty quick transformation, are an absolute scream. *Malí Npnaqs* is written in Salish and English, with a literal English translation structured as an aid for the Salish reader. The English syntax based on the Salish vernacular adds to the flavor of the story, and when read aloud, *Malí Npnaqs* will have children howling.—*Beverly Slapin*

Ashrose, Cara, *The Very First Americans*, illustrated by Bryna Waldman. Grosset & Dunlap (1993). Unpaginated, color illustrations; grades 1-2

From the *All Aboard Books* collection, this title oversimplifies and generalizes Indian peoples and their ways of life. Inauthentic illustrations and inappropriate text both romanticize and misrepresent Native peoples and traditions. The Indians all look exactly the same, while the white Pilgrims are well defined and individualized.

From the first page:

> Long, long ago, nobody lived in America. There were animals—huge woolly mammoths, big wildcats, bison—but no people at all…After hundreds of years, these first Americans were scattered across the country. They lived in big groups called tribes.

The picture, supposedly illustrating the Bering Strait theory, shows people walking across Alaska to North America, right behind a woolly mammoth and two bison. This would have been an impossibly long journey, and yet it appears that a family is just taking a walk.

What is more disturbing about this book is how the author minimizes the Native experience of colonialism. The last two pages of the book read (italics mine):

> For hundreds of years, Indians were the only Americans. Then about five hundred years ago, great ships began to arrive…The Indians tried to carry on with their way of life. But it was not easy… By 1900, the new settlers had claimed most of the country…Today, almost two million American Indians make *their* homes in *this* country.

The message here is that this is not Indian land, and never will be, that Europeans have taken this land and therefore Indians will have to like it or leave it. Not recommended.—*Sachiko Reed*

Awiakta, Marilou (Cherokee), *Selu: Seeking the Corn-Mother's Wisdom*, illustrations by Mary Adair (Cherokee). Fulcrum (1993). 336 pages, b/w illustrations; high school-up

For many years now, there has been a growing awareness among those who have not let themselves be blinded by greed, that we, the people of the Earth, are in a perilous condition. In this time, if it is not already too late, we are confronted with a clear choice: change our behavior, grow up, and begin to respect and care for our Mother and only home, or lose it all. In *Selu*, Awiakta speaks to this issue, and to all the others that have arisen from the insane acquisitiveness and lust for power with which the Earth and her peoples have been plundered over the last 500 years.

The heart of the book, and the center around which Awiakta builds her thesis, is the story of Ginitsi Selu; the gift of corn. Corn, that which has sustained life for so many of us on Turtle Island for unknown thousands of years. It is an extraordinary compilation of story, poem, interview, history, personal account—all the forms that words may take. Awiakta has chosen for her work the form of the Cherokee doublewoven basket, to "interweave in a pattern," a circular path to understanding and the application of ancient wisdom to our current situation.

> Reason for Making Our Journey:
>
> So we won't die.
>
> Neither will Mother Earth.

Should you now be thinking "mythology," or romantic longing for a time long gone and irrelevant for the world in which we now live, let me mention the work of Barbara McClintock, who in 1983 received the Nobel Prize in Medicine, for her work in corn genetics. (She makes an appearance here.) She, too, made her discoveries by listening to what the corn—zea maize—had to tell her. This is not a metaphor, but a real thing. Her paper, "A Correlation of Cytological and Genetical Crossing-over in Zea maize" was called a "cornerstone" of experimental genetics. Because she let the corn "guide and tell" her, McClintock was able to prove that

> what she called "transposition" takes place in genetic material. That genes, in short, "jump." And genetic changes are *under the control of the organism itself*... the organism that, in her own words, "guided and directed her work, that spoke to her."

Selu gave her body that we might live. It's a story. But story revolves around a real-life happening. There is a lesson here, if we can hold still long enough to learn it. Awiakta asks us to do that, to recognize that "we humans are truly sisters and brothers—one family in fact as well as philosophy." And that the words "Mother Earth" also are not a metaphor, but a real thing.

Awiakta tells of a conversation in which she was asked to sum up her work in a few sentences. "I'll do better than that," she said, and did in four words: "No respect, no food." I guess anybody ought to be able to understand that....—*Doris Seale*

Bania, Michael, *Kumak's House: A Tale of the Far North*, illustrated by the author. Alaska Northwest Books (2002). 32 pages, color illustrations; preschool-up; Iñupiaq

Kumak's House: A Tale of the Far North is "adapted," without attribution, from a popular old Yiddish story.

I have heard many versions of this story. My favorite is Margot Zemach's *It Could Always Be Worse*. In Zemach's telling, a poor man lives with his large extended family in a tiny one-room house in a crowded stetl in Eastern Europe, probably in the 19th Century. Thinking life unbearable, he seeks counsel from the rabbi, who advises him to bring the livestock, one by one, into the house. Soon the poor man's life becomes *really* hard. So the rabbi advises him to put the livestock back outside, thereby bringing peace and quiet into his house. This is a story that has served us well through the generations. In times that seem unbearable, we hear that it could always be worse—and we laugh. Zemach's story is rich in cultural context, and unstated historical context as well.

In *Kumak's House*, author Michael Bania changes the Jewish peasant to an Iñupiaq patriarch, the rabbi to an Iñupiaq elder, and the chickens, goose, goat and cow to Rabbit, Fox, Caribou, Porcupine, Otter, Bear, and Whale. Each time Kumak visits Aana Lulu she is busy working at some cultural task the author can then explain in her 1,172-word Author's Note (compared to 840 words in the entire text). Presumably to teach a lesson, Aana Lulu talks solely in metaphors, all about size—"Unhappy is the mukluk on too big a foot.... Unhappy is the parka on too big a body....Unhappy is

the hat on too big a head...Unhappy is the bush with too many berries....Unhappy is the ...." Is this supposed to be old Iñupiaq wisdom?

Both *It Could Always Be Worse* and *Kumak's House* ask young readers to suspend disbelief. Bringing farm animals into one's house is silly, but not impossible. Bringing a whale into one's house is not possible. Whales cannot survive on land. While I can envision a rabbi advising some poor soul to bring the livestock into his house, I cannot fathom an Iñupiaq elder telling someone to transport a whale into an environment where it would surely die.

Providing cultural context for a story is not the same as tossing in cultural snippets and straining credulity. Calling something a "folktale" or a "tale of the Far North" does not make it one. Unfortunately, this is probably going to be seen as another "multicultural" story used in classrooms to teach about the Iñupiaq.—*Beverly Slapin*

Bannon, Kay Thorpe, *Yonder Mountain: A Cherokee Legend*, as told by Robert H. Bushyhead, illustrated by Kristina Rodanas. Marshall Cavendish (2002). Unpaginated, grades 3-up; Cherokee

Paula Gunn Allen has said, "An odd thing occurs in the minds of Americans when American Indian civilization is mentioned: little or nothing." I would add that stereotypes of our peoples exist and grow because of what is fed to Indian and non-Indian children.

The author attributes the original "legend" of Yonder Mountain to the Rev. Robert H. Bushyhead, a Cherokee elder from whom she first heard the story. With an introduction from acclaimed Abenaki storyteller Joseph Bruchac, this book would appear to be authentic. It is not.

In this male rite of passage story, leadership of a tribe is passed on from one generation to the next by a series of trials performed by three young men. Two of the young men bring back gifts that will assist the people. The first brings back "sparkling stones" so that the people "could trade them for food" and "never be hungry again." The second young man brings back "healing plants" so that the people "will no longer be sick and suffer." The third young man goes to the top of "yonder mountain" and sees a "smoke signal… calling for help." He returns to his people with this story. "Chief Sky" determines that the people "need a leader who has climbed to the top of the mountain… one who has seen beyond the mountain to other people who are in need." And so the third young man is rewarded with tribal leadership.

While the lesson of *Yonder Mountain* is the importance of helping those in need, its glaring homogenous vision of Native people overshadows its message.

The author's language is archaic and stilted, belabored and dull, devoid of humor and reminiscent of images of Hollywood Indians fading sadly off into distant sunsets. The old chief, "Chief Sky,"

> had seen many summers and winters… he had led his people through long seasons of peace. He had seen their warriors go through great battles with enemies. But now his step was slow, and his hand trembled on the bow. He could no longer spot brother deer among the trees. He was no longer able to lead his people.

Cultural authenticity doesn't even make a cameo appearance. In traditional Cherokee matriarchal culture, power is shared and the Clan Mothers are the ones who decide who assumes leadership. In traditional Cherokee stories, there are girls and women. In traditional Cherokee stories, events happen in fours. And in traditional Cherokee stories, Christian analogies such as "going to the mountaintop and seeing beyond" do not exist.

So this is not one of our traditional stories. It's a story originally told by a Christian Cherokee elder to encourage young people to be of service to others. This is a good thing, but it doesn't make *Yonder Mountain* a "Cherokee Legend."

Rodanas' watercolor artwork, as is her usual style, is flat and unimaginative; her Cherokee subjects are dressed in Lakota-style fringed buckskin and beadwork, and the women and girls (all background figures) have little or no expression.

It's too bad that teachers will see Robert H. Bushyhead's and Joseph Bruchac's names and assume this book to be an authentic and accurate representation of Native storytelling rather than a white adaptation of a relatively contemporary Christian morality story dropped into an "old-days" setting.—*Carolyn Dunn*

Barber-Starkey, Joe, illustrated by Paul Montpellier. Harbour. Unpaginated, color illustrations; grades 1-3; Nuu-chah-nulth (Nootka)
Jason and the Sea Otter (1989)
Jason's New Dugout Canoe (2000)

One day, when young Jason is fishing in the sea, he sees an otter swimming among the kelp stems. He does not recognize this animal, so he asks his grandfather, who tells him a story about how plentiful otters once were, until they were overhunted for the fur trade both by whites and by Indians.

Jason goes back, day after day, to watch the otters play. One day he leans over too far, tips the canoe, and falls into the icy water. He is saved by the two otters he had watched, who stop the drifting canoe by what can only be described as little critter ingenuity.

This book will appeal to uncritical young readers who will learn that sea otters are cute and smart, that they were hunted to near-extinction but are now coming back, and that Nuu-chah-nulth youngsters don't know how to stay in a canoe.

From the very first line—"The summer sun was warm on Jason's brown back…"—it is clear that *Jason and the Sea Otter* is not written from a Nuu-chah-nulth perspective.

While it is true that sea otters were hunted to the verge of extinction by the global fur trade of the 19th Century, more recently they have rebounded to the point where their numbers are so out of balance that they are decimating whole red abalone and sea urchin beds up and down the West Coast of North America. We do not see sea otters—nor would we portray them in stories for children—as little heroes.

The animals and plants of the sea are illustrated richly and for the most part realistically, but the Nuu-chah-nulth people are not. In the "historic" scenes, they all look the same, down to their shapeless brown garb. In the contemporary pictures, Jason's body and features are practically cartoonish; he looks like nobody you'd want to know. Reflections of the past are distinguished by frames of pathetic ghostly "totem pole" imagery, showing characters with threatening teeth and large beaks. One guy looks like he's wearing a pineapple on his head.

The final illustration shows Jason, paddling home after being saved by the otters. He is not dripping wet and freezing and miserable, but dry and happy. He is smiling, while ghost figures of "ancient" Nuu-chah-nulth hunters in canoes, holding spears, hover in the clouds over him. The text reads:

> He lifted his paddle to start for home, still shivering with fright and cold, but as he turned to take a last look at his otter friend he was quite sure that it closed one eye and winked at him. As he headed home through the harbour entrance he was thinking about what an exciting story he would have to tell to his grandchildren when he was a grandfather.

What a trip to lay on a little kid! Youngsters do not think about becoming grandparents and telling stories—only grandparents think like that.

Jason and the Sea Otter, a not-so-thinly veiled conservationist morality play, badly written and badly illustrated, is definitely not recommended.

In *Jason's New Dugout Canoe*, our inept Nuu-chah-nulth lad, having been rescued by a sea otter in the previous book, fails to read the weather and pays for it by having his prized canoe destroyed.

This story—touted as exploring First Nations traditions and values through the making of a dugout canoe—crudely explores material technology but fails to recognize fundamental Nuu-chah-nulth values and traditions. Our canoes represent high inputs of scarce spiritual, social, technical and natural resources. Great ceremony is associated with their production, and great care is given to their use and preservation. This story notwithstanding, our canoes are rarely accidentally "lost" to sudden storms. In stormy weather, canoes are usually beached in the village. Learning to read the weather and the tides is a skill that youngsters have to learn before even getting a canoe. They practice with the canoes of family members until they can demonstrate that they can handle a canoe by taking care of it.

As in *Jason and the Sea Otter*, the illustrations here will probably engage little kids, but are inaccurate and unsuitable. Because the owl foreshadows death or harm to a person in many West Coast cultures, it was probably not a good idea to draw an owl to foreshadow the loss of a canoe.

Rather than sharing the canoe he and his uncle have just built, Jason muses about how other children could "learn about the freedom it could give them" if they had their own canoe, which he could make them if he grew up to be a canoe maker. Rather than reflecting Nuu-chah-nulth ethics and traditions, the author distorts them by making what is very much a communal activity into an individual one.

Inexplicably, this book comes with detailed instructions on "how to build a dugout canoe." The instructions begin with "Remove the bark from a cedar log and chisel out a section of wood from each end." This is a book for little kids, eh? Not recommended.—*Marlene R. Atleo/ʔeh ʔeh naa tuu kwiss*

Bartok, Mira and Christine Ronan, *Northwest Coast Indians.* Good Year Books (1996). 16 pages, color illustrations; preschool-grade 2 (Northwest Coast Nations)

This photoessay for very young children about the Northwest Coast Nations is oversimplified. That is because it's impossible to describe the lifeways of Northwest Coast Indian peoples in sixteen pages.

The first few pages read:

> The Northwest Coast Indians live in the Northwest United States, Canada, and Alaska. They live along the Pacific Ocean near rain forests. Many animals, birds, and fish live there too.

However, the photos show only trees, birds, the Pacific Ocean and an otter. But there are no Indians here. Are the rain forests, Pacific Ocean, animals, birds, and fish supposed to *represent* the Indians?

The following page shows a lone Indian woman cooking a dozen pieces of meat all by herself. The text reads, "Some Indian people hunt and fish for their food." While the contemporary photos are good, one wonders why almost everyone is dressed in regalia. Further, text such as "They drum and dance. Sometimes they even dance sitting down!" makes no attempt to explain anything.—*Sachiko Reed*

Beardslee, Lois (Ojibwe/Lacandon), *Lies to Live By*, illustrated by the author. Michigan State University (2003). 143 pages, b/w illustrations; grades 7-up; Ojibwe

Lois Beardslee is an Ojibwe woman—Anishinaabe—from the Great Lakes area. She is a teacher and writer, accomplished in basketry, quillwork and birchbark biting. You will see examples of this art throughout the book, as well her painting on the cover. There are forty-four stories in the collection. They are not "retold" myths-and-legends; if you are looking for secrets, revelations, look someplace else.

I have never met Lois Beardslee, but through these writings she comes across as a woman who knows what we have lost and what we still have and has come to terms with both.

In her introduction, she speaks of the "immediacy" of northern Woodland traditions.

> More pragmatic than mystic, our characters and the stories about them remained culturally intact because they are still applicable. They teach our children a system of behavioral guidelines and cultural values...teach them how to stay out of trouble or avoid being hurt...how to do things the right way, such as peeling a tree and building a temporary bark shelter....They...have evolved fluidly throughout the years, and continue to do so.

They remain relevant because they have never been anything else. The stories here are from Lois Beardslee's own life, seamlessly interwoven with the traditional stories of her people. There is a way of knowing that goes beyond the immediately provable fact. Our lives are embedded in that knowing. Our stories are part of that, and our lives are, inextricably, part of the stories.

Read slowly, one or two at a time. She is a beautiful writer; don't spoil it with haste. *Lies to Live By* is food for the heart, a book to come back to when your nerves are jangled, your brain scrambled, your heart aches, and you no longer know who you are.—*Doris Seale*

Beardslee, Lois (Ojibwe/Lacandon), *Rachel's Children.* **AltaMira (2004). 147 pages, high school-up; Ojibwe**

Rachel's story comes to us in the voice of an interviewer who wants nothing from her but her knowledge, her stories, and a piece of her spirit; who observes her life with the sense of superiority that comes from profound ignorance.

Rachel is frighteningly intelligent, and she brings the interviewer and the reader face-to-face with what it is to be an Indian woman in 21st-Century America; what it takes to live with the land and not off it, and the courage and unremitting determination required

to confront this country's social system and survive it. Scarred, but still alive.

Nothing is exaggerated; not the prejudice, not the hatred and deliberate cruelty, not the sheer stupidity that stunt Native lives. But there is also the beauty of true things; the way the pollen comes off the evergreens in the spring, "a great yellow cloud" borne on the wind, sweeping up and out, new life. And the intensity of Rachel's love for her children and her husband, and they for her.—*Doris Seale*

Beardslee, Lois (Ojibwe/Lacandon), *Waboseg (An Ojibwe story about Rabbits' ears),* **illustrated by the author. (1997), b/w illustrations; all grades; Ojibwe**

> Everyone knows that Waboseg (Rabbits) love wildflowers. In the warmest days of spring, when young Zweegun (Springtime) arrives from the south to coax old Biboon (Winter) back to his home in the north, the rabbits begin to nibble.

When Zweegun is doing her job, she brings warm southern winds, the days grow longer, the fish swim upstream and the sap moves into the branches of the trees. But girls just want to have fun you see, and Zweegun, being just a young girl, "kept forgetting about the job she was supposed to do." Zweegun's forgetfulness causes her friends the Waboseg to eat too many wildflowers, causing the Amoog (Bees) to make less honey, causing the Mukwag (Bears) to make a very difficult decision—and the Waboseg wind up with long ears.

Lois Beardslee is an accomplished storyteller and youngsters will want to hear this one again and again. Her illustrations complement the story.—*Beverly Slapin*

Beckman, Pat Ramsey, *From the Ashes.* **Roberts Rinehart/ Council for Indian Education Series (1996). 96 pages; grades 3-5; Shawnee**

Another white-boy-coming-of-age-story-with-an-Indian-theme. As the story begins, our young protagonist has just found the bodies of his mom and pop, killed by "renegade" Indians, and his brother has disappeared, presumably taken. The story is set in Ohio in 1794, as U.S. troops, led by General "Mad" Anthony Wayne, are laying waste to the lands of those Native peoples who had sided with the British against the colonists. While searching for his brother, Davey Joyce is grabbed by two "half-brothers" named White Wolf and Black Wolf. White Wolf is "lean and handsome" and Black Wolf is "swarthy and stocky." White Wolf is gentle, Black wolf is nasty; White Wolf talks, Black Wolf mocks, jeers, scowls, screams, shrieks.

White Wolf has an accident and Davey applies a tourniquet to stop the bleeding (because Indians apparently never knew about first aid.) The Wolf brothers take him home to their village where, after being forced to run the gauntlet, he is immediately adopted by Chief Blue Jacket and given a Shawnee name. Before you know it, the tribe has built him a house (the *whole* tribe). While Black Wolf continues to harass him, Davey becomes a warrior, leads the women to safety, frees a hostage, interprets at a treaty council, advises the chiefs in matters of war and peace, saves the American fort from the "renegades," and finds his brother.

Beckman probably read a book about Indians once, but it must've been a long time ago, because she gets a *really* lot of things wrong. For instance, she has a scene where "giggling girls pretended a buffalo leg wrapped in a blanket was their child." Now, I am trying to imagine this: a buffalo leg would weigh, oh, about 200 pounds. This would be a pretty big baby. Or is the author saying Shawnee girls had no dolls to play with, so their only form of amusement would have been to drag around someone's dinner? I cannot imagine any child wanting to cuddle up to a bloody piece of meat. Then there's the scene where "[a]n Indian mother was hanging her baby from a tree limb." Unless she's talking about infanticide, which was not a Shawnee practice, the author probably means that the woman was hanging a cradleboard *containing* a baby from a tree limb.

Then there's the battle scene, where Davey's about to scalp a soldier:

> [A]nother American soldier stormed up to him, waving his bayonet wildly. In a split second Davey straightened. His rifle was gone, but he still had his skinning knife. He grabbed for the soldier's hair, glassy eyes fixed on him. Suddenly Black Wolf appeared from behind, seized the soldier's hair out of Davey's grasp, and peeled his scalp away. "Whooaaa!"

What is the point of this? To show the Indian as more bloodthirsty than the white man? Or to save our hero from mutilating one of his own kind? In either case, pointless. And human beings do not come apart *quite* that easily.

There's also a lot purple prose: "His heart sang with the birds. Hope sprang up in him like the straight green rows of tender corn he had helped plant...." And lots of animal metaphors, so you know it's about Indians: "strength of a buffalo," "on cat-like feet," "her doe eyes softening," "snaking along."

Bad writing. Historical and cultural nonsense. Women are either controlling or helpless. Men are braves or savages or renegades. Prayers are chants. Dancing is "trotting, stomping, singing 'Yu-wooo, hi! he-hie.'" Not recommended, except as a bad example.—*Beverly Slapin*

Begay, Shonto (Diné), *Navajo: Visions and Voices Across the Mesa,* **illustrated by the author. Scholastic (1995). 48 pages, color illustrations; grades 5-up; Diné (Navajo)**

In his first non-fiction book for younger readers, Begay explores "facets of Navajo life that are rarely touched upon in Western literature." This is not a coffee-table book. It is not "American Indian wisdom," it is not "Mother Earth spirituality," it is not designed by those who are fascinated by Indians. The words tell the story of a life lived at such far remove from the clamor of urban society as to be nearly incomprehensible to those who inhabit that environment—although even here, what is called "civilization" impinges on the lives of the people.

A grandmother called Small Woman, so strong and gentle that she lived 113 years; the blessing of rain and how sweet the earth smells after a summer thunderstorm. An eclipse and a father who sang prayers for the sun's return. Tribal fair with its throngs of people—every size, every shape, every color. Ceremony that brings balance back to the world. And the things that come in the night, mysteries, to test that balance: "Sounds pounding from within/Threaten my spirit/More than the sounds on the roof."

And then there is that other world, the one that surrounds us, that requires us to make some sort of accommodation with its presence; the one, in fact, in which many of us live. The European hitchhiker of "Coyote Crossing," in the bed of the truck, "quietly sitting there, nibbling on his organic snack, oblivious to what just happened." The coal mines on the mesa with machines as big as buildings, the trucks, the trains, the jets, that disturb Grandfather's morning prayers. But "still we sprinkle pollen for another day/Still we have faith." Ancient truth still exists, "Like pictographs, like broken pottery shards/We have yet to see the picture whole." Still the spring comes, "For this generation, and many more to come,/This land is beautiful and filled with mysteries./They reveal themselves and their stories—/If you look carefully and listen...."

The pictures are magnificent, and there is much to see in them that might not at first be noticed. Look carefully at the pattern of earth and snow on page 12, for instance, and you will see a running horse, a man with what may be a dog—or something, a deer, a jackrabbit, Cousin Toad—the life of the land.

This is a strong and beautiful book. There is healing in it. Accept the gift as it is given.—*Doris Seale*

Benes, Rebecca C., *Native American Picture Books of Change: The Art of Historic Children's Editions,* foreword by Gloria Emerson (Diné). Museum of New Mexico (2004). 168 pages, color and b/w illustrations, b/w photos; high school-up

All children's books, no matter what the content, contain certain values, assumptions about life and ways of seeing the world that are encoded—purposefully or not—into the text or subtext.

From the 1920s through the 1940s, the Bureau of Indian Affairs hired white linguists to create orthographies for what had been oral languages; and white educators, writers and ethnologists to mine traditional Indian stories for "folktales." The result was a bilingual series called "Indian Life Readers"—new stories based on Indian experiences as these cultural outsiders perceived them.

These children's books were not "Native American" picture books. Rather, the stories used Indians as a theme but, with few exceptions, the individual writers had no real connection to the people they were writing about. Illustrated by young Indian artists who were going to school or living in communities and towns outside the reservations, most of the books nevertheless reflected more the Christian ethics of the BIA, the agency that oversaw their production, than the traditional values of the Indian children for whom they were intended.

And this is no accident. For the Indian children in the BIA boarding schools, brainwashing didn't come easily; the prevailing theory was that books with familiar images and familiar languages could be used more effectively to acculturate this captive audience of children. To some extent, this was marginally successful, producing children who could read and write in two languages, but belonged to neither the white world nor the Indian world.

All of this seems to have escaped the author of *Native American Picture Books of Change*. As an art collector and entrepreneur, Benes is very good at describing lines and brushstrokes, color, shading and light, but she is abysmal at analyzing the content of these books.

Of one of the very worst in the series, called *Five Little Katchinas*, Benes writes:

> In the story, when a little Hopi girl named Blue Flower goes to sleep, the five little carved kachinas that are hanging on the wall come to life in her dreams. They are Mudhead, who because his head is made of mud has no sense at all, Deer, Eagle, Corn Tassel, and Squash Blossom. The kachinas, predictably led into trouble by the obstreperous Mudhead, literally fall into their adventures, which range from trying to grind corn because they are hungry to setting a fire as they try to cook their food. This book about diminutive kachina dolls

is especially appealing. DeHuff skillfully combines elements of folklore and realism with whimsical tales of the playful kachinas.

Maybe one would have to be Hopi to know the intense pain and shame this reducing of their deities to diminutive little troublemakers—this mockery of their spiritual traditions—inflicted on the Hopi children forced to endure this at school. Apparently Benes has no idea. That *Five Little Katchinas* was illustrated by a young Hopi artist does *not*, as Benes writes, bestow "an authenticity that was lacking in national and regional collections of folktales." Rather, this "cross-cultural collaboration," this "bicultural movement" is merely a euphemism for a white attempt at cultural destruction, validated by the work of a hungry young artist.

Benes' writing is contradictory and confusing. Her afterword begins with this: "The bilingual picture books, designed to preserve Indian cultures while introducing different values, are multicultural statements." And ends with this: "As a multicultural expression that respects the cultural values and languages of Indian Native communities, the picture books were ahead of their time."

The cultural outsiders working for the BIA may have meant well in the creation of these picture books. Many are beautiful to look at, and the talent of several young Indian artists won public recognition. They later became mentors to a new generation of Indian artists. So the books have meaning and worth in a historical sense. But there also needs to be acknowledgment of the great damage that these books caused, and that acknowledgment is lacking here.

Gloria Emerson's beautifully written, insightful foreword about indigenous languages and story, her own experiences as an artist and educator, and the differences between the BIA programs and the Indian-directed language projects that came after ought to be developed into a book. "Somewhere in the beginning of the beginning," she writes,

> people shared the same languages of mountains, streams, spiders, swallows, coyotes. In those times, stories streamed like rivers into the hamlets and canyons and plains, wherever we walked and lived in this hemisphere.

> The stories were about mirth, myth, and metaphor; they taught ethics and histories, as well as lessons of survival and spirituality. These stories were ritualistically orchestrated and interwoven with the many elements of our natural and cultural landscapes because our ancestors were attentive to the spirits within all things, honoring them and moving in concert with the cadences of their richly textured landscapes. Our ancestors honored and respected complex cultural protocols. Certain

stories were told in their own seasons; gender differences were respected, and language that pertained to women or men was used in telling and retelling the stories; oratorical styles using gesture and motion were as important as words; rules of languages and languages of aesthetics were maintained, as was the communal consciousness of group, clan, village, extended families, and tribes; the exquisite relationships with the natural world were respected; and the spirits within all things animate and inanimate were honored.

Emerson's words elucidate an Indian perspective sorely lacking in Benes's culturally dysconscious writing.

But no doubt, *Native American Picture Books of Change*, which is beautifully designed and has received uncritically positive reviews, will sell well.—*Beverly Slapin*

Bennett, James, *Dakota Dream*. Scholastic (1994). 182 pages, grades 7-up; Dakota

A white teenager named Floyd Rayfield has a destiny. His destiny is to become a Dakota. That is his destiny. We know that is his destiny because the word "destiny" is used forty-nine times. He has a vision about this destiny. We know *that* because the word "vision" is used thirty-one times. His "vision" is about having been a Plains Indian in a previous existence, and he holds the Indians in "high esteem." This teenager has a "chosen Sioux name": Charly Black Crow. This name apparently has no significance. Our junior wannabe hero wears moccasins. He casually smokes a Calf Pipe, replete with eagle feather, which he calls a "ceremonial."

Floyd aka "Charly Black Crow" has been shuttled between foster homes and group homes for most of his life. One might suspect that this has something to do with his attitude. He escapes from his last group home placement and travels to the Pine Ridge Reservation, where he meets a man named "Donny Thunderbird," who takes him to meet the chief, a guy named Delbert Bear. The chief also fills in as a medicine man, probably because there are no other Indian characters in the book. The chief-cum-medicine man immediately sees that our hero is sincere, and in about five minutes, he's on his way to a vision quest, at a place he names "Mount Black Elk."

This "vision quest" is preceded by an impossible sweat ceremony, in which he is put, naked, without any preparation or guidance, into a sweat lodge, and left for hours. Every once in a while, an unnamed Indian woman (!) comes in to pour water on the heated rocks. Having finished his sweat, he is now ready for his vision quest. He is taken to "Mount Black Elk" and left again without

instruction, but with water, blue jeans, two t-shirts, a jacket, his "ceremonial pipe," a toothbrush, soap, a washcloth, his journal and two Bic pens, so he can write about his vision while he is experiencing it. (When a vision quest is a real thing, a blanket and some water might be as much as the young supplicant would be allowed.)

So he has his vision, which the chief interprets. Then the chief/medicine man decides not to adopt him or make him an honorary citizen of the Dakota Nation, but actually to enroll him, which, according to the chief, makes him an Indian. All this is done easily and matter-of-factly, without talking it over with anyone else, since there are no other Indians in the book. Donny Thunderbird, Delbert Bear, "Charly Black Crow," and Barb exchange "Sioux embraces," whatever they might be.

The author's interpretation of Dakota ways is disrespectful and flat-out wrong. The chief/medicine man "chants and mumbles" to the "four corners," rather than praying to the four directions; he casually smokes a Calf Pipe, and drinks while making ceremony: "Besides being a little drunk, he was mostly interested in doing the chanting and burning the sage."

Dakota Dream might have been good story. Our teenager, with all of his pretensions, could have come to Pine Ridge, where someone might have taken pity on him and explained to him that being Indian is a matter of blood and spirit, not of romance and imagination; and that sweats and vision quests are not games to be engaged in by adventurous non-Native teenagers. Of course, that would have required writing a completely different kind of book, from the beginning.—*Beverly Slapin*

Bernhard, Emery, *Spotted Eagle & Black Crow: A Lakota Legend*, illustrated by Durga Bernhard. Holiday House (1993). Unpaginated, color illustrations; grades 2-4; Lakota

"Spotted Eagle and Black Crow were brothers. Both were brave warriors, and both loved the same woman." So we know where this is going. Black Crow is jealous of Spotted Eagle and talks him into a horse raid on the Pawnee. On the way, Black Crow talks his brother onto a high bluff and down to a ledge where there are baby eagles, then drops the rope and abandons him. Black Crow goes home and marries Red Bird. But the baby eagles share their food with Spotted Eagle, and when they are grown, fly him to the ground. When he returns to the village he says nothing, because there is war with the Pawnee. During the battle, Black Crow loses his horse and asks his brother to forgive him, and take him up.

> "No," answered Spotted Eagle. "Long ago you swore to defend your people, to fight to the end.

Meet the enemy where you stand! Then, I will forgive you whether you live or die."

Black Crow dies a hero's death; Spotted Eagle marries Red Bird.

The author does cite his source: *American Indian Myths and Legends* by Richard Erdoes and Alfonso Ortiz (Pantheon, 1984). The bones of the story are here, but Bernhard's version is much abridged. Several changes have been made and conversations created; Black Crow and Spotted Eagle have been made brothers, rather than friends, to intensify the conflict. The raid that they made—disastrously—before coming to the cliffs is omitted, and sequences of events rearranged. This has none of the depth and richness of the original and Bernhard just could not resist adding a moral, blessedly absent from the Erdoes version:

> Both Spotted Eagle and Black Crow were brave warriors, but only one went the way of *wakan*, only one remembered the wisdom of things of the spirit...and in the end only one lived to give thanks to *Wakan Tanka*, the Great Spirit, and to the *Wanblee*, our winged brothers.

Well, at least we know that he knows three words of Lakota.

The illustrations are the usual Indian-like designs, mostly in pastels, and all the people have the same face. Read the Erdoes and Ortiz version; that's a good story.—*Doris Seale*

Bierhorst, John, *Is My Friend at Home? Pueblo Fireside Tales,* **illustrated by Wendy Watson. Farrar Straus Giroux (2001). Unpaginated, color illustrations; grades 1-3; Pueblo Nations**

In oral traditions, stories serve many purposes and transmit cultural values. Some stories tell how things came to be and explain the relationships between and among all forms of creation. Some stories illustrate the importance and interdependence of land, culture and community. Some stories are cautionary "trickster" tales about what constitutes proper and improper behavior. Some stories describe ordinary people participating in extraordinary acts of courage for the good of the community. Some stories are for everybody, some stories are to teach young people the responsibilities of adulthood, some are ritual or medicine stories told to certain initiates only, some stories are "grandmother" or "grandfather" stories, transmitted from grandparents to grandchildren. And some stories are just for fun. But for whatever reason and to whatever audience they are told, all told stories have certain cultural contexts and subtleties that are often not perceived by outsiders.

These nuances are generally either unknown or ignored by non-Native "retellers" and creators of "Indian stories for children." John Bierhorst's latest title is a perfect example of this kind of culture theft so prevalent in the "multicultural" children's book game.

Subtitled "Pueblo Fireside Tales" and described in the CIP data as "a collection of traditional tales originally told in the Hopi pueblos of Arizona," Bierhorst's versions are garnered from late 19th-Century anthropological texts (including Frank Hamilton Cushing's *Zuni Breadstuff* as a source for Hopi stories). They are apparently designed for non-Native children. All of the stories here, whatever their original intent, are, according to the book jacket, supposedly about "making and keeping friends." But this is not a traditional value among the Hopi, whose society of clan and familial relationships make it unnecessary for young people to have to go out and "make friends."

Further, most of the stories—how Coyote learns an easy way to make delicious food and winds up with short ears, how Mouse's habit of stealing food from the village gets her in trouble, how Beetle manages to get his fire built up without actually having to go and get the firewood himself, how Coyote attempts to get even with Snake and gets broken teeth instead—are clearly based on "trickster" stories, in which the animal characters model good behavior by behaving badly. The others are so truncated that one wonders what they're supposed to be about.

Bierhorst's narrative, in a futile attempt to sound "Indian," is contrived—"Mouse had two friends, Coyote and Beetle. They came often, to renew the breath of friendship." Also contrived, at the beginning of each story, is Bierhorst's "authentic recreation of a Pueblo storytelling session":

> One more story of the Grandfathers?
> *My word-pouch is empty.*
> Feel in the bottom of it, then.

Ha! Did you ever hear how Mouse was a doctor?
No, never.
Then listen.

Wendy Watson's style of illustration is totally inappropriate. Big-eyed animals with human expressions wear turquoise, their homes have pots with "Indian" zig-zaggy designs, the fires are on the ground rather than in a firepit, there is a strange-looking hogan (a traditional Diné, not Hopi, dwelling) inhabited by a snake inside a cave. And in one illustration, Coyote and Beetle, singing and drumming, eyes closed, mouths open, look like a mocking rendition of the beautiful Pueblo storyteller dolls made and sold all over the Southwest.

John Bierhorst has made a very nice living for a long time doing this kind of thing and he really ought to stop.

—*Beverly Slapin*

(Thank-you to Debbie A. Reese.)

Blake, Robert J., *Yudonsi: A Tale from the Canyons*, illustrated by the author. Philomel (1999). Unpaginated, color illustrations; grades 3-4

Yusi lives in a village in a canyon somewhere in the Southwest. We know this is an Indian village because "the people believed their whole canyon was alive" and "would take care of the people only as long as they cared for the canyon." And they wear their hair long. And there's a cow skull leaning up against a drum. But Yusi refuses to conform, wants to be different. So he spray-paints, carves and draws his name on the houses, the trees, the canyon walls.

So he gets ostracized for misbehaving, even gets renamed "Yudonsi" ("You don't see," get it?). He's not allowed to play his flute at a gathering,

> [f]or the people did not want the canyon to get upset. It is said that the canyon once got so angry that it moved its walls to hide the sky. Anther time, they say, the canyon conspired with the wind to make great rocks fall down upon the village.

So he decides to retaliate by painting a gigantic tag on the canyon wall. Predictably, the canyon gets angry again, and Yudonsi's tagging causes an enormous storm, endangering the whole village. But not to worry—Yudonsi all of a sudden "sees" that "everything is a part of everything," picks up his flute and plays "a song he had never heard before…the song of the ages." The canyon gets all happy again, and the storm stops.

What does any of this have to do with anything?

—*Beverly Slapin*

Bouchard, David, *The Song Within My Heart*, illustrated by Allen Sapp (Cree). Raincoast (2002). Unpaginated, color paintings; kindergarten-2; Cree

Cree elder Allen Sapp's stunning oil paintings are hauntingly beautiful remembrances of his childhood on the Red Pheasant reserve in Northern Saskatchewan. Sapp's painted stories honor his grandma, his Nokum, whom he represents as a quiet, introspective and calm white-haired elder. In almost every picture, whether she is feeding the chickens, or making bannock, or peeling potatoes, or telling a story, Nokum's figure appears much larger than that of the boy because she is deserving of that size, that huge respect. In a note at the end of the book, between two black-and-white photos—one of his grandma, and one of himself with his dad and his siblings—Sapp remembers his family with gratitude—"our old people have much to teach us if we will only listen." Although he never learned to read or write, he says, "my Nokum and my father Alex taught me to show respect, not only for the people but for everything that Manito has put on the earth."

Unfortunately, Bouchard's textual interpretation of Sapp's story—set in a sing-songy poem—is a noisy and chaotic intrusion into the relationship between this Indian child and his grandma. Bouchard's poem has the young Sapp saying, "I stood staring at my elder…," "I tugged with force on both her arms…," "I yelled out again, '[p]lease tell me what they're saying'." Indian children are taught to be quiet and respectful and to wait patiently for the elder to speak—not to yell, stare and pull on their bodies.

Bouchard's poem has Sapp's grandma saying off-putting, non-Indian things like "you should know," "that should be," "you should not" and "don't ever." Traditionally, elders impart advice indirectly, with a story, sometimes humorous, not with the "shoulds," "should nots," and "don't evers" that proliferate in non-Indian communication. Sapp's dedication, in contrast, states the essence of this traditional relationship between Indian grandma and grandson: "To Maggie Soonias, who encouraged me to paint and inspired me to do my best." That's what elders do, encourage and inspire.

And finally, the obnoxious "BOOM boom boom boom BOOM boom boom boom…" and "HEY hey hey hey HI hey hey hey" that make up the entirety of the endpapers and run along the bottoms of some of the pages—supposedly to accentuate the rhythm of the drum—further distract the reader's eye from the paintings. I can just see young non-Indian children wearing brightly colored paper feathers stuck into paper headbands putting their hands to their mouths and "chanting" (you know, WOO, woo, woo, woo).

After reading this, my nine-year-old daughter remarked, "The pictures tell the story better than the words." I'm tempted to cut out the artwork and throw away the book. Maybe I will.—*Barbara Potter*

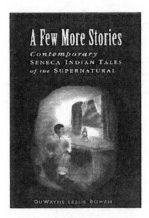

Bowen, DuWayne Leslie (Seneca). Bowman Books, b/w illustrations; grades 4-up; Seneca:
One More Story: Contemporary Seneca Indian Tales of the Supernatural, illustrated by Beth Clark (Seneca). (1991). 49 pages
A Few More Stories: Contemporary Seneca Indian Tales of the Supernatural, illustrated by Chris Terwilliger (2000). 65 pages

"The old folks always had time to tell us things," says Bowen in *One More Story*, "and on hot or chilly nights, they told us ghost stories." Then, as now, children "delighted in terror," and could hardly wait for day to end and the stories to begin.

Set in the Northeast Woodlands, Bowen's two collections contain narratives that are truly terrifying. In *One More Story*, a skeleton yells over the houses that were going to have boys killed in the next war, a little girl is saved from a flesh eater, hunters' bullets explode in front of a giant deer, the devil comes to play cards, a "peeker" receives his comeuppance from a large grey cat, a woman and a little girl are reunited in death, and an orphan girl's devotion is tested by two old people who may not be what they seem.

A Few More Stories is every bit as scary as Bowen's earlier book. Here, young readers will meet a shape-shifter caught in a jar with lightning bugs, a mysterious dark figure wearing a brim hat and poling a boat at night, the terrible Hah Ghone Dais—Long Nose—who roams the night seeking children, a giant snake who just wants to be left alone, talking horses and a devil and a killer rabbit, a "dew eagle," and a grandma and best friend whose love transcends death.

Beth Clark's and Chris Terwilliger's pen-and-ink line drawings perfectly complement these very short, very scary stories.—*Beverly Slapin*

Boyden, Linda (Cherokee), *The Blue Roses,* **illustrated by Amy Córdova. Lee & Low (2002). 29 pages, color illustrations; grades 2-up**
LaDuke, Winona (Anishinaabe) and Waseyabin Kapashesit (Anishinaabe), *The Sugar Bush,* **photographs by John Ratzloff. Rigby (1999). 16 pages, color photographs; grades 2-up; Anishinaabe**
McLeod, Elaine (Na-Cho Nyak Dun), *Lessons from Mother Earth,* **illustrated by Colleen Wood. Groundwood/Douglas & McIntyre (2002). 32 pages, color illustrations; grades 2-up**

These three contemporary stories for young readers and younger listeners are about relationships—between Indian elders and children, between the land and the humans who take care of the land. These relationships are described with varying degrees of success, and only one of them really works.

In *Lessons from Mother Earth*, a grandma shows her granddaughter the garden outside. It is not the cultivated kind of garden the child had expected; rather, it is down the trail, up the hill, along the creek. As they pick, the child learns what is ripe and what needs to wait, how and how much to pick, and the importance of not littering. All of this is a good premise for a story, but both Tess and Grandma are too self-consciously "Indian." The author is trying too hard, and there's no story in the story. What she probably wants to say is the creek *is* the garden, but the writing is stilted, and Grandma seems to be talking more to the reader than to her own grandchild:

> Tess, you must always take care of our garden. Never throw rubbish around. If you are careful and thankful, my granddaughter, our garden will take care for (sic) you. There is plenty for everyone to share if we don't destroy the soil.

There is none of the give-and-take humor, the fooling around, the feeling that Grandma and Tess enjoy being together. The story has been sacrificed to the message.

There is more of a story in *The Blue Roses*. Here, the relationship between adult and child centers around their garden and around one growing old and one growing up. All life is a circle. As in *Lessons from Mother Earth*, there are lost opportunities here. While the relationship between Papa and Rosalie is somewhat more realistic, the text is shallow in places and the presumption seems to be that young children are incapable of understanding complexities. Papa could have told Rosalie, for instance, that composted fish remains (not fresh "chunks of dead fish") eventually provide nutrients to the plants, rather than just saying, "Put in the fish and the plants will grow strong." And the gardening itself is very untraditional. Papa and Rosalie might have put in a Three Sisters garden, with corn, beans and squash planted together so that each depends on and is nurtured by the other. They could have planted the seeds in fours. In any event, it would have made more sense to distribute the seeds in a non-linear fashion and an Indian grampa would probably have told Rosalie planting stories as they worked. As well, *The Blue Roses* is way too heavy on straight rows, suburban houses and white picket fences, on metaphor ("nothing ever really leaves") and on Rosalie's obsession with death and dying and Papa's wrinkles.

In *The Sugar Bush*, Winona LaDuke and her daughter Waseyabin Kapashesit show young readers how maple syrup is made. But this is not "just" a book about making maple syrup—it's about friends and family and yesterday, today and tomorrow in the sugar bush. It's the different ways the Anishinaabe people are tied to the land:

> A hundred years ago, our forests were cut down. Strangers sold the wood to make money. Without our forests, my people were sad and lonely for our trees.

With luminous photos and clear, easy-to-read text—and without resorting to "Indian" metaphors—Wasey tells how the delicious maple syrup that family and friends enjoy on their pancakes comes from their beloved sugar bush. "When we're done," Wasey says,

> we have a big feast. We thank the sugar bush for the syrup. Then we eat! We like our syrup on wild rice pancakes. Akina minopogwad! It tastes good! My mother taught me that you can only cut down a forest once. But if you leave it standing, you can walk through it and taste its sweetness year after year.

—*Beverly Slapin* and *Doris Seale*

Bragg, Lynn (Métis), *A River Lost,* **illustrated by Virgil "Smoker" Marchand (Colville). Hancock House (1996). 32 pages, color illustrations; grades 3-5; Colville**

This beautifully illustrated book is an alternative to the best-selling *Brother Eagle, Sister Sky* by Susan Jeffers, though of course it's valuable on its own. Here, an

elder tells of a 1930s environmental disaster that all but wiped out the many tribes who depend on the salmon for subsistence: the construction on the Columbia River of several dams, the biggest being the Grand Coulee, and the consequent flooding of the Colville reservation riverside land. The river, along which the salmon and the humans had lived for millennia, was lost in the broad waters of Lake Roosevelt behind the dam. Since no salmon ladders were built on this high dam—the largest concrete structure in North America—the salmon who once came upstream to spawn now have all died out. Similar dam disasters have flooded the lives and homelands of Indian peoples all over North America.

Toopa (the Salish word for great-grandma) is a fictionalized representation of the elders of the Arrow Lakes Band of the Colville Confederated Tribes of Washington State who did not live the fifty additional years to see belated monetary compensation in 1995 for destruction of their tribe's way of life, the river, and the salmon on whom they depended.

Behind Toopa on the cover portrait, Virgil "Smoker" Marchand depicts Kettle Falls, from which the tribe was given a name—Kettle People—because the power of tens of thousands of years of falling water had scooped out rocks to look like kettles. Over Toopa's shoulders, both salmon and spirit salmon-people brave this power, going upstream to spawn. The young salmon hatchlings make their way downstream to live in the ocean, sometimes growing to forty-pound adult fish, who then swim back the one route around the circle of their lives in water to spawn in the place where they were hatched. Or so it was here for millennia; the circle of water and salmon life—and the lives of the peoples of this vast drainage basin in the Pacific Northwest, before the huge hydroelectric projects of Washington and Oregon.

When the river salmon could not climb the spillways of the Grand Coulee Dam, they died out in a few years, as will always happen if their upstream progress to their original hatching site is blocked, or they encounter polluted or muddy, shallow waters where they were hatched. Salmon do not—cannot—go to any other place but their headwaters birth-homes.

> Every summer my family camped at the Falls. When the salmon swam upstream to spawn, the water became so thick and matted with their red bodies that it looked as if you could walk across the river on the backs of In-Tee-Tee-Huh.

Toopa describes to her great-granddaughter how basket nets and basket-woven traps were extended across the bottom of the falls, where salmon who fell back on making their leaps were caught. Men stood on narrow wooden platforms out over the falls to gaff the fish; it was dangerous but very productive—the tribe was

> rich with salmon.... We traded for hides with the Plains tribes. Later we traded salmon for flour, guns, goods and tobacco from the settlers at the fort.

Toopa describes the feasting, the preparation of food, and the function of Kin-Ka-Now-Kla, their salmon chief who apportioned the catch to make sure all got a fair share; especially elders who might be in need of food because their own families had been decimated by the white man's wars, and by the diseases that accompanied confinement of the band, along with a dozen other tribes of mutually incompatible languages, to the Colville reservation in 1872.

Lynn Bragg worked with Colville elder Marguerite Ensminger to translate some of the words into Salish, and to oversee the telling of this important story. She presents it as Toopa's telling to Sinee-mat (the Salish word for great-granddaughter). All of Virgil Marchand's illustrations are wholly integrated with the story and tell other parts of it. Each is a full two-page spread, and each warrants discussion among young readers and adults.

One such picture shows the burning of the Indian houses that are soon to be flooded over as the dam is closed. Toopa's little cabin is not yet aflame, for she is one of the elders who refused to believe the white man could do this—so she had only a few hours to pack and move before the big, rapid final drowning of the land. Rising in swirls of smoke are spirits of the salmon, now a doomed species for this river. In the foreground are a deer and a raccoon. What will happen to them, when the swift floodwaters rise? Many animals will not escape. Many birds, their habitats and nesting grounds flooded, will not survive another generation, though adult birds can fly away (as some are shown doing).

On the last page, Virgil paints the high dam, spillways pouring tons of roaring, misty water down its steep, smooth high-wall surface. Made of mist-shadows, a band of tribal salmon people, as if on their way to salmon camp, are led into a dissolving future, by a mist-shadow eagle. In Virgil's illustrations, many eagles appear; often they have caught salmon for their own food and to feed their young. What will happen to the eagles when the salmon no longer come?

"Toopa died before my tribe received any payment for what this Dam had taken from us," Lynn ends.

> A few elders remember what life was like, when salmon traveled up the mighty River from the Ocean to the Falls. When they are gone, there will be no one left to remember this way of life.

This beautiful book can help the youth remember—as it

has done for Lynn's fourteen-year-old son. It can communicate with those far from the enormous manmade lake, on the shores of which—mostly at the town of Inchelium (to which this book is dedicated)—tribal survivors of their lost river now live. It communicates in a clear, beautiful, and personal way what the fake "Chief Seattle" book can only present in empty clichés based on false history. Where the paintings in *Brother Eagle, Sister Sky* are of people from distant tribes whose appearances and lives were quite different, *A River Lost* has beautiful watercolors by a young artist, born and raised in the dam-drowned area, poignantly recreating it from artistic imagination and the memories and words of surviving elders. Lynn Bragg, too, in her writing, has drawn on the remembered beauties and still-present sadness.—*Paula Giese*

Branford, Henrietta, *White Wolf.* Candlewick (1999). 95 pages; grades 4-6

White Wolf is a character study of a wolf, using Indians as background to provide conflict and move the plot. The wolf is the narrator of this strange book, which attempts to explore social history through his eyes. "Snowy" is raised by a white trapper and his son somewhere in the Northwest. His owners believe that the white wolf will protect them against the "heathen savages." But these unnamed people, in an unnamed place and an unnamed time period, kill the father, kidnap the son, and attempt to sacrifice the wolf so he can "travel to the spirit world" and "bring back the songs" to reawaken their dead ancestors. Just as knife is about to be put to throat, Snowy escapes, joins a wolf pack, and learns what it is like to have "sun on his pelt in the springtime and snow on his snout in the fall [and] live food with warm blood and running feet."

What young readers will learn from this book is easily stated: Wolves need to be free. Indians are savages.

In a carefully worded caveat behind the title page, the author says that she has

> created characters and situations consistent with the era portrayed in this book. To accomplish this, the author has occasionally used language which, while not reflecting her personal beliefs, gives the reader an authentic feel for the time and place depicted in the story.

Branford's stated attempt at historical accuracy notwithstanding, the fact that she mentions neither time nor place nor Nation of people gives her license to invent: value system, worldview, cosmology, naming, dance, ceremony, dialogue—and call it "Indian," to describe these unnamed people in a most stereotypical way and call it consistent with an era.

Much of the description of the people comes out of the mouth of the wolf: "Bears' grease coated the shining, sweating bodies of the people, giving off a rich, strong stink."

Here is a description of an "Indian dance":

> The flames blazed high, flickering on face paint, beads, and knives. Someone began to drum, knocking out slow patterns in the firelight. People began to fidget. One or two began to shake.... People stood up to dance. Some of them sailed like birds. Some swam like fish finning in the current, still and quiet while their world flowed past them. Some danced like deer, delicate and careful, stopping to listen to the drums. One man leapt and spun like a goat, his long hair swinging out behind him. A woman close by screamed and fell against her neighbor…

The author's note states:

> The Crow people did not live on the coast, like Sings-the-Best-Songs and Drums-Louder and the people of the Wolf Clan, but I have lent Chief Plenty Coup's words to Sings-the-Best-Songs because they are more beautiful and more apt than any I can invent.
>
> For the same reason I have lent him some of Chief Seattle's words as well. It was Chief Seattle who spoke about the memory of his tribe becoming a myth among the white men.
>
> For the rest of it, I've tried to take a little from several of the peoples of the northwest coast— Kwakiutl, Haida, Nuu-chah-nulth, and others. I cannot claim to know enough about their rich heritage to draw them, any of them, accurately. In any case, this is a work of fiction. But it is dedicated to them, and to the wolves whose hunting prowess they respected and admired.

Branford does not want to know enough about Indians to draw them accurately, yet she sees herself as qualified to write a children's book about them. Deborah A. Miranda uses the term "vengeful innocence" to describe the mindset of such authors who know the information is there, yet refuse to crack a book or ask questions. It is like a three-year-old, she says, having a temper tantrum, covering his ears with his hands and screaming "I CAN'T HEAR YOU! I CAN'T HEAR YOU! I CAN'T HEAR YOU!"

White Wolf could be useful as a tool to teach young people to think critically about racist writing in books for children, but I don't recommend that anyone purchase this title. It might further encourage the publisher.—*Beverly Slapin*

(Thank-you to Deborah A. Miranda.)

Brant, Beth (Mohawk):
I'll sing 'til the day I die: Conversations with Tyendinaga Elders. McGilligan Books (1995). 120 pages, b/w photographs; high school-up
Mohawk Trail. Firebrand (1985). 94 pages; high school-up
Writing As Witness: essay and talk. Women's Press (1994). 127 pages; high school-up

Reading Beth Brant's books again, I am struck anew by her courage, and the beauty and depth of her writing. She knows, more than anyone should have to, about the things that make us unacceptable, that separate us, but also about what brings us together and keeps us alive. The poems and stories gathered together in *Mohawk Trail* are about both.

From the opening "Native Origin"—the things that make us ourselves—through a quiet moment as a grandmother finishes a quilt pieced together by her daughters, to the humor and delight of "Coyote Learns a New Trick," the stories in the first part are about memory and wholeness. In the title story: "Late at night, pulling the quilt up to cover me, she whispered, 'Don't forget who you are. Don't ever leave your family. They are what matters.'"

In Part Two, "Detroit Songs," the world impinges. The stories are about the things people have to do to survive— or, in one case, not—and what it does to them. Part Three, "Long Stories," enters darkness. A woman who has lost herself learns, on the fifth floor of the county hospital, to be "good"—on the outside: "I have behaved well. I pretend to smile at the nurses and orderlies." But she takes another self home: "I am taking the woman home with me. It is our secret. She keeps me alive."

"A Long Story" is about two women, nearly one hundred years apart in time, who have their children taken away from them: in 1890, to residential school; in 1979, because the mother is a lesbian. A lot has been written about the horrors inflicted on children in the residential schools, not so much about the suffering of the parents. Brant writes about the devastating grief and unbearable pain in a way that no one who reads this story will forget. In "A Simple Act," two young girls discover the sweetness of first love together, only to have it trampled into the dirt in the name of "upholding the morality of the family."

A family loses the Indian things, in a basement fire: "False Faces. Beaded necklaces. Old letters written in Mohawk....Secrets brought from home. Secrets protecting us in hostile places." And in the end:

> I write because to not write is a breach of faith.
> Out of a past where amnesia was the expected....
> Out of a past, I make truth for a future....Ink on paper, picking up trails I left so many lives ago.
> Leaving my marks, my footprints, my sign.

There may not be words adequate to describe Brant's work. Certainly not in the lexicon of literary criticism. The extraordinary degree of compassion, tenderness, and clear-sightedness she brings to it must surely come out of a strength of spirit, honed by loss and tragedy, but unique from its inception. The essays in *Writing as Witness* go some way, at least, toward clarification of how it is that she is able to do what she does.

In her preface, Brant says,

> [W]ords are sacred. Not because of the person transmitting them, but because words themselves come from the place of mystery that gives meaning and existence to life.

In the essay entitled "The Good Red Road," she says, "The key to understanding Native women's poetry and prose is that we love, unashamedly, our own." I think with her it is a matter of honor, to get it exactly right, the right word in the right place; to say the truth, no matter what. The deep-seated belief among Native peoples, even today, that words are not to be used to lie with, is embodied in everything Brant writes.

Some of the essays are speeches that she gave at various times and places. Two favorites: In "From the Inside—Looking at You," given at a panel discussion entitled "From the Outside Looking In: Racism and Writing," Brant says,

> "From the Outside Looking In" implies that those of us on this panel are somehow on the outside of normal, the real and the truth. I must protest this abrogation of our thoughts and words to fit a white-defined framework of what constitutes racism and writing.

In the title essay delivered at another panel, "Native American Vision," she asks,

> Why are the words "Native" and "vision" used together so often? I expect it comes from the place that wishes to ghettoize and confirm our "quaintness" for the dominant culture.

She does have a way of getting right to the heart of the matter.

Brant's landmark "Grandmothers of a New World" is included, and "To Be or Not to Be Was Never the Question":

> Story is meant to be spoken—that has not changed. The written becomes the spoken whether by hands or mouth, the spoken enters the heart, the heart turns over, Earth is renewed.

In the early 1980s, Brant edited *A Gathering of Spirit*, the first anthology ever to be devoted entirely to writing and art by Native women. She said that "it changed the face of Native literature forever. It became its own entity. It became what it had to be—a brilliant and loving weapon of change."

It did, it was, and has been. Many who got their start there went on to writing carriers; some, to considerable fame. Since then, Brant has conducted writing workshops for Indian women, and edited other anthologies; *in a vast dreaming* (1995) was the first issue of *Native Women in the Arts*. The collection of conversations with fifteen elders from her reserve comes from her tenure as Writer-in-Residence at Ka:nhiote Library. It is a rich document. There's so much of living here, people's stories: "This is what we did, what was done to us, what it cost us, who we were then, who we are now. And now, we tell it to you, our daughter, so that it will not be forgotten"—continuity. There are pictures of most of the elders when they were younger—some *much* younger—continuity. We change, but we are still that person, not "living history." The title is from Eva Maracle, who was born in 1896. She said, "But I like to sing and I'll sing till the day I die." This book is a gift, not just to the Mohawk people, but to all of us.

In the old days, it was not those who sought power who were held in regard; it was those who worked for the good of the people—those who shared, those who gave back. Beth Brant has given so much to so many, made it possible for so many to find the courage to be who they might never have become without her. In *Writing as Witness*, she says,

> It is so obvious to me that Native women's writing is a generous sharing of our history and our dreams for the future. That generosity is a collective experience. And perhaps this is the major difference between Aboriginal writing and that of European-based "literature." We do not write as individuals communing with a muse. We write as members of an ancient, cultural consciousness. Our "muse" is *us*. Our "muse" is our ancestors. Our "muse" is our children, our grandchildren, our partners, our lovers. Our "muse" is Earth and the stories She holds....Our words come from the very place of all life....

Brant's writing is so important, so full of truth, but there is no ego in it, none of the arrogance of the gifted that some have learned too well from the literary establishment. She does not do it for herself. And that can give a person the courage to speak out of her own truth, and to say that truth without regard for the consequences. Brant makes no appeals to anyone's idea of what an Indian is supposed to be, or of what Native writing is supposed to consist. In that, she comes closer to the reality of what we are, and with greater clarity than may be comfortable to contemplate. She could not have chosen a better title for her book: *Writing As Witness*. We, Native people, are more various and more strange in relation to the dominant culture, than anything they could imagine for us; our cultures, our stories, how we think, how we feel, more real. Truth has always been an uneasy bedmate. Perhaps that is why Brant's work has been less well known than that of writers with far less ability. Fame was not what she was after, anyway; just to tell her story—and ours. In that, Beth Brant has been for many of us, and will be, a beacon burning in a dark night. Her integrity as a writer is a yardstick against which to measure ourselves.—*Doris Seale*

Brehm, Victoria, ed., *A Little History of My Forest Life: An Indian-White Autobiography by Eliza Morrison*. Ladyslipper Press (2002). 207 pages, b/w photographs and illustrations; grades 6-up; Ojibwe

This book is composed of a series of letters written by an Ojibwe woman of mixed parentage who was married to an Ojibwe man and raised a family in northern Wisconsin in the late 19th Century. Eliza Morrison put pen to paper out of a sense of obligation to the white family who had employed her and given her and her family charity. The people she worked for had pumped her for information about Indian life because they knew that this traditional life was "vanishing." Eliza felt a responsiblity to the people to give as much information as possible, and she seems apologetic for not knowing all that is expected of her.

Cultures are made up of many, many individuals. No one has all the pieces to a culture. But very often when queried by outsiders, we're expected to know it all. I wonder if the editor makes this assumption as well because she strongly distinguishes between "Indians" and people of mixed parentage when referring to these narratives. Although Eliza sometimes refers to Indians as "they," sometimes as "we," the editor may have seen this as more of an issue than Eliza actually did.

"Indian" is a word we use to describe ourselves and others, and sometimes we use it in the third person. For us, it's a term of recognition and comfort; for outsiders, including the people Eliza wrote for, it was a term of distinction.

Eliza Morrison's writing is beautiful, and without the flowery affect that was typical of white writers of the time. She describes in wonderful detail what was involved in an everyday hardscrabble life:

> Well but some people would be surprised to know twelve days after the birth of my little girl I took her in my arms and carried her for 8 miles over ruff trail. The last two miles it was hard, thawing made it hard walking. After being in the sugar bush one week,

> my husband went back to Spider Lake, what we call home. We left the ponies and cow and chickens. When he got there he could not find the ponies. They were gone. He found one of them but one he could not find untill the next day. When he found him he was dead.

While Brehm puts Eliza's letters into the kind of historical and social contexts that have not been addressed by outsiders before, her introduction is dispassionate and academic and best left to the teacher to read and interpret.

Young people will love Eliza's narratives; they're fresh and direct and unpretentious and they're not trying to pass on any lessons.—*Lois Beardslee*

Bruchac, Joseph (Abenaki), *The Arrow Over the Door*, illustrated by James Watling. Dial (1998). 89 pages, b/w illustrations; grades 4-up; Abenaki

Told in the alternating voices of two young men—Stands Straight, an Abenaki, and Samuel Russell, a Quaker—*The Arrow Over the Door* is based on an actual incident that took place between the Abenaki and the Quakers during the summer of 1777.

As British troops near Saratoga, Samuel Russell wrestles with his pacifism and the taunts of his neighbors, and Stands Straight—whose mother and brother have been killed by the Bostoniak—joins his uncle in a scouting party. Surrounding the meetinghouse, the party of Abenaki encounters a group of Quakers engaged in a "silent meeting." As Stands Straight and Samuel Russell sign their friendship to each other, an arrow—its head broken off—is placed over the door, and it is apparent that there will be no war in this place this day.

In an interesting author's note, Bruchac recounts the research that he and his sister, noted historian Marge Bruchac, conducted, notes how the several accounts of this historical event differ, and further denotes the changes he made in his telling.

James Watling's full-page black-and-white watercolors add dimension without detracting from the story.

Joe Bruchac is a gifted writer, and one of the things he does very well is breathe life into historical events. He has done so here. Stands Straight and Samuel Russell are real people with whom young readers will easily identify. *The Arrow Over the Door* is an excellent antidote to Elizabeth George Speare's toxic *The Sign of the Beaver*. —*Beverly Slapin*

Bruchac, Joseph (Abenaki), *Children of the Longhouse.* **Dial (1996). 150 pages, grades 4-6; Mohawk**

Here's a new idea—Indians have a life that doesn't revolve around the white man! People lived, loved, fought, played, laughed and cried without having to worry about the strange behavior of the English, Dutch, French, or "Americans." So much of fiction available for young people (and adults) focuses on the cataclysmic relationship between Indians and non-Indians that it's easy to forget that the Americas have a long history that goes back millennia before Columbus stumbled on these shores. Bruchac's *Children of the Longhouse* immerses the reader into the daily life of a village of Native people in 1491.

The children of the longhouse are Ohkwa'ri and Otsi:tsia, eleven-year-old twins living in a Mohawk town in the traditional homelands of what is now eastern New York State, near the Mohawk and Hudson rivers. They live with their Bear Clan relatives, their mother's people, in the great longhouse at Kanatsiohareke. The twins are brother and sister and reflecting the equal balance between male and female roles in Iroquois society, the book's chapters alternate between the events and perspectives of Ohkwa'ri and Otsi:tsia.

The story is simple—Ohkwa'ri inadvertently makes enemies of a group of older boys who try to bully him. Ohkwa'ri is singled out for an honored role at the upcoming Tekwaarithon, or lacrosse game, making the leader of the older boys, Grabber, even more determined to exert his dominance over Ohkwa'ri. During the lacrosse game, Ohkwa'ri saves Grabber's life and gains a grudging respect and acceptance if not quite friendship from Grabber and his friends.

But there is much more going on in and around this coming-of-age story. Bruchac seamlessly incorporates an impressive amount of information about precontact Mohawk culture, society, and beliefs. The reader is easily and almost subliminally immersed into traditional Mohawk life, including clan and family relationships, government, morality, spiritual beliefs, life cycle events, naming conventions, longhouse life, seasonal ceremonies, male and female roles, interactions with neighboring Nations, the prominent roles of women and the respect men accord them, and, of course, conventions surrounding the play and significance of the Creator's Game, lacrosse.

Deservedly praised for his picture books for children and "Keepers" series for educators with teacher Michael Caduto, Bruchac combines well-honed storytelling skills with his familiarity with Iroquois culture in this novel for the middle grades. His thoughtful afterword reveals the firm historical and archaeological foundation of his story (Kanatsiohareke was a real Mohawk village) and

makes it clear that this story did not end in the past. It continues today in the new Mohawk village of Kanatsiohareke on land acquired in 1993 by a group of Mohawks in their old homelands in the Mohawk River Valley.

This is an essential purchase for all New York libraries, and an exceptional addition to all school and public library collections.—*Lisa Mitten*

Bruchac, Joseph (Abenaki), *Crazy Horse's Vision,* **illustrated by S.D. Nelson (Lakota). Lee and Low (2000). Unpaginated, color illustrations; grades 3-6; Lakota**

Most of what has been written about the great Lakota visionary and war leader, Tasunke Witko—known to the whites as Crazy Horse—whether fiction or non-fiction, is of a speculative nature, and told from a non-Native perspective. What *is* known about his childhood and coming to manhood is carried in the stories of the Lakota people, from generation to generation. Because of its picture-book format, this is classified as fiction, but Bruchac tells the story of Crazy Horse's childhood, and the vision that was to direct his adult life, without romanticism, without feeling the need to flesh it out, so that it has more a feeling of truth than many of the multi-page volumes. The author's note gives some background and shows just how evanescent the "facts" about Crazy Horse's life really are.

Nelson says that his illustrations are influenced by ledger art, and one can see that. Although his paintings are much more detailed, with a wider use of color, they retain some of the iconographic quality. It's a good style for a young child's picture book, and quite beautiful, although not "traditional" in the generally accepted sense of that word. Another good thing about it is that Crazy horse is never shown full-face. As there was no image made of him in life, so there is no painting here that pretends to be a likeness.—*Doris Seale*

Bruchac, Joseph (Abenaki), *Eagle Song*, **illustrated by Dan Anderson. Dial (1997). 80 pages, b/w illustrations; grades 3-5; Mohawk**

Over half the Indian population in the United States live in cities and towns off reservations. Some families are second- and third-generation city-dwellers, but many are recent arrivals. Despite Indian centers and other support organizations, many Native families find themselves alone in a sea of non-Indians. For those who've recently left their homelands, this can be quite a culture shock. A child may find for the first time that he is the only Native in his class, or even in the entire school. When this is compounded by the usual lack of knowledge about Native America in general, and the specific cultures of individual tribes in particular, the adjustment for Indian kids can be rough.

Bruchac has written a brief novel about the experience of a fourth-grade Mohawk boy whose family has just relocated from the Akwesasne Mohawk reservation in upstate New York to Brooklyn, where his mom has taken a job as a social worker with the American Indian Community House. Danny Bigtree's father is an iron-worker in high-steel construction all over the country, and is often gone for weeks at a time.

Danny is having a tough time making friends in his new school. While basketball is the game of among the boys, Danny is a lacrosse player. The usual teasing of the new kid in class takes the form of racial taunting, as the boys call him "chief," ask him about his tipi, and want to know where his war pony is. Danny's attempt to respond with information about his people is met with ridicule.

The return of Danny's father for a few days gives Danny a chance to talk about his problems. Dad tells Danny the story of Aionwahta and The Great Peace, how former enemies joined together as allies, and how the Iroquois believe there is good to be found in all people.

When Danny's dad comes in to talk to the class about Iroquois culture and government, the visit goes well, inspiring Danny to assert himself, and Danny's classmates begin to look at him with more respect.

Bruchac's knowledge of his subject comes through in his book. Akwesasne is a Mohawk reservation in upstate New York, many Mohawk men are known for their skill as ironworkers and are based in New York City, Aionwahta and The Great Peace are keystone events in Iroquois history and culture, and the American Indian Community House is New York's Indian center. Mohawk words sprinkled throughout the story are accurate, and there is a brief glossary elaborating on the words used in the text. Each of the eight chapters is accompanied by a full-page black-and-white drawing of an event in the chapter, and are acceptable, if not exceptional.

Good fiction about contemporary Native kids is hard to come by, and *Eagle Song* is a solid addition.—*Lisa Mitten*

Bruchac, Joseph (Abenaki), *Fox Song*, **illustrated by Paul Morin. Philomel (1993). Unpaginated, color illustrations; grades 3-up; Abenaki**

Jamie is lying in bed, not wanting to open her eyes, wanting to "find her way back into the dream where Grama Bowman was with her." She remembers all the time she spent with her great-grandmother, all the places they went, all the things Grama showed her. She remembers, dreams the song Grama Bowman taught her: "It is a welcoming song....When you sing it, you will not be alone."

When Jamie gets up, she goes out to the tree where her Grama used to sit, leans against it, and sings the morning song. As she sings, a fox comes out of the woods. She finishes the song, looks away, and when she turns back, the fox is gone, but she knows then that she will never be alone.

An author's note tells that this is a family story; maybe the same fox that shows up in *Turtle Meat*. The book is a lovely thing; both writing and illustrations. "The fox yawned and sat down on its haunches. The same sun was bright on its coat and its eyes glistened." That's exactly what they do; sit down and yawn. Their ears go back a little, their eyes squint, and that yawn makes a sort of creaking squeak.

The illustrations are a perfect match, full of that indescribable autumn light; Jamie looks like an actual Native child. The relationship between Jamie and her Grama is full of the special love that often happens between child and grandparent, and is like no other. Although it was clearly not written to be "bibliotherapy," *Fox Song* is a book one could give to a grieving child, something that might really help.—*Doris Seale*

Bruchac, Joseph (Abenaki), *Skeleton Man,* **illustrated by Sally Wern Comport. HarperCollins (2001). 114 pages, b/w illustrations; grades 4-8; Mohawk**

There is a traditional story told among the Algonkian and Haudenosaunee peoples of the Northeast of a cannibal ogre who hides its face from the child it has stolen to fatten up. In some versions the fearsome cannibal becomes a skeleton after eating its own flesh, then kills and devours all of its relatives, and then goes looking for children to eat. The cannibal can be male or female. Sometimes there is a rabbit or other game animal whose life is spared and who then helps a child escape.

Told from the perspective of a contemporary youngster whose father is Mohawk, this terrifying young adult novel is rooted in one of these stories.

Soon after her parents mysteriously disappear, Molly—who is named after Molly Brant, an 18th-Century Mohawk Clan Mother—is placed in the custody of a strange man claiming to be her great-uncle. Each morning he leaves food out for her, and each night he locks her in a bedroom. And he hides his face from her. Having grown up with the traditional story and knowing who this stranger really is, Molly pretends to eat the food.

As she has been taught to do, Molly trusts her dreams, and it is those dreams—in which a helpful spirit rabbit appears—that present the way out. Through Molly's courage and fortitude, and her willingness to whisper "help" into the night, she destroys Skeleton Man and rescues her parents.

"There are still creatures that may look like people but are something else," Dad tells Molly. "The reason creatures like Skeleton Man do what they do is that they like to hunt us. The only way to defeat them is to be brave."

Bruchac's skillful weaving of old times and now-times will have young readers easily identifying both with Molly's terror and her courageous resolve to defeat Skeleton Man. They will learn that sometimes "something evil (comes) into the lives of good people and (they must find) a way to defeat it."

Comport's shadowy black-and-white charcoal illustrations perfectly match the horror of the story. On the cover, a translucent hand and arm—bones clearly defined—grabs onto a child's ankle as she tries to scramble up a precipice. She is missing one shoe. He is trying to pull her down.

In the old stories, Skeleton Man and other malevolent beings are usually defeated by the hero who is in some way strengthened by family and community. An important dynamic of traditional tales is that details are often changed to fit the appropriate teaching situation. In this case, Molly gains strength from her family, her traditional ways and her understanding of the story; and then seeks reinforcement from a trusted teacher and school counselor. This is an important thing for children to do; nowadays, Skeleton Man can be found lurking around the schoolyard.—*Beverly Slapin*

(Thank-you to Dovie Thomason and Awiakta.)

Bruchac, Joseph (Abenaki), *Turtle Meat and Other Stories.* **Duluth: Holy Cow! (1992). 119 pages; high school-up; Northeast Nations**

Of all Joe Bruchac's works of fiction, this might be my favorite. There are seventeen stories of varying lengths, all set, or growing out of, the Adirondack area that is author's home ground. His strong connection to the land is evident; in one sense, it is the protagonist. He writes of things that we have known for a long, long time—although sometimes we forget. In "Wolves," evil brings its own reward, and retribution, although it may take its time, is certain. And in "The White Moose," forgiveness.

"Bears" is a funny—and moving—story about something very serious: our responsibility to and for the other creatures of Earth. There are stories of courage, and not all of them have happy endings, but they all end *right*. Some of the things that happen in Bruchac's stories seem "impossible," but they are not. The problem is that too many have forgotten how to see.

"The Fox Den" is clearly a family story; "Notes From a Morning of Fishing," out of the author's own life. And "How Mink Stole Time" is a cautionary tale if ever there was one. Perhaps they all are. They remind us of things we forget at our peril.

Read endless times, these stories still have the power to move to tears, and laughter.—*Doris Seale*

Bruchac, Joseph (Abenaki), *The Winter People*. Dial (2002). 168 pages; grades 4-up; Abenaki

In the last ten years or so, historical fiction for young people has been used not only as literature, but to teach history as well. Perhaps the worst of these are the captivity novels, loosely based on the narratives of white people taken captive by Indians in the 17th through the 19th Centuries. For the most part, these young adult novels are lessons in white cultural and moral dominance over "Indian savagery."

The Winter People is an antidote to the poison being taught about Native peoples in these captivity novels. In the first few pages, the protagonist-narrator says,

> The English think we are bloodthirsty savages. I have heard this from the mouths of white captives surprised at how well we treated them. They did not expect us to honor their women, to show tenderness to their children. They expected us to act like beings with hearts of ice. They thought to see hundreds of white scalps hanging in our wigwams as we danced about the fire like the monsters in their nightmares. They had not expected houses of log and stone, or that we would dress much as they dressed and that our best dances would be not of war but of thanksgiving and friendship.

In the mid-18th Century, warfare raged between the French and the British colonial forces, each side fighting for hegemony over North America, and—for a variety of military and political reasons—alliances shifted between Native communities and their French and/or British allies. The Abenaki living in the mission village of St. Francis near the St. Lawrence River in Canada were strongly allied with the French and a small coterie of Stockbridge scouts were working for British Major Robert Rogers.

The Winter People takes place in 1759, towards the end of the period that became known as the French and Indian Wars. In a raid, the British soldiers led by Major Robert Rogers and called "Rogers Rangers" killed a number of people and burned down most of the village. It is in this setting that a fourteen-year-old soon-to-be warrior named Saxso sets out to rescue his mother and sisters, taken captive by Rogers Rangers.

Told in Saxso's own words, the story is rooted in land, culture and community. Saxso is a very real Indian person. He doesn't have any of the adolescent angst or self-importance that is so typical of modern white teenagers. He is valued as everyone else is valued. Saxso's strength and courage come not from imagining himself a hero but from relying on lessons learned from his elders, and the knowing that he is responsible to and supported by the community. He knows who he is and what he has to do.

What else is remarkable about *The Winter People* is that it draws on the oral histories of the descendants of the survivors of Rogers Raid to reconstruct through their eyes what really happened and how the community survived.

The title of the book comes from traditional stories about the monster cannibals called the "winter people," who have hearts frozen by greed, who hunt human beings, who eat human flesh and drink human blood. Saxso equates those who cause such damage to his community with these ogres. For this reader, there is an uncanny sense of parallel between past and present, and the modern-day Bostoniak with greedy hearts of ice who would consume us all.—*Beverly Slapin*

Bruchac, Joseph (Abenaki) and James Bruchac (Abenaki), illustrated by Jose Aruego and Ariane Dewey. Dial. Unpaginated, color illustrations, grades 1-3:
***How Chipmunk Got His Stripes*, (2001). Eastern Nations**
***Turtle's Race with Beaver*, (2003). Seneca**

In *How Chipmunk Got His Stripes*, the Bruchacs' rendition of this old story of how little Brown Squirrel becomes Chipmunk leaps right off the pages. As Bear brags that he is big enough and strong enough to keep the sun from rising ("The sun will not come up, hummph! The sun will not come up, hummph!"), Brown Squirrel taunts him ("The sun is going to rise, oooh! The sun is going to rise, oooh!"). Although he wins this round, Brown Squirrel also learns it's *really* not a good thing to tease people, especially *really big people* who've just lost a bet. And Bear learns that not everyone can do everything. Aruego and Dewey's vibrant pen-and-ink and water-color paintings are a perfect complement to this story.

Turtle's Race with Beaver, a Seneca story, has big-time redevelopment taking over the neighborhood, as Beaver overruns and enlarges Turtle's comfy little pond while Turtle hibernates. Turtle, generous creature that she is, offers to share her territory, but Beaver wants it all. Turtle accepts Beaver's challenge to race, the animals gather on the shore and choose sides, and—of course, Turtle wins, but not because she's a faster swimmer. Thoroughly humiliated, Beaver goes off to another pond, where he accepts another Turtle's generosity. In the versions I've heard, Turtle wins the race, Beaver gets a sore tail, and the two agree to share the pond. But this telling works also. I especially like the animals switching sides as the winner becomes apparent. Again, Aruego and Dewey's pictures, this time pen-and-ink, gouache, and pastel, suit the story. As with *How Chipmunk Got His Stripes*, youngest listeners will ask to hear this one over and over.—*Beverly Slapin*

Bruchac, Joseph (Abenaki), and James Bruchac (Abenaki), *When the Chenoo Howls: Native American Tales of Terror,* **illustrated by William Sauts Netamuxwe Bock (Lenape). Walker (1998). 135 pages, b/w illustrations; grades 4-6**

Based on traditional stories from the Northeast Woodlands, these twelve terrifying stories—"from the very distant past to very recent times"—are of ordinary and extraordinary heroes battling hideous monsters. In many of them, having a good heart and a clear mind and "standing up against their own fears" are what enables them to defeat their terrible foes. There are cautionary tales too, demonstrating what can happen to children who don't heed the advice they're given. Of course, in these stories the monsters win.

There is Stone Giant (Seneca), whose skin is hard as flint and who has an appetite for humans; Flying Head (Seneca), whose weakness is its insatiable appetite; Ugly Face (Mohawk), whose countenance is so awful that no one who has seen him lives to describe him; Chenoo (Passamaquoddy), the cannibal giant whose heart is made of ice; Amankamek (Lenape), the giant horned snake; Keewahkwee (Penobscot), the cannibal ogre who hides his face from his victims; Man-Bear (Oneida), a shape-shifter who hunts humans; Toad Woman (Abenaki), who lures people with her sweet voice. And more.

Each story is accompanied by a brief informational note setting that story in place and time, and a list of sources for oral and other written versions. There is also a helpful pronunciation guide at the end. Bock's pen-and-ink sketches give just enough detail to engage young readers; they are perfect and perfectly horrifying.

When the Chenoo Howls will teach youngsters, as the great Cherokee philosopher Thomas King advises, to "Stay calm. Be brave. Wait for the signs." This is a book that will enthrall reluctant readers, and children who love being scared in a safe place will not be able to put it down.—*Beverly Slapin*

Buffalo Bird Woman (Hidatsa) as told to Gilbert L. Wilson, *Waheenee: An Indian Girl's Story,* **illustrated by Frederick Wilson. University of Nebraska (1921, 1981). 189 pages, b/w illustrations; grades 5-up; Hidatsa**

Waheenee-wea (Buffalo Bird Woman) was a Hidatsa, one of the agricultural tribes living on the upper Missouri River. She was born in 1839, two years after the devastating smallpox epidemic that wiped out most of the allied nearby Mandan tribe and about half the Hidatsa people. The survivors consolidated and moved from the deadly site of the Five Villages some distance north, where they founded Like-a-Fishook Village (now drowned by the Army's 1948 Garrison Diversion Project). Waheenee's great-grandmother White Corn, and grandmother Turtle, told her many stories of these times (Waheenee lost her biological mother when she was six, but had three other mothers, the sisters of Weahtee).

In the early 1900s, Gilbert Wilson, seeking a Ph.D. in anthropology, was sent to the Hidatsa at Ft. Berthold reservation, and returned every summer for twenty years. He became very close to the elderly Waheenee and her family: Wolf Chief, her younger brother; and Goodbird, her son. Traditionally, the Hidatsa women were the agriculturaists, but Goodbird had attended the white man's schools and was a cattle rancher in the white style.

The importance of Wilson's work is that the Hidatsa people—with whom he became quite close over many years—tell their own stories in a lot of detail. It is clear that the family made drawings and models, reproduced tools, and showed Wilson how many daily life activities were done. Wilson's brother, an artist, often visited the reservation with him, making many sketches that were later reproduced as engravings in this book.

Waheenee tells many stories—some of which I've seen elsewhere—but differently, with warmer, plainer language, and she always gives a context in which she heard the story. Here's one about both her early hairstyle and child discipline:

> When I was naughty, my mothers usually scolded me, for they were kind women and did not like to have me punished. Sometimes they scared me by saying "The owl will get you." This had to do with an old custom.... Until I was about nine years old, my hair was cut short, with a tuft on either side of my head, like the horns of an owl. Turtle used to cut my hair. She used a big steel knife. In old times, I have heard, a thin blade of flint was used. I did not like Turtle's hair cutting a bit, because she pulled. "Why do you cut my hair, grandmother?" I asked. "It is our custom," Turtle answered. "I will tell you the story. Thousands and thousands of years ago, there lived a great owl. He was strong and had magic powers, but he was a bad bird..."

Owl appeals to the people he'd been harming for protection against their hero. He promises to help them by making children obey their elders in the future, if he can recognize them by their owl-ear hair tufts.

Other contexts for traditional stories include a hunting camp (Hidatsa men sometimes took wives along on hunting parties for pleasurable spring outings before the planting season). It's quite clear here that the storytellers are telling tall tales, capping and topping each other, to appreciative and joking remarks among all the listeners. A visitor drops in to the lodge and, seeing

Waheenee's puppy, tells her an Arikara dog story about how sickness and death came to the people via a white and a black dog.

Another time, Waheenee is fooling around with seed corn her grandma was shucking into a bowl, spilling a few grains. When her grandma tells her not to fool around with it, she complains they have plenty for her to play with—and her grandma tells her the story of one little forgotten nubbin of corn, whose moral is that none of this gift (which is alive, has a spirit of its own) is supposed to be wasted.

As a budding teen, Waheenee attracts the attention of the young warrior Sacred Red Eagle Wing, who attends her family corn husking (along with thirty other young men—husking was a kind of combination party and feast, and a way to show off to a family's girls). But somebody else shows up:

> I saw Red Hand looking at me, and I was glad I was wearing my elk teeth dress. "He is a young man," I thought. "Not a boy, like Sacred Red Eagle Wing."

She promptly forgets the younger man and starts a teen crush on the older one.

In her twenties, describing her life while married to her long-time husband, a Mandan, Waheenee makes it clear that any picture of a "squaw" doing heavy work, submissively walking behind hubby, is a white man's fantasy. Son of a Star is considerate, and chides her for trying to show off to the other women by taking up what he considers too heavy a load for her. She often mentions his little attentions, not the exploitation of women of the stereotype.

> My husband walked at my side if he talked with me. At other times he went a little ahead, for if enemies or a grizzly attacked us, he would thus be in front, ready to fight, giving me time to escape.

Waheenee's is a good story, filled with the details that give color and vitality to the life as it was. She ends

> I am an old woman now. The buffalo and black-tailed deer are gone, and our Indian ways are almost gone. My little son grew up in the white man's school. He can read books, he owns cattle, he has a farm. He is a leader among our Hidatsa people, helping teach them to follow the white man's road....But for me, I cannot forget our old ways.

"Often in summer I rise at daybreak and steal out to the cornfields; and as I hoe the corn, I sing to it, as we did when I was young. No one cares for our corn songs now," she says sadly.

Young readers will get a warm narrative of the ordinary lives of a peaceful people. Life is in the details, and those came out over many years of remembering, not quick interviews. Wilson says,

> Indians have the gentle custom of adopting very dear friends by relationship terms. By such adoption, Buffalo Bird Woman is my mother. It is with real pleasure that I offer to young readers these stories from the life of my Indian mother.

Minnesota Historical Society has published other books about the life of this Hidatsa family. All of them are highly recommended.—*Paula Giese*

Buffalohead, Priscilla, *Ojibway Family Life in Minnesota: 20th Century Sketches*, illustrated by Robert DesJarlait (Ojibwe). Indian Education Program, Anoka-Hennepin Independent School District (1991). 57 pages, b/w photos and illustrations; Ojibwe

This book is, according to the authors,

> ...a different kind of history book. It is not about important treaties, famous chiefs, or tribal governments. These are important topics, but excellent books about Ojibway political history are already available. Instead, this book focuses on the day-to-day lives of Ojibway families of the 20th century. National and tribal events are briefly covered to explain how these events affected family life. In the chapters which follow, you will meet some remarkable people. John Rogers tells how his family gathered snakeroot early in the century to trade to white people for sacks of white bread. Maude Kegg explains how she met her future husband at a logging camp. He got her attention by being a real pest...

These are essays, illustrated with many old photos, reproductions of Native family documents, news clips from the Minnesota Historical Society, and wonderful black-and-white circular drawings by Robert DesJarlait. Some of the essays are signed—for example, artist DesJarlait's "Nokomis Wakaigun (My Grandmother's House)" and his memorial essay on his father, Patrick DesJarlait, probably Minnesota's best-known Indian artist.

Chapter 1 sketches Ojibwe history of the migration and spread of the Anishinaabeg peoples around the Great Lakes; the seasonal round of traditional family life—sugaring, rice harvest, family lodges, naming and learning customs of young people. There's a piece about Wah-we-yah-cumig (Round Earth), one of AIM leader Dennis Banks's ancestors, that explains how the Mille Lacs traditionals were forced off their land in 1904 to go to what the U.S. intended to be a concentration camp for all upper midwest Indians, White Earth. He was a leader and orator in the attempt to resist this forced move, and communicated with others using an Ojibwe-Cree syllabary not as well known as Sequoyah's earlier Cherokee invention.

Chapter 2 (1900-30) deals with the agency trading posts, the employment of Indians as loggers (as their former lands were all being deforested by the timber industry), and changes made by the automobile.

Chapter 3 (1932-40) chronicles the effects of the Depression years—employment in the Civilian Conservation Corps, berrying, and selling crafts by the highway. This brought isolated Indian communities together for the first time. And there were some ironic aspects: Indian hunters were asked to provide game to feed the hungry poor in the Twin Cities, for example. Accustomed to being poor, jobless, and surviving with gardening, hunting and gathering, Minnesota's northern woodlands Ojibwe were able to provide help to those worse off than themselves during hard times. It is amusing to think of white people and government officials turning to Indians for charity.

Chapter 5 (1940-50) describes a period of coming together during which several Indian organizations—particularly the National Congress of American Indians—were formed. And World War II brought knowledge of the outside world to the reservations, via soldiers, victory gardens, and a home defense brigade of women, who drilled with the rifles and shotguns left by brothers and husbands who went to war, in case any of the enemy showed up in the north woods. The women passed a single pressure cooker among families and districts to do massive canning of victory garden produce more safely and quickly than with waterbath canners. A few elderly women still talk of that first pressure cooker with amazement and love as "the white man's best invention."

With all the young men away, some elders invented a wild rice threshing machine, paddles run off pulleys attached to car engines, to replace the strong young men, not available during wartime for the tiring task of "jigging," or dancing the rice to loosen its husks. Special mention must be given to Buffalohead's sketch of Mary Rogers Perez, an elder who was a wartime welder and defense factory worker. Later she became an actress at the Guthrie Theatre in Minneapolis, playing the parts of Russian, Spanish and other "ethnic" women. (Sir John Gielgud put on no plays about Indians during his directorship.)

Hard times eased up after World War II for everyone but Indians. The U.S. government adopted the post-war policy of termination and relocation—ending national sovereignty of reservations, and moving the Indian populations off their remaining land to cities. Chapter 5 (1950-60) deals with contrasting memories of childhoods on reservations, and desperate poverty and

exploitation in the cities. Chapter 6 (1960-90) discusses moving toward sovereignty and self-determination. The book ends with a memoir by Pauline Brunette, who uses quilts and crocheted afghans to tell a family history.

This book combines guidance and information from elders who lived through the events described, careful documentary and especially photo source research, and a focus on the kind of history almost never told. It is well complemented by another secondary school publication by Buffalohead: *Modern Indian Issues—Repatriation, Religious Freedom, Mascots and Stereotypes, Tribal Sovereignty, Tribal Government, Tribal Enterprises, Treaty Rights*. Together, these provide a substantial, accurate, interesting picture of 20th-Century Native life in the Northern U.S. woodlands. Though it centers on Minnesota's Ojibwe peoples, the clear, well-illustrated, and lively descriptions are good reading and good learning, both for Indian and non-Indian students everywhere.—*Paula Giese*

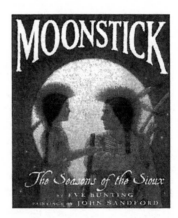

Bunting, Eve, *Moonstick: The Seasons of the Sioux*, illustrated by John Sandford. HarperCollins (1997). Unpaginated, color illustrations; grades 2-3; Dakota

During the long-ago "seasons of the Sioux," the young narrator's father notches a "moon-counting stick" at the beginning of each moon to mark the passing of the year—and to give Bunting a historical backdrop for her poetic interpretations of Dakota life.

The text's idyllic setting suggests life before contact with the whites (late 1700s or early 1800s, maybe), yet the pictures of women wearing beaded dresses, one holding a mirror, another whose braids are tied with red trade-cloth, and a pony hooked up to a drag suggest otherwise. People during this time did not refer to themselves as "Sioux," a French corruption of an enemy word; nor did they call containers "parfleches" or pony-drags "travois," both French names. Women did not sing strong-heart songs before a hunt; these were sung to encourage and honor a war party. Crows were not caught, put in cages and taught to speak. And children did not fly tethered pet birds like kites.

Each two-page spread, in dark, earth-toned colors and muted details, depicts a particular "moon" and the season that encompasses it. The pictures fit in well with the romantic tone of the text: Indians exist only in the netherworld of a cultural outsider's imagination. Even Sun Dance, a sacred event that should not be depicted at all, is given this superficial treatment, both in text and illustration.

Following twenty-six pages depicting a paradise on earth without war, famine, disease, murder, white depredation, theft of land, residential schools or forced assimilation, the young reader is jolted:

A balding Indian man with short hair, wearing a plaid shirt and overalls, looks sadly out of the windows of a barbershop. The shop is named "Two Buffalo," and the windowpanes resemble the bars of a prison. "Many moons have died," the narrator says, and "[m]any winters have passed." The reader will realize that the man on this page and the next is the boy who was running through the meadow on the previous page:

> My father is with the Great Spirit.
> The buffalo have gone
> and the eagles are few in the sky.
> Our lives are different now.
> My eldest brother works in a barbershop.
> His hair is white as winter snows.
> My wife does beadwork
> and I make headdresses of feathers
> that sell well.
> We do not hunt.

In the next spread, this old man, now a grandpa, tells his grandson not to despair, because

> One time follows another
> on life's counting stick.
> Changes come and will come again.

So Bunting's so-called "moonstick" is a literary device, a thirty-page metaphor, a "vision of a vanishing race." The reviewer for *School Library Journal* called *Moonstick* "a lovely, elegiac book, a romantic paean to a vanished existence."

There's more than a little resemblance here to Jane Yolen's *Encounter*. It is curious to see how much this sort of thing there is now that Native people have been taking back their lives, cultures, and ceremonies.

If Bunting knows anything about Native people at all, she must know that there is no reason for an elegy.

—Beverly Slapin

Burks, Brian, *Runs With Horses*. Harcourt Brace (1995). 116 pages; grades 6-7; Apache

Summary: "Sixteen years old in 1886, Runs With Horses trains to become a warrior with Geronimo's band of Apaches in the American Southwest."

It is apparent that the author seen "Dances With Wolves," hence the name of the young protagonist. The people who are called "Apache" were named "ahpachu," meaning "enemy" by the Zuni. They call themselves Ndee—"the People"—and would not have referred to themselves as Apache, as in "My son, you are not yet a Chiricahua Apache warrior." The name of the man called "Geronimo" by the whites was actually Goyathlay, or "One Who Yawns." His people at this time would not have referred to him as Geronimo, as they do in this book.

The grownups talk in metaphors to show how wise they are. Here's a particularly revolting sample:

> Your legs are your friends. You must teach them to run like the antelope. Then your enemies will not be able to catch you. Your eyes are your friends. You must make them see like the eagle so that you are a great hunter and your enemies cannot approach without your knowledge. Your ears are your friends. They will tell you what your eyes cannot see in the night. Teach them to hear the beetle that crawls on the ground. Then you will hear the snake slither in the grass and it will not be able to bite you. Your arms and your hands are your friends. They must be strong and quick like the cougar's.... Your mind is your friend. It will tell you what to do. Remember all that you hear and see. In your head will be the wisdom to survive all things.

I am thankful that Red Knife ends "your friends the body parts" here.

The coming-of-age rituals are as distorted. Our young hero must kill a deer, run three miles to the top of a mountain and back with his mouth full of water, fight a tree, roll a ball of snow until the ball becomes too big and heavy to be pushed, and, without flinching, place burning sage on both forearms until it burns to ashes. All within the space of about two days.

Jake Perea (Mescalero Apache), who teaches at San Francisco State University, says that Apache boys were trained for endurance in order to become warriors. Such training might involve lifting and throwing rocks to develop upper-body strength, running to build stamina, learning how to track game and what game to hunt. Training progressed according to the child's understanding and ability, not to some predetermined time scale. For instance, says Perea, "a young child would be given a bow and arrow. When he got older he would see how a bow and arrow were used. He might start to bring small game to a clan mother or grandmother. Then he would learn how to track game, and would be taught how and what to kill depending on what was needed by the people he was hunting for." Children would also be taught to run for endurance, with pebbles gathered at the base of a wash and put into the mouth to retain moisture. They were taught to pace themselves while running so as not to become mentally fatigued. The distance was not important. And, need it be said, that Apache people did not measure distance by "miles"? Snowfall in the desert is erratic at best, and it is highly unlikely that rolling snowballs would be part of an Apache youth's training. Tree-fighting was also a practice not engaged in, nor is that sage-burning-on-the-arm stuff. Perea says that young Mescalero boys were often interested in tatooing themselves. "The way to do this," he says, "was to get a cholla, a jumping cactus, and heat the spines and use them to make very small designs on the forearm, then to rub four wings salt bush on the cuts to help heal. But we would never use sage in that way—sage has always been sacred and would never have been used that way."

In *Runs With Horses*, Indians are savages. When they are not busy making animal-to-human metaphors, they shriek, yell, moan, and chant: "[T]he air was filled with the frenzied whoops of the warriors." They are wildly superstitious: "[Runs with Horses] was sure of his riding ability,... having been to a shaman who had performed a ceremony to give him the clinging ability of the bat."

And they are fiercely antagonistic:

> Many times he'd seen the warriors return from a raid with captives, either Mexicans or whites. With their hands tied behind their backs, the captives were given to the Apache women to be hacked to death with axes and knives as they tried to run away.

Nowhere here are grandparents, husbands, mothers, children. They do not play, joke, sing, love each other. There are no women to speak of. Nowhere here is a freedom-loving people, veterans of 250 years of guerrilla war with the Spaniards, desperately fighting the Mexicans and the U.S. to protect a way of life that had gone on for millennia. Nowhere is shown the atrocities perpetrated upon the Ndee people by the Mexican and U.S. governments, at the behest of land-hungry settlers, miners, and politicians.

Finally, the man called Geronimo is portrayed, not as a hero who would have preferred death to the loss of his land, but as a boastful drunkard with "cold, mystical eyes." *Runs With Horses* is beyond ugly.

Oh, and one last thing: The people called "Apache" did not castrate their war ponies.—*Beverly Slapin*

(Thank-you to Jake Perea.)

Burrill, Richard, *How Magpie Got His Yellow Bill*, illustrated by Chryssa Otto and Robyn Waters. The Anthro Company (1990). 38 pages, b/w illustrations; grades 2-up; Maidu

Looks like Burrill's alter ego, "Grizzly Bear Heart of the Mountain Maidu" is back, this time in a classroom teaching all about magpies, Maidu language, "special songs," what's in the yellow leather bag he carries, the California Gold Rush, and the "Old Ways" that Burrill—I mean Grizzly Bear Heart—defines as "Traditional life ways (philosophy) passed down by the Elders for keeping respect; learned from watching Nature; the Great Teacher and Spirit Behind the All Of Nature." And "The Four Rules of Life." Oh, and the "legend" of "How Magpie Got His Yellow Bill." All in thirty-eight pages.

It might seem (at least to the non-Native children and their teachers for whom this book is presumably intended) that Burrill knows his stuff. Even the Library of Congress Cataloging in Publication people seem to have been confounded, listing this title as "folklore-fiction." It's not folklore. Not even close.

In his preface, Burrill explains that he couldn't find a real California Indian story explaining why magpies in the Central Valley have yellow beaks instead of black beaks like all the other magpies in the world. So he made one up.

Burrill seems to have a problem, among other things, of worldview. In an indigenous worldview, all things are alive and related in a large general classification called living things, with a rich multitude of living things needed to make up the whole. Each kind of living thing has its own unique family and occupies its own special niche in creation, and this creates harmony and balance in the world. If that is your understanding of the world, then you understand the world in a whole, interrelated way and you don't need to chop up the world into classifications and sub-classifications in order to understand it.

It was the advent of the "sciences" and the academy in Europe that brought us the phenomenon of classification of species, sub-subspecies, phyla, genus and non-species. It comes from a worldview that compartmentalizes life, takes it apart, categorizes the pieces and creates a hierarchy of it—then devises scientific explanations of why certain sub-members differ from the "normal" members of its group.

There is no Indian story explaining how the magpie got its yellow beak because it was never an issue with us.

The magpie has a yellow beak because it has a yellow beak. The beak isn't what defines it or makes it unique. The magpie is unique because it was created to occupy its own niche in the scheme of creation.

Burrill's story of Magpie goes like this: Magpie is jealous of the other birds because of their beautiful colors, beautiful dances and beautiful songs. He has no respect for them and no respect for himself. He interacts with a "young Indian girl" by not listening to her advice. His jealousy gets the best of him:

> The angry magpie now thought of a terrible plan. He used his magic ability of seeing into the future. His heart was now evil, like the heart of Trickster Coyote.

Our creation stories do not have the animal people—the first people—interacting with humans, who haven't been created yet. Magpie doesn't have the ability to see into the future, and Coyote is a lot of things, but he's not "evil." Nevertheless, Magpie, in his mean-spirited jealousy, brings "many strangers here"—he sets the California Gold Rush into motion, leading to the genocide of the Indian peoples of California. So Creator teaches him a lesson by painting his black bill yellow.

This is just too weird. I thought we Indians had heard every explanation and obfuscation of the death and destruction that arrived with the white settlers, but blaming this all on a little bird must certainly be a new one! And to put this garbage into an illustrated children's book as a "legend," in the voice of an Indian character, is—I just can't say this strongly enough—just beyond ugliness, beyond racism.

Burrill probably spends a lot of time imagining Indians and fancying himself an "Indian expert." By creating a fantasy Indian world—by taking bits and pieces of real Indian languages and cultures and binding them up in his own biases—he doesn't have to worry about accuracy. By self-publishing all of his books, Burrill is not accountable to any real Indian people, contemporary or historical. He does not have to be concerned with what we want to share of our own cultures, what we want to teach our children and what we want the rest of the world to know about us.

In *How Magpie Got His Yellow Bill*, Burrill becomes a broker of Maidu language, yet he uses the language in a totally distorted cultural context, uses real Maidu language to legitimize his own fantasy stories in his own fantasy land of fantasy Indians.

This is a stupid racist book built on a stupid racist premise.
—*Robette Dias*

Burrill, Richard, *Protectors of the Land: An Environmental Journey to Understanding the Conservation Ethic*, edited by Regina Macias. The Anthro Company (1994). 353 pages, b/w line drawings and photos; grades 4-up; California Nations

Richard Burrill has taught me a lesson about the smarmy world of publications about Natives by non-Natives for non-Natives. The authors and publishers of newer works, especially so-called educational works, aren't dumb—they are catching on to the tell-tale signs of appropriation and racism in children's books. They have adjusted accordingly—not, unfortunately, by working to *end* those problems, but by figuring out how to present the same biases in seemingly "clean" form. Sorry, guys: When you're using the same rotten ingredients, wrapping them up pretty doesn't change the smell. Therefore, I present you with a few tools gleaned from my reading of *Protectors of the Land*, and hope that this review will also serve as a template by which to read other books which, beneath their pretty covers, are simply "recycled racism."

Some of these RR books seem to have the involvement, tribal knowledge and "blessings" of the Native peoples being discussed within the pages—for example, illustrations done by people identified by tribal affiliation, photographs of Native children in clothing and jewelry that is identified by tribal source, a bibliography of Native resources and informants. This can be deceptive. The problem here isn't whether or not the Native contributors are "authentic" or not (although believe me, I have issues with that too!), but the ways in which their information is portrayed and framed. In this case, Native contributors have their words, artwork and photographs coated within the sugary, patronizing, pseudo-Indian Hiawatha-speak of a character called "Grizzly Bear Heart." This guy narrates the entire book, saying things like, "I am of the Mountain Maidu." Now, any contemporary Indian would most probably say, "I'm Mountain Maidu" or "My tribe is called the Mountain Maidu." But that's evidently not "Indian" enough for Burrill. This is followed by,

Walk with me. Open your heart and listen. Open your heart and understand. You will learn about the family of earth spirits, plant spirits, animal-people and human-people. All is sacred Power... In the following pages, my friends and I will share with you our Old Ways...

This type of writing—choppy, short, full of loaded words such as "heart," "spirit," "sacred," "Power," and most importantly, those "Old Ways"—are straight out of a New Age wannabe's computer, not a contemporary Native person's mouth. Nowhere are there words such as "blood" or "swamp" or "mosquitoes"—all parts of the realities of outdoor Native life—or anyone's life—in an ecologically self-sustaining world.

It is not until page 319 (in the chapter notes), that we are told that "Grizzly Bear Heart" is a fictional character who "lives in the heart of California." Burrill defends this "literary device" by saying it allows him "to include insights and virtues of a bigger cross section of California Indian tribes." By creating the Indian "Grizzly Bear Heart" as "the heart of California," Burrill's representation becomes a new and improved Indian—sort of "Here, let me show you Indians how environmentalism is done." This is both appropriative and patronizing.

Question: Whose "Indian" is created by this "Grizzly Bear Heart" as narrator? Answer: Once again, the white man's Indian.

Because there is so little material available on California Indians, many educators, I imagine, will purchase this book to diversify their library collections with California Native perspectives and provide solid environmental curricula. However, much of the information here is culled from sources that are questionable at best. The material on the "Woman of San Nicholas Island," for example, merely retells the Scott O'Dell romance, which in turn recycles the Mission-era fable of a "Robinson Crusoe" girl who dies because she rejects the salvation of colonization. Material about Ishi, often the only Native Californian students or educators have any connection to, is boiled down to one short paragraph, and elsewhere Ishi is referred to as one of the last "stone-age" people. Hey, I'm no paleontologist, but I know damn well that the Stone Age ended quite a bit before Ishi came into Oroville in 1916. Surely a more respectful term could have been found to describe the culture Ishi's people lived within, and which was destroyed not because it ceased to function, but because white people hunted down and killed them.

The few real "environmental" articles are long and dull and provide little or ineffectual hands-on experience. Certainly better activities are available elsewhere.

These RR books may claim to address and "solve" real, vital concerns for readers—for example, attaining spiritual peace, wholeness of body and spirit, or sustainable ecological balance. The appeal to the reader is a sort of simplified, self-help manual for hugely complicated issues: How To Be One with the Earth, How to Communicate with Endangered Animals, How to Ease Your Fears of Environmental Melt-Down. But at the heart of such an approach is yet another way for white people to ask, "What can we get out of Indians this time? How can we, once again, make their images and lives serve us best now that we've really screwed things up?" Worse still, in Burrill's book are the curriculum lessons themselves, which distill some of the major illnesses of modern times into a one-page, "teachable moment" complete with directions for location, grades, length of time, group size, and materials.

One such example is Lesson 1:1—"How to Feel at Home in the Woods." The stated learning objective is ludicrous: "Students will be able to relate to the Yurok Indian way of feeling at home in the woods by using their senses (touch, smell, sound, sight, and taste)." I guess the senses are listed in case the teacher doesn't know what they are! But to state such an incredible—and impossible—learning objective as being able to "relate" to the Yurok way of feeling "at home in the woods" is no less than obscene. In one sentence, Burrill assumes that a people's entire history of place and survival skills can be learned by non-tribal children in a very short time; he restricts the Yurok people to a time and place in which they all possess some mystical connection with the natural world; and he trivializes the relationship between a people and the land. In other words, erase history, erase experience, erase place—none of it is necessary to "be Yurok." All you have to do is read this book and follow the formula.

Throughout the entire book, Burrill's pervasive message is that being Indian is 1) something that can be learned by reading and a few field trips, and 2) something that is totally located in the "woods." Burrill has distilled the teachings, stories, recipes and photos of real peoples into a how-to manual that avoids the necessity of ever meeting or spending time with elders or spiritual leaders, having a community, or even possessing a sense of "place" or a source of origin. Although Burrill writes about his experiences taking students on real trips into the woods, this book does not, and cannot, begin to take the place of such an experience—and that experience, itself, must be viewed with real skepticism if Burrill thinks his students are gaining true Indian knowledge on such brief and superficial outings. The book also ignores the fact that we—Native peoples—live in contemporary houses, utilize modern technology, and incorporate such materials into our daily lives in the most "Indian" act of all—constant adaptation to change, and the struggle to maintain our identity despite judgments imposed by outsiders of what is or isn't "Indian" enough.

So there you have them—all the elements of "recycled racism" in one book. Now, keep an eye out for the ones near you.—*Deborah A. Miranda*

Caduto, Michael J., and Joseph Bruchac (Abenaki), illustratons by John Kahionhes Fadden (Mohawk). Fulcrum. b/w illustrations; grades 2-7:
Keepers of the Animals: Native American Stories and Wildlife Activities for Children **(1991); 265 pages**
Keepers of the Earth: Native American Stories and Environmental Activities for Children **(1988); 209 pages**
Keepers of Life: Discovering Plants Through Native American Stories and Earth Activities for Children **(1994); 265 pages**

The "Keepers" series is a superbly written and illustrated presentation of Native philosophies about the environment.

These three books for Native-centered science include activities suitable for young elementary children through late middle school. This holistic philosophy is set forth by contrasting two kinds of learnings and wholenesses: that obtained by a "journey through the world of Native American beliefs" leading to an overarching, multi-tribal belief that "all things are connected as one." This part of the journey is conducted by means of story from many tribes, using the faculty of imagination. But the stories are only half the story.

> Science takes us on another journey, a different way of seeing than through the eyes of American Indians. Through intellectual and systematic study, science reveals the natures of the earth and humankind in intricate and intriguing detail. Slowly, through the centuries, a sense of order has emerged. Although the knowledge of science, in chronological age, is a child compared to the antiquity of American Indians, the wisdom from both has led us to some of the same lessons about the oneness of people and the environment.... The science of ecology, the study of the interactions between living things and their environments circles back to the ancient wisdom found in the rich oral traditions of American Indian stories. Time and again the stories have said that all of the living and nonliving parts of the earth are one and that people are a part of that wholeness. Today, ecological science agrees.

Bruchac, a well-known Abenaki storyteller and Caduto, a non-Indian ecologist and educator, together have created a useful educational resource for Native and non-Native students. It should supplement, but not replace, hands-on science. A skilled teacher can use some of the

activities as lead-ins to quantitative activities involving measurement, estimation, prediction, and other skills that are fostered in good elementary science programs. The science presented in the "Keepers" series is observational but not quantitative, and does not prepare children for quantitative science.

All the books in the "Keepers" series have an introductory two-page map showing precontact culture areas of North America, with tribal locations. In each book, activities are coded with small icons indicating which of several types they are. There is also a very rough indicator of appropriate age level—younger children or older ones. Also available for each book in the series is a book that contains the twenty-five or so legends from many different tribes, illustrations, and some background on each story; and an audiotape of Bruchac telling the stories.—*Paula Giese*

Caduto, Michael J., and Joseph Bruchac (Abenaki), *Native American Gardening: Stories, Projects and Recipes for Families.* **Fulcrum (1996). 158 pages, b/w illustrations; all grades**

Except for the fact that most schools don't meet in summer, when gardens take the most work and come to harvest, this book is full of excellent school science gardening projects. The book follows the holistic approach found in the Bruchac-Caduto "Keepers" Native-centered science series, with traditional stories from several tribes, explanations of traditional Native gardening practices, designs for traditional Three Sisters gardens from several tribes, and other activities. These range from cooking or drying what you grow to making gourd rattles and cornhusk dolls.

The gardening portion of the book includes choosing a site (most people will have little choice—backyard or nothing), planning and preparing the site, choosing seeds (with sources for getting traditional varieties from organizations trying to save these from the commercial hybrids that dominate the market), composting, combating pests naturally, and other topics fairly conventional to most organic gardening books, but treated here with a Native flair. The final chapter contains instructions for drying corn, beans and squash; and recipes for several traditional Native foods using those Three Sisters. Some of the recipes thought of as traditional contain no salt or modern spices, and may be too bland for our tastes. It is unlikely this is the way traditional cooks prepared them in the old days, but herbs and spices they used are no longer known or not readily available. The last two chapters—"Traditional Native Gardening" and "Native Harvests, Meals, Recipes"—end with a branching out section of further readings. If you have some land where you can plant and care for a garden, this book is highly recommended.—*Paula Giese*

Cameron, Anne, Harbour Publishing:
How the Loon Lost her Voice (1985), illustrated by Tara
Miller. 31 pages, b/w illustrations; grades 2-up
Lazy Boy (1988), illustrated by Nelle Olsen. 25 pages, b/w
illustrations; grades 4-up
Orca's Song (1987), illustrated by Nellie Olsen. 25 pages,
b/w illustrations; grades 2-up
Spider Woman (1988), illustrated by Nelle Olsen. 27 pages,
b/w illustrations; grades 2-up

Orca's Song is the story of a black being and a white being,
both female, from two different worlds falling in love
with each other and bringing forth an offspring that is both
black and white but physically belongs to the world of
only one of the parents. This story stretches the imagination as Orca, the killer whale and Osprey, the fish eagle,
fall in love. Olsen's cover illustration uses a Northwest
Coast artistic style that intermingles what looks like a bird
and a whale. The black and white line drawings accompanying the story line are naturalistic although framed
in circles that juxtapose "Northwest Coast style" throughout the book. This very "New Age" rendering of this
story, even with West Coast symbols, obscures any sem-
blance of the story it might be based on. "And because
these wonderful creatures are the result of love between
creatures of different worlds, they are capable of love
for all things." While transformation across species is a
traditional Northwest Coast theme, same-sex reproduction
is not—an underlying dissonance that Cameron cannot
calm even with a wave of sentiment about whales and
osprey and women becoming one in sound and water in
the second half of this book.

How the Loon Lost Her Voice is a variation on the story of
how Raven freed the daylight. It features Loon's role in
the time when all animals participated in freeing the daylight and the consequences. The tedious causal logic of
this story grates almost as much as the uncharacteristi-
cally rationalizing Raven, both reflective of Cameron's
stylistic renderings. Loon begins with a beautiful singing
voice and is reduced to a "sad cry that echoes across
the water…as a reminder of the time she lost her singing
voice…" While Deer loses antlers annually, Bear hibernates
in the fall, and Raven is entranced by shiny things, for
her heroic efforts Loon is robbed of her song. Loon's
lot seems rather inequitable, to say the least. Cameron,
again pointing us in the wrong direction, leads us to
conclude that Loon is content with her contribution
even though she is eternally sad. What kind of message
is this for children, for adults?

Spider Woman is a very powerful deity who appears in many
traditional stories to fix the world. But she is not "from"
the Northwest Coast. So, in keeping with her eclectic style,
taking a little from this story and a little from that and
throwing it all together, Cameron has made *Spider Woman*
into a sort of "road story." Here, Spider Woman actually
comes crawling from her home under the desert sand and
pops up on Vancouver Island to reposition the spindle/
world when it slips "from its proper hole," defeats the
"Birds of Torment" with the first lacrosse stick (soothing
human misery in the process), and forms an alliance
with the trees. And when she is done with all this, she
goes back underground to her desert home—where
"she could hear the patter of lambs' hooves on her roof"—
to wait and watch for the next slip of the firmament.

Lazy Boy is a jarring read, and probably the most con-
founding of all of Cameron's retellings. In it, she seems
to want to tell a sort of all-encompassing "how-it-came-
to-be-story" by mixing Northwest Coast cultural imagery
with Greek and American mythology, feminist under-
pinnings and bizarre anatomical technicalities. And the
story is full of useless details and conjectures that Cameron
seems to like to throw in. "Orca," for instance, "feeds her
own babies with milk from her breasts, as do women…"

Lazy Boy—supposedly nudged up to beach by Orca—is
a little like Snot-Boy, the Nuu-chah-nulth transformer.
He is a little like Blackskin, the Haida hero. He is a lot
like Atlas, from Greek myth. There's even some Paul
Bunyon thrown in. Yet, even though he is clearly magical
—all he does is eat and sleep and grow—the people
expect him to "do some work and begin to justify his
existence." (In our stories, supernatural persons don't
have human expectations imposed on them. That
would be a bad thing.) Then, catastrophes happen.
There is a flood, threatening to drown the village. Lazy
Boy fixes it by singing the water back to where it
belongs. Nature goes berserk again, as the trees grow
wildly, once more threatening the village. Lazy Boy
uproots the trees and neatly stacks them out of the way.
There's more. Some "Supernatural Uncles" come to visit,
a deaf girl is able to hear again. And this: "[T]he bird of
menstrual cramps squeezed through the hole, but Frog
Woman taught us the kneeling position to defeat the
cramps, so the bird was thwarted." What??

As in her other books—but more so in this one—Cameron exploits the big metaphors and ends up trivializing
our stories.—*Marlene R. Atleo/ʔeh ʔeh naa tuu kwiss*

Campbell, Maria (Cree/Métis), *Halfbreed.* **University of Nebraska (1973, 1982). 157 pages; grades 7-up; Cree/Métis**

Maria Campbell's *Halfbreed* is one of the most important works of Indian literature of the 20th Century. It's a hard book to read. Of it, she says:

> I write this for all of you, to tell you what it is like to be a Halfbreed woman in our country. I want to tell you about the joys and sorrows, the oppressing poverty, the frustrations and the dreams.

This she does, in detail, and with devastating honesty. Campbell starts with a quick overview of the history and situation of the Halfbreeds in Saskatchewan, after which approximately half of the book is devoted to her childhood, which seems to have been a happy one, up until the age of fifteen. In a two-room log house, the kitchen-living room was "one of the most beautiful rooms I have known." From her description, it sounds it. Here, with her parents, and later siblings—Campbell was the oldest—and her beloved *cheechum* (grandmother), who "tried to teach me all she knew about living," she enjoyed the richness of life in that house. Her father taught her how to trap, shoot and fight; her mother, cooking, sewing and knitting. She grew up on Shakespeare, Dickens, Longfellow and Scott, from the family book collection. There were gatherings of families and friends, stories told, tricks played on each other.

Campbell was only in her early thirties when her book was first published; she had already lived enough for ten lifetimes. Her writing is dense. In little over a hundred pages she manages to cover all of it. The hatred, the social, political and economic inequities that led to the downward spiral of her own life after a disastrous marriage at fifteen, are unflinchingly set down. She spares herself nothing. No one has spoken more precisely, more evocatively, of what mixed-blood people, and especially women, have faced, and do still.

When Campbell does at last begin to pull herself out of the quagmire of betrayal, alcohol, drugs and time on the street, it seems impossible that she will make it—even though we know she did, because she wrote this book; an act of courage if ever there was one. We are told that a friend said to her, "Maria, make it a happy book. It couldn't have been so bad. We know we are guilty so don't be too harsh."

Campbell can still say, "I am not bitter. I have passed that stage. I only want to say: this is what it was like, this is what it is still like." She has done that, unforgettably.
—Doris Seale

Campbell, Maria (Cree/Métis), *Stories of the Road Allowance People,* **illustrated by Sherry Farrell Racette (Timikaming). Theytus (1995). 144 pages, color illustrations; high school-up; Cree/Métis**

"I had hoped when I became a student of storytelling," Campbell writes, "that I would get old women teachers, but that was not meant to be. The old women were kind, made me pots of tea, cooked me soup and bannock, made me starblankets and moccasins, then sent me off to the old men who became my teachers." The eight stories here are some of those she learned. They range from funny to hair-raising, with a few stops in between. "Dah Song of Dah Crow" is about a man who went where he wanted, and did what he chose—"he makes damn good storytelling." He has a good heart, but you don't mess with him. He's a man who belongs to himself. There's a story about a man whose wife was a werewolf, one about a man who was given a song by Jesus—after they have a drink or two, some about injustice and hard times, and the occasional fitting retribution. "Jacob" is a tragedy worthy of a Sophocles, and one of the grimmest results I have seen of the government policy of taking Indian children away from their families, and holding them in residential schools for years at a time.

The Métis people have had it as bad as anybody, and these stories show it. But there is also the humor, and the tough-as-old-boot-leather quality that has enabled them to survive. Racette's illustrations perfectly capture this, and the nature of each character—of each story. As well as the full-page paintings, there are little embellishments here and there that help to make this a beautiful job of book making.

Campbell's book is quite unlike any other. These stories were not "collected." They are not taken from any old-time story-hunter's gatherings. They belong to real people, and have reality as told; and here, as set down. There is truth in every word.

And yes, it is written in dialect. Don't worry about it. Just start reading and the stories will pull you into their spell. This is the real thing. That's just the way they're told.

—Doris Seale

Carvell, Marlene, *who will tell my brother?* Hyperion (2002). 150 pages; grades 6-up; Mohawk

Unlike his older brother, Evan Hill was born looking like his white mother rather than his Mohawk father. In waging a struggle against his high school's Indian mascot, this sensitive, artistic teenager is following in his brother Jacob's footsteps, taking on a task that is "a matter of honor, a matter of respect." Journal entries that are quiet, moving, and very readable express Evan's deep shame and great determination as he tries to get the students, teachers, principal, and school board to listen to him. "I simply have no choice. I have no choice," he says. He addresses the school board in his "monthly plea for justice," and each month, the school board members look at the wall above his head. Or, as they condescendingly explain to him, "racism is a matter of opinion."

In the face of escalating name-calling, threats and even physical attacks by some of the students, Evan stands strong. "I simply have no choice," he says. When someone kills his brother's dog, leaving a paper-feathered headband on the bloody, mangled body, Evan asks his journal:

> Who will tell my brother?
> Who will tell him
> that the fear, the hatred, the cruelty
> were not kept for him or me
> or for my mother or my father,
> but shared with a creature that had no part
> in its own undoing?

"Let it be resolved from this day forth," the school board proclaims, "in honor of the heritage of this area, the Indian profile will continue to be the official mascot of this school." As Evan graduates, younger students carry in the school's "Indian" banner, and a handful of his friends stage a silent protest. He writes:

> I know my struggle is not over.
> It is a struggle which will continue
> as long as people see others as different.
> But I know I have made a difference.
> And I know I am no longer alone.

Carvell may be forgiven for the occasional use of terms such as "ancient," "proud solemnity," and "proudly serene." She wrote this fictionalized account of her own two sons' experiences, and if they are at all like Evan and Jacob, she has reason to be proud. I wonder what they think of their mother's work.—*Beverly Slapin*

Chambers, Catherine E., *Daniel Boone and the Wilderness Road.* Troll (1984, 1998). 31 pages, b/w illustrations; grades 4-6

This particular Daniel Boone story, set in 1827, takes the form of a narrative from Grampa Halliday of his exciting travels with Boone along the "Wilderness Trail." It falls into a genre one might call "manifest-destiny-for-kids." The use of words such as "wilderness," "new land," "elbowroom" and "unfriendly Indians" reinforce the idea, prevalent in so many history books, that this land was largely empty and free for the taking. We could add the word "settling"—read "civilizing"—a land in which the original inhabitants were of marginal significance.

Teachers who happen to have a class set of this book could have children use it for math, counting the number of times insulting references to Native peoples are used. Otherwise, recycle the paper.—*Beverly Slapin*

Chanin, Michael, *Grandfather Four Winds and Rising Moon,* illustrated by Sally J. Smith. Starseed (1994). Unpaginated, color illustrations; grades 3-4

The basic story here is a grandfather teaching his grandson some random values through a story about how an apple tree goes through her life more gracefully than a pine tree because she has faith, hope and charity. In the end, it turns out that the "Sacred Tree of Our People" under which these two have been sitting is that wise little apple tree.

There exist within this story the usual problems associated with certain non-Native writers who write about Native peoples: no specific Nation is given, only male characters are active in a physical form, the people are always transported to about the 1850s, and the real lessons being learned at that time (such as government lies) are completely ignored. However, the idea of the sacred tree of a Native Nation being one which in reality would not even have had enough time to grow that long in the depicted western U.S. setting is especially odd. And need I say that apple trees are not, and never have been, sacred to any of us?

The idea that the sacred tree of a people, about which a story from "long ago" is being told, is only at most one hundred years old shows a complete disregard for the time and spatial realities of Native Nations. For Americans in general, one hundred years is a long time because they are recent arrivals. But for us, one hundred years is nothing like a long time, because we have always been here. To disregard this ancient residency is to disregard the right to this land that we rightly assert as the First Peoples of this continent.

As an aside, typically one can say of this genre of fiction that while the text is dull, misguided, damaging, and culturally irrelevant, at least the artwork is nice. Not so here. For example, see Rising Moon on page 27. He looks like a troll.—*Ella Rose Callow*

Chimera, Donna, *WolfStar*, illustrated by Gregg Lauer. WolfStar Press (1996). 71 pages, color illustrations; kindergarten–grade 3

According to the jacket copy, this book is "[w]ritten to be read aloud in the oral tradition of storytelling," and from the author's note:

> WolfStar is an original fictional tale written in the spirit of and with respect for Native American values and the oral tradition. It is not derived from any particular indigenous North American tradition.

A child named Snowdeer meets an apparition named WolfStar, who is a "messenger of the Ancient Ones of the Star Nation." These Ancient Ones are concerned because the "braves" are always going to war. WolfStar tells her:

> The Great Spirit has stirred within you and brought you here to acknowledge that which is soon to be. Your purpose in this turn of the medicine wheel is a noble one. You are to be a new voice, one that speaks for the sisters of the tribe. Too long silent, the gentle and peace seeking voice of the she has been lost in the thunderous rumble of your brothers who seek resolution through competition and aggression against your neighbors.

So Snowdeer, egged on by WolfStar, decides to join the council of elders so she can talk the "braves" out of war. She is sent on three tasks to prove she is worthy: Get a claw from the Cave of the Angry Bear. Bring back a feather from the Place of the High Eagle. Retrieve the Sacred Arrowhead from the Liquid Fire.

She does. It takes seventy agonizing pages. Having learned the secret of everything that is from WolfStar, Brother Otter, Great Paw, and High Eagle, Snowdeer returns to her people—and gets killed. Her death teaches her tribe a valuable lesson. They decide to Give Peace A Chance. The End.

The writing is awful. This from WolfStar again:

> Do not fear your Self. Just as you merged as one with the river, you are the earth and the bear, you are the eagle and the wind, you are the arrow and the fire. Do not fear your Self. Love and appreciate these expressions of the same energy from which you emerged.

I keep on telling everybody. We gotta keep these blissed-out New Age Indian wannabes away from computers.

Lauer's pictures perfectly complement Chimera's text. They're really ugly.—*Beverly Slapin*

Clark, Karin, illustrated by Joe Silvey (Coast Salish), Karin Clark, and others. First Nations Education Division, Greater Victoria School District (1996). b/w line drawings; grades 1-4; Salish, Kwakwaka'wakw, Nuu-chah-nulth:
***First Nations Families*, 41 pages**
***First Nations Technology.* 25 pages**
***Grandma's Special Feeling*, 25 pages**
***Wait for Me!*, 33 pages**

This project was a collaborative effort between the Victoria Native Friendship Center and the First Nations Division of the Greater Victoria School District. Written in consultation with First Nations elders, students, parents, teachers and Native advisers in the school district, these little books demonstrate the traditional value of inclusion. The black-and-white line drawings are a joy because while individuals are visibly highly differentiated in their facial features, body types, clothes, likes, dislikes, living arrangements and housing, they are clearly First Nations people with diverse and expressive facial features.

> This is my mother. She likes to go to movies with her friend. This is my brother. He likes to cry. This is grampa. He likes to tell stories. This is my mother. She likes to do aerobics. This is my dog. He likes to scratch.

In the simple early reader called *First Nations Families*, children introduce the reader to all their relatives, and what they "like" to do. In an important plus, families are diagrammed, and silhouettes of a man or woman in the family diagram mean that that person is "out of the picture" for that child.

On the front cover is a circle of First Nations faces surrounding a traditional design in which the central figure has its mouth open as if speaking. The effect is an invitation. The back cover features a vocabulary list of phrases, verbs, and an assortment of nouns such as the terms for family members, types of housing, and games, that makes it easy to use as a high-interest or alternative text. This is an excellent book about the diversity of family that First Nations children experience in urban school districts.

Whenever Grandma gets that "special feeling," the children know they're about to pile into the van, "get out into nature," and get a lesson about how First Nations peoples used to live in the old days. In *Grandma's Special Feeling*, Grandma knows that the children need to be able to experience what she wants to talk to them about. While her tribal history is only hinted at by the bentwood box, the elongated-headed woman, and the particular type of canoe, it is clear by the illustrations that Grandma comes from the Northwest Coast. The black-and-white line drawings of the grandparents and children are followed by a progression of activities and artifacts clustered around a photo illustrating the tree, shrub, flowering plants, sedges or aquatics from which they are produced. While Grandma passes all this knowledge on to the children she also brings in cultural history about how respect was, and is, shown for the plants—how they are acknowledged for their contribution and assured that they will not be over-harvested. Inside the back cover is a visual and textual summary of the featured plants that makes this book easy to use in preparing classroom lessons.

Wait for Me! is a touching little book about the importance of noticing the world. Charlie's brother and sister call him "Turtle" because he's always stopping to look at something interesting instead of keeping up with them. Charlie is intensely interested in everything he sees and wants to share his interest with them, but they are impatient, in a hurry. Charlie, who has brought along his bucket, finds things everywhere on the way in the seaweed, the driftwood, the kelp, the sand, the waves, the tree, the air, the ocean, and by his uncle's smokehouse. When Granny asks Charlie what treasures he has found, he shows the whole collection; among which are items his brother and sister had lost. They come to admire him when Grandpa explains how noticing things can be very important and could even save a life. The interaction among the siblings—and their relationship with their grandparents—illustrates the theme of this story. While Granny knows Charlie's ways and draws him out, Grandpa draws the lesson from the conversation, confirming Charlie's perspective. The line drawings provide rich detail of the environment that Charlie notices on his seaside walk. The "Words to Learn and Use" lists in front and back make this a classroom-friendly reader. The front cover, showing Charlie calling to his siblings speaks the name of the book as an invitation to pick it up to read.

Are they still *really Indians* if they wear modern clothes, drive cars, live in houses, watch TV? The contentious question of whether or not the identity of a people is dependent upon a particular technology is answered effectively in *First Nations Technology*, a little book that delivers a big message: "Many things have changed for our people, but many things are still the same." The book is dedicated to Nella Nelson, a Kwakwaka'wakw woman who has worked for many years with the Greater Victoria School Board to assure First Nations children a respectful learning space. Illustrations of old-time and modern houses, methods of transportation, occupational activities and implements of the three major cultural groups of Vancouver Island are used to illustrate practices of the past and present—to show how cultural patterns have changed, and how they have continued. The appropriateness of technological accommodation is illustrated in many ways: children and adults, for instance, are shown wearing fashionable, seasonally suitable clothing for the Pacific Northwest, and on a facing page, dressed in ceremonial regalia. This well-done, deceptively simple little reader clearly depicts First Nations peoples as technologically adaptive while maintaining cultural identity —a critical message for First Nations children, and everyone else. The drawings are accurate in their cultural details and the juxtaposition of the digitalized images provides sort of a past/present feel.—*Marlene R. Atleo/ʔeh ʔeh naa tuu kwiss*

Cohlene, Terri, illustrated by Charles Reasoner. Rourke (1990). 48 pages, color illustrations; grades 2-3:
Clamshell Boy: A Makah Legend
Dancing Drum: A Cherokee Legend
Ka-ha-si and the Loon: An Eskimo Legend
Little Firefly: An Algonquian Legend
Quillworker: A Cheyenne Legend
Turquoise Boy: A Navajo Legend

The six in this series, all "written and adapted by" Terri Cohlene, written to a formula, illustrated in the same style (Indian faces, mostly in profile, with closed eyes, seeming to go through the motions asleep), printed to the same dimensions, are definitely not recommended.

Aside from mentioning the tribal source (sometimes incorrectly), Cohlene does not credit her sources. In each retelling, she has personalized the story to provide a sub-teen or child as hero. In most of the stories, she has thrown in that all-purpose New Agers' delight, the shaman. And she has eliminated the cultural teachings, moral or natural history, and reflections of the sacred number four.

Cohlene ends each book with a short formulaic non-fiction section, purporting to provide a brief history of the tribe from which the original legend was taken, and a map of where the people once supposedly lived, supposedly during precontact times. There's a bit about housing and clothing. There's a timeline of historical dates and a glossary of terms that might not be familiar to child readers. Pictures in these sections are generally good.

The history itself is awful. Cohlene can't always describe precontact history either because it isn't known at all—or *she* doesn't know it. In three of the books, 1890 is marked as "Native Americans lose Battle of Wounded Knee, ending major Indian Wars." In fact, as just about everyone now acknowledges, this was a massacre of Big Foot's band, which was on its way to virtual imprisonment at the Pine Ridge reservation when the troops opened fire and chased down and slaughtered the fleeing women and children. Cohlene's ghastly insensitivity is also shown in the Cheyenne timeline (*Quillworker*): "1861-64: Cheyenne-Arapaho War, Native Americans lose Battle of Sand Creek." Well, this was actually the war for the Plains, but Black Kettle's band, who had notified the fort they would be camped 40 miles away at Sand Creek, were not fighting it and had already surrendered. Colonel John Chivington's Colorado Volunteers, though they had been specifically told to leave Black Kettle's band alone, attacked before dawn and slaughtered most of them, with a great deal of female mutilation and brutality, so much so that it drew an official reprimand. Chivington's response? "Kill them all, big and small, nits make lice." And that was the "Battle of Sand Creek."

LITTLE FIREFLY: AN ALGONQUIAN LEGEND

This seems to have been taken from Charles Leland's 1884 collection of what he called "Algonquian Legends." Leland knew the term was a general one, not the name of a Nation (it is a pejorative word meaning "bark eater" applied by the Iroquois to some of their enemies). In fact, the story Cohlene took her "legend" from is a 19th-Century Mi'kmaq retelling—with an ironic twist—of the French "Cinderella." Leland and others collected, Leland says, enough of these French folktales retold by the Indians, especially the Mi'kmaqs, to "publish a veritable *Contes Populaires*." Cohlene doesn't mention the Cinderella aspect, about which Leland is quite clear.

In the original, for the abused child who is sickly and crippled, the old ways represent her only possible escape

from an intolerable life as a victim. The storyteller shows that no "fairy godmother" will show up to help her. There is no vision or other inspiration, although the teller remarks in passing, "It may be some spirit inspired her." Cohlene has her little heroine inspired, in great detail, by a vision-dream sent by her dead mother.

The original storyteller emphasizes the courage and determination of Little Burnt One. To prepare for her visit to the forest beyond the village, she attempts to clothe herself in stiff birchbark garments (there being nothing else available) and stiffened old torn moccasins. As she starts out of the village, she is mocked for her crazy garments. Cohlene does replicate this event, but the original storyteller's language is far more vivid.

The burnt child is able to pass the guardian spirit's test. Unlike everyone else, she sees that the Invisible One's sled harness is the Ghost Road (Milky Way) and another piece of his gear is the rainbow. In the original story, she is overcome with awe; the old religion—in the form of Nature personified—still has power. She is healed of her all-over burns by the guardian spirit and told she will be the wife of the Invisible One. There is no happily ever after. The original is a powerful, disquieting story.

Like the English lady who collected a Victorian-rewritten version in *The Red Indian Fairy Book* of 1906, Cohlene has missed the point of the story entirely, and her legendary construct is a trivial thing.

In the original, the way the storyteller plays against the fabulous lies of Perrault's durable bourgeois myth of happiness-from-wealth, beauty as fashion, and a Fairy Godmother who is wealth personified, is a subtle and interesting cultural transformation of French folk and fairytales commonplace among the Mi'kmaq who had intermarried and got along so well with the French settlers (Arcadians), until in 1750 the English expelled *them* in order to take their land. The actual history of the Natives (especially the Mi'kmaq), the French-Arcadians and the English of Nova Scotia is an interesting one; no hint of any of this is to be found in Cohlene's canned mini-history of "the (non-existent) Algonquian" tribe, though she includes pictures of Mi'kmaqs, indicating that her actual source was Leland, rather than the *Red Indian Fairy Book*.

QUILLWORKER: A CHEYENNE LEGEND

This one is from *American Indian Myths and Legends*, edited by Richard Erdoes and Alfonso Ortiz (Pantheon, 1984). Members of the Strange Owl family, who told it to Erdoes at Lame Deer, Montana, on the Northern Cheyenne Reservation in 1967, called it "The Quillwork Girl and Her Seven Star Brothers."

Had Cohlene been a bit more diligent in perusing the

source, she could have avoided making the mistake of naming the youngest brother (the story's hero) Wihio. In her glossary, Cohlene says that Wihio "means one with higher intelligence." Actually, Wihio is an *evil* and *stupid* spider spirit, whose name now is a Cheyenne slang pejorative word for "white man." In Erdoes' and Ortiz's book, Rachel Strange Owl tells another story, one about Veeho, another name for Wihio: "Veeho is like some tourists who come into an Indian village not knowing how to behave or what to do, trying to impress everybody," she begins it. "You know, I think you should stop fooling around, trying to impress people with your tricks," she ends it. But Cohlene probably didn't see this particular story, so she doesn't know she's given a pejorative name to her young hero.

Other aspects of cultural ignorance creep in. Since Cohlene doesn't understand that four is a sacred number, hence Native storytelling conventions usually award success only on the fourth try, she shortens from four to three the episodes with the hostile buffalo who demand the seven brothers give up the girl to them. Similarly, the children do not escape the buffalo herd into the sky until the youngest brother has made four shots with his magic arrows, pulling them higher—but again Cohlene truncates this to three shots. While in the Cheyenne version, Quillworker and her seven brothers become the eight stars of the Big Dipper (there are eight), and the youngest is last on the "handle," Cohlene gratuitously makes "Wihio" become the North Star.

Combined with a history section that denotes the massacre of a peaceful, encamped band of Cheyennes as a "battle," this story is insulting.

DANCING DRUM: A CHEROKEE LEGEND

This is another one Cohlene took from Erdoes and Ortiz, where it is titled "Daughter of the Sun," rewritten from James Mooney, a 19th-Century ethnologist, who compiled *Myths of the Cherokee*. The title is significant because although the story became mythic—an explanation of the permanence of death—it probably also records a real historic drought followed by relentless rains, an ancient environmental disaster. Unlike Cohlene's version, the original has the Sun's daughter's house at the zenith of the sky (not somewhere she goes during the night). It is at the zenith the Sun appears to pause and hang for an endless period of daily heat. In Cohlene's version, the daughter's house is located in The Twilight Zone.

In the original, people can't smile at the Sun, as they do the Moon, because they can't look directly at her without squinting—she is too bright, a natural phenomenon. In Cohlene's story, the people simply "twist their faces when they look up at the sky" for no particular reason.

Cohlene, true to her formula, creates a young hero—

Dancing Drum—to carry out the actions, which in the original are carried out either collectively by the people, or by individuals chosen by them. She gratuitously posits a wise "shaman" (who is made to be a woman). In the original, there is no such figure; the Little Men are the possessors of knowledge. All the people (not a solitary hero) ask them for help.

The sacred number four turns up in the original: four people are transformed into snakes by the Little Men's medicines. The first three fail in various ways that supply origin-explanations for some characteristics of various species of snakes. The rattlesnake, who mistakenly bites the Sun's daughter through impatience, now doesn't bite unless disturbed, and gives warning by rattling. Since this is all meaningless to Cohlene, she simply eliminates it. Dancing Drum becomes the *only* snake, bites the Sun's daughter by mistake, and the Sun's grief turns to endless cold.

The wise shaman pops up here with advice again. In the original, all the people go back to the Little Men, and, advised how to bring the Sun's daughter back from the dead, "the people chose seven men to make the journey."

When the spirit of the dead woman escapes from the basket in which she's being brought back to the land of the living, she turns into a redbird. The original story explains that bird's sacredness: "So we know the redbird is the daughter of the Sun. And if the party had kept the box closed as the Little Men told them to, they could have brought her home safely, and today we would be able to recover our friends from Ghost Country." Cohlene isn't interested in this or any other of the sacred mythic aspects of this story, so she omits them.

Cohlene's ending continues her process of starring a single hero: Dancing Drum, now a sort of rock star, "began playing his own song," which attracts the Sun's attention and cheers her up, providing the happy ending. The original story has all the people trying to cheer the Sun after they've failed to return her daughter to life. A "drummer suddenly changed the song" (which undoubtedly reflects a drumming change that would have occurred in the ceremonies accompanying this myth cycle), which captures the Sun's attention.

Cohlene has here changed an ancient, interesting ceremonial nature myth—which provided explanations of many natural phenomena—into a formula children's story, by eliminating everything that doesn't particularly interest her—or that she does not understand.

CLAMSHELL BOY: A MAKAH LEGEND

It appears that, here, Cohlene has combined several stories put down by Lushootseed elder and scholar Vi

Hilbert, who collected a number of Basket Woman stories in *Haboo, Native American Stories from Puget Sound* (University of Washington, 1985).

These Puget Sound stories have a common theme. Adults do not believe in child-eating cannibal ogres, but tell the stories to young children to enforce self-discipline on the curiosity and heedlessness that can get them in real and fatal trouble if they wander too far. In none of these stories is there an overt defiance of adults by the children. In most of the stories a boy is one of the children, not a mythic figure who emerges magically to help worried adults when the children have been carried off. The character flaw that usually causes the children's capture by the ogre is not disobedience but greed and selfishness.

In Cohlene's version—found in none of the originals— it's the children's overt defiance of elders' cautions that gets them captured by Basket Woman. The children are also lazy, stupid, and subject to her flatteries. They climb into her basket to get a free ride home, and help her "clear my bad name" with the people.

In all the real stories, the children escape together, without the help of adults or supernatural interventions. By refusing to panic, they either push Basket Woman into her own cookfire when she stumbles in her triumphant premeal dance, or trick her by flattery. In Cohlene's construct, Clamshell Boy appears magically in response to tribal grief at the kidnapped children, and affects the rescue through his cunning and strength. The real stories show that greed and selfishness cause trouble—*near*-fatal trouble for the selfish children and *true* fatal trouble for the ogre. Collective values—not individual heroism, natural or supernatural—are emphasized. Since raids to capture children for slaves were a fact of life in the precontact Northwest Coast, the stories teach that by sticking together and not panicking, and exploiting captors' weaknesses, there may be a possibility of escape. Neither the moral nor the practical survival lessons survive in Cohlene's construct; the cultural meanings are gone.

Not surprisingly, the mini-history here makes no mention of the long struggle of the Native peoples of Washington State (including the Makah) for land and fishing rights guaranteed by treaties. It presents the Makah in terms of "long ago," and says that nowadays they exist around this area and celebrate "Makah Days" to remind themselves of a vanished culture. Meanwhile, (down the coast at the Ozette archaeological site), digging brought "a cultural renaissance to Neah Bay" in the form of over 55,000 "artifacts."

The real cultural rebirth grew out of political and legal struggles marked by the Boldt decision on a lawsuit brought by the treaty tribes of western Washington (including the Makah), which determined that Native people retained the rights to fisheries and resource gathering activities, including commercial use of salmon. Decades of fish-ins, arrests, beatings, shootings, and raids on homes, preceded this decision, and followed it, too. No hint of this tumultuous history appears in Cohlene's canned fishy catfood one.

KA-HA-SI AND THE LOON: AN ESKIMO LEGEND

First off, there are no "Eskimo" people; that is a pejorative name meaning "raw meat eaters" applied to the peoples of the Arctic by other tribes. Inuit is the preferred name for those of the central Arctic; Iñupiaq is often the name preferred by those of the Yukon and parts of northern Alaska; Yup'ik is the self-name for those of western coastal Alaska, and Aleut for those of the westward-stretching island chain and mainland peninsula.

As usual, Cohlene cites no source, and I cannot find one for this alleged legend. I think it is concocted mainly from Tlingit-Haida stories, where there is a heroic figure often called Blackskin, whose deeds fit parts of Cohlene's construct. Of course, these people don't live in snow houses, and seals, walruses and kayak hunting—trappings of Cohlene's construct—are no parts of their culture. I think she probably reasoned like this: "Alaska=cold=Arctic, therefore Alaska Natives=Eskimos" and laid the igloos, parkas, and such onto Alaska Tlingit-Haida Blackskin tales she'd found.

Cohlene's story doesn't fit the cultural givens of any of the Arctic peoples. A boy who slept all the time, awakening only to eat, would have been seen as a drain on scarce resources on the harsh survival environment and his behavior would not have been tolerated. The non-Arctic Haida hero Blackskin on the other hand, does engage in this kind of behavior. He sleeps all day—so soundly no one can wake him when his skin chars from sleeping too near the fire—while he gains strength, not from some mystical loon (Cohlene's version), but by secretly exercising at night, longer and harder than the other young men do. In the much richer, more survival-favorable world of the Northwest Coast, this behavior would be mocked, but tolerated.

After Ka-ha-si has shown his strength by conquering walruses by hand and wrestling a giant challenger brought to his village by another tribe, Cohlene has him push "attacking mountains" back from the seacoast. As an Arctic legend, this is incredible. Lands of the Arctic Circle were under heavy glacial ice, quite recently as geological time goes. They're ground down flat. Cliffy shores are revealed only where lingering glacier is now retreating, rocky areas that do not support human—or much other—life. The Haida hero Blackskin, however, does tear a huge sea lion apart with his bare hands (to avenge an uncle whom the bull had killed) and, though I've found no such Blackskin tale, it would at least make geological sense for a Haida-Tlingit hero to push sea-coast mountains back into place. None of Ka-ha-si's deeds make sense for an Inuit hero; most of them have analogs in Tlingit Blackskin tales.

Cohlene ends her story by having Ka-ha-si, who is now a supernaturally strong character, hold up the Earth, like the Greek Atlas. This notion makes no sense for *any* Native culture. The idea that the Earth needs holding up from beneath is a European concept.

Cohlene's mini-history is even more than usually inaccurate. Although there is a map showing the common culture area of the Arctic Circle encompassing Canada, high Arctic islands and Greenland, her discussion and important dates concern only those in the U.S. area of Alaska. In the brief note about "Eskimos Today," she doesn't mention that in land claims negotiations begun in 1973, the *Canadian* Inuit people have obtained rights over a huge land area called Nunavut. Cohlene ignores the entire history of the Greenlandic people who obtained Danish home rule in 1979. As for Alaska Arctic Natives, there is no mention of the U.S. Atomic Energy Commission's gonzo plan to excavate a deepwater harbor with nuclear weapons, blowing up the Point Hope community. It was their opposition to this that eventually led to all-tribal court actions and the entire Alaska Native Claims settlement. Cohlene's take on all this? "[T]he (U.S.) government has allotted certain lands to them individually and as villages."

There is also no mention of the circumpolar alliance of Native peoples (including Arctic culture Natives from Russia, and the Sami from Finland and Sweden), representing the rights of all of them in the United Nations, and forwarding their environmental concerns, which are acute, as North Sea high-tech resource development moves into full swing. None of this is in Cohlene's "history"—it's Nanook of the North and mush, you huskies! all the way.

TURQUOISE BOY: A NAVAJO LEGEND

While the other five Cohlene constructs are based on what are often called "little tales"—instruction for children, entertainment stories and a couple created by chopping and mashing a number of such stories, this one is a distortion of a major sacred myth and associated song cycle—the Blessingway—part of the most widely revered of the great Diné sings, still alive and practiced among the Diné people today. That this is wrenched and trivialized into a little story for children is itself a new low in demonstration of cultural appropriation and ignorance.

Turquoise Boy is one of the twin sons of Changing Woman, a principal Diné creator-deity. Her sons have many names and functions—Turquoise Boy is also Enemy Slayer, Monster Slayer, and other names.

Everything is distorted in this story. Cohlene has Turquoise Boy bring horses of four colors "to make life easier for the people." Actually, horses in the mythic cycle here symbolize because of their beauty (especially when running), the life forces, primarily water: rain and the rare springs of the desert, but also plants:

> Sprouting plants being their ears, with their voices for me they are calling. Great stars, dark, being their eyes, with their voices for me they are calling. Waters of all kinds being their faces, with their voices for me they are calling. Great shell being their lips, with their voices for me they are calling.

These mythic horses are described at great length in this part of the song. Most of their description is of rain, storm, lightning, clouds, but also of the life these bring to the desert and the people, and the beauty of such storms with their life-giving water is emphasized. Horses galloping like thunder, manes and tails swirling like clouds or hanging down like falling rain, legs flashing like lightning—these are a metaphor for the sacred beauty of life that is sung of in the Blessingway, which invokes psychic and spiritual renewal, health, safety, and above all, balance among personal and natural forces, described as walking in beauty.

Important ceremonies of a living religion are not the stuff of a children's story about a teenager's going out and about on a maturity quest. Cohlene hasn't a clue as to what it's all about. It's kind of questionable if any non-Diné does. Luci Tapahonso, a very talented Diné poet, who is thoroughly at home in her own language and culture and writes beautifully in English as well, doesn't think the Blessingway can or should be translated, even by serious poet-scholars. While Cohlene's other books in this series are merely generally and culturally inaccurate, this one is a desecration.

Almost needless to say, Cohlene's mini-history is also poor. She does mention that American officer Kit Carson led a death march to "concentration camps," but not the slaughters and burnings that preceded this. And since there was only *one* concentration camp, Bosque Redondo, why not name it?

Then there's the ubiquitous "how they live today" pablum:

> Today many Navajo live in the traditional way, tending their flocks and practicing the old ways. Others have jobs in tourism, oil or other more modern careers.

Cohlene fails to mention some modern aspects of the Diné situation: not only do Peabody Coal and other corporate giants desecrate Diné land and foul the clear desert air, but they have played Diné and Hopi against each other, forcing hundreds of Diné families off their ancestral land. A short-lived uranium mining industry has left radioactive wastes in huge piles, and has already caused deaths in the Monument Valley area. Seepage from radioactive waste material into the water table and river threaten land and people for future millennia. So some Diné have the "more modern career" of working with geiger counters and environmental experts, trying to create temporary solutions to these mountain-sized problems left by white military and industry on their land. As usual, Cohlene totally ignores actual pertinent history—real, current Native struggles with white-caused problems.

Summing up: These are terrible books, some more than others; stories taken without credit and then distorted, accompanied by mini-histories that are not only inaccurate but racist as well. It is unfortunate that they seem to attract school buyers, some of whom think that attached mini-histories provide a nice cultural-historical context. As for the illustrations, Reasoner's style neither varies to suit the story nor the culture each was taken from. When I reluctantly gave these books the "kid test," I was asked, "Why are their eyes always tight shut?" Maybe because the characters couldn't stand to see what they were being put through.—*Paula Giese*

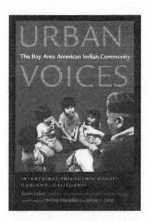

Community History Project: Sharon Mitchell Bennett (Pomo), Charlene Betsille (Yurok), Joyce Keoke (Lakota), Geraldine Martinez Lira (Lakota), Susan Lobo, Marilyn LaPlante St. Germaine (Blackfoot), eds., Urban Voices: The Bay Area Indian Community. University of Arizona (2003). 136 pages, b/w photos and illustrations; grades 7-up

During the 1950s the federal government, in an attempt to assimilate Indian families, implemented a policy of relocating Indian people to major urban areas. From the 1950s to the 1970s, thousands of Indian families moved from their home reservations to twelve major cities, where they were promised educational and vocational training. This separation from tribe and land—the very ties that gave them their identity and spiritual grounding—resulted in culture shock, loss of extended family support systems, and poverty for many Indian families. While a large number of Indian people, homesick and lonely, returned to their reservations, many stayed in the cities, creating intertribal communities and "friendship centers" to help each other survive in an alien place. One of the first such organizations in the country, the Intertribal Friendship House in Oakland, remains a gathering place for Indian people who are new to the city, as well as for "urban Indians" whose parents and grandparents came here half a century ago.

As the politics of the San Francisco Bay Area impacted the growing Indian community, events such as the occupation of Alcatraz Island became a focal point for Indian activism all over the country. It is the stories of this activism, along with the stories of the many other ways that Indian people came together in a new kind of extended family, that *Urban Voices* documents.

Lovingly put together by the Editorial Committee of the Community History Project, *Urban Voices* is more than a history or anthology. Rather, it is a "family album" of photos, told stories and reminiscences, drawings, poems, letters, essays, posters, newspaper clippings and songs. Both the history project and the book it birthed are unique in their breadth and scope.

From Darryl Babe Wilson's telling of the Song that created the galaxies and the land and the people who "left footprints in the sand…(and) sang and danced to all of the powers of the universe," to poems by the children of Hintil Kuu Ca School, to a letter from Hooty Croy on Death Row at San Quentin State Prison, to "Relocation: The Promise and the Lie" by Ray Moisa, to the bold in-your-face poetry of Esther G. Belin, to Rosalie McKay-Want's story of her arrival on Alcatraz Island during the occupation, to Sarah Poncho's recipe for frybread, to reminiscences by Millie Ketcheshawno and Bill Wahpepah, the voices here are many and varied. *Urban Voices* is a living thing, an honoring for everyone who dropped in to IFH for Wednesday night dinner and never left.—*Beverly Slapin*

Cossi, Olga, Fire Mate, illustrated by Paulette Livers Lambert. Roberts Rinehart/Council for Indian Education Series (1995). 87 pages, line drawings; grades 4-6; Pomo

A young girl finds a Saint Bernard puppy who has been abandoned in the forest by dognappers. She and the dog form a special relationship. The two become inseparable until the true owners of the dog locate him by chance and try to reclaim him. Girl meets dog. Girl bonds with dog. Girl almost loses dog. Girl gets dog back.

The author should have stopped here. For young readers, there's always room for one more coming-of-age-with-dog story. But the author makes her protagonist Pomo, and that was a bad idea.

Cossi tells the story as a first person narrative:

> I am a Pomo girl whose tribal name is Walakea. My given name is Yvonne, but when I am alone I often think of myself as Walakea.

What does she mean by "tribal name"? Surely, her "given" name would be Walakea. Who named her Yvonne?

Some "facts":

> I live with my family on an Indian reservation not far from the town where my brothers and sisters and I go to school. At one time all the land as far as we could see was ours. Now, we must stay within the boundaries of the rancheria set aside by the government as a reservation for our tribe.

This is just not true. No Pomo people (in fact, no Indian people at all) "must stay within the boundaries" of any-where. Many people live on reservations, many live off reservations.

Then there is the "Song of Fire." According to Walakea/Yvonne, there's a song that is part of her "tribal memory." It goes like this:

> I am the Great One, strong and all-powerful. I am the fire that glows in the hearthstone. I am the flame that lights up the heaven.

According to Yvonne/Walakea's grandmother, this means that

> In the center of your being there is a hearthstone. It is up to you to kindle the fire whose glow will warm the hearthstone and whose flame will light up the heaven.... Your heart is your hearthstone. Your mind is the heaven. The fire is your spirit. Someday it will burst into flame.

But Kathleen Smith, a tribal scholar who is Bodega Miwok and Dry Creek Pomo, told me,

> There is a part of firemaking called a hearth, made out of buckeye wood. Traditionally, we used a straight stick of willow and rubbed it very fast in the hands, a certain distance from the hearth, to create a coal. Then we would put tinder on it and blow on it softly. So there's a long, complex song about how this happens. The song acknowledges fire, which is an entity of itself. It has the ability to give warmth, but it also has the power to destroy, so it is something to be very careful and respectful

of. It's a very awesome power. The part about "I am the flame that lights up the heaven" and "the fire is at the center of our being" is not the way we think. What is important to tribal people is that we know our place in the world. We are part of the world. The world is not part of us.

That Walakea/Yvonne goes around looking for her "fire mate...the one who would complete the sacred circle of (her) being" has nothing to do with anything. When she finds the dog, she immediately realizes that he is her "fire mate." The pseudo-spiritual term "fire mate" is used thirty-two times in seventy-three pages, and "sacred circle of my being," ten times. This book is a parody. *Nobody* talks like this.

> When I was called Yvonne, I was just a girl living with her family on a reservation. But when I was called Walakea, I saw myself as an Indian princess, part of the spirit world that included the forest and all the creatures that lived there.

Indian princess?

In the fullness of time, there is a dog show. Yvonne/Walakea decides to attend with Zoll (the dog). She wants her people to be proud of her.

> When the day came...my family did everything to make sure I was a credit to myself and to our Pomo tribe. Mother made me a beaded shirt to wear. She tied my hair in braids and gave me a headband she had woven and decorated with Indian designs.... Margaret had loaned me her turquoise bracelet and Leona gave me a lucky charm to add to it.

What the author describes here is a combination of Northern Plains, Southwestern and K-Mart dress. Any modern child attending a dog show would probably be wearing jeans and a t-shirt.

Fire Mate is the creation of a non-Native writer who knows nothing about Native people and could care less. As Kathleen Smith says, "It's a lot of nonsense, a mishmash of romantic ideas; it turns Indians into storybook creations rather than seeing us as we really are. This is a real disservice to Indian people, and to children who think they are reading about us."—*Beverly Slapin*

(Thank-you to Kathleen Smith.)

Craven, Margaret, *I Heard the Owl Call My Name*. Doubleday (1973). 159 pages; grades 7-up; Kwakwaka'wakw (Kwakiutl)

It is possible for an author to put down, in truth and beauty, the lives of a people not her own. Such authors are few and far between. Margaret Craven is one of them.

Mark Brian is a young vicar, dying but not knowing it, assigned to minister to the bishop's "hardest parish," the Kwakiutl village of Quee ("inside place"), which the whites call Kingcome. He encounters a place of incomparable beauty and a people of ancient tradition and ceremony, of prefabricated houses and an alienated younger generation. In this place, and from these people, he learns of living and dying, of compassion and commitment.

Writing in the third person, Craven clearly and with great good humor sympathizes with the villagers. She describes how they take revenge on the intruders by serving them mashed turnips, and how they "cautiously confabulate" about the newcomer's "looks, his manners, even his clean fingernails." "He will be no good at hunting and fishing," Jim tells Chief Eddy.

> He knows little of boats. All the time he says we. "Shall we have dinner now? Shall we tie up here?" Pretty soon he will say, "Shall we build a new vicarage?" He will say we and he will mean us.

Craven has the handful of white characters doing and saying things that will have (at least) Indian readers chuckling. Such as the British anthropologist who insists on calling the people "Quackadoodles." "For the past century in England," she argues, "this band has been known as the Quackadoodles and as the Quackadoodles, it will be known forever." And there is the teacher:

> This was the teacher's second year in the village. He did not like the Indians and they did not like him.... The teacher had come to the village solely for the isolation pay which would permit him a year in Greece studying the civilization he adored.

Craven's writing is spare, simple, and beautiful, with understanding and compassion. Here, the swimmer, having laid her eggs, meets her end:

> They moved again and saw the end of the swimmer. They watched her last valiant fight for life, her struggle to right herself when the gentle stream turned her, and they watched the water force open her gills and draw her slowly downstream, tail first, as she had started to the sea as a fingerling.

After Mark has died, and the villagers have laid him to rest, she writes:

> Past the village flowed the river, like time, like life itself, waiting for the swimmer to come again on his way to the climax of his adventurous life, and to the end for which he had been made. Wa Laum. That is all.

I Heard the Owl Call My Name is a book of great beauty that can teach much, without polemic, for those who will listen.—*Beverly Slapin*

Creech, Sharon, *Walk Two Moons.* **HarperCollins (1994). 280 pages; grades 5-up; Seneca**

This is a poignant story revolving around two friends—Phoebe Winterbottom and Salamanca Tree Hiddle—whose mothers have disappeared, and the journey Salamanca makes with her grandparents to find her mother. The protagonists, Sal and Phoebe, are well developed as very bright thirteen-year-olds with overactive imaginations. Sal's goofy grandparents, too, are well drawn, as are some of the minor characters—such as Mrs. Cadaver, whom Sal and Phoebe suspect is an axe murderer; and Mr. Birkway, the hyperactively joyful English teacher with no sense of privacy.

This beautifully written and compelling story is deeply flawed by the "Indian" material that is thrown together with no cultural or historical context and really has nothing to do with anything actually Native. Neither does Salamanca, although frequently referring to her "Indian blood," and constantly repeating the overdone maxim about "walking two moons in another man's moccasins." (In chapter 44, the phrase is actually used nine times in four pages!) Most of what she says—such as that she was given her name because her parents didn't realize that the name of the "Indian tribe to which my great-great-grandmother belonged" was actually "Seneca"—is ridiculous.

When Sal and her grandma discuss whether to use the term "Native American" or "Indian," she recalls her mother saying that "Indian sounds much more brave and elegant" and that the "Indian-ness" in their background made them "appreciate the gifts of nature" and makes them "closer to the earth." Does the author really think that there is some kind of a genetic Indian-earth-nature connection?

There are episodes involving cross-cultural "legends," casual smoking and sharing of "peace pipes," someone referring to himself as an "American Indian person" (as compared to an American Indian chair?), and a dance described this way:

The Indians had formed two circles, one inside the other, and were hopping up and down. The men danced in the outer circle and wore feather headdresses and short leather aprons. On their feet were moccasins, and I thought again about Phoebe's message: *Don't judge a man until you've walked two moons in his moccasins.* Inside the circle of men, the women in long dresses and ropes of beads had joined arms and were dancing around one older woman who was wearing a regular cotton dress. On her head was an enormous headdress, which had slipped down over her forehead. I looked closer. The woman in the center was hopping up and down. On her feet were flat, white shoes. In the space between drum beats, I heard her say, "Huzza, huzza."

One wonders why the author did this; perhaps she wanted an "Indian" title and needed to make some kind of a context for it. Although Creech's characterizations are excellent, the way she manipulates the characters—and the child reader—is inexcusable. Not recommended. —*Beverly Slapin*

Crow, Allan (Ojibwe), *The Crying Christmas Tree*, illustrated by David Beyer (Cree/Métis). Pemmican (1989). Unpaginated, color illustrations; grades 1-2; Ojibwe

In this story, Allan Crow transmits an important instructional worldview characteristic of American Indians—allowing individuals to find their own ways of doing what is appropriate. Here, grandmother ventures into the woods with an axe to choose the family Christmas tree and returns with a tree her grandsons laugh at. She keeps her hurt feelings and disappointment to herself and goes with grandfather into town, returning to celebrate the holiday with the entire family. Much to her surprise, her grandsons have realized the love their grandmother must have for them to have worked as hard as she did to bring home a tree—scrawny as it was—by herself. Here is a lesson learned without a reminder by any adults, a wonderful holiday story everyone will enjoy and appreciate.—*Pam Martell*

Crowl, Christine, illustrated by the author. Tipi Press/St. Joseph's Indian School (1990). 19 pages, color illustrations; grades 2-4; Lakota:
The Hunter and the Woodpecker
White Buffalo Woman: A Storybook Based on Indian Legend

On the title pages, both of these are described as parts of "The American Heritage Series," whatever that may mean. St. Joseph's is, as its name suggests, a Catholic-run school, and their press has published some good books, some written and illustrated by Lakota people.

These are both very widely known stories. White Buffalo Calf Woman's story shouldn't be diminished to the status of a "legend"; it's an account of how the sacred Pipe came to the Lakota people. Moreover, this particular storybook very clearly cribbed from John Fire Lame Deer's 1967 telling, published in Erdoes and Ortiz's *American Indian Myths and Legends*. Where words have been changed, it's a disimprovement. Lame Deer says, for instance, "When a man takes a wife, they both hold the pipe at the same time and red trade cloth is wound around their hands, thus tying them together for life." Crowl's rewrite: "When a man and woman are joined in marriage, they will hold the pipe at the same time. Their hands will be wrapped together, thus binding them for life."

Crowl omits many things, such as Standing Hollow Horn saying,

> "Sister, we are glad. We have had no meat for some time. All we can give you is water." They dipped some wacanga, sweet grass, into a skin bag of water and gave it to her, and to this day the people dip sweet grass or an eagle wing in water and sprinkle it on a person to be purified.

There are many other omissions of this type. This results in clear, specific, and beautiful instructions about all the most important things, being reduced to a few generalizations that are not even very well expressed.

Crowl has made it more "storylike" by giving the two warriors specific names and some chit-chat. And they're both nice guys, one of whom gets zapped because he accidentally touches the holy Woman. In fact he got zapped because he had it in mind to rape the unprotected woman found alone on the prairie. This relates to the instruction of "respect for women" that was brought to the warriors.

I'm not Lakota, but I found this quite a distressing little publication. Whatever the intentions of those who put it together were, the end result is an awkward, ugly travesty. If any remain, they should be withdrawn from sale and respectfully be destroyed under the supervision of a Pipe keeper.

The other book, *Woodpecker*, is also cribbed from a story, but at least not a central, most important, sacred one. It's a toss-up whether it was taken from Lame Deer (it's the lead story in *The Sound of Flutes*) or Henry Crow Dog's in *American Indian Myths and Legends*, where it's titled "The Legend of the Flute." This too is a traditional story of which there are more versions than one. But it's been cleaned up, romanticized, turned from an adult story into a kid story, with pretentious language.

She stood there blushing, her eyes full of love. "Young man," she said swooning. "I am yours forever. Send your gifts to my father, no matter how small. You and I shall marry and make music together!"

I just can't understand why anyone would publish these things.—*Paula Giese*

Culleton, Beatrice (Ojibwe/Métis), *April Raintree*. Peguis (1984). 185 pages; high school-up; Ojibwe/Métis

In the best possible way, *April Raintree* can be hard to read because it comes from a hard place and reflects it, because the characters and their experiences live on its pages, and because it asks questions without flinching or holding back.

The story is one of two sisters, April and Cheryl Raintree, who fight the images, horrors and expectations imposed on them while trying to resolve their feelings about their heritage and each other. The girls are taken from their parents as young children and reared in foster homes—doing all they can to maintain the ties between them, especially after their parents' visits stop.

April is able to "pass" for white but Cheryl's Native heritage is more physically apparent. Throughout, their self-images are shaped in part by their coloring and the prejudices of others. To varying degrees both struggle with learned shame. But April begins as the sister ready to leave her heritage behind while Cheryl is more predisposed to fight for Indian people and maintain ties to the community.

April's aspirations lead her to marry into a wealthy white family that will not accept her (or Cheryl), and eventually she divorces her philandering husband. Meanwhile, Cheryl's future as an activist is derailed by her drinking in response to family traumas and the harsh realities of urban life.

The story heightens when April is gang-raped and later, when Cheryl is driven to take her own life. Neither episode is depicted gratuitously or without sensitivity, but both convey the pain and tragedy thoroughly and with unusual insight.

The book ends with the revelation that Cheryl had a son, Henry Lee, who was previously unknown to April. Readers may see in April and Henry a hope for a better future though they will understand the obstacles they face, the odds.

April Raintree is a triumph of contemporary realism—not simplified, not romanticized, not without layers, not lacking in rounded individuals. The writing is com-

pelling, pulling in readers and refusing to let them go. It offers no false comfort but embraces moments of joy and awakening.—*Cynthia L. Smith*

Curry, Jane Louise, *Back in the Beforetime: Tales of the California Indians*, illustrated by James Watts. Macmillan (1987). 134 pages, b/w illustrations; grades 3-up

"In reading through the many tales and fragments of tales recorded during the past century," Curry states in her author's note,

> I chose first those legends which could be woven together to tell the larger tale of Creation from the making of the world to man's rise to lordship over the animals, and then a selection of comic or trickster folktales which seemed to fit happily within that framework. In several instances, where a story was incomplete or lacking in detail which could be found in a second version from the same or another tribe, I have told a composite tale.

In other words, the title notwithstanding, these twenty-two stories are not "tales of the California Indians," but rather bits and pieces of different stories from different peoples lumped together. Worse, they are then changed to "fit happily" into the Christian framework of "man's rise to lordship over the animals."

This is a perfect example of what we mean when we call a thing "fakelore." It is just one more thing to be taken from us, mashed to fit into someone else's worldview, and packaged and marketed as "multicultural" for mass consumption by another people's children.

Our stories belong to the peoples and places in whom and where they originated, with people who understand their value and sacredness, with people who tell them in the roundhouse and keep them alive.—*Barbara Potter*

Curry, Jane Louise, *Turtle Island: Tales of the Algonquian Nations*, illustrated by James Watts. McElderry (1999). 146 pages, b/w illustrations; grades 3-5

This title has the superficial markings of an attempt to take Native sensibilities into account: the book uses "nations" instead of "tribes," indicating an awareness of the diversity of tribal relationships; it places "retold" in front of the author's name, indicating that she is aware that the stories did not originate with her; and each story is given a token tribal source. Unfortunately, this book also serves to illustrate one of the classic mistakes made when non-Indians attempt to tell Indian stories: the original is downgraded, from a story told by adults to adults—and whichever children happened to be around—about serious topics related to tribal relationships with people, the land, and spirituality (religion, shame, sexual exploits and mistakes, power, death, jealousy, greed) into entertaining "legends" or "tales" aimed at and marketed for children.

The sad result is *not* a "Native American story," but what is always called a "legend" or "tale" or "myth"—a Native story with all the guts taken out. We don't cut out the profound spirituality, disturbing violence or sex from the Five Books of Moses and call them "legends." We don't call other religious tracts "myths," if we are being respectful of the people to whom that religion is home. (And we certainly don't treat those materials as if they are suitable only for children: the full version of those stories is almost always available, while the full versions of Native stories are usually not.)

For example, the illustrations in this book are for the most part caricatures, nearly cartoons, of Indian people, while the language is simplistic and ruthlessly removes the signatures of some infamous Native characters. I almost didn't recognize Nanabush, he was so changed—the trickster-hero whose adventures are more familiar to me through Basil Johnston's *The Manitous: The Spiritual World of the Ojibway* and William Warren's *History of the Ojibway Nation*. I know Nanabush as a being full of ambiguity, the epitome of power: both good and bad, or (in less definitive terms) a being whose powers cross all boundaries, both human and spirit, useful and destructive, and whose use of sexual innuendo and crude jokes carry potent messages about human nature and psychology. Yet the stories in *Turtle Island* have so obviously been made "appropriate" for children that I found them infuriating to read.

Why? Why care if stories are tamed down for non-Native children's consumption? Isn't it giving those children a good dose of diversity, an exposure to Indians, a glimpse of another culture? And doesn't it make young Native children feel less invisible, more a part of the literary world? Well, no. What books like these do is perpetuate the same kinds of stereotypes about Indians that we have been battling since first contact: Indians are children. Indians are simple. Indians cannot function as mature human beings without intervention from a "great (white) father" source. Indians live according to ancient legends and stories that have no relationship to real life. Indians do not have a "real" religion. And so on.

It's a pretty book, and as such, I fear does far more harm than good.—*Deborah A. Miranda*

Cuthand, Beth (Cree), *The Little Duck • Sikihpsis*, illustrated by Mary Longman (Salteaux), translated by Stan Cuthand (Cree). Theytus (2003). Unpaginated, color illustrations; preschool-grade 3; Cree

There's this little mud duck—plain even by duck standards, but especially plain when he compares himself to the humans. Oh, how he admires the Cree whose camp is near the muddy swamp he calls home: "The camp was full of beautiful women and handsome men and playful, happy children, not to mention the fine horses and smart dogs." With his short legs, his "bumpy humpy beak" and plain black feathers, the little duck wishes he could be just like the Cree.

As he watches the humans prepare for a big dance, the little duck gets an idea—if he goes to the dance, maybe they will ask him to live with them. So he makes himself a dance outfit—using locally obtained (swamp) materials—and off he goes to the dance. But communication with humans is difficult, even when they speak Cree, Salteaux and Assiniboine—and try sign language—and the little duck just doesn't understand them. His attempt at dancing doesn't work out either, what with his short legs and all. As he pulls off his outfit and prepares for a life of utter loneliness, he hears "the sounds of many mud ducks calling, glorious wonderful mud duck words that he could understand!" And the little duck knows where he belongs, in his own body, in his own community, with his own duck people.

The pictures—rich watercolors in jeweled tones of turquoises, purples, blues, golden-yellows, and oranges—appear to glow, and the little duck's expressions, ranging from sadness to wistfulness to joy, are very real. The story is in Cree and English, and has a version in the Cree syllabary at the end.

This extraordinary and deep little story, with no stated "moral," will resonate with little kids. The reading moves me to tears, every time.—*Beverly Slapin*

Dadey, Debbie, *Cherokee Sister*. Delacorte (2000). 119 pages; grades 3-6; Cherokee

From the ersatz Indian designs on the cover to the cardboard characters, formulaic plot and implausible situations, this ridiculous marriage of *The Prince and the Pauper* with *Hansel and Gretel* ought never to have seen the light of day.

Allie McAllister, the white twelve-year-old protagonist, resembles more a whiny, self-absorbed contemporary suburban kid than a settler child in 1838. She complains about her chores. She complains about the boring sermons. She complains about not having enough time to spend with her friend. Even on the death march that history will name the Trail of Tears, she—complains—"I would have done a hundred chores without even being asked if I could just be safe at home again."

How does a whiny white girl come to get captured and forced on a death march meant for Cherokees? Because she *happens* to have a tan from being in the sun too much and *happens* to be wearing her Cherokee friend's buckskin dress and *happens* to have her dark hair braided *just before the raid*. But never fear—even though some 4,000 people died on the *real* Trail of Tears, Allie manages to get herself and her friend rescued by dropping the beads from her friend's dress along the trail.

Dadey's "fascinating" Cherokee heritage notwithstanding, she gets a lot of things wrong, including some of the Cherokee words she clumsily tosses in along with some Cherokee historical and cultural tidbits. "Tsi-lu-gi" does not mean "hello," for instance, it means "I have arrived." The word for "hello" is "'Siyo." And "bathing every morning" is not the same as "going to the water," which is a morning prayer, a thanksgiving, an acknowledgment that water is life.

The writing is as bad as the plot is preposterous. Throughout, in places where Dadey could have referred to people as "people," she calls them "Cherokee" or "Indian." Even the Cherokee characters call themselves "Cherokee," which they would not have done at that time. They would have referred to themselves as Tsalagi or Aniyunwiya, "Real People." And the dialogue: When Allie isn't complaining or obsessing about being white and not fitting in, she's telling the thugs who captured her that they're not being fair.

But even if it had been well written, this story is fatally flawed by Dadey's misinterpretation of what the Trail of Tears was about. It was not just a casual rounding up of people with dark skin and braids—it was a purposeful political dispossession of landed, acculturated, influential communities of people who were in the way of white expansion.

If Dadey is so "fascinated" by her "Cherokee heritage," why did she need to use a white protagonist to validate an Indian experience? *Cherokee Sister* is tortuously bland and stupefyingly boring with nothing good to say about it at all.—*Beverly Slapin*

Dalgliesh, Alice, *The Courage of Sarah Noble*, illustrated by Leonard Weisgard. Macmillan (1954, 1991). 55 pages, b/w line drawings; grades 2-3

Sarah Noble is eight years old in 1707, and living in Westfield, Massachusetts. Her father is going to the "wilderness," to put up the first house in what will be New Milford, Connecticut, and Sarah is going with him, to cook. "Keep up your courage," her mother says, "Keep up your courage, Sarah Noble." And she finds much to be courageous about—the strange sound that is the call of an owl, a fox calling to his mate, the howl of a wolf—John Noble has his musket ready for that one— and most of all, Indians.

> "The Indians will eat you," Lemuel said and smacked his lips loudly. "They will chop off your head," little Robert added, with a wide innocent smile... "They will skin you alive..." That was Lemuel.

Sarah is greatly afraid, even though her father has told her that these are "good Indians." When they reach their destination, Sarah and her father set up housekeeping in a cave, until the house can be built.

Chapter five is entitled "Indians!" And here they do arrive—a bunch of little kids.

> Sarah kept still as a rabbit in danger. The children came in, creeping nearer, creeping nearer, like small brown field mice...

Sarah is shocked to see that they are naked, "unless you could call that one small piece of cloth 'clothing.'" However, they turn out to be friendly, so all goes pretty well until it is time for John Noble to go back for the rest of his family. He tells Sarah that she is going to stay with "Tall John," father of two of the children she especially likes. "You have been brave," John Noble says, "and now you will have to be braver." "*You mean I am to live with the Indians?*" (Italics in the text.) Once she gets over that, Sarah starts to worry about the "Indians from the North," of whom even "Tall John" is afraid. But none of Sarah's fears are realized, and her family arrives safely.

The author tells us that "This is a true story, though I have had to imagine many of the details," and that might be part of the problem. It seems pretty unlikely that a child living anywhere in what would become New England in 1707—except maybe Boston—would be unfamiliar with owls, foxes, even wolves. And contrary to the mythology, there is no documented case of any human ever having been attacked by a wolf in North America. At this time, well away from any white settlements, that "one small piece of cloth" the little kids are wearing would have been hide—if it was anything at all. At one point, John Noble says, speaking about a piece of land, "The Indians have cleared it for a hunting ground." Now, I am trying to imagine how this would work. Did they just go out there and stand, and wait for something to go through, or what?

Such things simply indicate that the author saw no need to look into anything beyond what she already "knew" of the time period. On the other hand, the air of menace throughout the book is nearly tangible. The forest is always "The Wilderness." The trees are "angry dark trees" that

> seemed to stand in their path...trees dark and fearful, trees crowding against each other, trees on and on, more trees and more trees. Behind the trees there were men moving...were they Indians?

And it is in the Native people that the heart of the menace and strangeness lies. Although in fact *nothing* ever endangers this child, neither the animals nor the people, and there is *never* any need for all this courage, the author carries it to the very end. Having—finally—gotten it, that "these Indians are our friends," Sarah tells her doll, "...and they will tell us if the Indians from the north are coming...Keep up your courage, Arabella, keep up your courage." Although "Tall John" has become a friend, and Sarah has played many time with his children, when it comes time for her to stay with them, there is fear. John Noble worries, "Am I doing right to leave her?" Sarah

> was not saying anything, but her mind...was making pictures, trees...trees...dark trees...narrow paths through the forest...wolves...bears. Suppose her father never came back and she had to live with the Indians all her life?

As for the people themselves, we never see how *they* live. Although there are many children, there are no adults beyond "Tall John" and his wife. Where are the families, the band, the encampment, or village? The people have no Nation, they are just "the Indians." From this book, one would never know that they had a way of life, societal structure, and economy. In the illustrations, there are two distant views of one dwelling only, the "Indian house," but we never see inside. Much is made of Native names: "There is a tall Indian who...will help me. I cannot say his name, so I will call him Tall John." Sarah "could not say the long, long names of the children, so she called the boy Small John and the girl Mary." And on her first night in their home, she is faced with a dilemma: "Now she really had to stop and think. Was it right to pray for Indians? Did the Lord take care of Indians?"

Dalgliesh called her book a "story of faith and courage and friendship." Possibly that was her intent. Friendship does not call people out of their names just because they are unfamiliar. Friendship does not doubt the safety of a child with people who have shown you nothing but kindness. Friendship does not wonder if people are human enough to pray for. If words and pictures show people only as creatures of the wild, that is how children will think of them, no matter how much you speak of friendship. If there is something fearful about them, even after months of relationship, if you say their names are impossible, and slap other names on them—any old ones will do—and nobody objects, if you show nothing of their lives, then they have no identity that children can understand, no reality as human beings.

The subtext of *The Courage of Sarah Noble* is the same story that we have heard for 500 years. Indians were/ are primitive—wild. When not outright savage, Native peoples still have more in common with the creatures of the Earth and the birds of the air, than with the culturally and technologically superior Europeans. They aren't "civilized." And therefore no obstacle. This message is the one underlying everything children have been taught about indigenous peoples, not just in the Americas, but around the world, and it comes through in this book—loud and clear.

In fact, as a little research will quite clearly substantiate, we were—and are—hundreds of separate Nations—all with certain things in common, such as belief in the Creator, relationship with all things, and the sanctity of Earth and all life—but also, all varying greatly from one to another, in appearance and lifeways. Nothing was "wilderness." This was—and is—our home, and we belong to it deeply, in a way few non-Native people seem to understand. Some of us had "civilizations" as complex, if not more so, as anything the old world ever produced. (We also considered personal hygiene to be pretty important—something that records of the time indicate the colonists had yet to discover.) But it is always a mistake to judge any people solely on aspects of material culture. Native understanding of the web of life was sophisticated, with a spiritual connection to all creation that has yet to be equaled by any non-indigenous people, something that all must now learn—or else perish.

I am picturing the use of this book in a classroom situation, and I know what will happen, because I have been there. The white kids—at least those who are well-to-do—will be reinforced in their sense of entitlement and superiority to everybody else in the world. The poor kids will discover that there is someone they can look down on, too. They will all make fun of the Indian kids (not in front of the teacher, maybe, although I have seen that, too). The Native kids will be shamed— one more time.

The usual defense for a book of this nature is that we must understand it as a product of its time. This is true. *The Courage of Sarah Noble* was published in 1954, and it is very much a product of its time—a time that has come and gone. In a world where our divisiveness threatens the very existence of *all* human beings, of all life, there is no room, and no time, for such a story. I would give a child no book, rather than this nasty little thing—and I'm damn sure I don't want *my* kids reading it.—*Doris Seale*

Davis, Kenneth C., *Don't Know Much About Sitting Bull*, illustrations by Sergio Martinez. HarperCollins (2003). 128 pages, b/w photos, b/w illustrations; grades 3-5; Lakota.

In Davis' trademark question-and-answer format designed for report-driven third- to fifth-graders, this book is appropriately titled—he *doesn't* know much about Sitting Bull. There has been a lot written about this great visionary, philosopher and war leader, and some of it is pretty good. But from a look at Davis' sources—including Jewel H. Grutman and Gay Matthaei's *The Ledgerbook of Thomas Blue Eagle*, Albert Marrin's *Sitting Bull and His World*, and Stanley Vestal's *Sitting Bull, Champion of the Sioux*[1]—it can be readily inferred that he has not done his homework.

Davis' analogies and comparisons to contemporary culture fall flat. For instance:

> All people "count coups" (sic) in some way. Modern kids and adults can count coups (sic) with good grades, new toys, designer clothes, sports trophies, or money. We all want to succeed at something that shows off our skills and makes us look good. That's what the Lakota were doing.

No it wasn't. Counting coup was a demonstration of an individual's bravery. This has nothing to do with "good grades, new toys" or shopping malls. And, uh, Gatlings were *not* "very old-fashioned machine guns" in 1876, they are very old-fashioned machine guns *now*.

Frivolous questions and ridiculous answers belie Davis' pretended objectivity: "Did the Lakota really scalp people?" ("Yes," he answers, "although sometimes they chopped them up instead.") "Why did the Plains Indians like to fight? Why didn't they want peace?" ("It's hard for us to understand a warrior culture," he explains. "But the Lakota liked war.")

The question, "Why did warriors kill babies?"—and its answer—is reworded from of *Sitting Bull and His World*[2], which is reworded from *Sitting Bull, Champion of the Sioux*[3]:

> Since war was about honor and courage, you might think that Plains Indians would kill only warriors. In real life, it didn't work out that way. Some warriors would do anything to hurt and insult their enemies, so they would kill or kidnap the people their enemies were trying to protect—their families.

There is another section, also cribbed from Vestal's and Marrin's titles, in which Davis explains how "a dead enemy (or pieces of the enemy)" was dragged through a village in order to help a Lakota child overcome his fear of dead bodies. And another, from the same sources, describes how Sitting Bull and a band of warriors massacred an Assiniboin family. This. Never. Happened. It is documented otherwise.

Land theft is justified, again in Davis' "objective" way. "Different beliefs led to serious problems" and most people who went west "didn't mean to do anything wrong," Davis explains, but "[n]o one had ever seen a land as big and empty and free as the American West." Settling this "empty land," though, was not without risk. In 1862, for instance, "Indian war parties spread out for a hundred miles in all directions, killing and chopping up settlers, including teachers, missionaries, ministers, and children."

Don't Know Much About Sitting Bull has been praised as "a joy for students or history buffs," and "great for supplementary reading for students." Rather, it's a great piece of fiction—for Manifest Destiny buffs. —*Beverly Slapin*

NOTES

1 The first two of these titles are reviewed in this book.

2 Dutton, 2000.

3 University of Oklahoma, 1957.

Davis, Russell G., and Brent K. Ashabranner, *The Choctaw Code.* **Shoe String (1961, 1994). 153 pages; grades 5-up**

For a time in the late 1800s, after removal to Oklahoma, the Choctaw Nation adopted capital punishment to deal with rampant street crime, a result of the devastation caused by land theft and alcohol. After having been sentenced to death, a tribal citizen was allowed a time of freedom to take care of business and say his goodbyes, after which he was expected to—and did—report for execution. Sometimes, a condemned person would request to be executed by a friend, a wish that was granted.

In *The Choctaw Code*, the authors turn this piece of history that they clearly do not understand into a coming-of-age soap opera. The protagonist, a white teenager named Tom Baxter, whose family has just moved west to Indian Territory, is befriended by Jim Moshulatubbee, a Choctaw who has been sentenced to death for an accidental killing. With a few weeks left before the scheduled execution, Tom frantically tries to save Jim's life, "[b]ut at each dead end he finds Jim Moshulatubbee himself, determined to keep his word and uphold the honor of his people by accepting the sentence of the Choctaw code."

Jim Moshulatubbee is one of the "good Indians" who don't want to sell their land. He is at odds with a slimy bunch of "bad Indians" who are concerned only with their own self-interest. Jim is good-looking and educated. He is fluent in Choctaw and English. He owns books. He is neat and clean. His cabin is neat and clean. The clearing around his cabin is neat and clean. He is a good cook and a good hunter. He is honest and honorable and polite to white people.

It is clear that the authors have invented Jim to teach Tom about hunting, honor, dignity, loyalty, decency, and the necessity of washing up before dinner.

Although Jim speaks standard English, his speeches are so belabored and unutterably noble that by page 48, I was screaming, "Aarrrgh, shoot him already!" Here is an example:

> Tom, I want to explain. I want to and I don't know the words. I always hated men who could talk and talk, but now I almost wish I was one of them. Then I'd know what to say to you to make you know. I am a Choctaw, Tom, and I must follow the Choctaw way. The Choctaw code says I must not sneak away. I must use my year to live fully and right. Once the court sentenced me to die, there was no other way for me. My people believe that—I believe it. I lived my whole life believing it and I'll die believing it. It can't be any other way, boy. It will come surely and in its time, as winter does when the fall has gone. I

> don't like winter, when the trees are old-looking, and the animals lose their flesh; but I know it has to come.

Did someone say something about men who could talk and talk?

I am familiar with Brent Ashabranner's later works, most notably *Morning Sun, Black Star: The Northern Cheyenne Indians and America's Energy Crisis*; *Children of the Maya: A Guatemalan Odyssey*; and *To Live in Two Worlds: American Indian Youth Today*. Those titles were written with intelligence and integrity. I don't know what happened here.

—Beverly Slapin

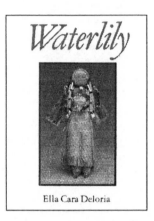

Deloria, Ella Cara (Dakota), *Waterlily.* **University of Nebraska (1990), 244 pages; grades 7-up; Dakota**

Ella Deloria, born near the end of the 19th Century, was the aunt of well-known contemporary Dakota scholar Vine Deloria. She went to college and became a research assistant to the famous anthropologist Franz Boas, who praised her to the skies privately and took credit for her work publicly. *Waterlily* is a novel, a life story of the Dakota people—those who had moved somewhat west to the prairie, out of the Dakota woodlands of Minnesota—as their lives were beginning to be disrupted by the *wasichu*. Told from a woman's viewpoint, it emphasizes the network of obligations and relationships that formed cultural unity.

> [I]deally, (a family) must be part of a larger family, constituted of related households, called a *tiospaye* ("group of tipis"). In the camp circle such groups placed their tipis side by side where they would be within easy reach for cooperative living. In their closeness lay such strength and social importance as no single family, however able, could or wished to achieve entirely by its own efforts.

In the atmosphere of that larger group, all adults were responsible for the safety and happiness of their collective children. The effect on the growing child was a feeling of security and self-assurance, and that was all the good. Almost from the beginning everyone could declare, "I am not afraid; I have relatives." To be cast out from one's relatives was literally to be lost. To return to them was to recover one's rightful haven.

Although the domain of scholarship was almost exclusively male until near the end of her life in the 1960s, Deloria felt that omitting the personal vitiated the life of the culture and reduced human emotion to statistical patterns. *Waterlily* is therefore her kind of Native-centered science monograph. *Waterlily* is a good story, and woven into it are the solidly based facts of actual plains life. The book's afterwords make good reading, too.

Deloria is a fine role model of a Native scholar for today's young women. The manuscript—apparently finished in 1947—was not published during her life, perhaps because of the death of Ruth Benedict, whose professional support was needed to impress publishers.—*Paula Giese*

Dengler, Marianna, *The Worry Stone*, illustrated by Sibyl Graber Gerig. Northland (1996). Unpaginated, color illustrations; grades 2-4; Chumash

This kind of book just wears me out, and this one made me immeasurably sad. It is a story of cultural emptiness filled by the romanticizing and appropriation of another, smaller culture that is not allowed to defend itself. In a brief "about the author" section at the back of the book, the author tells of finding her daughter asleep with a "worry stone" in her hand soon after Dengler's father has died. Her daughter tells Dengler that "holding the stone gave her dreams of her grandfather...which made her feel close to him and made losing him less painful." Evidently, Dengler felt that this touching story was unworthy of being told in its own right; perhaps her family does not have a strong ethnic background or traditions that could blossom into beautiful illustrations and details. So instead of telling her *own* story, Dengler tells—or pretends to tell— someone else's story: she invents a "Chumash legend"

and buries her own story inside it.

In a confusing disclaimer at the beginning of the book (which most parents and teachers will not read aloud to children), Dengler says:

> Most folktales are handed down from one person to another, from generation to generation and even from century to century. Some, like *The Worry Stone*, come directly from the heart and mind of the storyteller.
>
> Thus, the Chumash legend within this story is not authentic. I do hope, however, that it is consistent with the spirit of the People. For many years, I've walked their trails, joined their Solstice celebrations, and drawn strength from their mountains. I am grateful for their energy and their spirit, and I wish to pay them homage.

This making up of a "legend," saying you made it up, and ascribing it to a people anyway—is not paying homage to a people. It is appropriation, pure and simple.

Using Chumash images—of people, basketry, clothing, petroglyphs—presents an exotic and colorful background for a "how-it-came-to-be" story. Unfortunately, neither the story nor the illustrations hold up to scrutiny.

In a story within a story within a story, a lonely old woman and a lonely young boy become friends, as she gives him a worry stone and a story. The story she gives him is how her grandfather gave *her* a worry stone and a story. *This* story is the "Chumash legend" of how worry stones came to be. Or something like that. In the "Chumash Legend," a maiden named Tokatu waits around to be married to Akima. By the end of the first paragraph of this story, the "peaceful" Chumash all of a sudden get embroiled in a bloody civil war. This is so that Akima can die, but not before they "spoke the ancient vows and drank from the Cup of Life. Then, as the braves of the village danced around him, the Wind of Time carried off Akima's spirit." So Tokatu cries and cries, and when the Wind of Time carries off *her* spirit, her tears (you guessed it—*the Tears of Tokatu*) have become those famous worry stones that help troubled people.

Gerig's watercolors portray the physical beauty of the Chumash "maiden" as more like that of a well-tanned beach-babe Anglo-Saxon woman, with none of the features of a Native Californian. In the two paintings of Tokatu, she is seen first from the shoulders up, facing into a clichéd sunset as her lover is brought to her on a litter with just enough breath left to marry her and die. This image of Native womanhood facing the sunset of her future—without love, husband, children or hope— is a heartbreaking metaphor for all that California women have faced, but it is a representation of Native womanhood that is fatalistic and stereotyped. In the second illustration of Tokatu, we do not even see her face—she is now on the ground, prostrate with grief, hair spilling over her bare shoulders, in what is either a fetal position, or a sexy pose a la Playboy. Two beautiful Chumash baskets are placed in the illustration as well, so that we are able to identify this near-naked beautiful woman as Indian.

Returning to our story(ies), those worry stones, the Tears of Tokatu, become scattered all over the earth, and people rarely find them anymore. You may be one of the lucky ones. The end. Except we are left with a legend that isn't real, and an author whose own story serves as a reminder that cultural appropriation is most rampant in people who feel that their own heritage is not good enough, interesting enough, or financially lucrative enough.

To pass this lesson on to children is, at best, reprehensible. Not only is cultural ownership transgressed, but all of the real Chumash legends have been dishonored, and the seeds for future acts of racism and intolerance are sown.—*Deborah A. Miranda*

Dennis, Yvonne Wakim (Cherokee), and Arlene Hirschfelder, *Children of Native America Today*, with a foreword by Buffy Sainte-Marie (Cree). Charlesbridge (2003). 64 pages, color photos; grades 2-6

The intent of this book is to show that "Native children live in many different places, speak many different languages, and have many different cultures and customs." Twenty-two Nations and culture groups and three confederacies are represented here, as well as, briefly, "Urban People." Each profile gives location, a quick overview of the economy, cultural activities, political organization, typical skills, arts, crafts, points of interest, fun things to do, a little bit of history, and achievements of notable citizens of the Nation; and each closes with "More facts about..."

The photographs are of children engaged in a variety of activities, reflecting many different aspects of their lives. Some of them are dressed in regalia, some wear everyday clothes. Some of the photographs are clearly posed, others not. The latter tend to be the best.

There are great photographs of kids in this book. One question: Why are none of them named? The only people whose names are given are well-known adults, and of these, only one appears in a named photograph. The text speaks of Native children as very much a part of the 21st Century, doing 21st Century kid stuff. How much does it help the young non-Native reader, for whom this title is obviously intended, to see Indian children as individuals, rather than as generic "Indian," if they have no names? If there was reason for this, it should have been so stated.

It is good that the authors tell about such people as Mary and Carrie Dann, who have fought for years for Shoshone land rights in Nevada. Yet the discussion of land rights in general, the struggle to preserve languages and subsistence hunting and fishing; and broken treaties, pollution, damming of rivers and destruction of ancient forests, are brief if mentioned at all. And the tragic results of government depredations are not spoken of in any way that will give the reader any concept of the scope of these things.

It is understandable the authors would want to present a sunny picture in a book for children, as an antidote to so much that has gone before, but too often the book reads like a travel guide. "Have you been to Walt Disney World in Florida? You should visit the Seminole recreation park..." Or, "The canyons have the greatest concentration of wild desert palm trees in the world. Hollywood is always filming movies in the Cahuillas' back yard!" The device of "Did you know that..." is used constantly; it becomes very annoying. "Did you know that there was a Lumbee Robin Hood?" Or its variant: "Have you heard of the Wampanoags..." "Have you ever searched for a giant moose?" Children detest being talked down to, and there is a lot of that in this book.

Finally, one wonders why the constant exaggerated emphasis of questions and exclamations, where they are neither needed nor desirable, was seen as necessary. For example: "If you are Yurok, you'd better like fish!" and "Salmon travel all over, and sometimes the Lummi do, too!"

In sum: A good effort, only partially successful.

—*Doris Seale*

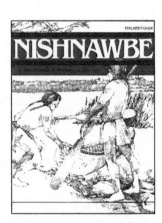

Deur, Lynne, *Nishnawbe: A Story of Indians in Michigan*, illustrated by Lori McElrath. River Road (1981, 1989). 52 pages, b/w illustrations; grades 3-5; Ojibwe, Odawa, Potawatomi

Illustrated mostly with maps, photos, old prints, and unattractive drawings (there are even photos of what appears to be a diorama!), Nishnawbe is an unsuccessful attempt to present an accurate history of the Indian peoples of Michigan. The opening sentence of this book declares that *Nishnawbe* "is a word used by Michigan Indians to mean 'Indian.'" Nishnabe, a Potawatomi word, can be spelled in many different ways, but it has one meaning—the people.

Unfortunately for the student readers for whom this is intended, inaccuracies abound on just about every page. For the most part, the author portrays the Ojibwe, Odawa and Potawatomi as a peoples of the past: they *had* plenty of meat and fish to eat, they *lived* in wigwams, they *built* sturdy snowshoes, they *moved* from time to time.... There is even this:

> Television shows and movies often show Indians as people who never smile. This is not a true picture. Indians loved to laugh, joke, and have fun. Games and sports were an important part of their lives.

Too bad we don't laugh, joke, and have fun anymore. I really miss that ancient part of our lives.

The few pages that address contemporary Indian people are patronizing as well:

> They have jobs in offices and factories. Some are storeowners, builders, nurses, teachers, lawyers, and artists. They live, work and play like everyone else.

We *are* just like real people! (Except we don't laugh or joke anymore, see above.) Of course, there is no mention of the important contributions of Native knowledge to medicine and science, just that Native Americans have "important ideas, like protecting the water, land, plants and animals around us." And except for two sentences about treaty rights, there is no mention of modern Indian issues, such as the effects of colonization, residential schools, repatriation, religious freedom, mascots and stereotypes.

Nishnawbe comes with a teacher guide. Neither is recommended. Instead, pick up three volumes of contemporary photoessays from Lerner's "We Are Still Here" series: *Ininatig's Gift of Sugar* by Laura Waterman Wittstock (Seneca), *The Sacred Harvest: Ojibway Wild Rice Gathering* by Gordon Regguinti (Ojibwe), and *Shannon: An Ojibway Dancer* by Sandra King (Ojibwe). And, of course, anything written by elder storyteller Simon Otto (Ojibwe/Odawa).—*Barbara Potter*

Dewey, Jennifer Owings, *Minik's Story.* **Marshall Cavendish, 2003. 143 pages, grades 6-9; Inuit**
Hill, Kirkpatrick, *Minuk: Ashes in the Pathway.* **Pleasant Company, 2002. 198 pages, grades 4-7; Yup'ik**
Sullivan, Paul, *Maata's Journal.* **Atheneum, 2003. 244 pages, grades 6-up; Inuit**

Three motherless "Eskimo" girls from the "top of the world" battle hardship, loss, cultural confusion, disease and the temptations of western culture—and somehow emerge strong, self-assured women. Minuk, Minik, and Maata are stylized aboriginal heroes, shaped by anthropology and the fantasies of the non-indigenous writers who conveniently kill off their mothers and expose them to every cultural challenge there is. Young readers who are not Native are likely to empathize with these characters; Native readers will be confused at best.

Maata's Journal is set in the Canadian Arctic in 1924. Maata is an Inuit teenager, writing a journal as she nurses a dying companion and waits for rescue on a remote Arctic island. Having lived a traditional community life on the tundra, traveling with the seasons to hunt game, eight-year-old Maata and her family are evacuated from their hunting grounds in 1915 to a Canadian government settlement. Here, she encounters marvels such as electric boats and houses with glass windows, and also the terrors of alcohol and family violence. After her parents die, Maata, who by now can speak English and proudly carries around a Webster's dictionary that she has been given by a white surveyor, is sent away to a residential school in Quebec. Upon returning as a young woman, she finds herself outside the close circle of family and community. As an "Eskimo" alone, Maata joins a mapping expedition where the nature of the land takes its toll, and the geographers become increasingly dependent on her knowledge of the land. Over a three-month period as she and one other survivor wait for rescue, Maata reflects on her life and the events of the expedition.

There are several problems with this book, the least of which is Sullivan's collapsing of history in order to justify his protagonist's leaving her community to become part of the mapping expedition. Inuit people were not relocated in 1915; that didn't happen until mainly in the 1950s in response to sovereignty issues. While Maata is old enough to be an adult in her community, Sullivan has her writing as if she were a child. Although this bright and educated person treasures her dictionary, for instance, she never actually writes the word "dictionary"; rather, she calls it "Mr. Webster's big word book" and "my wintertime book." Her views are too modern for 1924, and the author puts an unrealistic cultural responsibility on this young woman. She knows way too much about everything. People don't know everything about their own culture, especially a seventeen-year-old who has spent much of her childhood away from her community. And yet, Sullivan has Maata writing: "My father would have known…how to travel safely….[I]t is natural for the Inuit to know this in their own land." She would know, but apparently Sullivan doesn't, that cultural knowledge comes from teaching and experience, not instinct.

Twelve-year-old Minik's story is set in the mid-1800s, at the early onset of whaling along the Hudson Bay in the Canadian Arctic. When her mother dies in childbirth, the Dog Children (white whalers and priests) are said to have stolen her soul. Minik's grandmother warns her to keep away from the strangers:

> It is their stench. They stink. It's their eyes, watery and pale. Their voices are harsh and loud. Their bodies are covered with thickly matted hair. They carry black books in their packs and read aloud from the pages and speak melancholy words. The Dog Children lust after Inuit girls. Some take what they want without bartering. We are comic to them. They laugh out loud at us. They urge us to be like them.

Nevertheless, Minik befriends an outcast priest and tries to understand about her mother's soul and her own role in that loss to the community. Between the grandmother, who provides Minik with strategy; and the priest, who provides her with rationale, Minik achieves all the insight necessary to adapt to the new reality she must face and secure a future for herself and her children. This gives the totally unrealistic impression that it takes very little for a young person to adapt to an alien reality. All cultures have inherent in them adaptive strategies; cultures and communities—not just the appearance of two individual people—provide the framework that allows people to adapt. But the author fails to notice this dynamic—from out of what black hole does Minik's socialization come?

Dewey's Minik is a cultural expert as a child, blithely discussing the contents of medicine pouches—"amulet bags"—and casually talking about tattoos, taboos and shape-shifting:

> I flew. I did. I was the Spirit Bird of the Storm…. I saw a flock of snow geese, far below, and a fox, and ducks on the water, millions of ducks. I saw gulls and a baby whale dead and rotting on the shore.

This happens all through the book, and it's a real problem. There's no culturally respectful context because the author clearly does not understand the sacredness of the things and events her protagonist prattles on about. Outside of confiding to a grandparent or medicine person, children just do not talk about these things. If a child has a powerful dream or becomes another being, it's a matter of great concern for all and must be understood and dealt with. It's a very big deal.

Minuk: Ashes in the Pathway, part of the "Girls of Many Lands" series, is set in a Yup'ik village in 1890, as the first American missionaries come north. Twelve-year-old Minuk, bold and inquisitive, demonstrates all the characteristics that supposedly make her less than an ideal Yup'ik, i.e., quiet and demure. Yet poor Minuk is tragically heroic in the seemingly unending cycle of disease that wipes out whole families, villages and peoples. She becomes the liaison between the families and the health care system to which they must submit during the outbreaks, and after her mother dies of influenza, Minuk is invited to go south for training. But she knows that there is work to do at home, and she chooses to remain in the community.

Minuk is the ultimate cultural expert, even as a child. From the very first page—"When we were little girls, we were very carefully taught what our responsibilities as Yup'ik women would be when we were grown and had families of our own"—sets the stage for all the stuff that she knows. But little girls were not and are not taught these things all at once. Children are taught developmentally—not didactically—in the context of family and community relationships and work. By the author's taking these teachings out of the context of their relationships, one assumes that these little Yup'ik girls are all imbued with all the cultural expertise they need to know in order to bring young non-Native readers up to speed. On the first few pages, as Minuk's narration smoothly moves from "we" ("we would listen carefully") to "she" ("she had to get up early, as soon as she awoke") to "I" ("I would be a good woman"), the author sets up these expectations to draw young readers in:

> I would miss going to the Hoffs' very much. I would miss David, and jolly Miss Oakes, and joking with the boys in the morning when I dished out their oatmeal. I'd miss the magazines

and the catalogs, and the stereoscope and the mirror. I'd miss my dress with the white apron and the pocket, and I'd miss the soap.

Minuk's speech patterns, her articulation, are coolly and irritatingly differentiated—this kid just doesn't talk like an aboriginal child. She uses "I" too much; she thinks of herself as an individual. I don't hear aboriginal kids saying "I" at all; kids want to be part of the big "we," the group. That level of differentiation, looking at oneself apart from the group, especially in 1890, would have been seen as an aberration.

Hill projects her own imaginings onto her child characters. In her author's note, she says she "tried to imagine what it must have been like to first see mirrors, cloth, and writing, and to taste sugar and bread." So, of course, little Minuk echoes her sentiments:

> I wonder what our faces looked like the first time Panruk and I saw white people's underwear, sat on chairs, and looked through window glass. I wonder how big our eyes were!

It might be said that this is just what writers are supposed to do, but when they do it in a cross-cultural way that discounts and violates the integrity of the people they are writing about, it's a fraud, a smoke-and-mirrors seduction of the non-Native child reader. Hill may not fully understand what she's doing, but she is responsible nevertheless.

While purporting to tell a story through a Yup'ik child's voice, Hill's information comes "straight from the (non-Native) journals and documents of the time," and the rest comes from her (non-Native) imagination; she tells the story of adaptation, acculturation and loss from a non-Native cultural web.

She relentlessly and dismally elaborates and exaggerates all of the horrors of disease, dysfunction, destruction, disaster, and death. It's painful for us and our children to read over and over again about all of this because we don't have the distance that the non-aboriginal author does. She hasn't paid her dues in death and destruction as we have; she has the sort of repugnant social distance that makes it possible for her to write about it.

Our children, the legacy and the future of our peoples, are exploited by this kind of fictionalization of our lives, a genre that Alex Haley called "faction" because of the blurring between fact and fiction. Our children become caricatures for the storylines of the settler cultures that brought the destruction. Writers of this kind of juvenile "faction" could probably use some lessons in morality and ethics to understand the harm they perpetrate on our children. "Not only the heroine but the vanished society here feel alive in their complexities," remarked the reviewer for *Publishers Weekly* about *Minuk*. What appears to be "good stories" to the reviewers for *Publishers Weekly*, *School Library Journal* and the like, are a deceit that teaches deceit.

—*Marlene R. Atleo/ʔeh ʔeh naa tuu kwiss*

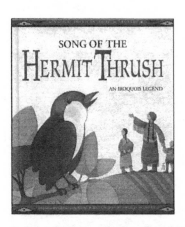

Dominic, Gloria, illustrated by Charles Reasoner. Troll; Rourke (1996). 48 pages, color illustrations; grades 2-3:
Brave Bear and the Ghosts: A Sioux Legend
Coyote and the Grasshoppers: A Pomo Legend
First Woman and the Strawberry: A Cherokee Legend
Red Hawk and the Sky Sisters: A Shawnee Legend
Song of the Hermit Thrush: An Iroquois Legend
Sunflower's Promise: A Zuni Legend

This is the second "six-pack" of "Native American Lore and Legend" by Troll and Rourke for school consumption. These six are "adapted and retold" by Gloria Dominic, following the same formula used in the 1990 series, "written and adapted" by Terri Cohlene, even employing the same cookie-cutter illustrations by Charles Reasoner. Unfortunately, due to the availability of the Troll catalog in schools and the inclusion of "historical information," glossary and bibliography, these titles can be found on entirely too many library and classroom shelves.

These slick little books have generic "Indian" border patterns on the covers and are done in bright primary colors, with an abundance of red and turquoise. "Indian motif" designs appear throughout the series: meaningless patterns, thunderbirds, stars, heartlines and feathers. The characters are wooden and monolithic, almost always shown in profile, with closed eyes and no mouths. The absence of mouths on the faces of Native characters from traditional stories is particularly significant as it graphically depicts the lack of Native voice in these appropriations of our oral stories. There is a difference between stylized art and stereotypical representations and these illustrations lack the life, vitality and accuracy found in stylized work by such Native artists as Virginia Stroud, for instance.

There is no mention of the source for any of these stories, other than that of a tribe, which is sometimes incorrect. It is intellectually irresponsible, not to mention unethical, to call a text an "adaptation" or a "retelling" without acknowledging the original source (preferably, multiple sources) of a cultural story. There has been enormous debate internationally in the near-decade since the first Troll series was published about the protection of cultural intellectual property and the necessity for respect and dedicated and rigorous research and discipline when working with materials across the cultures. There is no indication in any of these books that the author was involved in or is even aware of the critical issues associated with "adapting" Native stories. This is unacceptable laxness, especially for materials that readily find their way into classrooms and children's minds.

These versions of the stories lack the multiple dimensions and possibilities for interpretation and reexamination that are found in true tellings of the original stories. They are simplified and formulaic, and reduce the characters and events to the status of egocentric individuals in personal conflict, rather than the rich, complex, subtle stories that reflect cultural values and teachings and serve to reinforce and strengthen a community that knows and tells the stories.

Each book ends with a short section that seems intended to give a history of the "tribe" (never the Nation) from precontact to the present. The inclusion of this section is a major selling point with teachers, who try to link stories with cultures and to provide an introduction to Native peoples that encompasses the present as well as the past. That is why it is even more disturbing that this section, throughout the series, is so terribly done.

Maps of the original homelands of the peoples from whom the stories were taken are often inaccurate or based on anthropological theory, rather than where oral tradition says the peoples originate. There is the standard section on food, clothing and shelter, which is a part of most social studies units in the U.S. today. The descriptions of families, relationships and the responsibilities of woman and men in the communities are brief and unexplained, other than a mention in the "Iroquois" and "Zuni" books that "[l]ike other Native American societies, women played an important role.... This type of kinship is called matrilineal."

The glossaries contain short inaccurate definitions of words that have to do with particular spiritual beliefs and ceremonies. It cannot be overstated how inappropriate and disrespectful it is to intrude into the sacred ways of cultures—as Dominic has done—emphasizing the superficial, the sensational and the "exotic" with no understanding of the complex spiritual belief systems, ceremonies or societies for whom these are profound beliefs. These are the Native "religions" that have endured the government prohibition against their practices, the exploitation by New Age experience-seekers, and countless instances of misrepresentation. It would have been better to avoid mention of our spiritual practices altogether than to reduce them into senseless minibytes of misunderstanding.

Pictures in back sections contain glaring examples of inappropriate art and inaccurate descriptive captions. Most offensive, perhaps, is the inclusion of False Face masks, despite the requests made by the Grand Council of the Haudenosaunee (Iroquois) that these sacred masks not be represented in any illustration or other manner. Other examples are the illustrations of Katsina masks, Shalako pictures from 1897, a beaded "umbilical amulet" (though these were never in the form of an eagle), and Pomo fire dancers in 1912 dressed for a "spiritual ceremony." Although most of the photos come from museum archives, it is difficult not to think of how the families of the people depicted in those photos might feel about having them included in these books.

In the simplistic section at the back of the book called "The Pomo," one old photograph particularly stands out: a Pomo woman who seems to be trying not to look at the camera holds a baby's hand while a little boy looks on. The mother and her children are wearing ill-fitting western-style clothing, and she holds a load of sticks and kindling in one arm. The caption says "A Pomo family dressed in their Sunday best." Why "Sunday best"? This comment makes a mockery of the obvious poverty of this little family, and by extension, of all Pomo people.

Another photo, from the Shawnee book, shows "Shawnee kindergarten children dressed in their school clothes." These children are dressed in uniforms, most likely for one of the government- or church-run military-style residential schools that separated children from their families and cultures for years and caused grievous harm and trauma to children, families and communities. Nowhere is the residential school "experiment"—or the complex issues surrounding it—mentioned.

The "(X) Today" sections, which contrast the living and work situations of contemporary Native peoples, may have been intended to show the diversity of lifeways today. But a closer look at the choice of words reveals a racist perception of the place of Native peoples in 20th-Century America. For example: "(X people) live in non-Native cities (or "cities and towns with non-natives" or "many of the major cities in the U.S."), contrasted with, "though some continue to live on reservations" (or "small rancherías instead of on large reservations").

The discussion of careers and work is even more revealing: "Many (X people) still work recreating traditional crafts and ways," contrasted with, "while some follow careers in non-native industries, such as timber, tourism, the arts and sciences." A more graphic example of this attitude—"[they] celebrate the old ways through dance and ceremonies while working in non-native professions such as law, education and the arts"—is incredibly biased in its expectation that Native people conform to white definitions of work that has to be either "non-native" or "traditional."

The historical sections are so full of inaccuracy and ignorance as to serve no purpose. For instance, here is a sentence from *Song of the Hermit Thrush: An Iroquois Legend*: "Many believe the confederacy influenced our forefathers as they formed the government of the United States." Now, whose forefathers are these? To whom does the word "our" refer? Wording like this excludes Native readers who have stories of their own forebears, who were no part of the founding of the colonial U.S. government. Moreover, "belief" has little part in the relationship between the Iroquois and the roots of democracy, which is documented historical fact.

The major historical events in Dominic's capsule timelines are more of the same. In three of the six books, the timeline begins with "1492—Columbus Lands in the Americas" and in the other three, the timeline begins in the 1700s. This is not the beginning of the history or culture of any Native peoples. Dominic describes events with passive inert verbs that provide a simplistic rendering of complex events: explorers "land" and "sail," land is "ceded," treaties are "granted," tribes "sign over much of their land," homelands "become" states. The year 1849 is simply "The Gold Rush," with no reference to the impact of the greed for gold on the Native Nations from California to Georgia.

Perhaps the most offensive historical note is the very sanitized "1890—The Battle of Wounded Knee ends the Indian Wars." Even road signs and historical markers in South Dakota now call this "The Massacre at Wounded Knee," when troops used rapid-fire Gatling guns to slaughter unarmed people, mostly women and children and elders. It is sad to note that the strongest phrase in any of the timelines is "Extermination of over 13 million buffalo by white men." As with the earlier series by Cohlene, the insensitivity—no, outright racism—in the non-fiction sections of these books should be enough to warn any reader that the "retellings" that precede them have problems serious enough to disqualify them for classroom use.

SONG OF THE HERMIT THRUSH: AN IROQUOIS LEGEND

It is difficult to guess the source for this story, as it is unrecognizable as compared to the many acceptable versions available, particularly both the book and recording made by Tehanetorens/Ray Fadden, Mohawk elder, storyteller and teacher. It begins with an illustration of an "Iroquois" (which one—Oneida, Mohawk, Onondaga, Cayuga, Seneca, Tuscarora?) grandmother with her two grandchildren, "Dancing Flower" and "Dark Eyes." They are walking on a bright, summer morning when Grandmother decides to tell them a story. This is despite the fact that Iroquois peoples traditionally tell stories only in the winter. Immediately, this telling is in question because it's obvious the author doesn't know enough about stories in their cultural context to be "adapting" them.

The only similarity to the traditional story is the birds' flying high into the sky to find their songs. The flight in Dominic's telling is prompted by the "wise old" owl of the European tradition, who knows where the songs are kept by the generic "Great Spirit." In Tehanetorens' tellings of the story, the Good Spirit, who had created all things, walked the Earth to view all his creations and heard the good morning song of thanksgiving of a man. He noticed the silence of the birds and decided their song was missing from the Earth. So, the Good Spirit asked the birds if they wanted songs. When they said they did, he told them to fly in the sky as high as they could and that, when they could fly no higher, they would each find their song. The one who flew the highest would find the sweetest song.

In Dominic's version, all of the contentious, argumentative animals (with the exclusion of water animals, insects and amphibians) had to divide the forest "in order to live peacefully" and the sound of their voices "was not beautiful to hear." This is a distortion of the story and sends a peculiar judgmental message about diversity, as song after song is judged "not a lovely one… not a beautiful one," instead of the differing songs of birds of different natures. The birds who don't fly as high as "where the Great Spirit lives" are deemed failures, instead of finding the songs that are right for them. Only Eagle "succeeded where others failed."

The small Thrush, hidden on the Eagle's back, hears only one song when he enters the Spirit World or Sky World. This is unlike Dominic's version where he "sang each of the songs he heard…at last, he heard a melody so perfect…" After hearing it and learning it, Thrush returns from his "triumphant journey" and waits until night so that the other birds will be "too tired to chase after me." He then sings "the sweetest song he knows."

In Tehanetorens' version, which carries deep cultural values that resonate throughout this story, the small Thrush, on returning, has a very different experience and awareness. "Suddenly, the feeling of glory left the little Thrush, and he felt ashamed. He knew he had cheated to get his beautiful song....In shame, with dragging heart, he hid under the branches of the largest tree. He was so ashamed that he wanted no one to see him. There you will find him today. Never does the Hermit Thrush come out into the open. He is still ashamed because he cheated."

The hierarchy and competition and judgment of differences found in Dominic's version of this story have nothing to do with "Iroquois" or any other Native culture. Her Thrush is triumphant and deceptive and proud of his dishonest theft of song. This carries important messages about how the author perceives life, as imposed on a traditional story. There are no lessons here that are compatible with the community values of Iroquois people. If Dominic agrees with the quote from an "Iroquois" given on the first page of the book, "We...have methods of transmitting from father to son an account of all these things," she should never have ruined this story in her retelling.

FIRST WOMAN AND THE STRAWBERRY: A CHEROKEE LEGEND

Dominic could have gotten this story from James Mooney's *Myths of the Cherokee*, or from any of a number of text or recording sources. It begins with another of those standard "Indian grandmothers," telling a story to a granddaughter who, fortunately this time, does not have a ridiculous pseudo-Indian name. Before touching on the details, it is important to note that the greatest flaw in this "adaptation" is the taking of a profound story about conflict and resolution and man and woman (and many things) and making it "cute," simplistic and sanitized for children. This demonstrates a lack of respect for both the story and the children for whom it is intended.

The reasons for the conflict between First Man and First Woman are never given in traditional versions of this story, a Cherokee friend and storyteller told me. The reason for the fight has long been forgotten, so it becomes a metaphor for all fights. It is understood that this was a major conflict, not the foolish and trivial disagreement about which path to take at a fork while gathering tender roots for basketmaking. They travel in post-contact cloth clothing that is inaccurate for the people and that make the story seem more contemporary than the timeless traditional story it actually is. After the conflict, Dominic stretches the story by inserting inessential devices as the man going on a "quest" to find the woman. This action is not central to the sense or development of the story and

distorts and diminishes its flow and power, while introducing foreign elements of European folk tales. These extraneous details recur when the woman begins her return, gifting the same animals who had guided her husband as she seeks him in her parallel, gender-equity "quest."

In Cherokee story and culture, the mediator is called Creator or Provider, not the generic "Great Spirit" of Dominic's version. When "He" speaks in a "voice unlike any other," the text is accompanied by illustrations of eagles and/or thunderbirds, who are not associated with Provider/Creator in Cherokee stories. This "Great Spirit" entices the woman with grapes and cherries or European orchards, instead of the serviceberries of the Cherokee homelands. In the traditional story, the strawberry's scent slows the woman just long enough for the man to find her, instead of Dominic's creation of the woman searching for him in her "quest." And so Dominic ends with that gift of the "Great Spirit," which the woman learned to make into "sweet-tasting jellies and jams to eat all year round." Jellies and jams? With the processed sugar required? In a timeless traditional story? "These delicious foods were always there"? So as not to have to follow the seasonal calendar of thanksgivings and ceremonies? This is a classic example of how the power of a profound and sacred story can be stripped and remade into a culturally barren caricature. (Thanks to Gayle Ross for the help with this one.)

BRAVE BEAR AND THE GHOSTS: A SIOUX LEGEND

This story most likely comes from a version called "The Man Who Was Afraid of Nothing," told to Richard Erdoes and Alfonso Ortiz by John Fire Lame Deer, and which appears in *American Indian Myths and Legends*. Dominic chooses once again to make up clichéd, pseudo-Indian names; this time it is Brave Bear. She begins with "long ago in the land of ghosts, where it is always winter," far more of a description of setting than is usually found in our traditional stories. Moreover, she creates a separation between the world of human beings and the world of ghosts or spirits—this totally runs contrary to the Lakota way of looking at things. She creates a "supernatural" story based on a story told in a culture that believes there is nothing other than the natural world, cohabited by spirits and other beings. This is so she can add dialogue like, "I find it very easy to scare people. They are all frightened of ghosts, aren't they?" No, we are not. The ghost story genre into which Dominic tried to force this story is not typical of Native or Lakota stories. (And since the origin of the name "Sioux" is explained in the historical notes, and the correct names of the peoples—Lakota, Dakota and Nakota—are given, why not use them instead of calling this "A Sioux Legend"? Or was she unable to determine whose story this is?)

Although Dominic adds unnecessary seasons and setting descriptions that distract the reader and disturb the flow of the story, she follows the events in the version recorded by Erdoes and Ortiz fairly closely. There are four ghosts, though Lame Deer has his materialize as skeletons, and four encounters. She changes them from a game of hoop and stick and shinny ball to shooting arrows; from a skull drum and thighbone stick to a skull drum, stout stick and skeleton hand for a rattle—rattles and drums aren't played simultaneously by a single singer; from a ribcage used for sledding that ends up in a stream to spinning tops (?) made of teeth (?); and from being knocked to the ground and broken to a guessing game that results in a ghost's falling into a stream. It is hard to understand why she changed these details.

In Lame Deer's telling, it's a spider; but the significance of a trickster figure like a spider in a Lakota story seems to have been lost on Dominic. "The Man Who Was Afraid of Nothing" was arrogant and boastful, disrespecting the spirits of the dead. He was vain and egotistical and frightened children and women, upsetting camp life when he returned to camp on a skeleton horse. He was thoughtless and self-centered, mindless of the consequences of his actions and not shown as being related to others in the story. He was undone by a trickster spider and a little girl who could see his failings. There's a lesson in this.

But Dominic's "retelling" becomes just a silly story where the laugh is on the ghosts and, somewhat, on the man who finally admits to fear of "ants." *Brave Bear and the Ghosts* is offensive in a way that the others are not, as it would seem that a single version of this story was taken and changed just so it could be "owned" by the "reteller/adapter."

RED HAWK AND THE SKY SISTERS: A SHAWNEE LEGEND

This story rings with familiarity, but I was unable to find source material with which to compare it. Nevertheless it is troublesome, and based on the previous three stories with which I have some experience and background, I am entirely suspicious of this one. Here, Dominic continues to name her characters in pseudo-Indian style, this time "Red Hawk" and "Morning Star." A creation, addition and/or misinterpretation of this story has the hero on a bizarre "quest" demanded by his father-in-law, "Bright Star," to "kill one of each kind of bird and animal from the forest and bring them to me." This seems to be gratuitous and senseless, as the body parts of these slain creatures of Mother Earth are distributed among the stars, who turn into the animals and return to the forests of Earth. (Dominic never capitalizes Earth.) Why? What is the point or lesson or value that this story was and is meant to share for Shawnee people? I can't tell from this "retelling," which resolves itself as a sentimental romance.

SUNFLOWER'S PROMISE: A ZUNI LEGEND

Again, I was unable to find the source for this story. It is safe to assume that the characters' names, "Sunflower" and "Little Mole," are more fabrication. It is also safe to assume that the action of the story has been altered or that two stories have been combined to create this "adaptation," as the story of Coyote plunked in the middle of this story has elements that seem to mark it as a more traditional story. The main character, "Sunflower" is beautiful, rich and clever and "did not see why she needed a husband." That a young woman in a matrilineal culture would see no need for continuing her family and clan is unthinkable. If this is the lesson to be taught, then Sunflower would most likely be depicted as vain and foolish and a problem for her family, but here she is described as "content in the warmth of her family's devotion."

Her unlikely suitor is "plain" as the mole he is named after, has large ears, is "homely" and poor. This sets off warning alarms that suggest this has been shaped after a European folk tale, as the poor, homely Little Mole must outwit the creatures of the natural world who have become Sunflower's adversaries over the ownership of her garden to win her hand and devotion (and a castle from her father, see where this is going?) He goes through labors, trials, initiations and quests and emerges triumphant—save for being unable to defeat Coyote, who must be unhappy about being relegated to such a small part in this drama. The lesson is, of course, that clever men are preferable to handsome men. Can that be all? Despite limited experience with Zuni stories, I would suspect a lot got lost in this "adaptation."

COYOTE AND THE GRASSHOPPERS: A POMO LEGEND

I was unable to find a version from or about Clear Lake to check Dominic's version of this story. Perhaps my reluctance to do other than suggest interpretations and flaws in this story can serve as a valuable lesson. I have over twenty years of learning and studying stories of a few Nations (my own and near-dear friends and extended family), and that does not qualify me to interpret the stories of another people and their culture. These books lack that awareness or restraint.

I'd like to quote my friend, folklorist Barre Toelken (yes, Indians have friends who are folklorists and, sometimes, even anthropologists) who spent some 40 years living and working with Diné friends and family and Coyote stories before making the decision to return those important stories and no longer being an accomplice in their misunderstanding and abuse. He wrote in his introduction to Barry Lopez' *Giving Birth to Thunder, Sleeping With His Daughter* (Avon, 1977), "to get beyond Coyote's fascinating façade we do in fact need to know his local, specific tribal manifestations. And to know these, we need to know the tribal language, the tribal lore about storytelling events, and the local taboos concerning when a story may be told, by whom, to whom, and under what circumstances."

Coyote and the Grasshoppers does not meet any of these criteria. Although the story explains a feature of the land in the Pomo homelands, it lacks a feeling of place, a connection to the land that is vital to the stories of a people and a culture with strong ties to specific locales. The illustrations give lie to the text of the story. There is a drought, lakes have dried up, people, animals and plants are dying from lack of water—and yet page after page of Reasoner's illustrations have grassy, green rolling hills! We never know what act or imbalance created this disharmony and lack of water. We do not know why the people's prayers and songs—not "chants"—fail to call the rain. Instead, Coyote, in a selfless and self-sacrificing manner atypical of him, thinks only of the children and endures great hardship and effort to bring back the lake—with no ulterior motive! In truth, Coyote is more than the one-dimensional "naughty boy" he is in many characterizations. But this characterization is just as limited and senseless as the others. Here we have a more sentimental Coyote who is strong and unselfish. This is not a bad lesson for children; but choosing and reshaping a story to make the author's point is not a culturally sensitive thing, or even a wise thing, to do with Coyote stories that are taken out of context, out of season and out of culture.

Like the six Cohlene stories from Troll before these six, Dominic's are terrible. Troll/Rourke has some moral/educational responsibility to work closer with Native people to produce work of more accuracy and integrity for the schools and families looking for Native stories. These books are fatally flawed in different ways, ranging from near plagiarism to gross distortion and mixing of European folktale motifs with Native cultural stories. I showed these books to my child, who had just completed third grade. Before I could even warn her about them, she exclaimed, "You shouldn't tell or read Coyote stories in the summer!" and "Brave Bear is really Man Afraid of Nothing!" and "It's Lakota, not Sioux!" and "Daddy says those masks aren't supposed to be in books because they're holy!" I didn't have to tell her a thing. But I do have something to say to the authors of these books and Troll/Rourke: Don't insult our stories and cultures—Don't insult our children.—*Dovie Thomason*

Drucker, Malka, *The Sea Monster's Secret*, illustrated by Christopher Aja. Gulliver/HBJ. Unpaginated; color illustrations; grades 3-5; Tlingit, Haida

In *The Sea Monster's Secret*, the author throws together literary elements from different kinds of stories with cultural elements from the Northwest Coast and ignoring a cultural context, creates a perfect example of why outsiders ought not to write and illustrate children's books about cultures they don't know.

The author says that she learned about the sea monster by looking at a totem pole, which "hints at much more than it actually says." A totem pole doesn't "hint"; it organizes cultural meaning. There are symbols in sequence that are cues for whole stories, so someone from the culture sees a totem pole and knows the story it conveys. Drucker, on the other hand, looked for "clues" on a totem pole, found written versions, chose the outcome she liked best, and dragged the whole thing through her own cultural framework.

In this story, a young man proves himself to be a resourceful hunter, despite the constant nagging of his mother-in-law, when he kills a ferocious sea monster and puts on its skin.

This not a Tlingit or Haida story. While there are cultural elements here, the cultural context is missing; the cultural logic is lost. The relationships that provide the meaning between and among the cultural elements—hunter and hunted, young man and young woman, young woman and mother, young man and mother-in-law, her family and his family, individuals and society—aren't here.

In societies where scarcity and even starvation were often reality, there are stories where a person does not or cannot "fit in." There might be someone who is greedy. These stories pass on knowledge about the necessity of living in right relation to each other. Here, the young man is not having trouble hunting, he's not lazy, he's not anything out of the ordinary, except his ambitious mother-in-law's just giving him a hard time. The rationale for her fury has to do with lack of provision, but there is no hunger in this story. And, although there was a high level of specialization on the Northwest Coast—men hunted, made up songs, carved canoes and totem poles—here, it seems the only thing for a man to do is hunt. There is no reason for the mother-in-law's greed, either; she's just wicked because, well, she's a mother-in-law. There is no lesson here.

The metaphor, "getting into someone's skin," comes from the traditional stories of hunting societies of Northwest

Coast peoples where a hunter comes to know an animal by putting on its skin. Then, a certain sympathetic magic happens, and the hunter can become that animal or attain its attributes. So there are stories where people put on the skins of animals and become those animals. And when they become those animals, there is something to be learned.

Here, a young man traps a sea monster, puts on its skin, becomes the sea monster and journeys to its domain, where he learns—nothing. He does not become a hero, he does not bring back any hunting knowledge to his people, he just keeps dragging ever-growing catches back to his mother-in-law's door.

In traditional potlatching cultures, usually relationships were arranged. Marriages were political joinings of families, and matches based on "love" were seen as aberrant. So the problem between the young man and his mother-in-law would be a political problem between two families, not a personal problem the way it's set up here.

Both in text and illustrations, the female elder—the mother-in-law—complains and nags, while the young woman—the wife—is voiceless and ineffectual. She just sits there, at her husband's side, while her mother abuses him. And while there are cultural elements in the illustrations—there are cedars and totem poles, and the outfits are vaguely West Coast—the people do not look like they come from a food-oriented culture, except for the mother-in-law, and she's stereotypically huge as the visual clue of her greediness, another thing that's a real problem.

Traditional stories may contain underlying themes of greed, starvation, doing the right thing versus doing the wrong thing, being part of a group versus being an individual. Sometimes, people behave wrong—to teach right behavior. But we have never heard a traditional story in which belittling someone was a motivational strategy. In a traditional story involving elements such as social dysfunction and greed, the web of relations needs to make cultural sense and provide a teaching of some sort, to convey a moral principle. But here, we have no clue as to what that moral principle, that right behavior, might be.

"In some versions," the author says, "the young man dies when he tries to bring back more than one whale; in others, the young man is successful in his attempt. I prefer the second ending and have used it." Different endings serve different purposes, and just choosing one over the other doesn't make sense if it doesn't provide the cultural logic that conveys and illuminates the moral principle being taught.

—*Marlene R. Atleo/ʔeh ʔeh naa tuu kwiss* and *Beverly Slapin*

Duncklee, John, *Quest for the Eagle Feather.* **Northland (1997). 85 pages; grades 3-5**

I am immediately suspicious when I pick up a book about Indians, and I can't find the Nation. And when the author's note says something like this: "I have a continuing deep respect for Native people and their strong beliefs. This book is but one of my ways for showing that respect."

These ones live in a "village of stone houses on top of the mesa," they cultivate corn, beans, and pumpkins, and they allude to Spaniards ("the men in metal hats and shirts"), so they may be one of the "pueblo" peoples, maybe Hopi. Just a guess.

Three boys—Running Fox, Screaming Crow, and Quiet Water, a white boy adopted by whoever these people are—are assigned by the medicine man, Swift Elk, to "climb the Sacred Mountain to watch the eagle fly" and bring back an eagle feather for the Eagle Clan. Eagles are very important in Hopi culture, but not in this way.

So the boys go camping, bag some game, confront a cougar, kill an attacking bear, engage in some miscellaneous male bonding, ya-da ya-da ya-da, get to the top of the Sacred Mountain, watch the eagle fly, get the feather (because every time you see an eagle fly, a feather drops at your feet), discuss what they learned from the experience, and head on home. Happy medicine man. Proud parents. Quiet Water decides not to look for his white parents: "The eagle showed me where I belong. I belong here with the Eagle Clan. You, father and mother, are my family."

Generic Indians. Trite, boring writing. Illustrations of animals and feathers, no people. Foolish names supposed to sound Indian. Another ripoff in the name of multiculturalism.—*Beverly Slapin*

Dunn, Anne M. (Ojibwe):
Grandmother's Gift: Stories from the Anishinaabeg, illustrations by Annette Humphrey (Ojibwe). Holy Cow! (1997). 142 pages, b/w illustrations; grades 4-up; Ojibwe
When Beaver Was Very Great: Stories to Live By, illustrations by Sharon L. White (Ojibwe). Midwest Traditions (1995). 223 pages, b/w illustrations; grades 4-up; Ojibwe
Winter Thunder: Retold Tales, illustrations by Cynthia Holmes (Ojibwe). Holy Cow! (2001). 161 pages, b/w illustrations; grades 4-up; Ojibwe

Anne Dunn's books contain variations on numerous traditional Ojibwe short stories that have been told and retold for generations. These stories are examples of the oral storytelling tradition of the Ojibwe, and those familiar with these stories will note the unique versions Dunn tells and appreciate them for their variations. Stories that are handed down orally from person to person take on the characteristics of the storyteller and here, Dunn's stories provide a glimpse into her storytelling style.

Some of these stories are shared with listeners in the traditional Ojibwe teaching style at times appropriate to a specific situation to help strengthen a lesson that can be learned through the experience. Others of the stories are best told together or individually during a quiet time when the relaxed atmosphere of storytelling facilitates thoughtful reflection.

Most of the characters in these stories are animals common to the Ojibwe home areas of the Great Lakes. Looking through the eyes of animals allows us to see our own humanness in new ways and to think about and learn important ideas. Even though these stories are short in length, don't be tempted to rush from story to story without reflecting, whether you are a lone reader or reading to a group. There are many lessons to be learned from each of these stories if they are enjoyed in the same loving way in which Dunn writes.—*Pam Martell*

Ann Dunn dedicates *Winter Thunder: Retold Tales* to "all who appreciate the power of story; who find mystery in the common and magic in the ordinary." From the hilarious "How Grasshopper Tricked a Trickster" and "Coyote and the (sacred) Fry Bread" to the scary "Snowbird and the Windigo" and "Frog Vengeance," Dunn's third volume, forty traditional stories passed down to her from her mother, brims with kindness and insight, strength and beauty, and great good humor. —*Beverly Slapin*

Edmiston, Jim, *Little Eagle Lots of Owls***, illustrated by Jane Ross. Houghton Mifflin (1993). Unpaginated, color illustrations; preschool-grade 2**

The child in this story, of unknown Nation, is named Little Eagle Lots of Owls. We don't know who named him or what his name is supposed to mean. We do not know where the people are because the only other character is his grandfather, the "old chief." According to the illustrations, these two live in the desert, the Great Plains *and* the forest.

Little Eagle, etc., has a long name. His grandfather the old chief says,

> You have the sharp eyes of the eagle, and you can see many things. But your name is as long as it takes the moon to walk across the sky.

His grandfather is afraid that Little Eagle will forget his name, so he gives him a basket of something as a gift. The rest of the story has the boy trying to figure out what's in the basket. It turns out to be three owls sleeping together. "Little Eagle Lots of Owls," the old chief says,

"you have the sharp eyes of the eagle and you are as wise as the owl. Now you know your true name." And that's it.

The story, dialogue, and illustrations are truly remarkable. The boy and his grandfather look as though they dressed in the Halloween aisle at Toys R Us. The art is generic "Indian" designs—done, oddly enough, in batik. An example of the text:

> Little Eagle jumped up and down. He whooped and yelled and beat his drum. His rain-dance only made it rain. When he stopped, the sun shone again...

For many Nations, Creator sends Owl to bring people up to the Spirit World. I don't know any Native person who would even think of giving anyone owls for a gift, much less naming someone "lots of them."

Both author and illustrator, who live in England, are a model for ignorance. This is a truly awful book.—*Beverly Slapin*

Edmonds, Walter, *The Matchlock Gun***, illustrated by Paul Lantz. Dodd, Mead (1941), G.P. Putnam (1989), Penguin Putnam (1998). 50 pages, b/w and color illustrations; grades 2-4**

In 1941, Dodd Mead published the story of a young Dutch family who, in 1756 while living in the Hudson River Valley, is attacked by Indians. The book was awarded the Newbery Medal "as One of the Most Distinguished Contributions to American Literature for Children."

The father, Teunis Van Alstyne, captain of the militia, responds to a report of raiding and a call to gather, assuring his wife that "there's no real chance that the Indians will carry so far as this." Of course they do. The matchlock gun of the title is the huge Spanish gun, longer than a grown man, brought to "the wild America" by Great-Grandfather Dygert. It is the gun with which the Captain's son, young Edward, kills the Indians when they come.

Here is the description of the Captain and his wife, Gertrude:

> They were a young couple to have a ten-year-old son; they were handsome and high-spirited; he lusty and thick-set, a true Dutchman; she, showing her Palatine breeding, dark, brown-eyed, with black hair braided round her head, her slim body limber and quick about her work.

The climate of danger, the aura of gathering menace, are skillfully set:

> There was only the note of the wind in the chimney and the feeling of it on the roof, like a hand pressed down out of darkness. It was easy to think of it passing through the wet woods, rocking the bare branches where only the beech trees had leaves left to shake.

> Their fields were so small in all these woods. An Indian might walk onto the stoop before they were aware of his presence on the farm, if they were indoors at the time.

When the Indians come, they fulfill the expectations that have been created. They are horror, the ultimate nightmare:

> There were five of them, dark shapes on the road, coming from the brick house. They hardly looked like men, the way they moved. They were trotting, stooped over, first one and then the other coming up, like dogs sifting up to the scent of food.

This may very well be one of the worst descriptions of Native people in children's literature, certainly in the 20th Century.

Edward fires off the Spanish gun, killing three of the Indians, the cabin burns, Gertrude is wounded, but the family is saved. On their return, the astonished militia finds them so:

> Gertrude still unconscious, Trudy asleep, and Edward sitting up with the gun across his knees, the bell mouth pointing at the three dead Indian bodies....And in the creek valley they had found another Indian crippled and had killed him. But now while Teunis picked up Gertrude, the others just sat their horses and stared from Edward to the dead Indians...."Who shot them, Edward?" "I did. With the Spanish gun," said Edward. "You've killed more than all the rest of us put together!" Mynderse exclaimed.

Paul Lantz's lithographs are well matched, making the words of the text visually manifest. We see the sweetness, the rightness of the little family and their triumph over savagery. A dark, double-page spread of the monstrous Indians, back-lit by the explosion of the big gun, with Gertrude at the cabin door, looking over her shoulder in terror, a hatchet buried in her back, contrasts sharply with an earlier illustration of a light-filled autumn landscape. Gertrude stands in profile, her arm around her son, one hand on her heart. Edward's little sister stands with arms spread wide to take in the whole universe.

African Americans do not escape unscathed.

> Edward asked whether he should take the butter over to Grandmother Van Alstyne...."She can send Tom over to get it." Tom was the widow's head negro. Trudy asked, "Why haven't we any slaves, Mama?" Gertrude explained that all the place really belonged to Teunis, so that Grandmother's slaves actually were theirs...

This book was bad enough for 1941. Now it has been chosen by the National Endowment for the Humanities, in cooperation with the American Library Association, for its "We the People Bookshelf on Courage," in order "to encourage young people to read and understand great literature while exploring themes in American history." These brooks chosen are said to be expressions of themes "that are integral parts of American culture," and to represent "the rich texture of the American heritage." *The Matchlock Gun* is a perfect choice for this list, but perhaps not exactly in the way the NEH intended, because it eulogizes an American past in which the indigenous populations were regarded as sub-human, and every effort made to exterminate them.

That this book has been consistently in print for sixty-three years and is now on a recommended list says something about American culture that some might not care to look at more closely. As for "great literature," one of the requirements for inclusion on the list was that the books had to have been published before 1980. That eliminates some of the best writing for children of the 20th Century. On the subject in question, Louise Erdrich's *The Birchbark House* and any of Joseph Bruchac's young adult novels would have been better choices than this. This thing has outlived its time—if it ever had one.—*Doris Seale*

Ellison, Suzanne Pierson, *The Last Warrior*. Northland (1997). 140 pages; grades 6-up; Ndee (Apache)

In this coming-of-age story very loosely based on historical incidents involving Geronimo's band of Chiricahuas who are forced to surrender to the U.S. Army, young Solito yearns to go on four raids to complete his "ritual training" and become a "true Chiricahua Apache brave." After being imprisoned at Fort Marion, taken to Carlisle Indian School, and loaned out to a Quaker family, Solito is forced to kill a white man and (from the Northland publicity):

return to the old ways in order to survive. Soon he finds himself at odds with the army, a vengeful warrior from his tribe, and his own family, who ritually abandoned him at birth. Badly torn, Solito must face a brutal Apache outlaw—and bridge the gap between his two worlds—before he can clear his name, carve his own future, and prove his manhood to himself.

There are too many inaccuracies here to deal with. The self-name for the people called "Apache" is Ndee; "Solito" is a Spanish name, as is "Geronimo"; the "ritual training" and "four-raids-and-you're-a-warrior" stuff is absurd. The narrative, dialogue, and use of metaphor are abominable. *The Last Warrior* is an excellent example of what goes wrong when a writer superimposes her own value system over that of the people she is writing about. Ellison writes in the first person, yet she treats the Indian characters, including Solito, in a way that shows no insight into their beliefs and lifeways; they are all ignorant, superstitious and savage, but the one really "bad guy" is Solito's cousin, Scarred-by-a-Woman. This is how he got his name:

> Discovering a young girl in a barn sleeping beside her sick colt, Scarred-by-a-Woman chose to kill her instead of slipping away unnoticed. She clawed his face with all her might as he stabbed her, and her blood mingled with his as she died.

Ellison portrays the whites, on the other hand, as well meaning (though sometimes misguided). They include Captain Richard Henry Pratt, the founder of Carlisle. Native children were stolen away from their parents, clans, and Nations; beaten and worse for trying to communicate with each other; humiliated daily in word and deed; "loaned out" to white families who treated them as slaves; seeing their siblings and friends die of malnutrition, disease, and beatings; and finally, if they survived, released; suffering from what we call today traumatic stress syndrome—outcasts belonging neither to their own world nor to the white world. Few survived with body and spirit intact.

As a non-Indian with outsider values, and whether out of ignorance or by intent, Ellison has produced one more historical whitewash. Not recommended.—*Beverly Slapin*

Erdosh, George, *Food and Recipes of the Native Americans*. Rosen (1997). 24 pages, color photos and illustrations; grades 1-4

The cover art of *Food and Recipes of the Native Americans* features a color photograph of a young white woman and her young white daughter (who look like models) cooking together. The photograph is slightly overlaid by a ghostly reproduction of either a painting or drawing of "Indians" wearing a lot of feathers. The juxtaposition of these images is indicative of the book's target audience and approach.

This is complicated somewhat by the author's choice of a contemporary Seminole girl, Nancy, who appears invented for illustrative reasons, to guide readers through a culinary journey through various regions, seeking the foods and recipes of Indian people "before European settlers (SET-ul-erz) brought new foods to North America."

The inclusion of "Nancy" and a few references to contemporary Native people does cut against the too-frequent "Indians-as-extinct" and "what-they-left-us" themes suggested by the cover, but here the separation of present and past may confuse young readers.

Nancy supposedly lives "on a Seminole reservation (reh-zer-VAY-shun)" in Florida but is so overtaken with curiosity about historical Native recipes that her entire family goes on the road. This rather extensive and undoubtedly expensive trip involves her interviewing elders because "she thought they would know the most about the traditional (truh-DISH-un-ul)" foods of their tribes.

Among other things, "Nancy learned that there were many Native American tribes in North America." While it's important to emphasize to non-Indians that there are different Nations, one might expect Nancy to know that.

In a discussion of historical foods, the book features only five recipes: Indian Fry Bread, Pumpkin-Corn Sauce, Baked Sweet Potato, Indian Vegetable Mush, and Pinole. The false implication is that Native people prepare none of these foods today.

But the most memorable thing about the book is the distinction between words deemed to require pronunciation assistance, and words that do not—"hide (HYD)," "plain (PLAYN)", and "sacred (SAY-kred)" all were deemed difficult for young readers, but not Sokomish, Quileute, or zucchini.

This cookbook is part of a series, "Cooking Throughout American History," which according to the back cover includes a number of other titles that all begin with the words "food and recipes." Other titles are tied to historical people and events such as: the Civil War; the Pilgrims; the Revolutionary War; the Thirteen Colonies; and the Westward Expansion. Many of the inconsistencies in *Food and Recipes of the Native Americans* may have resulted as an attempt to tie this historical theme in with peoples living today and the foods we eat now.

Look for a cookbook that is more consistent and offers more recipes.—*Cynthia L. Smith*

Erdrich, Lise (Ojibwe), *Bears Make Rock Soup and other stories,* **paintings by Lisa Fifield (Ojibwe). Childrens Book Press (2002). 32 pages, color illustrations; preschool-grade 3**

These are original stories, designed to show the long-time relationship between humans and animals. The illustrations are very beautiful but they seem throughout the book to be generic "Indian" more than relating to any particular Nation. For example, in the illustration for "The Bears that Couldn't Hibernate," two of the women are wearing dresses that could be perhaps Lakota, while a third is wearing a dress with elk teeth that could be Crow.

The stories demonstrate something common to nearly every Native tradition; that we do not see ourselves as better or on a different level than all the other forms of life with whom we share this Earth. But the title story, "Bears Make Rock Soup," seems more to relate to an old European folk tale that has many versions, the most familiar of which may be one called "Stone Soup," most famously written and illustrated by Marcia Brown.

There have been through history stories of bears who found and protected children who have been lost. That appears here in "Bears Return the Lost Children." For many of us, bears occupy a special place. They are our teachers and the givers of medicine. In the words of Joe Bruchac, "they hold this fragile Earth on the Turtle's back between steadfast paws." It is good to see them honored here.

Consistently, it is bothersome that no specific Nation is ever named. For instance, in "The Naming Ceremony," not all peoples have clan affiliation in this way. Although the illustration shows in a lovely and delicate way the relationship of the people to their clan totem, what is this little boy in the middle doing playing with the deer antlers? Maybe the painting is meant to convey a feeling of mystery? Perhaps that feeling of mystery comes through most strongly in "Forest of the Deer Spirits," my personal favorite. Occasionally the author's strong feelings about what she is saying betray her into a certain awkwardness of language. In the story, "Last Respects":

> Eagle came to soar with a spirit as fierce and sharp-eyed as his. Canada Goose came because the heart of Deer Chief was as faithful and true as his. Loon came because the heart of Deer Chief was just as brave and strong and free as hers.

This collection is an odd thing. The stories are certainly not traditional. The writing is sometimes awkward. The illustrations cannot really be called "authentic." But the author's and the illustrator's feelings and intent come through clearly. (As an aside, it would be interesting to see what the text looked like before going through the editing process.) I think I like this book better than I ought to.—*Doris Seale*

Erdrich, Louise (Ojibwe), *The Birchbark House,* **illustrated by the author. Hyperion (1999). 244 pages, b/w illustrations; grades 4-up; Ojibwe**

> She was named Omakayas, or Little Frog, because her first step was a hop. She grew into a nimble young girl of seven winters, a thoughtful girl with shining brown eyes, and a wide grin, only missing her two front teeth. She touched her upper lip. She still wasn't used to those teeth gone, and was impatient for her new, grown-up teeth to complete her smile.

With these few sentences, the child stands before us, not complete, but already someone we begin to know. Omakayas lives with her family on Moningwanaykaning Island, in what is now called Lake Superior. *The Birchbark House* is the story of one year in her life, and it may be the single best book of its kind. Many non-Native children's writers have attempted historical novels with an American Indian setting—from the outside. It is hard to think of even one that is successful. Erdrich writes from within: the culture, the historical memory of the events she chronicles, are from a real world, one that actually existed and is, still, the past out of which we come and have our being, and that will hold our future.

Omakayas' year is a time of growth, and joy, of lessons learned—some hard—and of tragedy and loss. It is a time when only the tribal and family bonds, the traditions of acceptance and caring, enable the people to hold together and come full circle, to another spring. For Omakayas, the year ends in a stunning revelation that shows her just how deep the love that holds the universe together goes.

Although it is very clear here that one child is not valued above another, it is also clear that Omakayas has gifts. She is growing into her life; there is the promise of who she may turn out to be. She is also an endearing little girl, with a very good heart. And it is hard to leave her. For all that it is so simply written, this is a rich and multi-layered work, with a strong sense of relationship, the "at-oneness with" of Native life, sometimes referred to as being "in tune with nature," which, of course, is not the same thing at all. Nor, *Hornbook* to the contrary, is this even remotely like the Laura Ingalls Wilder books.

The Birchbark House is a strong and beautiful book, and it is highly recommended.—*Doris Seale*

Erdrich, Louise (Ojibwe), *Grandmother's Pigeon*, illustrated by Jim LaMarche. Hyperion (1996). Unpaginated, color illustrations; grades 3-5; Ojibwe

Erdrich is one of the Native writers known to the mainstream book world, as well as the Native community. This was her first attempt at a children's picture book, and it is a delight: "As it turned out, Grandmother was a far more mysterious woman than any of us knew. It was common knowledge that she had trained kicking mules. We'd often heard how she had skied the Continental Divide." But it's when she decides to sail away to Greenland "on the back of a congenial porpoise" that things really get interesting. "Every time I pass Grandmother's room," Mother said, "I hear noises."

But all was as usual; the petrified buffalo tooth, the Sun-tzu's horse effigy—you know, like that—except for the bird's nest with eggs in it, which proceeded to hatch. "'I can't explain this,' Mother muttered over and over, holding the nest and warming the hatchlings with her cupped fingers." And then there's Grandmother's stuffed pigeon—looking "very pleased with itself." Wait 'til you see what they turn out to be.

It is not as common as one might think, in children's book publishing, for words and pictures to be an organic whole. Jim LaMarche's acrylic and colored pencil illustrations are luminous, with a feeling of wonder that makes them perfect companions for a story that is quite out of the ordinary.—*Doris Seale*

Erdrich, Louise (Ojibwe), *The Range Eternal*, illustrated by Steve Johnson and Lou Fancher. Hyperion (2002). Unpaginated, color illustrations; grades 1-up; Ojibwe

Once there was a time, and that not so long ago, when the land owned us the way we now think we own the land. Outside the cities, it still does.

Louise Erdrich's second picture book comes from such a time and such a place, from her memories of visits to her grandparents' home on the Turtle Mountain Reservation in North Dakota. It is told in the voice of a little girl who might have been her mother.

"On cold winter days in the Turtle Mountains, I helped Mama cook soup on our woodstove, The Range Eternal." That stove warmed her when she came inside from doing her barn chores. That stove was, "the warm heart of the House," and of their lives.

> The Range Eternal was printed in raised lettering on the blue enamel of the door. I learned to write by tracing those letters in the air. I copied them down, with charcoal, in the margins of daddy's newspaper.

And at night, when the sweeping winter winds of the Dakotas hurled themselves against the walls of the house; when, "In the thick breath of storms, I heard the footsteps of Windigo....At the window, at the door," waiting, it was the stove that saved her. "The monster's snow fingers could not grasp through its heat....Safe, I looked through its door into pictures of long ago."

Because the Range Eternal is not only a stove. It is also "the range of the buffalo, who once covered the plains of North Dakota so thickly that they grazed from horizon to horizon." Also the range of all prairie life and the place where hawks and eagles drift on the wind, the place where a child could grow up in the warmth and safety of family and home. Inevitably, "poles and wires went up along the road to our house." Now there was light at the touch of a finger, and a new stove—which wasn't the same at all.

But a day comes when the little girl is all grown up with a child of her own.

> All things seem complete. Yet there are times when I feel something missing. My son cries out in his dreams....I long for a center of true warmth. It was not until I passed the broad window of a store that sold old things, that I knew what I missed. The Range Eternal. The Range Eternal.

So the Range Eternal came home. And now,

> Even in the city, I show my husband and son how the animals race back and forth across the walls....Together, we see again the old range, the vast range, the living range restored.

Because in the end, the land itself is eternal, no matter what we do to it, and will be here long after we are gone.

For this reader, the pictures are a perfect fit, conveying both the beauty and power of the land, the bitter cold of a Dakota winter, and the things that might move in it, but also the goodness of the life that can be found there.

This is a lovely and powerful book.—*Doris Seale*

Esbensen, Barbara Juster, illustrated by Helen K. Davie. Little, Brown. Unpaginated, color illustrations; grades 3-5; Ojibwe:
Ladder to the Sky: How the Gift of Healing Came to the Ojibway Nation (1989)
The Star Maiden: An Ojibway Tale (1988)

These are new-age "retellings" of a story or stories that Ojibwe writer and Methodist minister George Copway first put down in 1850. I have not seen the originals, but Esbensen's versions are hokey.

In *Star Maiden*, the people live in an idyllic sort of place, reminiscent of the garden of you-know-what:

> There were no wars among them. Summer was always in the air. The streams were clear and pure and filled with fish. And the earth was rich with everything the people needed.

No snake or anything to tempt them. So they see this star, and the chief sends his "braves" into "the far hills" to see what's going on. That very night, a "brave" with thunderbird underwear has a dream vision, of a "silver maiden" with a voice "like a thread of silver" who wants to live among them. She has to choose what form she will take. After many trials, she does. She becomes a star, and somehow, she and all her star sisters become water lilies: "Water lilies! They are the stars that fell from the deep sky…Touch them gently and remember."

Although the jacket copy gushes that the paintings are "beautifully framed with patterned borders, reflecting authentic Native American sources," and some of them are pretty, authentic they are not. The border illustrations are a mishmash, using elements of Plains parfleches and quillwork, Great Lakes beadwork, Dutch pottery, miscellaneous applique ribbonwork, and who-knows-what-else? And what are those outfits supposed to be? Whole otters on people's regalia? Feather headdresses? Thunderbird on the lead guy's underwear? Spirit beings surrounded by "silver light"?

Our traditional star stories have purpose. They teach direction and ways to navigate, they're tied to the seasons, and they have deeply spiritual significance as well. None of this comes through, either in Esbensen's ethereal googly-eyed "retelling" or Davie's wannabe romantic illustrations.

Ladder to the Sky is "retold" in the same way; it may actually be worse. This retelling includes a guide for pronouncing Ojibwe vowels, but includes few Ojibwe words. Instead, it is written in the self-conscious way of non-Indian retellers trying to sound "Indian"—you know, "spirit beings," "sky-kingdom," "run like the storm wind."

Ladder has the same idyllic setting as *Star Maiden*. And, in those days, all the men were strong and brave. They could run like the storm wind….The women in those times sang as they worked. Their clear voices filled the forest with melodies, and they walked with light step and straight back, even when they were very old.

Nobody ever gets sick, and nobody ever dies. The "shining spirit messengers" come down a magic vine (a la Jack and the Beanstalk?) to earth, and carry the old people up to the sky. The Ojibwe are forbidden by the Great Spirit to touch the magic vine (maybe they would steal the goose?). But comes a time of discontent: the people grow jealous of a young man who had become friends with a spirit messenger. This spirit messenger reads the young man's thoughts and takes him to the skyland against his grandmother's wishes. Granny climbs the vine to try to retrieve her grandson. The people find out and—"Ay-e-e-e!"—they are horrified, because she had disobeyed the Great Spirit. She falls, and brings down "pain and discomfort…disease and death" as punishment. But the spirits, "who seemed to be speaking with one silvery voice" (Esbensen really likes silvery metaphors), also give the people medicine and medicine people.

Ladder is every bit as belabored as *Star Maiden*, and even more Christian with its vengeful, punishing Great Spirit. Not recommended.—*Barbara Potter*

Eubank, Patricia Reeder, *Seaman's Journal: On the Trail with Lewis and Clark*, illustrated by the author. Ideals Children's Books (2002). Unpaginated, color illustrations; grades 1-4

Virtually all the children's books about the Lewis and Clark expedition to the contrary, it was not a scientific endeavor. All their journals and sketches of flora and fauna notwithstanding, the purpose of Meriwether Lewis and William Clark's famous search for a water route to the Pacific Ocean was a colonial expedition of expansion.

Throughout the expedition, Lewis and Clark and their "Corps of Discovery" met with tribal leaders representing more than fifty Native Nations, to whom they explained that their land now belonged to the United States, and that Thomas Jefferson was now their "great white father." The captains would then distribute some trade goods and a "peace medal" featuring the likeness of Jefferson and two clasped hands. The Corps would then march in formation and hold a sort-of show of military might. As can be expected, some of the tribes were not very happy about all of this.

The narrator in this terribly contrived picture book is Seaman—Lewis's Newfoundland dog—who keeps a journal as he accompanies Lewis and Clark on their "voyage of discovery." Seaman's "story" is a series of very short, simplistic, and oftentimes idiotic, descriptions of what he sees and hears. For instance:

> We named this river Teton River, but the Sioux call it "Bad River." The only thing bad are the manners of the Sioux! They carried my master on a painted buffalo robe to their camp. They placed him on a white buffalo skin where he smoked the peace pipe with the council chiefs. When we started toward our boat to leave, the Sioux grabbed the boat's rope to stop us. They wanted tobacco and our pirogue. When Lewis threw tobacco at the chief, they let us go. I was glad to get away. The Sioux eat dogs!

Seaman says that the Corps "named" a river that the Indians "call" something else, thereby legitimizing for young readers the renaming and invalidating the original (Indian) name. Seaman criticizes the Lakota for their bad manners, a word play on the original name of the river. But then he describes how the Lakota honored Meriwether Lewis by inviting him to sit on a white buffalo hide and join them in the smoking of a Calf Pipe. It would not be a stretch to imagine that the Lakota did not like Lewis's treatise on Manifest Destiny while smoking a Calf Pipe. It is known that a major argument ensued; and after a standoff in which weapons were drawn by both sides, the argument was ultimately settled by a gift of tobacco from the Corps to the Lakota, who then allowed them to leave. It probably seemed to the Lakota that Lewis exhibited his own "bad manners" in the way he responded to their attempt to honor him.

That "the Sioux eat dogs!"—especially since it's uttered by a dog—is bound to evoke a loud "eeeeyyyuuuu" from young readers. But on the topic of eating dog meat, the following entry can be found in Clark's own journal (January 3, 1806):

> [O]ur party from necescity have been obliged to Subsist some length of time on dogs have now become extremely fond of their flesh; it is worthy of remark that while we lived principally on the flesh of this animal we wer much more healthy and more fleshey than we have been Sence we left the Buffalow Country. (spelling and grammatical errors in journal)

It would seem that Seaman would have been in far more danger from the men of the Corps who had just "discovered" another delicacy than he would have been from the Lakota, who generally didn't go around eating other people's pets.

In other notable passages:

• Seaman "writes" that "[o]ne day (Sacajawea) made pem-

mican and gave me a piece. I ate the dried meat in it but spit out the nuts and berries. Phooey!" It is impossible to separate the ingredients in pemmican—they're all mashed and held together with fat. And besides, dogs *love* nuts and berries!

• Seaman "writes" of hearing an "Indian legend about the Spirit Mound. The legend says men only eighteen inches tall with huge heads live at the mound.... The men (of the Corps) walked for three hours before reaching the mound. They saw no men, but buffalo covered the prairie." To describe a Native traditional story this way negates a belief system at least as complex as Christianity.

• Except for Sacajawea and a few children, all the Indians are depicted as men. Did the Corps of Discovery encounter only male Indians? And even they are drawn and labeled, not as individuals, but as part of the general flora and fauna "discovered" by the Corps. Buffalo, bobcat, prickly pear cactus, elk, Sioux.

• Practically each page has an illustration of a place, plant or animal "discovered" and renamed by the Corps. Yet there is no writing about the traditional uses and significant scientific knowledge of the plants and animals taught to the Corps by their hosts. Because of the generosity of their Native hosts, the expedition was able to learn and utilize this life-saving knowledge time and again.

Finally, to save the best for last:

Seaman's Journal has a recipe called "Sacajawea's Pemmican." When Sacajawea made pemmican, she would have used local ingredients and traditional food preparation techniques. She would have pounded berries—such as raspberries, blackberries, blueberries, or chokecherries—into dried, flaked buffalo meat or venison, and there would have been some kind of tallow to hold it together and to preserve it. She could have, but probably would not have, sweetened it with honey. Among the ingredients in "Sacajawea's Pemmican" are dried cranberries (indigenous to parts of the Northeast) and peanut butter (indigenous to West Africa and imported to the Southeast and Caribbean with the slave trade). And young readers will be led to believe—because there is no note to the contrary—that Sacajawea used a measuring cup, blender, microwave, plastic-lined baking dish, and—a refrigerator.

This is what non-Indian children will learn from *Seaman's Journal*:

Indians were rude. Indians believed in "legends" that weren't true. Indians ate dogs like Seaman. Sacajawea was very nice.

This is what Indian children will learn about themselves from *Seaman's Journal*:

Indians are rude. Indians believe in "legends" that aren't true. Indians eat dogs like Seaman. Sacajawea was very nice.

Seaman's Journal is not recommended.

—*Barbara Potter, Beverly Slapin, Jane Waite*

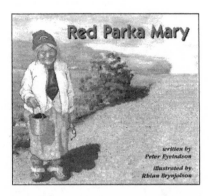

Eyvindson, Peter, Pemmican Publications:
Chester Bear, Where Are You?, 1988, illustrated by Wendy Wolsak-Frith. Unpaginated, color illustrations; preschool-up
Kyle's Bath, 1984, illustrated by Wendy Wosak. Unpaginated, b/w illustrations; grades 1-2
Old Enough, 1986, illustrated by Wendy Wosak. Unpaginated, b/w illustrations; grades 2-up
Red Parka Mary, 1996, illustrated by Rhian Brynjolson. Unpaginated, color illustrations; grades 1-3
The Wish Wind, 1987, illustrated by Wendy Wosak. Unpaginated, b/w illustrations; grades 2-3

Peter Eyvindson's children's books focus on everyday life issues that young (and we older ones also) think and ponder about. Who hasn't wished that summer's heat couldn't be relieved by a winter wind? *The Wish Wind* plays out our longing for change, a change in the weather or a change in our age, with an unspoken reminder that enjoying each moment for what it offers now is a precious part of life. *Old Enough*, about taking time to enjoy the young people in our lives, is a story many adults ought to read. What young child hasn't plotted to get out of taking a bath, when there are so many other things to do instead? The young protagonist in *Kyle's Bath* shows us the futility of trying to outwit one's mother. My young niece and nephew remind me each time I tuck them into bed (as my daughter did when she was young) of the importance of a special nighttime companion; this is portrayed so well in *Chester Bear, Where Are You?* My favorite Eyvindson story is *Red Parka Mary*, because the story made me feel more human about being hesitant to befriend people who are different from me, yet reminding me of all the precious family and friends in my life who probably appear unusual to someone who doesn't know them.

Eyvindson has a gift for taking familiar and everyday events and playing them through in a story that is easy to relate to, trust, and then examine the merits of my own personal reactions in similar situations. Yet the self-examination that is sparked by Eyvindson's stories feels comfortable and comforting. It was refreshing to see our faces in stories about everyday modern life, rather than just seeing our faces in stories specifically about Native people.

These are important books for families and classrooms of children to have as reminders that we're all feeling, dreaming, and at times afraid human beings just trying to make our way in life.—*Pam Martell*

Fitzpatrick, Marie-Louise, *The Long March*, illustrated by the author. Tricycle (1998). Unpaginated, b/w illustrations; grades 4-6; Choctaw

In 1847, an impoverished group of Choctaw, having learned of the potato famine in Ireland, made a gift of $170—the equivalent today of about $5,000—to the starving people there. This is a story of one dispossessed people reaching out to another—a story that, until now, had not been put into a book for young readers.

Narrated in the first person, *The Long March* is the story of Choona, a teenager who hears for the first time about his people's forced march at the hands of the U.S. government, from their ancestral lands in the east to "Indian Territory" in the west. And it is the story of his people's decision, a few years later, to share what little they had with starving strangers an ocean away.

The drawings, in what looks like pencil, are lovely. These are Choctaw faces. These are real people. But the weakness of this book—and its failure—is Fitzpatrick's attempt to tell this event through the eyes of a Choctaw child. Despite all of her research, the story is forced, the dialogue is strained. This is not an Indian worldview. For instance,

- "I was fourteen years old. When they called me a boy, I was insulted. When they said I was nearly a man, I was confused." In traditional tribal society, children know where they belong—adolescent angst is characteristic of a different culture.

- This story is told in the first person, but there are far too many "I's" to comprise an Indian speech pattern. On one page, there are actually fourteen "I's."

- It is hard to believe that a Choctaw child in 1847 would not have heard the stories of the "long march" during the 1830s. Elders, then as now, would probably have passed along the stories for the children and grandchildren to keep in their hearts forever.

- An elder telling a story probably would not have compared the people on a death march to a "great herd of buffalo."

- People on a forced march in the middle of the winter would not need—nor would they ask for—nor would they get—an explanation from their captors of "why the blankets and food the government promised did not come."

- On the last page, the old man whose boy's name was Choona, remembers the past with the oratorical skill of a white person trying to sound Indian:

> I wear white man's clothes. Some of my grandchildren's children do not speak Choctaw. Our great traditions seem fragile now. But that day as I watched Moshi ride away on his horse, I felt the eagle spirit race through my blood.

I don't know why Fitzpatrick chose to tell this story from the perspective of a people she knows little about. Had she chosen to tell this story from the point of view of her own people—the Irish—as recipients of this generous gift of food and friendship from another beleaguered people, it might have been stronger.—*Beverly Slapin*

Flood, Renée Sansome, *Lost Bird of Wounded Knee: Spirit of the Lakota*. Scribner (1995). 384 pages, b/w photos; high school-up; Lakota

History can be told through dates, battles, political figures; you'll find all those here. But this history is told through the sad life of one Lakota woman. Not only is there a perspective on events of the 19th Century, but there is a strong resonance with current problems of removal of Native children from their relatives and tribal cultural heritages.

Zintkala Nuni (Lost Bird) as an infant survived the Wounded Knee Massacre of 1890, only to be adopted by a white general as a political stepping stone for his ambitions, then later sent off to a miserable life at a Native residential school, being passed among many men, abandoned and betrayed, and dying at age 29 of diseases from which she had no immunity. The book is a story of how Lost Bird's body was traced by Pine Ridge Lakota relatives and reburied at the Wounded Knee Massacre Memorial Cemetery on the Pine Ridge Reservation in South Dakota. It has very great interest for Native children who were adopted away from their relatives and cultures, and also as a different look at the history of the Lakota people and the dispossession of their lands. This book is very highly recommended, especially for older Native youth who, for reasons perhaps more subtle than those of Lost Bird, feel removed from their culture and relatives.—*Paula Giese*

Freedman, Russell, *The Life and Death of Crazy Horse*, "drawings by Amos Bad Heart Bull" (Lakota). Holiday House (1996). 166 pages, b/w illustrations; grades 5-up; Lakota

"History is a set of lies agreed upon."
(Napoleon)

"Lying is done with words, and with silence."
(Adrienne Rich)

Tasunke Witko, Crazy Horse—along with Sitting Bull, Pocahontas, Sacajawea and Geronimo—captured the American imagination. He is a mysterious figure; it has been impossible to fit him precisely into any of the categories to which Native people are generally consigned. Crazy Horse was instrumental in handing the U.S. Army one of its worst defeats, but very little is actually known about him with any degree of certainty. Perforce, anything written about him must be more history than biography. In Freedman's case, it is also a work of the imagination.

There is so much one can say, by implication and innuendo, without really saying it, beginning with the statement, "Drawings by Amos Bad Heart Bull." Unless one knows better or turns to the information in the back of the book, one would get the impression that the drawings were created specifically for this volume. The way in which one says something is immensely important, especially when writing for young people.

> As white miners, ranchers, and farmers streamed into the West, it was the clear duty of the United States Army to protect the advancing frontier, and Indians stood in the way.

Given what they have been taught, this is not going to appear to young readers as anything but a reasonable statement.

> Thanks to...the written accounts of white men who came into contact with Crazy Horse, writers and historians have been able to reconstruct the story of his life.

Not the most reliable of sources. Perhaps Freedman's dependence on these sources accounts for the bias, both subtle and blatant, that is pervasive throughout this book. When speaking of the Native people, Freedman's tone, slightly derogatory, rather patronizing, is perfect for fostering distance—an "us-and-them" way of looking at what happened on the Northern Plains in the second half of the 19th Century, and to the people who lived there. Cast doubt on the facts just slightly (italics mine):

> "[T]he Indians protested again. They had not been told truthfully what the sixteen articles of the treaty really said, *they claimed*."

> "The Sand Creek Massacre, *as it was now called...*"

On the cholera and smallpox epidemics that caused terrible losses among the Cheyenne and Lakota: "The Sioux and Cheyennes blamed the whites for the epidemic. Some of them believed that white men deliberately introduced the disease among the Indians, and they talked darkly of revenge."

The facts: Misrepresenting the contents of treaties was a standard tactic with people who spoke little or no English. Sand Creek was a massacre. Black Kettle and his Cheyenne were under a flag of truce when they were gunned down; men, women and children. Spreading disease among the Indians was common; they had reason to believe it. Lord Jeffrey Amherst was the first, in the 18th Century, when he caused blankets that had belonged to victims of smallpox to be distributed among the people he wanted to eliminate. And it happened many times after that.

Make the Indians look ridiculous, or savage, or both: "They knew...how to put an ear to the ground and hear the distant rumble of hooves..." And, "Then they galloped off, yipping and yelling on their swift painted ponies." And, "[T]hey paraded through the village on painted ponies, singing war songs, wearing flowing crests of eagle's feathers and bright robes fringed with the scalp locks of their enemies." These are images straight out of Hollywood—and bad writing, besides. There is plenty of that. Just one, on the woman Crazy Horse loved, Black Buffalo Woman:

> She had soft eyes, black hair that shimmered like moonbeams as it fell in braids down her back, and a laughing smile that attracted young men.... For a few minutes he could smell the sweet-grass that perfumed her whitened deerskin dress and hear her shy, quick breathing inside the dark folds of the courting blanket.

Perhaps Freedman's next money-maker could be noble-savage romance novels.

Freedman seems to have taken Mari Sandoz as his primary source, and her *Crazy Horse: the Strange Man of the Oglalas* in

particular. Maybe he relied on that one a little too much, because a goodly amount of what he has written really is fiction. The chapters on Crazy Horse's young years are mostly based on generalized information about what a Lakota boy's life might have been like at the time, and are purely speculative. He certainly is not tentative about it; no "he might have," "perhaps he," "it was likely that"— just the imagined, presented as fact. Instances of this throughout the text: "As the days grew shorter, Crazy Horse looked in the faces of his people and saw the fear and loneliness of the hunted." At the Arrow Creek attack, Crazy Horse "wanted to show off his courage to Sitting Bull." Lieutenant Casper Collins and Crazy Horse "had some good laughs together as they compared the different customs of their two peoples." And, "As the Sioux leaders looked around them...the strength of their people made their hearts glad again."

Assigning thoughts, feelings and motivation to one's biographee is risky business, especially when writing about someone who essentially inhabited a different universe. Double that when your book is full of quotes, many unattributed, and not a single reference given for any of them. There is not a footnote in the entire 151 pages of text. Freedman's description of Crazy Horse's "quest" for a vision is purely his own imaginings of what this might be like, and fairly offensive to boot. The words, "the world ...where there is nothing but the spirit of all things," that he sets down as his own, are a direct quote from Black Elk.[1]

Apart from this, there are a number of things Freedman gets wrong. Crazy Horse and Hump were not young boys together. "[W]hen he was a boy [he] used to be around with the older Hump all the time. Hump was not young at the time, and he was a very great warrior, maybe the greatest we ever had until then...I think Hump knew Crazy Horse would be a great man and wanted to teach him everything." This is from *Black Elk Speaks*.[2] Freedman lists this book as a source; did he read it? He says that Crazy Horse's band was "Hunkpatila." "Hunkpatina, the Lower Yanktonai, belong to the Nakota; Crazy Horse was Oglala Lakota. Freedman says that "Crazy Horse struck up a fast friendship with Sitting Bull," which may well be true, but as with so many of his statements, without documentation, it is not subject to proof.

Akicita were not societies of warriors. They kept order in the camps, and watched over the people when they were on the move. Freedman persists in using "Sioux," which was never the People's name for themselves, rather than Lakota—which for most, has replaced the older Teton. "Witko" does not mean "holy." That is "wakan."

There is, of course a lot about the battles, conflicts over treaties and land-grabs, and demonstrations of Crazy

Horse's exceptional valor. There is no way to know how many of the stories ever happened—legends accrue around such a man. It isn't so much that Freedman plays fast and loose with what is known for a fact—although he does that sometimes, too, as, again, the way he says it. The Cheyenne "rode into camp howling like wolves"; the government's efforts "to buy the Black Hills peacefully"—is there another way to "buy" something?—is ended by the intransigence of the "hostiles."

There is considerable confusion surrounding the murder of Crazy Horse, and the events leading up to it. The two most important accounts are listed in Freedman's bibliography are *The Killing of Chief Crazy Horse: Three Eyewitness Views by the Indian, Chief He Dog, the Indian-White, William Garnett, and the White Doctor, Valentine Mc Gillycuddy*[3] and *To Kill an Eagle: Indian Views on the Last Days of Crazy Horse.*[4] Freedman finds them "unusual." Even here, the details vary. Getting past accusation, denial, the self-serving, and assertions of absolute fact from those in no position to know, some things seem to stay constant. There was some jealousy of Crazy Horse on the part of other leaders. There was plenty of doubt about how long their Eagle would stay caged, and whether he would become a locus of disaffection if he did. He was stabbed with a bayonet by a guard. It was not an accident. He was being held by some of his own people when he was stabbed. All else is written on the wind.

Freedman says that what happened "will always be uncertain....people who were there that day saw what they wanted to see..." That does not stop him from going into some detail about the trouble stirred up against Crazy Horse by others, and the murder itself, complete with quotes. "The officer of the day shouted, 'Stab him! Kill the son of a bitch!'" At this point, Freedman says, "Crazy Horse could not fight back because his arms were being held by one of his own people—just as he had seen in his vision." What he intends this to mean escapes me. What Crazy Horse said—or didn't say; who was there—or wasn't there; whether his father was with him—or wasn't; all, open to interpretation, depending on which source you're looking at.

The Life and Death of Crazy Horse adds nothing new. There is no original thinking, no attempt to provide for young readers a new and more truthful way of looking at the colonization of this country. It's a handsome book physically, from the soft focus, romantic jacket painting, to the large format, good paper, clear print and wide margins; a high-end item. But it has no heart.

I would rather have what Black Elk said:

> In his own tepee he would joke, and when he was on the warpath with a small party, he would joke to make his warriors feel good...everybody liked him, and they would do anything he wanted or go anywhere he said....He was a queer man. Maybe he was always partway into that world of his vision. He was a very great man, and I think if the Wasichus had not murdered him down there, maybe we should still have the Black Hills and be happy. They could not have killed him in battle. They had to lie to him and murder him. And he was only about thirty years old when he died.[5]

Here is some sense of flesh and blood, a glimpse of someone real.

Freedman's last sentence, as the Indians rode away:

> [The white men] saw them disappear into the hills, heading north in search of freedom, taking the spirit of Crazy horse with them.

So many things have been written, or done, or said, "in the spirit of Crazy Horse." The image to carry is this one: two old people, going away with the body of their son, to a place where he could never be found, and his spirit find peace "in the real world that is behind this one."[6]
—*Doris Seale*

NOTES

1 Neihardt, John G., *Black Elk Speaks: Being the Life Story of a Holy Man of the Oglala Sioux.* University of Nebraska, 1961, p. 85.

2 Neihardt, *ibid.*, p. 85.

3 University of Nebraska, 1988.

4 Johnson Books, 1981.

5 Neihardt, *op. cit.*, p. 87.

6 Neihardt, *ibid.*, p. 85.

Gaikesheyongai, Sally (Ojibwe), *The Seven Fires: An Ojibway Prophecy*, illustrated by Polly Keeshig-Tobias (Ojibwe). Sister Vision (1994). Unpaginated, color illustrations; grades 4-up; Ojibwe

In a touching and straightforward way, Gaikesheyongai tells of each of the seven fires, how she interprets each prophecy, and how each relates to Ojibwe life (and the life of all of us) today. Readers will feel Gaikesheyongai's presence as she shares a heartfelt, inspiring and philosophical discussion. As she explains the prophecies in simple, personal language that young people can easily identify with, they will come away with a lot to think about.

The First Fire, Gaikesheyongai says, "speaks of the time before colonialism." It was a time when the people welcomed the teachings that would help them to see everything around them as being sacred because their survival depended on the establishing of a way of life that was harmonious, not destructive, to everything they depended on.

The Second Fire, she says, was a "weakening of the ways," and the Third Fire was a time of migration. The Fourth Fire told of the coming of new "brothers and sisters from across the ocean." The Fifth Fire was lit when the people realized that the newcomers "had forgotten the sacredness of all things." These colonizers brought the seeds of oppression, control, the wiping out of the people's identity. The Sixth Fire was lit when most Ojibwe withdrew from their culture, traditional and spiritual values and practices. The Seventh Fire, Gaikesheyongai says, is the time we are living in now, "a new generation who would not let all the pain and anger and lies stop them from finding out the truth about who they are and what has happened." It is a time of looking back and looking forward, and "that choice is before us now."

The discussion of each fire is accompanied by a full-page watercolor-and-ink drawing, awesome in its simplicity and honesty. Both discussions and pictures will have children thinking very deeply about what was, what could have been, what has changed—and what is yet possible. This is a treasure of a book.—*Barbara Potter*

Garaway, Margaret Kahn:
Ashkii and His Grandfather, illustrated by Harry Warren (Diné). Treasure Chest (1989). 33 pages, color illustrations; grades 3-4; Diné (Navajo)
Dezbah and the Dancing Tumbleweeds, illustrated by Cathie Lowmiller. Old Hogan (1990). 82 pages, b/w illustrations; grades 4-5; Diné (Navajo)
The Old Hogan, illustrated by Andrew Emerson Bia (Diné). Old Hogan (1993). 32 pages, color illustrations; grades 2-3; Diné (Navajo)

I read these books with a highlighting pen and found myself highlighting just about every line on every page; they're that bad.

ASHKII AND HIS GRANDFATHER

Ashkii is a six-year-old who goes to "summer sheep camp" with his grandfather. I have never heard of such a thing as "summer sheep camp." People go out with their sheep every day. If a family can afford it, they have a winter home and a summer home, to which they move all their stuff and all their animals. They have a sheep dip at the chapter house, and they stop there long enough to dip the sheep and then move them home.

Most Diné do not have quarter horses; they ride mixed-breed horses, mostly mustangs they have caught and tamed. Diné sheepherders do not wear spurs.

On the range, "Ashkii wished Grandfather would talk to him, but he knew he had to wait for Grandfather to speak first. That was the way of his people." Diné children talk to grandparents whenever they feel the need to talk with them; but they don't babble and they don't interrupt, and they are quiet when they sense that an adult doesn't want to talk. They learn this social skill through observation. Later, Grandfather tells Ashkii,

> Grandson, I'm proud of you. You did not keep chattering just to hear yourself talk. You left me alone with my thoughts. You will be a fine sheepherder.

Diné don't commend children for doing something they should do. Children know by non-verbal communication whether a relative is happy with their behavior or not; it does not have to be explained.

Particular plants are referred to by their Diné name; "locoweed" is not one of them. Diné refer to specific animals by name; they don't call them "wildlife."

All a shepherd needs is a horse, a good sheepdog and a stick to control the sheep and keep coyotes and wild dogs away. Sheepherders don't refer to their job as "responsible"; rather, it's an important job and it's understood that sheep are valuable.

Ashkii draws while he's watching the sheep. Grandfather tells him that "each day's picture has gotten better and better." Grandparents don't put a value judgment on something a child has drawn, and Ashkii wouldn't need his grandfather to validate what he has done. Grandfather goes on and on about how Ashkii needs to go to school so that his teachers can help him become a good artist. Most Diné children can draw better than their non-Native teachers; it is a natural ability to be nurtured, not taught.

Every night, Grandfather reminds Ashkii and Chee how important it is to go to school and to learn their ABCs and their numbers. A Diné grandparent might tell the children that they need to get a good education, but the whole concept of school usually has a negative connotation because most parents had very negative experiences at the residential schools. They don't value the experiences; rather, they value education. Moreover, specific skills such as ABCs and numbers are not valued; a grandparent would speak about skills that would help them in life.

When Ashkii and Chee run away, the principal sends someone to their home. Usually school staffers do not visit children at home because they could not *find* their homes. And the principal is "kind and understanding" here, also not typical characteristics. Usually the principal would punish them for things they hadn't even done, much less let them off the hook.

What's this about "at last the day came" when the teacher let the class draw pictures? Children draw every day in kindergarten; this doesn't make any sense. And a school art show? With ribbons? It's unacceptable to reward certain children and not reward others; rather, the school would probably display all the art.

DEZBAH AND THE DANCING TUMBLEWEEDS

Dezbah is a twelve-year-old who dreams of becoming the first Diné girl to win an Olympic gold medal. Then she gets hit by a truck and finds herself unable to walk. Her teacher, who is white, visits her every day, and teaches her all about (white) classical literature, (white) classical music, and ballet. Out of devotion to "Miss Julie," Dezbah casts aside her backward Diné values, "overcomes her adversity," and becomes a talented ballet dancer.

Diné children generally do not aspire to "win" at individual competitions. They do not work out on homemade tracks each morning. Rather, they run east, as far as they can, toward the sun, to greet the morning.

The Diné reservation is so flat one can see for many miles, and there's no reason why a person would not see a pickup coming on the highway. There are no ambulances on the reservation; Diné bring injured people into town themselves. The family would probably hold a Healing Way or Blessing Way Ceremony first, then deal with the doctors afterwards if that didn't help. It would not be up to a white doctor to suggest that the family hold a ceremony.

Teachers do not go out daily to tutor children on the reservation. Homes are usually far from the schools, and there are no addresses or signs. Dezbah would not tell Coyote stories to her teacher, nor would she share the stories of her grandfather, because it would be inappropriate to do so with an outsider.

Dezbah's mother would not "glance shyly" at the teacher. Diné do not stare into other people's faces, but that is different from being shy.

Diné children do not have "their curiosity aroused" by seeing someone read. Although the traditional way is storytelling, Diné read not only in English, but also in their own language. Also, books are given to Diné children because they often can't afford to buy them.

"All I know is Navajo music I hear at powwows," Dezbah confides to her teacher. Most music is done in ceremony, and there aren't many powwows out in that area.

Then there's the Healing Ceremony, more accurately called a Healing Way or Blessing Way. The ceremony would not take place in the way in which it is described here, and furthermore, white people would not be invited

to this or any other ceremony. The things that take place are sacred and would not be discussed with an outsider. Dezbah wouldn't be sitting on a Pendleton blanket; she'd most likely be on a sheepskin. Pendleton blankets are expensive; they are given away at marriages and funerals.

Diné girls don't engage in a lot of negative self-talk as Dezbah does, because it could come true. It is also very unlikely that Dezbah would worry about being brave. Bravery is a concept that is instilled in Diné children as a way to behave. For instance, one does not cry or otherwise show emotions in public.

Diné grandparents do not talk down to their grandchildren.

I don't know of a Diné who is interested in ballet. It has no useful value and it's not part of the culture. Diné by nature are very conservative in dress. I don't know any Diné who would be caught dead in a tutu.

Dezbah gets a sheepdog as a pet. On the Diné reservation, where resources are scarce, every animal has a useful purpose; there are no such things as "pets."

Dezbah's mother brings "out a beautiful Navajo style blouse and skirt...made of light blue cotton dainty floral print." Traditional Diné clothes are very elegant; they're made from velveteen and satin. Only everyday clothes are made of cotton.

Dezbah wants "Miss Julie to be the first to know of (her) recovery" and tells everyone "not to tell Miss Julie until (she does)." The first people who would know would be her immediate family, her extended family, and the medicine man. Her teacher would find out when she saw her walking.

Dezbah's twelfth birthday would be a family and community celebration, not a "birthday party" as non-Native people know it.

Dezbah "(flings) herself into her beloved teacher's arms." It is considered inappropriate for Diné to display affection in a public way.

A dance teacher from New York City moves to town and opens up a dance studio. This is so unlikely as to be ridiculous. Who would be her students?

"The girl had the stature of a classic ballet dancer. Her head was small and her neck long. She had long legs..." Diné aren't built that way; for the most part, they're short and stout.

"[S]even people living in a one-room hogan left no room for warm-up and limbering exercises," so father fixes up the old shed to become an area for Dezbah to practice dancing, even builds her a barre. Vanity is not a Diné value, nor do they have the time or money to put into something as frivolous as ballet. When it's the end of the month and you're down to stirring flour into your coffee for breakfast, you're not going to spend time worrying about a mirror.

"Ballet is probably one of the most esthetic forms of expression," Dezbah says, "it's very thrilling when every part of my body moves to the music." For Diné, dance is not a "form of expression"; it is used in ceremony, it is prayer.

Before Dezbah goes to New York, her parents discuss the possibility that she might "lose" her Diné culture. People do not "lose" their culture. Despite the best efforts of the U.S. government to destroy indigenous cultures, we have managed to survive.

THE OLD HOGAN

An old hogan is sad because her family is moving to a modern house. The whole book explains the old hogan's feelings.

At the beginning, the old hogan "feels the spring wind whip the sand around her gentle curves." Diné do not speak of sexual characteristics when they speak of the female gender, or in this case, of a female object.

"The old hogan has been happy and content all these years." The concepts of happiness and contentment are not thought of, and Diné do not attribute emotional characteristics to houses or material things.

"They are chanting, 'We're going to move, we're going to move. We're going to live in a real house, a real house, A REAL HOUSE.'" Diné think of the hogan as their home, the concept of house is irrelevant, and they certainly would not "chant" about moving from one place to another.

The question, "What is a real house?" is irrelevant. Where we stay is our home. Moving to a house with six rooms, a bathroom, with running water and electricity is not something to celebrate, since Diné are being pushed off their land into prefabricated, spiritless "houses."

"'The family does not love me anymore,' thinks the old hogan and feels very sorry for herself." Self-pity and reminiscing about the past's being better than the present are not Native concepts. To think that a hogan's feelings about traditional life is more significant than the culture of a people is absurd.

That the old hogan thinks about what it would be like to have everyone gone, and how sad it would be is ridiculous. Unless they have been relocated to a city far away from the reservation, Diné have a hogan in the area where the family lives. Many important ceremonies and traditions are carried out at the site.

"If the old hogan could cry, there would have a pool of tears on the earthen floor." Crying is not something that Diné speak of or bring to the attention of someone else. Grief is usually expressed alone. Neither the concept of a broken heart nor that of a "bride and groom" is Diné.

The author of these books, who allegedly spent seventeen years teaching on the Diné reservation, has little or no understanding of Diné ways and, what's worse, no respect. I shudder to think of what effect she's had on the children she's taught.

I would be embarrassed to share any of these books with any child from any culture, Indian or non-Indian. Cultural concepts cannot be taught by a person who does not understand them.—*Linda Baldwin*

Gardner, Sonia, *Eagle Feather*, illustrated by James Spurlock. Writers Press (1997). 30 pages, color illustrations; grades 3-4

This is a Really Inspirational Story with a Really Deep Message wrapped around a Really Generic Plains Indian Theme.

An adolescent named Little One, who is an orphan and has been blind since birth (thereby providing double pathos), is "coming into manhood" and about to receive a new name "honoring his Vision Quest." I am not sure why a teenager would still be named Little One, which is a baby name. I am also not sure why a vision quest would be honored. During his Vision Quest (with the help of his guide wolf), Little One hears the cry of an eagle, who speaks to him "about the special gifts he possessed" and drops a feather at his feet. The manhood and naming ceremony follows. I am not sure why this one is done by committee; a name is usually given by an elder, a family member or a medicine person.

Besides the pathos, there has to be conflict. So the antagonist, Running Horse, speaks "hurtful words" that "pierce Little One's heart," prompting the elders to speak of Little One's phenomenal gifts: "Little One can smell and feel...when the wind tells us we must seek shelter... warns us when the snow will fall so we may gather and prepare for winter." I am not sure why no one else in the tribe can do this. The elders tell Running Horse that Little One "has the keen ears of a deer" and "much like the eagle,...possesses the power and wisdom about things we cannot see." I am not sure why describing us as having the attributes of animals is so important to white people who feel the need to write about us.

The conflict is resolved and Little One is given the name Eagle Feather, One Who Sees in Darkness. I am not sure how an eagle feather is related to seeing in darkness, but why trifle? In the end, Running Horse

> learned to look beyond his own blindness and appreciate the special gifts that Eagle Feather possessed. Through their friendship Running Horse discovered the meaning of true vision— vision that can only be seen with the heart.

For readers who have gotten this far and still don't get that this is a parable about physical blindness and moral blindness, vision and *vision*, there is the endpage, which could be perfect for one of those greeting cards whose message is so profound you want to barf: "True vision soars when embraced in the enduring winds of encouragement." I am not sure what this means, and I'm a pretty smart person.

The author's and illustrator's acknowledgement of the "Native American community for allowing us the privilege of using a Native American theme" notwithstanding (and I can only imagine what *that* conversation might have been like), this is a Really Bad Book.—*Barbara Potter*

Gerber, Carole (Cherokee), *Firefly Night,* **illustrated by Marty Husted. Charlesbridge, 2000. Unpaginated, color illustrations; preschool-2; Ojibwe**

Here's yet another book "inspired by lines from Longfellow's Hiawatha," so get your junk-o-meter cranked up. The sing-song, sickening-sweet text describes a nighttime journey of a young Ojibwe ("Chippewa") girl through the woods, accompanied by fireflies and woodland animals, to her "sleeping place."

Longfellow's version is bad enough: "Wah-wa-taysee, little firefly,/Little, flitting, white-fire insect,/Little, dancing, white-fire creature,/Light me with your little candle,/Ere upon my bed I lay me,/Ere in sleep I close my eyelids."

But Gerber's version is even worse: "Firefly, guide my way to sleep/in the forest, green and deep./Shine your light above my head./Lead me to my cradle bed./Wah-wah-taysee, firefly;/name for you from Chippewa./Flash your golden signal bright/as the evening turns to light."

Name for you from Chippewa? Is this the way Indians are supposed to talk?

Here is a little girl, four years old maybe, dressed in a Peter-Pan-inspired sleeveless buckskin dress, out at night, accompanied only by a bunch of woodland animals, going through a forest, across a lake, into a marsh, through the forest again, and finally arriving home, where her mother waits. Is all this because Indians are supposed to just naturally know how to get places, even when they're young?

The illustrations not only strain credulity, but are downright ridiculous: One needs a paddle, not a ricing stick, to paddle a canoe; grizzly bears have not ever, *ever* lived in the Great Lakes Region—nor have nocturnal butterflies, nocturnal kingfishers or red flowers that bloom at night. And turtles do not come out to sun themselves under the moon, either.—*Barbara Potter*

Gone, Fred (Gros Ventre), *The Seven Visions of Bull Lodge as Told by His Daughter Garter Snake,* **edited by George Horse Capture (Gros Ventre). University of Nebraska (1992). 125 pages; high school-up; Gros Ventre**

The story of the recovery of this important book is in a way as captivating as the story of A'aninin (Gros Ventre) spiritual leader Buffalo Bull Lodge (1802-1886) told by his daughter, the Pipe Child, Garter Snake (1868-1953). Trying to retrieve a destroyed history, Horse Capture found a reference to a 1930s WPA writers project, in which tribal citizen Fred Gone had been supported as a writer, to record the history of the last Pipe Keeper, Bull Lodge, as told by his daughter before her death at 86.

After considerable efforts, Horse Capture was able to repeat the visits Bull Lodge made to seven high buttes in Montana to pray for the visions that guided his life. Bull Lodge was a well-known healer and the last Sacred Powers Keeper of the Feathered Pipe of the tribe. Horse Capture tells of his own attempts to get this and other tribal materials reprinted and circulated among the people of his tribe, and to start a tribal museum to make available to the youth their own cultural and historic heritage. He mentions his reluctance to say much about the WPA tribal writers' projects that preserved tribal personal accounts of history that could still be recorded in the 1930s and 1940s: "If you look around, you see countless books on the American Indian. But do the Indian people really benefit from any of them? It is doubtful."

In this book—retrieved first for tribal people, and second for its sales contributions to scholarship funds and funds to restore more of the stolen and scattered cultural materials—is told the story of a sacred life. Garter Snake memorized the stories her father told and was an excellent observer of the ceremonial and healing events at which she, as Pipe Child, was present, including causing storms and stopping them, which Bull Lodge did on occasion. Although he was a noted warrior and political figure, this book is his story of a life devoted to the sacred. It is told, gathered, and edited by Native people of the tribe, an excellent model of what can be done by Native people working together, even when the work is done decades apart. Horse Capture, in his introduction, tells also of reprinting and making available to tribal citizens a dictionary of the language and a history of the people. He is seeking to create a tribal museum also.

One hopes that more money becomes available for illustrated works that preserve and present those parts of the culture that have been stripped away from the People of the White Clay. In particular, there is no mention by anyone involved with the book of the whereabouts of the Feathered Pipe. Even though according to its own prophecies about itself, Bull Lodge was the last recipient of its sacred powers, I wish it would be returned to its tribe from wherever it is now, if—as I guess from lack of any mention of it after Bull Lodge's death—it has probably been taken for a collection somewhere. The book is highly recommended; its purchase will help to rebuild the nearly-destroyed Gros Ventre or A'aninin culture, but it is also a well-assembled, unified story of a spiritually interesting life, well told by Native people for Native people.

—Paula Giese

Goodbird, Edward (Hidatsa), as told to Gilbert Wilson, *Goodbird the Indian: His Story*, illustrated by Frederick N. Wilson. Minnesota Historical Society (1914, 1985). 78 pages, b/w illustrations; grades 5-up; Hidatsa

Goodbird was Buffalo Bird Woman's son, born in 1870. He lived until 1938, through the move forced by the Dawes Allotment Act, from Like-a-Fishhook Village to the clan town of Independence on the Ft. Berthold North Dakota reservation. This book is Goodbird's own life story, of forced changes amid surviving traditions, covering a period when the people's culture was nearly destroyed—with special attacks on religion—and they were supposed to become farmers on high-arid plains as the reservation land was allotted.

Goodbird's mother tells her own life story, the most complete story of precontact traditional agriculture ever recorded. Goodbird is in the transition: born during a buffalo-hunting journey, he becomes a successful rancher for a time, then the first Indian Christian minister on the reservation. Wilson, an unusual anthropologist who's been ignored by professional scientific types, spent twenty years in North Dakota with the Hidatsa clan that adopted him in 1906, preparing a trilogy of life stories, told by Indian people themselves, for young people. The only publisher he could find (in 1914) for the first one—Edward Goodbird, Son of Buffalo Bird Woman, whose life spanned the old ways and the new—was a women's missionary society.

In the long introduction, Mary Jane Schneider, professor of Indian Studies at the University of North Dakota, tells some of the historical background and explains some distortions the church publishers introduced—including the title:

Nowhere in the narrative is Goodbird presented as "the Indian." He is always Goodbird, one man doing his best to cope with the upheaval of social and economic changes. Furthermore, although the title pages of both Goodbird and Waheenee (his mother's autobiography) indicate "as told to" Gilbert Wilson, in neither book is Wilson an active presence. That is the charm and strength of the books—there is reality and immediacy to the subjects' lives.

Schneider compared Gilbert's field notes on his conversations with all the Hidatsa and what he published. She finds that there was some rearrangement—these stories were told in many conversations over years—but the editing was minimal. It does appear that there was considerable church editing or censorship of Goodbird's personal religious history.

But the reality of Goodbird's story still comes through in a non-artificial way. Goodbird points out that the original spiritual traditions had already become corrupted by incorporating Christian ideas. (As we might see it, and as he apparently did even when recounting his youth from the viewpoint of having become a Christian minister):

> My father explained to me, "All things in this world have souls or spirits. The sky has a spirit; the clouds have spirits; the sun and moon have spirits; the trees, grass, water, stones, everything..." We Indians did not believe in one Great Spirit as white men seem to think all Indians do. We did believe that certain gods were more powerful than others. Of these was It-si-ka-ma-hi-di, our elder creator, the spirit of the prairie wolf, and Ka-du-te-ta or Old Woman Who Never Dies, who first taught my people to till their fields,...Anyone could pray to the spirits, receiving answer usually in a dream....[But] a man might have mystery power and not use it wisely.

Goodbird was a strong character. He became a leading rancher, since farming the allotted lands was not possible, everything always died. He even made up a posse and retrieved some Indian cattle a local white rancher had stolen. At this time, although the treaty payments were paid in head of cattle and equipment, the Indians didn't own them, the government did. Goodbird describes how as Assistant Farmer for the Indian agent, he goes around inspecting what his neighbors are doing: Have they built a barn as prescribed? Have they laid in two tons of hay per head of cattle? But in the 1909 taking of the northeastern rangeland of the reservation and giving it to white ranchers, the government thought they would put the Indians out of the cattle business. They abolished Goodbird's job. Goodbird, a Christian by then through school and perhaps choosing some religion over none (all demonstrations of Indian religion were being heavily suppressed) took a job as a missionary at Independence. He reports another kind of motivation:

> My uncle Wolf Chief says of the Christian way: "I traveled faithfully the way of the Indian gods, but they never helped me. When I was sick, I prayed to them, but they did not make me well. I prayed to them when my children died; but they did not answer me. I have but two children left, and I am going to trust to [the Christian] God to keep these that they do not die."

But Wolf Chief's last surviving child, who was in college, died about the time Goodbird's first grandchild was born. For Wolf Chief, and perhaps others, the tragedies were perceived as failures of spiritual powers rather than things done or caused by the white man—even as the more overt suppressions and Christian proselytizing were going on.

Still, some of the old ways come through. The people want to build a better chapel instead of the log cabin, so they take up a subscription among themselves to buy lumber.

> Wolf Chief wanted to give us the land for our chapel, but the Indian commissioner wrote "No, you may sell your land but you must not give it away." So we bought the land for a dollar an acre; but Wolf Chief gave the money back to us, outwitting the commissioner after all!

Damned curious: all sorts of Indian land was given away—huge acreages to be farmed or ranched to make money—for churches on reservations all over. Here the Indians have to run a kind of scam to build their own church, which they are running themselves, even though it is an established well-known sect.

Goodbird ends his story:

> I own cattle and horses. I can read English and my children are in school. I have good friends among the white people, and best of all, I think, each year I know God a little better. I am not afraid.

But the white man hasn't been very kind to Goodbird's descendants. Before his death in 1938, much more land had been taken; ten years later, the dam that was to drown all the good land, the heart of the reservation, the Missouri Valley of the millennia-old cultures of all three tribes—Mandan and Arikara, as well as Hidatsa—was being built. Though perhaps overly focused (due to the church publisher) on Goodbird's religion (with some of their own interpretations), the book was also guided by Wilson's life-long intention that the Indian people tell their own story, to tell their history and lives as they themselves saw and lived it.

There's considerable overlap in this book with the much more detailed and polished old village life story of Goodbird's mother, *Waheenee*, that Wilson published thirteen years later, not long before he died. Various passages attributed to Goodbird in the present book were in fact told by Buffalo Bird Woman. Others come from her brother (Goodbird's uncle) Wolf Chief. Wilson intended to make these autobiographies for young people a trilogy, but Wolf Chief's life story was never published. It exists in Gilbert's extensive field notes and reports and in several anthropology papers he published before his death.

Goodbird's autobiography, despite the occasional bits of church-imposed censorship, and the tilt toward Christianity it had to have given the only publisher for it Wilson could find (as well as by Goodbird's own adaptation to the enforced white man's road) is still interesting reading for young adults, and for many adults as well.—*Paula Giese*

Grace, Catherine O'Neill, and Margaret M. Bruchac (Abenaki), *1621: A New Look at Thanksgiving,* **photographs by Sisse Brimberg and Cotton Coulson. National Geographic Society (2001). 48 pages, color photos; grades 4-up; Wampanoag**

Produced in collaboration with the Wampanoag Indian Program at Plimoth Plantation, *1621* weighs Wampanoag oral traditions and English colonial written records against the popular myth of "brave settlers inviting wild Indians over for turkey dinner." Stunning photographs by Sisse Brimberg and Cotton Coulson, accompanied by thoughtful text by Margaret Bruchac and Catherine O'Neill Grace, walk the young reader into the dual perspectives of Native peoples and English colonists in Patuxet/Plymouth. The text, written for a young audience but not solely for children, also offers insights into the relationship of the Wampanoag people to their traditional homelands, and survival into the present. As well, *1621* addresses the harsh reality of the subsequent colonial history. "Considering this history and what came on in later centuries," the book concludes, "Native people do not share in the popular reverence for the traditional New England 'Thanksgiving.' To the Wampanoag, the holiday is a reminder of the arrival of the English in their homeland, a presence that brought betrayal and bloodshed." Especially important is the chronology at the end of the book; teachers who want to engage their young students in critical thinking will read this section first.

Abenaki scholar Margaret Bruchac is an accomplished writer, and it is clear that she respects the intelligence of the young readers who are asked to consider that there may be more than one way of looking at history. Also to be thanked are the Mashpee Wampanoag people who created the traditional outfits and wore them for the October 2000 recreation of the 1621 harvest feast, which was documented for this book. *1621* is an excellent tool for un-teaching the myth of "The First Thanksgiving."

—Beverly Slapin

Gravelle, Karen, *Soaring Spirits: Conversations with Native American Teens*, photographs by the author. Franklin Watts (1995). 128 pages, b/w photographs; grades 7-12

Here, Gravelle interviews and photographs seventeen American Indian teenagers from reservations in the United States and Canada. As the young people talk about the things that matter to them—family, community, school, dating, music, sports—Native and non-Native readers will readily identify with them, and will learn about modern Indian issues.

The voices of the teenagers, their personal issues and struggles, and the issues of their families and peoples are all here:

> "We're no different from other people except for our culture, and the way that our ancestors lived and our dark skins," Kristy says. "We are into heavy metal, pop, rap, and all this other kind of stuff. People think that because once all of our tribes-people had hair down to here and wore headbands and moccasins that we're different from everybody else. But it's not like that anymore. We're definitely normal people!" she adds.

> "I don't like the way people treat Native Americans," Fawn says. "Like on TV, they don't show us as we are. They show us as barbarians who go around killing the whites. As people who are just doing bad things. They always show the white people as good guys. Like cowboys and Indians—the Indians were always the barbarians, and the cowboys had to go kill them."

But while the young people speak in an interesting and candid manner, Gravelle is clearly looking through an outsider's lens:

- The 2 million Native Americans who currently live in the United States are proof that Indians are far from dead and gone.
- [T]he parents of some of the young people in this book are employed as firefighters, school-teachers, engineers, nurses, restaurant owners, government employees, artists, fishers, office workers…
- Because Native Americans don't pitch tipis in their front yards or dress in buckskin and feathers…many non-Native people don't realize that they have Indians as their co-workers and neighbors.
- Like teenagers from other ethnic groups, Native American teens enjoy dancing to popular music too.

Too bad. Gravelle clearly had good intentions.

—Barbara Potter

Green, Timothy, *Mystery of Coyote Canyon*, illustrated by the author. Ancient City Press (1993). 137 pages, line drawings; grades 7-up; Diné (Navajo)

Mystery of Coyote Canyon is formula young-adult-coming-of-age-novel-using-Indian-themes. White boy, recovering from trauma of parents' divorce, vacations with uncle, a national park ranger, on Diné reservation, where he meets Diné girl. The two investigate bizarre occurrences in a place called "Coyote Canyon," and solve eerie mystery. Adventure almost kills them. Intrepid teenagers. Ghosts. Grave robbers. Superstitious Navajos.

The girl's grandfather talks like this, apparently to demonstrate the author's knowledge of Diné spiritual beliefs.

> My whole life I have walked the medicine path…I learned about the Diyin Dinée, the Holy Beings. I was taught the Beauty Way stories of White Shell Woman and her twins: Monster Slayer and Born-for-the-Water. I learned the ways of walking in harmony with Mother Earth and Father Sky.

It is hard to imagine circumstances in which a Diné elder would talk about such things. Grandparents do not embarrass grandchildren, especially in front of white people. Diné do not "feel rich according to how many songs [they] know."

This is not the first book to imply that white environmentalists will save the land on which Native people lived so successfully for thousands of years. But Anna's statement that—

My uncle Kee says our people are destroying the land by overgrazing their sheep on it. He says they need to be taught soil conservation and ecology.

—totally ignores the fact that Peabody Coal's strip-mining has done more damage to Dinétah than a thousand years of sheep-grazing could possibly accomplish.—*Beverly Slapin*

Green, Timothy, *Mystery of the Navajo Moon*, illustrated by the author. Northland (1991). Unpaginated, color illustrations; grades 2-4; Diné (Navajo)

Wilma Charley is a Navajo girl who likes to dream and also likes horses a lot. She wakes up one morning to find that the "Navajo Moon" had left her a "diamond star." The following night, a magical white pony—a "silvery steed of a thousand dreams" with a "diamond-studded mane"—magically appears and takes her for a magical ride "across the glittering vaulted sky," until she falls off while reaching for a moonbeam. Waking up the next morning to the sounds and smells of breakfast, Wilma wonders if she had been dreaming. But when she finds a magical moonflake next to her magical diamond star, she knows her magical dream was real. And now, every night, Wilma sings to the "night-mantled heavens":

> Oh Navajo moon
> My secret boon,
> Bring to me a gift this night…
> Bring to me my pony to fly,
> And I will hang my moonflake
> in the sky.

Full-color pictures in shades of blue, brown and purple pastels alternate with text pages framed with borders in colors that complement those in the illustrations. Besides a clunky, social studies-like introduction, a later reference to frybread—and of course the "Navajo Moon" in the title—there's no Diné sensibility in this overwrought little book. Not in the pictures, not in the text. There's a hogan, but where are the sheep? Where's the rest of the family? Who's

cooking breakfast? The magical white horse is really unattractive and the land bares only a vague resemblance to Dinétah.

One suspects that this was more of an attempt to showcase the author's art while producing a "multicultural" book rather than to tell a good story.—*Beverly Slapin*

Greene, Jacqueline Dembar, *Manabozho's Gifts: Three Chippewa Tales*, illustrated by Jennifer Hewitson. Houghton Mifflin (1994). 42 pages, b/w illustrations; grades 3-5; Ojibwe
Leekley, Thomas B., *The World of Manabozho: Tales of the Chippewa Indians*, illustrated by Yeffe Kimball (Osage). Vanguard (1965). 128 pages, b/w illustrations; grades 4-up; Ojibwe

Both of these books are "retellings" by non-Indian authors of traditional Ojibwe stories. Greene researched the "tales and myths of the Chippewa people" through several sources, most of which were also written by non-Indians.

The tone of *Manabozho's Gifts* is disturbing; neither author nor illustrator apparently cares about accuracy or authenticity. Ojibwe people are portrayed as people of the past, the women haul water in southwestern-style earthen jugs instead of birchbark containers, Manabozho dreams of woodland spirit dancers wearing feather headdresses, and wild rice grows along streams instead of lakes.

Describing what she did to "How Manabozho Stole Fire," Greene says,

> In this story, I have changed the season to emphasize life without fire. I used dramatic fiction to create Manabozho's magical words to transform his shape ["Once as a man,…now as a rabbit. A rabbit, a rabbit will I be."] and command his canoe…

While casually admitting to using "dramatic fiction" in her retellings, she does not admit that her retellings belittle the content and lessons of the original stories.

One of the sources Greene uses is Leekley's book, a collection of thirteen "tales of the Chippewa Indians" that, according to Leekley, "have been treated with some freedom." Although he has "tried to keep the stories… Indian in mood as well as in event" (whatever that means),

> [O]f course I did not write these tales for Indians: I set out to make them interesting to American boys and girls generally. In so doing I had to rearrange and edit them, because, told the way the Indians tell them, they seem more like story material than finished stories.

Here is a small sample of Leekley's "improved" retelling, this from "The Theft of Fire":

Manabozho knew now why he looked foolish. He turned himself back into an Indian very quickly. Sure enough, his skin didn't hurt. His hair wasn't scorched any more. In fact, like most Indians, he didn't have much hair at all!

Our stories are thousands of years old and cannot be adapted or changed by most non-Indians without damaging their essence. Good intentions (if there are any here) are not a substitute for cultural and spiritual knowledge, and these authors appear to have neither.

Rather, for real Waynaboozhoo (Manabozho) stories, told with beauty and strength, hold in your hands *The Mishomis Book: The Voice of the Ojibway* by Ojibwe elder Edward Benton Banai. You'll see a world of difference.
—*Barbara Potter*

Gregory, Kristiana, *The Legend of Jimmy Spoon*. Harcourt Brace (1990). 165 pages; grades 4-up; Shoshone

Based on a historical incident, this novel of a twelve-year-old Mormon boy taken by a band of Shoshone to be the adopted brother of Chief Washakie is a combination of history, ignorance and very poor writing.

A white child taken in adoption would not be likely to be mercilessly harassed, especially not two years later. Acts of blatant cruelty and violence toward women and children were not a sanctioned part of traditional tribal culture. Here, the people are portrayed as unreasonably and relentlessly cruel to their white adoptee. After more than two years, a boy threatens: "I'll take that white devil into the willows so we can have another pretty scalp to dance with." Even the medicine man snarls at him: "I would be happy if the little white devil dies."

The narrative and the timing are not believable. For instance, Jimmy Spoon, like the rest of his settler family, is afraid of Indians: "[E]very night they went to bed in fear. Would they be killed in their sleep? Or would the terrible sound of the drum wake them in time?" Yet after only eleven days of living with the Shoshone, "He felt like a real Indian. If only he could wear a feather in his hair."

The author uses the words "brave," "squaw," and "papoose" over and over, both in the narrative and in the dialogue. These words are derogatory, and they are not Shoshone. Neither is "Happy Hunting Grounds" a Shoshone term.

While the Shoshone characters speak the all-poetical dialect of the "noble savage," ("You will journey north, four suns…you will wait for my return, maybe fifteen sleeps"), Jimmy speaks modern English and, in fact, has concepts totally foreign to a Mormon child in the 1800s. (Warfare was "a waste of energy…would there ever be peace?") At one point, after Jimmy has prattled on about

equal rights for women, Washakie answers, "A boy who is patient learns much…. An owl listening from his branch has more wisdom than a magpie who chatters all day long."

As with many novels of this sort, it is the white outsider who can soon run things more efficiently:

Jimmy discovered how hard it was to get things going. He had wanted to leave by dawn, but it was quite another matter to pack up ten saddles and nine travois, then round up the horses and direct fifteen women, thirty-five children, and three elders.

In the old days, it was the women's responsibility to set up and break camp and "get things going," a job that they conducted with speed and expertise. And it would have been unheard of for anyone to be directing elders.

In what is described as an "Indian funeral" for the war chief's young son, "three horses were killed to bury with the boy so he could ride to the Happy Hunting Grounds," and the horses are later "buried on the beach below." If a warrior had died, his favorite horse was sometimes taken to the bier and there killed, so that it might join him in the Spirit World. This would not be done for a child. The rest of the description smacks more of a Christian open-casket funeral than a Native one.

Peoples of the Plains had a relationship with their horses such as never has been seen, yet the author portrays them here as incompetent:

[T]he racing grew louder and wilder. By sundown two Indians had been trampled to death, and a bucking horse had kicked a woman with her cradleboard, killing the baby. For several days the cries of mourners pierced the air.

But probably the worst thing the author does here is to portray, through the protagonist's eyes, a Nation of people as merciless savages:

Bonfires dotted the valley under a moonless night. Drums pounded. A high-pitched singing rose in the night air, making Jimmy shiver; the voices sounded like a wail. In the center of camp, warriors circled the largest fire…. To Jimmy's horror, some held spears in the air, dangling scalps from a recent raid on a wagon train. Jimmy clamped his hand over his mouth and swallowed the bile rising in his throat. He had heard about such things, but he hadn't thought friendly Indians killed people. A sickening, sweet odor brought tears to his eyes. He was afraid and angry at the same time….But now this—this atrocity!…Jimmy felt ashamed for having had so much fun among people who could be so savage. He counted six scalps, all caked with blood. One was a woman's long red hair, one a girl's blond pigtails, four were men's scalps, three dark, one gray. Jimmy thought about his family. His little sister wore pigtails, his uncle Lefty had gray hair. Molly's hair was long and flowing. He pictured their house pierced with burning arrows and his mother crying for help....He hated himself for thinking that living with Indians would be carefree.

In truth, there was no honor in killing women and children. In all wars horrible things are done. It would have been good if the author had said that atrocities happened on both sides. The numbers of Native people killed by whites so far outnumber those of whites killed by Indians as to boggle the mind. How could any child read something like this and think Native peoples were (and are) anything but savages?—*Beverly Slapin*

Griese, Arnold, *Anna's Athabaskan Summer,* **illustrated by Charles Ragins. Boyds Mills (1995). Unpaginated, color illustrations; grades 3-4; Athabascan**

Anna, an Athabascan child of about ten, waits for summer to come, when she and her family can return to fish camp on the river. That is where her people have returned for millennia, fishing for salmon, drying berries, and preparing for winter.

This could have been a beautiful book. It is not. The author, speaking in a child's voice, oversimplifies and misrepresents traditional Native lifeways. Some of these misrepresentations are subtle. For instance, at fish camp, Anna's mother tells her to "[t]ake Grandmother to the place she loves and sit with her." It is highly unlikely that a mother would tell a child to "take" Grandmother somewhere. More probably, Anna's mother would say, "Go for a walk with Grandma," or Grandmother would say, "Let's go for a walk," or Anna would say, "Grandma, wanna go for a walk?" and they would go off together. Here, the author implies to the reader that elders are to be taken care of by young people. This is in contradiction to tribal tradition: Elders may be physically frail, but they are nonetheless in charge.

While they are sitting together, Grandmother sees two ravens and says, "Old Grandfather, bring us luck." Anna asks why, and Grandmother explains, "Our people say that Raven made the world. That, even though he plays tricks, he can bring luck." A child of Anna's age would most likely have heard stories about Raven even before she was old enough to understand language, and she would know why Raven is addressed that way. More importantly, she would not ask her grandmother questions like that. Finally, Raven's relationship to people is much more complicated than this dialogue would have it. Probably, Grandmother, seeing the ravens, would tell Anna a story.

In another place, Anna challenges her mother:

> One day, I ask Mother: "Grandmother says we must show respect for all living things. Then why do we catch and kill the salmon?" Mother brushes the hair from her face and answers, "Our people believe living things die gladly for us. But we must show respect by killing only what we need and by returning to the river fish bones and other things we cannot eat."

It is understandable for a young child to express compassion for an animal, but this is not the way that Indian children are taught to relate to adults. Traditionally, they are taught by example to assist and learn from their parents and grandparents, not to confront them. In any event, a child that age would know that Salmon, a most sacred of fishes, gives his life so that humans and other animals can survive. As a thank-you, the people return the bones to the water. By inserting this discussion, the author uses an Indian child as an instrument to set up lessons for non-Native children. While his intention might have been to educate, he does the opposite. Finally, real people don't talk that way; the dialogue is too self-conscious and stilted.

Although the author "has been involved with the Athabaskan people since 1951, when he moved his family from Miami, Florida, to Tanana, an Athabaskan village in interior Alaska," he has apparently failed to learn from and understand the stories of the world he writes about. No matter how well meaning his intention, it is disrespectful to presume to speak in the voice of someone whose lifeways, language, and deepest beliefs are contrary to one's own.

In an apparent effort to educate non-Native children, the author has created a false story about Native people and their relationships with each other and the world. As a white parent, he could have told a story about his own children, newly transplanted from Florida, asking those same questions. That would have been appropriate for them, and it might have made a good story. —*Beverly Slapin* and *Janet King*

Grifalconi, Ann, *The Bravest Flute: A Story of Courage in the Mayan Tradition,* **illustrated by the author. Little, Brown (1994). Unpaginated, color illustrations; grades 2-4**

Summary:

> It is New Year's Day. A Mayan boy wakes up to face his great task. He will lead the parade of highland farmers across the mountains to the big town. But for him, this annual celebration of renewal will be a test of his courage and spirit....

In the Mexican highlands towns of Chiapas, where many Mayans live (and a peasant revolution's been going on for some years now), they did and do have fiesta parades, town Societies of Weavers and such. Presumably every year some kid flutist leads the fiesta parade and has no difficulty making the route.

But not this kid. With all the villagers behind him,

> [H]e staggered slowly down into the valleys, and up again, [a]nd he knew he could not stop.... Unsteady by now and tired, the boy worried.... He made his tired legs take one shaky step and then another, advancing slowly...Only a few more steps...The boy's head begins to spin in a fever of exhaustion. He feels his sweaty hands and knows he is beginning to shake all over.

Had enough yet? This is one of the dumbest kid stories I've ever come across. There's no cultural content in it to talk of accuracy; I downcheck it on grounds of super-outstanding dumbness. All the agonizing of the nameless "Mayan boy" who fills the role one year is incredibly silly (as well as boring). Even if the kid is outta shape, it boggles the mind to call it "courage" that he manages the route that everyone covers annually, and maybe more often— they used to have a lot of festivals.

I dunno what's wrong with this woman, Grifalconi. I recommend she read *I, Rigoberta Menchú*, the autobiography of a Mayan hero and Nobel Laureate. Then maybe read *Children of the Maya: A Guatemalan Indian Odyssey*, about the refugees from the CIA-backed terror who've settled in Florida and 150,000 who didn't make it, who have been killed. Find out about courage. Then half an hour of aerobic exercise a day, walk maybe a couple miles, quit smoking, get herself in shape to follow a parade—uphill, even—without fainting or whatever the problem here was.—*Paula Giese*

Grossman, Virginia, *Ten Little Rabbits,* **illustrated by Sylvia Long. Chronicle Books (1991). Unpaginated color illustrations; preschool-grade 1**
Kusugak, Michael (Inuit), *My Arctic, 1, 2, 3,* **illustrated by Vladyana Krykorka. Annick (1996). Unpaginated, color illustrations; preschool-up; Inuit**

Although both of these are counting books, they are very different from one another.

Ten Little Rabbits has received several awards. It has been favorably reviewed in all of the major journals, can be found in most bookstores, and is featured on many "multicultural" lists and in catalogs. Long's earth-toned ink-and-watercolor pictures are pretty and her rabbits look like rabbits.

But it shouldn't be necessary to tell people that counting rabbits dressed as Indians is no different from counting Indians. It objectifies people. Same faces, different blankets. As Teresa L. McCarty writes,

> The book's implicit suggestion that children will learn to "count by diminutive-ethnic-group characters" is perverse and patently racist. That the author and the illustrator appear completely unconscious of this and choose to portray their characters as "cute" little animals reveals an especially insidious and societally acceptable form of racism. It is difficult to believe any writer, illustrator, or publisher today would accept or promote equivalent portrayals, for instance, of American Jews or African Americans.[1]

There are some who would ask, "but are the pictures authentic?" They're neither authentic nor accurate. There's no cultural relevance, no connection between each illustration and a people's way of being in world. Even if the pictures were not contrived, the impact of this book—"rabbits as Indians"—on impressionable little kids is what makes it toxic.

Neither Long's lifelong "fascination with Native American cultures" nor her reading of *Watership Down*, which together "inspired a series of Native American rabbit illustrations that later became the basis for this book"[2] excuses what she and Grossman have done.

On the other hand, *My Arctic 1, 2, 3* is an example of a counting book that simply and beautifully reflects a people's connection to the land.

"I grew up in the Arctic Circle," Michael Kusugak writes.

> When I was a little boy we hunted seals, caribou and whales….We do not hunt animals all the time. Mostly, we watch them. We look at their tracks. We see how their coats change with the seasons. We watch what they hunt for food. We see how they hunt. In this book I want to show you some of the animals we have watched and the other animals that they hunt. Watching animals is fun.

My Arctic 1, 2, 3 is clearly more than a counting book. Unlike *Ten Little Rabbits*, it shows the relationships between the humans and the animals and between the different animals in an environment that demands that this relationship be understood. Each two-page spread, in luminous watercolors and ink, shows a certain number of animals on the left, and the animals they hunt on the right. The story comes full circle at the last spread that shows, on the left, Kusugak's extended family picking "millions of berries (that) ripen in the fall" and on the right,

> One lone polar bear walks along the shore, thinking of seals. It sees the berry pickers and says, "Never mind. They do not look like very good meals." It continues on its journey, looking for what it might find…

There are words in Inuktitut for the animals themselves, and the last four pages, "The Arctic World of Michael Kusugak and His Family," place all of the Arctic animals in the context of their relationship to the humans and each other. From start to finish, this is a beautiful book.
—*Beverly Slapin*

NOTES

1 McCarty, Theresa L., "What's Wrong with *Ten Little Rabbits?*," *The New Advocate*, vol. 8, no. 2, 1995, p. 98.

2 From the endnote.

Haegert, Dorothy, *Children of the First People*. Tillicum Library (1989). Unpaginated, b/w photos; all grades; Northwest Coast Nations

Children of the First People is the result of four summers that photographer Dorothy Haegert spent traveling up and down the British Columbia coast, taking pictures of Native children in their villages. The text, with the exception of the introduction, is formed from interviews with elders of the villages, who shared their stories of Native life, and how it was when they were young.

The reason I think this book is so valuable, even though it was not written specifically for children, is that few non-Native children in areas away from reservations think that Indians still exist, much less have lives that are in many ways not so different from their own. Kids are always interested in pictures of other kids. These beautiful photographs give quite a different impression of Native life than the one usually acquired from textbooks. And for Native children, nothing could be better than to see themselves and their lifeways portrayed truthfully and with respect.

Children of the First People can be a valuable tool for human understanding. The words of the elders are a bridge to the past; the faces of the children are right now.

—*Doris Seale*

Haley, Gail E., *Two Bad Boys: A Very Old Cherokee Tale*, illustrated by the author. Dutton (1996). Unpaginated, color illustrations; grades 2-3; Cherokee

Let me first say two things. I don't tell this story publicly. It's part of the long creation story that is told in ceremony every year at Green Corn time. An elder once told me that the Earth needs to hear these stories, but how, when and to whom they are told must be respected.

The second thing is that, in order to tell a good story, you have to know that the story is alive. You have to make it comfortable in your interior landscape. Most Native stories that find themselves wandering around in the psyches of non-Native storytellers and writers would be in a place as foreign to them as Mars would be to the average Earth-dweller. That's where you'd find something like *Two Bad Boys*.

Gail Haley's retelling of our sacred story about Kanati and Selu mirrors the Christian myth about Adam and Eve, the Garden of Eden, and how work came into the world.

In Haley's version, First Man (Kanati, the Hunter), First Woman (Selu, the Corn Mother) and Boy lead an idyllic life, until Boy's reflection in the river springs to life and becomes Wild Boy, Boy's alter ego and trouble-making playmate. Wild Boy tempts the well-behaved Boy into mischief, involving freeing all of Kanati's game animals from a cave and discovering Selu's secret source of vegetables. And because of the two bad boys' disobedience,

> Since that time, people have had to hunt for their meat, plant their vegetables, and *work* in this world.

All of the major review journals praised this "cautionary tale about two bad boys whose actions change the world forever." *Publishers Weekly*, for instance, called it "conscientiously researched," and from *Kirkus Reviews*:

> The transgression of moral authority and the dual nature of existence are themes which have echoes throughout western literature; this Cherokee legend confirms the universality of human nature.

But *Two Bad Boys* is not, in any way, *at all*, "a very old Cherokee tale," nor is it, in any way, *at all*, what our story is about. There are layers and layers of meaning in this most sacred story that are contained in essential elements that Haley did away with in order to make it a "children's story." The entire process of eliminating what makes the story sacred is what makes Haley's version a desecration. *Two Bad Boys* is the cultural equivalent of retelling the Easter Story and leaving out the crucifixion. It's that insensitive.

"Sge, sge! Sge, sge! My story rattle has sounded; it is time to begin!" Haley begins. Turtle shell rattles are not green, blue, yellow and white—and our turtle shell rattle is not a story rattle. It is carried by our traditional healers, one of whom was Yunini (Swmmer), who told the story of Kanati and Selu to anthropologist James Mooney. Haley probably saw the photo of Yunini holding his turtle shell rattle in Mooney's book and figured it was a "story rattle."

Throughout *Two Bad Boys*, Haley changes our story to reflect her own Christian values. For instance, in our traditional story, the two boys spy on Kanati while he is hunting. They see him release the animals from the cave, and know how he always manages to find game. But in Haley's version, Wild Boy, knowing the answer, asks Kanati where he finds such good meat, and Kanati responds:

> Ah, my son…[I]t is the way of the Hunter to know the secrets of the four-leggeds and the winged ones. It is the proper way of young boys to accept what they are given and not ask so many questions.

The Christian concept that "children should be seen and not heard" is not an aspect of traditional Cherokee culture, nor is it in our stories.

From the very beginning Haley homogenizes and sanitizes all of the essential elements of our story. She glosses over where Wild Boy comes from. In our traditional story, Wild Boy is born from the blood of a piece of game that Selu was washing in the river. In *Two Bad Boys*, Haley has him just coming up out of the river to play with Boy.

In our story, Kanati and Selu catch Wild Boy and adopt him. Haley says in her story, "Ku! We all wish they had not; for although they had captured him, they could not tame him." That's editorializing and it's not Cherokee. We would never say in a story that we wish something had or had not happened. The story is as the story is and it explains several important things.

Haley's delineation of the two boys as good and evil with the evil boy always leading the good boy astray is not in our traditional story either. In our story, Wild Boy makes suggestions and the boys go off together and do their mischief. The moralistic tone Haley inserts in order to make the boys the focus of the story is completely at odds with our traditional story. Over and over again, she does this.

In our story, when Kanati discovers that the boys have released the game animals, he goes into the cave and kicks the covers off four jars. The boys are immediately covered in swarms of bedbugs, flies, lice and gnats, and they get stung. Then, Kanati says to them:

> "Now, you rascals," said he, "you've always had plenty to eat and never had to work for it. Whenever you were hungry all I had to do was to come up here and get a deer or a turkey and bring it home for your mother to cook; but now you have let out all the animals, and after this when you want a deer to eat you will have to hunt all over the woods for it, and then maybe not find one. Go home now to your mother, while I see if I can find something to eat for supper."[1]

Haley's version:

> "You two bad boys did not heed my words," he shouted. "Now I must go away. And you will have to track the animals and bring them down with bows and arrows. This you have brought on yourselves." And he strode off to the Western Land of the Darkening Sun.

In our story, the boys go straight home to their mother who feeds them with corn and beans while they await Kanati's return. Instead, Haley has the boys "cold as well as hungry," having to "hunt every day to find enough meat just to stay alive." During the long hard winter, they spend "many hours staring into the fire and regretting what they had done."

The final part of our story—that Haley so desecrates here—is the hardest part to talk about. In our traditional story, when the boys see Selu making food from her body, they are horrified. They immediately decide that she is a witch and that they must kill her. As soon as she comes back into the house, she sees them and knows their minds. She allows the boys to kill her and sacrifice her body into the ground. She gives them detailed instructions on how to do this so that the corn will always grow and Selu will always continue to feed her people.

The whole rest of the story—Selu's death, the preparation of the ground, how the corn grows from her blood—is very, very sacred. What happens after Kanati comes back and finds Selu gone is incredibly beautiful and powerful. This told story can—and often does—go on for hours.

The blood, the pain, the very real elements involved in two sons' turning on and killing their mother—all of this represents a very sacred powerful aspect to the reverence in which we hold corn. Corn is never taken for granted. Corn is alive.

But here is how Haley disrespects and trivializes our story: After the "two bad boys" figure out how Selu produced the food, they do the same.

> But when they came down the ladder, Selu was waiting for them. "You two bad boys," she cried. "Because you have helped yourselves, our lives must change forever." With a wave of her hand, the building pulled loose from the earth and flew away to the West.
>
> "The corn and beans in your basket are all that you have left. From this time on, you must dig the earth, plant the seeds you hold, then tend and harvest the plants when they are ready," she told them.
>
> Then Selu flew away to join her husband in the Western Land of the Darkening Sun. Since that time, people have had to hunt for their meat, plant their vegetables, and work in this world.

A children's book about the Easter Story, in which the author has left out the crucifixion because it is too bloody, would have been thoroughly trashed by professional reviewers. No question about it. Yet Haley's superficial, Christianized, abominable retelling of what is without doubt one of the most powerful and sacred stories we hold, went unchallenged; and in fact, was highly praised.

No one has the right to do this. This review was a very painful thing for me to write.—*Gayle Ross*

NOTE

1 I am quoting from our story of Kanati and Selu as told by Yunini (Swimmer), a traditional Cherokee healer and storyteller, to James Mooney, who published it in 1900 in *Myths of the Cherokee*. All of the stories that Swimmer told to Mooney are the most complete, the most detailed, of any in Mooney's collection.

Hamm, Diane Johnston, *Daughter of Suqua.* **Albert Whitman (1997). 154 pages; grades 4-6; Suquamish**

In the early 1900s, Young Ida Bowen, her family, and their people face the changes brought by allotment, residential schools, and related assimilationist efforts.

Daughter of Suqua stands out for its characterization. The relationship between Ida and her grandmother is particularly strong and complex. Gentle but not romanticized. Each character is depicted as a person, each with his or her own perspectives and personality. Their community is not without problems, but it has internal mechanisms for coping with them. Young readers will become emotionally invested and gain a greater appreciation for the surrounding history and setting.

The upcoming allotment and, for Ida, residential school, are the primary changes looming over her family.

> If going to the allotment was for their own good, like Teacher said, why was no one happy about it? Why did it feel like being put in the corner at school? In the corner you couldn't see anyone; your back was turned for shame. All of Suqua was being sent to corners.
>
> "If it's to be a frame house with finished lumber, we'll have to sell trees from the allotment to pay for it," [Father] said after a while.... "To sell the trees I'd have to ask permission of Mr. Simpson".... "I don't like having to ask permission," Father said. "It's as though we were children."
>
> "There is talk of changing the law so that allotments can be sold to outsiders," he said, thinking out loud. "By selling the allotment we could buy a house somewhere and not have to farm."... "If we begin to sell off the reservation, though, it will be the end of the Suquamish," he argued unhappily. "Now it is only the land that can keep us together as people. We must hold onto it!"

For all of its intense effects, the allotment policy that resulted in loss of lands for many Native peoples is not frequently explored in children's literature. Perhaps it lacks the visual imagery of other tragedies. However, it is an important piece of the history and should not be ignored.

With regard to Ida's upcoming departure for residential school, young readers will appreciate her desperately not wanting to leave her family and community, which is already undergoing unwelcome and significant change. At this point, it is unclear to Ida what to expect at the school. She hears conflicting stories, including that some children die there. The adults wonder at and grieve what is happening though they do not yet know all of the long-term costs.

"But the children go away!" said David. "The *paesteds* separate all our people! What will we be without our children?"

With engaging characters and simple but engaging prose, *Daughter of Suqua* reflects the historical period and draws young readers into Ida's story.—*Cynthia L. Smith*

Harper, Jo, *The Legend of Mexicatl*, illustrated by Robert Casilla. Turtle Books (1998). 31 pages, color illustrations; grades 1-4; Mexica

First off, it was hard for me to tell whether this story was supposed to be about the Mexica (Aztecs), or if it was really about Jesus. The story is about a boy, Mexicatl, who is called upon by a generic "Great Spirit" to eventually lead his people to their promised land. Upon flippng open the book to the first page, I was struck by how much the first illustration appears like so many nativity scenes that one would expect to find in a church. Although this will probably make the book appealing to Catholics with Mexican roots, it does not tell us anything about the Mexica people. There are many accounts about the journey that the Mexica took from Aztlán to what is now Mexico City. Some of these are Native accounts while others are colonial Spanish stories. Amidst all the academic argument and speculation, all the contradiction and inconsistency, the author seems to have found it very easy to put forward her version of a "glorious triumph of faith and courage."

There is something subtle and maybe even insidious about the Christianization of what is not a Christian story. Rather than honor the culture of which the real legend of Mexicatl is a part of, it suggests that there is something that needs to be improved by rewriting it and that the Mexica people can be redeemed only by being compared to early Christians. I think that Friar Bernardino de Sahagún, on whose colonizing works this particular version is based, would have been envious that he did not think of manipulating the legend in this way. No doubt he would have put it to good use in his efforts to stamp out from the Mexicas any trace of their Native worldview and spirituality.

The one good thing about this book is the illustrations by Robert Casilla, whose wife and son were the models for Mexicatl and his mother. The skin tones are realistic, the facial features are not exaggerated, the people look like real people. The illustrations are actually better than most you would expect to find in children's books about Aztecs, Mayas, or Incas. Still, this in itself is no reason to buy the book.—*Marco Palma*

Harjo, Joy (Muscogee-Creek), *The Good Luck Cat*, illustrated by Paul Lee. Harcourt 2000. Unpaginated, color illustrations; grades 1-3

Everybody knows cats have nine lives. Not everyone may know that some cats are good luck. Woogie is one who is, "but Woogie's nine lives, for all her good luck gifts, went fast." Climbing up into the car engine to curl up and keep warm. Running right out in front of a car. Getting spun (briefly) in the dryer. Then there was the dog. And a cat fight. And the boys with a BB gun. Smuggled into the car—because "I wanted to take her to the powwow with us"—and forgotten. Oh, yeah, falling out of a tree. "I thought cats always landed on their feet. Woogie landed on her head."

But the worst was when she didn't come home. She was gone for four days. But the cat came back. "Her left ear was bitten in half, but she was purring and singing as if she had never left." "Aunt Shelly said...'She has more than nine lives.'...I know Aunt Shelley is right."

It is not easy to draw good pictures of cats. Lee captures that essential "catness," and the humor in situations that could have been disastrous. Anyone who has lived with a cat—child, or adult—will recognize all of this.—*Doris Seale*

Harrell, Beatrice O. (Choctaw), *Longwalker's Journey: A Novel of the Choctaw Trail of Tears*, illustrated by Tony Meers. Dial (1999). 133 pages, b/w illustrations; grades 4-up; Choctaw

Ten-year-old Minko Ushi and his family are caught in the removal (Trail of Tears) of their Choctaw people from their ancestral lands to Indian Territory in 1831. Shortly into the story, Minko, his father, and a pony named Black Spot travel ahead to build a home for their family at the journey's end.

Along the way, they meet a man named John Turner. He has learned their language from his grandparents, who had fled slavery and were given refuge by some Choctaw people. Minko and Itilakna, his father, also encounter a refreshingly unsympathetically portrayed missionary, a wolf pup appeased by jerky, a racist but desperate white man, and government bureaucracy.

The reunion with their people is a sad one as many lives were lost, including that of Minko's grandmother. It looks for a while as if Grandfather may die as well and that Mother will never recover emotionally. But Grandfather does live on to pass down more of his wisdom to Minko. Mother later regains hope with the new baby she's carrying. And Minko receives the name "Longwalker."

Unlike many other authors who frame such events as inevitable or unattributable, Harrell—through her characters—doesn't hold back on rightfully blaming greed, racism, and the Jackson administration. The inclusion of John Turner is a plus, if only because it is unusual to see non-white characters from different communities interacting in children's literature. While it seemed a bit convenient that he would appear when he did and with his unique family history, no doubt such seemingly random connections occur. Perhaps fiction too often tries to create order where there was little, especially around historical tragedies. Also, readers see that the Nation will rebuild in Indian Territory, weakened and mourning but also committed to a future.

This is not a "how-the-Indians-all-died-what-a-shame" story. In fact, *Longwalker's Journey* is based on a true story from the author's own family, which takes readers with Minko along a parallel but largely separate trek from the rest of his people.

What works less well are a few ways in which the story appears to be framed perhaps to make it more accessible to the cross-cultural audience. The role of the pony Black Spot, based on a real pony that accompanied the author's great-great grandfather on his journey, is expanded to serve as a metaphor. In the novel, Itilakna observes,

> You know that Black Spot has a mind of his own. I think he knows what he must do, but he does not always like it. He is rather like the Chata people, don't you think? He has been through a great deal, but still he is full of life and spirit and he challenges us, defies us to break him.

The courage of the characters is sufficient to show their determination and vitality without relying on Black Spot. To the extent that the pony does illustrate parallel traits, young readers could most likely appreciate that on their own. So many writers use an animal as a metaphor for a Native person or people that it's become a cliché (though often in a more insulting way than here). The pony also seems to offer some comic relief from the more serious themes and events in the book. While that's generally welcome, it appears here to be overdone.

In addition, Itilakna refers at one point to his ancestral homeland as "this place the whites call Mississippi." It's unclear why he would say that in speaking with his own family. Young readers can refer to the 1831 map (charting the trail of the Choctaw and the trail of Minko and Itilakna) is included at the front of the book.

Despite the subtitle, this isn't really a novel of the Choctaw Trail of Tears, so much as the novel of a young boy, his father and the pony who traveled ahead of it. The motivation here is not to shelter young readers, but to expand and retell a family story within the historical context. This adds a certain freshness to the book. The downside is that readers don't become especially attached to the char-

acters who suffer most, the grandparents and Mother. This mitigates the emotional impact of the book and therefore full appreciation of what happened to the Choctaw people. For those specifically looking for books related to the Trail of Tears, this one might be offered along with another that pays as much attention to historical detail but also places the protagonist more squarely in the moment.

Yet especially after reading the author's note, which traces what aspects of the story are part of family history, it's clear that the heart of this story—a Choctaw family's survival of the Trail of Tears and rebuilding in Indian Territory—is important and lovingly rendered.

—*Cynthia L. Smith*

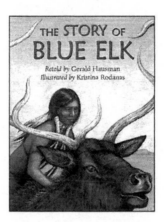

Hausman, Gerald, *The Story of Blue Elk*, illustrated by Kristina Rodanas. Clarion (1998). 32 pages, color illustrations; grades 1-4; Taos Pueblo

"Libraries looking for legends of the Pueblo Indians will find this a useful version," says Ilene Cooper in her review of *The Story of Blue Elk* for *Booklist*, one of the key journals librarians use when purchasing books. But the story Hausman tells here is not a Pueblo legend. Rather, as Hausman says in his author's note, it is his combined version of two distinct stories, one about "the magic of the flute" (which he heard from a noted Taos flautist), and one about "the magic of the elk" (which he heard from a noted storyteller from Santo Domingo Pueblo).

In one story, a boy who cannot speak falls in love and finds his voice in a red cedar flute. In another story, an elk gives himself to a hunter and lives again in the hearts of the villagers. In Hausman's version, a boy's birth is marked by the visit of an elk. Named for the elk, Blue Elk is unable to speak, but eventually gains a voice through a cedar flute he makes after the elk is killed by a visiting hunter.

A people's stories are created with purpose and meaning. They are often complex and subtle and convey significant teachings. I can't think of them as numbered motifs folklorists find in books like *The Storyteller's Sourcebook* by Margaret Mead MacDonald—motifs indexed for storytellers to take and use as they please.

I have additional concerns around the author's embellishment of the details of what has become his story. It is not unusual for a young person in one of our stories to have a special relationship with an animal, but Hausman employs the romantic and hokey Indian-as-one-with-nature theme to the point of absurdity.

> Blue Elk watched as the great elk eclipsed the sun, coming closer and closer, until he felt its flowery breath on his face and smelled the sweetness of jumbled cliffs, sun paths, cloud-washed ponds. The breath of the mighty elk, warm with bark, bud, and scrub, was good, and it passed between them as a bond of love, an unbreakable link in the necklace of their lives.

Later in the story, there are nonsensical plot elements. A "hunter from the far west" visits Blue Elk's village and tells them about a fine elk he had killed because the elk "gave me his breath." The hunter laments that he was so far from home that he could not share the elk meat with his people. But—what did he do with the meat? Leave it to rot? In Hausman's story, that is apparently what happens, but at my home, or in any other Pueblo home, that would not happen. Nobody would do that. When a hunter brings home an elk or deer, we honor the spirit of the animal. And we don't kill an animal unless we can take it home.

Rodanas may have visited Taos Pueblo, or studied photos of the village as she created the illustrations. Her colored pencil and watercolor pictures of the land are generally good, but the dark illustrations lack the brilliant quality of light typical of New Mexico, and the people appear thick and heavy, as though they were carved from wood like the cigar store Indians used by merchants during colonial times and standing in front of tobacco stores and pawn shops today. Also, Rodanas shows a young woman at the river, getting water in a black jar. While the illustrations clearly place this story in Taos, the black pottery was developed in San Ildefonso, not Taos, and it was not around at all prior to the 1950s. And, she seems to have forgotten something very important: For the most part, her Pueblo houses don't have doors!

Despite the favorable reviews in the book review journals, the illustrations that set the story in Taos Pueblo, and the Library of Congress Cataloging-in-Publication data that labels the book "Pueblo Indians—Folklore," The *Story of Blue Elk* is not one of our traditional stories. It is just another in a long line of books that gets consumed as though it has something special to say about us. It doesn't. Avoid it.—*Debbie A. Reese*

Hayes, Joe, *A Heart Full of Turquoise: Pueblo Indian Tales*, illustrated by Lucy Jelinek.   Mariposa (1988). 75 pages, color illustrations; grades 3-6

As a Pueblo woman whose life's work is writing and teaching about images of Native Americans in children's literature, I am so troubled about this collection that it is difficult to know where to begin, or even where to place my emphasis.

In the introduction, Hayes says that he learned these stories by reading books written by anthropologists and others who collected the stories decades ago from the Pueblo Indians. From those collections, Hayes says he "got the basic idea of the stories, and then made up my own way to tell them. Sometimes I changed a story, adding new characters, or dropping out some incidents." The seemingly innocent statement "Sometimes I changed a story…." speaks volumes about how Hayes and other storytellers from outside the culture see our peoples. What, specifically, did he change in each story? Did he, like Penny Pollock's version of the Turkey Girl story, make changes that fundamentally alter the stories, and by doing so, misrepresent the values of the Pueblo peoples? If he did, then it is disingenuous to call this a collection of Pueblo Indian tales.

In his "Notes on the Stories," Hayes says that he adapted several of the stories with permission from the American Folk-Lore Society. Pause to think about that for a moment. Ask yourself why Hayes contacted the American Folk-Lore Society. Shouldn't permission reside with the Pueblo peoples? Ask yourself: Whose stories are these?

Last year, I learned that there were songs recorded at Nambé in the early 1900s and housed in the Archives of Traditional Music at Indiana University. When I asked for copies, I was told that I had to write to someone for permission to get a copy of these songs—our songs. Even the governor of our Pueblo had to get permission to obtain a copy of our own songs. There is a long tradition of Native peoples being seen as "less than," and in that perception, our songs, our stories, our art have been seen as free for the taking. And that's what outrages me about people like Joe Hayes.

In his adaptations, he has mixed elements from several stories, added incidents to "make the story more complete," changed endings to be "happy" and "more conclusive," and generally, made the stories conform to his own style of storytelling. In my view, this common practice of "professional" storytellers is akin to going into someone's home, taking some of their most precious items, repainting them, and then selling them off using the names of the original owner as the hook for the consumer. Doesn't anyone see that this is wrong? We must begin to call it what it is—theft.

In the note for the Turkey Girl story, Hayes indicates he's heard a Navajo version, a Tewa one, and a Zuni one. The Tewa Pueblos are in the northern part of New Mexico, far from Zuni Pueblo, and they don't speak the same language. Why does Hayes' retellings in a collection of "Pueblo" tales contain a Navajo source? Hayes apparently does not think it is wrong to mix these very different traditions, but I do, and others who work with children should care about that, too.

Except for the vaguely Pueblo houses, Jelinek's black-on-turquoise line drawings are generic "Indian" illustrations, done with little or no attention to detail. In this regard, they suit the stories.

Those who live, work, or travel through New Mexico know who Joe Hayes is. Those who read or study children's literature know who Joe Hayes is. The back cover of the book says he is "soon to be a legend." Indeed, he has enjoyed a large measure of success with his storytelling. Through his performances, books, and audiotapes, Hayes is, unfortunately, becoming a legend. It is, sadly, The American Way. Take. Use. Make money, and never mind who or what gets stepped on along the way.—*Debbie A. Reese*

Heath, Kristina (Mohican/Menominee), *Mama's Little One*, illustrated by the author. Muh-he-con-neew Press (1996). Unpaginated; color illustrations; preschool-up; Mohican
Joosee, Barbara, *Mama, Do You Love Me?*, illustrated by Barbara Lavallee. Chronicle (1991). Unpaginated, color illustrations; preschool-up; Inuit
Scott, Ann Herbert, *On Mother's Lap*, illustrated by Glo Coalson. Clarion (1972, 1992). 32 pages, color illustrations; preschool-up; Inuit

These three titles in very different ways portray a mother's love for her child. In *Mama, Do You Love Me?* the emphasis is placed on talking, as an Inuit child tests the limits of her mother's love. Mother's answers ("I love you more than the raven loves his treasure, more than the dog loves his tail, more than the whale loves his spout") are pushed ("What if I put salmon in your parka, ermine in your mittens, and lemmings in your mukluks?"), and finally, the child ends up on Mother's lap with a doll on her lap, and Mother declaring, "I will love you forever and for always, because you are my Dear One." While this kind of thing might be almost believable in another cultural context, this is not typical of the way Inuit children and their parents communicate.

Lavallee's watercolors are a weak attempt at imitating an Inuit art style. The nuances, the delicate details are not there and the cultural context is wrong. A child is shown playing with masks. There's a flapping tent for shelter in deep snow. Happy little puppies are loosely tied to a sled. Joosee's glossary contains numerous errors as well. For instance, ravens and crows are not the same bird called by different names; they are different birds. Ravens (the birds) do not play an important part in Inuit culture; Raven (the Being) does.

Despite all of its critical acclaim, *Mama, Do You Love Me?* is *Runaway Bunny* redux with a contrived "multicultural" overlay.

On Mother's Lap also takes place in the Arctic, but its emphasis is more on "show" than on "tell." Michael's favorite place is on Mother's lap cuddling with her in a small rocking chair, a place made cozier as he adds—one by one—a dolly, a toy boat, a blanket, and a puppy. Each time he climbs back onto Mother's lap, "back and forth, back and forth, they rock." When baby cries and Michael declares that there's no more room, he soon finds out "there is always room on Mother's lap."

Glo Coalson's calm pastels in muted earth tones and turquoise do not try to imitate anyone else's style. There is cultural context here, such as a clothesline inside the house and mukluks and a reindeer blanket and a doll wearing a parka, but there is no pretended expertise, no glossary, no screaming "multiculturalism." Youngest children hearing this story will repeat, "back and forth, back and forth they rocked" as they enjoy the quiet of the moment.

Created for the author's children and "for all the children of the Mohican Nation," *Mama's Little One* is based on an old Mohican tradition, described in a text by Hendrick Aupaumut, a Mohican historian and diplomat from the late 18th- and early 19th Centuries. "The head of each family," Heath writes, "would wake the children each morning and teach them the ways in which to please the Great, Good Spirit. This was done until the children were grown." In *Mama's Little One*, Heath has interpreted Aupaumut's teachings—and illustrated them—to appeal to a modern audience of little ones. With realistic dialogue and simple colored pen-and-ink drawings, Heath portrays mother and child, in a new morning, quietly talking with one other about what is to be done in the day. It's a lovely little book that teaches a lot.

—*Beverly Slapin*

Helly, Mathilde, and Rémi Courgeon, *Montezuma and the Aztecs*. Holt (1996). 96 pages, color photos, color illustrations; grades 4-up; Mexica (Aztec)

This title is part of Holt's "W5" (who, what, when, where, and why) history series, originally published in France under the title *Cortés et son temps*. The stated goal of the series is to bring history to life for young readers, and the text brings in culture as well as history and biography.

Beginning with the Chinese epigraphy, "A picture is worth a thousand words," the mostly full-color illustrations include photography, drawings, maps, cartoons, modern paintings, and antique prints. The text of each double-page spread covers a different topic, ranging from aspects of Aztec cultural and spiritual life, to the establishment of Tenochtitlán, to the military campaigns of Cortéz and the exploitation of the Yucatán peninsula, to the lives of Moctezuma (the correct spelling) and Cortéz themselves.

Unfortunately, the goal of this book is belied by the sloppy writing and editing, inconsistent and illogical design, and most important, the condescending Eurocentric perspective that stereotypes and demonizes every aspect of the powerful and rich Mexica (Aztec) culture. A few of the more egregious examples:

- The cover bears the legend, "Quetzalcoatl, Huitzilopochtli, and other words you can't pronounce." We can pronounce these words just fine. To whom does the "you" refer? Certainly not to Mexica children.

- On the first page is a photo of a "Mexican salad." The salad, in a large clay bowl, consists of tomato, corn, beans, peppers, and pieces of cactus—with the thorns on. While nopales are part of the traditional Mexican diet, do the authors really think they were/are eaten this way? Also in the salad are cards with very odd statements from children and adults about Mexica people, such as: "It was hot where the Aztecs lived so they ate chili." What is the point of this?

- A headline for one of the spreads says, "The Gods Are Like Germs: They Are Countless, Invincible, and Hyperactive." The accompanying text does nothing to explain what this might mean. The illustration shows a naked Aztec man kneeling, looking into a microscope. Although the Mexica honored many, many aspects of nature, how is referring to them as "hyperactive" and "germs" in any way educational? And while the Mexica were technologically advanced for their time, they did not have microscopes.

- Another headline, "Eat Your Heart Out," leads one of several gory references to blood sacrifice, accompanied by an equally gruesome set of images. Here, the text reads in part:

> The body was cut up: the skin stuffed with cotton, went to decorate the façade of the palace where the priests lived; the right thigh went to the emperor; the head was impaled on a stake; the blood was smeared on the statues of the temple. The rest was eaten by the family of the man who had captured the victim or was thrown

to the wild beasts kept in the palace.... the smell of decaying flesh and coagulated blood was masked by copal incense.

What was the source for this? We don't know. It was likely based on turn-of-the-14th Century Spanish apologists for the destruction of the Aztec empire. Human sacrifice was an important part, but not the only aspect, of Mexica culture and cosmology. How can putting this inflammatory and prurient text alongside a sarcastic headline encourage any serious interest in the study of such a complex culture?

- The section called "The Garland Wars: They Only Sound Pretty" is accompanied by the cartoon image of a grinning Jaguar warrior, down on one knee, presenting to a smiling Olive Oyle lookalike a bouquet— of severed limbs. The Flowery Wars, as they are more commonly known, were an institution in which the sole purpose was to settle land disputes between neighboring Nations by seeing who could take more captives. The emphasis was—unlike today's warfare— not on killing the enemy but on attaining a higher rank and recognition from one's own people.

- "The Aztecs Never Discovered the Wheel, But Their Children Played with It Every Day," says another headline, which is accompanied by a photograph of an Aztec toy with four wheels. What does this incongruous headline mean, then?

- At Moctezuma's crowning, after self-mutilation ceremonies, the authors state that "he had sacrificed several quail on the altar; then with a gold incense burner he had waved incense toward the four corners of the earth to symbolize his power and authority." At the beginning of indigenous events, now as then, whether it is a birth, wedding, planting a garden, or dinner, there is an honoring of the four directions—and Mother Earth and Father Sky—to ask their blessings for the undertaking at hand. Power and authority rest easily only on those who honor the givers of life, and not even Moctezuma would have put himself above the forces of nature.

- Perhaps the most offensive image is the one that accompanies the section on Doña Marina or La Malinche. It is a color photo of a beautiful young Indian woman (most probably from Guatemala— which is nowhere near Mexico City—and most probably Maya, not Aztec). Over her mouth are placed the words, "Translation by Doña Marina" as if she were wearing a gag. What is this image supposed to suggest to our daughters—that they should be silent? That their role in life is blind obedience to those who would "conquer" them? The text states that Doña Marina was Cortez's willing "mistress and closest advisor," but in fact, there are many stories in our culture about La Malinche and no one knows for sure what the truths are.

Although there are Aztec scholars in Mexico today—and over fifty variants of the original Aztec language, Nahuatl, that are still being spoken by over a million people—there is nothing in this book from a Native point of view. The racism in the artwork and text is just appalling; page after page after page suggests to young readers that the Mexica people were conquered because of their savagery and backwardness. Further, there is no attribution for any of the illustrations, no source notes, and no recommended bibliography. Apparently, the authors do not expect young readers to do further research on any of the many topics covered here.

In a review of the "W5" series for the *Minneapolis Star Tribune*, Professor Jane Resh Thomas of the University of Minnesota writes:

> A species of seductive, expensive, glitzy, inferior nonfiction has emerged. Reference books for kids ought to exemplify clear thinking and principles of excellent writing. But a competent teacher would reject a student paper modeled after Montezuma and other titles in this series.

We couldn't have said it better.—*Judy Zalazar Drummond* and *Marco Palma*

Hewitt, William, *Across the Wide River.* **University of New Mexico (2003). 96 pages; grades 5-up; Ho-Chunk (Winnebago)**

By using a fictional narration of a young Native protagonist, *Across the Wide River* purports to reveal actual Native sentiments. Instead, it reveals the sentiments and prejudices of the non-Native author.

The major events of the novel actually occurred in Sioux City, Iowa, during what has become known as the "Korean Conflict." In 1950, a Ho-Chunk (Winnebago) U.S. army sergeant and World War II veteran, John R.

Rice, was killed in battle. Returned to his family a year later, his body was refused burial in the local "whites-only" cemetery. Because of the activism of Evelyn Rice and the Ho-Chunk community, the controversy drew national attention—and embarrassment—to Sioux City and President Truman arranged for Rice to be buried at Arlington National Cemetery with full military honors.

Hewitt, a historian who previously researched and wrote about this incident, has turned this painful part of history into a coming-of-age, walking-in-two-worlds young adult novel whose young mixed-blood protagonist—the son of John and Evelyn Rice—encounters prejudice, swims across the Missouri River in order to test himself, finds out who he is, and "confirms his worthiness in the eyes of his peers."

From the beginning, this story is full of stereotypes, the most blatant of which is the interpretation of Indians as somehow possessing of "warrior" genes, an assumption that draws parallels between Native Americans as warriors and Native Americans as soldiers. The fact that Indian people have served and continue to serve in the U.S. military in far greater proportion than any other ethnic community is a complex and sometimes divisive issue in Indian Country, and there are no easy answers. A book that addresses the issues of how the notion of being a warrior by serving in the military became imposed on Native people has yet to be written.

Amid the ever-present images of dreamcatchers and soaring eagles, Grandfather Rice tells young John stories of Crazy Horse and Geronimo and other warriors. Like other Indian elders in the imagination of white writers, he speaks in metaphors when he has something important to say: "You are an eagle. You will circle until you swoop down and stand where you want." Here, Grandfather seems to be advising young John that the child can choose his ethnicity, who he is. This is an outrageous assumption that children of mixed parentage have these kinds of options, and to put these words in the voice of an elder shows a casual disregard for all that is imposed on mixed-blood children and all that Native people deal with on a daily basis.

Moreover, young John discusses his parents in a way that more reflects the author's prejudicial thinking than that of an Indian youngster. After an experience with his cousin in which he is accused of shoplifting, John says, "I immediately thought of my parents and how hard it must have been for my mother to be married to an Indian." It is more likely that an Indian kid in these circumstances would lash out at a society that causes him to be suspect because he's brown, or to realize the difficulty his parents must have had as a mixed couple in a society that refuses to acknowledge them.

Why does young John undergo a sweat ceremony/vision quest "to strengthen (his) Winnebago side" that was "somehow weakened" by his father's death? Why does he fast before going into the sweat lodge? Why does he go on vision quest in a sweat lodge? By inappropriately merging two distinct events, the author has invented yet another generic-romantic "Indian ceremony" for young non-Indian readers to learn about. That he inserts a vision quest at all in this story, and that he hopelessly mangles it demonstrate his casual disregard for Indian lives. No one ought to have to read about themselves in a way that diminishes their value as human beings.

There's more. Why does Grandfather Rice constantly use the word "wasichu" to refer to white people? "Wasichu" is not a generic "Indian" word for white people; it's specifically Lakota. Why is young John's Indian name "Coup Feather"? This is an odd choice of a name for a young person. Was he given the name because he did something heroic? Was he given the name at birth and if so, why? There's no explanation, no context other than the name fits in with the "warrior" theme of the book. Why does young John think in metaphors, such as "I leaned my head out the open window and... soared as an eagle, effortless"?

As a non-fiction accounting of the struggles of the Rice family and the Indian community against discrimination in the 1950s—discrimination that continues today in everyday indignities, large and small—the story had the potential of educating young readers, Indian and non-Indian, about an important piece of history. The story is about racism, but ironically the author displays his own racism and ignorance in the telling of the story, giving the illusion of a Native point of view when it's not.

The "wide river" is the heavy-handed metaphorical gulf between the Indian and white communities, and between what the author perceives as the opposing forces in the heart of a child of mixed parentage. But no matter how well meaning Hewitt might be, he can't break through the barriers to see from an Indian perspective.

What troubles us most is that the Rice family is neither thanked nor acknowledged here. If they were not asked for permission to use their names in a work of fiction, they should have been. If they read the manuscript and saw it as offensive, changes should have been made. If they did not want to call further attention to themselves, then that should have been honored and the project dumped. As it stands, the author is exploiting a real family and a real incident.—*Beverly Slapin and Lois Beardslee*

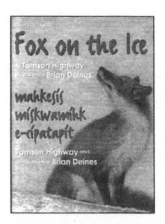

Highway, Thomson (Cree), illustrated by Brian Deines. HarperCollins. Unpaginated, color illustrations; all grades; Cree:
Caribou Song/atihko nikamon (2001)
Dragonfly Kites/pimihákanisa (2002)
Fox on the Ice/mahkesis miskwamihk e-cipatapit (2003)

Set in the far north of Manitoba, close to the tree line, this bilingual trilogy of picture books called "Songs of the North Wind" are the stories of two young Cree brothers, Joe and Cody, their mama and papa, and their huskies and black dog, Ootsie, who live along Reindeer Lake. There is no TV here, or the toy section of the Christmas catalog to look at—just the vast expanse of snow and bush and what might just be the most beautiful land there is.

All day, Joe likes to play the accordion and sing the caribou-come-here song: "Ateek, ateek! Astum, Astum! Yo-ah, ho-ho! Caribou, Caribou! Come, come! Yo-ah, ho-ho!" And Cody, Cody really likes to dance—"He danced on the rocks, he danced on the ice, he even danced under the full silver moon."

On a spring day, the family stops for lunch of whitefish and bannock in a meadow surrounded by forest, and while their parents drink their tea near the fire, the two boys wander off to sing and dance for the caribou. And then suddenly, a thousand, no, two thousand, no, ten thousand caribou thunder out of the forest, "fill[ing] the meadow like a lake." To say what happens next is to spoil this wonderful story that will leave young readers "laughing and laughing and laughing."

On a winter afternoon, with a clear sky and the sun so bright that the "snow sparkle[s] like diamonds," the family goes ice fishing. After lunch, as the children play and the huskies happily doze in the sun, Papa sets the nets. Their peace is shattered when the huskies notice a fox with "fur as bright as flames" and take off after it, dragging along Joe and Mama, and leaving a dilemma for quick-thinking Papa—and clever Ootsie—to solve.

In the summer, Joe and Cody remember the baby animals they have fed and named—they even named the ants—

but the dragonflies were their favorites, because the boys flew them like kites and then let them go. And at night, the boys

> dreamed they jumped so high that they didn't come down. Off they flew with their dragonfly kites into the gold and pink of the northern sunset, laughing and laughing. Until it was time to wake up.

These beautifully designed books, with spare and lyrical text in Cree and English, are filled with Deines' vibrant full-page oil on canvas paintings. In muted natural tones of browns, grays, blues and greens, the earth, snow, brush and water are very real, as are the family and the animals. The exuberance on the faces of the children, the worried mom, the scrubby bushes and caribou moss coming up through the snow, Ootsie's goofy-happy tongue-hanging-out expression and the nonchalant grin of the fox, the thundering herd of caribou kicking up bits of earth and clumps of snow, sunlight shining through the ice and the luminous dragonflies—all of this places the young reader right in the middle of the action.

And knowing that these stories are drawn from memories of Highway's childhood in the 1950s—before he and his brother were sent to residential school—makes these lovely little stories all the more moving.—*Beverly Slapin*

Hill, Kirkpatrick, *The Year of Miss Agnes*. McElderry (2000). 115 pages; grades 4-6; Athabascan

As a "native" Alaskan, the author brings the experience of thirty years of remote teaching and living to this seductive and well-written story. But the smiling faces on the dust cover obscure the double-edged blade of "cross-cultural education" that cuts to the bone in the name of progress and humanity.

The story, told by ten-year-old Fred, a Native Alaskan girl with a boy's name, is about the year—1948—the children spend with "Miss Agnes," an eccentric and dedicated white teacher who comes to the bush and "opens the door to the world" as she infuses the children with Greek myths, Robin Hood, geography, time lines, microscopes, and opera. Miss Agnes even wins over Fred's "mamma," with whom she is juxtaposed in this story. While "mamma" is the argumentative grump, a "hard-luck person" who is "kind of mean," and sees schooling as useless, Miss Agnes is the loving, progressive, forward-looking individual who sees the promise in each of "her" children.

Throughout, there are comparisons between Fred's indigenous culture and that of Miss Agnes. The unspoken—but nevertheless strong—implication is that, while Native people merely *survive*, white people *think* and even *philosophize*. For instance,

> Grandma makes the sinew thread for sewing out of that big hump on the back of the moose, and she tans the moose hide with rotten moose brains. Boy, does *that* smell bad.

On the other hand,

> With Miss Agnes the world got bigger and then it got smaller. We used to think we were something, but then she told us all the things that were bigger than us, the universe and all that, and then all the things that were smaller. Too small to even see. So people were sort of in between, not big and small, just in between. That was a really interesting thing to think about.

Hill's story focuses on the themes of illiteracy, child poverty, deafness, single parenthood, elder dependency, urbanization, and poor material conditions; and ignores the rich cultural history and cosmology that have enabled a people to survive and thrive for millennia in what is seen by some as a harsh, unforgiving environment. While it is probably a good thing for children to know about the world, real education must be based in common values rather than merely common geography. The true survival of the Freds and Bokkos of Native Alaska must include respect for identity, heritage, and family that this story denies.—*Marlene R. Atleo/ʔeh ʔeh naa tuu kwiss*

Himango, Deanna (Ojibwe), *Boozhoo, Come Play with Us*, photographed by Rocky Wilkinson (Ojibwe). Fond du Lac Head Start Program (2002). Unpaginated, color photographs; preschool-up; Ojibwe
Jaakola, Lyz (Ojibwe), *Our Journey*, illustrated by the author. Fond du Lac Head Start Program (2002). Unpaginated, color illustrations; preschool-up; Ojibwe

"Boozhoo, Whitney. Boozhoo means hello. Boozhoo, Samanthia. Agindaaso means read. Boozhoo, Rebecca. Mazina'igan means book." With Ojibwe words and color photographs of the Fond du Lac kids doing what little kids do, this beautiful board book will appeal to little kids everywhere.

Our Journey uses two Ojibwe words that require no translation; their meanings are obvious from the context and the illustrations:

> Anin to the East, Anin to the South, Anin to the West, Anin to the North, Anin to the Sun, Anin to the Earth, Anin to the One who gave me my birth! Miigwetch to the East, Miigwetch to the South, Miigwetch to the West, Miigwetch to the North, Miigwetch to the Sun, Miigwetch to the Earth, Miigwetch to the One who gave me my birth!

The paintings are of the people living in their traditional way and in traditional dress: winnowing wild rice, weeding corn, playing, being together. The paintings are lovely, the words have a nice rhythm. Designed with Indian children in mind, this book will also work well in non-Native settings.—*Doris Seale*

Himmelman, John, *Pipaluk and the Whales*, illustrated by the author. National Geographic Society (2001). Unpaginated, color illustrations; kindergarten-grade 2; Chukchi
Schuch, Steve, *A Symphony of Whales*, illustrated by Peter Sylvada. Voyager (1999). Unpaginated, color illustrations; grades 3-4; Chukchi

During the winter of 1984-85, some 3,000 beluga whales became trapped in an opening in the ice pack near the Senyavina Strait of Siberia. For several weeks the people of the Chukchi Peninsula and the crew of the icebreaker Moskva worked to save the belugas. The icebreaker cut a twelve-mile-long channel through the ice pack from the open sea to the whales. But the whales refused to follow the ship to open water until scientists aboard the Moskva lured them to freedom by playing classical music over a loudspeaker.

Both books, fiction, are "inspired" by this event, and both are very similar. In each, the author has created a young Native girl as the focal character—Glashka in *A Symphony of Whales* and Pipaluk in *Pipaluck and the Whales*—who discovers the trapped whales and plays the pivotal role in their rescue. In both stories, the villagers set up camp near the whales, chipping away at the ice while they await the rescue ship. When it finally arrives, it is only the child protagonist who can figure out a way to lead the whales back out to sea.

It is young Glashka's dream of the singing of the whales, singing that she has heard "from the earliest time she could remember"—singing that the "old ones of her village" determine is the voice of Narna the whale, a long time "friend to our people"—that enables her to hear the "eerie moans and whistles" of the trapped whales.

While it's Glaska's mystical dreams of the songs that enable her to bring about the rescue, Pipaluk's songs come from a more emotional Disney-like place. With sadness at the sight of a young calf in whose "large dark eyes" she sees "a reflection of the stars," she begins to sing. "It was a song for the little whale with the stars in its eyes. Soon, others joined in the singing. The whales grew silent as they listened."

In both books, the plotting is far-fetched and the writing is trite. At the scene of thousands of whales struggling to breathe, pushing their young calves to the surface, "Pipaluk knew the whales sensed the danger they were in."

With the rescue accomplished, Glaskha's dream songs become "something like a whole symphony of whales." As Pipaluk comes ashore,

> The whale with the stars in its eyes swam up to her. Pipaluk knelt down and stroked its head. "Stay out of holes in the ice," she whispered. The whale gave a quiet whistle and joined its family in the sea.

A word about the illustrations. While Sylvada's heavy oil paintings emphasize the changing light patterns, bitter weather and texture of clothing and land, Himmelman's cartoonish watercolors trivialize the land and the community, not to mention the whales.

Both authors have taken an awesome story of a community's commitment to save the relatives they depend on for sustenance, and another community's willingness to help—and turned it into a romanticized tale of an individual child's heroism that stems from some special mystical relationship. As it stands, both A *Symphony of Whales* and *Pipaluk and the Whales* are an unforgivable condescension to the child reader—*Barbara Potter*

Hirschi, Ron, *People of Salmon and Cedar*, illustrated by Deborah Cooper. Cobble Hill (1996). 42 pages, b/w photographs, color illustrations; grades 4-6; Northwest Coast Nations

Ron Hirschi grew up in the Pacific Northwest, where he was once Fisheries Biologist for the S'Klallam people. That background shows in this historical/cultural/environmental work. The book begins with a welcoming speech attributed to "Chief Seattle" (his name was Seealth). In six chapters, Hirschi shows how the lives of the Northwest Coastal Peoples were deranged by the coming of the whites. The richness of the sea and their lands acted as a magnet for the greed of those who came to exploit it for their own purposes, without regard for the results. It's the usual story: suppression of customs and spiritual beliefs, spread of disease, destruction of sources of livelihood. But Hirschi also writes of the ways in which people have worked to take back their ceremonies and the fishing rights theirs by treaty, and have fought against deforestation and destruction of fishing stocks due to pollution, overfishing and dam building, particularly the salmon, which are to them as the buffalo are to the peoples of the Plains.

For someone who knows so much and means so well—*does* so well—it is hard to see how Hirschi can say some of the things he does.

- On welcoming the first salmon: "The celebration holds the importance of Christmas, Hanukkah, or the Fourth of July." Actually, it bears no resemblance to any of those.

- "They more or less knew how to have the forest and use it too." More or less?

- A potlatch is "like a Christmas party with Indian costume." Ouch.

- In the chapter, "Welcoming the Salmon People," Hirschi says that "most" of the coastal Indians regarded the salmon as people. Thereafter, *every* time he refers to salmon people—and he does it a lot—he puts it in quotes. Very Annoying. At one point, he says, "You may not believe that salmon are people. Lots of Native Americans don't think that is true." That. Is. Not. The. Point.

On the other hand, he'll say, "All parts of the earth are sacred. The air we breathe, the sand beneath our feet, and the birds in the air...[I]t is especially easy to see how sacred thoughts surround the towering cedar trees." And, "Much has been lost because of the loss of words...."

I don't know about this guy. I think his heart gets it, his brain just hasn't caught all the way up yet.

And then there are Deborah Cooper's illustrations. The first good thing is that her people *look* like Indians. The colors are good, and the full-page designs for each chapter amplify the text. For cedar: in the center, trees. Around them, cedar bark clothing, basketry, a bentwood box, a carver at work, an ancestor pole, a baby sleeping in a basketry cradle, and a canoe. She doesn't get everything right. Some of her designs are a little off, and we could have done without a picture for the Christmas-Hanukkah-and-Fourth of July thing; Santa holding a little kid, Uncle Sam waving in the background, a small boy lighting a Menorah, and a happy smiling Native holding a carving of a salmon. And there's no way you'd need all the towels in the potlatch picture, unless you were planning to open a bathhouse. By and large, Cooper does better than this, but the piece de resistance is a double-page spread of the salmon people. Naked people are walking into the water, where they are turning into salmon. A beautiful young woman, not yet a salmon, is lying on her tummy in the water with her arms folded over a rock, with

a come-hither expression on her face. There are what I thought were salmon-mermaids, before I read the text. One man is holding a bath towel, strategically placed. Now where did he get that?

I don't like the Indian people bringing back the traditions and "sharing their wealth of knowledge, rich heritage, and generous ways with all who will listen" kind of comment, and some of the travelogue aspects of Hirschi's writing. But even with its flaws, this a lot better book than many, and it carries a serious message: "Today, more than 175 separate stocks [of salmon] are either gone or endangered," and [A]lmost 90 percent of the original forest is now gone."

The 1948 photograph of a parade of eighteen-wheelers, each carrying a section of tree bigger than the truck itself, is worth at least a thousand words. One could give Hirschi a lot for telling the truth about so many things. From a S'Klallam tribal citizen: "All is not well. There are visible and invisible warning signs that we ignore at our own peril."—*Doris Seale*

Hirschi, Ron, *Seya's Song,* **illustrated by Constance R. Bergum. Sasquatch (1992). Unpaginated, color illustrations; grades 3-up; S'Klallam**

This book was made possible in part by a grant to the Port Gamble S'Klallam people from the National Park Service Historic Preservation Grants to Indian Tribes for the preservation of their language. In it, Hirschi tells, in the first person, the story of a little girl who is learning some words from her Seya. In her voice we are told some things about the land, what lives there, and some of the ways of her people, using S'Klallam words for land formations, animals, plants, sea creatures. It's a simple, appealing little book, beginning with a morning walk down to the sea, where "I hear the sounds of S'Klallam words Grandmother (Seya) taught me," ending with sleep and a "dream of the seasons past. Starlight and shadows dance in my mind and the words of Seya's songs—Skio, Skaatl, and Kloomachin—swim with the tiny salmon resting in the river, waiting for a new spring." Well, it's a dream...

An afterword gives further information about the S'Klallam people and the challenges they have faced since the conquest. A glossary of S'Klallam words includes instructions on how to try to say them. I'm not so sure about Hirschi's suggestion that the few remaining Seyas will be happy to help "you" in "your" search for words.

The pictures are pretty, but the illustrator has taken a certain amount of artistic license with them. This child is not going to be standing in the water, fully clothed, playing with the salmon eggs. It is hard to picture a medieval sand castle being built on the beach here, and the clams steaming beside a most unusual-looking canoe are lying on top of the seaweed, not under it. That won't work very well. And the illustration for the dance (kwoieishten) is pure fantasy. There are three figures. The one on the right wears a mask of some kind. On the left, an androgynous figure clothed in what looks to be beach grass dances with a rattle. The central figure, the drummer, is morphing into the smoke from the fire, against a star-speckled night sky.

I think these people meant well, and Hirschi is to be commended for his commitment to the preservation of the People and the creatures of the Earth—which he has demonstrated over and over in many books for children. This just seems a little romantic for so serious an effort as the preservation of the language of an entire People. —*Doris Seale*

Hogan, Linda (Chickasaw), *Power.* **W.W. Norton (1998). 235 pages, high school-up**

What happens when one people's power is another people's broken law? How does a person who is witness to a power that is simultaneously "right" and "wrong," "good" and "bad," remain sane? In Hogan's latest work, that person is Omishto, a Taiga teenager who watches her Aunt Ama track, shoot, and kill a sacred golden panther in what is left of their Florida homeland. Here, Hogan is once again in her lyrical element, describing the land and the people she loves:

> Except for swamps and bogs, the land takes in all the water. It is a thirsty land. It is also an honest land. It doesn't lie or hide anything. Neither does Ama. Everything she is, everything she is about to do, is clear in her face and in her movement and in her words. The way everything is open to view when sunlight comes down through the hole where all life entered this world.

Emotionally and physically torn during the hunt, ragged from a hurricane that has just exploded across Florida, Omishto can and cannot understand why her beloved aunt is committing this act. Stunned, she says,

> [W]hat I believe now is the force of the storm, the mighty force of it, and the cat lying dead or half dead in the bushes and trees and that what we are doing is wrong but I know that we are compelled to do it.

Omishto knows, too, that this killing will lead to the inevitable:

> The police will ask what I know about it. Not because they care but because it's a law, because you can't kill one of them.

Ama and Omishto endure a court trial: Ama as the accused killer, Omishto, Ama's dearest relative and young heir, as the witness against her. Eventually, a tribal court is held, too, and once again, Omishto's heart is torn by her allegiances, her need to survive, her own passionate integrity, and her fear of making a mistake.

Hogan encapsulates the paradox of colonization in her tale, juxtaposing the aboriginal power that arises out of an uncontrolled and unknowable source against the colonial power whose domination rests on an obsessive knowing and controlling, a refusal to acknowledge the possibility of an equally powerful, but different, cosmology.

Omishto witnesses these two powers—the elemental power of Ama's ability to communicate with the panther and the abusive power of a culture that hunts the panther to near extinction, then declares it "endangered." So Ama's killing of the cat, whether an act of indigenous ritual or a crazy woman's post-hurricane madness, is something to be punished.

Power questions not just ecological and environmental justice, but the politics of power between tribal and U.S. government laws and the personal struggle to stay alive in a world we know we are "never meant to survive." Like the Makah Nation in Washington State, the Taigas in *Power* believe they have the right to a ceremony that may help heal the world, even if it requires the death of an animal protected by the Endangered Species Act.

In this context, Hogan's brilliant novel expresses the risks tribal peoples face when they access power after centuries of colonization. Among those risks: Will they remember the ceremony correctly? Can they find a path into the song that is required, or must they create a new song? Will that song suffice, or will it cause still more upheaval? If the tribe is divided about renewing the ceremony, how will it heal that wound? What will happen if, after all the preparations and personal sacrifices, the colonizer says, "No"? Says, "We know best how to deal with this"? Says, "We have always said you are savages—uncivilized, incapable of leaving behind superstition—now we can prove it"? Can an indigenous people so battered by the "civilization process"—lost or damaged languages, lifeways, familial connections, land bases, livelihoods and, often, self-respect—can that people take a stand in the face of one more colonial attack?

It is all of these excruciating questions, traced in one girl's mind, that makes *Power* critical and essential reading for high school-age readers. Listening at Ama's trial to two Taiga elders of the Panther Clan who have been called to testify, Omishto thinks,

> Together, the two old women don't say enough to condemn Ama, not enough to free her either. But even so, the crack in that container, that jar of history, opens and it breaks. It widens between two halves of a single world. And now I feel that the breaking is all that's left. I can't put it out of my mind, any of this, and I too am broken and divided.

When tribal citizens are called upon to testify against their own power, "the breaking is all that's left." Can that brokenness be endured? It would be easy, as Omishto's mother and others do, to walk away, to submit to the power of colonization, to deny that an older, uncontrollable, unknowable power exists. Who wants to risk ridicule, impoverishment, loss of personal freedom, financial sanctions? And if this attempt to heal the world fails . . . who could live with that shame? Yet Ama can—and does—face such risks: "She walks like a strong woman chasing her God and I'm surprised how fast she moves," says Omishto of Ama during the pursuit of the panther. It awes me to conceive of such a woman: someone who, seeing a power greater than herself, hurries after it, trusts it to lead her, knowing her actions can save, or devastate, all that she loves.

In our Native belief systems, our cosmologies, it is not a contradiction to call an animal "grandmother," to recognize and honor its sacred kinship, and to kill it. As exemplified by the media frenzy and racism that accompanied the Makah whale hunts in Neah Bay over the last few years, this is something I have come to doubt that white people can understand. At the same time, as our land and our bodies change, our cosmologies undergo tremendous movement and stress, and we must find ways to continue to honor power in our diverse ways, coping with an oftentimes ravaged land, and the decimated beings who live here with us. Hogan wrestles with this painful love within the pages of Power, and opens pathways for her readers to explore on their own.

Power does not presume to speak for all indigenous peoples faced with such awesome work, and it does not supply any "answers." However, it demands respect for power, and teaches us that the hard work of the spirit is the only work that matters. I am grateful to Linda Hogan for tracking this panther to places I am not sure I can go myself.

—Deborah A. Miranda

(Note: The "Taiga" people do not exist as a Native Nation. Linda Hogan created them in order to communicate to readers the complex and surrealistic experience of being colonized. In this, I hope she has succeeded, inasmuch as anyone can communicate a concept this difficult to people who may not be living it. This is not a technique I would recommend to most authors, Native or non-Native, because of the incredibly inept representations we already have of Indians in the American imagination. In my mind, few people have earned the authority and the right to push the boundaries when talking about spiritual survival, and Linda Hogan is one of them. As a teacher of creative writing and as an Indian woman, I am continuing to think about the ways that Native writers can use the English language to articulate the experiences of being Indian.—D.A.M.)

Hogan, Linda (Chickasaw), *Solar Storms.* Simon & Schuster (1995). 351 pages; high school-up

Linda Hogan is known as much as a poet as a novelist. And though in *Solar Storms*, her multi-layered story is intriguing, it is the music of her language and the power of her voice that most distinguishes the book. The reading is an experience.

In many ways, it is the story of coming home to a land, a people, a family, and one's self. To the ties between women through love and grief and anger and generations. It's the healing of young, red-haired Angel's interior scars, those that mirror the ones on her face. And it's an unfolding of the stories behind the mutilation and the secrets to slow-born understanding.

> And then Agnes walked out of the mist toward me, a woman old and dark. I knew who she was by the way my heart felt in its chest. It recognized its own blood.

> It was during this change of seasons that I began to see. To see that there were three women and myself, all of us on some kind of journey out from that narrowed circle of our history the way rays of light grow from the sun.

And so Angel grows to know her grandmother, her great-grandmother, and the woman who is not her mother but who was once her father's wife. She learns her own mother's tragic story and seeks the beginning of their tale.

One of the biggest opponents is a hydroelectric dam, this made more poignant after the narrative's observance of the relationship of water to life. It is somehow a symbol of the greater forces struggling against them:

> Auntie stood up to speak. "We've been here for thousands of years." Her hands shook with anger. "We don't want your dams." She sounded calmer than she looked and I was proud of her.... But

after she spoke her strong words, the man called us remnants of the past and said that he wanted to bring us into the twentieth century.

Unlike so many novels that paint Native women narrowly, as shadows or even burdens, Hogan celebrates her characters for who they are. They have been marked at times by sorrow, but that is not their whole. Humor, wisdom and kindness can be found in many of the tensest moments. And while the trials between men and women are depicted with force, so are the moments of connection, reconciliation and respect: "Even if the white men didn't pay attention to Auntie, the young Indian men did. They loved her."

There are good books that grab readers and carry them fast. This is a good book for savoring, reading over and again, aloud even. Aloud and then contemplated.

When Hogan speaks of cooking, take the time to smell it. When she talks of the land, let it rise up beneath your feet. When she slices into your heart, cry with her. Carrying with you whatever wisdom you may glean.—*Cynthia L. Smith*

Jacobs, Shannon, *The Boy Who Loved Morning,* illustrated by Michael Hays. Little, Brown (1993). Unpaginated, color illustrations; grades 3-5

The author's note, more of a caveat actually, says that her "story grew out of my great love and respect for Native American spiritual traditions, especially those teaching the connection of all life. It does not depict any specified tribe." Her qualifications for writing this? She "loosely based *The Boy Who Loved Morning* on her extensive travel experiences and on research about Native American culture."

Hays' pictures—of tipis, geometrical border patterns and ghostly buffalo—hint that the location might be the Great Plains, although there are also "mesas." There are prayers to the "Great Spirit." There is talk of buffalo "disappearing quickly," so the time is probably around the mid-19th Century.

A boy of about ten, called "Boy" because he has not been given a name yet, has a flute, a gift from his grandfather. Every morning, he greets the sunrise with a song. He also has conversations with his animal friends, Coyote, Crow, and Snake. He doesn't appear to have any human friends. "Boy" eagerly awaits his "naming ceremony":

> After his family presented names to the council, a final choice would be made at the ceremony in two moons. A person's naming was a very important event. Sometimes the choice of a name could affect a person's future.

While he's waiting for all this to happen, he discovers that his music has the power to call up morning light. So he decides that, at his "naming ceremony," he will "call for a full sunrise at midnight." The long-awaited

day of the naming ceremony arrives, and "the camp overflowed" with people, including Aztec dancers, women and a little girl wearing contemporary fancy shawl outfits and some Pueblo people with hand drums. The people, impressed with Boy's music, break into a wild dance:

> People stood up, feeling the wild rhythms. One by one they began dancing to Boy's fast music. They leapt and kicked and pounded the earth as fast as stampeding buffalo.

Boy becomes so enchanted with himself that he makes the sun shine at midnight. His grandfather, shamed, takes the flute away, and Boy goes off to a mesa to ponder what he has done. His animal friends help him to understand that pride goeth before the fall, or something like that. Boy promises Grampa that he'll never do *that* again, whereupon Grampa asks Boy to choose a name. Does. Chooses "Morning Song." Grampa agrees. "Boy" is now and forever known as "Morning Song," "a very good name for a boy who loved morning."

No Native child would live to be ten without a name. What do you do, yell "boy" and every kid in the camp turns around? Naming can certainly have its ceremonial aspects, but it isn't a party; people don't come for miles around and span centuries. Names are not chosen by committee, nor are they picked by little kids. A name may be chosen by parents, by a respected elder, or by a medicine person. There might be a giveaway to honor the person being named or the person giving the name. In the course of a lifetime, as events and responsibilities change, a person may be given several names.

The basic storyline is that a child has medicine that allows him to alter the rising of the sun. He comes to understand that to use this medicine is to disrupt the natural world for his own gratification. Mastery of medicine of this kind is a great gift that the child would have likely been taught how to use in a good way. Such things are not unheard of. But our concern lies here: A sideline to the story is that the grandfather has been inattentive to the child because the whites are invading the land. Why does the author see this child's gift of altering the natural world in a less immediately damaging manner more important than the white settlers' slaughtering the buffalo by the millions and by so doing, destroying the environment of the child's people? At the very least, the author could have made this connection. Her failure to do so expresses a willful decision to trade the realities of a time and the lessons they could teach for a false construction of a people and a lesson that hits less close to home.—*Beverly Slapin*

(Thank-you to Ella Rose Callow.)

Jeffers, Susan, *Brother Eagle, Sister Sky*, illustrated by the author. Dial (1991). Unpaginated, color illustrations; preschool-up; Suquamish/Duwamish

Susan Jeffers has over the years produced a number of beautifully illustrated books for young children. For her 1991 title, *Brother Eagle, Sister Sky*, she chose to illustrate the speech attributed to "Seattle" and generally called "How Can One Sell the Air?" The Suquamish/Duwamish "chief" Seeathl has because of his speech become a sort of new-age icon—a thing that he might regard with a certain amount of irony. Since as Jeffers points out in the afterword of her book, nobody knows for sure what Seeathl really said, she has felt free to further adapt "Chief Seattle's message."

It does seem to be agreed that the man said something. In an article entitled "Chief Seattle's Speech(es): American Origins and European Reception," Rudolf Kaiser examines four versions of the speech, with a view to determining which, if any, might be the most accurate. In this work he points out that "[t]wo short speeches by Seattle that are recorded in the National Archives in Washington, D.C., bear no resemblance to the texts of the speech popularized under Seattle's name," and that "the first published version of the now-famous speech was presented to the public by a Dr. H.A. Smith in 1887, more than thirty years after the chief is said to have delivered it."[1] Kaiser further states that, while we can "take it for granted that there is at least a core, a nucleus of authentic thinking and, possibly, language in the text, as Dr. Smith was able to base his version of the speech on 'extended notes' in his diary, taken on the occasion of the delivery of the speech," it is also impossible to determine "the degree of authenticity of this text, as Dr. Smith's notebook has not been found."[2] This article extends to more than thirty-five pages, and is well worth the reading.

In any case, this speech was not, as Hornbook would have it, a "beautifully environmental statement,"[3] but an elegy. Seeathl was speaking at a time when all life as he had known it seemed to be close to an ending, and his words carry a clear warning. When Seeathl says, "We may be brothers after all. We shall see," he is not talking about brotherly love—or the environment.

> Even the white man... is not exempt from the common destiny... Every part of this country is sacred to my people....and the very dust under your feet responds more lovingly to our footsteps than to yours, because it is the ashes of our ancestors...And when the last red man shall have perished...the streets of your cities and villages... will throng with the returning hosts that once filled and still love this beautiful land. The white man will never be alone. Let him be just and deal kindly with my people, for the dead are not altogether powerless.[4]

Make a "beautiful environmental statement" out of *that*, if you can. Not particularly suitable material for a picture book either, one would think. Jeffers' take on this?

> When the last Red Man and Woman have vanished with their wilderness, and their memory is only the shadow of a cloud moving across the prairie, will the shores and forest still be here? Will there be any of the spirit of my people left? My ancestors said to me, This we know: The earth does not belong to us. We belong to the earth.

Although *Brother Eagle, Sister Sky* was a children's bestseller for months—it had, as of June 1992, sold more than 300,000 copies[5] and by the end of 2003, had almost doubled that number[6]—the book did not come out to universal praise. Patricia Dooley, reviewing in *School Library Journal*, said, in part: "Alas, her entire stock of characters appears to have come from Sioux Central Casting," and notes that the text is

> not well served by images that ignore the rich diversity of Amerindian cultures (even Seealth's own Northwest people) in favor of cigar-store redskins in feathers and fringe. Where Jeffers' book is used, it should be supplemented with others more sensitive to Native American heritage.[7]

As she has changed the words to suit herself, so Jeffers has drawn pictures that, with the exception of what may possibly be a carved canoe on the title page, have nothing at all to do with any aspect of Northwest Coast life. In a letter of reply to Dooley's review, Jeffers indignantly states that her research for the book was "extensive," and that "Mag La Que, Miyaca, Mahto-Topah and Bear Woman—all Lakota Sioux—edited the text and drawings and sat for portraits."[8]

That. Is. Not. The. Point.

Native Nations are not interchangeable. All the research in the world doesn't mean squat, if it isn't about the right people!

We know of course that the Plains warrior is *the* image of

"Indians" for most Americans. One can surmise that it seemed logical to Jeffers to buy into that ready-made romantic imagery, rather than to do the work necessary to accurately portray the culture of the man whose words she was using. But even granting Jeffers her "research," what are we to make of the California poppies that appear here? And the painting of the Trail of Tears? And the man and woman riding up through birch trees? (This one is amazingly reminiscent of the work of Bev Doolittle, a well-known painter of Native subjects.) And the approximately-Great-Lakes-style canoe floating on a lily pond?

Having heard about this book before seeing it, my sense of shock was great when confronted with the cover illustration—not of Seeathl, but of Two Moons, Cheyenne. (Some very small print opposite the title page says only that the jacket art is "based on a photograph by Edward Curtis.") A photograph of Seeathl does exist. In it, he seems to be small; he is undeniably old. He is seated, plainly dressed, turned in upon himself. One can see how that picture wouldn't have fit very well with these words:

> With a commanding presence and eyes that mirrored the great soul that lived within, the Chief rose to speak to the gathering in a resounding voice...

Throughout the book, in both text and illustrations, it seems to have been Jeffers' *intention* to portray Native people as gone:

> In a time so long ago that nearly all traces of it are lost in the prairie dust, an ancient people were a part of the land that we love and call America.

Well for one thing, Seeathl lived several hundred miles west of any prairie; for another, this is 1854 we're talking about, not 40,000 years ago. And for yet another, Seeathl's people are still living, right where they have always lived, although in greatly reduced territory. And they deal with clear-cutting of their forests, pollution of their waters, and battles for fishing rights, along with the struggles they share with all the rest of us for a bare decent life, the well-being of our children, and survival as Native Nations.

In many of the pictures, the people are translucent, ghostly presences. On the jacket we see the stripes of the boy's shirt through Two Moons' hands. On the endpapers, the Native man is spirit, but the animals are "real." The canoe floats not *in* the lily pond, but above it. In the water itself float two disembodied faces. A double-page spread is literally a bunch of ghost riders in the sky. (And it's hard to say what the bird painted on one shield is supposed to be, but it looks like a pigeon...)

The last picture in the book is extraordinarily disturbing. A ghostly, nuclear Native family looks on benevolently at the family—white, of course—that has replanted the denuded land with little trees. The Indian man's hand is raised in blessing. The woman holds a cradleboard—in which there is no baby.

For people who so loved—and still do—the land to which they belonged and fought so long and hard—and still do—to protect, this book is an insult. If Jeffers had given one thought to how *Brother Eagle, Sister Sky* would affect Native people, she must surely have dismissed it as unimportant. Could she possibly not have known that the government would not have been "buying" anything from Seeathl or his people? Does she know that, although Seeathl had a city named for him, Native people were not allowed within its boundaries? Had she cared to, Susan Jeffers could have done a book that was also beautiful within its heart, one that dealt more honestly with the realities of Native life and history, one that would have had some meaning for our children as well. We would have honored her for that. Of course, it probably wouldn't have made so much money...

I have heard, although I do not know of any personally, that some Native parents have given this book to their children, because at least the people in it are beautifully drawn, and as human beings. I find it tragic that we should have to reach after such cold comfort.
—*Doris Seale*

NOTES

1 Swann, Brian and Arnold Krupat, eds., *Recovering the Word: Essays on Native American Literature.* University of California, 1987.

2 Swann, *ibid.*, p. 506.

3 "The New Didacticism," *Hornbook*, January/February 1992, p. 5.

4 For the purposes of this review, we have chosen to use the first version of the speech, since there is some evidence that this is as close as anyone will ever get to what was really said.

5 *Publishers Weekly*, June 1, 1992, p. 22.

6 572,806, according to the publisher (phone conversation).

7 *School Library Journal*, September 1991, p. 228.

8 *School Library Journal*, November 1991, p. 88.

Johnston, Norma, *Feather in the Wind.* **Marshall Cavendish (2001). 192 pages; grades 5-7; Lenape**

A few years ago, a California landscaper driving back from a job found a battered skull in a roadway. At first, he told a reporter, he thought the skull was the remains of a Native American from the last century. It didn't seem like anything significant, he said, and he thought about taking it and putting it on his bookshelf. Instead, he turned it in to the sheriff, and when he found out whom the skull belonged to, he broke down and cried.

He was overwhelmed at the fact that what he had thought was an Indian skull actually belonged to a missing seven-year-old girl, the focus of a widespread search.

I thought about this story while reading *Feather in the Wind*, a bizarre and profoundly disturbing young adult novel about a white family, "not-quite-human" DNA, ghosts and Indian bones.

When fourteen-year-old Becca's grandmother dies, the family moves with grandfather to an old Dutch family homestead in New Jersey, in what was once traditional Lenape territory. There she discovers an 18th-Century ghost, a Lenape young man whose people were massacred while he was away on a vision quest. She also discovers that she, her mother, and her grandfather have the ability to communicate with this ghost because Pappy's DNA—enhanced by a nuclear occurrence years before—has affected his daughter and her daughter. Now, besides her usual teenage identity crisis, Becca has the additional burden of helping Little Hawk's spirit find peace.

There are two things that Little Hawk's spirit wants: to have his people's bones properly buried, and to have his own bones placed with those of his mother.

This story takes place in the year 2000. It seems odd that an Indian spirit would ask a white family to bury his bones and rebury those of his people. Johnston's rationale is that the family discovers that one of their "many-times-great-grandparents" was Lenape, and this "Ancestress" turns out to have been Little Hawk's mother.

Johnston creates a science fiction in which exposure to nuclear radiation can cause genetic mutations that can enable people to communicate with ghosts. But she sets it in a context of contemporary New Jersey and introduces very real issues, such as discovering and dealing with Indian remains. By making her only Indian character a ghost and referring to Indians in the past tense only, she infers that all the Lenape, and by extension, all the Indians in New Jersey, no longer exist.

Carla Meninger of the Lenni Lenape Historical Society said that, had Johnston bothered to call her, she would have suggested this: "If I had found bones and realized they were Lenape, I would have just quietly buried them without telling anybody. If a white family had found Lenape bones, I would have told them to give them to us for reburial. There are three state-recognized Lenape groups in New Jersey. The family in this book could have and should have contacted the group nearest to their home and turned the remains over for reburial."

It is inconsistent with Indian beliefs and ethics that a person would request that his mother's bones be disinterred so that his bones can be buried with hers. It is inconsistent with Indian beliefs and ethics that a person would allow anyone to touch his medicine bag, much less open it and take out the contents. And it is inconsistent with Indian beliefs and ethics that a person would, under any circumstances, *at all*, permit a white family to handle his people's bones, bring them into their house, carry bone chips around with them, submit them to DNA testing, and finally, to bury them in their back yard. Becca's family may be very nice, but this does not negate what happened to *Little Hawk's* family. It is totally inappropriate for a white family to make any kind of spiritual, moral, ethical or cultural judgments about what is required to bury Indian bones. And not only is it unethical and immoral to disinter bodies, it's also illegal.

Given the efforts that Native people have been making to retrieve the bones, pieces of bones, and sacred objects from museums and other collections, what Johnston has done here is particularly reprehensible.

I doubt that, had this story been about the bones of a white person, it would ever have been published. As it stands, white children will once again be reinforced in their belief in the "otherness" of Indian peoples, and Native children will once again be violated in their sense of self.
—*Beverly Slapin*

(Thank-you to Carla Meninger and Dovie Thomason.)

Jones, Guy W. (Hunkpapa Lakota), and Sally Moomaw, *Lessons from Turtle Island: Native Curriculum in Early Childhood Classrooms*. Redleaf Press (2002). 175 pages, b/w illustrations

There are many "multicultural" teacher resource books on the market, and many classroom activity books targeting Native Americans. Most are garbage. Written from an outsider perspective and purporting to teach "us" about "them," these books encourage non-Native kids to "play Indian" by making vests out of paper bags and headdresses out of feather dusters.

It should not be necessary to have to tell teachers why counting rabbits dressed as Indians is offensive. Or why an arts and crafts book that has children recreating sacred objects out of toilet paper rolls is insulting. Or why a book about an animated miniature Indian owned by a white child and housed in a cupboard is not a good thing. But teachers are buying these books, so it is necessary. In *Lessons from Turtle Island: Native Curriculum in Early Childhood Classrooms*, long-time educators Guy Jones and Sally Moomaw examine the problems, present clear alternatives, and encourage teachers to include appropriate materials and strategies in countering deeply held stereotypes about Native peoples.

Traditional teachings begin with stories; sometimes the story *is* the teaching. In *Lessons*, each chapter begins with heartfelt stories from Guy's and Sally's lives and experiences.

Following an introductory chapter that effectively examines the many issues and problems in early childhood classrooms in the portrayal of Native peoples, the authors focus on five cross-cultural themes—children, homes, families, community and environment. Within these themes, they discuss such issues as cultural similarities and differences, appropriate and inappropriate children's literature, and appropriate and inappropriate activities. For each recommended literature selection the authors suggest ways to extend the curriculum, including activities in the areas of dramatic play, art, music and cooking, as well as literacy, math, and social studies. Finally, there is an extended section that includes clear guidelines for teachers in selecting class guests, literature, materials and toys; a bibliography and discussion of recommended and not-recommended books and materials; and an excellent resource list.

I hope that after reading *Lessons from Turtle Island*, teachers will take careful inventory of what they have and use in the classroom, think of different things to do with their recycled feather dusters, paper bags and toilet paper rolls, and throw out the garbage that oppresses Indian children. Now there is no excuse.—*Beverly Slapin*

Katz, Welwyn Wilton, *False Face*. Margaret K. McElderry (1987). 196 pages; grades 6-up; Haudenosaunee (Iroquois)

This book is a mixed bag, and gives credence to the statement that a little knowledge is a dangerous thing. Award-winning author Katz' familiarity with both London, Ontario and the nearby Grand River Iroquois reserve is both obvious and accurate, but her knowledge of Iroquois people and culture is superficial, and riddled with inaccuracies and flights of fancy.

Laney McIntyre, a white girl, and Tom Walsh, a schoolmate of Mohawk and Caucasian parentage, are thrown together by their accidental mutual discovery of an ancient Iroquois False Face mask in a neighborhood bog.

Laney's divorced parents, both of whom have intense but divergent interests in archaeology, express keen interest in the mask from their different perspectives—one is a university professor of archaeology, and the other is an antique dealer. Tom feels the mask should be returned to the Iroquois whose ancestors created it. This sets up a number of issues involving archaeology and Native rights that, despite the book's 1987 publication, are still hot issues today. The repatriation of Indian grave goods and artifacts is a federal mandate in the U.S. today that museums nationwide are being forced to confront. Katz does a decent job exploring them here.

But when it comes to understanding Haudenosaunee culture, and even more impertinently, False Face masks, Katz creates a fantasy world full of evil spirits and imagined bigotry unrecognizable to this reviewer at least, and more than likely the residents of the Grand River Reserve in southern Ontario. Contemporary "creative license," the common justification given by authors when confronted with inaccuracies, is nothing more than an excuse for being too lazy to fully research their subjects beyond common stereotypes. Such "creativity" is both irresponsible and harmful, especially in a novel like this one, where actual places and contemporary people are involved.

The False Face Religion, an ancient tradition dating from the epochal battle between the Good and Evil Minds when they created the Earth, is still practiced today in Haudenosaunee communities throughout the U.S. and Canada. A key feature is the wearing of False Face masks. They are not evil, and they do not influence the wearer or "owner" of the mask to do evil. But that's exactly what Katz would have the reader believe. This entire book, although well written and exciting, takes this "ancient evil Indian spirit" theme as its central conflict. Katz creates an Iroquois "god" who is embodied by the mask. Its evil influence is felt by Laney and both of her parents, compelling them to believe in "evil ways" in their tug of war over its final disposition. Mom the antique dealer wants to sell it to a collector for big bucks, while dad the archaeology professor thinks it belongs at the university.

And then there's Tom Walsh, the hapless half-breed. Fourteen years old, he has spent his entire life until three months ago growing up among his father's Mohawk relatives, part and parcel of the Haudenosaunee society on the reserve. As soon as his father dies, his mother (who has also lived on the reserve with her husband and son) moves them off the Grand River reserve to the town of London, Ontario. Although he has lived with both of his parents his entire life until his father's death, Tom suddenly sees his mother as "a white woman," rather than as his mother. Even more astounding (people in this book are very mercurial when it comes to their interpersonal relationships!), Tom has instantly become an outcast among his own relatives at Grand River, immediately recast into the stock character of the half-breed who belongs in neither the white nor Indian worlds.

Although Indian kids of mixed blood raised away from their people can certainly experience identity problems, this is rarely the case with mixed-blood kids who have been raised their entire lives among their own people on their own reserve, as Tom was. Yet again, Katz has Tom, he of the cheekbones "sharp as axe heads," face outright hostility when he goes home to see his people.

Not only that, but the house that Tom's family have lived in on the reserve now has "two filthy older children" in the yard. The new siding is "splattered with mud," and the vegetable garden is a "mass of dying weeds." Why is this? Because Tom's white mother isn't there to keep it looking nice any longer? And because the Indian family living there for the last three months is running it into the ground? That is certainly the impression the reader gets.

When Tom goes to the longhouse to ask for help in handling this old mask (ownership is mutually if uneasily shared by Laney and Tom), he happens upon one of the Doorkeepers, a longhouse official. Now this is the same longhouse that Tom had been attending with his father his entire life, and where he learned the tenets of the longhouse religion. By Katz' own stereotypical descriptions, Tom has the looks of someone one would expect to have posed for the Indian nickel, with his cheekbones "sharp as axe heads." After 14 years as a longhouse participant, Tom's would be a familiar and accepted face in that locale. But no, the Doorkeeper dismisses Tom as "the white woman's son." (!) In three months, "[t]he Reserve was a foreign place, and he was a foreigner in it." (!!) Come on! Many Haudenosaunee are mixed-blood, and often "look" more white than Indian. But it hardly makes them less Indian or rejected by their own people. And just because people move off the reservation doesn't make them not Indian any more! Or severs them from all relationships with their relatives.

This is perhaps Katz' greatest insult in the book and it functions on several levels. It implies that to be a "real Indian," or acceptable to Indian people, you must (a) live on the reserve, and (b) be a full-blood. This certainly fits the picture of the "white man's Indian"—the image that springs to the minds of most non-Indians when they think of what an Indian is.

In a lengthy author's note, Katz explains how she came to write this novel, and states that she attempted to be accurate "with only a little leeway." Unfortunately, her "leeway" deeply flaws a book that could have been much better, given the research that she describes having done.

But she even misunderstands the information she did look at. For example, the Haudenosaunee were not driven south to what is now North Carolina as Katz states, and have never lived in North Carolina. She also states that "the Canadian government gave them several reservations." Reservations are not land "given" to Indians; they are lands retained by Native peoples after giving the bulk of their lands to the Canadian or U.S. government. Also, there was no "Canadian" government at the time the Grand River Reserve was created. Dealings were with the English king. Finally, although Katz talked with several museum officials and individuals in Ontario and consulted a couple of ethnographic studies on the Iroquois, she could have avoided a lot of these gaffes if she had talked with the Haudenosaunee themselves at Grand River. Not recommended.—*Lisa Mitten*

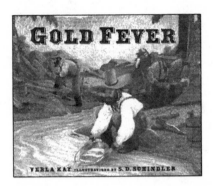

Kay, Verla, Putnam. Unpaginated, color illustrations; grades 1-2:
***Gold Fever*, illustrated by S.D. Schindler. (1999).**
***Iron Horses*, illustrated by Michael McCurdy. (1999).**

> What's a farmer to do when he sees hundreds of miners heading west to get rich? Join them! Jasper is off to California with dreams of gold that will fill his pans to overflowing. He has his shovel, his pick, and lots of energy—but finding gold isn't easy....Experience the hopes, dreams, and realities of the thousands of forty-niners who, like Jasper, decided to go west and seek their fortunes during California's Gold Rush. (from the jacket, *Gold Fever*)

In hindsight, let's make the Indians invisible. No, stick with me for a minute. You'd be surprised at how convenient this is when it comes to children's literature! For example, writing a children's book about the Gold Rush in California could be a harrowing, tricky task without invisible Indians. We'd have to talk about the starvation of thousands of Indians, the devastation by diseases such as tuberculosis and smallpox, syphilis, alcoholism, and unpleasant door-to-door assassinations of Indian servants working in Spanish or American households (the picture book illustrations alone would be full of skeletons of Indian children, exploding heads, blatant racial violence right there in living color...uh, dead color...); we'd have to sketch the laughter of white men's faces (and portray women honestly—waiting, patiently, on the home farm) as they massacred whole tribes or villages whose territory happened to "encroach" on possible gold fields; there's even the possibility that we might have to deal with the whole idea of "whose land" the gold was found on in the first place! Plus, the mere thought of Indians would lead to questions about the environmental impact of ripping up mountains, pouring dirt and cyanide and mercury into spawning streams, and other authentic but unnecessary historical details. Now all that would really detract from the story, don't you think?

> Welcome aboard! Travel back in time to the days when the transcontinental railroad was forged across our great nation. Two companies took the challenge of laying track where only wagons had gone before.... It was high drama all the way. Workers had to blast through rocky outcrops while hanging in baskets. Trestles had to be built over deep ravines. At night workers had to sleep in tents on top of railroad cars or in barracks buried in snow. But the promise of easy travel from coast to coast made the hard work worthwhile. (from the jacket, *Iron Horses*)

Best of all, the strategy of making Indians invisible works for books about the Great Transcontinental Railroad Race, too! With those Plains and Rocky Mountains tribes completely avoided, with the "minorities" represented instead by hard-working Irishmen and ridiculous-looking Chinese men willing to hang out in baskets next to explosive materials, we perpetuate the concept of Manifest Destiny quite well. The land must be illustrated as barren; not a sign of "previous" life—not a bird, not a buffalo, wolf, bear, fish—nothing but strong happy white men. Oh, okay—a few horses, a dog—those domesticated European animals fit the bill, as long as there's a white man riding the horse, and the dog is clearly happy in his domestication. We want to portray *civilized* here. We want *tame, controlled, conquered*. It's just too hard to do that with Indians in the way.

Trust me on this: just don't talk about Indians, and eventually, they all go away. (P.S.: on the off-chance that you have an Indian student in your classroom or visiting your library or bookstore who asks where all the Indians are in these books, just smile and say, "For heaven's sake! These are only *children's stories*, you know. Don't take things so seriously!")

Now, about that picture book series on World War II. First thing we do, we get rid of those inconvenient Jews...
—*Deborah A. Miranda*

Keeshig-Tobias, Lenore (Ojibwe), illustrated by Polly Keeshig-Tobias (Ojibwe), translated by Rose Nadjiwon (Ojibwe). Sister Vision. Unpaginated, b/w illustrations; preschool-grade 2; Ojibwe:
Bineshinnh Dibaajmowin/Bird Talk, 1991
Emma and the Trees/Emma minwaah mtigooh, 1996

Both of these books focus on mothers and daughters living in urban areas, and the ability of mothers to soothe those things that are strange and scary in their daughters' lives.

Bineshinnh Dibaajmowin/Bird Talk, which is based on an incident in the life of the author's daughter Polly, shows how hard things can be for Indian children when they are away from the support of their full families and are no longer surrounded by their Indian communities. When Polly comes home from school saying she doesn't "feel like an Indian" and doesn't "look like an Indian girl," her mom gently draws her out, letting her tell of the pain of her first encounter with racism. The solution is traditional and very modern—Momma and daughters talk about the loneliness of being away from the home reserve and relatives, about Christopher Columbus, about Anishinaabe language, and about the incident that caused such a deep sadness. "As for cowboys and Indians," Momma says she will talk to Polly's teacher, and then takes her children out for ice cream—a near universal, if temporary, antidote.

Emma and the Trees/Emma minwaah mtigooh demonstrates a traditional aboriginal way—without using violence—of "breaking" a young child's tantrum by calling her attention to the trees.

> "Look, Emma. Look," Mother said. "The trees are waving to you. The trees are saying *Don't cry Emma. Don't cry.*"

And now,

> [E]verywhere Emma goes she says *Hi trees. Hello trees. How are you? Isn't it a nice day?* All the trees wave back at Emma. And they say *Yes, Emma. It's a beautiful day.*

The deceptively simple black-and-white line drawings by the author's daughter beautifully convey all of the emotions in the stories—from the pain of a little girl's encounter with racism, to the frustration of a mother dealing with a crying toddler, to a child's realization that she and the trees really *do* know and recognize each other—and are perfect. Both stories are charming and the option of reading them in English or Ojibwe (or both) makes these books a special treasure for bilingual households or school settings. Maintaining our languages is an important aspect of assuring that future generations know about and appreciate our cultures.—*Pam Martell*

Keeshig-Tobias, Polly (Ojibwe), *The Illustrated History of the Chippewas of Nawash*, illustrated by the author. Chippewas of Nawash (1996). 90 pages, color illustrations; grades 6-up; Ojibwe

This is an engaging book packed with creatively presented facts. The story begins as two Indian teenagers arrive home from school complaining that history class is "sooo…b-o-r-i-n-g," and that they have to write an essay about a person or event in Canadian history. Their gramma encourages them to write about their history, a history that is not written in the history textbooks. The teenagers then learn their own history through oral tradition—their gramma's stories. As the stories progress, the teenagers, as well as the reader become intensely involved with the oral history of the Chippewas of Nawash.

The reader's attention is captured, not only by the relevance of the history to the teenagers, but also by the colorful illustrations and comic book format. Keeshig-Tobias' line drawings focus on the faces and emotions of the people and bring the stories and their struggles to life, and her writing makes history anything but b-o-r-i-n-g. She backs up all her facts in a comprehensive appendix filled with maps, references, a glossary of Ojibwe words, and a discussion of treaties.

The Illustrated History of the Chippewas of Nawash is a refreshing example of how dedicated, knowledgeable writers can make history interesting and engaging. Highly recommended.—*Barbara Potter*

King, Edna (Ojibwe) and Jordan Wheeler (Cree), *Adventure on Thunder Island*. James Lorimer (1991). 95 pages; grades 4-up; Ojibwe, Cree

Adventure on Thunder Island is a collection of four short stories for kids. The narrative complexity and reading level of the stories increases from the opening story, "The Troll" to the final story, "Pigeon Bridge." Jack Waboose meets a troll and trades a golden walnut for a Frisbee; Milton Whitehawk takes a walk in Ebony Forest and meets a ghost with unfinished business; Jessica rides a raft in a storm and is washed ashore on Thunder Island where she is taken care of by Thunderchild; and Troy accepts a dare from his new non-Indian friends to catch birds on Pigeon Bridge and gets trapped himself. In these contemporary stories, the supernatural is everywhere and the characters are believable; young readers will identify with the social struggles and adventures of the young characters. The authors skillfully include Ojibwe or Cree words in each story.

This book is Ryan- and Rachel-approved, and I highly recommend it as well.—*Barbara Potter*

King, Thomas (Cherokee), *Green Grass, Running Water*. Bantam (1994). 470 pages; high school-up; Blackfoot

> So. In the beginning, there was nothing. Just the water.

Water is everywhere in Tom King's *Green Grass, Running Water*. It puddles up around the tires of a red Pinto. It waits for First Woman to plunge from the Sky World. And for Changing Woman. And for Old Woman. It laps at the manmade shoreline of Parliament Lake behind the Grand Baleen Dam in Alberta; overflows the women's room toilet in the Dead Dog Café. Jolly waves tossing, it rocks a small boat full of men who beg to be rescued by one Young Man Walking on Water. It soaks through clothing, squishes inside shoes, soothes a world-weary Native Studies professor as she sinks down into a bath. . . .

But you get the picture.

Treaties that were supposed to last "as long as the grass grows and the water flows" may now be worth less than the paper they were written on, but that water is still flowing. And it makes its presence and its power known to King's cast of characters—and by extension, to anyone lucky enough or wise enough to enter their world. Or worlds. You see—

> Coyote was there, but Coyote was asleep. That Coyote was asleep and that Coyote was dreaming. When that Coyote dreams, anything can happen. I can tell you that.

And I can tell you this. All through this novel, things happen that nobody expects, including the first-time reader. But when the stories are all told, when the tributaries run together, when the confluence is joined at last, we look back and see with crystal clarity where the border crossings, the interwoven conversations, the tour bus and the John Wayne videos have been carrying us.

Carrying us: with windblown prairie grit in our nostrils, and in our ears the harsh click of a forbidden camera at the Sun Dance. The book is extraordinarily sensory—especially visual. If you find yourself casting the various story lines as if they were movies, you're not alone. According to the book jacket of King's latest novel, *Truth & Bright Water*, someone is making a film of *Green Grass, Running Water*. How, I can't imagine. But I'll be first in line at the multiplex, and if they give the role of Babo to anyone other than Whoopi Goldberg—well, it will still be a good story. Even if it's not the Truth. As King reminds us, there are not truths, only stories.

Green Grass, Running Water is often called a comic novel, but to do so both understates the case and misses the point. Yes, the reader may laugh out loud at the "punch line" of a situation King has been setting up for several chapters. And there's the ongoing dance of names and identities, and even some wild slapstick, comedy at its most basic and physical. But there are also moments of acute sorrow with roots deeper than prairie grass; moments of joy; of anger, and of horror. It is a mystery in the sense that life is mysterious: we mortals can only guess around the edges of its meaning. King's writing is thoroughly grounded—in traditions, yes, but also in subversions.... Well, that's another essay, or maybe a dissertation.

Green Grass, Running Water is a journey to take more than once. On its final page, King seems to invite us to begin it again. Those who take him up on the invitation will find still more humor, more heartache, more layers, more mystery, more Coyote dreams. And of course more water. There is water everywhere.

"That's true," I says. "And here's how it happened."

—Jean Paine Mendoza

King, Thomas (Cherokee), *Truth & Bright Water.* **Atlantic Monthly (1999). 266 pages; high school-up; Blackfoot**

Questions of what is "true" and "real" permeate Tom King's *Truth & Bright Water*, much the way water percolates through his previous novel. King's adolescent protagonist, Tecumseh, lives on the border of Canada and the U.S. His life and the lives of those around him also seem poised on boundaries

of their own. Here, certainty is as elusive as the trio of feral dogs (or are they?) known as "the Cousins," who appear and vanish seemingly at random. As elusive—and perhaps as dangerous.

"Telling the truth is always chancy," Tecumseh tells us. He's talking about the responses honesty gets from his mother. But everyone around him seems to live by that motto, too. His community is full of the half-explained, the partially understood, the incomplete transaction. And as for asking questions to get things clarified—no one tells him outright to stop, but just see how often he gets an answer! (Some of the most humorous moments in this book—and there are many—are the parallel conversations the boy has with his neighbors and family.) Meaning-making is no simple task around Truth and Bright Water.

Bright Water and Truth are separated by the Shield, a river with multiple personalities. Truth is a railroad town on the U.S. side, Bright Water a reserve town in Canada. They seem, from a distance, to be connected by a modern bridge big enough for cars to cross, but for reasons that were never explained to the residents, the construction crew pulled out when the job was nearly done. The almost-bridge remains, not exactly unusable. Kids occasionally try to cross it on foot, and it comes in handy for target practice.

In this split community, Tecumseh will learn to drive (more or less), get a job (such as it is), and meet a girl (sort of). Typical summer activities for a boy of sixteen in Canada or the U.S. But this is no typical summer. Tecumseh and his cousin Lum have seen a woman leap off a cliff into the river and disappear. Soldier, Tecumseh's dog, has found a small, gleaming human skull with a red ribbon laced through the eye sockets. His mother's sister, globe-trotting Auntie Cassie, has come to visit. Another near-legendary former resident has bought an old landmark overlooking the Shield but won't come in to town. And Native people from near and far (not to mention foreign tourists) are arriving for the annual Indian Days celebration, presided over by Lum's evil-tempered father, Franklin.

King's skill at creating relationships between his characters stands out in *Truth & Bright Water*. His depiction (through Tecumseh's eyes) of an unhappy family trip will resonate with any reader who has ever been trapped on vacation with folks unable or unwilling to stand one another's company. The boy's adolescent pout at being taken to Waterton Lake instead of a mall is dwarfed by the deep, nameless but inescapable discontent that divides his parents, the two people on whom his life depends.

King also peels back layers of the relationship between Tecumseh and Lum to reveal what it's like when your best friend embodies "a walk on the wild side." The brutality

Lum faces at home has given him the impetus to become the fastest runner around—and made him a little dangerous in his own right. Yet Tecumseh is his willing and nearly constant companion.

A lot goes on in this book, and I won't kid you, some of it hurts. King invites us to take a hard look at what it means to be separated by invisible boundaries from everything to which we need connection: family, community, history, myth, the land. Everything, perhaps, except imagination?

He is still playful, still ironic. Witness a harrowingly funny driving lesson, a herd of iron buffalo, foreign tourists "playing Indian." Keep track of the sub-subplot of the quilt Tecumseh's mother has spent years stitching. Meet his employer, an artist who discovers that scenes of Native life bleed through the old landscape paintings he'd been hired to restore. Then there's Lucy, a First Nations Marilyn Monroe fan who insists her idol must have been Native, and is on her own cheerful beauty-parlor quest for blondness.

Truth & Bright Water is different from Tom King's previous work in many ways. In *Green Grass, Running Water*, he troubles the boundaries between human "reality" and the bigger picture that is often called "myth." In *Truth & Bright Water* he stirs up the dark secrets humans keep, or try to keep, from others and from themselves.

The Truth/Bright Water community is a place where meanings are continually tested and contested, and truth is ultimately a matter of consensus. (Or is it?) Identity is fluid in a mutable container. Coincidence is actually confluence. When things are not as they seem, there is a world of possibility—for joy and hope, for mystery and for believing, for pain and struggle, for comfort and redemption. —*Jean Paine Mendoza*

Korman, Susan, *Horse Raid: An Arapaho Camp in the 1800s*, illustrated by Bill Farnsworth. Smithsonian Institution (1998). 31 pages, color illustrations; grades 4-6; Arapaho

What better way is there to promote the Smithsonian Institution's Museum of Natural History than for Smithsonian to publish a children's book about its own "Native Cultures of Americas" exhibit? *Horse Raid* does exactly this. Here, Kevin, a contemporary child of unstated Asian ancestry, discovers his bravery through a fantasy journey in the museum's display of traditional Arapaho life. As he and his friends marvel at the museum's "life-like figures," Kevin wonders "what life would be like for the Indians."

"The museum walls fade," and Kevin, now inexplicably called "Yellow Bear," is suddenly helping the Arapaho men unload buffalo meat and skins. He is invited to a horse raid and manages to steal an enemy chief's horse. This not only gains him respect for his bravery, but also initiation into the Kit Fox society. After learning all of the traditional songs and dances (in one day!), Kevin takes part in the Kit Fox ceremony, gifts his cousin Wolf Moccasin with the horse he has captured, and—finds himself "back in the museum."

While Kevin's fantasy adventure may give him the courage to join the soccer team, the story is absurd. Boys were not rewarded for jeopardizing the safety of the community and were certainly not initiated into an adult society. Inexperienced children would not only be a danger to themselves, but to the entire tribe. This would never be allowed.

The names used in this story are ridiculous and the illustrations are inaccurate. It is almost impossible to ignore not only Kevin's Asian features, but also the fact that he is called "Yellow Bear." What is the point of this? Are Asian people still being referred to as "yellow"? Kevin's fantasy of Indians in this story perpetuates the notion that Indians exist only in museums, and contemporary non-Native kids can gain courage by "becoming" Indian. Not recommended.—*Sachiko Reed*

Kotzwinkle, William, *The Return of Crazy Horse*, illustrated by Joe Servello. Frog, Ltd. (1971, 2001). 35 pages, color illustrations; grades 3-up; Lakota

In 1948, Korczak Ziolkowski, a sculptor, decided that it would be a good idea to carve a statue of Crazy Horse to go along with those presidents in the Black Hills of South Dakota. Since then, he—and now his family and associates—have been engaged in this endeavor. So this book is not about Crazy Horse; it is an ode to the blasting of Thunderhead Mountain to create the enormous Crazy Horse monument.

While the Indians were alive, "roaming on the plains below" Kotzwinkle tells us, the mountain "dreamed in the sun." Now that the Indians are dead, save a few, "the mountain slept on—for the time of a mountain is not the time of men." The mountain continues to lie dreaming in facelessness, waiting for someone to give it shape, to let Crazy Horse out of it. "One day," the mountain "felt a rumbling inside itself. Then the mountain learned it was not just a mountain, but a great Chief too." The rest of the book describes the sculptor's "relationship" with the mountain as he blasts away tons of the awesome granite: "It's not easy to be friends with a mountain."

Considering the disasters with which this project has been plagued, that is probably an understatement. (Ziolkowski himself once went over a cliff on his 'dozer—and lived to tell the tale.) "Friendship" is not a relationship with a mountain. The relationship that the Lakota people have with this mountain, and all of the Black Hills, is one of deep abiding respect, and great sorrow. In the past, the Black Hills provided everything the people needed. Now, it is continuing to be destroyed by gold miners and tourists.

When—or if—the Crazy Horse Memorial is completed, it will dwarf that hideous tourist trap, Mount Rushmore. The author uses the support of Henry Standing Bear to indicate Native approval of the project, saying that he and Ziolkowski see Crazy Horse emerging from the "shapeless" mountain; that the sculptor's explosions will set him free. According to Kotzwinkle, this is what the mountain wants. This is what Indian people want because the site of the memorial has become a center of Native American activity. It's even what Crazy Horse wants because he wore a stone behind his ear, and told his people "I will return to you in stone."

It is true that Native people have been given work here. But Crazy Horse was held in great honor in his lifetime, and is to this day. He never accepted adulation; this "artwork" is the antithesis of what he stood for, and what he stands for now, not only to the Lakota, but for Native people all over this land. Neither those responsible for it, nor the author of this book, have understood the least thing about him. Both are profoundly disrespectful of the man and the place; a place that has been sacred for thousands of years.

In life, Crazy Horse never allowed his photograph to be taken or his image to be painted. It is impossible to imagine that he would have allowed a huge "likeness" of himself to be carved out of the Black Hills. There are verbal descriptions; none of them even remotely resemble what is "emerging" out of Thunderhead Mountain.

A mountain is not "asleep" until someone—a human—comes, "to give it shape." It is not faceless and shapeless to begin with. A mountain is itself. And the Black Hills were never given up. By the Fort Laramie treaty, they belong to the Lakota people forever. The struggle over the Black Hills continues today. To this day, the Lakota have refused payment offered by the U.S. government for the stolen land. *The Return of Crazy Horse*, with the artist's imaginative images of the Lakota leader on the cover and inside, is probably selling very well at the Native American Education and Cultural Center at the Crazy Horse Memorial. Too bad; it's one more crass rip-off of the Lakota people and the land.—*Robette Dias*

Krantz, Hazel, *Walks in Beauty*. Northland (1997). 182 pages; grades 7-9 Diné (Navajo)

According to the author bio,

> Hazel Krantz is a former elementary school teacher and the author of a dozen books for

young adults. The several weeks Hazel spent on the Navajo Reservation, attending several traditional and community functions, became research for *Walks in Beauty*.

One of the many problems with books like this is that a visit of a few weeks—or even a few years—is not enough for an outsider to understand the complexity of a way of living, a way of thinking, and an entire cosmology very different from her own. As is to be expected, by superimposing her own assumptions, worldview, and experiences onto her Diné characters, Krantz does an injustice to Diné children and perpetuates more of the same old stereotypes of Indian peoples.

The dialogue is wrong. The ceremonies are wrong. The relationships are wrong. The values are dead wrong. Errors are found on every page, but I will limit myself to a few of the worst:

- People do not pray to "chase away heavy thoughts" and certainly do not pray in both Diné *and* English.

- People do not avoid marrying within a clan to "prevent inbreeding."

- It is highly unlikely for a grandfather to name his granddaughter "Walks in Beauty," words from a prayer. If, in fact, that did happen, it would not be because she was physically beautiful, "slim and graceful." Besides, slimness is not considered an attribute of beauty in Dinétah.

- A teacher, even a white teacher, would probably know better than to ask a student to "share one of the chants you have learned."

- It is unheard of for Diné young women to talk about the coming-of-age ceremony, kinaaldá, as a bore or unpleasantness to be put up with, as in "that dumb old kinaaldá":

  > "It's the pits," wailed Lola. "I have to do all that stupid running and lying down and listening to those dumb chants. It's from the dark ages."

- Diné young people do not speak casually about *chindis*, ghosts.

- When a young person is sent on a vision quest, he goes to communicate with the spirits, to find out what they have given him to do in life. This is a spiritually, physically and emotionally demanding time. Needless to say, it is not a time to send psychic messages to his girlfriend:

  > His stomach was empty but he did not feel hunger....he felt a lightness, like the down of thistles, floating in the thermal winds. Anita felt all that. She went deep into his thoughts. He was

finding Navajo and further inside that Navajo he found a man. All men. Not just Navajo. Mankind. He required Anna to respond. She, too, searched within and found Navajo and then went further and found a woman, any woman, all women. Womankind.

• Traditional elders do not obsess about their weight.

• And one more time. Weavers do not leave an "imperfection" in their rugs to "allow for the escape of their souls." It is a reminder that only Creator makes perfect things.

All of this is too bad, because Krantz writes reasonably well, and she understands the ways that teenagers behave and speak and relate to each other. Just not Diné teenagers.

Educator Evelyn Lamenti (Diné) commented to me about this book:

> No matter how long they stay, there is no way that someone can pick up everything embedded into our language, our way of being with the seasons, our environment, all of which dictates a belief system that has been passed on from generation to generation. It is highly unlikely that anyone visiting as an outsider can interpret a way of life of a culture that's entirely foreign to their own upbringing. It just makes me so angry that they feel like they can come to the reservation and talk with a few people and then write a book, thinking that they're doing research, thinking they can learn the belief system and cultural values. They have never lived it and they will just never know. This is just another book for her, but this is our lives.

—Beverly Slapin

(Thank-you to Evelyn Lamenti.)

Krudwig, Vickie Leigh, *Searching for Chipeta: The Story of a Ute and Her People*. Fulcrum (2004). 119 pages, b/w photographs; grades 7-up

Outside of Colorado, there's little known about Chipeta, the second wife of Ouray, a controversial 19th-Century Ute leader appointed "chief" by the U.S. government. In Colorado, one doesn't have to search too far to find Chipeta: there is Chipeta State Park, Chipeta Sun Lodge and Spa, Chipeta Golf Course, Chipeta Elementary School, and even Chipeta potatoes.

But *Searching for Chipeta* is not about a search; it's merely an example of why it's probably not a good idea for cultural outsiders to write historical fiction about peoples whose lives they don't understand.

Krudwig's writing is full of clichés ("her heart ached for justice and at the same time she felt a stab of guilt…"), bad travel brochure writing ("The sun was beginning to rise in the east, shrouding the earth and sky in a golden hue"), out-of-place idioms ("unlit lodge," "brother-in-law," "stepmother"), descriptions that scream "otherness" ("brave," "maiden," "brown skin," "dark eyes," "almond-shaped eyes"), lots of speculation about her subject's actions, thoughts and motivations ("Chipeta's hands trembled with excitement," "'Ayee' cried Chipeta"), portrayal of her subject as both hyper-spiritual ("Chipeta gave thanks to Creator," "Now, the fifteen-year-old prayed to Creator," "the thought of wandering spirits frightened her") and hyper-emotional ("her heart beat frantically," "her heart pounded wildly," "her heart overflowed with joy," "her heart beat like a drum"), and middle-class 21st Century sensibilities ("She would not allow anything else to ruin her day.")

The author describes mundane, everyday occurrences with mind-numbing detail ("Chipeta stopped for a moment to remove a tiny pebble from her moccasin…She slowly unlaced the leather ties of her moccasin and slid it off her foot."), while brushing off more important things ("Not only had she taken over Ouray's household, she was now his wife, and…").

This reviewer will spare the reader the agony of a line-by-line critique. Here are a few more problems.

• The author pretends expertise while getting practically everything wrong:

> When food was scarce, they had learned to harvest the seeds, berries, roots, and insects that Creator had made. When shelters were lacking, Utes used trees and their branches to make wickiups to keep them out of the elements. Like Magpie, the people were able to adapt.

If seeds, berries, and roots were available, then the animals that eat them would be around, too. Besides, berries ripen in the spring or summer, not the winter, and there would most probably be a winter store of dried meat. So food was rarely scarce. If materials to build wikiups were available, then shelters would not be lacking. People built them. That's what you do when you need a place to live.

• The author pretends sympathy for Chipeta while being dismissive of her culture:

> Women had always been considered inferior and when it came to important tribal matters, they did not sit at councils with the men. Their place was at home.

Women had all kinds of important and key roles to play within the culture. While Chipeta may have been the only woman to attend treaty negotiations, to surmise that women were "considered inferior" is a huge leap over the credibility gap.

• And while pretending sympathy for the Utes, she validates the settlers' and government's land grab:

> Greedy prospectors screamed for justice. They did not think it was fair for the Utes to have the mineral-laden lands to themselves.

Here, Krudwig changes the discourse from living on the homeland that contains the bones of a people's beloved dead, to simple possession, to "having it to themselves."

Finally, something that has always bothered me about this kind of writing: While some people have epicanthic folds—folds of skin over the upper eyelids that partially cover the inner corners of the eyes—no one in the history of human creation has ever had "almond-shaped" eyes.

Unfortunately, *Searching for Chipeta* will probably be adopted by the Colorado schools. If this title were not dreadfully written, it would merely be dreadfully boring. As the great philosopher Joel Monture once said about another book (and I paraphrase), "The best thing about it is that it ended."—*Beverly Slapin*

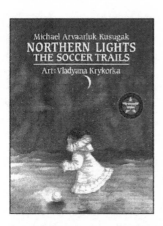

Kusugak, Michael Arvaarluk (Inuit), *Northern Lights: The Soccer Trails,* **illustrated by Vladyana Krykorka. Annick (1993). Unpaginated, color illustrations; kindergarten-grade 3; Inuit**

Kataujaq really loved her mother. In the spring they went fishing together; in summer they went for walks. They did everything together. But that was a long time ago.

> One day, a big sickness came. So many people were sick. Kataujaq's mother coughed and coughed and they sent her away, way down south in an aeroplane.

And she never came back.

Kataujaq is "almost a big girl now," but she has never stopped missing her mother, and sometimes she cries. *The Soccer Trails* is the story her grandmother tells her, to help her understand where her mother is now, and, perhaps, to feel the pain less keenly. This book is an honor to Inuit belief; it would also be a beautiful way to help a child who has suffered a similar loss:

> Sometime when the moon is out and the stars are twinkling brightly in the frosty air, you should go outside and take a look. Maybe you will see the northern lights way up in the sky. They really are the souls of people who have died and, like us, they like to go out and have a good time. They love to play soccer. And if you look closely, maybe you will see someone special whom you thought had gone away forever. That special person has not really gone away at all. It is the most wonderful thing.

—*Doris Seale*

Lacapa, Kathleen (Mohawk) and Michael Lacapa (Apache/Hopi/Tewa), *Less Than Half, More Than Whole,* **illustrated by Michael Lacapa. Storytellers Publishing (1994, 2001). Unpaginated, color illustrations; grades 4-up**

A huge issue for Native people is that of "blood quantum." Apart from New Age wannabes whose "great-grandmothers were Cherokee princesses," there are many for whom the question of who's a "real" Indian is a serious one; whether as mixed-blood—the polite term—or "half-breed"—not so nice. Because we are colonized people, with all that that implies, the mixing has run the gamut from rape to happy and successful marriages.

In their book, the Lacapas have dealt with a child's questions about who he is in the nicest possible way. Tony, Scott, and Will are skipping stones down by the water. When the boys see the perfect stone and grab for it, they also see their reflections in the water; Scott with his yellow hair, Will with his dark skin and hair, and Tony somewhere in between. Will says to Tony, "You're not like me. I'm all Indian. I think you're only half or less than half." At this point, Tony's mom calls him, but he takes a side trip to his Grandma Doris's house, wondering, "[L]ess than half. What does that mean, less than half?" Her answer is that he is special, like the butterfly. At home, he asks his brother and sister, who tell him he is part Indian and part Anglo, and not to worry about it. It is not until dinner that evening at Grandma and Grandpa's house on the reservation, that he gets an answer that has meaning for him.

Too full of food, he goes to lie down in Grandpa's room. Looking in the mirror, he asks himself, "Why am I less than half?" Grandpa, who has followed him in says, "I like what I see....You are not like anyone else." Tony sees the pictures around the mirror, of people of all sizes, shapes and colors. Grandpa shows him corn with many colors: "This corn is like you," he says, "It is one of great beauty because of its many colors. And just as the corn with its many colors is a gift to the people, so you are a gift from the Creator....You are a whole beautiful person." When Tony looks into the mirror again, he sees someone who, "like the corn, was more than whole."

This is an honest, wonderful book, graced with Michael Lacapa's usual beautiful illustrations. The setting of a warm, loving family may not be every child's situation, but it carries a word for all such children to remember: no matter who your parents are, you are "a whole beautiful person."—*Doris Seale*

Lacapa, Michael (Apache/Hopi/Tewa), illustrated by the author:
The Flute Player. **Northland (1990). 42 pages, color illustrations; kindergarten-grade 3; Apache**
Antelope Woman. **Storytellers Publishing (1992, 2003). 42 pages, color illustrations; grades 4-up; Apache**

A long time ago, a boy and girl met at a hoop dance and became "very, very interested in one another." The boy was a flute player.

> She told him, "Maybe someday I will hear you play your flute when I go to the canyon...When I hear you play your flute, I will place a leaf in the river that runs through the canyon. When you see the leaf float past you, you will know that I like your song."

Tragedy strikes, but don't be too sad, because

> Today, we go to the canyon, down to the cornfields and the river. We sit and listen to the echoes of the canyon and watch leaves fall into the river. Some say, "Listen to that beautiful sound. It sounds like the wind, blowing through the trees." But we smile, and know that the girl still likes the flute player.

In the valley among her people lived a beautiful young woman who was strong and knew how to do many things. Many young men came by, but none interested her, until the day one came who was not like the others. He talked to the people, and helped them, and said always, "Remember to respect all things great and small." And each night he left the village. Following him one evening, the young woman learned that his story was stranger and more beautiful than she could have imagined. They married, but in the end, because of the intolerance of her people, the young woman joined her husband in his world, forever.

> Since then, we have learned to honor all things great and small. So today, my son, we honor the antelope by never hunting or killing them. For out there among the antelope are Antelope Woman and her children and they are a part of us. Now as we hunt, my son, we must be thankful to the creator, who gives us all things great and small and who teaches us to honor them all.

These are exceptional books, with truly beautiful illustrations. They also show the value of stories being told by people who know what they are doing. In Lacapa's words, "This is our spirit in print."—*Doris Seale*

Larrabee, Lisa, *Grandmother Five Baskets*, illustrated by Lori Sawyer (Creek). Harbinger House (1993). 60 pages, b/w illustrations; grades 4-up; Muscogee (Creek)

Making a traditional basket is not easy; it's not meant to be easy. When our elders teach us how to make a basket, they teach us what materials to gather and in what season, what to offer in return for what we take, what songs might be sung or words might be said, how to prepare the materials, and finally, how to weave. But especially when they work with young people, what they are teaching is respect, caring, perseverance, commitment and generosity.

Sarah McGhee was the name of the elder known as "Grandmother Five Baskets" because she took on the responsibility of teaching the girls of the Poarch Creek community of Hog Fork, Alabama, the "lessons of the five baskets."

Now, Anna's twelve-year-old daughter is ready, and her mother remembers all that Grandmother Five Baskets had taught her more than twenty years before: As a child she had tested herself. She had completed five pine needle baskets, each holding a different lesson. When her enthusiasm faded, she had found the strength to win against the boredom. She learned that not all are able to finish what they start, and she learned that "the lows follow the highs...as surely as day follows night." And she learned that time itself is a valuable teacher.

Sawyer's softly shaded pencil illustrations convey both the gentleness and the lessons of the story. The people are very real, comfortable and comforting; the woods and stream look like woods and stream; and the baskets are drawn with the kind of detail that comes more from familiarity than from museums.—*Judy Dow*

Lasky, Kathryn, *Cloud Eyes*, illustrated by Barry Moser. Harcourt Brace (1994). Unpaginated, b/w illustrations; grades 2-4

I don't know how Kathryn Lasky got hooked up with James Crumley, author of the pulp mystery "Milo Dragovitch" series. In his book, *Dancing Bear*, according to the jacket copy, "Detective Milo Dragovitch spends too much time boozing until he gets caught up in a case involving two-bit criminals and an old lady on the run."[1] Somehow, she (Lasky, not the old lady) became enthralled with Crumley's prologue, a cockamamie "Indian legend" he made up about a "young man of peace, Chil-a-ma-cho, He Who Dreams Awake" (Milo Dragovitch in a previous life?). Through a series of supernatural occurrences and rituals, he (Chil-a-ma-cho, not Crumley or Milo) convinces a bunch of bears to share their honey so as to allow the Indians to "bring sweetness to the teepees."

Bear with me (pun intended). I'm trying to imagine the author's (Lasky's, not Crumley's) thoughts here: "Indians. Dances with Wolves. Dances with Bears. Indians. Multi-culturalism. Indians. Ooooh."

A young Indian dreamer is called "Cloud Eyes" because

> He could hear spirits and listen to the language of the animals. He could read the meaning in both the clouds of the sky and the clouds of the smoke that rose from the sacred pipes.

His wish is "for a way to bring the sweetness back to the lodges." The bears, you see, are greedy, ripping up the "bee trees" and stealing all the honey. So Cloud Eyes takes out his "sacred pipe" and begins "to read the shapes in the smoke." Does. "Great-grandmother Bee" appears, teaches Cloud Eyes the bear dance. He kills a bear, eats some, cures the bear skin and goes off to dance with the bears. Does. Bears, exhausted from all the dancing,

fall asleep, whereupon the people sing songs of thanks and make "the sacred smoke that calmed the bees." Bees get calm. People get honey. Bears wake up. Cloud Eyes dances some more. Bears behave themselves.

> The dance seemed familiar to the bears, as if they had danced it in a faraway time and place, as if it were a dance from a dream. And then the bears became as calm and gentle as the bees.

In honor of Cloud Eyes, the people give up honey during the first moon of each summer. Sort of like Lent.

> These were called the days of the bear dance, before the first harvest of the honey, when the air was filled with sacred smoke and the songs of thanks stirred in the wind.

Lasky's references to juniper, chokecherries and camas roots sets this story somewhere in the Great Plains. But there's a lot of, let's say, cultural dissonance here.

If the "sacred pipe" Cloud Eyes is using is a Calf Pipe, who gave him permission to do so? Only specific people under specific circumstances use Calf Pipes. They are not the possessions of individuals. How is Cloud Eyes able to get enough smoke out of the pipe to read? Calf Pipes are used to pray with, the smoke of their contents is not "read."

> The smoke gathered into clouds, the dying trees seemed to melt away, and the forest turned to sky.

Sounds like there's more than kinnikinnick in that pipe.

Who is "Great-grandmother Bee" and why is she teaching a human how to steal honey from her own creatures? Why doesn't Cloud Eyes give "Great-grandmother Bee" a gift in thanks for all her teachings? A Native young man would know, but apparently Lasky doesn't, that reciprocity is absolutely required for a transition of knowledge. And why is no gift left for the bees? I've been told it's really hard to kill a bear with a knife, even if the bear's asleep. And why on Earth would Cloud Eyes soften the bearskin by rubbing it with the bear's intestines? Brain tanning is the traditional process, and that smells pretty bad, but intestines? *That* smell might wipe out all the bees, not to mention everyone else in the area.

This book is *so* not recommended...—*Beverly Slapin*

NOTE

1 Random House, 1983.

Lawson, Robert, *They Were Strong and Good*, illustrations by the author. Viking (1940, 1994). Unpaginated, b/w illustrations, grades 2-3

Originally published in 1940 and republished in 1994, *They Were Strong and Good* is described by the author as being "the story of my mother and my father and of their fathers and mothers."

> When my mother was a little girl there were Indians in Minnesota—tame ones. My mother did not like them. They would stalk into the kitchen without knocking and sit on the floor. Then they would rub their stomachs and point to their mouths to show that they were hungry. They would not leave until my mother's mother gave them something to eat.

Look very closely to find what was changed in the 1994 edition:

> When my mother was a little girl there were Indians in Minnesota. My mother did not like them. They would stalk into the kitchen without knocking and sit on the floor. Then they would rub their stomachs and point to their mouths to show that they were hungry. They would not leave until my mother's mother gave them something to eat.

This illustration is of a Black woman—a bandanna-wearing "mammy"—brandishing a broom at two Indians who are running away with stolen food.

In another section, the 1940 text reads:

> When my father was very young he had two dogs and a colored boy. The dogs were named Sextus Hostilius and Numa Pompilius. The colored boy was just my father's age. He was a slave, but they didn't call him that. They just called him Dick. He and my father and the two hound dogs used to hunt all day long.

And the 1994 text reads:

> When my father was very young he had a Negro slave and two dogs. The dogs were named Sextus Hostilius and Numa Pompilius. The Negro boy was just my father's age and his name was Dick. He and my father and the two hound dogs used to hunt all day long.

This illustration is of a Black youngster dressed in rags, carrying two dead animals, walking behind his young white master. Several other illustrations also show Black people dressed in rags, in various positions of servitude.

They Were Strong and Good received the Caldecott Award in 1941, which even for that time period is a little surprising, given its stereotypical and derogatory depiction of both Native and African-American people. The 1994 edition is not improved by its minor textual changes. It was a horrid little book then with its sense of white entitlement and superiority and it's a horrid little book now. In order for some children to be proud of their cultures, *must* other children be made ashamed of theirs? —*Beverly Slapin*

Littlechild, George (Cree), *This Land is My Land*, illustrated by the author. Children's Book Press (1993). 32 pages, color illustrations; all grades; Cree

George Littlechild is a Canadian Cree artist, whom the publishers mis-describe as "a member of the Plains Cree Nation." Actually, he was born at Hobbema Reserve (Alberta), and it's possible his mother lost her citizenship through George's father, considered a white man (despite some Mi'kmaq ancestry), under Canada's Indian Act. Prior to repeal of this portion in 1986, an Indian woman who married a white man lost citizenship and had to leave the Reserve, with all children (who also lost their citizenships), though Indian men who married white women did not.

Littlechild tells half of an ancestral story (his mother's side) with a frontispiece of small photo portraits of Cree ancestors, that go back to great-greats. The rest is told in exciting, expressive paintings and collages, with short narratives about their personal meanings to him on facing pages. A picture of his green-eyed mixed-blood brother is entitled "Urban Pain Dance." He explains how "both of our parents died violent deaths on skid row," and a life "like being in prison" in the city is "why I put bars in the background of this picture."

Cities can be liberating if you come to a new one as an artist and find friends and inspiration. In "The Indian Artist Visits New York, New York," a tiny photo of Littlechild not dressed up Indian is backed by huge colorful skyscrapers painted with a child's innocent eye and brush-strokes. A knocked-for-a-loop pink horse, Littlechild's alter ego, (who shows up elsewhere in several paintings) stretches his neck along the street, looking up and exclaiming a thick-brushed "WOW" at the scene. "I loved the tall buildings, the crowds of people, the huge stores, the fancy restaurants. And the art! It was amazing." Here, Littlechild discovered the freedom to paint expressively, not to follow the rules for what and how Indian painters "should" paint.

He paints pain—but also pride, joy, laughter. "Are buffalo fuschia-pink and gold? Of course not, but...it's good medicine to laugh," he says of one very striking image of a buffalo-masked dancer.

With his family, in its history and personally, Littlechild has danced the pain dance imposed on Indian people. But "In Indian Country we are closing the circle by healing ourselves. We are very hopeful and the future looks promising."

Pictures and narrative are an antidote to stereotypes of "Indians," galloping the plains or sitting wisely around campfires, showing us with broad strokes and bright colors that there is Indian life in most every major city today. A pain dance still for all too many, but a spiritual circle too, broadening to encompass more in a dance of beauty.—*Paula Giese*

Littlesugar, Amy, *A Portrait of Spotted Deer's Grandfather,* **illustrated by Marlowe deChristopher. Albert Whitman (1997). Unpaginated, color illustrations; grades 3-5; Ojibwe**

A Portrait of Spotted Deer's Grandfather is Littlesugar's fictional homage to George Catlin and the other white artists who roamed Indian Country in the 1800s to capture on canvas the visions of a vanishing race. Imagining Catlin's 1836 visit to an Ojibwe community in Minnesota, Littlesugar has a boy, "Spotted Deer," trying to get his grandfather, "Moose Horn," to sit for Catlin:

> "Grandfather," he said, "you are so handsome. On the Medicine Painter's canvas cloth you would live forever!" But Moose Horn was not so sure. "Why should an old man give away his face?" he asked. "If I give my face to the Medicine Painter, he may take my spirit. If I lose my spirit, I will not be able to find my way to the village of the western sky one day."

But after a prophetic dream and a prayer, Moose Horn is convinced that the so-called "Medicine Painter" "stands in the way of [the] wind—[he is] a man who might keep us from blowing away forever." So he goes off to sit for Catlin.

> [W]hen the people looked at the picture of Moose Horn, they could see that it was just as he was— with the wisdom of dreams and the courage to face the western sky....And on that canvas cloth, Moose Horn would live forever.

The idea that being the subject of a painting can confer individual or tribal "immortality" is not a Native concept and never has been. A number of things motivated people to sit for portraits, including curiosity—and payment.

When we look at old European portraits, there is no implication that the subjects were incapable of keeping their own histories alive. But Littlesugar's book has Indians recognizing Catlin as the white savior, the preserver of traditional Indian knowledge and culture, whose paintings "might keep (them) from blowing away forever."

By the early 19th Century, Indian people were embellishing their lives with beauty every chance they got. Even patching of canoes was done artfully, in patterns. Painted drums and parfleches, carvings and wood implements, quillwork and beadwork, pottery and basketry were traded up and down the continent. People appreciated different styles of art, but they certainly weren't worshipful of or awestruck by Catlin's slightly different technology— and they certainly didn't see this non-Indian technology as superior to their own.

Most troubling is Littlesugar's depiction of Indians as superstitious and fearful, this stealing of spirit stuff, as if they never looked in the water and saw their own reflections. Moose Horn's fear that his spirit will be stolen and never "reach the western sky" changes when he acknowledges "the wisdom of his dreams" and finds "the courage to face the western sky." Littlesugar's text could not make the people sound more stupid, simple or superstitious.

Littlesugar's less-than-cursory research has her referring to the Great Spirit as "Manito," which she apparently thinks is his name; having Moose Horn talking about his dream to a large crowd and going into the woods to pray, rather than praying where he happened to be; using stilted language with pseudo-poetic speech patterns no self-respecting Indian this side of a grade-B western would use; and choosing "Indian" names that are not Ojibwe. And, moose don't have horns, they have antlers.

DeChristopher's oil paintings are dark and depressing, without light or saturation. In twenty paintings, many of them double-page spreads, not one Indian is smiling. While the Ojibwe patterns on people's outfits are some-what detailed, the faces remain, for the most part, muted or blurred. This is somewhat odd, given that the subject is portraiture. And. Moose Horn's "purple war belt" looks like a wampum belt, which is from a different Nation entirely. Jingle dresses are a fairly recent phenomenon, very late 19th or early 20th Century; and deChristopher really doesn't know how to paint woodlands, birch trees, wigwams, or horses.

This is a profoundly offensive book, whose subtext is a sense of white entitlement and superiority.

—*Lois Beardslee* and *Beverly Slapin*

Lossiah, Lynn King (Cherokee), *The Secrets and Mysteries of the Cherokee Little People, Yuñwi Tsunsdi',* **illustrated by the author. Cherokee Publications (1998). 151 pages, b/w illustrations; grades 4-up; Cherokee**

I've dreamed about the Yuñwi Tsunsdi'—the Cherokee Little People—for as long as I can remember. These men and women are full of magic and mysticism, mischief and compassion. They are helpful to the Cherokees, and have always had a special place in my heart.

As a child, I was told stories about how they cast spells on strangers who disturb them and how they sometimes steal the playthings of children, then bring them back. How they love to dance and sing and "make music." How their little footprints are found in the cornfields where they have helped elders harvest corn. My granddaddy told me that the Yuñwi Tsunsdi' understand the importance of harmony in the world and teach us about this harmony.

This book is written and illustrated by Lynn King Lossiah with the cover and title page art by her equally talented husband, Ernie. The Lossiahs, who live on Quallah Boundary, take the reader on a journey into the mystical world of the Cherokee Little People. In her introduction, Lynn says that she has gathered this material both from personal reports and from accounts given to James Mooney, a noted anthropologist who lived for several years among the Cherokee in the late 1800s.

In the chapter, "Who Are the Little People?" Lynn tells of the clans of the Yuñwi Tsunsdi'. The people of the Rock Cave Clan, who have made themselves invisible "because of the constant invasion of their privacy," live in caves on the sides of mountains and bring the Cherokee people medicine plants. The people of the Tree Clan, whose companions are snakes, live in the huge trunks of old trees whose large roots "act as private entrances." Those who are of the Laurel Clan help to nourish the plants; their job has become more difficult as "man keeps adding to nature's destruction." These little ones teach us not to take our needs too seriously and to share with others, always. Those of the Dogwood Clan are very delicate in physical strength and emotions; they look only for "the good and beauty in everyone in all things."

The chapter "Cherokee Women and the Yuñwi Tsunsdi'" tells how these little beings sometimes watch over Cherokee babies:

> A new mother walked softly into her baby's bedroom to watch her sleep...But she stopped, stared, when she saw a little woman no more than two feet tall peering into the crib. She was slender, with long black hair that fell over her shoulders. She wore a simple white dress that seemed to glow. The woman stepped away when the mother saw her, and a moment later she had vanished.

Of course, there are many who doubt that these magical, mystical people actually exist. But as they stand on their reasoning and look for proof, those of us who do believe are sitting back and continuing to enjoy the wisdom and gifts of the Yuñwi Tsunsdi'.—*MariJo Moore*

Lunge-Larsen, Lise, and Preus, Margie, *The Legend of the Lady Slipper,* **illustrated by Andrea Arroyo. Houghton Mifflin, 1999. Unpaginated, color illustrations; grades 1-3; Ojibwe**

A version of this traditional story is used as part of the Red Cliff Wellness Curriculum in Red Cliff, Wisconsin. It tells of a time long ago during a bitter winter when so many people became ill that the medicine ran out, and many died. It tells of a runner who volunteered to go to the next village to seek medicine, but he, too, became ill; and his wife went in his place, leaving the village without telling anyone. Her thoughts about her sick husband and her suffering people gave her the strength to push through the snow and cold. The next morning the people heard a voice calling from the woods, and found her lying in the snow. Her feet were swollen and bleeding from the frostbite, but there were medicines in her bundles. They carried her back to the village and wrapped her feet in warm skins. The winter passed and many of the sick recovered. The people honored the young woman for her devotion to her husband and the village. She lived a long and full life, and when she died the first lady slipper flowers grew where she was buried. "Now when you see this beautiful flower in the spring," this version ends, "remember the kindness and devotion of this young woman."

There is a similar version told by Ojibwe elder and scholar Basil Johnston, and it appears that the authors have leaned heavily on it. But the liberties that Lunge-Larsen and Preus take in retelling this beautiful story make hash of it. Their story is overly dramatic, there is way too much extraneous detail and somewhere along the way, they lose the message. The woman has become a little girl and her husband has become her older brother, who is "as strong as a bear, as fast as a rabbit, and smart as a fox," and because of this he is chosen to be the messenger for the village. At the end of this book, the little girl is given a name that means "'Little Flower,' because although she was as strong as a bear, fast as a rabbit, and smart as a fox, she was also as lovely and rare as a wild spring flower."

In our creation stories, animal people—because they are the first people—sometimes have the attributes of the humans who follow them into this world. In our teaching stories, we don't describe humans as having the attributes of animals. Only outsiders retelling our stories do this.

In Basil Johnston's telling, the young woman, "oblivious to the cold, almost indifferent to the snow crusts, and anxious only to get medicines for her husband and the people of her village,...ran swiftly over the drifts." That's it. Here's what Lunge-Larsen and Preus do:

> Trees lashed about in the wind, rattling their branches. Falling snow stung her face. "Mash-ka-wi-zin," it hissed. "Be strong." [Question: Why would the wind encourage her while stinging her face?] The girl bent her head and stalked like a bear into the storm. [Question: Don't bears around here hibernate in the winter?] The snow tugged at her, but she charged through it, plunging into the wind.

The ice encourages her too, telling her to go quickly. So she runs like a rabbit, "skittering and slipping" *on the same ice that encouraged her*. The drama continues on the way back.

> Suddenly, the snow collapsed around her and she was buried up to her arms. She kicked and punched at the snow. That was no use. She churned her little legs as fast as she could, as if to run out of the snow. That only dug her in deeper.... "Nib-waa-kaan!" the snow around her whispered, "Be wise!" Yes, she must be smart like a fox who *thinks* his way around the trap. [Question: Wouldn't a person who grew up with snow know how to move in the snow without getting stuck?]

This drama of the little-Indian-girl-bravely-fighting-the-elements goes on for eight pages, plus the illustrations, including some weird-looking northern lights that resemble seaweed. Besides the really ugly watercolor pictures "inspired by Ojibwe patterns and beadwork," there's also a liberal dose of Ojibwe words, presumably to make the story more authentic than the original (and to heighten the drama); guilt and worry (to heighten the drama), a confusion between "medicine bundle" and "bundle of medicines," and more.

I didn't want to go on. I wanted to yell, "Stop it! Stop it! I can't stand it!" But I bravely trudged through this book. I had to. My people needed me to do this.—*Barbara Potter*

Marcos, Subcomandante Insurgente, *Questions & Swords: Folktales of the Zapatista Revolution*, illustrated by Domitila Dominguez (Mazateca) and Antonio Ramirez, Essays by Simon Ortiz (Acoma) and Elena Poniatowska. Cinco Puntos (2001). 112 pages, color illustrations; grades 5-up; Maya

On the back of this book's striking cover appears a little tag: "The sequel to the infamous STORY OF COLORS." And that's what it is, plus more. "Infamous" because *The Story of Colors*, Marcos's previous book, encountered a blatant attempt at censorship—by the National Endowment for the Arts—before it was even published. The attempt failed, and the publicity guaranteed that book an extra print run.

Like that book, *Questions & Swords* is illustrated by "Domi" (Domitila Dominguez) who again gives us a stunning range of colors, moods, and imagination. The text is a more complex, even elusive creature than the first Marcos volume, with several voices to be heard and ambiguities to ponder.

"The Story of Questions," which is bilingual, brings us old Antonio again with all the same wisdom, charm and humor we have a right to expect from his role in the previous book. But this time his words to Marcos defy even "el Sup" in a conversation about who Zapata was. To answer that question, Old Antonio tells the story of two gods who were opposites but really one, and struggled to resolve their differences with many questions about how to walk together, which path to choose. He draws out a profound message:

> [Q]uestions are for walking, not just standing still and doing nothing...[W]hen true men and women want to walk, they ask questions. When they want to arrive, they take leave. And when they want to leave, they say hello. They are never still....[T]o know and to walk, you first have to ask.

When Marcos asks how this defines Zapata, old Antonio replies that Zapata speaks of two Zapatas who are really one and both were the same road for all true men and women to follow. A reader can be left wondering if perhaps this whole story is about leadership, the need for flexibility and openness. Or perhaps it is a lesson in dialectics? Or both? What matters is that we have been captivated by vision with deep indigenous roots.

The other major piece in the book, "The Story of the Sword, the Tree, the Stone & the Water," also stars Old Antonio. It is an "ethical metaphor," as author Elena Poniatowska says in her short essay following that story. When those four different sources of strength go into battle, water triumphs in the end. Similarly, as Marcos observes, the Mexican government's February 1995 offensive against the Zapatistas made a lot of noise but like the sword, ended up rusting in the water and growing old. The water follows its own path and never stops.

The book then offers a short piece by Acoma poet and essayist Simon Ortiz, "Haah-ah, mah-eemah/Yes, it's the very truth," in which he speaks about the effects on indigenous peoples in the United States when word spread of the 1994 Zapatista rebellion: "[T]he news from the South was good news!" All over the Western Hemisphere, he says, Native people have had to survive against 500 years of deadly foreign domination but they have maintained a sense of continual cultural identity that is the essence of Existence. The signal from Chiapas is clear and Simon Ortiz dares to dream, as he says, of what might happen: "What if Indians throughout the Amercas rose in united force to seek the return of their land, culture, and community? Think of it!"

Mexican author and journalist Elena Poniatowska closes the book with the eloquence that has made her work respected and loved for decades. "Can a book explode like a bomb?" she asks. "Can it change minds? Should a government feel threatened?" The answer could not be clearer.

The idea of books having such power sustains El Colectivo Callejero (The Street Collective), dedicated to expressing left political thought through art in Mexico, whose main founders are Antonio Ramirez and Domi. "Old Antonio," indeed, we might suspect. And perhaps it is no accident that Domi, whose work makes this new book so vivid, so strong, bears the same first name as Domitila Barrios de Chungara of Bolivia. A tin miner's wife representing the "housewives' committee," she electrified the UN Tribunal on Women in 1975 in Mexico with her cry of "Let me speak!" to the mostly middle-class women present. In *Questions & Swords*, Domi's art is also an unforgettable outcry.—*Elizabeth (Betita) Martinez*

Marcos, Subcomandante Insurgente, *The Story of Colors/ La Historia de los Colores*, **illustrated by Domitila Dominguez (Mazateca), translated by Ann Bar Din. Cinco Puntos (1999). Unpaginated, color illustrations; grades 5-up; Maya**

This enchanting bilingual book for children and adults with the imagination of children is a story in more than one way. As told by old man Antonio in the jungle to his friend Marcos, it's the story of how the world, born black and white with gray in between, took on a rainbow of color. For this, as Antonio relates, we can thank a bunch of cranky gods who got bored with the way things were so they went looking for other colors to brighten the world for the people. Red, green, blue, and on they go, finding new colors in ways both goofy and supremely logical. My favorite is how yellow was born: from a

laughing child. One of the gods stole his laughter, making it the seventh color—what else?!

Today we see the macaw bird with every color in its feathers, representing this bright new world. As Marcos tells us, it struts about "just in case men and women forget how many colors there are and how many ways of thinking, and that the world will be happy if all the colors and ways of thinking have their place." With that reminder of the wisdom so often found in indigenous cultures, the book says "FIN"—The End—in a swirl of pipe-smoke.

The illustrations by Domi (Domitila Dominguez), an indigenous artist born in Oaxaca, are as original and unpredictable as the tale itself. Both refuse to romanticize, westernize, or stereotype the culture and worldview of Chiapas' indigenous people. Anne Bar Din's English text is on the same wavelength; she is very adept in her resolution of translation-defying phrases and presents no problems other than an occasional Spanish-ism (better than anglicisms!).

Appropriately, Subcomandante Insurgente Marcos stays in the background while old man Antonio tells the story. But he is there in meaningful small ways: lighting his pipe, commenting on human idiosyncrasies, and dropping reminders that people often make love ("a nice way to become tired and then go to sleep"). The gods in this tale are often not godlike but instead bumbling and stumbling around. Refusing to be pompous, enjoying a light irony, the style of this wonderful story constantly reminds us of who the author is.

That identity gave birth to the story about the story. In November 1998 Cinco Puntos, a small publisher in El Paso, Texas, won a $7,500 National Endowment for the Arts grant after going through a yearlong approval process including several review committees. With these funds, Cinco Puntos planned to pay half the cost of printing *The Story of Colors*. But NEA Chair William Ivey abruptly cancelled the grant.

Ivey said he was "concerned about the final destination of the money"—meaning some might go to Zapatista rebels or Marcos himself (even though the grant proposal had stated no part of the grant would go to Marcos, who had formally waived his rights). Recent attempts by Congressional Republicans to eliminate the NEA were obviously in the front of Ivey's mind.

But Ivey's blatant censorship backfired. News articles about it appeared in major media and Borders put in an order for 1,000 copies of the book. Another grant came almost immediately from the Lannan Foundation, a public arts organization, and it was twice as big as the cancelled NEA grant. The book went back to press for another run.

Like the Zapatistas themselves, *The Story of Colors* has become a symbol of truth overcoming lies, courage overcoming cowardice, and passion overcoming prejudice. Ever since they rose up on New Year's Eve of 1994 in armed rebellion against 500 years of brutal colonization, naming themselves for the hero of Mexico's 1910 revolution, they have stood for all indigenous peoples. They have also stood for the universal dream of human liberation and true democracy. Subcomandante Insurgente Marcos, their main spokesperson, has been that most dangerous kind of leader: a soldier with the soul and voice of a poet.

The NEA, trying to disclaim political censorship as the motive for canceling that grant, said the book didn't fit into the "mainstream" of children's books. True enough—and grounds for celebration. Its originality, its voice coming from a culture so long ignored or despised, is its great strength. There may be parents concerned about the references to smoking or lovemaking. Without dismissing such concerns, let me just say: these cannot begin to equal the assault on young people by mass media images that equate smoking with sophistication, or love-making with sexual activity wherein somebody has to conquer somebody. Let parents talk with their children about these issues, if they wish, and never forget that this is a folktale—not MTV (thank the gods).

The Story of Colors is about the joy of seeing the world around us with new eyes. It is about the way that very ancient peoples can often see very far. It is about the holy power of harmony and balance among the many forms of life on our planet. It is a gift, this book: food for hungry spirits.

We the orphans of opportunity
have dared to pass through the door opened by the Zapatistas
and cross to the other side of the mirror
where everyone can be the same
because we are different,
where there can be more than one way of living
where rejection of the present system
exists together with the desire to build a new world
in which many worlds will fit.
—from the Zapatista movement

—Elizabeth (Betita) Martinez

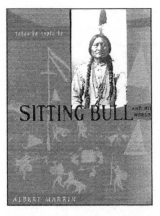

Marrin, Albert, *Sitting Bull and His World.* Dutton (2000). 246 pages, b/w photos, b/w illustrations; grades 5-8; Lakota

It is absolutely astonishing that anyone could, at the beginning of the 21st Century, write a book that incorporates nearly every stereotype and misrepresentation about Indian peoples ever uttered. Albert Marrin has.

His book contains six and a half pages of bibliography, only half a dozen titles of which are Native sources. The rest are the tried and true collection: archaeologists, anthropologists, and Indian experts. Marrin can hardly have claimed to have added anything new to the body of information already available on Plains societies in general, and Sitting Bull, Tatanka Iotanka, in particular. What he has done is create another apologia for westward expansion and the destruction of Native cultures and lives, as well as what was probably the richest land mass in historical times.

> In the winning and losing of the West, each side acted according to its own beliefs and customs. Few people deliberately set out to do wrong. By the standards of their own societies, most individuals acted decently and responsibly. In this, both Indians and whites showed their common humanity. I hope to bring home that truth by telling a uniquely *American* story through the life of a fascinating human being. For the first Americans, no less than the later arrivals to these shores, share a common land and a common history and, now, a common destiny.

> Indians and whites lived in separate worlds.... Having almost nothing in common, each used the standards of their own society to judge the other. This opened the way to misunderstandings and, finally, to countless tragedies.

There was no misunderstanding. To paraphrase Red Cloud, the white man kept only one of his promises to us. He said he would take our land, and he did. At the investigation after the Sand Creek massacre, Colonel John Chivington, when asked to account for what he had done, said, "Kill 'em all, large and small, nits make lice." And

General Phil Sheridan publicly remarked, "The only good Indian I ever saw was dead." By using terms such as "common humanity," "common land," "common history," "common destiny," "decent and responsible" and "misunderstandings" to link together Indian peoples and whites —by pretending to be objective—Marrin whitewashes the genocidal assault by whites on the Indian peoples of this hemisphere.

After misrepresenting Lakota spirituality and belief systems, Marrin engages in inappropriate and defamatory speculation about Sitting Bull's motivations and character:

> Native Americans believed that the Great Spirit —God—visited people in dreams. During such visits He might give them magical powers and show them the future. Others might say that Sitting Bull believed so strongly in his mission that he convinced himself that the Great Spirit had chosen him before his birth. Or, perhaps, he made the story up simply to show his devotion in a dramatic way. For whatever reason, he spent his entire life "studying" his people and serving them.

This statement shows no understanding at all of Native cosmologies, spiritual practices, or the responsibility such a leader would carry to his people, the land, and the Spirit World.

For 500 years, the people in the Americas have been regarded as heathens because we did not have a "religion." Marrin takes every opportunity to dwell, in loving detail, on themes of mindless and bloody savagery. Artfully, he couches these themes in a sort of pseudo-sympathetic language:

> Youngsters had to overcome their natural fear of dead people. To help them, warriors paraded between the lodges with enemy heads, ears, hands, and feet skewered on sharp sticks. Sometimes they dragged dead bodies through camp by ropes tied to their feet. Parents encouraged their sons to shoot the bodies with arrows and crush their skulls with rocks....We do not know how Slow reacted to his very first sight of a dead enemy. We do know, however, that when he was ten, warriors dared the boys to touch the bloody remains of a Crow warrior. Slow went first, winning praise as the bravest boy in camp that day.

In actual fact, from time to time a dead enemy might be brought into camp, particularly if he had been especially brave, and the young boys might be encouraged to count coup on the warrior. (Counting coup was done with a stick, specifically designed for this purpose, called a "coup stick." Among all the Plains cultures, it was considered a far braver act to count coup upon an enemy rather than kill him.) Had Marrin not decided to empha-

size (or invent) these gruesome details, that is all he would have had to say.

Further, Marrin states,

> Plains Indians also killed, scalped, and mutilated women and children for the sake of honor. That made sense to them. Since men fought desperately to defend their families, warriors believed that killing loved ones in front of their defender showed courage.

There was not, there has never been, any honor to be obtained by killing women and children. In a battle, they might die, but no warrior would deliberately claim the death of such ones and expect to be honored for it.

> By their early teens, boys would sneak away in groups of three or four to experience killing people for themselves.

What?! If any kids were sneaking off, it was to go hunting, not to find someone to kill. This, by the way, was *not* generally looked on with approval by their elders. Sometimes teenagers would sneak off and go on a horse raid by themselves, and the results were frequently disastrous to them.

Marrin's spin on Lakota life in general is always designed to portray it in the most negative way possible.

> Boys were destined to become providers, protectors, and warriors. Slow grew up knowing that one day he would have to kill, and go on killing until the day he died.

> White people did not bring war to the Great Plains. Long before they arrived, the Plains tribes themselves participated in what seemed an eternal cycle of violence....Later, even as they fought white invaders, they continued to expand their holdings by conquest.

One misconception still commonly held about Native Nations was that they all had one chief. In fact, there were a variety of leaders. There were war leaders, hunting leaders, and peace chiefs. People fought for various reasons. Peace was important to survival; to hunt, to make clothing, to raise children, to have ceremony, to plan for the future, all activities that were made difficult if not impossible by the invaders. Because it was an invasion, as truly as any of those that happened in the recently ended war-torn 20th Century. Marrin mentions none of these.

When Marrin does refer to a Native source, he deliberately distorts it.

> If Plains Indians hunted to live, they lived to fight. War was part of Slow's mind-set, his expectations of life, ingrained in him from infancy. The idea that people should prefer peace to war would have

struck him as strange. Peace, to him, was merely a time between wars.... Success in battle was the true measure of a man's worth; courage the supreme virtue. Victory in battle brought the greatest rewards. These were not material things, but the admiration of his people. Only the successful warrior, Slow knew, could advise others, speak in tribal councils, and become a chief. No woman would marry a man who had not proven himself in battle....

Of course, warriors died. That was natural, and the younger they died, the better....

Fathers repeated proverbs such as "The brave die young." "Son," they would say earnestly, "I never want to see you live to be an old man. Die young on the battlefield. That is the way a Lakota dies."

The footnote for this information cites Luther Standing Bear, from *Land of the Spotted Eagle*. What Standing Bear really said was this:

Then but a mere child, father inspired me by often saying: "Son, I never want to see you live to be an old man. Die young on the battlefield. That is the way a Lakota dies." The full intent of this advice was that I must never shirk my duty to my tribe no matter what price in sacrifice I paid....If I failed in duty, I simply failed to meet a test of manhood, and a man living in his tribe without respect was a living nonentity. My ancestors had been brave men. There was not an enemy they feared—not even did they fear death. So if I were not afraid to die I would then dare to do whatever came for me to do....

Contrary to much that has been written, warfare with the Lakota was not a tribal profession. They did not fight to gain territory nor to conquer another people....As a matter of fact, the philosophical ideal of the Lakota was harmony, and the most powerful symbol was that of peace. So powerful was this symbol that the wise men or chiefs had but to present it to the warriors and they obeyed its mandates, no matter how reluctant they might be.

One could almost say that this book was written with criminal intent. To cite every instance would be a review as long as the book itself. There is, however, one other issue that must be dealt with, and that is the "battle" of Wounded Knee, because it was such a watershed event for Native people; and was for all extents and purposes, the end, the place at which, finally, we were truly conquered.

Two weeks after Sitting Bull was murdered by government troops and Native police, the 7th Cavalry—Custer's old command—was called in. Big Foot's band of Minneconjou Ghost Dancers was coming in to surrender. The band consisted mostly of women, children and elderly men.

They had been disarmed. It was about 40 degrees below zero, the people were starving, and Big Foot was dying of pneumonia. There are conflicting reports of what happened next. But when the bluecoats opened fire, some 300 women, children and elders were killed. As far as anyone has been able to determine, the bluecoats who were killed that day died from what is now called "friendly fire." From reports of the time, it is clear that Custer's men were out for revenge, and they got it.

And yet Marrin has chosen to place the full blame for what he calls a battle on the victims themselves:

Meanwhile, the warriors were growing restless.... A medicine man called Yellow Bird made matters worse...[H]e walked around the seated warriors, blowing on an eagle-bone whistle. Occasionally he paused, threw a handful of dust into the air, and reminded the warriors of the power of their ghost shirts.

Yellow Bird immediately threw a handful of dust in the soldiers' direction. Then it happened. Warriors sprang to their feet, pulled rifles from under their blankets, and aimed at the soldiers.... Both sides fired at once....The warriors could not have been thinking clearly or aiming carefully. Every one of the bullets that missed a soldier slammed into the lodges behind them, striking women and children.

Warriors escaping from the council area followed close on the fugitives' heels. Now mixed up with women and children, they handled their Winchesters with deadly effect. In reply, the Hotchkiss guns poured a murderous fire into the ravine. The shells exploded on all without regard to age or sex. Troopers also rode along the rim, firing downward with carbines and six-guns. Since both warriors and women wore ghost shirts, they could not be told apart amid the smoke and confusion. Warriors also shot at the troopers from between the women and children. They were not deliberately using them as shields, but the soldiers fired at innocent people in order to get at the warriors.

Accounts of the massacre, both by people who survived it and those who arrived at the scene immediately afterwards, are available and totally refute Marrin's interpretation. His use of language hints at objectivity, but it doesn't change the truth of what happened. All the even-handed language in the world does not change the fact that Wounded Knee was a massacre:

Whites refer to the events at Wounded Knee as a battle. Native Americans have another name: the Wounded Knee Massacre. In some sense, both are right—and wrong. It was a battle because the Lakota killed and wounded one in eight white soldiers, a heavy loss even by the standards of twentieth-century warfare. Yet it was also a massacre, because the soldiers fired into a village and then into a ravine crowded with women and children.... Whether we call it a battle or a massacre,...

There are people still alive whose grandfathers fought Custer. There are people still alive whose parents survived Wounded Knee; they are called the Wounded Knee Survivors Association and they are located on the Pine Ridge Reservation in South Dakota. Marie Not-Help-Him was the president not very long ago; she may still be. They know what happened at Wounded Knee, because they hold the stories in their memories. As well, there is an association of descendants of Sitting Bull at Standing Rock Agency, North Dakota. There is no evidence that Marrin contacted any of these people. Nor did he use sources such as Charles Eastman's *Indian Heroes and Great Chieftains* or *Indian Boyhood*, Luther Standing Bear's *My Indian Boyhood* or *My People the Sioux*, or Zitkala-Sa's *American Indian Stories*. All three respected Indian authors were contemporaries of Sitting Bull's.

Readers ought not to consider this a historical biography of Sitting Bull. It is not. Rather, *Sitting Bull and His World* tells far more about its author than it does about its subject. *Sitting Bull and His World* has received a number of starred reviews and even awards. It doesn't deserve any of them. It is no better than any of the yellow journalism about Native peoples that came out of the 19th and early 20th Centuries. To consider this book worthy of an award is shameful.—*Doris Seale* and *Beverly Slapin*

Martin, Rafe, *The Rough-Face Girl*, illustrated by David Shannon. Putnam (1992). 30 pages, color illustrations; grades 3-6; Mi'kmaq

In this story, originally a Canadian Mi'kmaq storyteller's reworking, sometime in the mid-19th Century, of a French-Canadian Cinderella, a young girl is tortured by two elder sisters, to the indifference of the townsfolk and her widowed father (there are no step-sisters in this story). At the edge of town lives an Invisible Being, who will marry whatever girl can truly see him. All the girls, including the elder sisters, try, by guessing at what they can't see, but fail the tests put to them by the Invisible Being's sister—namely, to describe bits of his gear.

The victim-girl dresses herself in an improvised odd homemade costume imitating old-time clothing as best she can with birchbark, refuses to obey her sisters who try to stop her, and is not daunted by jeers and hoots of the villagers. She passes the test by seeing that the Invisible Being's bowstring is the rainbow and sled runners are the MilkyWay. She is cured of her horrible burns and marries the Invisible Being.

Though Martin does not cite his source, it is clearly Carles Leland's *Algonquian Legends of New England*; or *Myths and Folklore of the Micmac, Passamaquoddy, and Penobscot Tribes*, 1884, reprinted by Dover in 1992, and by several publishers in Canada and England. Contrary to the original title, all the Mi'kmaq materials were collected in Canada, not New England, by Rev. S.T. Rand, a Baptist missionary to the Mi'kmaq there. In a prefatory note, Martin says the story "in its original form is part of a longer and more complex traditional story." This is not correct. Martin misunderstood some of Leland's long, complex footnotes.

Martin gives his story a romantic interpretation, by filling in various blanks the 19th-Century storyteller deliberately left. He places the story long ago and far away, although the storyteller did not use the conventional Mi'kmaq story-starting formula ("N'karnayoo, Of Old Time") for this, and probably was referring ironically to the present situation of the Mi'kmaq people in some then-contemporary Indian Town of drunken, indifferent, dysfunctional idlers.

Martin cleans up the story, which in the original has the older sisters deliberately torturing the youngest, with intentional burnings—which all the villagers know about and don't prevent or interfere with. (In Martin's version, they just make her tend the fire; sparks snapping out from it do the burning.) Neither does the girl's father, who's put off with a transparent lie that she keeps falling into the fire. The girl's name—Oochigeashw— is given her by the indifferent, hostile townsfolk in mockery of her burns. The girl in the original story is small for her age, weak, and sickly. She is a family child abuse victim. No supernatural help—no rich Fairy Godmother supplying clothing and coach and horses to attract the Prince—only her own efforts can change the situation.

Martin—and especially illustrator Shannon—makes the girl's father a sympathetic nice impoverished old guy, and deletes the Mi'kmaq storyteller's implications that the burnt girl turned to him for help, in vain. The original storyteller has the older sister call her a "lying little pest" when she begs for some beads, strongly suggesting that she has tried to tell of her plight and been ignored.

In the original, the girl makes what the storyteller describes as a costume "of the old days" of birchbark. "Of the old days" just refers to the garments, not that birchbark ever was used for this purpose. Contrary to Martin, the bark is not said to be stripped from dead trees (which would be impossible). Even fresh-stripped bark will result in something like a tunic and leggins made of cardboard. The storyteller's mention of incising designs on it is probably a reference to the one-time practice of recording pictorial mnemonics for sacred songs and stories on birchbark scrolls, not to decorations. When, oddly costumed and starting on her way, she is jeered at by the townsfolk, the original storyteller stresses her resolution, but unlike Martin, does not say she has faith in herself, instead "it may be some spirit inspired her." Unlike the Cinderella story, there is no question of impressing or charming the Invisible One. The necessity is to pass his guardian-sister's test by proving the girl can really see him. Since everyone has always failed this test, there is no reason for the victimized girl to believe she will do any better at it.

Martin and Shannon impose a certain interpretation, as the girl is on her way to the Invisible Being's lodge at the end of the village:

> [S]he alone, of all in the village, saw in [the beauties of nature] the sweet yet awesome face of the Invisible Being.

This is shown: a double-page spread, with the Invisible Being's face created from birds, tree branches, clouds, edges of mountains. For this book, he is all the powers of Nature personified. To the acculturated, despairing villagers, he is invisible; not to the girl.

Martin minimizes the girl's awe, reverence—and fear—when she actually sees the rainbow and stars that are part of the Invisible Being's gear. Martin neglects to mention that these are *symbols of death*. The "spirit road of stars" is the Milky Way, a road traveled by the spirits of the dead, and is perhaps best translated as the Ghost Road. The guardian sister makes medicine to remove the girl's burn scars; Martin has her merely wash them away in the lake.

Martin gives the story a much more romantic ending than does the original storyteller, having made the Invisible Being remark on how beautiful the girl is, saying he'd seen so from the start, i.e., her inner beauty. Actually (in the original), the Invisible One is never really very enthusiastic. When he finds the girl in the wife's seat, "So, we're found out!" he tells his sister. "Yes...and so they were wed." That's it.

Since the Invisible One's supernatural symbols (rainbow and Ghost Road) are symbols of death, the original story doesn't really look that much like Cinderella snagging the Prince and living happily ever after. The victimized little girl may be escaping her miserable life into death. The happily-ever-after convention is enforced artistically on the last page of *Rough-Face Girl*, with the Invisible Being now shown as a conventional warrior, paddling the girl off into the sunset.

Shannon's pictures—several of them two-page spreads—are very fine. One bears a major share of the romantic

interpretation of this story: that the burnt girl (unlike the dysfunctional townsfolk) sees the beauty and power of nature (which constitutes the Invisible Being). Others characterize the haughtiness of the two elder sisters and the madness of the birchbark attire the little girl makes for herself.

The puzzling features that give the original story its eerie power: unmotivated family malice, general village hostility to the girl, the mystery of the Invisible One—all suggest a storyteller who created a parable about the old ways of life (250 years in the past for the Mi'kmaq people at the 1870 time of this telling) in conflict with the form of life in a dysfunctional Indian Town, a despairing remnant of centuries of subjugation. But Martin and Shannon insistently force the romantic interpretation, closer to the European Cinderella than this more powerful, disquieting tale.

It is inexcusable for Martin to identify this as "an Algonquin Indian Cinderella." Though the teller's name is not given, the source clearly specifies that the tribe is Mi'kmaq. Algonquin is not a tribe; it is an ethnographer's mistake, an Iroquois pejorative meaning "bark eaters."

—*Paula Giese*

Max, Jill, ed., *Spider Spins a Story: Fourteen Legends from Native America.* **Northland (1997). 65 pages, color illustrations; grades 4-up**

"Jill Max" is a pseudonym for Ronia K. Davidson and Kelly Bennett. Their book is "the result of their interest in exploring the recurrence of the spider as a unifying thread in the literature of diverse Native American cultures," and it *looks* really good. All the illustrations have been done by well-known Indian artists, and some of them are lovely. In the Preface and the "Story Sources," all kinds of people are thanked for telling stories, and for giving permission for use of the stories and the changes the authors have made to them.

In fact, this thing is a mess. "Jill Max" may be listed as

editor; Davidson and Bennett are not editors, they are authors. They have retold the stories with their own additions, omissions and rephrasings, and the texts are anglicized out of all rhythm and sound of true Native storytelling.

Each tale has a little introduction. These are most notable for the number of things "Jill Max" gets wrong. Here are some:

- "How the Tewas Found Their True Home" "illustrates Grandmother Spider in her customary role as the 'Earth Goddess'." Grandmother Spider is not an earth goddess.

- "The Osages are a Sioux tribe...Osage legends are simple teaching stories," and they "have no alphabet and have always relied on the power of storytelling." Just for the record: the Osage belong to what the anthropologists refer to as the "Siouan linguistic family." Which is not a tribe. Given that north of Mexico and prior to 1492, we were all people from an oral tradition, *none* of us had an "alphabet." We all have one now, though.

- The Muscogee were "a sedentary people"—in front of their computers, one presumes—and "the Navajos call themselves Dineh." No they don't; they *are* Diné. They got called Navajo by some other people.

- "Achomawi mythology has no religious significance." That is absolute rot. There is not a People on the face of this Earth that has no spiritual beliefs. Well, maybe there are, but you will find them in cities and government offices, not among the Native peoples of the world.

A small sample of "Jill Max's" writing style might be appropriate here:

> The Achomawi Indians who lived along the river were worried, too. It had been raining so hard for so long that the Achomawi men couldn't hunt or catch fish. The Achomawi women couldn't dry hides or cook. And the Achomawi children couldn't gather roots or berries. "Shaman, we must do something to stop the rain," the Achomawis said to the medicine man. The Shaman put on his finest blue-jay feathers and picked up his turtle-shell rattle. Chanting loudly, his seed-pod and shell anklets jingling, the Shaman danced his finest stop-the-rain dance.

Native stories don't go like this; the one who tells and those who listen already know who they are. "Shaman" is a term from the Tungusic peoples of Siberia, and not a word in any Indian language.

- In their notes for "How the Half-Boys Came to Be," the authors say it is "part of the Kiowa sacred cycle. Some Kiowa believe it's sacrilegious for the sacred cycle stories to be published, printed, or talked about by non-Kiowa." However. "The sections appearing here...have been previously published, and permission has been granted for their use." Ladies. Just because someone else has the sense of entitlement, lack of respect, and just plain bad manners to do it, doesn't make it right.

- For "Wihio Meets One of the Little People," there is a lesson in the Cheyenne language. This is "both a white man's story and a spider story. Though many believe wihio means 'spider,' it actually means 'sod dweller' or 'earth lodge dweller' which is what the Cheyennes called white men. The word for spider is not wihio, but *vihio*." Say, what?

- The "Lakotas" are not "part of the Sioux family," they are Lakota. Stories about dreamcatchers are not "shared by almost every Native American tribe." Dreamcatchers are Ojibwe in origin, and most of the stories about them have been made up by non-Native people.

"Jill Max's" Preface begins:

> Sadly, Native Americans have been denied knowledge of their distinct tribal histories and cultures....It is only recently that many people of American Indian ancestry have had the opportunity and freedom to reconnect with their roots. To this end, we have added details about clothing, dwellings, landscapes, and hunting-and-gathering practices to the legends in this book, so the reader may experience the stories more fully.

The implication is clear. We are no longer "real" Indians, but only people of American Indian *ancestry*, without knowledge of our own traditions; because "different storytellers tell varying versions of the same legend" anyway, so how the stories are set down becomes mostly a matter of opinion. (I'm not sure how "Jill Max" squares this with all the "authentication" listed.) Well, we lost some things, but not everything. It is presumptuous of "Jill Max" to assume that we need two white women to teach it back to us. And it is interesting to note that none of the artists here is listed as Hopi, or Diné, etc., but as of Diné "descent," Cherokee "descent"—every one of them: descended.

About the "permissions" to tell the stories and to change them: Some of the people cited in this regard are known to us. In no case did they tell these women stories, give them permission to use them—or to change them. Pick it out of the Preface and the Editor's note: Traveling "extensively, collecting Native American crafts and studying various cultures"—at the Central Library in Tulsa and the Gilcrease Museum, from Alice Marriot's *American Indian Mythology, Kiowa Voices, Vol II: Myths, Legends and Folktales*—*this* is where they got their stories. What they did with them is their responsibility and theirs alone.

(It's not at all surprising to note that "A few of the story-tellers we worked with wished to remain anonymous.")

Spider is greatly respected by Native people, both as an animal, for its wisdom and artistry (look at a dream-catcher and you will know where the idea came from), and also as a sacred being. But there is a great distance, and no "unity," between Grandmother Spider, a spirit being of power and mystery, and Iktomi. Iktomi is a trickster figure, more akin to Coyote and the African spider figure, Anansi, and I don't think I would call Iktomi stories "legends." He can appear as both spider and man; "Jill Max" says, "As a man, he is handsome and beautiful and always wants to do good things." No he isn't, he just *thinks* he is, and who he wants to do good things *for* is mostly himself. If he does accomplish any-thing good, it's pretty much by accident.

Spider does not spin these stories; that is the work of Ronia K. Davidson and Kelly Bennett—without much regard for the good names of the Native people the authors say helped them do it, or for the artists who illustrated their work. One can only assume that they and the publishers just took it for granted that no Indians would read the book, and nobody else would know the difference. Produce a pretty book, get well reviewed (it did), make a lot of money. That's all that matters.
—*Doris Seale*

Mayo, Gretchen Will, illustrated by the author. Walker:
Big Trouble for Tricky Rabbit! **(1994). 38 pages, color illustrations; preschool-grade 2**
Here Comes Tricky Rabbit! **(1994). 38 pages, color illustra-tions; preschool-grade 2**
Meet Tricky Coyote! **(1993). 32 pages, color illustrations; preschool-grade 2**
That Tricky Coyote! **(1993). 32 pages, color illustrations; preschool-grade 2**
Earthmaker's Tales: North American Indian Stories About Earth Happenings **(1989). 96 pages, b/w illustrations; grades 3-up**
More Earthmaker's Tales: North American Indian Stories About Earth Happenings **(1989). 48 pages, b/w illustrations; grades 3-up**
Star Tales: North American Indian Stories About the Stars **(1987). 96 pages, b/w illustrations; grades 3-up**
More Star Tales: North American Indian Stories About the Stars **(1987). 42 pages, b/w illustrations; grades 3-up**

Mayo, an elementary teacher and children's book illus-trator-writer, has combined and homogenized a number of Native trickster myths from different tribes for two trickster animal figures, Rabbit and Coyote. The stories are written in the kind of simplified language with child-appealing sound effects children's circle library readers might use, but Native storytellers do not. Some of the tales are credited to a particular teller (often the Native informant of an anthropologist recording the tales), some are made into a mishmash from several tribes. Although the Coyote tales are not quite so homogenized as the Rabbit tales, each story here is a filtering down of a teller's anthro-collected version.

The illustrations are small cartoon-style pastels that don't show any Native perception. The animals are not de-picted as wearing clothing, but they are anthropomor-phized as the tales require.

The anthropologist's note at the end of both Coyote books says that the author

> has taken care to tailor her selections to a young audience and has wisely limited the panoramic perspective that got Coyote into so much trouble over the generations.

Translation: She has dumbed-down and sanitized all complexity, ambiguity, and cultural content out of these tales. I do not think this is a good idea for children's or any other literature. For Native stories, it entirely distorts them, a process generally begun by the anthros who "collected" them. The prose is condescending, crude and babyish, with wooden prose and lots of onomatopoetics and exclamations of the type that an untalented writer inflicts on young children.

This style is not typically true of Native storytellers, who do not cater to limited word counts, short sentences and other such devices, but build children's vocabularies and stretch their minds with complexities and ambiguities. these books embody the complexities, integrations with living cultures and environments, and multiple levels of meanings that give them their appeal to all ages, not just young children. Too, Mayo's combination of unrelated legends from widely different tribes and times into one continuous story guarantees that everything that authen-ticates their tribal meanings is gone. Cultural distortions aside, this is the type of book occasionally given me as a child by some distant relative I really hated.

Mayo has done a better job retelling the nature stories (*Earthmaker's Tales/More Earthmaker's Tales*) and the sky stories (*Star Tales/More Star Tales*) than she did with the trickster stories. There are fewer stories homogenized from several different—quite different—tribal sources, and the literary style is less dumbed-down. However, these stories (in general, legendary explanations of various natural phenomena) are retold from 19th- and early 20th-Century anthropological or folkloric collections; and, com-pared to living stories still told, culturally alive, by actual Native storytellers, don't have much life. And Mayo's black-and-white wash illustrations are unattractive, often poorly reproduced, and un-Indian in style and concept.

The maps are identical in *Earthmaker's Tales* and *More Earthmaker's Tales*, and only in a general way indicate locations of the tribes from whom the stories were taken. Mayo defines geographical locations such as Cascade Range, Mississippi River, Pike's Peak in the glossary, but does not indicate them on her map. It is truly bewildering that the glossary defines such terms as "coal—a black mineral which burns and is used for fuel" (not by Natives, it wasn't), fog, rainbow, blizzard, sleet, mosquito, swan, tornado, warrior, wolf. On the other hand, no pronunciation guides are given for Native names or words used in the stories.

Most of the stories in *Star Tales/More Star Tales* relate to various constellations, usually not identical with constellations named in Western culture. It would have been better if the books had contained star maps marking off the various Native constellations, but this would require knowledge Mayo apparently doesn't possess. The maps in both books are the same and don't reflect the tribal locations of where the stories come from. The bibliographic notes do not contain complete citations by means of which earlier versions could be located. In comparison to some nighttime star tales I've heard told outside, with the glittering skies as backdrop, Mayo's versions are poor, thin stuff. This seems the likely result of mining anthropological lore by a non-Indian writer who doesn't have much literary talent.

Several of these star stories can be directly compared to versions in print, generally by small Indian-owned publishers. For example, the Iroquois tale of how the Pleiades came into existence is told by Mohawk elder and storyteller Tehanatorens/Ray Fadden at much greater length, with great literary flourish and detail, and beautiful authentic illustrations by his artist son, Kahionhes/ John Fadden. For several others where comparisons are possible, the Native version is in every sense preferable, not just for "authenticity," but for quality—better stories, better told, better illustrated.—*Paula Giese*

Mayse, Arthur, *Handliner's Island*, illustrated by Nola Johnston. Harbour (1990). 152 pages, b/w illustrations; grades 4-up; Kwakwaka'wakw (Kwakiutl)

Historically, handlining was a basic type of peripheral fishing requiring only a boat, a set of oars and minimal fishing gear. In the 1940s, mainly older men, children and First Nations families engaged in handlining as an easy entry into the cash economy.

Handliner's Island is the story of three young people—two non-Native, one Native—trying to contribute to the perilous finances of their grandparents by earning money fishing. How they learn from each other and how they each contribute to the success of the season is the basis of the story. Poaching and gender rivalry come in to round out the plot, somewhat.

While Mayse is clearly intimately familiar with the nuts and bolts of commercial fishery in British Columbia in the 1940s, the story is labored, clunky and totally predictable with semi-developed characters and a highly contrived plot. More troubling, Mayse's writing reflects the racial attitudes of most non-Native people of that time. While this might be acceptable in dialogue (if it is done well), it is not acceptable in the narrative.

For instance, the author constantly and consistently describes Mayus, the Native youngster, in negative and stereotypical ways. Mayus is "dark and brooding" with "raggedy-clipped black hair," his face is often "carefully blank," he gets spooked at a burial ground, he eyes people "darkly," he's an "insatiable eater" who finishes the last of a stash of meat with "unthinking greediness." And he says "In'yan" a lot, and inexplicably refers to English as "white-man's talk."

Mayse also uses Mayus' character as the vehicle for cultural snippets, which the author throws in as asides, discounting story, ritual and ceremony:

> Mayus was far removed in spirit from the frolicsome raccoon which his Kwakiutl name, bestowed at a long-ago potlach gathering of the bands, signified.

Further, the author contrasts cultural value systems around fishing by creating conflict between the Native and non-Native characters in a way that demeans Native lifeways:

> "Where's those salmon trimmings?" [Mayus] demanded.
>
> "I burned 'em," Paddy answered. Then, puzzled, "Why? What's wrong?"
>
> "Well," Mayus said, eyeing him darkly, "you sure fixed us proper. We should have put the head an' the backbone an' all back in the sea, so's the rest of the salmon would know we respected them, and treat us right."
>
> "That's another of your Indian things, huh?" Paddy was unimpressed.
>
> "Yeah," said Mayus, biting off his words. "It's an Iny'an thing. Pretty important thing, too."
>
> Mayus turned abruptly from the fire. He plodded off toward the shack, hands jammed in pockets and head down.

Only a little worried, Paddy watched him go. Okay, so he'd broken one of Mayus's cockeyed Kwakiutl rules! But could anything like that hurt their fishing chances?

The author also interprets Indian ethics in a condescending and racist manner:

> Mayus loosed a jubilant war-whoop.[!] He shook the minnows off his rake and scrabbled them into his bait tin.
>
> "We're in business!" he shouted across the water to Paddy. "Want some?"
>
> With a sudden warmth, Paddy knew that the offer was instinctive—part of the Kwakiutl philosophy that refused to hoard and that took open-handed generosity for granted in a friend.
>
> "Thanks," Paddy called back. "But I'd better learn how myself."

Through Paddy, the author interprets Mayus' generosity as "instinct." And, if he knew anything about Indian manners, he'd know that it is rude to refuse a gift.

And finally, Mayse even treats the salmon disrespectfully. When the salmon begin their run, the author calls them "wild and hungry pirates" and "suicide-bent" and "rampaging coho" "swarming thick as thieves."

Although there is a lot here that is accurate about the nature of handlining and commercial fishing, this story promotes negative attitudes about Native lives and ethics. Not recommended.—*Marlene R. Atleo/ʔeh ʔeh naa tuu kwiss*

MacGill-Callahan, Sheila, *And Still the Turtle Watched*, illustrated by Barry Moser. Dial (1991). Unpaginated, color illustrations; grades 1-3; Lenape

Another of the legion of environmental stories for children with an Indian slant. This one has the rather novel approach of being based on an actual carving at the New York Botanical Garden. The author creates a history for this turtle figure by pretending it was carved by a Lenni Lenape (Delaware) to be the Creator's eyes. The centuries pass—as, once again, so do the Indians (a recurrent theme in this genre)—and the turtle puzzles over the changes in the land as forests are chopped down and the overgrowth where he now resides becomes a hangout for teenagers with boom boxes and spray paint. Finally, he is "rescued" by an archaeologist and placed in the Botanical Garden. A rather depressing story, whose point is never really made clear.

The art is depressing, too—and flat-out wrong. Lenni Lenape never dressed in Grecian-style robes, they did not use Calf Pipes, and children did not run around with

eagle feathers in their hair.

And the dialogue is tacky:

> Here at our summer lodge...I will carve the turtle. He will be the eyes of Manitou the All-Father to watch the Delaware people and he will be our voice to speak to Manitou. In summer you will bring your children to the rock to greet the turtle and they will bring their children. And Manitou will bless our land with plenty, our people with straight bodies and strong arms, and peace shall reign beside our fires.

Not recommended.—*Lisa Mitten*

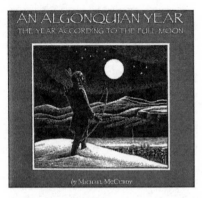

McCurdy, Michael, *An Algonquian Year: The Year According to the Full Moon*, illustrated by the author. Houghton Mifflin (2000). Unpaginated, b/w scratchboard illustrations; grades 3-up

First of all, let's look at the obvious: There are thirteen full moons—not twelve—in a year. Next, from the first line in the introduction: "Native Americans have long had the custom of assigning descriptive names to each month's full moon." Assigning names is not a "custom"—it is language, it is culture. And third—still from the introduction:

> But regardless of the name of the particular month in which a tribe carried out its daily chores, its labor remained basically the same— a struggle to survive in an often hostile land.

Why is this almost always the way outsiders describe our ways of life in the old days? We never regarded our lands as "hostile"—we loved our lands and lived in a good way. We worked and we also had fun. Just like people do today. Why is this so hard to understand? Add this perspective to other sweeping generalizations about "Algonquian" peoples, add highly inaccurate artwork, and you have *An Algonquian Year*.

JANUARY—"HARD TIMES MOON"

January is a harsh month for the winter-bound northern Algonquian people...These animals must be hunted down and killed for their meat and fur while the Algonquians are housed in their secluded winter quarters.

The people are housed in their secluded winter quarters because it's too difficult to hunt in January. We hunted for most of our meat and furs before winter set in because there was too much snow to get around easily.

The Abenaki name for this moon is Alalmikos, the Greeting Maker Moon. Does this imply "hard times"?

Next, the author refers to a "small cluster of dome-shaped wigwams." Here is an example of inappropriate generalizing of large geographical areas. For instance, the Abenaki of Vermont use the word "wigwam" to describe the shelter we lived in, while the Wampanoag just south of us in the Massachusetts area call this shelter a "wetu."

The picture that goes with this text shows a person wearing snowshoes on what appears to be hard ground with very little snow. If these were winter-bound northern people as the text states, there was lots of snow in January, and we wore snowshoes—to navigate the snow.

FEBRUARY—"SNOW BLINDER MOON"

Again the author talks at great length about hunting and drying meat. If any hunting occurred during this time, we simply cut the meat into chunks and froze it in the snow or dropped it into the lake in big pieces until we needed it. It would be very difficult to dry meat in February.

The Abenaki name for this moon is Piaodagos, the Makes Branches Fall In Pieces Moon, because there is lots of snow falling, causing the branches to break. There was so much snow it was extremely difficult to for us to hunt; we hunted in this moon only when our survival was threatened.

MARCH—"SAP MOON"

"Life seems to stir again in the northeastern lands," McCurdy says. Does he think we all died when it got cold?

Tapping trees cannot be assigned to a specific time. This is an event that occurs when the warm sun is up in the day and there are cold nights. This may be February, March or April, and the location of the tree also makes a difference. A maple tree in the mountains may not be tapped until several weeks after one in the valley. Further, while northern Algonkian-speaking tribes tapped maple trees, southern Algonkian-speaking peoples did not. And, tapping is hard, exhausting work; it was certainly not the "carnival-like atmosphere" that McCurdy describes.

"The Algonquian tribes will one day show the white settlers how to make maple syrup," McCurdy says, yet the illustration shows a metal pot hanging over a fire. Was this before or after we showed the white settlers how to make maple syrup?

The Abenaki word for this moon is Mozokas, the Moose Moon. *Now* is the time to hunt Moose; they're easier to track and there is a great need for their meat after the long winter. Now, we also give thanks to Sigwankas, the Abenaki word for the moon between March and April—the Spring Season Maker Moon, which McCurdy leaves out altogether.

APRIL—"SPEARFISH MOON"

The picture shows bare-skinned men spear fishing in an open river and refers to Abenakis and Micmac (Mi'kmaq) fishing. This ice doesn't leave many of the rivers around Vermont until late April to mid-May. The lakes don't usually free up until the beginning of May and then the rivers follow. It would be a rare year to see men fishing, without heavy clothing, on an open river in April around here, and it would be even rarer in the lands of the Mi'kmaq.

The Abenaki word for this moon is Sogalikas, the Sugar Maker Moon. This is when the peoples of the Northeast finish up the harvest process, boiling the sap.

MAY—"PLANTING MOON"

In the Northeast, we did not plant our gardens at this time because of the frost. I have friends who live by the Canadian border who have in most years only thirty to thirty-five frost-free days a year. Plants have to be covered to protect them from the frost on the remaining days of summer.

The picture shows a man gardening alongside the women. This would not have been true for most Northeastern tribes. The only thing that men grew and maintained was tobacco, and this was in an area away from the women's garden.

The Abenaki word for this moon is Kikas, the Field Maker Moon. This is a time when the fields are prepared, but not yet planted.

JUNE—"STRAWBERRY MOON"

"Algonquian tribes love wild strawberries," McCurdy says. That's like saying, "Negroes love watermelons." Wild strawberries (and watermelons) are delicious to many, but to say it like this is offensive.

The author says that strawberries, thimbleberries, blackberries, shadberries, raspberries, and elderberries all come ripe within this month, and that they all grow in natural clearings, or fields that we allowed to lie fallow.

Elderberries grow in open fields, but early shadbush grow in swamps and open woods, mountain shadbush grow on upper slopes and ascend to alpine areas, raspberries grow in low and medium elevations and some in the mountains. They do not all come ripe in June; we are lucky to see elderberries ripe by September.

The Abenaki word for this moon is Nokahigas, the Hoer Moon. Here, McCurdy is correct; we did continue to cultivate the rich soil in our gardens during this moon.

JULY—"RIPENING MOON"

Here the author gets parts of this right—"The men spend much time tending their tobacco plants in special gardens that are set apart from the food crops." Then he screws the whole thing up with some strange-sounding spirit-thing:

> The rising smoke from a pipe is visible evidence of the Algonquians' desire to contact the spirit powers above. By smoking a pipe, an Indian asks for support from the spirit powers and demonstrates his commitment to those spirits.

This is insulting, and shows no understanding of our complex and beautiful belief system.

Although the platform with children shooing away crows appears accurate, the rest of the garden scene is not. In the Northeast, we did not garden in neatly weeded rows, but rather in scattered areas around tree stumps and trees, in small mounds with other plants such as beans and squash planted in between the mounds. This was to shade the ground from the weeds, to maintain the moisture content of the ground and to help prevent predators such as raccoons from stealing the corn.

The Abenaki name for this moon is Temaskikos, the Grass Cutter Moon. This is when we harvest our sacred sweetgrass.

AUGUST—"GREEN CORN MOON"

The corn is not ripe for everyone in August. The Green Corn celebrations are in August for some and September for others. We did not hang our babies, bound in cradle-boards, on nearby tree branches. We hung the *cradle-boards*. This is an important distinction.

"The women make baskets from birch bark," McCurdy says. Not in August we don't; we harvest the best birchbark, the strongest bark, in the spring when the sap is flowing. Summer bark is very lightweight and is good only for repairing or emergencies. The baskets in the picture look like Japanese bamboo baskets. We can and do use them for harvesting now, but we didn't before contact.

We often dried skins over a slow fire, because the smoke makes them somewhat waterproof. The pores of the hide fill with soot and become plugged. But I don't understand what the author is calling a "smudge fire." I hope he doesn't mean smudge purification, which is something else entirely.

The Abenaki word for this moon is Temezowas, the Cutter Moon, referring to harvesting.

SEPTEMBER—"HARVEST MOON"

Some of our tribes lined our food cellars with birchbark. But tribes who lived where there are no birch trees used other materials that contain the same anti-bacterial properties. The Pequot around the Connecticut area, for example, lined their food cellars with a kind of anti-fungal grass.

The Abenaki word for this moon is Skamonkas, the Corn Maker Moon, because most people are now harvesting their corn.

OCTOBER—"HUNTER'S MOON"

Not all Algonkian-speaking peoples eat bear. To the Abenaki, bears are sacred and some people don't eat them.

Killing a moose and returning it to the village is a big job. An average size moose is about 1,500 pounds. Usually women came with the hunting party for the purpose of preparing the moose meat on site, and then transporting it back to the village. To suggest that it would take a "couple of days" to carry a moose back to the village, as the author says, is an understatement.

The Abenaki word for this moon is Penibagos, the Leaf Falling Moon.

NOVEMBER—"BEAVER MOON"

"Someday, when the European settlers arrive," McCurdy says, "the pelts will be traded for the white man's goods."

It would have been more accurate had he said, "After the Europeans arrive and stay awhile the beavers are almost on the brink of extinction." Or how's this? "Someday when the European settlers arrive, plants, animals and people will be destroyed, made extinct or relocated."

The Abenaki word for November is Mzatanos, the Freezing River Maker Moon.

DECEMBER—"TOMCOD MOON"

In the picture we have a fishing scene with one guy wearing what appears to be a wolf skin and someone else wearing a coat made of some kind of beaded fabric. And there's another of those Japanese bamboo baskets. "The pleasant summer activities are long past,"

McCurdy says, "as the Algonquians settle in for the long, cold winter." His implication, I suppose, is that pleasant winter activities didn't exist for us. In reality, such fun activities as sledding, snowshoeing, and a good game of snow-snake gave much pleasure to the long winter.

The Abenaki word for this moon is Pebonkas, the Winter Maker Moon.

I don't know why McCurdy uses the present tense when he is clearly describing peoples before contact. I also don't know why he refers to many peoples, using words and describing lifeways of one or two specific Nations. I don't know why he uses twelve moons instead of thirteen, why he makes sweeping generalizations and why his pictures don't reflect the realities of the Algonkian-speaking peoples. And finally, had he identified a Nation, a people, and explained the significance of each moon for that people, he might have given a clearer picture of what was happening. And it would have been good if he knew what he was talking about.—*Judy Dow*

McDermott, Gerald, *Arrow to the Sun: A Pueblo Indian Tale*, illustrated by the author. Viking (1974). Unpaginated, color illustrations; grades 2-5; "Pueblo"

Arrow to the Sun won a Caldecott Medal for McDermott's illustrations. They are striking and it's easy to see why the Caldecott committee selected this book for the award. I like the art, but there are many things I don't like.

The child in the book (referred to as "Boy") is taunted because he doesn't know who his father is. In a traditional Pueblo, that isn't likely. The concept of "illegitimate" doesn't fit with our ways of caring for children. They aren't born to a single family, but into a large, extended family of aunts and uncles, grandparents, and siblings who cherish and love the newborn.

But the thing that bothers me most about the book is that the boy has to go into four different kivas to face "trials" that will prove him to be the son of the "Lord of the Sun." In these kivas, he has to fight serpents, lions, bees, and

lightening. The battle scenes are vibrant. The fierce-looking lions have sharp teeth. One of the serpents opens its mouth wide, ready to bite the boy as he climbs down the ladder into the kiva. Clearly, McDermott doesn't know what goes on in kivas. A kiva is a place of gathering, a place to learn, a place to worship. It is not unlike a synagogue or church or meeting house. Thanks to McDermott, many non-Native children probably think that kivas are scary places.

McDermott says this is a Pueblo tale. I wonder which Pueblo—there are nineteen in New Mexico. Nowhere in the book does he tell us where he heard the story.

Some scholars of children's literature write about the universal themes in this book and refer to Joseph Campbell's work. Underlying themes and messages. I'm sure that's all very well and good for those scholars and their careers. As for me, I don't care about those underlying themes that they see. All I see is a gross misrepresentation of our ways of thinking about children, and our way of worship, and I'd just as soon this book disappeared from schools and libraries across the country. No book is better than a book with this level of misrepresentation.—*Debbie A. Reese*

McGinnis, Mark, with Pamela Greenhill Kaizen (Lakota), *Lakota & Dakota Animal Wisdom Stories*, illustrated by the author. Tipi Press (1994). 27 pages, color illustrations; grades 2-up; Lakota, Dakota

As a Lakota grandmother, I am interested in any children's books that may contain Lakota language, lifestyle or characters. Since I grew up hearing many stories from relatives and storytellers around South Dakota, I was eager to see what this book was about.

These stories were quick to read through. After reading the first story, I had a feeling of disappointment. Not because my expectations were too high, but because the tone of the stories was "scolding" and just about each had a judgmental ending. For instance,

> "So, now you reap the punishment of your idleness," said the hard working Mouse. "This is the way it always seems to be with the lazy and careless. But I will lend you a packing bag. Now go to work and see if by hard toil you can regain some of your wasted time."

And,

> "You have been disobedient, so from this day forth the Crane's wing tips shall remain black, and so shall it be with all this tribe of Crane to remind them of how they had to sweep coals and soot with their wings to remain warm."

In our traditional stories, choice is available, accountability for one's decisions is valued, and love is bestowed. Our stories were and are structured for individual interpretations; children get out of a story whatever they need based on where they are on their journey. They are not led by the storyteller's telling them that an animal is "idle," "lazy," "careless," or "disobedient." And we don't tell our children what to think.

I attended and graduated from St. Joseph's Indian School where Tipi Press is located and this book reminds me of the harsh lessons and shaming we continually underwent. I recognize this as the influence of Christianity into our Lakota world once again, and I recognize this has infiltrated much of what is said and written about our traditional ways. This book like many others, is written by someone outside of our culture, interpreting then solidifying through his own vision of the world and then slapping the label of "Lakota Wisdom and Oral Tradition" on it. This is not a book I would want my grandchildren to see.—*Lakota Harden*

McLellan, Joseph (Nez Percé), Pemmican Publications. Unpaginated, color illustrations; grades 2-up; Anishinaabe:
The Birth of Nanabosho, illustrated by Jim Kirby, 1989
Nanabosho Dances, illustrated by Rhian Brynjolson, 1989
Nanabosho: How the Turtle Got Its Shell, illustrated by Rhian Brynjolson, 1994
Nanabosho, Soaring Eagle, and the Great Sturgeon, illustrated by Rhian Brynjolson, 1993
Nanabosho Steals Fire, illustrated by Don Monkman (Cree), 1989
Nanabosho and the Woodpecker, illustrated by Rhian Brynjolson, 1995

McLellan's children's books about the Anishinaabek people of the Great Lakes regions present a written portrayal of one of the traditional teaching styles of the Anishinaabek, who have used storytelling throughout time. Though stories told for enjoyment and entertainment were and are often planned, stories told for instructional purposes were and are spontaneously told as the situation and context warrant. I grew up in a household where stories were told for all sorts of reasons, but the stories I

remember most are the ones that were told to help me think about important ideas or values that I was expected to hold. Reading McLellan's books is like a visit home.

These are all Nanabosho stories and *The Birth of Nanabosho* is an excellent starting place for understanding him. McLellan portrays the Anishinaabek great teacher in his many faces: as a naïve and innocent childlike character discovering the meanings of life in *Nanabosho and the Woodpecker* to the gift-giver in *Nanabosho: How the Turtle Got Its Shell* to the student and teacher in *Nanabosho Dances*. Just like the lessons taught in similar indirect ways to Anishinaabek children throughout their growing years, McLellan weaves in the important messages without directly telling the reader the specific lesson that Nanabosho learns.

The beautiful illustrations add the type of depth and wonder that attracts readers of all ages. I am especially fond of *Nanabosho, Soaring Eagle and the Great Sturgeon* because of the story itself and the way in which illustrator Rhian Brynjolson maintains the multiple story lines. Growing up in an Anishinaabek family I had the opportunity to spend time and learn with my siblings and cousins by participating in activities with my grandparents. In this story, Winona and her cousin Bonnie spend the day fishing with their mishomis, grandfather, while Winona's brother Billy learns how to do laundry. As the story begins, the reader meets each of the characters and travels along with Winona, Bonnie and their mishomis as they head for a day of fishing and hear the story of *Nanabosho, Soaring Eagle and the Great Sturgeon*. Though the story focuses on Winona and Bonnie, Brynjolson's illustrations keep the reader informed of the progress Billy is making on his own project to learn to do laundry, including a hilarious illustration of a distraught Billy and a washer with soap bubbles flowing from the washing machine onto the floor. McLellan begins with a glossary of Ojibwe story vocabulary, and ends with factual information about sturgeons. Each of McLellan's books is wonderful and I'm sure readers will identify their own favorites to share again and again with family, friends and teachers.—*Pam Martell*

McLerran, Alice. *The Ghost Dance*, illustrated by Paul Morin. Clarion (1995). Unpaginated, color illustrations; preschool-grade 3; Lakota

By the last decades of the 19th Century, the indigenous populations of the Americas were essentially conquered. Their lands had been taken, their sources of survival cut off or destroyed. Ill-fed, poorly housed and clothed, they were facing starvation. In 1888, Wovoka, a Northern Paiute, saw in a vision that if the People danced in a certain way, the land would roll back, taking the white men with it, and all would be as before. Word of his vision came like the blessing of water to a dry land, giving hope where there had been only despair. Called Ghost Dance because part of Wovoka's message was that the dead would live again, the movement spread quickly: West Coast, Great Basin, the Plains. This made the white settlers very nervous. Soon they were screaming for armed intervention, leading ultimately to the assassination of Sitting Bull and, a few days later, the massacre of more than 300 Lakota on December 29, 1890, at Wounded Knee Creek in South Dakota. The figures vary, depending on who's talking; those who wish to see it as the "last battle of the Indian Wars" giving the lowest figure—around 150—as though this somehow made what happened less awful.

What kind of mind would find anything in this out of which to make a picture book suitable for young children? This is how it works.

Alice McLerran has taken a terrible and shameful episode in U.S. history, one that reverberates even to this day, and made it into an environmental fable. She says that she first heard about the Ghost Dance in an anthropology class and "never forgot the powerful story....As I began to see the relevance of the Paiute vision to concerns today, I immersed myself into historical accounts and pondered how to make this Native experience accessible and meaningful to young readers." Her book was lauded everywhere when it came out, no one seeing, apparently, a lack of equivalence between people dancing for their lives and being massacred for their efforts, and an environmental lesson. *School Library Journal* gave *Ghost Dance* a starred review for its

"optimistic and hopeful vision of environmental healing," and recommended it to teachers "seeking a poetic call-to-action" for environmental preservation.

McLerran's "story" is short, a mere 441 words. In it she tells how Native people "lived in sunlight" until the white men came and cast a shadow. But they brought "swift horses" and "guns more true than arrows," and these things were seen as good. The people learned too late that the white men "wished to own the earth": "Oh, for the days of the grandfathers!....Ghosts now, all ghosts."

McLerran says that it was "Tavibo the prophet, Tavibo of the visions" who first "dreamed" the dance: "The song was strong...but bullets sang more loudly."

> One day the sun died in the sky and in that darkness hope was born again. Wovoka, he who was Tavibo's son, to him the vision came....But once again the music failed, and many died.

An awful thing happened and this is the sole reference to it: "many died." For McLerran's purposes, it is irrelevant that unarmed, defenseless people, under a white flag of truce, were butchered, shot down like prey animals, with the wounded left to freeze to the ground. The real importance is the "vision-song." "Yet still the vision calls" and if "all hold to the dream," "we" can call it back. "Tavibo, Wovoka, teach us to dance! The time has surely come."

> Maybe if we all dream.
> Maybe if we all sing.
> Maybe if we all dance.

The end.

In the back pages, McLerran hopes for a "joining of purpose across political and cultural boundaries. I see the century-old Paiute vision as an oracle still offering healing. It is not a vision that failed; it is one yet to be realized." I wonder if the ghosts of Wounded Knee would agree with her—or any of their descendants, who still ride to heal the tears of seven generations.

Paul Morin is an accomplished artist, with awards and recognitions. His paintings for Joe Bruchac's *Fox Song* are particularly beautiful.

These illustrations, seen from an outside place, may be artistic. They also were praised by *School Library Journal* as "evocative" paintings, that "glow with the golden colors of the sun-drenched prairie." They do not glow, they are dark. Dark, and disturbing. Even the first two paintings have a sunset, valedictory quality. The Native people are seen through this darkened, sinking-down light. Perhaps in that sense, Morin's work may, perhaps unintentionally, more truly fit what actually happened than does the text.

Sometimes it is hard to tell what he is symbolizing; one

illustration resembles European cave painting more than it does, say Chumash rock art, or the petroglyphs found all over the Americas.

The People killed at Wounded Knee were Lakota—although that is nowhere mentioned—Pte Oyate; buffalo people. For them and many other Nations beside, buffalo are wakan, "animal representation of the sun."[1] It is not a good thing to take a "ceremonial buffalo skull" from the "western door" of a sweat lodge, and plunk it down as background for the title page of a book. Even if it is about Indians. *Especially* if it is about Indians.

A double-page spread is of "found and historical objects": On the left, bullets, a metal disk stamped "United States Tobacco Co." These things rest against a bullet-holed wall that stretches across the pages. In the center, a dreamcatcher is pinned to the wall, like the flayed skin of an animal. Then an unidentifiable object, perhaps from a long bone, the thick end wrapped, the narrow end tipped in metal. In the right background, what is probably a reproduction of an old map of "Indian territory"; in front of that, a piece of leather bearing the punched design of a church—the one at Wounded Knee? Lower right, a braid of sweetgrass burnt at one end, two bunches of sage, and, in total darkness, something hanging, wrapped in string, with seeds and what might be red beads. Below all this a rifle, running the width of the illustration.

For the artist, these objects and the others may "symbolize the 'sacred hoop' of the nation"; be an "epic universal statement." For the Native observer, they speak only of defeat and death. And the sacred herbs do not mitigate the effect. If anything, to see them used in this way only intensifies it. And it does take a certain amount of ego to refer to one's own work as an "epic universal statement." Isn't that usually decided by the viewers?

Of whose "hoop" does he speak? *His* nation does not have a hoop. The sacred hoop was ours, and it was broken. Wounded knee was a human event, not an ecological disaster. A People's dream died there. We may have a new one, our hoop may be mended—although there's some duct tape, here and there—but our life will never be what it would have been if we had been left alone. This book is a brutally insensitive appropriation of a human tragedy. To dedicate it to "all First Nation (sic) peoples who are rediscovering traditional ways and spreading these teachings" is an astonishing act of hubris. —*Doris Seale*

NOTE

1 Momaday, N. Scott, "The Great Fillmore Street Buffalo Drive," in N. Scott Momaday, Storyteller (audiotape). Lotus Press, 1989.

Medearis, Angela Shelf, *Dancing with the Indians*, illustrated by Samuel Byrd. Holiday House (1991). Unpaginated, color illustrations; grades 1-3; Seminole

I would never have known by looking at the strange cover that this book was based on a specific tribe, my tribe, the Seminole. Inside, it starts out with what seems to be some real family history and the reality of the alliance of enslaved Black people with Seminoles, but then it goes *way* downhill from there. The rhyming verse degenerates into absurdity and stereotypes—along with the illustrations: Wheeling... Whooping... Fiercely painted... Untamed...

> Warriors stamp and holler,
> an angry cavalcade.
> I draw away from them,
> a little bit afraid.

The leaping, kicking, twisting figures make a mockery of any real Native dancing (and it's certainly not Seminole dancing!). The "costuming" is a weird combination of different eras of Seminole and Creek dress, and stereotypical "Indian" dress. There's just enough touch of reality that people might actually think this book is OK., but the stereotypes just keep on coming, haunting us all. Sadly, this book is from an African-American author and illustrator. It seems clear that Angela Madearis meant to pay tribute to a people who helped her ancestors during a terrible time. Unfortunately, Medearis' good intentions have resulted in a book that is embarrassing and disappointing, and maybe scary for the picture-book audience for whom it is intended.—*Adrianne Micco*

Merrill, Yvonne Y., *Hands-On Latin America: Art Activities for All Ages.* Kits Publishing (1997). 87 pages, color photos, b/w illustrations; grades 3-up; Aztec, Inca, Maya

I can't imagine why anyone would want to use this book. There's no information on the pieces children are being taught to make. Any child or teacher with an inquiring mind would ask: Where were the originals of these pieces made? Who made them? For whom were they made? What were their uses? As a teacher who does project-based teaching I found myself looking for at least photos of the original pieces and any kind of information to answer these questions. And as an Indian woman I can't in good conscience tell my culturally diverse students that they're "Latin American art pieces." That is just not enough.

The food page in particular ranks up there in bad taste. I teach my students that what people ate and thrived on was what grew in their areas and that the availability of food was usually why people came to a certain area. The author's statement—"Here are some of the foods that were new to the world with the Spanish conquests"—is ungrammatical and confusing and sets the tone for the European-American "us-versus-them" perspective that permeates the entire book.

A few glaring misses: The map shows the continent of South America, Central America and a little of Mexico, but does not include the United States or Canada when in fact, some of the art work is purely North American, north of Mexico—the luminarias for instance. The Aztec symbols are referred to as "designs" when in fact each had and has great importance relating to specific aspects of a belief system. The historic pieces relating to belief and ritual—such as Aztec headbands, medallions and rattles—are shown as craft objects, devoid of meaning, easily constructed out of paper, pasta, paint and canning lids. Each design on each piece had a specific meaning; rituals associated with them were sometimes known by all, sometimes known only by initiates. In any event, they were not simply things for children to copy and play with.

To give this book "educational" value, Merrill has incorporated what she considers important to know on several full pages and after many of the craft instructions. These "facts" mostly range from strange to unintelligible to ridiculous. In a paragraph labeled "Health Care and Hygiene," there is some useful information, followed by this:

> The New World natives had an impressive knowledge of the human body, derived largely from human sacrifice and body dissection. Mesoamerican "surgeons" used sharp obsidian knives and were skilled in drilling for brain injuries.

Sacrificed bodies were considered holy and were not defiled by dissection, nor were they used for educational purposes. The "impressive knowledge" in science and medicine was derived from the need to better the human condition, and trephining was done to relieve pain and pressure on the brain. By surrounding the word "surgeons" with quotes, Merrill implies that people were *not* surgeons, but rather "primitive" people poking around with sharp instruments.

A page about the Maya is illustrated with a drawing of a person's head, with arrows pointing to "knotted hair," "crossed eyes," "filed pointed teeth filled with jade," "sloped forehead," and "tattoos." Above the drawing, Merrill writes, "[A]rcheologists know the Maya had an unusual beauty code." Her use of the word "archeologists" is incorrect; people who interpret archeological finds to theorize about their cultural relevance are called "cultural anthropologists." There was always a purpose or reason for everything that was done; in this case, it

might have been beauty, spirituality, status or class. Using the term "unusual" here is patronizing, as is "beauty code." The picture Merrill shows may well be that of someone belonging to a warrior society, possibly jaguar, whose members personified certain cultural icons. In any event, it's made to look like a frivolous beauty style filtered through a modern European sensibility. This is not a good thing to do.

In "New World Influences," Merrill writes: "Though their governing power was quickly eliminated, the New World resources and knowledge forever changed the European lifestyle." Can anyone tell me what this means? Finally, my favorite "doesn't-quite-make-it" quote:

> In most cases they called themselves by their indigenous name: the Chimus or Chancas of the Inca empire, the Mixtecs or Toltecs of the Aztec empire.

What else on Earth *would* they call themselves? Would they use Spanish names they had never heard?

The "Art Today" section is surprisingly good, mainly because there is no history to mess with. Most of the items are highly visible in modern culture and have become popular to display and make. However, there are better sources for teaching students that include photographs of actual pieces with accurate histories that allow children to learn about the original peoples of this hemisphere in a respectful, non-racist way.—*Judy Zalazar Drummond*

Miller, Montzalee, *My Grandmother's Cookie Jar*, illustrated by Katherine Potter. Price/Stern/Sloan (1987). Unpaginated, color illustrations; grades 1-3

Summary: "Grandma passes on the stories of her Indian people to her grandchild as they eat cookies together from the cookie jar shaped like an Indian head."

On the cover, an Indian grandma, facing front and looking stoic, has one arm around her granddaughter's shoulder. The granddaughter is nervously looking back over her left shoulder at a shelf, on which rests a cookie jar—a creepy, disembodied "Indian head," replete with five feathers and four stripes of "war paint." To the left of the cookie jar floats a ghostly Indian rider chasing two buffalo.

The child is clearly afraid of the cookie jar: "It sat at eye level on the dark shelf in my grandmother's kitchen, waiting for me, as it always did. The head seemed to laugh at my fear."

What does this fearsome thing have to do with an Indian grandparent passing on culture to her grandchild? Does anyone really think that a healthy positive relationship would be based on a gruesome object? Would such a thing be the focal point of a story about a family of any other culture? Say a "Negro head" cookie jar or a "Jewish head" piggy bank?

Somehow the child's fear of the cookie jar turns into "Indian pride" when her grandma tells vague, generic "stories" about their people's past. But they are not really stories, they are a few strung-together clichés about "painted dancers" and buffalo hunts:

> I could almost feel the Indians' fear of the people who took the land away… I felt Indian pride and understood Indian honor. I longed for the ancient ways.

What pride? *What* honor? *What* ancient ways? "Then one day Grandmother was gone. Grandfather came to me with the Indian head." At this point, I had to look to make sure that the "Indian head" was that damned cookie jar and not Grandma. Grandpa says, "the jar is full of Grandma's love and Indian spirit." Is Grandma actually *in* the jar? Has Grandma fallen victim to the haunted Indian head?

The last illustrations show the child holding the cookie jar and looking beyond it to Grandma's disembodied head floating among the clouds.

The illustration of this "cookie jar" pulled me back inside the curio shops and museums in 1950s Nevada. There, as a young child, I first saw the bodies of dead Indians on display. I remember walking up to a glass case and looking into the hollow eyes of a dead Indian man. I remember being filled with sadness and horror.

My Grandmother's Cookie Jar has nothing to do with passing on any useful information. This short, macabre and nauseating story, complete with ugly and stereotypical pictures, promotes disturbing feelings and offensive ideas about Indian families and cultures. It is disrespectful to the memory of Indian grandmas everywhere. We are, once again, in life and death, a stereotype, a myth, a possession to be used for entertainment. This is a nightmare being passed off as a children's book.—*Adrianne Micco*

Momaday, N. Scott (Kiowa), *House Made of Dawn.* **University of Arizona (1968). 212 pages; high school-up; Pueblo**

Momaday, a Kiowa, was raised in the southwest. This novel, his first, won a Pulitzer Prize in 1969—the first by an Indian writer. But its literary significance—why it won this prestigious award—is why this book marks a watershed in Indian literature. There have been straightforward narrative novels by Indian writers before and since, usually attempting to capture in fictional form something of the lifeways of a tribal people, or displaced peoples' experience. Momaday was the first to show that Indian writers can use sophisticated literary techniques to convey both Native cultures and modern Native lives. His work remains one of the best examples, as well as the first, of stylized form; the majority of Indian novels are still straight narratives.

The story of Abel, a Pueblo youth raised traditionally in the self-contained world with its meaningful customs, sacred events—and the boredom and lack of a future that leaves him envying eagles and longing to fly away himself—is told by an interleaving of disconnected interior monologues from a variety of characters, some of them untrustworthy. It's full of flashbacks, forwards, and side glances. To figure out plot and events, the reader has to fit these monologues together like a puzzle. In the end, certain key pieces are left missing, a mystery that keeps the story always before the reader's own inner eye, turning in the circle of its basic structure.

The book starts "now," sometime in the early winter of 1952. The distantly seen figure of Abel, smeared with ash, is running a sacred endurance race. We later learn this race of the dead is actually held late every November. At the end of the book, Abel's grandfather has just died— running off in dreaming that same race, where he excelled as a young man, beyond his pain of illness and age, chasing the dark shadow-figure of death. After Abel has prepared his body for burial, he goes out in the snowy dawn to join the blackened runners, who may be metaphoric, imaginary. To me, Abel's run means survival of the people and the culture, despite the hard times of Termination and Relocation, which have just started. Yet there is also an implication that Abel will run into the shadows beyond his own pain, drink himself to death. Abel has no real connections, as his grandfather had, to the timeless traditions. He has no remaining relatives. He loves no one and no one—except an abandoned lover in Los Angeles—cares about him.

At the end, he is running—as at the beginning—on a song. It is not a song of his pueblo's traditions, which he has not involved himself in since killing the eagle whose ceremonial confinement and degradation he couldn't stand. The eagle, trapped for traditional sacrifice, reminded him of himself, trapped on the reservation. He leaves, joins the army, becomes a war hero, but can't make it afterward either on the reservation or off it.

It's not clear why he and the albino man he kills hate each other—that's one of the missing puzzle pieces. It's possible this man was the baby born to his grandfather's woman—the reason he abandoned her. It's not at all clear why he is supposed to be a symbol of absolute evil. The role of the old crazy priest—whose diaries we read—indicates something is going on that resulted in the albino's birth. The crazy old woman—possibly his mother—may be the beloved, wildly sexy woman Abel's grandfather abandoned when her child (who might not have been his) was born with something wrong.

The misremembered scraps of song Abel runs on at the end are not from his pueblo's traditions, which he doesn't know much about. They are bits of the Navajo Beauty Way he picked up from his one friend, Benally, talking and drinking in the L.A. hills after his parole from prison. Yet, the feeling is strong: he is running into life, not his and his people's long death:

> The people of the town have little need. They do not hanker after progress and have never changed their essential way of life....They have assumed the names and gestures of their enemies, but have held on to their own, secret souls, and in this there is a resistance and an overcoming, a long outwaiting.

The story doesn't unfold as a chronicle. It is extracted like puzzle pieces from tangles and time-cuts among incomplete inner thoughts of the unreliable characters. The mysterious albino evil figure, whom Abel—drunk after his World War II sojourn in the outside world—kills during a Pueblo ceremony, is a central mystery, never solved. Another mystery figure is the L.A. Sun Priest, Momaday himself, a combination hype artist and word-struck preacher, who purveys a central part in Momaday's later, more accessible book, *The Way to Rainy Mountain*, as a miniature sermon, preached to dispirited Indian people at a mission in L.A.

Literary reviewers described the book as the story of a post-war Indian man's "descent to hell" caused by his war years away from the timeless beauties of his tribe and his exposure to a senseless and violent alien culture. In this view, Abel is modeled on Ira Hayes, a young Pima war hero who became a drunk on his return and drowned in two inches of water. That's an oversimplification; it is much more than that. The hell is that the beauties of the ancient culture are not in fact timeless; they are dying. Abel was wild to get away

from where he felt as trapped by tradition as the eagle. Benally remembers the wonder of being in the center of everything, but says that's only true when you're a kid. The old people, the old ways are dying, and the reservation is actually a place of poverty; there is nothing for young men there. The vividly conveyed (but ultimately impenetrable) human mysteries, and set-piece visual images, give the book most of its power.

Advanced high school students can follow it, the passages themselves are not difficult reading. For those not experienced with complex literary form, teacher help with the time scheme will be required.

None of its force has been lost over thirty years. *House Made of Dawn* is—for its groundbreaking form and its enduring power—the most important literary work by a Native writer to date. No person of any culture can claim to be educated who has not read and pondered it.

—*Paula Giese*

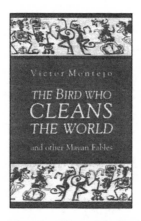

Montejo, Victor (Maya), *The Bird Who Cleans the World and Other Mayan Fables,* **translated by William Kaufman. Curbstone (1991). 120 pages, color illustrations; grades 5-up (younger for read-aloud); Maya**

To my knowledge, this is the only collection, done by a Mayan person, that has been translated into English. The stories were transcribed from the Jakaltek-Maya language—one of twenty-one still spoken in Guatemala—by Montejo, whose purpose was to show

> [T]he creativeness of the Mayan people [and] to leave a testimony to the values of respect, unity and understanding that exist between the people and their natural and supernatural environment.

Some of the stories are obviously from more recent times; some are very old. Some are so old that they don't make "sense" in the commonly accepted European meaning of that word. These are the ones that stick in the mind, teasing it into understanding.

The illustrations are from the Late Classic Maya Period. A note tells us that they were mostly taken from ceramics, and that the colors have been enhanced, as they had become faded with age. Should the pictures seem rather enigmatic, these notes also explain what we are seeing.

The hand of the anthropologist or "adapter" being notably absent from them, the stories read well. Montejo says, "These stories...are also expressions of a millenarian tradition that has come from the deepest soul of the Mayan people." One can feel that, and it gives the stories a haunting quality beyond their apparent simplicity. Knowing something of recent Mayan history adds to this: "People can destroy themselves by not recognizing the value of all living creatures on earth with whom they should coexist."

The Bird Who Cleans the World is highly recommended.

—*Doris Seale*

Moore, MariJo (Cherokee), *red woman with backward eyes and other stories*. Renegade Planets (2001). 95 pages; grades 7-up; Cherokee

Author MariJo Moore, like the best of Indian writers, knows the power of story, the magic of words. In *red woman with backward eyes*, her female protagonists dance around and through past, present and future; honor the ancestors, the elderly and the children; and even in the depths of alcoholic despair, still know who they are. Like the famous Cherokee "double-wove" baskets, MariJo Moore's words weave around, through and around again, teasing the reader into understanding what may not always be apparent the first time around.

In these ten short stories of contemporary Indian life, middle readers will find alcoholism and family dysfunction and loneliness, and the poverty that breeds and feeds them. But they will also find the strength and tenacious spirits of those who refuse to give up, no matter what. And they may come to know the incomparable beauty of the four gifted red words braided into Suda Cornsilk's hair—respect, share, remember, and persevere.

A lonely young girl communicates with one of the Nunnehi—the one she knows as "red woman with backward eyes"—who shows her the way back to her mother on the other side. A young girl named Siren hears the voices of the Old Ones, who give her instructions that will temporarily get her mama out of a dilemma. The prayer songs of a "crazy" woman, known to the other prisoners as Singing Martha, comfort and teach another woman. Grandmama Toinetta has killed many a chicken in her time, but she finds she is no match for the rooster named "Old Tsa Tsi." Rumors have it that

"stranger than most" cousin Addy May Birdsong could sneak into people's houses and change the course of their dreams. An old woman prepares to join her husband who has gone to Spirit. Hownetta, a medicine woman whom people think is "strange in the head," can see through the eyes of the dead.

All of the girls and women in *red woman with backward eyes* are of the spirit and of the blood. They come from MariJo Moore's ancestral stories, dreams, experiences, and "spiritual intuition." And they are a precious gift, an invitation to come into "the place where hummingbirds and cacti hold tiny hands and speak of their similarities." Wado, MariJo.—*Beverly Slapin*

Moreillon, Judi, *Sing Down the Rain*, illustrated by Michael Chiago (Tohono O'odham). Kiva Publishing (1997). Unpaginated, color illustrations; grades 2-4; Tohono O'odham

At home, we have the bringing-down-the-rain ceremony, done every year in late July or early August. There's a lot of ongoing preparation for the actual ceremony. The headman sets the time of the ceremonies in each village, says the blessings, and takes care of the songs. All know and take care of their different responsibilities, including the children. This is all to say that our rain making is a very complex, very involved ceremony.

What Judi Moreillon has done here—her stated intent—was to create a choral reading out of our rain-making ceremony. She has taken elements of this sacred event, this religious ceremony, and made it into something for kids to recite. This is as inappropriate as, say, kids reciting the Catholic communion:

> The wafer and wine
> That tastes so fine…

We appreciate a thing for the way we see it, for the way it is. Growing up on the O'odham reservation, I used to complain about the heat, and my father would just say, "S-h-h-h-! That's just the way it is, you don't have to talk about it." Here, Moreillon talks about it, adding commentary that is out of place and messes up the image. She doesn't allow the words and pictures to sit with us. For instance, rather than "The life-giving clouds float over the mountains to bring cooling water"—which is our observation—she writes:

> The life-giving clouds, enormous and white
> Float over the mountains, a beautiful sight
> The bountiful clouds, that precious rainfall
> To bring cooling water, for one and for all

After the ceremony, it begins to rain. It's for everybody, everything, we know this, we don't say it. Just as the desert is hot. That's just the way it is, it doesn't need to be said. That's the way it is, until the rains come. But to have to describe and verbalize everything, using certain words to fill up a line and just add fluff and rhyme—"enormous," "beautiful," "precious"—trivializes the events and our observation of them.

It bothers me that Moreillon uses words such as "magic" and "mystical" to describe elements of a ceremony she doesn't understand. That the rains come after our ceremony is not "magic" or "mystical," it just is.

I don't know if Michael Chiago painted the pictures before or after Judi Moreillon wrote the poem. While the rains are extremely important, Moreillon implies that the desert is dead until the rains come ("the earth seems alive… the desert *will* thrive"). Chiago's art shows how alive the desert really is—the plants, the animals, the clouds, the ollas, the baskets, the ladies with their scarves, Tabletop Mountain—all are here. When I look at these paintings, I'm home.

Non-Native children and their teachers are not going to see what I see in these paintings, nor are they going to understand our ceremony from this poem. This kind of rhyming is not what O'odham kids hear when our stories are told. Non-Native kids need to be given an opportunity to hear people's ways of telling stories that may be different from the usual sing-songy forced rhyming that they are used to and comfortable with.

I would much rather have seen Chiago's work paired with the words of our elders.—*Carol Pancho-Ash*

Morgan, Pierr, *Supper for Crow: A Northwest Coast Indian Tale*, illustrated by the author. Crown (1995). Unpaginated, color illustrations; grades 1-2; Makah

Supper for Crow is a classic rendering in the Makah/Nuu-chah-nulth tradition. Pierr Morgan, who is non-Native, provides the cultural and situational context for her telling in an author's note that reveals that she lived in Neah Bay and learned to weave baskets with the elder, Isabelle Ives, who first told this story. Morgan situates herself in the genealogy of the tellings of this story and demonstrates that she knows how stories about Raven teach:

> His skills as a trickster…inadvertently make him one of life's greatest teachers. Even Mama Crow, who still gets tricked now and then when she isn't paying attention, knows that no amount of talk can make up for a good jolt of firsthand experience.

Morgan does not westernize the story by moralizing at the end. Our storytelling traditions usually do not provide explanations or quick solutions because our stories demand that the listeners (or readers) think creatively.

Morgan's detailed illustrations are a delight; they give the flavor of the Cape Flattery location of the Makah (where many of us have been potlatch guests) complete with vegetation, Tatoosh Island, and details such as float balls, mottling on the rocks and the action of the canoes in the surf. The illustrations also do affective work in this story: in the foreground there is highly expressive interaction between deception and greed, represented by the Crow family and Raven, while in the background the arrival of potlatch guests represent sharing, goodwill and cooperation. This device both differentiates and at the same time makes visible the two parallel threads of the story.

The author, who acts as narrator, "travels" through the illustrations as a ladybug, a spectator, a device that places her in the picture but not as part of the story. We particularly like the subtle visual joke of Raven's spoon with the handle in the shape of a human being. This story originates in a society based on cooperation about essentials of life, such as food, which requires a high level of mutual trust; only personal experience can truly teach the subtle lessons about life's essential relationships. When she realizes she had been duped, Mama Crow provides her children with a first-hand opportunity to learn this. The feeling is right about this book. *Supper for Crow* is highly recommended.—*Marlene R. Atleo/ʔeh ʔeh naa tuu kwiss,* and *Marcia Fenn, Karen Frank, Trudy Frank, Coral Johnson, Nora Lucas, Patricia Mack, Connie McPhee, Patricia North, Della Patrick, Tracey Robinson, Marlene Watts and Pam Watts*

**Morris, John and Kathy Morris, *Jumping Mouse and the Great Mountain: A Native American Tale*, illustrated by Charley E. Burns (Yurok). Flame of the Forest/Bamboo Books (2001). Unpaginated, color illustrations; grades 1-3
Steptoe, John, *The Story of Jumping Mouse: A Native American Legend*, illustrated by the author. Lothrop, Lee & Shepard (1984). Unpaginated, b/w illustrations; preschool-grade 3**

Although the Morris' *Jumping Mouse and the Great Mountain* is an obviously retooled version of John Steptoe's beautiful *The Story of Jumping Mouse*, the two are as different as day is to night.

In Steptoe's telling, a young mouse sets off to find the "far-off land." On his way he meets various beings in need, to whom he gives away pieces of himself. For his unselfish and loving spirit, he is transformed into an eagle and told he "will live in the far-off land forever." The luminous drawings, in black and white, are a perfect complement to the story.

The Morrises' book, on the other hand, so kills the subtlety that it's difficult to imagine that this could ever have been an Indian story. "As dawn broke over a magical world," they begin,

Jumping Mouse began his daily routine. He was not in a particularly good mood this morning, nor were the other mice from his burrow. This day, as every other, they would rush into the desert to compete for a few scarce seeds.

This little mouse is *really* unhappy with his life, especially "the daily drudge of foraging for food." "I am not sure what," he says, "but certainly there must be a greater purpose to our lives." "You ask what mice are destined for?" another mouse answers. "I'll tell you: to eke out a living in this dry desert, or to end up as food for hawks, snakes, coyotes, and bobcats."

Steptoe noted that in his version of the story he had made certain changes and additions to the story he had heard. However, they did not violate the spirit of the story or a Native understanding of the nature of life. The Morrises' version is so contrary to the Native understanding of the balance of life and the acceptance of the way things are that it is absurd for them to call it "a Native American Tale."

So the little mouse goes off toward the place that Steptoe calls the "far-off land" and the Morrises call the "fabled land of the Great Mountain." Here is how Steptoe describes the little mouse's generosity and how it is reciprocated:

> Jumping Mouse was saddened by the wolf's story. He told him about Magic Frog and Eyes-of-a-Mouse. "I have a little magic left," he said. "I'll be happy to help you. I name you Nose-of-a-Mouse." The wolf howled for joy. Jumping Mouse could hear him sniffing the air, taking in the mountain fragrances. But Jumping Mouse could no longer smell the pine-scented breezes. He no longer had the use of his nose or his eyes. "You are but a small creature," said Nose-of-a-Mouse, "but you have given me a great gift. You must let me thank you. Come, hop along beneath where the shadows of the sky won't see you. I will guide you…

Here is the Morrises' version:

> He was very sad to see such a powerful and intelligent animal suffering. How could he be so selfish? Flooded with respect for Coyote, feelings of compassion filled his heart: he wished with all his being that Coyote could have her leg back. Mystically and magically, the world began to spin, and in a moment it was over. Jumping Mouse had lost one of his legs, and Coyote stood…. "What have you done little mouse? Given me your leg? Are you crazy? You must be! Certainly I shall eat you now." Jumping Mouse gazed at Coyote. "Without my leg I cannot complete my journey up the Sacred Mountain. I have lived a good life, and am not afraid to die." With that Coyote grabbed him in her mouth, and

gently set him upon her back. "Not yet, little friend. First, you must complete your journey. I shall take you…"

Here, wolf of Steptoe's story has been changed to Coyote, the sense of smell has been replaced by a leg, and a beautiful story about reciprocity has become an exchange of body parts.

In an afterword. "About Jumping Mice," the Morrises write,

> Shy, nocturnal and typically occupying a home range of less than half an acre, the jumping mouse is an obvious choice to represent the challenges involved in the journey of transition from childhood to adulthood in Native American stories.

This is not what the story is about. It is purely and simply the story of a small creature with a generous spirit whose goodness is ultimately rewarded beyond anything he expected. As that, it conveyed something that was and is a very important part of Native belief.

Charley E. Burns' vibrant color illustrations may be appropriate for the Morrises' adaptation, but they too do not fit the original nature of the story.—*Beverly Slapin*

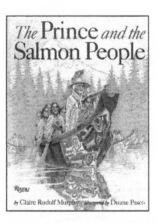

Murphy, Claire Rudolph, *The Prince and the Salmon People*, illustrated by Duane Pasco (Klallam). Rizzoli International (1993). 48 pages, color illustrations, color photos; grades 2-5; Tsimshian

Duane Pasco is a Seattle artist, carver, and art teacher of Port Gamble Klallam ancestry. His work was part of the rediscovery of traditional art that began to take place in the 1960s as younger artists strove to revive the dying traditions from the last few remaining artist-elders and intensive study of museum pieces. His large black-and-white drawings are aesthetically interesting, realistically accurate and (despite children's love for color in books) will generally hold the attention of the seven- to ten-year-olds for whom this book is intended.

Claire Murphy, who has lived in Alaska for twenty years, says she took the model for this story from "recordings made by anthropologists Franz Boas and William Beynon in the early twentieth century," probably the Boas publication *Tsimshian Mythology*, published by the Bureau of American Ethnology in its 1916 Annual Report. Murphy combines elements taken from a number of unrelated stories into one smoothly told narrative, losing the purposes of the originals the process.

Murphy is motivated by environmental concerns. "Overfishing, concrete dams, polluted rivers, and hatchery fish contribute to the lowered numbers of North Pacific salmon," she says, apparently believing that in some way modern industrial culture may be derailed by adopting the values in these old teaching stories. This aim has led to a certain wrenching-about of the traditional content of these stories. Murphy adds characters—like a slave boy and the inevitable wise old "shaman"—present in no versions (in some, there is a younger brother who is told to put the salmon bones in the river but is careless). She wants the boy-prince to be a hero; it wouldn't do to have him greedy and selfish, so he steals dried salmon from his mother on behalf of a hungry young slave—a noble motive, rather than personal greed.

Murphy's villagers—via that wise old shaman—know they are supposed to perform various ceremonies, and to return salmon offal to the river. But they forget! They get involved in other things! As—we have forgotten! But the original stories are mythic tellings of how these kinds of knowledge first came to the people, not metaphors for cultural change under industrial capitalism. So, since the villagers forgot the ceremonies—kind of like, uh, forgetting causes industrial pollution and big dams—the salmon stop coming for the villagers because they aren't honored. As the pollution, dams, overfishing have led salmon to stop coming nowadays....

It doesn't work at all, despite the Procrustean wrenching around. Modern industrial capitalism has to make its own survival myths—if it can. It cannot recycle myths and legends of Indian cultures. All that is accomplished is to remove the possibilities of cultural learning from the reworked myths.

The original stories are double-faceted teaching stories. On the one hand, there are spiritual and moral values of the culture: showing respect to the important food fish, the salmon; sharing, not being greedy and selfish. On the other, there are practical matters. Return of salmon bones and offal to the river has *practical* value (village sanitation) and not holding dried salmon more than a year is practical also: it may spoil. (Salmonella, which will infest any oily food, such as unrefrigerated mayonnaise in hot weather, is named after its discovered origin in spoiled salmon.)

Murphy either has no sensitivity to these practical teachings, or considers them unimportant in view of her larger environmental intentions, irrelevant in the age of flush toilets, sewers that make it all vanish—into lakes, rivers and water tables—and modern canning and refrigeration.

Murphy's story is smoothly told. The photos (mostly of Tsimshian art objects from several museums) add cultural value and considerable interest to the book. A large, clear map at the end identifies traditional territories of Northwest Coastal tribes.

But river dams are generally outside of our control and so are industrial sewage disposal and farming-caused water and air pollution. "Respect and honor for the salmon" isn't going to have any impact on the political and economic causes of these problems. But it remains a favorite theory of New Agers that various shallow imitations (often with some homegrown shaman presiding) of Native stories and rituals can substitute for more difficult and less interesting long-range commitments to political action. That, coupled with scientific research, might eventually actually have some effects. Cultures, traditions, oral literatures—these should be studied for their own sake, not wrenched into tortured forms to serve some other purpose.—*Paula Giese*

Native American Culture Series, Rourke Publications (1994). 94 pages, color photos and illustrations; grades 4-6
McCall, Barbara, *Daily Life* **and** *The European Invasion*
Prentzas, Scott, *Tribal Law*
Sherrow, Victoria, *Spiritual Life*
Sonneborn, Liz, *Arts and Crafts*
Wood, Leigh, *Child Rearing*

This series on traditional Native American lifeways attempts to present an overview of the variety of cultural institutions found among Indian peoples of the United States. Most of the books focus on customs in the major cultural regions of the Plains, West, Southwest, and Eastern Woodlands, with examples from specific tribes. *Daily Life* talks about the gathering and farming of plants, hunting, fishing, homes and clothing; while *European Invasion* is organized by invading colonizers (Spanish, English, Dutch, and French). As with most attempts to encompass such a vast diversity of cultures into such a brief overview, this series is only sporadically successful. Despite a stated goal of providing "more accurate images of Native Americans [to] enable [the reader] to challenge the stereotypes," illustrations are often dated and contribute little to the reader's understanding. The captions in several of the books describe the "Native Americans" in the photographs or painting, rather than identifying the tribe or even the regions, as is done in *Child Rearing*, and at least one illustration (p. 50, *Arts and Crafts*) has absolutely nothing to do with its caption.

Two photographs of human remains—a burial site in an archaeological dig, and body parts around a burial scaffold—are particularly offensive. Coming as they do in the *Spiritual Life* volume, they reveal a basic lack of respect and understanding of the very subject being written about. Actually, this topic would have been better placed in the *Daily Life* volume, since the author correctly states that "spirituality is much more closely tied to daily activities than is typical of most regions, particularly in modern times."

Generalizations ("All remaining tribes of the East were forced to relocate to a place called Indian Territory"—*European Invasion*); inaccuracies ("By the 1500s, there were hundreds of thousands of Native Americans already living here"—*Spiritual Life*—there were actually millions; "Today, St. Augustine is the oldest city in the United States"—*European Invasion*—should read "European City"); misunderstandings ("Tribes did not name themselves"—*Daily Life*); omissions and inconsistencies (a discussion of wild rice harvesting in *Daily Life* fails to mention the Ojibwe, one of the largest groups involved in this activity; while Ojibwe prayers connected with ricing are described in *Spiritual Life*); and biased terminology ("men of less warlike tribes"—*Daily Life*), are scattered throughout the books.

Use of the past tense is pervasive. Efforts to inform the reader that these are peoples who exist today and still carry on many of the activities being described are uneven from book to book. A glossary appears at the end of each book, but there are inaccuracies there, too. For example, a reservation is not, as the glossary states in all five volumes, "a tract of land that was set aside by the United States for a group of Native Americans," but the *retention* by individual tribes of a portion of their own lands. This seemingly minor but very fundamental difference is important in helping to convey the relationship between Native Nations and the United States. This series is not recommended.—*Lisa Mitten*

Nechodom, Kerry, *The Rainbow Bridge: A Chumash Legend*, illustrated by Tom Nechodom. Sand River Press (1992). Unpaginated, color illustrations; grades 2-3; Chumash Wood, Audrey, *The Rainbow Bridge*, illustrated by Robert Florczak. Harcourt Brace (1995). Unpaginated, color illustrations; grades 2-4; Chumash

Both of these books trace their origins to an oral telling of a legend by Russell A. Ruiz, which appears in *The Chumash People: Materials for Teachers and Students*, a publication by the Santa Barbara Museum of Natural History. The Museum identifies Ruiz as "a Santa Barbara historian," who told this story to Ros Perry in 1980, but does not tell us if Ruiz is Chumash or other Native Californian. This is a concern for me, particularly in light of the made-up "legends" that are so popular in children's books today. Because all four of the people involved in these books—both authors, both illustrators—are non-Native, I am concerned that the legend itself may be far from the original intent. Although the legend is famous as a Chumash story, neither author actually connects the story to a Chumash person in any way except by content. This leaves the way open to many interpretations and appropriations of the story. As Wood says in her "Storyteller's Note," she has "taken artistic liberty with the original legend by adding characters and expanding the tale into a story form," while the Nechodoms thank the Museum, in very small print, for permission to "adapt" Ruiz's version of the story.

The story is a lovely one—the Chumash people begin on Santa Cruz Island, become too crowded, and are led over a rainbow bridge to the mainland. Some of the people look down, become dizzy, and fall into the water, where the goddess Hutash quickly turns them into dolphins so they won't drown. In the Nechodom book, a young Chumash boy is told this legend by his grandfather; in the Wood book, the legend is told straight out, with a Chumash girl and boy as friends who take part in the "exodus" to the mainland.

Looking at the Ruiz version of the story in comparison to these two much more "polished" versions is interesting. Ruiz's first sentence is, "The first Chumash people were created on Santa Cruz Island. They were made from the seeds of a Magic Plant by the Earth Goddess, whose name was Hutash." This is given to us as fact—no doubts, no "once upon a time" framework, no elaborate creationism.

Wood's story begins,

> On the island of Limuw, where the heavens touch the sea, Hutash the earth goddess walked alone. The birds and sea lions, flowers and trees all were her friends, but still Hutash was not happy. The earth goddess longed to share her island home with people made in her own image.

Can you say "King James Version"? Suddenly what has been a factual historical event has become a retelling of the Christian creation story. The illustrations in this book are also rich oils, reminiscent of those "Tales from the Bible" books so popular when I was a child. The biblical tone is carried out throughout the book, as the story becomes more a "legend" and less a part of Chumash history.

The Nechodom book puts even more distance between the story and the telling of it by having a grandfather tell "legends." The storytelling is secondary to the reader's invitation to identify with Limuw (yes, the island's name is given to a person) as a regular kid who likes to swim, play with dolphins, hunt, and so on. In the accompanying illustrations, no one looks too friendly or happy; the human faces and expressions are almost obliterated. What I assume are Chumash petroglyphs are used as borders or backgrounds on many pages, I suppose to tell the reader that yes, this is a real Indian story with real Indian *stuff*. Such drawings are, however, sacred; to simply throw them into a children's book as decoration ignores their deeper, spiritual powers.

I wonder what it is about this story that draws non-Native authors and illustrators? Do they see a thin line between Indian and animal identity? This country has long likened Native peoples to "savages" or animals without souls or morals. Of course for us, the relationship between animals and humans is spiritual, and would never be seen as an insult. But for the dominant culture, a story in which Indians "fall" and become animals fits into the Christian fear of The Fall and all the religious symbolism inherent in an Edenic loss. Such a story also appeals to the more contemporary non-Native fetishising of marine mammals such as dolphins and whales, and thus fits in with an "ecological" mindset. Again, we regard animals as a form of "people," but this does not preclude a necessarily practical and spiritual relationship in which animals are hunted and eaten—with proper ritual and thanks, of course. At any rate, these two books frame a Native story in another people's worldview, which appropriates both the power of the original story as well as the validity of orality as real history. Not recommended.—*Deborah A. Miranda*

Neitzel, Shirley, *From the Land of the White Birch,* **illustrated by Daniel Powers (Ojibwe). River Road Publications (1997). 30 pages, b/w illustrations; grades 3-5; Ojibwe**

From the Land of the White Birch is a collection of three "retold" Ojibwe stories, or to be more precise, a mishmash of story elements from different peoples, and said to be Ojibwe. Neitzel does not credit her sources, but these stories bring to mind elements from Nanabosho (Ojibwe), Wisahkecahk (Cree), and Gluskabi (Abenaki) stories I have

heard. Further, rather than tell the stories of beings who sometimes appear to be humans with human foibles and sometimes can—and do—do remarkable things that change the Earth and her creatures, Neitzel's characters *are* humans. I wonder if she thinks that children are unable to comprehend stories of the supernatural? *Our* children have been doing just that for (at least) thousands of years. Besides, Neitzel's stories are very poorly written.

This storybook is accompanied by a teacher's guide, in which the Ojibwe are treated as a people of the past. The author presents her own, surely original, way of looking at things. Two examples:

"Storing food was a problem for the Indian people since they had no refrigerators or freezers." In the old days, storing food was *not* a problem. We dried food. We froze food. We ate fresh food.

"Today people enjoy visiting the beautiful hills and lakes where the Ojibwa lived." "People," as opposed to Ojibwe? We *still* live here.

The detailed lesson plans, suggesting such teaching activities as having children create their own "how and why" stories, teach nothing about our people—other than that our belief systems are trivial. Neitzel also suggests, presumably seriously, that children buy several kinds of nuts and dried fruits, mix them together, and "have an Ojibwa snack."

Very definitely not recommended.—*Barbara Potter*

Nelson, S.D. (Lakota), *Gift Horse,* **illustrated by the author. Harry N. Abrams (1999). Unpaginated, color illustrations; grades 3-up; Lakota**

"The thing I remember most from my early days is a horse....[S]he was the blue-gray color of a thunderstorm, and her back was a blur of white spots, like hailstones raining down." Foregone, that she would be named Storm. Horse and boy become as one; giving him his name, Flying Cloud. Surviving a blizzard together "taught me to think before acting." Pleased with that, Cloud's mother begins a Warrior's shirt for him. He cries for a vision, hunts buffalo, saves the life of a companion, participates in a raid on the Crow to get back stolen horses.

Flying Cloud and Storm shared many adventures.

> The one thing I will never forget from my early days, so long ago, is the horse with eagle feathers tied in her mane...I can still see the two of us riding across the endless prairies of our youth, like a hailstorm and a flying cloud.

The story moves in a circular fashion and has very much the sound of an old, old man telling it; lost for a little time in his memories. Nelson says it comes out of his wondering what it was like for his great-great grandfather whose name was Flying Cloud. His illustrations are full of color and motion, clearly conveying this young joy in his life, and all the things that made it wonderful for him. The pictures are not only of the adventures but also of the life of the People.—*Doris Seale*

Nez, Redwing (Diné), *Forbidden Talent*, "as told to" Kathryn Wilder, illustrated by Redwing Nez. Northland (1995). Unpaginated, color illustrations; grades 3-4; Diné (Navajo)

Ashkii lives with his grandparents on the Diné reservation, where his favorite thing to do is paint. He thinks about painting all the time, but his grandfather tells him that "painting for fun and frolic is forbidden" because it is "not the Navajo way." Ashkii, little reality tester that he is, challenges every taboo he comes across, paints everything that will hold still, wins a blue ribbon in an art contest, and finally gets his grandfather's approval.

Trying to figure out what part of this is Redwing Nez's story and what is Kathryn Wilder's muddled cross-cultural thinking is a puzzle, because there are so many things here that are just plain wrong.

The word "forbidden" is used throughout, even though it is not a word we use. It doesn't make any sense to tell a child not to paint unless a specific reason is given. We encourage our children to paint and express themselves creatively, which is different from copying sandpaintings or other things that might be part of our belief system.

Here are some more problems:

> "The Ancient Ones made too much art," [Grandfather] says, "and they are no longer here. Painting for fun and frolic is forbidden."

Here, Grandfather implies that the Ánaasází carvings were frivolous, and somehow that is connected to why they disappeared. On the contrary, these pictures were used as a form of communication, to tell stories, to impart history.

> Something calls from outside. Is it Coyote? The dogs don't bark. I hear it again. Owl? To the Diné, Owl is bringer of bad news....When morning comes, my cat yawns and stretches beside me. I stretch, too. "I guess Owl's message wasn't for me," I say. "I didn't have any bad dreams."

Coyotes don't call. Owls don't sound like coyotes. Owls don't bring "bad news." An owl heard in a particular way—not just hooting or flying by or through dreams—is a harbinger of death. This story indicates that Ashkii thinks the owl is bringing a message for him; he would have no way of knowing this.

Since "Owl came and nothing bad happened," Ashkii decides not to pray and to use clay for paint to see what the consequences might be. There are no consequences for painting with clay, and what's the point of deciding not to pray—to test his own powers, to see if Owl will go away, or stay? If the implication is that Owl is warning him of trouble, that's not Owl's job.

> Grandfather makes sandpaintings, and he is teaching me how. "It is the Navajo way," Grandfather says. "It serves a purpose, and helps to keep the universe in balance."

Children are not taught to make sandpaintings; it takes years of training and only certain people are taught. Sandpaintings are used for healing, not to "keep the universe in balance."

> The sheep and Yellow Dog drink from Owl Springs, but I'm forbidden to. An owl drowned in here a long time ago, making the water bad. But I heard Owl calling in the night and I didn't pray in the morning and nothing has happened. "I'm going to take a drink," I tell Yellow Dog.

This is absurd. There's not enough water on the reservation for an owl to drown in. Streams are just a few inches deep. There are wells, with covers so that nothing falls in. If the water is bad for some reason, everyone would know not to go there—including the animals.

It's quite possible that young Redwing Nez tried to paint designs on the animals, but it's highly unlikely that a sheep would stand still for such a thing. And a smiley face is hardly a Navajo design...

> I decide to climb up behind the spring, where the Cliff People lived—*Ánaasází*, Ancient Ones, we call them. Grandfather has told me not to go up there, because if I disturb the spirits of the Cliff People they may become angry....But I want to see the patterns they made on the pots. And today seems like a good day to go, since Owl called and I didn't pray and I drank the bad water and nothing has happened.

What does Ashkii think the "angry" spirits are going to do? Are they going to fight him? Are they going to throw something at him? People are taught to respect areas especially where the spirits are at, and you just leave them alone. It's not "forbidden," it's just that, out of honor and respect, you let it be.

> The next day, Grandfather and Grandmother leave for town while it is still dark....I take out my school watercolors and paint on paper and cardboard. I draw sheep and horses and dogs and my cat, who watches me...."When do you think Grandfather's coming home?" I say to her. "What would he say if he saw this?"....I hide the paintings. Outside, the sun is already high in the sky. I run to let the sheep out. They are hungry and thirsty, but none are sick. I am not sick either, but I am confused. I do everything forbidden and nothing bad happens.

A Diné child would not be left home alone. When people go someplace, they all go together. A grandfather, especially a medicine man, would not allow a child to feel unsafe, unclear about situations, or confused. He'd do everything he could to make a child comfortable.

Still testing, Ashkii goes outside and "brands" all the sheep with a branding iron dipped in paint. He even paints his grandfather's horse and chips designs into the side of a water tank. Finally, he 'fesses up to Grampa, whom he finds at home—painting.

> "The ability to draw and paint is a gift given by the Creator," Grandfather says. "It must be used wisely, for a purpose. Maybe for healing, maybe to show others the way of our people, maybe to earn money for a family." He pulls a small leather bundle from inside his shirt. "We offer thanks for all things, even for what we don't understand.

That is the Navajo Way. Today you may not understand why your talent is forbidden, but someday you will. Owl will be there to remind you to use it wisely."

I don't understand why his talent is forbidden, either. And Owl does not give understanding or approval—elders do.

> Today it is still dark when I get up....I don't want to wake Grandfather, yet. In the early light I see the shape of Mother Earth to the east. I think about how I will paint that someday, but right now I have something to do. I take Grandfather's leather bundle from inside my shirt. Yellow Dog leans against me in the dark as the wind scatters the cornmeal to the Four Directions....Inside, I touch Grandfather's shoulder. "Wake up, Grandfather. Today is a special day."

Say, what? It's still dark, then it's light, then it's dark again? Grandfathers are usually awake to greet the dawn; why is he still asleep? Typically, a bundle is made specifically for an individual, so how did Grandfather's bundle get inside Ashkii's shirt? Did he give Ashkii permission to use it or did Ashkii steal it? We offer corn pollen, not corn meal, to the morning light, so it wouldn't be dark when this happens. What's going on here? No wonder the kid's confused; I am, too.

"Forbidden" is a strong word for children. Usually, we model certain behaviors because they're respectful and we explain the natural consequences of negative behaviors. And we encourage children to develop their natural talents, rather than tell them that what they're doing is "forbidden."

In "A Note on the Story," Kathryn Wilder writes about Redwing Nez's development as an artist, and this paragraph is especially telling:

> While in government boarding school, Redwing became fascinated by the pictures he saw of famous artists and their art. What stood out most to him was that the artists had blue eyes. He thought his brown eyes were the reason he was forbidden to paint, and he considered his blue-eyed cat, as far as he knew the only one on the Reservation, sacred, and hoped her blue eyes would rub off on him.

Like many Indian children in residential schools, young Redwing Nez probably internalized the racism he experienced there. All the artists he studied had blue eyes. He had brown eyes. He was "forbidden" to paint. Was it because he had brown eyes instead of blue ones? Of course it was. Could Kathryn Wilder have taken Redwing Nez's story about being "forbidden" to paint at a residential school and made it into a preposterous story about a confused Diné child who is "forbidden" to paint by his grandfather because it's not "the Navajo Way"? If this is so, it would account for the plot centering on a non-existent tradition based on a made–up belief system. If this is so, it is unforgivable.

Redwing Nez's colorful oil paintings—and his story, whatever it might really have been—have been made into a mockery of Diné people and traditions.—*Linda Lilly*

Nicholson, Robert, *The Sioux: Facts, Stories, Activities*, illustrated by Maxine Hamil and Zoe Hancox. Chelsea House (1994). 32 pages, color photos and illustrations; grades 3-5; Lakota

This little book is difficult to review due to the astonishing amount of inaccuracies crammed into its thirty-two pages. Part of the "Journey Into Civilization" series, *The Sioux* is described as "a lively and fascinating introduction to the dramatic history of the Sioux. Full of interesting facts, detailed illustrations, and clear photographs, this book offers real insight into how the Sioux lived...."

Among the "detailed illustrations" is a two-page map, supposedly of North America, but actually of the U.S. with a little of Canada on one end and a little of Mexico on the other. In this whole area, there are only seventeen Native Nations named. One of them, Nez Percé, is illustrated with a figure of someone from the Northwest Coast with a totem pole.

The "clear photographs" add to the confusion. For instance, the traditional headdress is actually a contemporary one, replete with satin ribbons and beadwork; the cradleboard, described as "made from leather or wood" appears to have been made from quilled deerskin with a checked cotton-lined interior; and the moccasins, described as "often decorated with beadwork" are actually quilled.

The author has a propensity for superficial and hopelessly mangled "interesting facts." The Great Spirit is Wakan Tanka, not "Wakan Taka" and the Black Hills are Paha Sapa, not "Paka Sapa." The piece about the sweat lodge combines different rituals. To say that "[m]en would not eat for several days and sit inside the sweat lodge until they had a vision" is absurd. Sweat lodge is part of the *preparation* for hanbleceya; the vision quest does *not* take place *in* the sweat lodge—which serves more than one purpose in the life of the people. Nobody stays in the sweat lodge "for several days."

And, here is an example of the author's "insight":

> Nowadays the Sioux and other tribes are confined to small reservations. With few buffalo left, they have learned how to farm or are unemployed. Some try to live in traditional style, and make a living out of tourism. However, without room to wander, their old lifestyle has almost disappeared.

It would probably take thirty-two pages to say all that is wrong with this book, and on one level, it isn't worth thirty-two words. On another, of all the peoples who make up America's very unmelted pot, the least is known to the general population about the original inhabitants. With the series title, "Journey Into civilization," the tone is already set. The Dakota word wasicuna, "to civilize," based on the word for the white man, wasicu, does not imply becoming anything better than you were before, but simply to become white, or more like the white man—which is a very different thing.

The comments on the way in which Native peoples live today carry a number of distortions that will not be obvious to most students—and teachers—using this book. Not all "tribes" followed the buffalo; the "Sioux" are not "confined" to reservations "without room to wander." The alternative to buffalo is not either farming or unemployment. Many of the Lakota-Dakota-Nakota people—to give them their real names—live off-reservation a good share of the time, and all across this land, from New England to California. And are employed in as many kinds of work as the majority of the U.S. population. Living a traditional lifestyle and tourism are mutually exclusive. The traditional way of life is not a living museum for the edification of tourists. If by "old lifestyle," Nicholson means living in tipis, and wearing regalia every day, then yes, we don't do that. On the other hand, neither do white people still dress as in colonial times, live in log cabins—or use outhouses. As for our cultures and traditional beliefs, it is amazing how much of that is still with us, given the history—and most of us prefer to keep them to ourselves. This entry in the Chelsea Juniors Series contains neither bibliography nor author information, so one can only assume that Nicholson is either sublimely ignorant or venal. And there is this to consider: Someone wrote this. Two people illustrated it. Someone thought it was a good idea to publish. Someone drew up a marketing plan. And teachers are buying this book to use in classrooms.—*Doris Seale*

Orie, Sandra De Coteau (Oneida), *Did You Hear Wind Sing Your Name? An Oneida Song of Spring,* **illustrated by Christopher Canyon (Cherokee). Walker (1995). Unpaginated, color illustrations; preschool-3; Oneida**

In traditional ways of teaching, elders sometimes pose questions and children go off to find the "answers." This gentle, beautiful book teaches in just that way: taking us from morning to night, each two-page spread asks a question or two ("Did you see Sun's face in the Buttercup? And did you see Sky's blue in the wildwood Violets?") that evokes an image and invites children to stop and contemplate all the beauty of what is, even in the city, even in an "empty lot."

The illustrations, for the most part, are vibrant and lovely, despite the big-eyed bunny rabbit and the Bambi-like deer. I especially like the dewdrops on the snail's shell, violets and spider webs.

Simply, without polemic about "saving the environment," Orie has made a beautiful song of thanksgiving, a celebration of the circle of seasons and of life. As a read-to for very young children, this song teaches that Earth is sentient, Being is sentient.—*Beverly Slapin*

Osborne, Mary Pope, *Adaline Falling Star.* **Scholastic (2000). 169 pages; grades 3-5; Arapaho**

Told as a first person narrative, *Adaline Falling Star* is a fictionalized story about the mixed-blood young daughter of Kit Carson and an unnamed Arapaho woman. After her mother dies, the child is brought to live with abusive white relatives, escapes, and runs off to find her father.

From the very first paragraph, there are serious problems:

> The night I was born on Horse Creek, the sky rained fire. Dogs howled and growled. Arapaho warriors put on red war paint and did a death dance.

Why? Where did Osborne get this stuff?

Despite the fact that Indian people had complex social systems, sophisticated scientific knowledge, and spiritual and cultural beliefs that were as profoundly religious as any brought by the people who came here, Osborne has Adaline voicing sweeping generaliza-

tions about her own people, such as "The Indians do not have the knowledge of Science."

The words that Osborne has put into the mouth of this Arapaho girl have nothing to do with what the life of an eleven-year-old Indian girl would have been really like—not the thought forms, not the feelings, not the attitudes, not the speech patterns, and certainly not this ignorance of her own people.

Throughout, Osborne invents Indian verbiage, such as "Land-Behind-the-Stars," "Great Holy Spirit," "Rain Spirits," "Tree Spirits," and "Ghost Spirits." Among the Plains peoples, it was customary under certain circumstances to sacrifice skin as a prayer in times of great need. In order to advance the plot, Osborne has Adaline "mutilating" herself to express her grief. This was not something done by children.

And this is how Osborne, through Adaline, describes Sun Dance:

> I'd have to grow up and be a warrior—decorate my body with eagle feathers, dance the secret Sun Dance. Some of them torture themselves during the dance to show how brave they are. They hang themselves from a pole by leather thongs pulled through their chest muscles. I could do that. I'm brave enough.

Sun Dance is the central sacred ceremony of the Plains peoples. Its purpose is not to demonstrate bravery. It is a pledging, a sacrifice, a thank-offering for the good of the community. LaVera Rose (Lakota), also writing for children, says that Sun Dance "participants offer Wakantanka the greatest gift they have—their flesh and blood." This is something that young non-Native readers can understand. What they will come away with from Osborne's writing is that Indian people were and are the epitome of barbaric savagery.

In a positive novel about a Native child's finding her place in the world, it is possible to portray the settler mentality, their hatred of Indians, without resorting to an unrelenting barrage of racist terms, such as "evil," "devilish," "heathen," "sinning," "mongrel," "half-breed," "half-red," "half-Injun," "savage," "Injun," and "redskin," along with the many references to scalping and murder by Indians—and none by whites. It just takes empathy for Indian people, of which Osborne shows none.

One can only assume that the author's purpose in writing this book was to demonstrate again, as with so many other young adult novels about Native peoples, that European culture was in fact far superior to indigenous cultures and lifeways and therefore the destruction was justified. I can't imagine what other reason she would have had for writing this.—*Beverly Slapin*

Parish, Peggy, *Let's Be Indians!*, illustrated by Arnold Lobel. Harper & Row (1962). 96 pages, b/w illustrations; grades 1-3

My book is called *Lets Be Indians!* by Peggy Parish. This book is about crafts and projects you can make. One of the chapters in this book is called "Wampum" and in it she tries to explain about all "Indian's" money. She gives you three steps to make a wampum necklace using dyed purple macaroni. (A long time ago where the heck would they get the color purple?) On page 24 there's a chapter called "Moccasins" and in it there is a picture of a dog (with a feather and band on his head of course) chewing on a pair of socks. In this chapter she says to make "Indian" moccasins out of a pair of socks. The drawings in the book are done by Arnold Lobel.

This book's got so many stereotypes I can't believe it. What I don't like about the title is that it says "let's be Indians" but it doesn't say what kind. It's like there is just one kind of Indian, not Hopi, Apache, Karuk, Hoopa, Yurok and so many more I can't put down because it will take too long and my writing will be boring. Another reason why I don't like the title is because nobody can be an Indian who isn't. They can try, but they won't get very far. In the chapter "Headband" the author says, "One of the first things you need to be an Indian is a headband." I don't think a headband can make you Indian.

The cover picture is worse. It has three kids, each with feathers sticking out of a headband. Even a dog sitting next to them has a feather and band. They all have a blanket wrapped around them. I don't have a blanket wrapped around me all the time and I'm Indian. I don't like the other pictures in the book because all the people in the pictures have a headband and fathers and bare feet. I don't have bare feet all the time.

The things in the book you can make are stereotyping Native Americans and as you read it she makes it sound like there are no more Native Americans living. On page 29 in the chapter called "Corn" it says, "The Indians USED corn in many ways. One thing they USED it for was for making jewelry." I don't like it when she uses the word "used" because to me it sounds like there are no more Indian people. I'm Karuk and I know people from my tribe that still use burden baskets to put acorns in, but she says on page 32 that "Indian women USED TO gather roots, nuts and berries."

Where does the author get this information?!!!! She says that it is important for Indians to walk quietly because if they were hunting the animals would go away and they would have no meat. If a white man was walking trying to get meat wouldn't he have to walk quietly, too?

In the chapter "Pottery" on page 38 the author says, "Indians made their dishes and pots from clay." All Native Americans don't make their dishes and pots from clay. I know some do, but she says "Indians" do.

Some of the chapters in this book are "Bow," "Arrows," "Quiver," "Tomahawk," "Shield." I wonder if the author thinks that these are the most important things for any Native American. I don't know anything about shields or tomahawks because those things are things from different tribes, NOT MINE.

Think about what this lady said on page 49:

> The Indians believed that illnesses were caused by evil spirits. To cure an illness, the medicine man danced around the person who was sick, singing a chant, and wearing as scary a mask as possible. He hoped this would chase away the evil spirits.

Judge for yourself, but I just want to tell you that to me this sounds like medicine men just sort of hope all the time and don't really do anything. It sounds like she doesn't really believe in what they do.

This lady wrote this book a long time ago I know, but then I ask why is it still around and in our school library? The author makes me feel like she is making fun of Indians because when I read it I feel like she is making fun of me.

This book is disgraceful and stupid and mean towards Native Americans and it gives people false information on Native Americans. To people that like this book and believe it I feel sorry for you.—*Nisha Supahan*

Paulsen, Gary, *The Night the White Deer Died.* Delacorte (1990). 104 pages; grades 6-up

Janet, a fifteen-year-old white girl who lives with her mother in a New Mexico artists' community, is haunted by the recurring dream of an Indian "brave"—"a warrior out of time, from before, with a shield and a small fighting headdress and no clothes except for a breechclout"—standing poised, ready to shoot a white deer drinking from a pool of water in the moonlight.

There are few characters in this book, none of them developed. There's Julio, a Chicano student who likes Janet, maybe. He's described as "arrogant" four times in this book ("his eyes were arrogant, black and distant"), although he doesn't say or do anything to warrant that description. Actually, he doesn't say or do anything at all, except hand Janet a pitcher of iced tea on a hot day. We know he's Chicano because he's called "macho," and he doesn't use contractions. "It is for you," he says, handing Janet the iced tea.

Then there's Janet's mother. She's a sculptor, chink, chink, chinking away while Janet is busy with her fantasies and teenage angst. She doesn't say much, except for an occasional "Is there something you want to tell me, dear?"

Then there's fifty-three-year-old Billy Honcho. We don't know his Nation, but we know he's a real Indian because he refers to himself as "Indi'n" and says "tscha" a lot. Also, he's an alcoholic, begging wine money from tourists: "Wanna take a picture of an Indi'n?...Good picture of Indi'n...blanket, braids, everythin'."

> He looked indescribably old and filthy, with a blanket wrapped around his head and upper body that had once been flannel but now looked like greased canvas. The wrinkles in his face were caked with dirt, as were his fingernails, and his eyes had the deep red-yellow that comes from acute alcoholism, and as she studied him out of the corner of her eye, he started to lean-fall over her.

Janet takes him home along with a stray dog she picks up and, over the mild objections of her mother, feeds them both. Thus begins a strange friendship.

Strange writing, too.

> That was before Janet met Billy and learned of wars that never were but should have been fought by braves that never existed except in dreams; before she learned that all things beautiful are sometimes ugly and that many ugly things are just waiting for beauty to come to them.

Janet and Billy and the dog hang out together. At some point she realizes that Billy is the "brave" in her dream "because of the look she'd seen in his eyes." He sends her a "kachina" that he says he won in a poker game with a Hopi. He sings a "Navajo rain chant" ("Hey-*uh*, hi-*uh*, hopa-*hi*, hey-*uh*"). He takes her home to his pueblo. He shows up in the middle of the night, dressed in full Plains regalia:

> He was a warrior, dressed in buckskins bleached white and made whiter by the moon and covered with such intricate beadwork that it looked painted on the leather, with a chest shield of quills and

beads in the shape of an eagle with wings outstretched, and all down the length of each sleeve was a ribbon of quills and more beads. His braids were clean and braided with leather strapping worked into the hair and bits of ermine fluff at the ends, and on his back in a case was a short bow and a few arrows, and he was more than beautiful, more than stunning. He was something from the past, something real and alive from the past of all men...the flute music ended and the flute came down, and he disappeared like a part of the moonlight.

Well, Janet's mother knows what *that* means, because she read it in a book ("the flute and the finery definitely mean courting. It's an old ritual, the way braves have always courted maidens."). The next night, he shows up in the same outfit, this time with two ponies. They go off together.

They ride to a mountain somewhere. He tells her a story:

> It is the ritual story always told in courtship between a young brave and the maiden who rode his pony.... Now we would sit for a day and another night, and I would go and kill a deer, and you would eat of it, and when we went down the mountain, we would be married.

Oh.

Then he tells her more stories. They are truly remarkable. I do not mean this in a good way. Then she realizes she loves him.

> She loved him. Not so much him, and it was not so much gushy love, but she loved what he was when he told the story, loved not just what he was but what he should have been, loved what he could have been if the time had been right for him.

Then he sends her away. Then she goes home and has that dream again, only this time the "brave" kills the doe, and both disappear.

The jacket describes this book as a "timeless love story fraught with spiritual connections." In other words, the author may have intended all this to mean something. Beats me what.—*Beverly Slapin*

Penner, Lucille Recht, *A Native American Feast*, Macmillan (1994). 99 pages, illustrated with prints, woodcuts, and drawings; grades 3-up

A Native American Feast is a soup of historical snippets, "charming" legends, quaint and curious culinary customs, reworked recipes and bad writing.

I've never heard this woman talk, mind you, but she reminds me of a teacher I once had as a child. She had a way, by raising her voice to an almost operatic pitch, of pretending to make the most boring lesson sound exciting. Well, Penner does it too, in writing. For instance, after the obligatory paragraph about buffalo disappearing and Indians dying, along with their traditions, she says cheerily, "But *one* tradition that survived was *cooking* and eating *special foods*." (Italics *mine*.)

Her "quaint and curious culinary customs" are going to seem pretty yucky to child readers. Here is a delightful sampling; they may have a little trouble equating all this with the statement that "We are the heirs of Native American cooks who were the first to prepare some of our favorite foods."

> Slices of raw buffalo liver, dipped in the salty juices of the beast's gall-bladder, were considered a great treat.

> [C]aribou eyes were a special treat, usually saved for the children...

> The Cheyenne loved nothing better than a fat puppy, nicely boiled.

> Some tribes cooked ants together with berries and pine-sap....Caterpillars and crickets were eaten raw or roasted. Other people collected the larvae of flies, dried them, and cooked them in soup....Cherokee cooks made soup of yellow jacket grubs, fat, and water. Beetles, locusts, wasps in the comb, fleas, and even lice were added to soups and stews.

> [T]hey gathered worms, pinched off an end, and squeezed out the insides. Then they braided the worms, baked them in pits, and finally fried them to make a popular dish.

> Plains women also cooked food in the stomach of a freshly killed buffalo. They filled it with meat, berries, and water and hung it over the fire. After serving as a pot for several meals, the stomach began to fall apart. When that hapened, the cook simply served it, along with its contents, at the next meal. Sometimes the emptied body of a whole animal was used as a storage or cooking container.

Luther Standing Bear, writing in 1928, has a slightly different perspective on this:

> After all the soup and meat was cleaned out of the bag, it was then cut up and eaten. This was a great saving in dishwashing, as there were no pots to wash and our dishes were very few.[1]

For the history, in that voice again,

> The first Americans were always on the move, looking for things to eat. They hunted animals and gathered wild plants. They knew which greens and roots were best, and which nuts, seeds, and berries. When all the nearby food was eaten, they had to find a new home. Slowly, people figured out that they didn't have to chase their food. They could make food come to them. They could grow it!

This is condescending as hell—and inaccurate. Not all Native peoples were nomadic. Many had been agriculturists for centuries. And the first Europeans to reach these shores would hardly have survived without Native knowledge and generosity. Penner's bibliography includes "scholarly" items such as Reader's Digest's *America's Fascinating Indian Heritage*. So we know she didn't just make this stuff up....

The problem, of course, is that Penner, in the tradition of much "multicultural" writing, shows no respect for peoples and worldviews other than her own. The point is not that the world's peoples did not and do not eat differently from one another. The point is that a people's legends, lifeways, spirituality, intelligence and ethics, are not stuff to be trifled with, disrespected, served up in such a book and handed to children as truth. Not recommended.—*Beverly Slapin*

NOTE

1 Standing Bear, Luther, *My People the Sioux*. University of Nebraska, 1975, p. 22.

Philip, Neil, ed., *A Braid of Lives: Native American Childhood.* **Clarion (2000). 82 pages, b/w photos; grades 5-up**

British writer Neil Philip's collection of childhood reminiscences is a second compilation of Native oratory, writing and archival prints. As with his first collection, these are for the most part from the early 20th Century, and predominately from western Nations.

It seems that an effort has been made to pair illustrations with narratives; many of the photos reflect the Nation or at least the region of the speakers, and some are well matched to the story. For instance, Luther Standing Bear's story of how he was given an American name is appropriately paired with a photo of Carlisle students in math class, and Zitkala-Sa's story of how she resisted the cutting of her hair is paired with the infamous "before-and-after" pictures of Apache youngsters at Carlisle.

But making heavy use of Edward S. Curtis's prints such as "Offering the buffalo skull" and "The morning bath" have nothing to do with the text, and many of the other photos are contrived as well. There is a photo of two little boys, probably under three years of age, sitting atop a Hopi dwelling. One is holding an adult-sized bow and arrows and looking straight at the camera. The caption reads, "The sentinels." Two other photos show young children wearing full Plains headdresses; one is called "A Cheyenne warrior of the future." There are no words from Geronimo in this book, but there is a photo of Geronimo wearing European-style clothing, paired with a Chiricahua story about disciplining children by calling in a "fierce-looking" old man. Geronimo loved children and would never have done anything to hurt or terrify any of them.

The Indian Nations are identified first with the names by which they are commonly known, which is often a corruption of a derogatory name given to them by enemies, and only then by their real names. Similarly, the Indian speakers and writers are usually identified first by their English names and then by their Indian names. It would have made more sense—and would have been more respectful—to have used their own Indian names first.

The narratives and writings themselves do give an interesting picture of traditional childhoods and worldviews different from those of the readers for whom this book was probably intended. Paired with the available portraits of many of the speakers themselves, this book might have been more than a standard treatment of old-time postcard-Indians. For a more real picture of what it was and is like to be a Native child, Patricia Riley's excellent anthology, *Growing Up Native American* (Morrow, 1993) would be a better choice.—*Beverly Slapin*

Philip, Neil, *Weave Little Stars Into My Sleep: Native American Lullabies*, photographs by Edward S. Curtis. Clarion, 2001. Unpaginated, b/w photos; kindergarten-grade 2

Neil Philip has made a career out of mining versions of Indian "myths and legends," songs and prayers that he's found in old anthropological collections, rewriting them and combining them with old Curtis photos for the benefit of young white readers and their white teachers who will think there is something of value here. They will be wrong. Philip says in his notes to this book,

> In adapting lullabies for this book, from the great wealth available, I have allowed myself some liberties with the source material....In some places I have added material that is merely implied in the original, or...have reworked the sense of the original into English verse. But I have tried not to transgress the spirit or the meaning of any of the source texts.

Attempts notwithstanding, he failed. An especially egregious example of what Philip has done can be seen in what he calls a Hopi "Owl Kachina Song," a "free rendering" of a "lullaby" from Natalie Curtis's "free English translation" in *The Indians' Book* (1907). This is how it goes:

> Owls, owls,
> Big owls and small,
> Are staring
> And glaring,
> Children, at you all!
> Listen to them hooting,
> Tu-whit, tu-whoo.
> Look up from your cradle boards—
> They are looking at you.
> What are they saying?
> This is what they are saying:
> "If you cry,
> Old Yellow-Eyes will come,
> Old Yellow-Eyes will come
> And gobble you up."
> What else are they saying?
> This is what they're saying:
> "If you're naughty,
> Old Yellow-Eyes will come,
> Old Yellow-Eyes will come
> And swallow you whole."
> So sleep, children, sleep,
> Sleep and never cry
> For the Old Yellow-Eyes
> Will pass you by.

According to a Hopi friend, this is not a traditional song. A Katsina song is not a lullaby, and this is neither. You're not supposed to have babies in the vicinity of Katsinam, he said, because you don't want to have new life disturbed by these powerful spirits. It's like leaving children around uncapped medicine and then singing about how pretty the little aspirins are, and how good they taste.

In the Hopi belief system, the Katsinam represent power and medicine and you don't lull babies to sleep by scaring them to death. Women don't sing like that and women aren't part of the Katsinam environment. And finally, Hopis don't use cradleboards.

Any self-respecting professor of folklore would flunk a college student for trying to get away with this kind of stuff. Way not recommended.—*Beverly Slapin*

Pielle, Sue (Sliammon), with Anne Cameron, *T'aal: The One Who Takes Bad Children*, illustrated by Greta Guzek. Harbour (1998). 26 pages, b/w illustrations; grades 3-5; Sliammon

The "One Who Takes Bad Children," the One who lurks in the forest beyond the village, away from the cultural world, is ready to devour children who stray. Such is the universal theme of this collaboration between Cameron and Sliammon storyteller Sue Pielle. This story is a retelling of a traditional legend about how mosquitoes came into being as a result of the slaying of that One by the children she had imprisoned.

The story centers on a brother and sister sent by their parents to fetch the grandmother to help their mother with the birth of their sibling, now on the way. The sister and brother are caught in the woods by that One and brought to where It has imprisoned other children who have violated cultural custom, that is, were "bad." But these children had been instructed to violate custom by their parents as a life-saving necessity. While it does not save them from that One's power initially, their resourcefulness and cooperation brings the death of that One, freedom for the captured children and a reunification of the family.

This text does not distinguish well between types of "bad." It is possible that oral renditions by Pielle effectively draw these distinctions but the issue of "bad" as a relativistic cultural/moral evaluation may be questionable without a cultural interpretation. The black-and-white illustrations are crude and unattractive. The children are illustrated as distressed for most of the story and even when they are happy they look pained. The message of this story is confounded: good can come out of bad and bad can come out of good. But the cultural hows are not explicated. Pielle's cultural storyline comes through strongly in the collaboration, especially in bringing forward the ungendered nature of legendary figures such as *The One Who Takes Bad Children*, which has been a problem for Cameron in earlier works. But this text is still dominated by Cameron's literary style. It is hoped that future work by Pielle would allow her Sliammon voice to be better heard.—*Marlene R. Atleo/ʔeh ʔeh naa tuu kwiss*

Plain, Ferguson (Ojibwe), illustrated by the author. Pemmican. Unpaginated, color illustrations; grades 2-up; Ojibwe:
Amikoonse (Little Beaver), **1993**
Eagle Feather—An Honour, **1989**
Grandfather Drum, **1994**
Little White Cabin, **1992**
Rolly's Bear, **1996**

I always feel like I'm having a personal visit with Ferguson Plain when I read his books. "Grandfather always shared his stories," he begins *Grandfather Drum,*

> when Mother Earth was preparing for her long sleep and all the animals of the forest were getting ready for hibernation....I always enjoyed the cool months because...Grandfather would sit beside his wood stove...I would sit with him and listen for hours.

All of these stories demonstrate how we respect our elders,

how social relationships develop between a young person and an old person, and how traditions are passed on from generation to generation. The black-and-white pen-and-ink illustrations of elder and child foreground the detailed, complex backgrounds in which animal spirits both observe and become part of the story. In some of the stories, as the child, now a man, remembers his elder, the elder is portrayed as present in the child's memory—he has shape and form, just not substance.

Merged with the personal tellings of Plain's memories are some of the lessons he learned as he became an Ojibwe man. I found many opportunities to talk about my own family's Ojibwe world view as I read Plain's books to my niece and nephew one lazy summer afternoon as we sat resting from the heat and activity of our day together. The stories, as well as the detailed illustrations, inspired questions and thoughts from my eight-year-old nephew and nine-year-old niece, whose usual questions focus more on "why?" and "how come?" But their questions and our discussions, as we read Plain's books, were thoughtful and complex. We talked about the ability of music to calm. We talked about the influence of grandparents in our lives. We talked about how powerful we feel when someone in our lives honors us and spends time with us. We talked about what it is to share stories about our lives. There is something very special about an author whose work creates such meaningful opportunities between adults and children.

I have read Ferguson Plain's books with mixed groups and have had the same opportunities for thoughtful dialogue, though I needed to provide a bit more detailed information and answer questions about the Ojibwe ways of seeing the world. These are books that should be read thoughtfully in situations where everyone can examine the illustrations carefully to take in their great depth.—*Pam Martell*

Amikoonse, the Little Beaver, had always lived with the boy. They were great friends. They went everywhere together, and Amikoonse had never known any other way of life. Then one day, while Grandfather was telling stories, an open front door presented an opportunity that he could not resist, and Amikoonse ran.

The story tells how Amikoonse finds himself lost in a world that is far different than he had known, and how he finally comes to his own place of belonging. It is no cute little retold animal "legend," and much of the meaning is carried in the powerful illustrations. Plain is an accomplished artist, who continues to grow in stature. *Amikoonse* is a good addition to his work.—*Doris Seale*

Polacco, Patricia, *Boat Ride with Lillian Two Blossom*, illustrated by the author. Philomel (1988). Unpaginated, color illustrations; grades 2-4

Polacco says this tale—of two human kids and a goat taken for a rowboat ride in the sky by "an old Indian lady who lived in the woods"—is a story her father had told her and her brother when they were children: "It was a moment and a story that have always been with me."

There's not much to the story; the illustrations are attractive. On the flying ride, Lillian Two Blossom, who has come from nowhere, and whom the kids describe as "ancient" and "mussed up" with a "raspy" voice, suddenly becomes young, her hair and clothes become much more fashionable, and her voice, "soft and soothing." She shows the children various sky animals: "great spirit fish" who make it rain, "unseen wolves" whose howl is the "voice of the wind," "spirit caribou" who carry the sun, raccoon-ish creatures who bring the night, and the "polar-bear spirit" who carries the moon. Then the boat comes down and she's "ancient again in her mussed-up clothes." Then she disappears again.

For all its cultural authenticity, Lillian Two Blossom could have been "an old Armenian lady who lived in the woods" or "an old Dutch lady who lived in the woods" or "an old guy who arrived long ago in a flying saucer." Too bad she wasn't. The story has nothing to do with any Native reality, including our spiritual lives. And it's especially disrespectful to our elders.

In a prefatory note, Polacco seems to be saying that Michigan is a state rich in Indian lore, because there are a lot of Native place names. Actually, Michigan holds only a few surviving bands on tiny reservations, whose land and almost all their culture had been stolen by the time of the author's father. The author considers "an old Indian lady who lived in the woods" an exotic hook to hang a kid story on, and give it a pretense of reality, because Indians once lived in Michigan. Maybe an old Indian lady did live somewhere around, doubtless not doing any too well unless she had grandchildren to take care of her needs.

This book is a sad departure for an author who has done a number of beautifully presented titles for young children. Perhaps having stepped out of her own culture was the problem. Not recommended.—*Paula Giese*

Pollock, Penny, *The Turkey Girl: A Zuni Cinderella Story*, illustrated by Ed Young. Little Brown & Co. (1996). Unpaginated, color illustrations; grades 2-4; Zuni

In today's classrooms, teachers use Native American "myths and legends" to teach about Native American peoples. Unfortunately, most of what is published provides children with additional misinformation. Pollock's story about Turkey Girl is a good example. Subtitling it "A Zuni Cinderella" and changing important details of the told story—a story, by the way, much older than the European "Cinderella" story—make this children's book appealing to a large segment of American society, but it is worse than worthless as a vehicle to learn about the Zuni people.

Pollock makes her protagonist a dirty, poor, outcast orphan who lives alone and is treated as a detested servant by the people in the village. In the story as told by the Zuni people, she is not an orphan, she does not live alone, and she is not detested. Instead, she lives in the village with her sisters who care about her. These are not small changes Pollock has made; they are significant ones that completely change the values and worldview of the Zuni people.

In doing so, Pollock presents the Zuni as a society with a hierarchical class system that doesn't care for its children. In reality, there may be differences in wealth, but there isn't arrogance and mistreatment of those who have less. And the concept of "orphan" does not exist in the Pueblo cultures. Children are born into extended families. If a child's parents die, there are grandmas and grandpas, aunties and uncles, brothers and sisters, all of whom continue to be the child's family.

This is only a little of what Pollock gets wrong in her retelling. There is much more that could be included here such as relationship between humans and animals, social gatherings, responsibility, and land formations—all of which she changes to make her version of the Turkey Girl story mirror Cinderella.

Pollock cites the work of Frank Hamilton Cushing, a white ethnologist who lived among the Zuni in the late 1800s, as the source for her story. Had she done her homework, she would have read the scholarship critical of Cushing, some of which is directed at his romanticizing of the Zuni language. Pollock uses the same romantic prose throughout her retelling, but at least Cushing didn't change Zuni culture and worldview in his version in the ways that Pollock has.

Teachers have options today about what they bring into their classrooms, and Pollock's book should not be one of them. Instead, look for "Turkey Girl" in Pablita Velarde's collection, *Old Father Storyteller* (Clear Light, 1989). She is from San Ildefonso Pueblo, where they also have a Turkey Girl story, and she is faithful to it and her people in her telling. You can also read "Turkey Maiden," in *The Zunis: Self-Portrayals*, by the Zuni People (University of New Mexico, 1972). This volume contains stories from the major Zuni storytellers in their language, translated into English by tribal member Alvina Quam. Another Zuni version is "The Girl Who Took Care of the Turkeys," told by Zuni tribal member Walter Sanchez, translated by Dennis Tedlock, a scholar of Zuni oral tradition, in Tedlock's Finding the Center (University of Nebraska, 1972). No Disney fluff here, just an Indian way of seeing the world.—*Debbie A. Reese*

Pollock, Penny, *When the Moon Is Full: A Lunar Year*, illustrated by Mary Azarian. Little, Brown (2001). Unpaginated, color illustrations; kindergarten-grade 3

A lunar year has thirteen full moons, but Pollock's "lunar year" has only twelve full moons, to correspond with the months of the Roman calendar. If this isn't confusing enough, she bestows so-called "traditional Native American names" on each of the twelve full moons, to five of which she adds sometimes bizarre, always sweeping, generalizations about Native peoples. For instance, January is allegedly called "the Wolf Moon," which Pollock explains by saying, "Native Americans believed that wolves became restless in January." Where did she get this?

Tying this all together is an assortment of stupefyingly amateurish short poems. For example,

> Full moons come,
> full moons go,
> softening nights
> with their silver glow.

> They pass in silence,
> all untamed,
> but as they travel,
> they are named.

Now, the idea of wild untamed moon(s) seems a little incongruous, since our moon is a large hunk of rock, so it has to be assumed that Pollock just needed something to rhyme with "named." Also, we only have one moon, so this "full moons come, full moons go" just adds to the confusion.

Azarian's hand-colored woodcut illustrations feature big-eyed animals with human expressions in contemporary scenes. Only one shows humans—two generic figures, facing away from the reader, holding hands and looking at the moon.

Bringing up the rear is a question-and-answer section, framed by a generic "Indian" design. One wonders, for instance, where Pollock got this one:

> Why do full moons have names? The Native Americans kept time by the Moon. They knew that every month had a full moon, so "many moons" meant many months. They chose names that reflected something special about each of these time periods. The elders passed along the names, mainly through storytelling.

The question-and-answer format here is especially misleading because it carries a false sense of authenticity. So young readers, rather than being motivated to think critically, are simply handed questions and—wrong answers.—*Beverly Slapin*

Prusski, Jeffrey, *Bring Back the Deer*, illustrated by Neil Waldman. Harcourt Brace Jovanovich (1988). Unpaginated, color illustrations; grades 2-4

It is winter. The boy's family awaits his father's return from hunting. There is a new baby in the lodge. The boy's grandparents are also there. The mother is worried.

There is very little food. "'I will hunt,' said the boy, trying to sound brave. 'I will bring back the deer.'" There is ritual preparation and advice. The boy is sent out. "*Winter*, he thought. *Tonight* I face it alone." He sees the wolf and follows it. The wolf leads him to the deer. Faster and faster he runs, until he realizes he *is* a deer. "*In one great leap....I, I am across. Running....Running on four legs! My antlers cradling the moon. Cradling the moon as I run.*" He finds himself outside the lodge. The wolf and the buck are standing there. When his mother reaches out to the wolf, it is a human hand she touches, not the paw of a wolf.

According to the jacket copy, Jeffrey Prusski is a computer programmer, "but his real interest has always been in 'learning to see the magical potential in the world.'" Apparently in his search, he has come across the idea of shape-shifters; for this book, he has created a whole family of them. We know that his grandmother is an owl, because she sits, "Watching everything. Like an owl, her head would turn, and her eyes would see. Even in darkness." And also because in the illustration, she is pictured with a barn owl sitting on her head.

The belief that certain people can take on animal shape is as old as humanity. *Bring Back the Deer* is Prusski's romantic, pseudo-poetic imagination of how this might be. His choice of an Indian setting might be because he thinks we are the only people left who are "primitive" enough for this. (He is a member of the Society for Creative Anachronism.)

Any knowledge of *actual* "ancient ritual," preparation for such an initiation, or what shape-shifting means in Native cultures, is totally absent. Practical realities: In a Northern Woodlands winter, dressed as he is, this child would freeze to death, particularly after he falls into a frozen stream. No capote—no outer wrap of any kind—nothing on his head, nothing on his hands. We're tough, but not *that* tough. But he sure looks pretty. Long, flowing black hair, long orange-trimmed scarf to match his wind band. And Neil Waldman's pictures *are* pretty; Peter Max-1960s, flower-child-new-age pretty; long flowing lines; bare, coal black trees against pastel snows, clouds and skies. Not very Indian, but pretty.

You know, one thing I'm wondering about: what *did* they eat?—*Doris Seale*

Purdy, Carol, *Nesuya's Basket*. Roberts Rinehart/Council for Indian Education (1997). 110 pages; grades 4-6; Maidu

Another classic literary move by non-Native writers: the first-person account of a "traditional" pre-invasion or contact experience. I'm not sure why this is such an attractive literary device, especially if the story is a recreation of the racial and inherently sexual violence of invasion and violation. The argument that authors have some sort of poetic license doesn't hold much water when the same authors are also banking on a certain level of authenticity from their historical research and ethnological/anthropological style. In other words, these kinds of books want to have their cake and eat it too: they want the freedom of fiction, but they also want the readers to feel they've had an authentic peek into an unfamiliar culture.

There are Native customs that can be observed and reported; but there is no way to know the interior life of a member of a community, culture and time period to which you have never belonged. To write a book like this is purely a leap of imagination and cannot be anything else. Thus, a book such as *Nesuya's Basket* veers wildly (and to me, ridiculously) between ethnological detail and "explanation" of Maidu culture and customs, and a totally fictitious internal monologue that Purdy has decided to appropriate for a young Maidu woman.

The biographical information asserts that Purdy's "interest in the natives of California began when she learned that the circular depressions near her home were remains of Indian houses." As with many non-Native enthusiasts, Purdy chose to create her own vision of the past, rather than deal with the more difficult questions of the present and future. The romanticism of the story—which involves feuding women, adolescent romance, traumas of declining elders (a symbol of the "vanishing Indian"), and unfaithful wives—sounds more like a modern-day American soap opera than the workings of a successful society. I am not an expert on Maidu history or culture, so the most I can say is that Purdy seems to have done quite a bit of research in the typical anthropological databases. What she's done with that data is another story.

However, Purdy's preface gives "fact" after "fact" without telling us where these "facts" spring from, and in fact no references are given anywhere for the hundreds of statements such as, "The Maidu believed the epidemic was caused by poison air sent through the valley by a shaman of the neighboring Sierra Miwok tribe..." Where did Purdy come up with this "fact"? Whose data is she using—a huge question—and how reliable or encompassing is that data? When was it gathered? Under what circumstances? From whom? In what language? By presenting such a statement in her authority as "author" to the children reading this book, Purdy performs a very complex move in the continuing colonization of the mind. When Purdy writes, "The Maidu *believed*," she disallows the Maidu any intellect or powers of analysis. They *believed*—an act without volition or care, almost instinctual, requiring no rationale—and furthermore, what they believed is patently obvious as primitive, childish, magical thinking. *Poison air*? How can we translate what that phrase might mean in the original language, the connotations, the history, the expertise of the person passing the phrase on? Would a Native informant have told a white anthropologist that she actually believed the whites were responsible for such a disease? Who is Purdy to use such a phrase with no background information? The over-simplification is staggering.

But my argument is not that non-Natives can never write about Natives. Instead, I argue that writers who are fascinated by another culture (Purdy says she was "hooked") are able to write most accurately from the point of view and perspective they know best—*their own*. There is no reason Purdy cannot research and write about her own fascination with the Maidu "remains" she found near her house. Obviously it made her think; but did it make her ask questions of herself, such as: *How do I feel about living on colonized land? What happened to the people who lived here? Do they have descendents who might be interested in these remains? What can I write about this experience that is authentically from within myself, rather than a projection of what I think happened?* These kinds of questions would help produce work that is both beautiful and honest—Purdy's skill as a writer is clear—without the taint of voyeurism and appropriation that continue to plague first-person "In-dian" accounts. If good intentions are what drive the authors of such books, then surely the effort to ex-amine one's own cultural limitations *and* advantages is well worth doing. Despite these good intentions, I can-not recommend this book for either Native or non-Native children.—*Deborah A. Miranda*

Raczek, Linda Theresa, *The Night the Grandfathers Danced*, illustrated by Katalin Olah Ehling. Northland (1995). Unpaginated, color illustrations; grades 3-4; Ute

Autumn Eyetoo is very exited. She is going to participate in the Bear Dance for the first time, and she is all dressed up. But nobody will dance with her. She is very upset: "It just wasn't fair!...The beautiful clothes she had been so proud of now felt dusty and hot." Oh, misery, a wallflower! When Autumn notices the very old men of the tribe, she decides it would be an honor to dance with one of them. Her friends tell her nobody does that, but being the independent little feminista that she is, "Autumn faced them with fierce eyes," and off she goes. "Her first Bear Dance had begun—the one her people would remember as the Night the Grandfathers Danced."

I don't know how old you need to be to do the Ute Bear Dance, and I wonder if the Cat Man is seen as a humorous figure, but I guess Raczek does know some things about it. Except for the author's note, the only reference

to the nature of the Dance is made when the old women try to push the young girls into joining it: "Autumn blushed. She was still a young girl, and had no plans to get married yet."

The illustrations, done in batik, are technically accomplished—and awful. Some attempt has been made to show authentic dress, but the people resemble those life-size, folk-art dolls that you see here and there, and they all have faces like Cabbage Patch dolls. All the faces are uniformly dark reddish brown. In fact, that seems to be the predominant color, along with other autumnal shades—which seems odd for an event that takes place in the spring. I am puzzled as to why someone thought this was a good idea.—*Doris Seale*

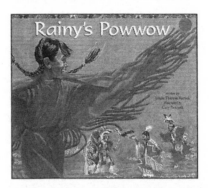

Raczek, Linda Theresa, *Rainy's Powwow*, illustrated by Gary Bennett. Rising Moon/Northland (1999). Unpaginated, color illustrations; grades 3-4

Rainy's Powwow is described as a "tale of self-discovery and acceptance." And that it is—in a convoluted way—about a girl's searching for her own style of dance at the "Thunderbird Powwow." On the inside flap of the dust cover, we are told that this "engaging story celebrates a vanishing way of life." From beginning to end, *Rainy's Powwow* just doesn't work. It just doesn't have the rhythm it purports to have found, and thus becomes another example of how not to write about Native peoples.

Lorraine—"Rainy"—is worried that she will never find her own style of dance, and will therefore never be given her ceremonial Indian name. So she goes around to several dancers and asks them how they feel about their particular dances. They tell her. Finally, an eagle feather drops, it is determined that the eagle feather is for Rainy, the Powwow Princess names Rainy "White Plume Dancing," and Rainy finds her dance.

From the introduction, to Grandmother White Hair and Uncle Eagle's soaring, through Rainy's quest for her dance style, finding it, and then receiving her name, the writing is stilted with stereotypical description, and the dialogue is belabored:

"When I dance," [Grandmother White Hair] said, "I am filled with reverence for Mother Earth. I walk slowly, with great respect. My moccasins touch the ground so tenderly, *touch-step, touch-step*. I carry the fan of sacred eagle feathers like a living being and offer my prayers for all the world."

In fact, all thirteen pages of text struggle so hard for authenticity that it seems that every word is trying to teach us something. (I hate stuff like this. Even my ten-year-old told me the story didn't make sense.)

Yet the teaching is, for the most part, wrong. Even the main premise—that Rainy "didn't' come from a powwow family" and had no "relatives who could help her learn to dance" is wrong. Powwows are gatherings of a community in which relations are reckoned by more than blood—there would most likely be someone in the community who would take on the responsibility of being Rainy's "auntie," who would make her outfit and teach her to dance and bring her into the circle. Who made the outfit she's wearing? And the part about Rainy's being named by the Powwow Princess is ridiculous— that's not how a young woman, or anyone, is given a name. Name giving is a very big deal. It would not be done on the spot, with no preparation. There is usually an honor dance. There is usually a giveaway.

Children grow into understanding of terms and concepts if these are used correctly and often. Here, the author (and/or editor) probably felt that young readers would not understand certain terms like veterans, regalia, outfits and inter-tribal and has opted for simpler—and inaccurate—terms like "soldier," "costume" and "song for all tribes."

Native veterans have always been known as veterans, not "soldiers." (I hear the word soldier and immediately look for a uniform. There are no uniforms in this book.) "Regalia" and "outfit" are the proper terms for a dancer's attire; "costume" is not. Jingle dress cones could be made of silver, but more than likely are made of a less expensive metal. But gold? Hardly. An "intertribal" is a song for all peoples of all Nations and is always announced as an "intertribal," not a "song for all the tribes." Also, it is customary to give an offering when one gathers medicine. This oversight belies the author's understanding of "to give" which is an important theme in the story.

There is a three-page "Glossary of Powwow Terms and Dances," which could have been made better use of, but for the most part it's okay. But here again we run into some weird warps, tell tale signs of the outsider telling us how it is with "the Indian." The brief introduction tells us that "the powwow is a special event that gathers modern Indians of different tribes, all with languages and customs as foreign to each other as to non-Indians." (Now, why *wouldn't* the Indians be "modern"?

And powwows have been going on a heck of a long time—the only foreigner here seems to be the author!)

The description of the "traditional dancer" is another example of what is wrong here: "These dancers create their outfits from nature—furs, buckskin, quills, shells— and materials that were available from the early Europeans, such as beads, cotton, trade cloth, and ribbon." Which century is she talking about?

I appreciate the author's intent, which I assume is to boost the self-image of a disenfranchised Native child, maybe the author's own adopted Native children. As well, there is always the added bonus of educating non-Native readers. That having been said, it is too easy for an outsider to interpret what she has seen and experienced and in the process misrepresent the knowledge and worldview of Native peoples. People ought to write about what they know. *Rainy's Powwow* unfortunately becomes the confused child the story was probably intended to help.—*Lenore Keeshig-Tobias*

Rappaport, Doreen, *We Are the Many: A Picture Book of American Indians*, illustrated by Cornelius Van Wright and Ying-Hwa Hu. HarperCollins (2002). 31 pages, color illustrations; grades 2-4

Thirteen two-page spreads with large text and full-color illustrations introduce young readers to sixteen Native people whose lives somehow impacted the place that has come to be called the United States. Both text and illustration highlight one incident from the life of each person in a sort-of "snapshot," while a sentence or two at the end of each piece describes what happened after. It is impossible to represent 500 Native Nations and 500 years with short stories of sixteen individuals, and it's apparent that Rappaport tried.

But the title itself is an anomaly, and the separation between the non-Native author and the people she's writing about lends to a lot of the contradictions inherent in this book.

Whether or not it was the author's intention, *We Are the Many* is not targeted for young Native readers. In her introductory author's note, for instance, she uses the words "they" and "their"—referring to Native people— eight times in the first paragraph alone. And the sentence, "Think of this book as the start of your journey to learning about American Indians," is a clear indication that "we" are going to learn about "them."

The book is designed, using pipestone and turquoise for the main colors, to look "Indian." But the writing reflects the textbook version of Indian history, rather than a Native perspective. For instance, in the story about Tisquantum (Squanto), Rappaport writes,

From a small deerskin pouch, he took out the precious gift of corn seed. He planted four seeds in each hill. Good farmers plant extra seeds to guard against beetles and crows and cutworms, he explained.

While this is how William Bradford, governor of Plimoth, may have understood Tisquantum's advice, it seems highly unlikely that Tisquantum explained traditional Wampanoag agriculture in just this way.

On the same page, Rappaport writes:

> In early December 1622, the Pilgrims invited Tisquantum and other Wampanoag Indians to a harvest feast to thank them for their help. Today Thanksgiving is a national holiday celebrated on the fourth Thursday in November.

It would not have taken many words to state that the Indian people whose generosity saved the Pilgrims' lives were rewarded by the theft of the land and seed corn, near total destruction of a way of life, and death from white man's diseases and guns.

The author may not have felt that it was a good idea to say all this in a book for young children, but it may have been a better book if some of the realities of Native-white relationships would have been touched on. As it is, the story of "the first Thanksgiving" as written down in textbooks is largely a myth.

There is a lovely illustration of Wilma Mankiller leaning against a shovel while working on a water pipeline, rather than the more familiar portrait of her sitting at her desk. But the text stating that this Cherokee leader "completed many projects to make her people more self-reliant" belies that fact that the Cherokee people *were* self-reliant before the U.S. government marched them off the land and onto a barren reservation in Oklahoma. And despite everything, still are.

The piece on the Navajo code talkers is the best in the book. Written clearly and with examples, it describes how the "brilliant code (that) was never broken by the enemy" was based on the Diné language. This is different from other books for young readers that describe the code as *being* the Diné language.

While Rappaport's choices in general are those who have come to mean something to white people, the addition of contemporary people who defied the white conquerors (for instance, Richard Oakes, Anna Mae Pictou Aquash and Leonard Peltier) would have made this book more meaningful to Native children. And the work of a gifted Indian artist such as Michael Lacapa would have added depth to the pictures.

Finally, books like this where the emphasis is placed on individuals ("American Indians of achievement") are misleading, since the individual was and is always considered to be less important than the wellbeing of the people. This is not to say that Native people did not or do not have heroes, but the heroes tend to be different from those considered important by the dominant culture.

Rappaport thanks many people for help with pronunciation of words from Indian languages. Had she sought advice from Native elders and tribal historians—and taken that advice—*We Are the Many* could have been, even on a young level, a more balanced and more realistic work.—*Beverly Slapin*

Red Shirt, Delphine (Lakota), *Bead on an Anthill: A Lakota Childhood*. University of Nebraska (1998). 146 pages; high school-up; Lakota

As a little girl, Red Shirt wanted glass beads to make a ring, to replace the metal washer that had to be cut off after it made her finger swell. She knew there would be beads, because the ants collected any they found, and took them home. Thus the title: how she has strung together the beads of her childhood, and the words of her people.

> These stories...are what I remember; "Weksuye" meaning "I remember"; "Ciksuye" meaning "I remember you"; "Miksuye" meaning "remember me."

Red Shirt's descriptions are vivid, especially of her very early childhood. Her book has what must surely be among the best of opening sentences:

> I remember how I once followed an ant home. When I was a child, I was able to do things that seem preposterous to me now. But as a small child, I stayed close to the ground and imagined all sorts of possibilities.

I was hooked, and flipping through the book before doing this review, I found it impossible not to just re-read the whole thing.

Red Shirt says that she has done this writing "primarily for the joy of remembering what was good in my life." There is also an underlying sadness, the sadness where "[i]t was as if we awoke in the night, in the middle of a nightmare, from which we have not yet awakened." Her mother is a very strong presence here, so much of the words that Red Shirt finds, and carries: "We lived in a world where words were heeded." There is so much of the land and the wind, "the wind whose essence my people had tried to capture in song and prayer."

Birth and death, loss and tragedy—and healing.

> It is there, in the He Sapa [Black Hills]...We retain even now our connection to the spirits that live there....These are things that will always be ours, because they belong to no one but the Creator.

The last chapter, "Sitting on Red Cloud's Grave," is a farewell to childhood, a farewell to innocence. In high school, Red Shirt was one of four students chosen by the math teacher to go east for the summer and teach Lakota at a New Jersey school. It was a turning point. "I didn't realize...that I would never really unpack my suitcase on the reservation again." The coming of AIM "was a loss of innocence" for the people in her community: "I remember the way it was before they came and the way it was after." After the occupation of Wounded Knee, "chaos came and settled in our midst." When she was shot in the chest in a random shooting, Red Shirt realized she could not stay; "I was no longer safe there." Thinking about sitting on the three-foot high block of cement that covers Red Cloud's grave, "I wonder, now...if I was like a young sapling grafted onto an ancient tree..."

One runs out of superlatives. Delphine Red Shirt has the rare gift of remembering what it feels like to have been that child, and the words to tell how it was. Reading it anew, I realized again what a remarkable thing that is.—*Doris Seale*

Red Shirt, Delphine (Lakota), *Turtle Lung Woman's Granddaughter.* **University of Nebraska (2002). 242 pages; high school-up**

One time, Delphine Red Shirt and her mother were driving toward Rosebud. It was a cloudy August day. They were going south on State Highway 63, southeast of Eagle Butte. Suddenly

> [A]n eagle that had been hovering over us dove down, and its wing hit the left side of the car. The great bird rose again and flew away. After the shock of feeling and hearing its wing hit the car on my side, I looked again, but it was gone. You can hear the sound of its wing hitting the car, on the tape in the recording we made that day.

It was on that tape that Turtle Lung Woman's granddaughter began to tell her story to her own daughter. This book is that story.

> The time it has taken me to tell her story, the effort I have put into the translations, the dreams I have had in that process....I brought joy into my mother's life by having her relive all the good that was in her life....What follows is her story, in her words.

There are a number of chronicles of Native women's lives; several are "as-told-to," filtered through the anthropological consciousness. There is nothing at all like this. No other chronicle uses the language in this way. Before she even begins, Red Shirt gives us a Lakota orthography and pronunciation guide. It is needed, because the ways in which Native languages

have been written down quite frequently have little to do with the way they are actually spoken. And her mother's language is used extensively throughout the story, so that one can see the beauty of the words, and how they carry meaning and connotation in a way not familiar to those who speak only English.

The story is remarkable. Turtle Lung Woman, Kheglezela Chaguwi's, long life—1851-1935—began at a time when it was still possible to live in a traditional way. And she lived through changes so vast they can scarcely be com-prehended. In all that time, this woman belonged to her own spirit.

> Friend
> what you say is true
> the chiefs
> are gone
> so I myself will
> try.

There are such poems, interspersed throughout the text.

I do not want to try to say too much more. There is no real way to convey the power and the beauty of this book, to say what a remarkable treasure it is. You have to read it. From Turtle Lung Woman to her granddaughter; from Wiya Isnala to her daughter, the story becomes living memory. Through Delphine Red Shirt, it comes to us, a gift, certainly for those of us who are Native, but also for all with clear sight and open hearts.

—*Doris Seale*

Reinhard, Johan, *Discovering the Inca Ice Maiden: My Adventures on Ampato.* **National Geographic (1998). 48 pages, color photos and maps; grades 4-up; Inca**
Vande Griek, Susan, *A Gift for Ampato,* **illustrated by Mary Jane Gerber. Groundwood (1999). 107 pages, b/w illustrations; grades 4-6; Inca**

Incredibly detailed, close-up photos of a frozen Inca mummy, a fourteen-year-old who lived about 500 years ago, send shivers up my spine. I don't think I'll sleep well tonight picturing the little frozen girl clutching her dress tightly to her body. Why was she buried on the rim of a volcano? Was it human sacrifice, as the author states and describes in great detail? Or was it something else? I feel like he's taking me on a very invasive tour of this young woman's death, relishing the blood-curdling "sacrifice" aspect of the whole tour de ice force.

Young readers will love *Discovering the Inca Ice Maiden*; it is easy to read, almost as if the author were telling a tale to a fourth- or fifth-grader, and the gruesome pictures will totally capture their interest. Strange that violence, mutilation, and human sacrifice are what make our children want to read. And it is this kind of information that the education system mandates in their social studies frameworks.

Reinhard takes us step by step on this "discovery" (I think "encountering" is a better word). It reminds me of Donald Johanson's writing about "Lucy," the "Australo-pithecus Afarensis" woman he encountered in Hadar, Ethiopa. He stumbled on Lucy's remains in much the same way Reinhard stumbled on the "Ice Maiden" by being in the right place at the right time, or as Johanson says, "I guess I'm just lucky. Luck plays a big part in this business."

I found myself studying the many maps and photographs with a magnifying glass to sift through the grains of pumice, the volcanic ash, and the ice floes to see if I could uncover anything myself—the photographs from the National Geographic team are that clear and compelling.

Two years ago in Tampa, Florida, I toured an exhibit that had been confiscated as part of a smuggling plan gone awry. It was being displayed for a short time before being sent back to Cuzco. All of this is to say: What is the right way to handle cultural invasion? Ask a "leading authority" about human sacrifice in ancient Inca civilization? Send the mummy to Johns Hopkins for x-ray techno-games-analysis? Hurry back to the site to make sure no "robber" gets the prize before "you" can cart it down the mountainside? You know, ethical things like that. Still, the story is compelling and I couldn't put it down. But I am pretty sure I'm going to have nightmares involving feathers and gold and silver statues—all very, very cold.

It was only a matter of time—one year, to be exact—before Reinhard's finding found its way into a young adult novel. It happened in *A Gift for Ampato*, Susan Vande Griek's heavy-handed, badly written, Eurocentric recreation of Inca society 500 years ago.

Timta and her friend Karwa are both selected to be "chosen ones," young girls groomed for life in the sacrifice pool of the Great Inca. Chosen to become the ultimate sacrifice, Timta does not want the honor, saying to her friend,

> I cannot see myself among the gods, Karwa. I only want to stay here among my people and the llamas in this stony valley. Oh, Karwa, you are so good, so believing, so sure of things. Why can't I be like that?

Karwa lets her off the hook by answering,

> I think we are each as we are, Timta. What is right for me maybe is not what is right for you, no matter what the priests or women say. I would gladly go to the gods for my people, for you. Can you see that, Timta? Do you understand? I would go for you.

At the same time, Riti, whose own daughter had been sacrificed the last time the gods were angry (the volcano was letting off minor eruptions) has had it with these people. She packs up her things, loads them on her llamas, and is leaving for the coast when she meets up with the runaway Timta, saves her from the guards, and together they head down the mountain to a new life away from human sacrifice and false gods.

Maybe young Inca women *were* rebellious of family and society in those days. Maybe they *did* run away from responsibility. Maybe they *did* think of themselves as individuals rather than as citizens of a highly defined society. Maybe they *would* let a friend take their place at the most important event in their lives. Maybe they *did* possess the same values as modern American middle-class teenagers who are products of over-permissive parenting and a materialistic culture. Or, more likely, maybe the author decided that young readers couldn't possibly relate to teenage citizens of a society in which emphasis is placed on the welfare of the group rather than that of the individual. In any case, this book just doesn't work.

Why is the idea of human sacrifice seen as something to which today's young people cannot relate? Why are gory details that both fascinate and repel young people—and set into a fake social context—seen as worthwhile reading? If this concept were discussed in terms relevant to young people—like Buddhist monks who believe in something so deeply that they are willing to give their lives; or like young men and women being sent off to die in wars they do not understand—maybe then the term "human sacrifice" would make more sense.
—*Judy Zalazar Drummond*

Rinaldi, Ann, *The Second Bend in the River.* **Scholastic (1997). 280 pages; grades 4-6; Shawnee**

The Second Bend in the River is a historical young adult novel based loosely on some real-life people and events. More essentially, it's an expansion of what some have claimed (and others disputed) may have been a friendship that gradually grew into a romance between a white girl named Rebecca Galloway and the well-known Shawnee leader, Tecumseh. The author's note reads, "Clearly the actuality of the romance is up for conjecture, but I have found more evidence that it happened than evidence to dispute it." (The character Rebecca says, "By firelight, I thought. He would look good dancing by firelight." In terms of mythology, it's vaguely Pocahontas-esque.)

Various events in Tecumseh's life are reported by Rebecca, a first-person protagonist who is mostly distant from him—both geographically and in stage of life. But because of that distance, the reader is not taken to those critical and sometimes poignant moments. Instead, much of the story revolves around the day-to-day life of Rebecca and her family.

Tecumseh himself is appealing to Rebecca in part because he is portrayed as a peacemaker and not an angry one. He refers to

> "Peace at the cost of my people's destruction." It was said in a becalmed way, with no bitterness.

From her point of view, he's a good Indian and occasionally a great man. Among other things, he promises Rebecca that he will protect white women and children as well as white men who surrender to him, against "massacre." When he does intervene in such a way, readers may see it as a credit to Rebecca or their love rather than to his personal convictions and beliefs.

At various points in the story, Rebecca is portrayed as racist, culturally insensitive and clueless. However, even as a young child she is shown as a more than fit match for Tecumseh—orator, military strategist, philosopher, and diplomat—and lectures him on the proper use of English grammar. Rebecca's primary conflict is whether to choose a life with her fellow whites in "civilization" or with Tecumseh and his people in "savagery," and Rebecca's voice does repeatedly put it in these terms.

Rebecca's choice between white "civilization" and Tecumseh is drawn with hints of parallels between each world. For example, Rebecca reports,

> The chasing out was called campaigns. My daddy took part in the campaign of '82. And he'd be the first to tell you that the Indians weren't treated fairlike. He got mooded up thinking on it sometimes.

There are also references to marauding whites, other violent behavior on the part of whites, and statements like: "We've got ourselves to fear more than the Indians" from Daddy.

In comparison, the Indian "savagery" is largely shown through references to off-screen events, back-story (Tecumseh "had been a young boy, he said, when he had seen his people torture and burn a white man"), the numerous (upwards of ten) baby-killing references, and Molly Kiser, a white woman who'd "been taken by Indians as a child. And never wanted to go back to her own people, though she'd had the chance."

Molly herself is, Rebecca tells readers,

> the most miserable excuse for a woman I'd ever seen. She wore dirty buckskins and had a tooth missing in front, and she was long past the age where it would grow back. Though up close she didn't appear as old as she did at first. George said she was only twenty . . ."

(It's difficult to believe dental care was especially advanced in white towns in the early 1800s either.)

Molly is a mirror to Rebecca, both white and female and confronted with the question of whether to live with whites or Indians. At the end of the book, Rebecca refers to Molly as a friend.

Much of this is an effort to show, through Rebecca's limited first-person point of view, her journey from racism to love and friendship. And Tecumseh does tell Rebecca, "The white man thinks many things of the Indian that are not true." But although Rebecca tells readers that the whites were not innocent victims of Indian savages, it is difficult to compare "weren't treated fairlike," stealing of land, or even violence with the pivotal symbolic and repeated image: the killing of white babies.

One might imagine a paragraph in which Rebecca reviews the falsehoods she had embraced about Native people and the truths she found to replace them. Or even a clarification in the author's note explaining that Rebecca had been misled about certain aspects of particular Native societies and offering the actual information.

What is of great concern is a different kind of parenthetical comment in the author's note: "[A]lthough Indians were known, in the heat of battle, to smash babies against trees and kill them." This follows a disclaimer that a baby killing integrated into a real-life battle, "Indian attack" in the novel's back-story, did not actually occur.

The bibliography lists several sources, most published before 1960 and few published in the late 1800s or early 1900s. It is not uncommon for researchers to use the oldest sources they can find in an effort to find those least distorted by reinterpretation or time. What must, however, be considered in looking at many seemingly scholarly sources supposedly about Native peoples is the context in which they were written. Many of these books were crafted in the tradition of an American mythology that dehumanizes Indian people in an attempt to justify their treatment by the United States government and many of its people. All of this is to say that it would not be surprising if a researcher could find sources that falsely claim Indians—all Indians—had engaged in any number of inhuman behaviors.

However, it would be difficult, if not impossible, to prove such a thing once actually happened, certainly beyond the "reasonable doubt" standard. But here, there is no mention of a particularly deranged individual or even a sort of warfare atrocity in a specific context. It is instead a sweeping condemnation of "Indians." All Indians. Millions of individuals from thousands of Nations across the Americas. In contrast, it is well known that there were numerous instances wherein white children were adopted into and raised within Native communities (like the Molly Kiser character).

Caution must be used in evaluating a claim that (1) encompasses any people in their entirety, (2) is made about a historically persecuted people, and (3) fits into a negative and persistent stereotype. Not recommended.

—*Cynthia L. Smith*

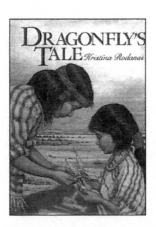

Rodanas, Kristina, *Dragonfly's Tale*, illustrated by the author. Clarion (1992). 32 pages, color illustrations; grades 2-4; A:shiwi (Zuni)

There are many versions of this story written by cultural outsiders[1], just about all retold from the one recorded in 1884 by Frank Hamilton Cushing, a supremely egotistical ethnologist who lived for a time at Zuni before his expulsion.[2]

The told story on which *Dragonfly's Tale* is based is very long and has many, many layers. It is a teaching story: The People's purposeful wasting of their food supplies shows disrespect to the plants, the rain and the earth. Their refusal to feed the Corn Maidens disguised as poor old women shows both a failure to honor strangers and a lack of compassion. Only three people—two children and a poor old woman—show them kindness and generosity. While the People's greed and wastefulness bring drought and famine, the generosity of the old woman and the two children, in different ways, are blessed and transformed. This is also a creation story that teaches about the kinship between the humans and the elements and the various corn Beings; of how dragonflies came to be, how they are related to the sacred corn, and how they are to be honored.

Rodanas says that she has "simplified Cushing's version and added some details of my own. That is the way of storytellers. I think the Ancient Ones will understand."

"Simplify" she does. The old woman's offer to the Corn Maidens of the last bit of her food and the Corn Maidens' reciprocity—gone. The Corn Maidens' visit to the hungry children and how their relationship becomes sacred—gone. The uncle's acknowledgment of his desertion of the children and his recognition of who they have become—gone. The relationship of the dragonfly to the Corn Maidens and to the sacred corn—gone. The transformation of the children—gone.

Rodanas has taken a very beautiful story and made it into, as a reviewer from *Publishers Weekly* calls it, "a valuable lesson about respect for the environment." *Dragonfly's Tale* is so far removed from the told story as to make it useless, except as an example of cross-cultural story mining thinly disguised as multiculturalism. Not recommended.—*Beverly Slapin*

NOTES

1 An especially well-known one is Tony Hillerman's *The Boy Who Made Dragonfly*. Harper & Row, 1972.

2 For a hilarious account of Cushing's years at Zuni, see Phil Hughte's *A Zuni Artist Looks at Frank Hamilton Cushing*. Zuni A:shiwi Museum, 1994. This is a book of cartoons emphasizing Cushing's "dress, his eating habits, his taking a bath, and his interactions with fellow Zuni... in the secular as well as sacred realms of life in the pueblo."

Rodanas, Kristina, *Follow the Stars: A Native American Woodlands Tale*, illustrated by the author. Marshall Cavendish (1998). Unpaginated, color illustrations; grades 1-3

There are many versions of this story about how the animals decide to divide time and share the warm and cold seasons and how all this results in Fisher becoming the North Star, but this one is completely unique.

The story usually begins something like this: "Long ago,

in one part of the world it was always summer. The birds and animals did not want to share summer with anyone. In the other half of the world, it was always winter. The animals in this part of the world wanted to find summer, but they did not know where to look."

But from the very beginning of Rodanas' retelling:

> It was I, the Quiet One, who was chosen to watch and to listen so that one day I could tell you this story. Many years have gone by since the time of the Everlasting Snow. I remember the winter sky was dark with clouds. Heavy snow covered the hills and fields, and the rivers had turned to ice. The wind howled like a hundred hungry wolves…

Rodanas milks this for all it's worth. Can't just *tell* the story, has to belabor every detail to make it appear more authentic than the original.

There are other things that are equally perplexing. Why does she turn the animals who are hoarding summer into humans (even though this story is supposed to be *before* the humans arrive)? Why does she have her animal characters refer to the humans as "dangerous creatures"? Why does she have the humans fearful of the animals, crying "Manitou! Manitou!….A powerful spirit is angry with us!"?

And if that's not bad enough, the pictures are worse. There are birchbark tipis she alternately calls "wigwams" and "huts" and "lodges." There are semi-naked Indians dancing around the fire (you know, hop-hop-hop).

Despite the book jacket copy that gushes, "[Rodanas'] work has been praised for its authentic and respectful representation of the cultures of which she writes, as well as for its luminous illustrations and lyrically written stories," this is a book to be seriously avoided.—*Beverly Slapin*

Rodolph, Stormy, *Quest for Courage,* **illustrated by Paulette Livers Lambert. Roberts Rinehart/Council for Indian Education (1984, 1993). 103 pages, b/w illustrations; grades 4-6; Blackfoot**

A physically disabled youngster named Lame Bear, son of the chief, is full of self-pity. (Who wouldn't be with a name like that?) His leg was broken in a riding accident when he was a child, so he spends much of his time bemoaning his misfortune:

> Lame Bear hated his leg. The other boys laughed and called him "old woman." The shame was unbearable! A young Blackfeet's entire childhood was spent developing himself into a strong and courageous warrior. Lame Bear's pain and shame kept him away from the games and hunts of the other boys. He sighed. Was he destined to spend the rest of his life helping the women gather roots,

berries and firewood? The thought sickened him…. Bitterness grew in him as he walked across the open meadow. Why did the spirits do this terrible thing to him? What had he done to deserve the suffering and humiliation?

The medicine man decides that it's time for the boy to go on a vision quest. He does, and finds a spirit horse to guide him, goes off by himself to find wild horses, captures a "prized stallion," outwits and outruns some enemy Flatheads, finds out that "strenuous exercise had strengthened him," and returns to camp a hero.

We don't know when this all takes place, possibly in the early 1800s. We do know that, in any Native camp, hunting, war, and illness did take their toll. There might have been other people with disabilities, and it would have been no big thing for a child to have a broken leg. But the child would have had a place in the community; he would not have been ostracized or shamed, and would not have had to prove himself any more than anyone else.

As with the other books in this series, the narrative is the usual Indian-speak: "The hearts of father and son were full," "The spirits have nothing but evil for me. I might as well be an old woman."

The illustrations are trite and boring; one wonders why the boy is wearing an eagle feather, having done nothing to earn one. Once again, men are either "braves" or "warriors," women are non-existent, except as objects of derision; and there is no cultural context to speak of, except the generic Plains Indian vision quest and horse-stealing. Not recommended.—*Beverly Slapin*

Runningwolf, Michael (Mi'kmaq), and Patricia Clark Smith (Mi'kmaq), *On the Trail of Elder Brother: Glous'gap Stories of the Micmac Nation,* **illustrations by Michael Runningwolf. Persea (2000). 128 pages, b/w illustrations; grades 5-up; Mi'kmaq**

During the creation times, when the world was being populated by plants, animals and humans, Gluskabi sets an example for behavior—both good and bad—and, as Elder Brother, creates the conditions in which all beings are to survive. As the embodiment of the Great Spirit's power—one story goes that he created himself with what was left over after the Great Spirit was finished creating—Gluskabi walks about, fixing things up, helping out, sometimes not.

The five Nations belonging to the Wabanaki Confederation —Mi'kmaq, Maliseet, Passmaquoddy, Penobscot, and Abenaki—hold similar versions of these traditional stories. Although I've heard all of these stories before, it seems to me that some are Mi'kmaq, some are Abenaki and some are Penobscot.

Further, I'm not clear as to why the authors, who include a glossary of Mi'kmaq and other Wabanaki words, in the text use the incorrect spelling for Mi'kmaq and Gluskabi and use English words for place-names. I wonder how much of this was the authors' doing and how much was done in the editorial department. Had they not attempted to put Mi'kmaq words in the text, it would have been a lot better, but this is unsettling for people like me who are learning Abenaki, one of the Wabanaki languages.

The woodcut illustrations are unsettling to me as well. They are beautiful, but in the creation period, people were probably not walking around wearing beaded clothing, fabric hoods, and what seems to appear in several pictures as a German silver brooch. And since some of these stories take place in the ocean and around open ocean waters, large dugouts rather than birchbark canoes would have been used—these little canoes portrayed in the pictures would have been quickly destroyed in the rough Atlantic Ocean.

Although these stories are condensed versions of our traditional stories, the book is a good collection and the stories generally read well. But it ought to be made clear that these are Wabanaki, rather than just Mi'kmaq, traditional stories.—*Judy Dow*

Sabuda, Robert, *The Blizzard's Robe*, illustrated by the author. Atheneum (1999). Unpaginated, color illustrations; grades 2-4

The "People Who Fear the Winter Night" fear the winter night because it's so cold, and they especially fear Blizzard, "who can destroy anything with its icy winds and snow." When Blizzard's robe is destroyed by sparks from a little girl's fire, she decides to make a new one. She does, and stands up to her ignorant, superstitious people who want to destroy the new robe. In thanks, Blizzard gives them the Northern Lights.

Sabuda doesn't say that this story is based on anything and he carefully avoids saying who these people are. The conical tipi-shaped dwellings with reindeer outside could be Saami lavvu, or they could belong to any number of people living in the Siberia area. Or, since Sabuda calls the dwellings "yarangas," they probably belong to the reindeer-breeding Chukchi of Eastern Siberia, who are neighbors of the Inuit peoples.

But whoever the people in this story are, they are clearly not "people who fear the Arctic night." Created to showcase the author's batik artwork, *The Blizzard's Robe* is an "original origin tale" with cultural overtones that are not at all authentic; a crass ripoff of the Arctic peoples.

—Beverly Slapin

(Thank-you to Nathan Muus of the Saami Baiki Foundation.)

Sanderson, Esther (Cree/Métis), *Two Pairs of Shoes*, illustrated by David Beyer (Cree/Métis). Pemmican (1990). Unpaginated, color illustrations; all grades; Cree/Métis

Today is a special day for Maggie, for she has been given *two* pairs of shoes for her eighth birthday, black patent leather shoes she had admired in a store window, and beaded moccasins her grandmother made for her. Along with the two pairs of shoes comes this advice from her grandmother: from now on, she "must remember when and how to wear each pair," indeed the challenge that all ethnically diverse people face in today's world. Esther Sanderson tells a simple story with an important message as she captures the special opportunities available to Indian people who live in both tribal and dominant society. It's also a really nice story showing the warmth of family life and relationships. *Two Pairs of Shoes* is a must-have for all mixed-culture families and schools.

—Pam Martell

San Souci, Robert, *Song of Sedna*, illustrated by Daniel San Souci. Doubleday (1981). Unpaginated, color illustrations; grades 1-3; Inuit

All the circumpolar Arctic peoples were entirely dependent for survival on sea mammals: seals, walruses, narwhals, and whales. Few plants, and no woody ones, no trees, grow above the Arctic Circle. Driftwood and usable stone are rare. Bone and sinew were the most important animal parts for the tools of survival. For light, warmth in winter homes, and very small amounts of cooking, the people used sea mammal fats in stone dishes with moss wicks. Sinew and hide formed most clothing, and the hulls of the one-man kayaks from which sealing and fishing were done during the few months of the year that were always daylight (from April to August), when ice breakup occurred and some water was open. For both summer kayak or winter ice hunts, waterproof overgarments or animal intestines were a necessity.

Thus the sea mammals were the basic necessity of life for the peoples of the Arctic, who call themselves Inuit, the largest group (Iñupiaq, Inuvaluit, Yup'ik, Aleut are other self-names). It means the same as the self-names of just about all Native peoples: "the people." "Eskimo" (what the San Soucis call the people of their story) was a pejorative name meaning "raw meat eaters" applied by Natives of the sub-Arctic.

For all the Arctic peoples there is a story like the one of Sedna that the San Souci brothers have debased. Some aspects differ: the girl is sometimes an orphan thrown callously overboard to lighten a load, for example. What is common to all stories is the betrayal by close kin, the murder, by throwing the girl into the frigid waters. And by chopping her fingers off, first at the topmost joints, as she clings to the edge of the craft trying to save herself from a death hypothermia, certain within minutes. As she tries again to cling with bloody part-hands, her father, relatives, fellow villagers, or mother chop off the finger-stumps down to the knuckles, and she sinks to the bottom of the sea.

The bloody finger fragments become the sea mammals on which the people depend for every aspect of life and survival. Her cold, dead, but animated body beneath the sea is the controlling spirit of these sea mammals. Sedna is the most powerful and dreaded of the entire Arctic pantheon of spirits and deities (most of whom are hostile or at least malicious).

She hates all of humankind, the people who betrayed and murdered her. She wants revenge. She wants the death of all humanity. When this desire becomes strong, when she remembers what they did to her, she sends away her former bloody finger-joints, and the people starve or freeze. Their only hope, then, is that an angkok, a man of spiritual power will send his spirit underwater and cause the woman to relent. In some versions, he does this by killing a variety of monsters that are her underwater companions. In more gruesome versions, small undersea crustaceans plague her, eating her cold, dead flesh. Because of her clubbed, fingerless hands, she cannot pick them off herself. The angkok can, and saves her from the intolerable pain and fear of their eating. In temporary gratitude, she may bring back her sea mammals, and the people may survive. Or she may not and they may not. Small winter camps of the dead were sometimes later found: all starved.

Surviving in the toughest environment human beings have been able to inhabit, the people did not see the forces of nature—arbitrary, uncontrollable and dangerous—as in any respect kindly or benevolent. There was no formal worship; spirits were feared and propitiated. Stories for entertainment featured lots of bloody violence, often for reasons that seem humanly as arbitrary as the potentially fatal forces of nature seemed.

To make culturally accurate children's stories out of the myths and legends that helped peoples live in this environment is not possible if these children's stories must somehow feature kindly or benevolent creatures, forces, deities. Nature is Not Always Nice, but an unrealistic nice-ness is apparently what is being pushed by publishers and consumed by educators and parents in modern, middle class culture.

For this, the San Souci brothers have made a mockery of Polar cultures. Their Sedna is, to be sure, flung overboard by her father when she has fled a husband who, she learns, is a powerful (and presumably malignant) spirit, who sends a storm after their umiak as they are fleeing him. But he doesn't chop her fingers off—too gruesome for kids—the necessary and universal element of the human betrayal that creates the sea mammals. The sea mammals in the San Souci brothers' version already exist. They and some handy nice cold-water guardian spirits escort her to an underwater throne where they tell her to Be Nice in her new power. She proceeds to do so, which pleases a non-existent deity of justice, made up by the San Soucis as "the most powerful being of all," and the brothers end with an alleged joyful song of Sedna that is actually a hunting song.

The illustrations are all wrong. Trees—both evergreens and huge deciduous ones—are shown flourishing in the snow—here above the tree line! Sedna's dreams of romantic love are why she refuses local suitors and settles on a handsome drop-in who fits these dreams. Romantic love is a completely alien concept in most cultures, and never more so than here, where a woman is an economic necessity for the survival of the hunter.

The deserted spirit-husband chases escaping Sedna and her father riding a scaled sea serpent that, more than anything, resembles the prow of a Viking war craft. The father's umiak is shown with sail. (Sails were not used. There was nothing to make them out of, and Arctic winds are hardly dependable for maneuvering among ice floes and complex currents around rocky headlands.)

Clothing, facial and bodily conformations of the supposedly Arctic peoples make them physically resemble the peoples of the warm, wooded Northwest Coast. A totem pole out in the middle of nowhere and Northwest Coast-style formline fish on prefatory and title pages reinforce these culturally alien lifestyles imposed on the Arctic people, who had and have an entirely different style in their art of bone- and stone carving and did not build totem poles. No wood, remember?

The New York Times Book Review called the pictures— which are the least authentic part of the book— "realistic illustrations [that] complement the haunting text and contrast well with the mythical quality of the story."

This sort of cultural travesty—distortions of supposedly up-for-grabs cultural heritages by any story miner—is the general rule for commercially concocted stories-about-

Natives for children. What is most notable of this book is that (in addition to various other awards by educational bodies) the National Council for the Social Studies has designated it a "Notable Book." This is supposed to mean that the book in question is one from which children can learn real facts about the history and culture of the people who story is told—or retold, reworked, remodeled. That does not happen with the *Song of Sedna*.

Two decades of sales success for this book is a strong indictment of the disregard for and total ignorance of Native realities among the publishing, educational, reading and reviewing authority, across the board in the U.S. and Canada, where this book is also widely distributed.—*Paula Giese*

San Souci, Robert D., *Two Bear Cubs: A Miwok Legend from California's Yosemite Valley,* **illustrated by Daniel San Souci. Yosemite Association (1997). Unpaginated, color illustrations, preschool-grade 2; Miwuk**

This is a retelling by cultural outsiders, of a Miwuk story of how the mountain called Tu-tok-a-nu'-la (later to be known as El Capitán) came into being.

From the very first page, the author's perspective is clear:

> Many snows have come and gone since this story was first told by the Miwok, whose name means "people" or "humans." They lived in a place they called *Ah-wah'-nee*, which is now known as Yosemite Valley. The Miwok believe that in the old days, the residents of *Ah-wah'-nee* were "animal people"— creatures that were part animal and part human.

This condescending introduction oversimplifies the role of stories, Indian cultures in general, and Miwuk cosmology in particular.

Miwuk cosmology is a complex system that explains the physical and spiritual world inhabited by the first people to prepare it for humans and to create rules—guidelines—for the right way for living in balance and harmony. That is very different from "creatures that were part animal and part human." What the author implies is that Indian peoples lack sophistication and real intelligence, because anthropomorphizing of animals—and seeing them as real—is not what intelligent people do.

In some of our creation stories, the animal people have characteristics of both the humans and the animals they embody, even sometimes the plants, because they are the first people. Some culturally appropriate depictions of our stories show human bodies with the head and tail of a skunk for example, or the head of a bird. Other depictions may show animals wearing clothing, and still others may show four-leggeds walking upright, or bird people walking on the ground. Our stories and belief systems are complex; they have content and context. They are very different than what the San Souci brothers have produced here.

I first heard the story of Tu-tok-a-nu'la from a Miwuk storyteller while I was a student. I have forgotten her name now, but the story she related to us was a teaching story. In her telling, we learned what foods to harvest at what particular time of the year, and the appropriate and inappropriate ways of relating to one's mother. She also cautioned us not to abuse this story. It was clear to us that she was sharing a story of her people, but she was not "giving" the story to us. She told us not to write it down or state or imply that it was ours to share with others. This elder wasn't just telling the story of how El Capitán was formed; she was teaching culture to a group of Indian college students.

In the San Souci version, two "playful" grizzly bear cubs wander off and get stranded at the top of a stone slab that, over time, grows to become a mountain. One by one, the animals—including "clever" Badger and "agile" Mountain Lion—try to rescue the cubs, but it is only tiny Measuring Worm who is able to scale the nearly vertical wall and bring them down.

The narrative, designed to appeal to non-Native youngsters, has the bear cubs racing, wrestling, playing hide-and-seek, and generally being mischievous. In the story I know, the little bears were supposed to be out gathering food and got distracted. They were more than "playful," a concept that leads young readers to see them in only that limited way. And since the first people had qualities of the animals and of the humans, they had the full range of human capacity. In our stories, they aren't just described in whatever particular attribute the animal happens to have. Rather, their behaviors inform the stories. By labeling the animal people "clever" and "agile," for instance, the author here limits the human capacity of the animals in a way that our stories don't.

In the San Souci book, the animals are dressed like "Indians." The women animals wear fringed buckskin skirts and necklaces that look like pearls (!), and the male animals wear loincloths and headbands, sort of generic "Indian" outfits. The little worm has a generic southwesterny "Indian" zigzag pattern all over him, and the red-tailed hawk, probably because the illustrator couldn't figure out where to put the loincloth, wears an abalone shell on a leather cord. And the bear cubs do not look, at all, like grizzlies; they look like overstuffed toy teddy bears.

In the story I heard, the measuring worm finds the bones of the two little bears and can't bring them down, so it is Eagle who scoops them up and brings them down. In another version, Measuring Worm brings the little bears down. For some stories—and this is one of them—there are many different told versions. But the way the story is told, and who tells it, and for what purpose, remain the same. A Native teller might embellish the story with details of rich family life. If there is dialogue, the dialogue is real. The storyteller would insert the dialogue to communicate something, illustrate something about how life is. In the story I heard, Bear instructs her children about what to gather. She talks the way real people talk with one another in a family.

Not so in the San Souci book. The dialogue is contrived. Mother Bear scolds her children and tells them not to go too far, so of course they do. Mother Bear then goes from one animal to another, asking for help in finding her children. In our story, the animal people all come together and decide how best to remedy the situation.

Many of our stories teach us who we are and how we came to be. Many teach us how the land we belong to came to be. Many teach us the rules for living in a good way. Some of our stories are simply told, but they are not simple—they are encoded in such a way as to remind us of our original instructions. For the most part, our elders tell traditional stories to transmit traditional culture. Even if a particular story is passed on, say, from the Miwuk to the Karuk, there's still a coherent cultural context.

The subtitle "A Miwok Legend" notwithstanding, *Two Bear Cubs* does not transmit Miwuk traditional culture. Nor does the section entitled "About the Miwok People," which conveniently relegates the Miwuk people to the past so as not to have to deal with contemporary Indian issues. Rather, the San Souci brothers continue to mine our stories in much the same way that the "forty-niners" mined our land for the gold—and their "story-mining" is just as deadly.—*Robette Dias*

Savageau, Cheryl (Abenaki), *Muskrat Will Be Swimming,* **illustrated by Robert Hynes. Northland (1996). Unpaginated, color illustrations; grades 3-4; Abenaki**

Jeannie lives with her grandfather by the shore of the lake. It's a wonderful place. There's so much to see and hear: polliwogs, ducks swimming, the great blue heron, a muskrat, and the cry of a loon. But the kids at school call the people who live there "Lake Rats," and the place where they live, a shanty town. Jeannie tries to tell them what a good place it is to live, and they laugh at her. "We wouldn't swim in that water," they tell her. "It's dirty, it smells. Bloodsuckers and snakes live in it....You Lake Rats are crazy." So Jeannie grows silent, like the turtle in its shell.

Grampa responds to her sadness; first, by telling her how as a child he was called "frog" because he was Indian and French, and then with the story of how Muskrat—a lake rat—brought earth up from the bottom to put on Turtle's back, so that the Woman who fell from the sky could have a place to stand. "That night, I dive into the waters of my dream. My body is covered with fur, and I dive down, and down, and down....my paws scrape the bottom, and I shoot up through the water into the light."

When morning comes, Jeannie asks Grampa to take her out on the lake, where she tells him about the dream, and then dives into the lake. "It feels as if my lungs will burst, but I know I can do it. I kick as hard as I can, and finally my hands scrape the bottom and close over the soft mud." When the mud dries out, Grampa puts it in a leather pouch for her.

> So I don't worry anymore when the kids call me a Lake Rat. I know who I am, and I know about the lake, that we are part of it, and it's part of us....[T]he lake will lap against the shore while the moon looks down, and somewhere, Muskrat will be swimming.

The picture of Skywoman falling makes her look more like a model posing on the runway, and that of Jeannie in her dream is so much a white person's idea of what shape-changing might consist of that it is a little disconcerting. In it, Jeannie is not the muskrat. She seems to be wearing a muskrat skin on her head. Otherwise, the illustrations are lovely, and reflect the gentleness of the relationship between child and grandfather.

Cheryl Savageau is a poet, and it shows. This is one of the most beautiful stories I have ever read. For this reader, the words "Muskrat will be swimming" have become a mantra for the times when all we can do seems futile.—*Doris Seale*

Sawyer, Don, *Where the Rivers Meet.* **Pemmican (1988). 147 pages, high school-up; Shuswap**

Where the Rivers Meet is primarily the story of a Shuswap teenager named Nancy. She lives in a community targeted by racism, opportunism, and hampered by bureaucracy. This manifests itself in many ways.

Her school, for example, is "close to The Heights, the white enclave located just above the highway and as far from the reserve as possible." To get there, Nancy and her neighbors have to travel a train bridge that lacks a pedestrian walkway.

> The band's suggestion that a simple walkway and handrail be installed was flatly rejected. "The expenses would run several thousand dollars," the letter read, "and we are under no obligation whatsoever to provide such a facility." After all, she thought angrily, only Indians live over there anyway.

At the beginning of the story, Nancy is sometimes defiant, sometimes resigned. At school, a teacher named Quigley terrorizes and humiliates the students, especially the Indian kids. Nancy feels powerless and fearful despite wanting to protect her classmates. Disparity in academic achievement between Native and non-Indian students is clearly linked to institutional unresponsiveness and hostility. The Indian students are taught from the earliest grades that lack of achievement is tied to their identity.

Yet the depiction is not unilateral or without subtlety. One teacher, Bernice Wu, is something of a mentor. But when Nancy brings up the issue of the bridge—seven people dead—in another classroom, her young teacher informs her that there is no time for such a discussion, that the topic is not in the curriculum, and that she should turn to her band anyway. Nancy speaks up to the extent she can and burns inside when she feels she can't.

One of the more interesting relationships in the book is between Nancy and her father, who struggles with alcoholism. Despite his drinking problems, it's clear the two have a strong relationship. Frustrated, she exchanges words with him after he questions her for defending a woman cheated at the local store. But their caring cools the debate.

> "Does the drinking make you feel stronger?" she asked softly. "No." Her father spoke slowly without anger or apology. "It just helps me forget what I've lost."

This father is no clichéd "drunken Indian." He is an individual who does care about his daughter and his community. And he grows to recall the stories and ways of his youth—hampered in his own cultural education by the residential school imposed on his family—but determined to be part of his people's future.

The story touches on harsh realities like suicide and attempted rape. Like the cheap government housing with its cheap wiring that leads to fires and death. Like Nancy's decision to leave school with so little time left before graduation because she feels that it and the town are crushing her inside.

"There's so much sadness," she stammered. "So much loss." Bessie hummed for a few moments. "Yes," she said, in slow soothing tones. "Yes, so much sadness. But like the river, we're still here. We're still here."

And so the story turns as Nancy goes to Mrs. Schmidt, an elder whose grandparents managed to mostly keep her out of the residential school (as much as possible). At first, Nancy doesn't know how to talk to Mrs. Schmidt, and asks her father for advice. Mrs. Schmidt herself, for all of her wisdom, is not a cardboard figure, but one capable of both being stern and sharing humor.

Through Nancy's experiences with Mrs. Schmidt and her own, she begins to find the balance within herself to better cope and even impact the world around her. She becomes part of a student movement to reform the school and its curriculum—and perhaps build an altogether new one.

In another book by another author, readers might be conditioned to see the unlikely and disproportionate triumph of the individual so prized in European tradition. But here, Nancy stands as one of her people to advocate for change.

The story is compelling and well written. It should hold young readers' attention and give them plenty to contemplate.—*Cynthia L. Smith*

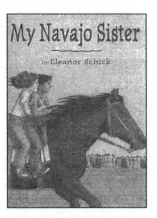

Schick, Eleanor, *My Navajo Sister*, illustrated by the author. Simon & Schuster (1996). Unpaginated, color illustrations; grades 2-5; Diné (Navajo)

As a little girl, Schick visited Window Rock and became friends with a Diné child named Genni. This story is a fictionalized account of their time together. The author wrote this book "as a letter to the real Genni, who lives and works in Window Rock, Arizona."

The pastel illustrations, rendered in colored pencil, don't capture the vividness of the land or the people of Dinétah.

The places the girls walk to explore—including the Kayenta area, Canyon de Chelly, the western pass outside of Window Rock—are many miles apart from each other.

Eleanor Schick's short visit to Dinétah does not allow her to understand all that she thinks she does. Although well meaning, this story is seen from a non-Diné perspective, so it can't help but be full of inconsistencies and misconceptions.

> Genni, when I came with my family to live on Navajo land, you made me feel welcome. You invited me to your home and on the very first day I visited, you gave me a basket.

Typically, when you meet a person for the first time, you're building a relationship and gifts are not a part of the initial interactions. The friend is brought in and introduced to the entire family. Food may be a part of the introduction. You're getting to know each other. In the picture, Genni is giving Eleanor a basket with a wedding basket design. This is something that is not given to a child. The picture also shows a cradleboard being used in a play situation. A cradleboard is not used for play. There is a process that takes place before it is used, and after it's used, it's carefully put away for the next infant.

> We climbed the canyon walls and collected shells left by the sea—maybe thousands or millions of years ago. You told me that the spirits of your people from long ago still live there. You called them the Ancient Ones.

As young children, you are told not to hang around places that spirits inhabit, as there is a certain respect afforded the spirits. Tourists go there because they don't understand or respect these places. Ánaasází is the Diné word for Ancient Ones, the relatives of the Pueblo peoples. Ánaasází sacred places are not found in the Window Rock area.

> One time we couldn't help falling asleep in one of the caves. When we woke up, we told each other our dreams. Yours was that the Ancient Ones came to visit us. Mine was the same, and they welcomed me to Navajo land. You smiled when I told you that, like you already knew.

No one sleeps in caves, especially if there are spirits in that area. It's extremely hard to believe that two children would have the same dream, except if it's telling them to get out of the damn cave!

> We stayed at your grandmother's ranch. You showed me her horses, running free in the canyon. We wanted to ride them.

Our horses are used to work and to ride. They don't run free; we keep them in corrals, unless they're out grazing and they're watched closely. We don't want them to run away and join the wild horses.

> "We'll ride Yago together!" we decided. Your brother warned us not to. We laughed and told him not to worry. He saddled up Yago, but he warned us again.

A family who owns horses teaches a child early on that horses have temperaments and are to be respected. A young sister would not defy her much older brother, especially when it comes to safety. Why is Genni doing this, why are two little girls sitting on one saddle, and why is the brother allowing this to happen?

> Going home, Yago galloped so fast and hard, he threw us both. We got hurt, and we were scared to come home, because your brother had warned us. Still, your cousin Eunice cleaned our cuts and scrapes, and no one scolded us.

The elders and parents certainly would have something to say! Although this would be considered a natural consequence, there is more to it than that. The disrespect towards the older brother and towards the animal would be addressed.

> You teased me for eating just vegetables and fruits, and your mother named me Sparrow, saying, "She eats like a bird!" All the family said, "That's your Navajo name, now." And from that day on, it was.

The author thinks she is being given an "authentic" Diné name, when in fact she is given a nickname. Traditionally, Diné children are observed for a long time before they are given names that identify who they are. It's the maternal grandmother who gives a name, not a bunch of people sitting around eating.

> Later that winter, your cousin Tina got married. We sat on the hogan floor while the medicine man chanted blessings. Everyone ate some cornmeal from the wedding basket.

During a Diné wedding ceremony, we sit on cushions or blankets or sheepskins. Medicine men do not chant, they pray and sing. Only the couple eats the cornmeal.

> I remember how you and I spilled the whole bowl of punch, trying to carry it by ourselves. We hoped the wedding guests wouldn't see how we laughed and laughed, because we were so embarrassed.

Everything is set up before the feast begins and the menfolk carry the heavy items. Our young people are taught to behave appropriately at major events, such as weddings. To do otherwise is rude and disrespectful to the families.

The next day, Tina's mother gave us each a gift. Mine was a silver bracelet with turquoise, more beautiful than I had ever seen. She said, "It is our custom to give gifts from the wedding dowry to the women of the family who make the wedding feast." That day she said I became one of the women of the family.

The connection between the wedding and the friendship is confused here. Actually, the man's family provides gifts such as horses or sheep to the woman's family. Those gifts are given prior to the wedding to ask the woman's family's blessing for the marriage. It's not a dowry. Sometimes we joke about it; we say to an in-law, "Where's my sheep?" Unless she was adopted, Eleanor would never be considered part of the family. And a child is not a woman.

> I hold the basket now, remembering your soft voice....I wear the silver bracelet.

What has Eleanor's family given to thank the Diné family for their hospitality? What is Eleanor's family's relationship with the Diné family? There is not one word, not one picture, of Eleanor's family. How did Eleanor get to Window Rock? From where?

> A second year is passing now, and I am growing strong in the knowledge of what we shared.

What knowledge? What sharing? What did Eleanor give to the Diné family? Where's the reciprocity? What has Eleanor learned that she thinks is making her strong? Why is this all about Eleanor?—*Linda Lilly*

Schneider, Antonie, *The Birthday Bear*, illustrated by Uli Waas. North-South Books (1996). 48 pages, color illustrations; grades 1-2

Sally and her brother David, who has a penchant for Indian adventure stories, visit their grandparents' home in the country to celebrate David's seventh birthday.

Wearing feathers, "war-whooping" and brandishing a tomahawk, the children jump out of the bushes and ambush their grandpa, who tells them that "all the land around here used to belong to the Blackfoot Indians." Follows a short question-and-answer session that exacerbates, rather than ameliorates, the problem:

> "Are there any Indians now?" asked David.
> "Sure," said Grandpa.
> "And do they wear headbands with feathers like ours?"
> "Some tribes wore headbands with feathers a long time ago," said Grandpa. "Now most Indians dress just like you and me."

> "For my birthday let's all wear feathers like those long-ago Indians," said David.
> "Okay," agreed Grandpa. He took a piece of fishing line, tied it around his head, and stuck in a duck feather. "How do I look?"
> "Great!" said David.

There's more of the same. When a bear attacks the birthday cake, David doesn't even notice because he's under the table, engrossed in an adventure book—about Indians. Grandma bakes a new cake, and Grandpa presents David with a "real Blackfoot Indian birthday present"—a salmon, which they roast, and the birthday party is a success. "This is a true story," the reader is told: "It happened almost exactly the way I told it."

I looked back to the verso page several times to check the year of publication. This is a very disturbing little book.—*Beverly Slapin*

Schwartz, Virginia Frances, *Initiation*. Markham, Ont.: Fitzhenry & Whiteside (2003). 268 pages, b/w illustrations; grades 5-8; Kwakwaka'wakw (Kwakiutl)

Set on the West Coast of North America during the 15th Century, *Initiation* is the story of three young people. The Salmon Twins are Nanolatch, the first-born son, a chiefly Kwakiutl heir; and his sister Nana, the second-born daughter. Noh is a Salishan slave, a young woman who had been trained to be a spiritual leader. The twins represent both ambiguity and potential. On the one hand, the twins are two who should have been one, and on the other, they hold the promise to mend the breaks in nature. The story begins with Noh's vision of the destiny of the twins, and she becomes inextricably entwined with their fate and the survival of the Kwakiutl.

Unfortunately, the combination of the author's imagination and abysmal writing has resulted in a quasi-feminist critique of what is perceived to be a patriarchal society by someone who doesn't understand the language, the culture or the time period.

The message is a mishmash of modern environmental conservation ethic and the myth of the necessity of self-sacrifice in order for the salmon to survive. In the end, the Salmon Twins disrupt their society in order to bring about a supposed mythic prophecy.

Initiation exploits both the historic Kwakiutl/Salish conflict and the traditional Kwakiutl/Nootkan (Nuu-chah-nulth) kinship relations. In the author's note, Schwartz says, "We are far removed in time from precontact society, which had an oral tradition." The author assumes that, because of this, the reader can never know what life was really like then. The intertwining oral histories of the Kwakiutl, Nootkan and Salish peoples and the evolution of their relationships through time belie such an assumption. The three peoples survive still, and maintain orality and ethnography and cosmology. The peoples know their own precontact histories; having an oral tradition does not mean there is no history.

The author's note is less of a caveat than a statement of entitlement. Apparently for her, the unknown easily (and rightfully) becomes the imaginable:

> While I tried to provide authenticity in depicting the precontact life of the Kwakiutl, I still had to remain true to my characters, who created their own world and understood it through their viewpoints. Certain aspects, like their names, tattooing, the Salmon Being chant…are my own interpretations. The ceremonies and rituals in the transformation potlatch have been altered and simplified to suit this story.

At the risk of being obvious, let me state: Her characters are fake. They did not create their own world and they do not have viewpoints.

The author's narrative is inconsistent. She represents the world in one way and then contradicts this representation elsewhere. Here are two examples:

> My brother Nanolatch is "He Who Leaps with the Salmon." Nana means "Salmonwife" but no one ever calls me that. It is my sacred name. When you say it aloud, you set the spirits loose. You can never predict what will happen then.

If "Nana" means "Salmonwife" in the Kwakiutl language, the two names are the same, and it would be her sacred name. And yet, characters refer to Nana as "Nana," her sacred name. If this is her sacred name and nobody's supposed to say it, why does everyone call her that?

> What can I do but chant the songs that only the salmon from this river know, songs Grandmother sang to me when I was little? Lines you cannot write down or tell anyone.

Nobody knows these songs but the salmon, yet Grandma (probably not a salmon) sang them to Nana. Nana, who belongs to an oral tradition, somehow is able to conceptualize writing.

Some Northwest Coast peoples see themselves in terms of their animal ancestors, the salmon. Salmon are sacred beings as well as relatives. The author, apparently not understanding the difference between mythological aspects of a belief system and the physical attributes of humans, mixes them up. The result is that the characters here continually describe each other in animal terms; for instance,

> Nanolatch gleams beside the fire like a wet seal….His body is as streamlined as a muscled salmon.
> He turns pale, like a fish's underbelly.
> My chest heaves like a snared fish.
> I leap into the waterfall like a fish.
> I twist inside, like a hooked fish, unable to swim away.
> I am weighed like a slab of salmon….I am a catch, the biggest fish in the tribal sea…
> She is like a fish out of water.
> She is narrow and lean like a fish skeleton.
> She is like a fish caught and flung to shore.
> So smooth and curved, she glides like a fish through waves.

Because the author doesn't know the structure of the Kwakiutl language and thought patterns, her vocabulary in the descriptions and narrative remove the people and actions from the particular place and time about which she purports to write. Many of the terms and concepts she uses were not in precontact aboriginal vocabulary; for example, "potlatch" is Chinook jargon, part of a postcontact trade language. Similarly, the use of measures such as feet, miles, hours, years, are post-contact. The generic "totem" poles to which the author refers, rather than being specific records of events, lineages and activities, reference nothing. People did not and do not describe each other as having "black eyes," "high cheekbones," and "bark-brown skin." Constant use of "tribe" instead of "people" objectifies the group, and "totem," "taboo," "chant" and "the Way" lack substance and evoke no particular cultural meaning. Nor does "evil," a postcontact judgmental word, used here over and over.

The main characters speak and behave in ways that are more reflective of the author's own biased cultural lens than that of traditional Kwakiutl and Salish society.

Each Kwakiutl community has a respected spiritual leader, a doctor. He consults with the world of spirits and with the head people, conducts ritual, does what needs to be done to help the community maintain cosmic balance. In *Initiation*, Shilka (the "shaman") is thoroughly unlikable, physically repugnant, and a person to be feared.

> He roams in the woods most days, collecting herbs and chanting to trees. They say he had a vision once of the sea rising and blood dripping off its edge. He opened his mouth and drank all the blood, saving the sea from foulness. Perhaps that is why we never get too close to him. His breath reeks of rotting teeth. Around his neck he has strung a charm of ten dead birds, decaying. He can say and do whatever he wants. Everyone obeys him, even my father.

In Kwakiutl society, the social leader (or "chief") collaborates with the spiritual worker in determining what's best for the people. His leadership is built on consensus and influence, and depends on the good-will of the community. The children who grew up with him would see him in a number of ways: as father or uncle, as leader, as husband. In *Initiation*, the twins' father is called only "Father" or "the chief." He is stubborn and autocratic, he barks commands, he has absolute power:

> My father's words shake the earth. "We leave today!" His words bang like drumbeats against my chest. An order to be obeyed. His voice is always final.

Before being captured and enslaved by the Kwakiutl, Noh was being trained in spiritual work by her Salish mother, who was a spiritual leader. Taken as a slave, she is given to Nana, to whom she becomes friend and protector. As an outsider with an inside track, she has a kind of cross-cultural vision that enables her to know more about the spiritual aspects of Kwakiutl culture than the Kwakiutl themselves. She can even—and does—communicate with the ghosts of the Kwakiutl dead. While everyone else appears to be in denial—even the "shaman"—Noh is the only one who knows what Nana has to do to bring back the salmon:

> She is the Salmon Being the Kwakiutls had long awaited. The one to sacrifice. The one to dive beneath the spring river. To return. It is the Way.

A Kwakiutl chiefly heir would have been taught to be humble. It is a requirement of the office. He would have been taught to seek consensus, and to be a good listener. He would have been taught to work with the spiritual leader, and be generous in spirit. If at any time he showed signs of arrogance, he would have been socially sanctioned. An elder male relative or his grandmother would advise him and help him attain proper social management skills. By puberty at the latest, he would have been behaving properly. In *Initiation*, Nanolatch is so distanced from the social

space he is being trained to occupy that he behaves totally inappropriately: he is disrespectful, self-absorbed, arrogant. He does what he wants, when he wants:

> I splash into the ice-cold river. With my bare hands, I lift a fallen salmon high. They can't tell me to wait. I won't anymore. I won't be still. I won't listen. My time is now. I will be the fisherman First Uncle was.

He disrespects the spiritual leader:

> Behind Shilka's back, I walk bowlegged to imitate him, frowning. We must do as this shaman says, even though I am the chief's son.

And he acts the glutton at his own family's potlatch:

> Hot clams slide into my mouth. Ten fish skeletons are all that remains on my plate. We must fill our bellies full until they ache. It is expected at potlatch. I toss my head back and laugh, for Nana always teases me that I eat each night like I am at potlatch.

Blood ties are strong among the Kwakiutl, where in one generation the women marry out and in the next they marry back, so they have close relatives in several West Coast communities. Many rivers run through the Northwest Coast Nations, and through these marriage arrangements, the feast and famine cycles of precontact fisheries were smoothed out. A Kwakiutl girl would be acculturated in her role and status early on, to see herself as an integral part of the community. She would expect—and see as normal—her marrying outside the community. It just wouldn't be seen as a big deal. She would be trained in these relationships by her grandmothers and aunties, who, by example, would demonstrate proper behavior for young Kwakiutl women.

In *Initiation*, Nana is the daughter of a Nootkan mother, so she has relatives in the Nootkan community. Yet, throughout the book, she exhibits extreme hostility to girls and women,

> The women remind me of sea turtles, the way their eyes turn to watch me. Their bodies sag in layers of thick skin like whale blubber.

extreme dissatisfaction with her role in the community,

> Have a successful Initiation or fail, the end is the same for all Kwakiutl girls. We will marry some boy we did not choose and leave this village. A wish twists sharply in my belly—not to be born... female, but to be male.

and in general, complains, complains, complains:

> I am prey, caught in a spider's web. Every time the spider creeps, he makes me whirl around and

around. My life is spinning without me. I cling to the web with my hands and feet. I look for a place to leap.

To be female in this village is to be a slave to men's demands. It is to have our spirits slashed before they have begun to soar.

Everyone abandons me. Even the spirits.

In the end, Nana fulfills what she sees as her "destiny," sacrificing herself to bring the salmon back:

A million voices are calling me, chanting the ancient songs of the salmon. Words I once sang to them, words I told no one. They swell in my ears so I hear nothing else. I lift my arms up to the sky to touch the spirits swirling there. I pull them down into my chest, until they fill me.

But here again, the reader is being set up. Nana has "joined the salmon" not to save her people so much as to escape a pathetic existence as a "Nootka wife." As with everything involving Nana, this is all about her. Besides, a *real* Kwakiutl young woman doing this would have left her people more destitute because social relationships were seen as far more important than one salmon run.

It is likely that reviewers from outside the culture will praise *Initiation* as "well researched," "sensitive," and representative of precontact aboriginal life. It is not any of these things.—*Marlene R. Atleo/ʔeh ʔeh naa tuu kwiss*

Scribe, Murdo (Ojibwe), *Murdo's Story: A Legend from Northern Manitoba*, illustrated by Terry Gallagher. Pemmican (1985). 44 pages, b/w illustrations; grades 3-up; Ojibwe

Stories that help explain why the world is as it is, and help us understand the worth of important values such as cooperation, are gifts that ought to be shared. Murdo Scribe's story provides this opportunity. People all over the world have stories that explain the pattern of the stars. Here, Scribe shares the story of the Big Dipper, his version of the traditional legend of the indigenous people of the Manitoba area of Canada. The characters of the story are the animals who face the challenge of living in the northern climate and living in harmony with one another. This story has suspense, and unforgettable characters that illustrator Terry Gallagher captures in detailed pen-and-ink drawings. This book was voted favorite, among a collection of American Indian books, by the fourth graders I read to because of the "adventure and suspense." It's an important book for family and school collections, as well as for people who like to hear many people's stories about the stars and constellations.—*Pam Martell*

Sechelt Nation, illustrated by Charlie Craigan (Sechelt). Nightwood/Harbour. Unpaginated, b/w illustrations; grades 1-3; Sechelt:
How the Robin Got Its Red Breast: A Legend of the Sechelt People, 1993
Mayuk the Grizzly Bear: A Legend of the Sechelt People, 1993.
Joe, Donna (Sechelt), *Salmon Boy: A Legend of the Sechelt People*, (1999).

The Sechelt Nation is a Coast Salish people living on the Sunshine Coast of British Columbia from Gower Point to south of Powell River. They are the first First Nations people to gain control of their own affairs. These attractive little books allow the Sechelt to provide an authorized version of three of their traditional stories. The illustrations by the talented young Sechelt artist Charlie Craigan that alternate between stylized motifs and realistic line drawings of the action are the best feature of the books.

Craigan's great-great grandfather is the chief who hosted the naming event told of in *Mayuk, the Grizzly Bear*. On the occasion of the naming of his great-grandson, a grandfather tells the story of three brothers who were hunting up in the inlets. One was ambushed by a grizzly bear. The other brothers came to his rescue, killing the grizzly, but not before the first was terribly wounded. He was brought home and treated with Indian medicine. To celebrate his survival this grandfather named his great-grandson Mayuk after the bear so that he would have the attributes of that animal. That this book is a story within a story within a story within a story is a common Northwest Coast oral history device.

How the Robin Got Its Red Breast relates an early time in the history of the Sechelt people. Groups of people were living in caves trying to keep the families fed and warm. Young men set out to search for food. The grandfather left in charge of the fire soon flagged and the fire grew dim. The resident brown robin found everyone asleep the next morning with the embers barely lit. He fanned the embers with his wings until he heard the young hunters return. As they entered the cave, he flew out. They noticed his new red breast. The robin's red breast is a sign even today of how he saved the Sechelt people from sure death in those early days. The story provides a strong cultural rationale for Sechelt children to be thankful to and respectful of resident robins on the Sunshine Coast.

In *Salmon Boy*, Donna Joe tells this story of her people with a poignant clarity. Joe has the advantage of fluency in the original language of the stories and also training in education that has resulted in a rendering of import-ant cultural sensibilities usually lost in translation. The basis of this story is the premise that all things are equal and due acknowledgement of who they are, respect in the fullest meaning of the word.

A swimming boy is abducted by a giant chum salmon and swept into the salmon world. Here he witnesses an annual round of life activities and learns about the special requirements of salmon life. When the boy returns to his people with the salmon run, he shares with them what he has learned: that the salmon must be treated respectfully so that they and the people will sustain each other.

While retaining the sacred quality of First Nations story-telling, *Salmon Boy* brings myth into the present in its lesson about what needs to be done to ensure that the salmon will always come back. Charlie Craigan's black-and-white drawings take us into the shadowy world of the salmon. The multiple salmon on almost every second page give the feel of traveling in a school of fish. This little book is highly recommended as a model for how the messages of First Nations mythology, vital for today's children, can be art-fully told.—*Marlene R. Atleo/ʔeh ʔeh naa tuu kwiss*

Sewall, Marcia, *People of the Breaking Day*, illustrated by the author. Atheneum (1990). 48 pages, color illustrations; grades 1-3; Wampanoag

Although it is entirely a product of library research, Sewall has chosen to write this book in the first person plural ("We are Wampanoags, People of the Breaking Day...").

Some background: Massasoit, father of Metacom ("King Philip" of King Philip's War) had made the big mistake of befriending the Plymouth Pilgrim colony, but Metacom, less trusting, bided his time, signing treaties and stalling around while building an intertribal alliance. Betrayed by an Indian informer for the whites, Metacom himself was captured, killed and dismembered, with parts of his body taken as trophies; his head was on display in the town of Plymouth for more than twenty years. Metacom's wife and children were sold into slavery for thirty shillings each. The outcome of the "war" was "the virtual extermin-ation of the Wampanoag, Nipmuc and Narraganset tribes...the cruel pattern of racial conflict had now been firmly established in the New World."[1]

Dates are not given, but the romantic, untouched life depicted in the book has to be just a few years before this tragedy occurred, because "[o]ur great sachem is Massasoit [and] Wamsutta, Massasoit's oldest son, one day shall lead our people." Actually, Wamsutta was summoned before colonial officials for questioning, and died shortly thereafter of what the Indians thought was poisoning. His younger brother Metacom then became the last sachem in the period of defeat for the New England Native allied forces. So the book's time frame, so carefully unmentioned by Sewall, is some-where in the middle 1660s, with the last war, "King Philip's War"—1675—yet to come.

But plenty had already been happening throughout New England. The slaughter of the sleeping Pequot village at Mystic, Connecticut, had occurred in 1637. Various troops and irregulars were marching around on their own, as were ship captains with on-board troops given "Indian duty" shore leaves. Land acquisition frauds were proceeding apace. Traditional Indians didn't like the missionary zeal to convert the "heathens," and the "praying Indian" (i.e., Christianized) towns found they weren't safe against white rampages, either. Whenever Indians committed— or were accused of committing—some alleged infrac-tions of colonial law—such as Puritan "blue laws" about not working on Sundays, or dress codes—they were dragged before colonial courts.

The picture presented under the rubric of "we, us" is therefore false, knowingly false, since Sewall has obvi-ously read the same books that I have for her research. All that I have said above is so much a matter of public record that she could not possibly have been unaware of what was going on in this historical time frame. No Indian in the area was ignorant of what was going on. It was a continuing and expanding disaster, and everyone could see that. Massasoit would come to realize that his youthful friendly help to a scraggly little group of poor, incompetent whites had led to their multiplication like cockroaches overrunning the land.

Sewall's idyll is full of clambakes, hunting, making med-icine out of water lily roots, playing games with neighbors, and so on, but she ends her book with what she presents as customary funeral rites:

> Those who survive us will blacken their faces
> and mourn and leave our house empty forever,
> never to mention our name again. So it has been.
> So it will always be. Aque'ne [peace].

This seems to be a composite of traditions from several cultures, not necessarily Native. It is an ironic ending, an irony that neither children nor most teachers will appre-ciate, because of Sewall's removal of Wampanoag people from the context of a pivotal point in their history, falsely portrayed as a time of peace and ignorance of what was shortly to be upon them, by one who believes she has the right to say "we"; in effect, to speak for the dead.

History is not taught in American schools; we have social studies. A true book about the past (including true fiction, true poetry) therefore must carry its basic foundational historic structure with it, into the intellectual, moral, and ethical vacuum that is American education. Sewall's book does none of this. A part of that truth would be to say that the Wampanoag people, in spite of all that was done to them, are still very much with us. This is something that even children living in Massachusetts do not always know. Those who work at Hobbamock's Village, near the reconstructed Plimoth Plantation, are standing on land that has been Wampanoag territory for a very long time.

It is an obligation upon all who would write of this past, on whatever level, to acknowledge the ghosts, the reality of leaking through memory. Sewall has totally failed to do that. So my "utmost good faith" toward this book is like that which the Northwest Ordinance extended to "the Indians." You can look that up.—*Paula Giese*

NOTE

1 Waldman, Carl, *Atlas of the North American Indian.* Facts on File, 1985.

Shaw, Janet, "American Girls Collection," illustrations by Bill Farnsworth and Susan McAliley. Pleasant Company. Color illustrations; grades 3-6; Nimíipuu (Nez Percé)
Book 1—*Meet Kaya: An American Girl.* 2002, 70 pages
Book 2—*Kaya's Escape! A Survival Story.* 2002, 72 pages
Book 3—*Kaya's Hero: A Story of Giving.* 2002, 73 pages
Book 4—*Kaya and Lone Dog: A Friendship Story.* 2002, 81 pages
Book 5—*Kaya Shows the Way: A Sister Story.* 2002, 73 pages
Book 6—*Changes for Kaya: A Story of Courage.* 2002, 70 pages
***Kaya and the River Girl.* 2003, 48 pages**

Little girls have been playing with dolls for as long as we have been human. If you are a Native mother, you would be hard put to find a doll to give to your daughter that would come near to being a representation of herself unless you made it. And that is what makes this Nimíipuu (Nez Percé) doll in the "American Girl" series so enticing. It's too bad that the Pleasant Company did not produce something that genuinely transmits the Nimíipuu culture.

This series of stories taking place in 1764 could have been worse. The young protagonist has a name, a family, and friends. In the course of the series, she grows and matures. The author does not represent the Nimíipuu people as savages. But whatever information she got from her advisors is filtered through a white consciousness and further adapted to fit the mold of this formula historical fiction series. All life-threatening conflicts are resolved by the end of each story, and all moral and emotional conflicts are resolved by the end of the series. This writing style is an especially bad thing in historical books about Indian people, whose conflicts—over, for instance, water and land rights, the government's theft of treaty funds, the issue of sports mascots—are ongoing. And books conceptualized as teaching tools—or worse, books enlisted in the cause of selling a product—usually result in writing that is stilted and boring. This series is no different. Some of the problems:

• Indian parents and grandparents lecture so that the author can convey information about the people. Besides being culturally dissonant, this breaks the cardinal rule in literature of "show, don't tell."

• Anachronistic wording such as the Lakota word "teepee" and the French words "travois" and "parfleche" are used throughout, even in dialogue. Nimíipuu words during that time period might have been translated as "dwelling," "pony drag," and "carrying bag."

• By having Kaya talk in similes and metaphors, comparing all her thoughts to nature—"her thoughts whirled like smoke in the wind," "she glides over the ground like the shadow of an eagle," "her feelings were all tangled up like a nest of snakes"—the author misses the subtleties of Indian language and thought patterns. Throughout, faces are "dark" and "gleaming," eyes are "dark," cheekbones are "high," expressions are "fierce," and Indian characters "cock their heads" in thought.

• Traditionally, Nimíipuu names given to children had to do with ancestors, place, and responsibility; and names were changed several times during a person's life. Unless the baby was dying and had to be named very quickly, naming was done after great consideration, often by an elder or holy person. It's unbelievable that any 18th-Century Nimíipuu mother would name her baby for the first thing she saw after giving birth—this is a stereotype that goes back even further than Will Sampson's joke in "One Flew Over the Cuckoo's Nest."[1]

• Swan Necklace was the English translation of a Nimíipuu leader's name, but one wonders why—and in some cases, how—the author came up with names for characters such as "Speaking Rain," "White Braids," "To Soar Like An Eagle," "Light On The Water" and "Bear Blanket." Did she research traditional Nimíipuu name giving or did she just spin the wheels for authentic Indian names?[2]

- One can understand the author's quandary in not wanting to use "Tonto-speak," but sign language, a visual-gestural form of communication, has a different syntax than spoken languages and does not translate into standard grammatical sentences. Here, Kaya signs to Two Hawks: "But there's hardly any game up this high. We'd still have nothing to eat."

- A prepubescent Indian girl in 1764 would not have had a relationship with her father that included physical touching. Generally, girls stayed with their mothers or aunties and grandmas; and boys stayed with their fathers or uncles and grandpas. Unless it was an emergency, it is not likely that Kaya would have ridden behind her father on a horse, holding onto him. Nor is it likely that she would have "put her arms around his neck while he held her tightly against his chest for a long time."

- Horse-stealing raids were not the same as raids to capture women and children, nor were they done at the same time. Nor would raiders feed captive children "only scraps from their meals." Captive children were taken into adoption, often given to a family to take the place of children who had died, and treated as well as the other children.

- The "enemy tribe" is unnamed; in any event, people from horse cultures did not whip or otherwise abuse their horses. Previously owned horses were accustomed to being ridden and wild horses were gentled—not "tamed"—by their owners.

- Hunters would not have brought back buffalo to camp and given "the meat and hides to the women." Rather, the camp moved to the hunting grounds so that the women could butcher the meat right there.

- Kaya's sightless sister, "Speaking Rain," as all Native children, would have been taught to take care of herself. She would not have to hold hands while walking with someone, nor would she be constrained from picking berries or gathering firewood, nor would she ask questions about things she could figure out for herself.

- The people all look alike, they are all the exact same tone of brown, and their facial and physical features are the same, too. In pictures where the women and girls are sitting, they're sitting in the wrong position. Indian women in this time period would not have sat with their legs crossed, nor would they have sat with their legs up, hugging their knees.

- *Kaya and the River Girl*, a 2003 tack-on to the series, is the most stupefyingly contrived of all of them. Here, Kaya loses a spontaneous foot race to a girl named Spotted Owl, who is from the "River People." For twenty-one pages, Kaya obsesses about losing the race: she's angry and miserable, her pride is injured, her feelings are bruised, her voice is grim and cold, she struggles with her shame. Finally, when the two girls come together to rescue an elder woman named Elder Woman, they become great friends.

- The non-fiction sections at the end of the books, called "A Peek Into the Past," are uneven. While some parts convey good information, particularly the residential school story in *Kaya's Escape!* and the story of the Dalles Dam in *Kaya Shows the Way*, other parts are rife with error. For instance, in *Meet Kaya*, the author states, "Early white explorers, including French fur trappers, mistakenly believed that all Nez Percé wore shells through their noses and gave them that name." How could anyone look at someone and "mistakenly believe" him to be wearing a shell through his nose? The Nimíipuu people were called "Nez Percé" by the French because they pierced the septa of their horses' noses so that the horses could breathe better and run faster.

- By setting these books in 1764—before white encroachment—the author and publisher were able to sidestep the nasty parts of what happened to the Nimíipuu and to relegate some of the history to the "Looking Back" sections. The series oversimplifies and sanitizes Nimíipuu history, and by doing so, makes history more palatable to the contemporary sensibilities of the young non-Native girl readers for whom this series was conceptualized.

The *Kaya* series exactly illustrates the problem with which we are constantly contending: It's almost impossible to tell another people's story in a believable way, no matter how good one's intentions may be and no matter how many cultural advisors there are. And writing to formula is never a good idea.—*Beverly Slapin*

NOTES

1 The punch line is too raunchy for this publication. Rent the movie.

2 Thank-you to Tom King, *Dead Dog Café Comedy Hour*. Canadian Broadcasting Corporation, 1997.

Shilling, Arthur (Ojibwe), *The Ojibway Dream*, paintings by the author. Tundra (1986). 48 pages, color paintings; high school-up; Ojibwe

Sometimes it is hard to say anything. A thing can be so completely itself that there isn't any place to take hold of it. That is this book. You can talk about form, and line and color, and those terms are meaningless. You could say *The Ojibway Dream* is the perfect marriage of word and picture, and that is true, but the words do not "explain" the pictures; if anything, the paintings explain the words. But truly, they cannot be separated. The poet, the artist, the visionary, go out and bring back messages for us. They say things that we cannot say for ourselves.

> The dream transforms life. For a bright illuminated instant the shackles of everyday eyes are shattered, and the gracefulness of life is laid bare. All things begin here. Mine would be the Ojibway dream.

So this is about Shilling's life, and work—and our history.

> I have survived the fire and wrath of the white man. His long and dying shadow has stretched over the whole earth and universe. I feel I'm a firefly in the terrible jaws of a dying bear.

On each double-page spread, a few words, opposite a painting. The paintings are shocking in their intensity and their beauty, and you need to look carefully, to see everything that is in them. They are a kind of lifeline, but who knows if that will be enough? "There is not enough color to subdue the shadows within me."

Arthur Schilling died, sadly too young, from a heart condition resulting from childhood rheumatic fever. The jacket copy calls this book "a memorial to a magnificent artist." So it is, and the people who put it together deserve great credit for just letting it be what it is. A great treasure.—*Doris Seale*

Silvey, Diane (Sechelt), *Little Bear's Vision Quest*, illustrated by Joe Silvey (Sechelt). First Nations Education Division (1995). 32 pages, color illustrations; grades 1-4; Sechelt

Diane and Joe Silvey of the Sechelt First Nation dedicate their beautiful book to a girl child of the community who has passed on. The story begins in mythic time and features Little Bear, who is preoccupied with himself. Now, preoccupation with oneself is antithetical to the friendships, harmony, and peace required for community living. Overtures of friendship by the other animals are rebuffed with taunting and insults by the haughty Little Bear. Grandfather perceives there is a problem, confronts Little Bear and cuts through his protests that it is the fault of others who are jealous. Grandparents who have much life experience can see the problems children are having and help to nip them in the bud. Grandfather, knowing what to do, sends Little Bear to the island to search his heart. Traditional remedies sometimes take time, and although a parade of land and sea animals come to him, Little Bear remains haughty. It takes time, sometimes a long time. In isolation Little Bear comes face to face with himself and gains insight.

The classic First Nations coming-of-age saga has been captured here: the transformation of an aloof self-centered spirit into a person fit to participate in the communal life of the village. One to whom Grandfather lovingly says: "Welcome home Little Bear, welcome home." The illustrations richly complement the story. The landscape is a colorfully painted background on which the spirit motifs of animals gambol. The transformation of Little Bear is indicated by the changes in his spirit motif.

This book is a visual joy and a textual treat. The section of notes at the end of the book provides a valuable and easy-to-use guide through the culturally significant aspects of the story, and the discussion guide will help students develop meaning for each of the traditional values the story teaches. This teacher- and parent-friendly book is highly recommended.

—*Marlene R. Atleo/ʔeh ʔeh naa tuu kwiss*

Silvey, Diane (Sechelt), *Whale Girl*, illustrated by Joe Silvey (Sechelt). First Nations Education (1996). 21 pages, b/w illustrations; all grades; Northwest Coast Nations

The partnership of Diane and Joe Silvey of the Sechelt First Nation brings to life this story of learning about the balance of good and evil from a First Nations perspective. The cover illustrations of the Sea Serpent and the girl transforming into Killer Whale encircle the Killer Whales at play with the young Peta, perfectly foreshadowing the story to come. In the Northwest cultures of the Kwakwaka'wakw, Nuu-chah-nulth, and Coast Salish, the Sea Serpent may be known by different names but in all are the symbol of transformation and transcendence, signifying the potential of both good and evil. Sea Serpents have poor vision but since they are very powerful they manage to use others to do their bidding. While the Killer Whales are playmates to Peta they also do the bidding, however reluctantly, of the Sea Serpents. Through her friends the Killer Whales, Peta learns of the scheme of the

Sea Serpents to devour her people. She plans to warn the people riding on the whales, only to succumb to the deep and be transformed into a Killer Whale herself.

This story contains many classic traditional elements. Killer Whales mediate between water and land forms. Good and evil is everywhere; the tension between the two is mediated by the will of people who have to make choices. Sometimes people are transformed by such choices, even if the choices are the right ones. The Killer Whales as mediators make explicit the dynamic between good and evil in a way that does not merely tell about but graphically illustrates the dilemma. The beautiful black-and-white line drawings have an intensity that speaks of the tension and action, effectively complementing the text. This book is recommended for all ages.

—*Marlene R. Atleo/ʔeh ʔeh naa tuu kwiss*

Simmons, Marc, *Millie Cooper's Ride: A True Story from History*, illustrated by Ronald Kil. University of New Mexico (2002). 56 pages, color illustrations; grades 3-6

Set on the Missouri frontier during the War of 1812, this is the story of how a brave young settler girl saves the lives of her family and community from an Indian attack. When her family and friends living at Fort Cooper are besieged and about to be massacred by Indians allied with the British, twelve-year-old Millie Cooper volunteers to ride to nearby Fort Hempstead to get help.

According to the foreword, the British "sent their agents to stir up Indian tribes on the frontier and persuade them to attack American settlers." In times of warfare, Indian Nations coalesced into traditional and political military alliances, with leaders making military decisions no less complex than those made by their white enemies. To suggest that Indian "tribes" were "stirred up" and had to be "persuaded" to attack American settlers greatly oversimplifies the situation.

In many ways this story is reminiscent of Walter D. Edmonds' *The Matchlock Gun*, originally published in 1941. The Indians are illustrated, in word and picture, as hideous, war-whooping, unthinking savages, lurking behind trees, menacing and attacking the besieged innocent settlers. There is not one word, not one picture, about the settlers' encroachment on and destruction of Indian land. The whites are fighting for land and freedom. The Indians want to kill them.

The writing is truly godawful:

> That evening at the supper table, Colonel Cooper said to his wife, "The situation looks bad for us. I fear this is the beginning of many bloody attacks

upon our people." "Oh, mercy. I pray that isn't true," replied Mrs. Cooper…. "Dark days lie ahead," [Colonel Cooper] concluded.

Upon entering the thick trees, Millie disappeared from the settlers' view. Her father had been right. The Indians were busy eating and napping.

The illustrations, besides showing the Indians as a mindless and terrifying threat, whooping and hollering and storming the fort on foot, are also extremely unattractive. And since the American flag is depicted with fifteen stripes, one wonders about the accuracy of the other drawings.

More than anything else, *Millie Cooper's Ride* resembles a 19th-Century piece of propaganda for Manifest Destiny. Simpleminded, grossly one-sided, and artistically unappealing, this picture book is not suitable for children of any age.—*Beverly Slapin*

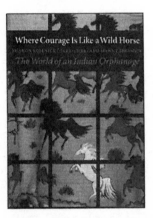

Skolnick, Sharon/Okee-Chee (Apache), and Manny Skolnick, *Where Courage Is Like a Wild Horse*. University of Nebraska (1997). 148 pages; grades 7-up; Apache

It was over forty years ago that the child who later became known both as Okee-Chee and Sharon Skolnick, together with her sisters, were removed from their parents and became wards of the state of Oklahoma. Shuttled back and forth between foster homes and orphanages, Okee-Chee and her nearest sister ended up at the Murrow Indian Orphanage at Muscogee where they stayed for a year before finally being adopted. It is here that the stories of a tough, courageous, resilient nine-year-old child take place. The twenty-six stories comprise Okee-Chee's memories of her family and her year at Murrow.

Okee-Chee's cover painting is luminous. There are horses of many colors and patterns. Some are black, some white, some golden, some brown with white spots, some red with purple spots. There is a blue one with dark blue spots all over. There is one with a turquoise line running down its face and turquoise spots on its rump. All have long, flowing manes. On the front cover the horses are enclosed by dark, heavy bars; on the back cover, they are running free. I wonder which horse belongs to the child, Okee-Chee.

In the introduction, Skolnick says:

> I remember fragments only: hugging and rocking my sobbing little sister in a dark closet for what seemed like hours, until her diaper leaked and the smell sickened us. Loud, angry voices beating me about the ears; belts and callused hands beating me on the butt and back; a slap that knocked me into a steam radiator, scalding my arm.

The beginning of each chapter, called a "photo," begins with these fragments of a conscious experience or dream, in the present tense. This "photo" is followed by a story, usually in the past tense, with added details, descriptions and dialogue. The photos and stories together are compelling and hauntingly describe a child's pain and torment.

There is a story about when Okee-Chee is asked by the other children to kill a dying cat to put it out of its misery. She is asked to do this because she is Apache and it is assumed that Apaches just naturally know how to kill. She asks the cat's forgiveness and then kills it quickly with a rock to the head. The story is entitled "When Only An Apache Will Do."

Some people say that to put a story on a page is to change forever its meaning, purpose and intent. Some people might say that there is something sacred about a family's story too, that it should stay with the family, and when that story is forgotten, then its purpose is done. Some people also say that to tell a story, a painful story, brings healing. Okee-Chee has been encouraged to find her voice, and I hope this has brought her healing.—*Beverly Slapin*

Slipperjack, Ruby (Ojibwe), *Honour the Sun.* Pemmican (1987). 211 pages, high school-up; Ojibwe

I read this book at a particularly hard time for my family. I was spending hours and hours each day at the hospital with my sister-in-law who subsequently passed away, leaving my ten-year-old nephew and seven-year-old niece alone with my brother, their father. Reading *Honour the Sun* helped renew my belief that all life experiences make us strong and help us become who we are to be. My greatest hope for my niece, nephew and brother has been for them to become more of who they are as they learn to live without such an important person in their lives.

Ruby Slipperjack's story, written in seasonal journal form, is about six years in the life of a child growing into womanhood on a small isolated Ontario reservation in the 1960s. It is very representative of the experience of many of us who grew up during the 1960s on Indian reservations. It will be hard for some to believe that many of us had no electricity or indoor plumbing, and engaged in old-style subsistence hunting and fishing during this era. But the story does not dwell on material poverty, on what one might consider a difficult childhood. Rather, the story focuses on Owl's growing up in her family, on the influence of family on who we become as adults. The story is candid, yet not depressing even when difficult times are shared, even when her mother begins drinking. The parenting style of Owl's mom in Honour the Sun reminded me of my own growing up, of the adventure, the family life. I would hope that readers will be able to focus on the good things in Owl's growing up—a close family, area to roam and explore, knowing who you are.

As a sixteen-year-old returning home for a summer visit, Owl knows her mother's words will always guide her:

> "Honour the Sun, child. Just as it comes over the horizon, honour the Sun, that it may bless you, come another day…"

Honour the Sun is a must-read for anyone wanting to understand more about the lives of American Indian people during the social transitions of the 1960s.—*Pam Martell*

Slipperjack, Ruby (Ojibwe), *Little Voice*, illustrations by Sherry Farrell Racette (Timiskaming): Coteau Books (2002). 246 pages, b/w illustrations; grades 4-up; Ojibwe

She lost her father two years ago, in a logging accident. Now her family is poor and kids make fun of her green eyes and her teacher doesn't understand her. She's got a boy's name. And ten-year-old Ray feels that her mother, with no money to speak of and two younger kids to care for, is much too busy for her.

When she gets to spend summers helping her grandma, an elder and healer in a small northern Ontario community, Ray learns how to paddle a canoe, put up and take down camp, hunt, fish, trap, and harvest berries and herbs. Under the careful tutelage of her grandma, "Naens"—"Little Voice"—also learns about silence and compassion and watching her hands grow older. Now fourteen, she is becoming someone who will one day be a "strong green-eyed medicine woman"—someone who knows that there are different kinds of school and that "time would bring what it needed to make things happen," someone who can take the knowledge of the past and bring it into the future, someone who is finding her voice.—*Beverly Slapin*

Sloat, Teri, *The Eye of the Needle*, "based on a Yupik tale as told by Betty Huffman," illustrated by the author. Dutton Children's Books (1990). 30 pages, color illustrations; grades 1-3; Yup'ik

Huffman and Sloat were teachers for more than a decade in Yup'ik villages in West Coastal Alaska. Huffman told this story based on a Yup'ik tale, and undoubtedly enter-tained youth and elders alike. The traditional story—which I haven't been able to trace—would have had a somewhat different emphasis, with a moral instructional purpose opposing per-sonal greed and selfishness, that is absent here.

This is just a funny story, with the little boy, Amik, eating more and more and larger and larger sea creatures (instead of bringing them home to his grandma). He goes home without any catch for grandma, drinking up an entire stream on the way.

He's too fat to get into the underground sod house. Grandma holds up a magic bone needle and tells him to push himself through its eye. Since it's magic, he does. And the needle makes him disgorge a great flood: all the water and all the sea creatures he had greedily swallowed, right on up to a gigantic whale, and a full-size whaling ship none the worse for its sidebar Jonah-con-finement. A fine feast on all the disgorged whale, fish, seaweed, crab, fish eggs, seal, walrus...is had by all the villagers—except for Amik, who is no longer hungry.

The story's joke quality lies in its repetition of increas-ingly improbable beasts that—

G-U-L-L-U-U-M-M-P! Amik swallows. Each time he repeats that Grandma would be proud of his increas-ingly larger catch-animals—but each time swallows them whole. It's actually a pretty funny story to tell aloud.

Little, if anything, will be learned about Yup'ik culture from this story, but then, from the story about the *500 Hats of Bartolomew Cubbins* you would not learn a great deal about the fur trade. (Hats were made of beaver-fur felt. Could those endless hats have caused the appar-ently insatiable demand?) Or theories of rulership (the king gets mad because every time Bartolomew doffs one, a new and more splendid hat appears on his head; Cubbins is magically unable to show proper def-erence to royalty). *500 Hats* is a joke story with a bit of anti-royalist bite hidden in it.

Needle is a joke story with no bite at all in it. Whatever moral bite there once must have been in the Yup'ik original about greed and selfishness has been entirely suppressed in American children's book Niceness. Amik suffers no consequences other than being unable to take part in the feast due to a temporary lack of appetite.

Neither the storyteller nor the children's book reteller— both Americans—noticed that there may be some sort of ethical, moral or even environmental problems caused by persons whose uncontrollable greed and selfishness cause them to gulp down ever larger portions of the world. Greedy Amik could really signify "American expansionism" or maybe even "average American" if we were able to get serious for a moment about this little story. I cannot help wondering: was the original Yup'ik storyteller making ironic play on the Biblical "It is easier for a camel to go through the eye of a needle than for a rich man to go to heaven"? Native storytellers often play with bits of European story, sometimes crafting a story that subtly needles the white man and leaves their Native audience in stitches—but without the original, I can't tell if that was true here.—*Paula Giese*

Smith, Cynthia Leitich (Muscogee), *Indian Shoes*, illustrat-ed by Jim Madsen. HarperCollins (2002). 66 pages, b/w illustrations; grades 2-5; Cherokee-Seminole

Reviewer caveat: I am an unreconstituted Cynthia Leitich Smith fan. Receiving one of her books is cause to drop everything, put my feet up and read.

Review:

Unlike contemporary stories of Indian families written by non-Native authors, *Indian Shoes* is mixed-blood-walking-in-two-worlds-dilemma-free. No dreamcatchers, no Indian rituals, either. Instead, here are six stories about a Cherokee-Seminole youngster named Ray, secure in the loving care of his Grampa Halfmoon and his extended family in Chicago and rural Oklahoma. From trading his own high-tops so that Grampa can have a pair of moc-casins, to overcoming a really serious wardrobe dilemma, to finding a creative solution to a dreadful haircut, to caring for their neighbors' many pets on Christmas Day, to midnight fishing and finding out that contests are not always about winning, these stories are goofy, quirky, laugh-out-loud funny, and poignant, sometimes all to-gether. *Indian Shoes* is about belonging to family and com-munity, about helping neighbors, about learning life's lessons, and about sometimes feeling different but most times knowing who you are in the world.

I can imagine Ray Halfmoon as an adult, sitting around the kitchen table with his own children, and saying some-thing like this: "Did I ever tell you about the time that Grampa Halfmoon gave me a haircut, turned out looking like a lawn-mower accident?"—*Beverly Slapin*

Smith, Cynthia Leitich (Muscogee), *Jingle Dancer,* **illustrated by Cornelius Van Wright and Ying-Hwa Hu. Morrow (2000). Unpaginated, color illustrations; grades 1-up; Muscogee (Creek)**

Jenna is a confident, exuberant child with a large extended family, including a grandma and aunties and neighbors who appreciate and encourage her. Like other Indian children, she wears jeans and watches TV, and especially likes to bounce-step along with the videotape of her jingle-dancing grandma.

Jenna's heart beats "to the brum, brum, brum, brum of the powwow drum," but there's not enough time to mail-order tins to make the cone-shaped jingles she needs for her regalia so that she can dance Girls at the next powwow. So Jenna must find another way to make her dress sing, and she does, by borrowing jingles from the dresses of her women relatives and friends. Just enough jingles to make her dress sing, but not so many that their dresses would lose their voice. And in return, she promises to dance for the women who, for one reason or another, can't.

The soft watercolor illustrations by Cornelius Van Wright and Ying-Hwa Hu are a perfect complement to this gentle, poetic story of balance and community and reciprocity and joy. *Jingle Dancer* is a gift from a gifted writer, lyrics to a song of encouragement to all of the Indian youngsters who enter the dance circle.—*Beverly Slapin*

Smith, Cynthia Leitich (Muscogee), *Rain is Not My Indian Name.* **HarperCollins (2001). 139 pages; grades 5-9; Muscogee (Creek)**

This is a young adult novel with heart. The characters are real. Smith deftly tackles such dominant society icons and artifacts as football mascots, fake dreamcatchers, Elvis, Anime, Pez, cigar-store Indians, and Barbie, as seen from a contemporary Indian cultural context. And there are no vision quests and no mixed-blood identity crises—"walking in two worlds"—that white authors love to write about. Cassidy Rain Berghoff is not troubled by who she is; rather, she's bothered by

other people's perceptions of Indians:

> At school, the subject of Native Americans pretty much comes up just around Turkey Day, like those cardboard cutouts of the Pilgrims and the pumpkins and the squash taped to the windows at McDonald's. And the so-called Indians always look like bogeymen on the prairie, windblown cover boys selling paperback romances, or baby-faced refugees from the world of Precious Moments. I usually get through it by reading sci-fi fanzines behind my textbooks until we move on to Kwaanza.

Written in the first person, each chapter begins with a refreshingly non-linear journal entry. In both journal and narrative, we see Cassidy Rain, called "Rainy Day" by her mom, as a smart teenager with an acerbic wit. Like most teens, she's critical of her looks:

> Here I am, average height, average weight, with bottle-cap boobs and eyes pinched at the corners. Nobody's impressed that I can look out the window and get a tan.

But she's not obsessive:

> Being a mixed-blood girl is no big deal. Really. It seems weird to have to say this, but after a lifetime of experience, I'm used to being me. Dealing with the rest of the world and its ideas, now that makes me a little crazy sometimes.

Rain Is Not My Indian Name is about a mixed-blood four-teen-year-old coming to terms with the sudden death of her mother and more recently, with the sudden death of her best friend, her might-have-been boyfriend. In allowing herself to grieve, she comes to know the fragility of the life that we're given. "I reached down," she says, "and snapped off a spray of Queen Anne's lace, desperate to touch something pretty. Not even caring that it would kill the bloom."

"Back when I was seven," she writes in her journal, "I didn't have to think about what I believed and where I belonged. I just did." As a tiny spider scrambles over her bare foot and the sun brings long shadows, Cassidy Rain is growing into what she will become.

I hope young readers will see in Cassidy Rain's story the interconnectedness of life and death and a delicate sprig of flowers, the birth of babies and the harvesting of rice, believing and belonging, what it is to build bridges and cause them to fall. I hope young readers will see and relate to a very real young person, sometimes tentative and fragile, sometimes steadfast and tough, finding her place in the world.—*Beverly Slapin*

Smith, Ray (Cree), *How the Mouse Got Brown Teeth*, **Whitstone, Dean (Cree),** *How the Birch Tree Got Its Stripes.* **Translated and edited by Freda Ahenakew (Cree), illustrated by George Littlechild (Cree). Fifth House (1988). Unpaginated, color illustrations; preschool-3; Cree**

These traditional stories were written down in an intermediate course in Cree in 1982. For this publication, they have been translated and edited by Cree elder and scholar Freda Ahenakew.

Mouse tells how a boy caught the sun in a snare by accident. No one could bite through it to free the sun, although all the animals tried. In the end, it is the most humble of all creatures, the mouse, who accomplishes what no one else was able to do.

Birch Tree is a Wisahkecahk story. In this one our hero, in his usual fashion, does something completely dumb, then blames someone else for the consequences. The stories are well and simply told. Together with the illustrations by Cree artist George Littlechild, they make two very appealing books.—*Doris Seale*

Sneve, Virginia Driving Hawk (Lakota), *The Chichi Hoohoo Bogeyman*, **illustrated by Nadema Agard (Cherokee/Sihasapa Lakota). University of Nebraska (1975). 63 pages, b/w illustrations; grades 4-6; Lakota, Hopi**

Sneve may have been the first to do a story about modern Native children from a Native perspective. *The Chichi Hoohoo Bogeyman* is about three little girls—cousins—visiting their grandparents one summer. Mary Jo lives nearby, Cindy and her family are from Pine Ridge. Lori is the youngest. Her Mom is Hopi, and the family is in the process of relocating from the Mesa to Aberdeen, near her father's new job. The trouble starts when Mary Jo's older brother screams "Look out! A chichi!" behind the girls in the evening twilight, scaring them half out of their wits. This leads to a real ghost story, and a later discussion between the cousins of chichis (Lakota), hoohoos (Hopi) and the bogeyman (Anglo): a chichi hoohoo bogeyman. Cindy and Mary Jo find this screamingly funny. Lori is not so sure.

Cindy is a pistol, always ready to lead the others into trouble. Lori is the most timid; Mary Jo, a commonsensical kind of kid, lands somewhere in the middle. Eventually, Cindy gets herself and her cousins into some real trouble when they do something truly frightening—for which she swears Lori and Mary Jo to secrecy. Neither girl is comfortable with this, and it all comes to a head in a night of nightmare and hysterics: Cindy runs away.

Sneve has created a close-knit, loving family. Everything is sorted out in the end, and the chichi hoohoo bogeyman turns out to be something utterly different. The girls have done something they were told not to. One might say this was a cautionary tale for them; when somebody tells you not to do something, there might be a good reason for it. Agard's drawings suit the nature of the story, delineating the character of each girl, and illustrating the family as a whole sorting the mess into healing. —*Doris Seale*

Sneve, Virginia Driving Hawk (Lakota), *Enduring Wisdom: Sayings from Native Americans,* **illustrated by Synthia Saint James (Cherokee). Holiday House (2003). 32 pages, color illustrations; preschool-grade 3**

Culled from a variety of printed sources, these sayings are divided into five categories: "Mother Earth," "The People," "War and Peace," "Spirit Life," and "Enduring Wisdom." Some of the sayings are old, some are new; the ones without attribution in the text are Sneve's own. Useful source notes provide context for each saying. I am not a big fan of "wise Indian sayings" taken out of context. They smack a little too much of the thought-for-the-day kind of thing; something to say, "oh, isn't that nice" to—and forget the next minute. This is not in any way a bad book; I don't think Sneve could do one, and some of the quotes are thought provoking, no question; worth hearing, worth remembering.

The picture-book format makes it a hard call as to audience. Kids don't particularly like this sort of thing; teachers doing mul-ti-cul-tur-al love it. The CIP headings practically guarantee the book's loss in library stacks: "Indian philosophy-North America-Juvenile literature," and Indians of North America-Quotations-Juv." An intrepid librarian might just bite the bullet and put it with "Indians" in the j970s.

The real problem is the pictures. Saint James was a particularly unfortunate choice of illustrator. Her trademark brown faces with no features are a bad way to portray Indians, who are already invisible enough. One reviewer found the bright, primary colors a perfect match for the text. They are not. The slabs of pure, flat color make the people into static, iconic figures. Without the accoutrements associated with Indians—braids, bows and arrows, wind bands, eagle-feather headdress, and so on—they could not have been identified as Native people. The illustrations have their own beauty. They are just not appropriate for this book. I don't think Sneve's editors have done very well by her. Maybe she would disagree with me, but I think she deserves better.—*Doris Seale*

Spalding, Andrea, *Solomon's Tree*, **illustrated by Janet Wilson. Orca (2002). Unpaginated, color illustrations; grades 2-4; Tsimshian**

Masks that are danced with are usually made to represent and remember certain kinds of experiences. Masks are symbols of important, intimate, spiritual, personally significant experiences. Sometimes there is personal trauma involved. Sometimes dancing masks can symbolize and evoke the insight or embodied experience of a whole clan, sometimes a whole tribe. Masks don't "tell" a story; rather, they remind each person of the elements of the story, the experience.

On the surface, *Solomon's Tree* has all the elements of an interesting story. A young boy develops a special relationship with a maple tree outside his house. He knows this tree as a living being. When a storm uproots the tree, the boy is devastated. With the boy's uncle's help, the tree lives again through its transformation as a mask, and by owning and dancing with the mask, the boy retains his relationship with the tree. The illustrations are well done and colorful. There is a photograph of the real mask, made by a well-known Tsimshian carver who also contributed the Tsimshian design elements for the book. The author gives the background to the story, and acknowledges the carver's contributions. Andrea Spalding, Janet Wilson, and Victor Reece seem to have collaborated well together.

Maybe, but there are some troubling aspects both to the story and the way it was created.

Elders have historically seen masking activities as spiritually potent and generally not appropriate for young people. Traditionally, young people don't dance until they're able to manage the spirituality of dancing and masking—you don't toy with it. Masks are not toys. That's probably why the cover copy says, "The mask itself will be handed down to Victor's son, Solomon." Yet somehow, the "Solomon" in the book is given the mask and, with his relatives looking on, dances with it.

Having experienced a mask-making workshop taught by Tsimshian carver Victor Reece, the author decided to write a children's book featuring a mask. "While Andrea carved in Victor's workshop," the cover copy says, "she became aware that she had received a cultural gift, one that she is honored to be able to pass on through her story." This "cultural gift," the inspiration of a cultural outsider, became, not the story of Victor Reece's son, Solomon, but the story of another "Solomon," the "Solomon" of Andrea Spalding's imagination.

The problem here is this: When a story is written about a white child, it is seen as a story about an individual. When a story is written about an Indian child, the story is seen—and often taught—as social studies. The Indian child in a children's book written by cultural outsiders is more often than not objectified, generalized, moralized, and—in a word—stereotyped. So this story is not about a child, it's about the Tsimshian people.

Do Tsimshian children develop unrealistic relationships with trees? Do Tsimshian people make masks for children

to dance with in the process of grieving for trees? In the interests of leveling the cultural playing field for children through storytelling, this may seem like a minor detail, but it matters a great deal.

Author and illustrator acknowledge Victor Reece and his family, writing, "Our grateful thanks for your contributions to bridging our cultures. May the bridge grow stronger and wider so more people can dance across." While this is something the author may not have understood, her "bridge" is paved with the spirits and cultures of generations of Aboriginal children.—*Marlene Atleo/ʔeh ʔeh naa kwiss*

Speare, Jean E., ed., *The Days of Augusta*, photographed by Robert Keziere. Douglas & McIntyre (1973, 1992). 80 pages, b/w photos; grades 6-up; Shuswap

Mary Augusta Tappage was born in the closing decade of the 19th Century, in the Caribou country of British Columbia. She was ninety years old when she died in 1978. In her eighties, she "shared with Jean Speare the memories of a lifetime." Out of that sharing came this book.

Born into a time of turmoil, Augusta lived to see Native life change beyond all reckoning. Her paternal grandfather came from the Red River Valley after the arrest of Louis Riel; her maternal grandfather was William Longshem, chief of the Soda Creek Indians. When she was four years old, Augusta was taken away to school at St. Joseph's Mission:

> What I never could understand, we weren't allowed to speak our language. If we were heard speaking Shuswap, we were punished.... And now we are supposed to remember our language and skills because they are almost lost. Well, they're going to be hard to get back...

Augusta married a white man, so she became "non-status." Her husband died when she was young, followed soon by her oldest son. She took what work she could get, and raised her children, as well as taking in others who needed a home.

The Days of Augusta is the story of a life lived, by most standards, on the bare bones of existence, and the photographs bear this out. They are sharp and intimate and yet in no way invasive, in no way do they deny Augusta her strength and her dignity. If Augusta resisted the changes, the difficulty, of her life, "it was with a fraction of the energy she gave to each day's living, for she lived every day to the full extent of her physical and mental strength."

Augusta's life is no metaphor for anything. It is just her life—lived to the best of her ability, in the time when it was given to her. If she knew heroic leaders she does not say so, she was not a "hero" herself, except insofar as all people of her generation who survived and remained whole were heroes. They were our elders. Whatever we have of life and our traditions we owe to them. Augusta never in her life left the Caribou country, and in the end she said, "Life was good. I have not been altogether idle."—*Doris Seale*

Spence, Peggy D., *The Day of the Ogre Kachinas,* **illustrated by Janet Huntington Hammond. Roberts Rinehart/Council for Indian Education (1994). 42 pages, line drawings; grades 3-4; Hopi**

Judson Honyouti is nine years old. Sometimes he forgets, sometimes he's careless, sometimes he loses his temper, just like other children. But since he is Hopi, his parents get out the big guns, and the "Ogre Kachinas" come to straighten him out. The Kachinas threaten to take him away. His parents defend him by giving the Kachinas gifts and telling them the good things he has done. The Kachinas go away. Judson behaves (and never goofs off again for the rest of his life, the reader presumes). And they all live happily ever after.

Hopi—as all peoples—have a complex way of seeing the universe and the mysteries of life. Katsinam, and the people who portray them, represent unseen powers, sacred and mysterious. There are a lot of them; the many prayers, songs, stories, and other sources of knowledge about the sacred powers of Katsinam, are learned by and passed down to only certain initiates. Certain Katsinam perform certain functions; one of them is to discipline unruly children after their parents and grandparents have thrown up their hands.

But without showing any understanding of or respect for Hopi sacred ways, this story becomes a recitation, told to "educate" non-Indian children about the exotic ways of the Hopi. The author is an outsider; her writing is stilted and flat: "Judson Honyouti was a Hopi Indian. He wanted to follow the ways of his people." The artist, also an outsider, has "illustrated books, greetings (sic) cards, menus, postcards, brochures, catalogs, and posters." This is not a qualification. Not recommended.—*Beverly Slapin*

(Thank-you to Michael Lacapa.)

Steiner, Barbara, *Whale Brother,* **illustrated by Gretchen Will Mayo. Walker (1988). 28 pages, color illustrations; grades 1-3; Inuit**

Omu, who wants to be a carver, lives in an igloo (snow dome), which means he is in the central Arctic, and it is winter. He trades his spear—which he just happens to carry around—for a harmonica to a trader. We can stop there a moment and note that no traders (and no one else, either) visited the central Arctic in winter during the period—before World War II—when Inuit people built winter igloos. It's the winter night there then! Kids didn't fossick around looking for things to do and giving away valuable survival possessions; survival occupied all the people—except infants—in this toughest of environments.

Anyway, Omu can't play the thing, so when pops reprimands him for making noise in the igloo, he goes outside (into the 40-below dark) and plays this metal instrument. Kids and adults make fun of his artistic and musical ambitions, so Omu swipes a kayak and goes off by himself. Somehow there is no shore ice. He makes friends with a pod of Orcas who (unlike dolphins) aren't the least friendly to humans, and certainly don't hang around shallow bays to get killed by the people, who greatly value their flesh, fat and bones.

One day when he's playing around in the valuable kayak he sees one of the whales beached. Instead of telling his people about this bonanza, he stays away from home, keeps it alive for five days (by pouring water over it from a large pouch he happens to have handy), and plays his harmonica for it. This wouldn't work, because a beached whale, even a small orca, dies of its own weight maldistributed on land, but never mind. So then another orca tosses him a walrus tusk, which he carves into a likeness of Skana, that takes in the spirit of the dead whale. He returns home and says he's sorry his parents worried. Actually they'd more likely be grieving than worrying; the kid's gone five days they would certainly assume he was dead, and in fact he *would* be dead if it were really the Arctic—but he had to stay with this dying whale, his bro. The parents show no interest in the whale. (Arctic Natives would have been off at once in an umiak to get as much as was left before birds and other scavengers got it.) Instead of supposing he must be some kind of evil spirit to have taken off so oddly and survived, they praise him for the fine carving and his newfound talent at playing a metal harmonica without freezing his mouth.

Whale Brother is a white lady's fantasy that bears no relationship to Native life in the Arctic, Native customs, Native values, Native stories. Steiner's little moralistic tale has nothing to do with Inuit life nor Inuit art, except to deny and falsify everything it's about. This beautifully illustrated book is an example of a depiction of Native life by a person who, knowing absolutely nothing about Inuit people's living conditions in the past or present, has created a mini-legend about a white suburban family in brownface and furs.—*Paula Giese*

Steltzer, Ulli, *Building an Igloo,* **photographed by the author. Holt (1981). Unpaginated, b/w photographs; grades 3-6 (younger for read-aloud); Inuit**

First you find some really good snow. Then you have to check the depth. Make a circle as big around as you want your igloo to be. You're going to need a saw for the blocks, and you'd better outline before you saw, so they'll be the right size and shape.

For Steltzer's book, Tookillkee Kiguktak and his son Jopee, Inuit from Ellesmere Island, demonstrate how it's done. They make it look easy, and making things out of snow is a perennial favorite thing to do for young children, the age group for which this was written. With these instructions, one could probably build an igloo. The photographs are crystal clear, and the text is concise. But Steltzer's intent is not only to entertain. In a land where the Arctic winter begins in September and lasts until June, being able to build an igloo and do it right would have high survival value. Today, Inuit people live in houses, but her book shows something important about a People who have lived successfully for thousands of years in one of the most demanding environments on Earth. Tookillkee Kiguktak still builds igloos on hunting trips: "It is evening. Father and son settle down inside. They look out on a frozen ocean. Tomorrow will be a day of hunting."

—*Doris Seale*

Strete, Craig Kee (Cherokee), *The Lost Boy and the Monster,* **illustrated by Steve Johnson and Lou Fancher. Putnam (1999). Unpaginated, color illustrations; grades 2-5**

Craig Kee Strete is the author of several children's books, adult novels, plays, and one of the funniest science fiction stories I have ever read. His style is quirky and idiosyncratic, never more so than in this original tale.

"Old Foot Eater was an awful old monster. Even the other monsters said so....Well, my goodness, he liked to eat little children's feet!" There's a boy who has been lost for so long that he no longer remembers his name, although he is called Snake Brother and Scorpion Brother by creatures to whom he has been kind. Because of that kindness, they help him to escape when the monster catches him, and to defeat it: "The lost boy with two names got away, and from that day on he never felt lost again."

Although this doesn't even pretend to be a "traditional" story, there's a real Indian feel to it. It comes; you see it; it's gone. No explanation, no "And that is why..." Only a little strangeness that worms its way into your mind and stays there.

The artists are not Native, and the illustrations certainly cannot be said to be "authentic," but they seem right for the story; more than a little weird. And the child has a beautiful face.—*Doris Seale*

Strete, Craig Kee (Cherokee) and Michelle Netton Chacon, *How the Indians Bought the Farm,* **illustrated by Francisco X. Mora. Greenwillow (1996). Unpaginated, color illustrations; grades 2-4**

"In days not so long ago, a great Indian chief and his great Indian wife lived on the homeland of their people." One day a government man came and told them that they had to move, and in the new place, they would have to farm, "and then everyone will be happy." Also they would have to raise sheep and pigs and cows. "Lots of them," said the government man. Problem was they didn't have any—and no money to get them with. "That's not my problem," said the government man, "[b]ut you will be in big trouble if you don't get some." "If you ask me, we already are in big trouble," said the great Indian wife. So she tells her husband to get in his canoe and go see what he can find. "The great Indian chief knew his wife was very clever," so he goes. He sees a lot of stuff, but it all belongs to somebody else.

He's going along, when he sees a moose. "How would you like to come home with me and eat better things than twigs?" says the great Indian chief. "That sounds good," says the moose, and gets into the canoe. "It was a very big moose and a very small canoe."

By the time he gets home, he has a beaver and a bear, too. He's riding the moose, because it is also a very big bear, and the canoe sank.

A week later, the government man shows up: "You promised to raise sheep and pigs and cows, but you don't have any!" "Not in the house," says the great Indian wife. "In the barn," says the great Indian chief. "But I wouldn't go out and look at them now if I were you. I just fed them..."

I'm not going to tell you what happened, but think beaver, bear and moose, just been fed... This is a very funny book, and the illustrations are perfect. They carry the same characteristic deadpan Indian humor as the text. I will tell you this much: This one, the Indians win.

—*Doris Seale*

Stroud, Virginia A. (Cherokee), *Doesn't Fall Off His Horse*, illustrated by the author. Dial (1994). Unpaginated, color illustrations; grades 3-up; Kiowa

Saygee ("youngest one" or "little one") wants her Grandpa to tell her a story, "but which one? He was a living book." Close to one hundred years old, her great-grandfather remembers a far different world. He sits on his bed, watching the setting sun, and Saygee knows not to interrupt him. When he is ready, Grandpa tells her how he got his name.

"To this day," says Grandpa, remembering, "I have no idea which one of us began talking about stealing ponies from the Comanches camped south of us. But for days all we talked about were the ponies and the raid." Inevitably, the thought precedes the deed. In the last dark hours before dawn, the boys take off. They get the horses, but are discovered. In the ensuing chase, "Grandpa" is shot. Bleeding and near to losing consciousness, he still manages to stay mounted, and hold onto his prizes. "Later," he says, "I was told that my hands had to be pried from the ropes attached to the ponies that I'd pulled across the prairie."

Badly hurt, the boy is cared for by his relatives—very effectively. When he can sit up, four elders arrive to discuss the matter with him and the other boys; in essence, to give them what-for. The boys could have endangered the whole camp: "We are not at war with this enemy. Stealing horses is a war deed only!" And most importantly, "No one is permitted to make decisions on his own without the counsel of the tribal leaders." On the other hand, what they had done was very brave. Also the horses were needed. And then the elders give "Grandpa" his warrior name: Doesn't Fall Off His Horse.

This book is not written from a distance, not from the outside looking in. It is a true story, told to Stroud by her adoptive Kiowa grandfather, Grandpa Steve: it's his story. Stroud's characters are true-to-life, as are their relationships and interactions, between the great-grandfather and Saygee, and in the way in which the elders deal with the boys' transgression.

What makes this book unique are Stroud's paintings. She doesn't just put in enough characters to illustrate the action of the story, which is what we ordinarily see. Her pictures are full of people, just as an encampment would have been. Little kids sit on a pony, moms and older girls cook, take care of babies, work on animal hides. When the boys take off, there are kids and ponies all over the place. When they return, people come running out; their great concern for this badly hurt young one clearly visible. In word and art, Stroud has captured life as it was.

The story is over. "Want your light on, Grandpa?" asks Saygee. He doesn't answer. Saygee "could see that he was with his memories again; he was with Doesn't Fall Off His Horse."—*Doris Seale*

Stroud, Virginia A. (Cherokee), *The Path of the Quiet Elk: A Native American Alphabet Book*, illustrated by the author. Dial (1996). Unpaginated, color illustrations; grades 3-4

Stroud, a well-known Cherokee artist, has taken a different tack for ABC books. Although structured as an alphabet book, this is really a story, for older children able to understand somewhat abstract philosophical concepts, with one of Stroud's charming, highly stylized illustrations on every page. The publishers recognize that it really isn't a learn your ABCs preschoolers book, and call it verbal mnemonics, 26 ways (one for each letter of the alphabet) for the child to "connect to nature."

A medicine woman, Wisdom Keeper, takes a little girl, Looks Within, for a learning walk on a path that is shown them by an elk, but is really "a way of looking at life," not a particular forest path. Stroud says she learned these various teachings from such nature walks over a six-year period with an unidentified medicine woman. Some things she really didn't learn right.

We don't bruskly ask cedar permission and start snapping its branches; cedars are very sacred. Someone gathering cedar will pray, bury or sprinkle or burn tobacco, and often give the cedar some other gifts of respect. Burning cedar is not an "I-is-for-incense that helps our prayers ascend" (if anything, that's tobacco smoke); it is a smudge that purifies people and premises before or at the start of ceremonies (the smudging might be the only ceremony, a cleanup).

I got kind of upset about "M-is-for-medicine-wheel," which the publisher even features to illustrate the catalog page for the book. This is a tipi-sized circle of small stones they happen upon in the woods. Wisdom Keeper tells the child it's a Medicine Wheel; she can sit in the center of it and perhaps have vision. Actual stone medicine wheels are very large constructions up on high, barren places of the Northern high plains and Rockies. They were solar and star-rising observatories. Some later became memorials to honored dead chiefs. Small circles of stone found all over the prairies are tipi rings, just left when no longer needed to hold down the tipi covers against the high winds of open camps. They have no spiritual significance, and there are no tipi rings in the woods anyway.

If you find some kind of odd stone construction and you don't know who built it or why, you might sprinkle some cedar to purify it, but should not try to pray there. Good altars are disassembled when done with (so they won't be defiled or used for bad medicine).

I still remember all the grief that some obviously non-Indian people caused us a couple of years ago when they found in the woods our old sweat lodge frame and fire pit. They conducted some kind of ceremony there for themselves. They had assembled a sort of stone collection that had a lot of fake Indian symbols painted on the rocks (bright yellow and blue enamel). We had taken some teenage kids there for a sweat that visiting Canadian elders were going to conduct. Instead, they made us clean up the place, singing and praying fiercely all the while, in purifications (smudging, prayers, offerings) we all took part in, for three days. The fourth day we had to go quite far away and build a new lodge. If not for those stupid rocks we would have just purified the place as usual and gone ahead, I think.

I love the artwork (I'm a big Stroud fan)—but Wisdom Keeper's philosophy unfortunately is a mixture that seems rather more new-agey than Native; a certain strain caused by trying to shoehorn a story into alphabetics like "K-is-for-(corn) kernel." HEY! What is a corn kernel doing lying on the ground in the woods? And "Y-is-for-yarrow"—but, uh, yarrow is an herb that's an immigrant, medicine from Yuropean Tribal Lore. Well, she could have, um, lessee, Y is for Yup'ik (no relevance), Yonder, Yow, Yellow maybe. Yep, ABCs is a very difficult form of literature.—*Paula Giese*

Swamp, Jake (Mohawk), *Giving Thanks: A Native American Good Morning Message,* **illustrated by Erwin Printup, Jr. (Cayuga/Tuscarora). Lee & Low (1995). Unpaginated, color illustrations; preschool-up; Haudenosaunee (Iroquois)**

"To be a human being is an honor, and we offer thanksgiving for all the gifts of life." Among the Haudenosaunee (Iroquois), a prayer of thanksgiving is said at the beginning and end of meetings and social events, and whenever people are gathered together. The thanksgiving address, which acknowledges and thanks Creation, is also said as a morning and evening prayer. The prayer is not memorized; rather, whenever it is said, it is changed according to how a particular speaker feels at the moment. Sometimes all Creation is thanked together, and sometimes thanks is given to each element of Creation. John Kahionhes Fadden (Mohawk) told me, "Every day we are alive—even if we are not feeling well or we're in a bad mood or we have a flat tire—we give thanks to all the elements of Creation. We take comfort in knowing that, when we pass on, these things will continue."

Giving Thanks is Chief Jake Swamp's adaptation for children of the Thanksgiving Address, called here a "Native American Good Morning Message." His simply worded address—"We give thanks to green grasses that feel so good against our bare feet, for the cool beauty you bring to Mother Earth's floor"—is accessible to the very youngest listeners, who can agree, talk about it and add their own personal thank-you's.

What is omitted here is the traditional call for group acknowledgment after each thank-you, something like the formal, "We bring all of our minds together and give thanks," or the simple, "We all agree," or "Don't you agree?" It would also have been nice if the Mohawk text could have been placed next to the English text rather than relegated to the back.

Printup's flat planes, saturated acrylics and highly stylized figures are bold and filled with color and light. Each two-page spread shows as aspect of the Earth's bounty—pristine skies and oceans, rivers, lakes and streams; snow-capped mountains, grasses and trees; butterflies, hummingbirds and geese and all manner of four-leggeds; sun, moon, winds and thunders; and, of course, the all-important foods that sustain us—all are to be recognized and thanked.

Unlike Susan Jeffer's *Brother Eagle, Sister Sky*, which a *Publishers Weekly* reviewer suggests "would pair well" with this book, there are no disappeared Indian ghost riders in the sky here lecturing about the "environment." Rather, there are only human beings acknowledging an awesome gift and an important responsibility. *Giving Thanks* is a very beautiful book.—*Beverly Slapin*

(Thank-you to John Fadden.)

Talltree, Robert (Ojibwe), *The Legend of Spinoza, the Bear Who Speaks from the Heart*, illustrated by Stephanie Roth. Universal Tradewinds (1995). Unpaginated, color illustrations; grades 2-4

The Legend of Spinoza, the Bear Who Speaks from the Heart is a combination of soporific writing with loony fantasyland illustrations, created to market a stuffed toy bear and all of its accoutrements. The book, the bear and a cassette player and tape are part of a package of therapy-related material for sick children. Somehow, we don't know quite how, company decision-makers felt "a strong tie to Native Americana and Native American spirituality"—and this "Indian legend" was born.

This "creation story"—how Spinoza came to be—is set in an unnamed "ancient Indian village" of tipis and wigwams somewhere in the Northeast Woodlands, where the chief's young son, sent out to gather medicine plants, gets into a number of adventures, unwittingly chews on a poisonous herb and slips into a coma. Dad doesn't know what to do and neither does anyone else except the medicine man who instructs him to listen to his heart, so he goes out to the woods and encounters a "Spirit Tree" and a "white stallion." Goes home where he dreams the magical toy bear into existence. Magical bear cures boy, grateful tribe honors bear, bear leaves to help others. But not before this:

> [H]e often spoke about the beauty that lies within each of us and compared us to the flowers—each of us different, yet needing to share one another's unique gifts. He even spoke about how life is like the passing of the seasons—how as each season comes, in its time it must go....[Crooked Moon] began to understand how important it is to believe in yourself and to follow your dreams... that love can heal, and that it doesn't matter how small you are if your heart is big.

Gag. Spinoza looks and behaves like a cross between Winnie-the-Pooh and Teddy Ruxpin on downers. And everyone in this tribe has the same goofy grin—they're all probably on drugs, too.

Some questions: Why would anyone send a little kid out alone to gather medicine plants and why would a parent allow a child to eat something poisonous? Why doesn't anyone know how to treat the ingestion of poison? How would nightshade, a poisonous plant from England, show up in the Northeast Woodlands in "ancient"—precontact—times? What is a "Spirit Tree" and why would it throw branches at the chief? Why would a child who lives in the woods be afraid of squirrels and why does he have a Thunderbird painted on his chest? Where'd the white stallion come from and how did he manage to gallop through the woods without knocking his rider off? How would the tribe know about a Portuguese philosopher and why would he come to them as a teddy bear? Why would an ancient people revere a stuffed toy bear and how would a stuffed toy bear know enough to impart all necessary traditional knowledge to an ancient people?

And why would anyone think that such a stupid story, ridiculously illustrated, is worthy of publication?

—*Jane Waite, Barbara Potter, Ryan Potter, Rachel Potter, Jean Paine Mendoza, Beverly Slapin*

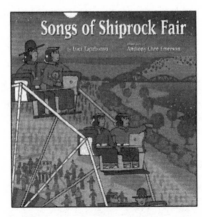

Tapahonso, Luci (Diné), *Songs of Shiprock Fair*, illustrated by Anthony Chee Emerson (Diné). Kiva Publishing (1999). Unpaginated, color illustrations; grades 2-up; Diné (Navajo)

Nezbah wakes up early on the first day of Shiprock Fair. She is very excited; no school, and everybody is going. Tapahonso's text incorporates many of the aspects of the fair: agricultural exhibits, Yeibicheii dances, relatives camping out in the yard, carnival rides, food, parade, powwow, more food, the last-night blessing of the Yei dance. Then it is all over, and "Nezbah is sleeping. She is smiling. She is dreaming of the next Shiprock Fair." That's how it is. You wait, and wait, and then it's over, much too soon.

Emerson's illustrations are wonderful. All the color, all the excitement; you can practically taste the frybread and stew. People of all ages celebrate this time of being together. Everybody looks happy. There will be stories to tell tomorrow—and the next day, and the next.—*Doris Seale*

Tapahonso, Luci (Diné), and Eleanor Schick, *Navajo ABC: A Diné Alphabet Book,* **illustrated by Eleanor Schick. Simon & Schuster/Aladdin (1995). Unpaginated, color illustrations; preschool-up; Diné (Navajo)**

In this ABC book, each letter represents a certain aspect of Diné life: land, relationships, weather, animals, clothing, cultural objects and food. The pastel color-pencil drawings are rich in detail, but as in Schick's other books, they do not fit the brightness and beauty of Dinétah.

While the pictures provide culturally appropriate images, there is inconsistency about what descriptive words correspond with the letters of the alphabet; some are in English and some are in Diné, and there doesn't seem to be a reason why a particular language was used to illustrate a particular word. For instance, the reader is led to believe that "A" for "arroyo" is a Diné word. But the Diné word for "arroyo" is "bikooh" and should be under "B," with "arroyo" as its English (actually, Spanish) equivalent. Similarly, while "H" is for "hooghan" (home) and "I" is for 'I'íí'á (sunset), "G" for "grandma" should be "S" for "shimasani."

A glossary gives the Diné equivalent and pronunciation for each English word, and the English equivalent for each Diné word. Each of the words is explained in the context of Diné culture. There are 21 English words depicted, and only five Diné words, which seems strange for something called "a Diné alphabet book."

The note about the pronunciation guide states that the "written Diné language is a phonetic language, meaning that the spoken word is pronounced very much the way it is written." This is not so. Diné is not a phonetic language—there are several different levels of sounds including gutteral sounds, and the meaning of the word depends on how it is pronounced. That's one of the reasons the Japanese military was not able to break our code in World War II.

The jacket copy invites the reader to "[c]ome and learn all about Navajo life through objects and words in this special alphabet book." Would an alphabet book describing objects from the dominant culture (you know, "A" is for "apple," "B" is for "ball") invite readers to "come and learn all about bilagaana life through objects and words in this special alphabet book"?—*Linda Lilly*

Tappage, Mary Augusta (Shuswap/Métis), *The Big Tree and the Little Tree,* **edited by Jean E. Speare, illustrated by Terry Gallagher. Pemmican (1986). Unpaginated, b/w illustrations; preschool-grade 3; Shuswap**

Jean E. Speare edited a book about Mary Augusta Tappage's memories of her life as a Shuswap/Métis woman in a time of many transitions for Indian people. *The Big Tree and the Little Tree* is one of the stories Mary Augusta Tappage

shared with Jean Speare. The characters in this story are two evergreen trees, the older nurturing in its own way the growth of the younger tree, who comes of age in this story. The story focuses on the ideas of respect and appreciation for the valuable role elders play in helping younger ones grow. But unlike many of our traditional teaching stories, the lesson learned by the younger tree is told in the final pages of the story. This was unnecessary and a disappointment to me. I read this book to my eight-year-old nephew and nine-year-old niece and stopped reading before the summary lesson. They got the message just fine. I would suggest reading this book in this manner in situations where you want the listeners to think through the wonderful values portrayed in the book itself. I wonder if Mary Augusta Tappage chose to tell the story with the lesson so defined, or if Jean Speare modified the telling to conform to a more non-Native style.—*Pam Martell*

Tehanetorens/Ray Fadden (Mohawk), *Legends of the Iroquois,* **illustrated by John Kahionhes Fadden (Mohawk). Book Publishing (1998). 111 pages, b/w illustrations; grades 4-up; Haudenosaunee (Iroquois)**

Ray Fadden has been working since the 1930s to preserve the stories of the Onkwehonwe, the Original Peoples. The list of his accomplishments is long. He is a man who is held in high regard by many more people than those of the Six Nations. It is not possible in the space of a short review to detail his seminal influence or the importance of his struggle for adequate and relevant education to Iroquois young people, but an essay at the end by Nadine Jennings gives a good overview.

This collection of familiar Haudenosaunee stories is made unique by the fact that they are also told in pictographs. A brief foreword, "The Great Peace," tells of the formation of the League of the Six Nations, the Haudenosaunee. It is followed by a short essay on picture writing and many pages of translations of the symbols themselves, including those for each of the clans of the Six Nations.

The first story, "An Akwesasne Hike," is illustrated by Joan

White, a seventh-grade student at the Mohawk Indian School in Hogansburg, New York. The collection includes "Thunder Boy," "The Flying Head," "The Story of the Great Bear, the Big Dipper," "Why We Have Mosquitoes," and others somewhat less well-known. None are watered down and that in no way lessens their appeal for young readers or audiences.

The non-pictograph illustrations, as always from this artist, expand the meaning and power of the stories. The beauty and mystery of the cover painting is especially compelling.

This is an important book and is highly recommended.
—*Doris Seale*

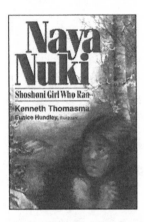

Thomasma, Kenneth, "Amazing Indian Children Series." Baker Book House. b/w illustrations; grades 3-5:
Amee-nah: Zuni Boy Runs the Race of His Life, illustrated by Jack Brouwer, 1995
Doe Sia: Bannock Girl and the Handcart Pioneers, illustrated by Agnes Vincent Talbot, 1999
Kunu: Winnebago Boy Escapes, illustrated by Jack Brouwer, 1989
Moho Wat: Sheepeater Boy Attempts a Rescue, illustrated by Jack Brouwer, 1994
Naya Nuki: Shoshoni Girl Who Ran, illustrated by Eunice Hundley, 1983
Om-kas-toe: Blackfeet Twin Captures an Elkdog, illustrated by Jack Brouwer, 1986
Pathki Nana: Kootenai Girl Solves a Mystery, illustrated by Jack Brouwer, 1991
Soun Tetoken: Nez Perce Boy Tames a Stallion, illustrated by Eunice Hundley, 1984
The Truth about Sacajawea. 1998 (not part of series)

> White men who have tried to write stories about the Indian have either foisted on the public some bloodcurdling, impossible "thriller"; or, if they have been in sympathy with the Indian, have written from knowledge that was not accurate and reliable. No one is able to understand the Indian race like an Indian.—Luther Standing Bear, 1928

Generations later, Kenneth Thomasma's books embody the very problems Standing Bear wrote about. Using historical events as a background, teacher-turned-author Thomasma has produced a formulaic series called "Amazing Indian Children." He also conducts writing workshops, storytelling assemblies and school programs, according to his press packet, "dressed in an Indian elk hide suit, complete with obsidian knife." Choosing to represent Indian children, families, cultures and histories, he says his program "makes those Indian children proud of their heritage and restores self-respect to them that should never have been taken away."

As a teacher, Thomasma could easily have accessed books by Luther Standing Bear/Ota K'te, Charles Eastman/Ohiyesa, Gertrude Bonnin/Zitkala Sa and others who wrote of their own lives as Indian children in the 19th Century. Instead, he visited historical sites, read accounts by non-Native scholars, spoke with Native elders "to get the details right," and added his own "speculations and educated guesses." Does all of this qualify Thomasma to produce a series of children's books about Indian children? Does it qualify him to interpret another people's stories? Does it make his books a way of teaching "all kids what it was like to be an Indian child" or make "Indian children proud of their heritage" and restore "self-respect to them"? Can an outsider enter a community, speak with a few people and then understand enough to be the legitimate voice of its children?

Thomasma may believe so, but it is *not* the voices of Indian children we hear in these books. Thomasma's "amazing Indian children" are disadvantaged and struggling and heroic, and generally engage the sympathies of young readers. In *Naya Nuki*, one of the most popular books in the series, the main character is taken outside of her culture, away from her family, and put in a solitary cross-country trek with the odds of surviving stacked against her. She and her friend Sacajawea are "Shoshoni Indians," and their lives, even before their capture, are described as hungry and desperate and ever wary of the "fierce... warlike tribes from the prairie." But would *she* have thought of *herself* and *her people* as "Shoshoni Indians" or "Indians" at all? Wouldn't she have thought of her people as Aqui Dika, their self-name, usually translated as Salmon Eaters (not Snakes)? Or, simply, wouldn't she have used the terms "we" or "our people" or "our family"? From the first chapter, she even calls her friend "Sacajawea," even though this did not become her name until years after their capture, when she was traded to the Arikara! Our young protagonist wanders through the entire story in a disembodied, out-of-culture state, seeing "Indians," measuring the snowfall in inches and feet, counting the days and knowing "November" was near. She doesn't think of her family often or comfort herself with a child's memories that would make the family she longed to return to real to the young, empathetic reader.

When not fearful of the pursuit by inexplicably "warlike" tribes, she is wary of "wild animals"—wolves, grizzly bears, coyotes and buffalo—and "fierce" weather. While much narrative is spent laboriously explaining (sometimes strangely, as when she makes "beautiful new moccasins" from untanned rawhide) various survival skills and close familiarity with nature, there is a fear of the "wilderness" that is not characteristic of the experience of an Indian child at that time. Her ability to survive, identify food and medicine, and recognize weather changes is described, not as the result of learning from relatives in an unbroken tradition of living with the land, but as instinctive. She "senses" and knows with no logical reasoning or teaching, seeming more like a part of the fauna of the "wilderness" than a child of people who knew the land intimately for millennia. She remains one-dimensional—an "amazing Indian child"—without ever being fully realized as a person and a citizen of a Nation.

The author's voice becomes particularly alienating and offensive in his descriptions of ceremonial practices, which he turns into "pleasing the spirits of the hunt" or "angering the evil spirits of the dead." And, of course, "chanting" for the "Great Spirit." The rumbling of thunder, for instance, is explained as: "The Great Spirit surely must be angry. The heavens seemed to roar." Surely these are not the thoughts of an Indian child in 1800. There is no sense of the worldview of her people. Why doesn't Naya Nuki remember the traditional stories she'd heard that taught her relatedness to the land and all of the creatures of the land? The only stories mentioned are stories of war parties and battles, of heroic "braves" who are never just men or fathers or uncles.

These problems may seem trivial compared to the hateful images of "sneaky, lurking, blood-thirsty, war-whooping savages" of the sort of literature Standing Bear observed as early as 1928 and which remains a concern today. But they still deny Indian characters in children's books the full humanity necessary for non-Indian children reading them to view our complex cultures and for our own children to recognize themselves and their communities in what they read.

Some may still ask, "But are these good books for my child or my classroom?" As literature, they are inconsistent and defy logic. The "heroic" deeds of the young protagonist are "thrilling," but unbelievable. My daughter—who is both the same age as "Naya Nuki"—and I read some of Thomasma's books together. Unlike most of her classmates, she *has* parents with a buffalo robe on their bed, so she was incredulous when she read of a young girl running for five hours with a buffalo robe bundled

on her back and then floating across a river with it! An undernourished child running a 10K race with a robe so heavy it's a struggle for an adult to move it from shelf to bed! Amazing, indeed!

My daughter found the books "easy" to read, "never once having to look up a word in the dictionary." Despite being described as "intermediate reading, ages 9-13," they are written at a third-grade level and the writing is simple and choppy. This from *Naya Nuki*:

> She could travel swiftly alone. She could run fast
> if she had to. She could hide in time of danger.
> She could climb trees to escape wild animals. She
> could find her own food. She could do it alone.
> She would do it alone.

As is probably true of most young readers, my daughter admired the children in these stories for their bravery and felt concern for their disadvantages, particularly the young Zuni boy born with a clubfoot, who is the main character in *Amee-nah: Zuni Boy Runs the Race of His Life*. Again, this is a "fictional story based on the life of a boy who actually lived," although the boy who came to be known as "Nathan" is never fully identified. Permission to tell this story did *not* come from the person or family whose life Thomasma depicts; rather, it came from the son of missionaries who had told Thomasma the story when he was a young camp counselor in Michigan.

Amee-nah, which means "lazy," is the cruel "nickname" given to him because "he never went to sheep camp. He never ran in the stick races. He never played any games with the other boys." This is the name that taunting bullies, his mother and only friend—and the narrator—use. It makes no sense except to dramatize their change to calling him Nathan (which, we're told, means "gift from God") after his foot is "miraculously" healed thanks to the intervention of the mission school's coach and his philanthropic doctor friend. Throughout the story, the only ones who pray for the boy are the people of the mission school—Thomasma doesn't mention the spiritual beliefs and practices of the Zuni people that often co-exist with Christianity. Thomasma's telling of the traditional story of Dowa Yalanne uses the spelling common in the Catholic schools, rather than the traditional spelling. Despite the often laborious demonstrations of "research" that slow all of Thomasma's books, he mentions only briefly the need to fast before the traditional stick races and eating only "paper bread," which he never calls piki. Instead, the young runner

> wondered if paper bread really did any good. It
> was just a paper-thin bread made from cornmeal.
> It surely couldn't satisfy a hungry appetite.

There is no mention of the significance to Zuni people of

corn or this special bread or the stick race. The lightning strike and rain during the stick race are not put in the context of Zuni belief, but serve only as dramatic background for one boy's "amazing" victory. Here, the rain is just an element that makes the race treacherous, with no link to growth or nourishment or a good life. Ameenah seems as much a stranger to his own culture as the young non-Indian readers of these books. Nothing of this book gives those readers any understanding of the people Thomasma presumes to represent.

My daughter said the only thing she learned about the Zuni from this book was that they are good runners, and that she learned "nothing new" about history. She guessed that the children who went to mission schools must have really liked it because the "white teachers were so nice to the Indian kids." To leave this impression, without ever mentioning the devastating effect on cultures and individuals of the mission or residential schools, is worse than mere omission. To choose as his hero a boy who is unable to be worthwhile or whole until saved by white agencies is an unacceptable image for the experiences of Indian children.

With no mention of the Pueblo Revolt of 1680, Thomasma cites World War II as the singular event that taught a Zuni boy "the high cost of freedom," and mentions in another book that the Nez Percé "have gone on to defend the United States against enemies of our freedom. *They* have earned *our* respect and admiration" (italics mine).

Despite the good counsel of people from the Shoshone, Zuni, Blackfoot, Nez Percé, Salish-Kootenai, and Winnebago Nations, and despite the fact that the heroic children and happy endings carry the young reader along, Thomasma's books are filled with errors of fact and perspective. His condescension is obvious in his prefaces and epilogues where he depicts Native Nations as "a proud tribe" (Zuni), "a very proud people" (Kootenai), "proud of their past" (Nez Percé), and "a very special group" (Shoshoni). It would seem that we hold a monopoly on pride and specialness.

All of Thomasma's books are problematic and cannot be recommended on any level. As an Indian, a parent and a teacher, I want better for my daughter and all children.—*Dovie Thomason*

Thurlo, Aimée and David, *The Spirit Line*. Viking (2004). 216 pages, grades 6-8; Diné (Navajo)

Crystal Manyfeathers, a fifteen-year-old Diné (Navajo), is outspoken in her disdain for all the traditions in which she has been brought up. Yet Crystal, who is the most accomplished weaver on the reservation, must prepare for her kinaaldá, her womanhood ceremony, because that is what her mother, now deceased, would have wanted.

Although her best friend, Henry Tallman, is a traditionalist, studying to be a hataalii, a healer, she decides to weave a large rug without the traditional "spirit line." When Crystal dreams about Spider Woman and the unfinished rug is stolen just before her kinaaldá, she must figure out what to do. As is typical of this formulaic sub-sub-sub genre one could call "young-person-coming-of-age-with-an-Indian-theme-fiction": (1) the protagonist exhibits behaviors opposed to those of her own culture, (2) the question of what could cause her to feel so disconnected is not addressed, and (3) the culture itself is depicted in a way that makes no sense.

- A young Diné woman raised traditionally would not consider her home "the middle of nowhere," nor would she feel "suffocated by her father's traditional culture." This is her world. Even if she were to move to the city, she would be tied to the land that would always be her home. The "culture of her ancestors" would be her culture, and she would not think of it as "dead."

- Traditional Diné weavers incorporate a small opening or break—sometimes a light-colored piece of yarn woven into a border—as an acknowledgment that only Creator makes perfect things. It's also a personal reminder to keep one's heart "open" to learning. Crystal decides not to weave in this "spirit line" because she doesn't believe in traditional ways. But she wouldn't be weaving if she were not a traditionalist. Weaving is a sacred gift; it's a way for Diné to embed the culture, it's a constant reminder of why and how things are done.

- Crystal's father and her other relatives wouldn't openly criticize her. Diné don't criticize their children's choices, nor do they impose their beliefs on their children. Rather, they allow them to learn about life in their own way and make decisions about their lives that support their own beliefs.

- A visit to a medicine person for assistance is not a casual thing. The whole family would be involved. They would arrange for the visit and pay in cash, food, sheep, goats, blankets, rugs. A person who does not believe in traditional ways does not consult a medicine person. A young woman would not just go for advice and then decide not to follow it.

- A person would not express to the medicine person how she felt as a result of the ceremony. Rather she would take in the experience and think about its significance. More than likely, it would be the medicine person giving follow-up instructions.

- A kinaaldá is held to welcome a young woman into the circle of women. It is a blessing and an honoring, and physically rigorous, not to mention expensive. A young woman's female relatives would not go through all the work and expense to arrange a kinaaldá if the ceremony "didn't mean much to her," nor would they have one if she weren't ready or if they couldn't afford it.

- There's a lot of ado about addressing people only by their nicknames, since "Navajo names are supposed to contain power, and using them too much burns up your energy." Friends or relatives call each other by first names or nicknames or relationship names. Traditional Indian names are generally not used, except in certain circumstances.

- Despite Crystal's assertions that "traditionalists believed that even a single mistake by a healer during a Sing could cause the gods to ignore their efforts or, in some cases, make everything worse," Diné healers take their jobs very seriously, but if someone makes a mistake, there's something done to redeem it.

- While many Diné don't have personal computers, they have computers in school. In Rough Rock and Chinle and other places, every classroom has computers, credentialed teachers, and good bilingual and bicultural programs that teach cultural and academic language, as well as other subjects.

And:

At home, Diné know each other as Diné, the people, not "Navajo," a word used with outsiders. Diné generally refer to their homeland as Diné Bekayah or Dinétah, not "the rez." Diné do not call white people "Anglos"; the Diné name for white people is "bilagaana." "Crystal Manyfeathers" and "Henry Tallman" are not Diné names. It's inappropriate for a Diné to discuss matters of spiritual significance with an outsider, especially a trader. Not weaving in a "spirit line" would make a rug less, not more, valuable. Schoolteachers do not teach weaving as part of "home economics." A medicine pouch is not the same thing as a purse. A medicine pouch carries spiritual medicine; a purse holds spare change. And you don't take a picture of a medicine pouch, even if it's a device to move the plot. Boyfriends and girlfriends do not sing sacred songs to each other. Nobody, not even a gang member, would steal from a medicine man. Healing a minor itch does not usually call for a prayer. Diné don't joke about death in any way. The term "walk in beauty" is not used casually; it is part of a prayer. Nobody I know has ever heard of a Diné deity called "Beautiful Flowers, the Chief of all Medicines." There are all kinds of good songs, some used for protection, some used for specific blessings, but there is no such thing as a "Good Luck Song." The word "luck" is not part of Diné vocabulary or belief.

The authors appear to have relied on several Diné sources, particularly Monty Roessel's excellent photoessays,

Kinaaldá: A Navajo Girl Grows Up (Lerner, 1993), and *Songs from the Loom: A Navajo Girl Learns to Weave* (Lerner, 1995). But a quick comparison between these titles and *The Spirit Line* shows that the authors don't know enough about Diné culture to write about it, even with help. In *Songs from the Loom*, for instance, Spider Woman instructs Changing Woman to leave a small opening in her rugs:

"If you don't leave an opening," she said, "you will close in your life and thoughts. You will be unable to learn anymore."

Here is the Thurlos' version of Spider Woman's instructions via Henry (Junior) Tallman:

I'm sure you were warned about Blanket Sickness and Spider Woman when you first learned to weave. If you omit the tribute due her, Spider Woman will leave cobwebs in your mind and trap your thoughts inside the pattern of your rug. Why would you ignore that—particularly after Spider Woman herself came to warn you?

It's not the role of Diné men, even medicine-men-in-training, to talk to a young woman about weaving. It's especially not their role to lecture her. If her mother had passed, her women relatives—grandma, aunties, sisters, female cousins—would make an extra effort to support her. They would teach her what she'd need to know as a woman and what she'd need to pass on to her own children.

Once again, while young white middle-class readers will readily identify with the young protagonist here, cross-cultural authors have manipulated them into thinking they are getting something real. And the reviewers joined in, writing that *The Spirit Line* "contains accurate portrayals of Navajo customs" (*School Library Journal*), is "filled with well-integrated cultural details of Navajo life" (*Booklist*), and that "Navaho beliefs, traditions, and rituals are woven throughout the story line, and readers…gain an appreciation for the traditional ways of (Crystal's) people" (*Kliatt*). With the critical writing that Indian reviewers have been doing for years, there is no longer any excuse for ignorance.—*Beverly Slapin*

(Thank-you to Linda Baldwin, Gloria Grant, and Linda Lilly.)

Tingle, Tim (Choctaw), *Walking the Choctaw Road: Stories from Red People Memory.* Cinco Puntos (2003). 142 pages, b/w photos; grades 6-up; Choctaw

There are storytellers and there are tellers of story; Tim Tingle is the latter. The twelve stories here read like told stories, with a fluency of timing and rhythm. These are stories of ordinary people doing extraordinary things as magic brings healing, shape shifters test bravery, tragedy leads to courage, and true friendships develop in the worst of places.

Choctaw women make magic so that enslaved people can cross Bok Chitto and get to freedom's side. The medicine and wisdom of an elder woman—"keep working to the good"—give a boy the courage to defeat a shape-shifter. A youngster carries the memories of his mother, and her bones, as he continues with the okla nowa, people walking, on the Trail of Tears. A widowed woman with a healing stone shows a young boy that you don't have to be blood to be family. A child at an Indian residential school, unable to attend his brother's funeral, finds that "wherever you are, you can always find one decent person." A twenty-year war between father and son is resolved, and when Mawmaw regains her sight, there is no more "saltypie."

In a brief preface, Tingle sets each story in time and place and acknowledges the person or family with whom the story resides.

The stories are put down chronologically, but linearity isn't always a good choice, especially when the stories are related to each other. I would like to have seen "Saltypie" first, followed by the "Trail of Tears," and then have the stories circle back in time and come around to the present. Some of the historical photos scattered throughout the book, such as Mawmaw and one of her grandchildren on her front porch, are beautiful, but many have little to do with the story in which they are placed. I would also like to know something about Norma Howard, whose awesome painting graces the front cover.

But overall, these are evocative tellings by and for the Okla Homma, red people, clay people "kneaded out of this place," people who, as Tingle says, "reached across boundaries to offer a hand to those in need." Written in a down-to-earth, accessible style, these stories will especially appeal to cynical young people who don't especially like to read.—*Beverly Slapin*

Troughton, Joanna, *How the Seasons Came: A North American Indian Folktale*, illustrated by the author. Bedrick/Blackie (1992). Unpaginated, color illustrations; grades 1-3; Ojibwe

> Once the world was always cold and when the wolf's son fell ill he could not be cured, until the wolf and his brave friend the fisher went on a dangerous journey to bring down spring, summer and autumn from the land above.

Actually, this is not a myth that "comes from the Algonquian Indians of the north east U.S.A." It comes from the Ojibwe Indians in Northern Minnesota, which I will note in geographical reference is "near Winnipeg," if that helps.

A dozen or more versions of this tale were collected in my home state by William Jones—a citizen of the linguistically related Fox tribe who had become a student of Franz Boas, and traveled northern Minnesota in 1903-1905. While this publication (*Ojibwa Texts*, American Ethnological Society, 1917) was a bit delayed, copies of the hard-to-get material have been circulating among Native curriculum developers in Minnesota and Wisconsin since the early 1970s when someone got hold of it and the new invention of photocopying did the rest. There are quite a number of children's versions, some of them in our language, some in English, some in facing pages of both.

Some have fallen into the hands of non-Indian story-miners, and it seems most likely it is from one of these that Troughton actually cribbed her tale. Since the Algonquian "tribe" is an invention of ethno-linguists (it is a pejorative word meaning "bark eaters" applied by the Iroquois to some of their enemies), it's hard to imagine how "they" got credited with it, but in the story-mining industry anything is possible. One thing characterizes all the versions I've seen (none attributed to "the Algonquian tribe of the north east U.S.A." to be sure): they don't begin with Daddy wolf seeking help for his sick son. That seems to be something Troughton has added for kid appeal.

This is also not a "myth." We distinguish those (major religious import, creation stories, major moral and ethical) from "little" teaching stories which (like this one) answers kids' "why" questions. Actually, in the Big Picture, it was Nanabosho who freed Summer from her captivity by Winter, but that's another story.

In *this* story, it is said, the "birds of the seasons" were always above the sky, it was always winter.

The birds were captured. Some say by a village of grizzly bears. The animals do plan to free them, and Fisher (Odjig, an animal made almost extinct by the peltry trade, because its hide was worth twice the price of a beaver hide) is their leader. In most versions, the animals do not jump up toward the sky; they travel a long way and cross a lake. Fisher leads the animals—in good war-band leader fashion—to bite holes in the canoes and paddles of the villagers who have captured the birds of—not three seasons—but only summer. After releasing the birds—they are hidden in birchbark makuks, boxes, Fisher is nearly caught but escapes into the sky, where he becomes the constellation generally called the Big Dipper. Sometimes he's hit by an arrow in the tail, just as he's reaching freedom in the sky; the arrow point through the tail becomes Polaris, the North Star.

In Troughton's version, the birds are in budgie-like cage confinement somewhere up above the sky. The animals all try to jump up there, but only Fisher is "long and skinny" (fishers are kind of like weasels), so he makes it, does the job, but gets shot by some really ugly people who come running up and are called "the Thunderers." Animkeeg, Thunderbirds, never take human form, and don't socialize that much with people or animals. In their cages, like so many canaries or budgies, the birds sing various poems roughly based on Diné prayers, particularly the Blessing Way.

Troughton's Fisher dies up there above the sky, his body falling across the hole he punched in it jumping up there, his corpse blocking his entry hole, so the birds can't fly back Upstairs. The corpse turns into some kind of stars-or-other, thus dumping the astronomy part of the teaching story—a particular constellation and (arrow version) conceptual explanation of the observed natural phenomenon: Dipper/Fisher and whole night sky seem to revolve nightly about the Pole Star (because it's pinned by the arrow). Not in Troughton's version. The father wolf and his child look up at the stars, sad scintillant memory of Fisher's self-sacrifice, bringing the warm weather that has allowed the small wolf to heal.

Actually, Native peoples have always had a pretty sophisticated sense of science. There is neither cultural learning nor validity in *How the Seasons Came*. And this author is a whole mult-cult industry—she's done eleven more books in the *Folk Tales of the World* series by Bedrick/ Blackie.

—*Paula Giese*

Turner, Ann, *Red Flower Goes West*, illustrated by Dennis Nolan. Hyperion (1999). Unpaginated, color illustrations; grades 2-4

This is a poignant story about the adventures and hardships of a settler family on their journey to California to take part in what has become known as the Gold Rush. Using young James as the first-person narrator, there is just enough detail here to convey to young readers what this experience might have been like for settler children. The pencil illustrations, in muted shades of grey and brown, are very, very evocative, with a red geranium virtually the only touch of color. The faces are the faces of real people.

Because it is so evocative, one scene in particular stands out. Someone who is described as "an Indian" saves Pa from drowning. In thanks, Ma offers him the "red flower," the family's beloved geranium that Ma had dug up from their garden and carries in a wooden box to travel with them. Rather than accept the gift, he "smiled and shook his head." In the Native way, a gift is accepted; not to accept a gift is considered rude. While the text describes the Indian man as smiling, in the picture he has a "stoic" expression. And finally, this is the only mention of Indian people in the whole story. Going west at this time period, the family would have met Indian people from many different Nations. While *Red Flower* is the story of a settler family, and no children's story can or even ought to reflect everyone's perspective, at least something ought to have been said of the effect of the Gold Rush on the peoples on whose lands the settlers were encroaching.

If not for this important omission, *Red Flower* would be highly recommended. As it stands it is not.—*Beverly Slapin*

Umpherville, Tina (Cree/Métis), illustrated by Christie Rice. Pemmican Publications. Unpaginated, color illustrations; grades 2-4; Cree/Métis:
Jack Pine Fish Camp (1997)
The Spring Celebration (1995)

Narrated by a child named Iskotew, these are two stories about life in Brochet, a small village in northern Manitoba, "where the winters are long and bitterly cold." As the days get longer and warmer, Iskotew and the other children look forward to the spring celebration, when they can play with all their friends on this beautiful warm Spring Sunday.

Every summer, Iskotew—she is named "little fire" in Cree because of her bright fiery red hair—and her family and friends go to work at the fish camp, where she learns, among other things, about shopping on credit (what seems to be free has to be paid for) and sharing with bears (who don't mind eating rotten fish).

Christie Rice's watercolor paintings with pencil overlay, in subdued tones of blue, brown and green, suit these gentle little stories perfectly. Although the details are muted, readers can always tell which of the people is Iskotew. Hint: Look for the one with the red hair.

—*Beverly Slapin*

Urrea, Luis Alberto (Chicano), *Vatos,* **Photographs by José Galvez (Chicano). Cinco Puntos (2001). 95 pages, b/w photos; high school-up; Chicano**

When I was first asked to review this book, being seriously feminist I thought: Men, men, men, why do I want to spend time on a book of photos of men? Especially the notoriously super-macho young types called "vatos" (street slang for dude, guy, pal)? Then I opened *Vatos,* glanced at just a few pages, and it was a matter of "Wow! Wow!! Wow!!!" all the way through.

The photographs offer a marvelous variety of humanness, a range of age and lifestyle, an unending combination of playfulness and seriousness. Many photos contain several moods and dimensions in a single image. These are more than pictures of people, they are pictures of relationships. They give us a world many of us never know; once known, through this book, it is haunting. Luis Alberto Urrea's "hymn to vatos who will never be in a poem" is the perfect verbal accompaniment to Jose Galvez's imagery. How can a few words simultaneously evoke such sadness and celebration? But they do, and every line is a snapshot in itself. For those who know little of Chicano urban street life, an education awaits you.

The mix of poverty, racism, despair, courage, absurdity and beauty, arrogance and self-mockery can be found in many cultures of the oppressed. But people of Mexican origin grown in the United States seem to have a claim to collective uniqueness that has usually been romanticized or ignored. This book commits neither sin. It is simply rich and powerful in the reality it presents.

Galvez's thirty years of photographic experience, and the composition genius he developed, have made that possible. He was lead photographer of a *Los Angeles Times* team that received a Pulitzer Prize for their portrayal of Latinos in Southern California. They were the first Chicanos to receive a Pulitzer. Goes with the book, doesn't it? Just another bunch of vatos the Anglo world finally noticed. Gracias, Jose, your book is a gift to us all.

—Elizabeth (Betita) Martinez

Van Laan, Nancy, *Rainbow Crow,* **illustrated by Beatriz Vidal. Alfred A. Knopf (1989). Unpaginated, color illustrations; grades 1-3; Lenape**

Rainbow Crow is a new and supposedly improved version of an old Lenape story of how the first snow grew so deep it buried the animals, and how Crow brought fire to earth, melting the snow. A consequence of Crow's bravery is the loss of his melodic voice and brightly colored feathers.

The first sign of trouble is in the author's note, where Van Laan speaks of her long-term intrigue with "Crow, also known as Raven," because of the bird's size and temperament. Uh, most amateur bird watchers know that crows and ravens are very different birds of different sizes and different temperaments. And in our traditional stories, Crow and Raven are two very different Beings.

The illustrations are troublesome, too. The watercolor paintings of lavender and bright green birds and tropical-looking foliage do not even come close to the images of Eastern Pennsylvania, part of the traditional homeland of the Lenape people.

As for the story itself, Van Laan's adaptation completely destroys what might have been a beautiful traditional story. The jacket copy describes a "poetic retelling... perfect for reading aloud," but the story is far from poetic. Several times within the story, the animals talk to each other in moronic, rhyming chants:

> Scritcha, scritcha, screetcha, scratcha,
> Yippa, yappa, yow hi yowl!

and

> Aiya, aiya, aiya, aiya,
> Rain, Rainbow Crow,
> Stop the snow, Crow.
> Fly to the sky high,
> Rain, Rainbow Crow,
> Aiya, aiya, aiya, aiya.

I imagine that Bill Thompson, in whose family this story resides, is deeply embarrassed for having given Van Laan permission to "adapt" it. And I can't imagine why Van Laan could possibly think that her retelling will please a "wide, new audience" when, most likely, the traditional version of the story has been enjoyed for hundreds, if not thousands, of years.—*Barbara Potter*

Van Laan, Nancy, *Shingebiss: An Ojibwe Legend,* **illustrated by Betsy Bowen. Houghton Mifflin (1997). Unpaginated, color illustrations; grades 2-4; Ojibwe**

The diving duck who lives by the lake could fish even in winter, "for Lake Superior is much too large to freeze over, as most lakes do." So North Wind, or "Winter Maker," as Van Laan likes to call him apparently because it sounds more Indian, freezes the waters of Lake Superior solid and Shingebiss needs to find a way to fish through the ice. So despite Winter Maker's threats, the little duck is determined and courageous and finds a way to adapt to his environment, surprise, surprise. As much as Winter Maker tries to do him in, he finds ways to get what he needs. He succeeds four times, but "seeing Shingebiss so brave and content made Winter Maker angrier than ever…. 'I will find a way to defeat you.'" This goes on and on, and finally, Shingebiss wins.

What really bugs me about this is that this "Winter Maker" acts more like a christian god than one of our sacred beings. In our story, North Wind and Duck go back and forth, teasing each other, as we do when we're fond of each other. But here, Winter Maker wants to punish duck because duck is challenging him. In the end Winter Maker ends up leaving "in a blinding whirlwind of sleet and ice," but it's the end of the season anyway.

As many non-Native "retellers" will do, Van Laan finds no problem with throwing in elements of other people's stories, in this case, the Abenaki story about how spring defeated winter. This is not part of our story, and it just doesn't make sense here.

In an apparent attempt to redeem herself, Van Laan says in her author's note that "tobacco and gifts were taken to an elder in the Grand Portage Chippewa Band to ask for an understanding of this story." She didn't ask permission, just understanding, and why she didn't understand it I don't know.—*Barbara Potter*

This story was originally published by Henry Schoolcraft in 1841 in his book, *The Indian in His Wigwam.* Schoolcraft's wife was Ojibwe, and he collected a lot of stories and songs from his in-laws. However, Schoolcraft was a product of his time and his linguistic limitations. He was writing for an early 19th-Century white audience, so the English language is flowery at best, leaning heavily toward the cultural prejudices of the times. His wife didn't read and write in English, so she couldn't exactly look over his shoulder and correct his errors. His bloops, fumbles and outright fabrications therefore remained intact and mistaken for fact based upon direct observation. Schoolcraft remains an unshakable, unquestionable source into the present among many non-Indian readers and "scholars," contributing to a phenomenon that I refer to as "Buckwheat Anthropology." While the information recorded is invaluable, it should be put into the context of an era of conquest during which Native Americans were depicted as childish and incapable of managing the resources of their territories within the scope imagined by the conquerors.

It is obvious that, at the time this story was recorded, Schoolcraft had a hard time understanding the concept of Winter, or *Biboon*, as we call him, as an animate character. The storyteller must have kept saying, "Look, it's this guy who makes it into wintertime, all winter long…." This is about as close as one can get to Schoolcraft's rendition of the name Winter, or *Biboon*. It is a matter of understanding the structure of a language, what sounds right, what doesn't. And Schoolcraft didn't quite.

And neither does Nancy van Laan. Her name for *Biboon*, "Kabibona'kan," is just that sort of garbled almost-Ojibwe. It's a little bit like translating the term "ice cream" into Ojibwe, using the USDA legal description. That's the way I feel about her glossary in general. Some of the words are about as accurate as if Schoolcraft's wife had interrupted him while he was reading a book about astronomy, and then asked him a question about his anus.

I am dumbfounded that this non-Indian had the audacity to invent her own glossary. She does indicate in fine print in the back of the book that she brought "tobacco and gifts" to a Chippewa elder to ask for an understanding of the story, but I must admit that I would have like to have been a fly on the wall during that particular conversation. It must have been a landmark event in the field of cultural confusion. I wish I had a nickel for every time a non-Indian author comes to an Indian with specific non-contextual questions for cultural information and then unwittingly, non-maliciously misuses that information.

Van Laan also borrowed Schoolcraft's mid-19th Century cadence and culturally loaded writing style. The result is yet another Indian story told in stilted English that makes Indians sound childlike and simple. We do not refer to the distant past as "the way-back time." If we did, we'd all flunk out of Freshman Composition 101. For Van Laan to impose this crude language style upon us is to promote the proliferation of destructive stereotypes for her own economic benefit. The too-frequent result of this subtle stereotyping is that non-Indian educators often assume that Indians can't communicate about anything without a non-Indian to transform our words and ideas. Many people also assume that we can't possibly interpret our own cultural material, because our styles don't fall into the accepted norm for Indian stories. Norms change. Just ask Rosa Parks.

Also, I'm not sure I agree with Van Laan's translation of Shingebiss as merganser. Things vary from one community to another, and most people just don't have a name for every single duck. But in my family, we used the name *Dzhiinigipizh* to denote a smaller duck with more distinct markings. We had a child's song about the character, which we translated as "Digger Duck." We had even invented a modern verse to the song: "*Dzhiinigipizh* ate my hockey puck." My family still uses *zhiishibonh* for merganser. It is the maiden name of one of my aunts.—*Lois Beardslee*

Vennum, Thomas, Jr., *Wild Rice and the Ojibway People.* **Minnesota Historical Society, 1988. 358 pages, b/w photos; grades 7-up; Ojibwe**

As the salmon is to the Northwest Coast peoples, as the buffalo to the peoples of the Plains, so is wild rice to the Anishinaabeg.

Mahnoomin, wild rice, is a grain that grows in shallow lakes and along the margins of some rivers in the Great Lakes region. In the early fall, *mahnoomin* bears plentiful grains that still are harvested from canoes poled through the standing reeds. This method leaves enough reseeding grains to fall later, when the last of the head shatters. A few grains fall into the water when the stalks are pulled into the canoe with one stick, struck gently with the other. Traditionally, rice chiefs observed the rice and declared when it was ready: ripe enough that the dying reeds would not be hurt by canoes crisscrossing the beds, but the stalks would spring back up later to deliver their remaining grains to the mud for the next year's crop. And the people gave thanks for it.

The rice is woven into Ojibwe culture through legends and ceremonies; *mahnoomin* was the center of Anishinaabeg existence. Harvest was a time when families came together to work, hunt, fish, and socialize before the long winter; then broke up into smaller family units to support themselves on the winter hunting of a particular woods range. When prepared by drying, parching and husking, mahnoomin is richer in nutrients than all cultivated grains; caches of *mahnoomin* can remain viable for years.

Vennum's book is divided into eight sections: The plant itself, *mahnoomin* as food, in legend and ceremony, methods and social life of the traditional harvest, the rice camps and the society they were part of. The last chapters— the economics, the law, and the future—take *mahnoomin* into the second half of the 20th Century. World War II was the beginning of the end for this millennia-old tradition. As young men whose strength was so important in the traditional method of hulling, were away at war, the older men developed machinery for threshing and parching.

This technology evolved into small rice-processing plants and to the death of the rice camps. People drove to the rice lakes, got a day's harvest, and drove home, giving it over to the processors, who dry, parch, and thresh the rice with simple mechanical setups. The emphasis changed from a social and ceremonial occasion—gathering and celebrating the food that was the center of life—to getting a big harvest for cash.

Because most of the traditional beds were not included within reservation boundaries, wild rice supervision fell under state and provincial control in the U.S. and Canada, the cause of great resentment from the people for whom *mahnoomin* is a gift. The prospects of mechanization attracted the interest of giant food corporations, several centered in Minnesota.

Vennum discusses the effects that forcing Great Lakes Indian peoples onto reservations has had, including the legal struggles around aboriginal hunting and gathering rights reserved to the peoples in 19th-Century treaties. In Wisconsin, a suit by two brothers who challenged the state's right to regulate winter ice-fishing resulted in a Supreme Court ruling that upheld these treaty rights on state and federal lands. The main struggle there centered on tribal spear-fishing, and Vennum points out that a similar struggle may develop around wild ricing, too.

Once commerce entered the picture, there began to be lobbying for scientific support. The Minnesota legislature funded the University of Minnesota to research "taming" the wild rice—make it cultivable in artificial paddies less sensitive to environmental conditions, and growing in thicker grains with looser husks for mechanical processing. By the 1970s, much commercial "wild" rice was "tame" or paddy rice, grown by white farmers in the economically depressed areas of northern Minnesota. Some tribes formed their own marketing collectives, but these have never been able to compete in price with paddy rice, so their limited sales have been to tourists and a few non-Indian city health food co-ops.

Federal agricultural price-support law has resulted in devastating industrialization of the paddy rice. Chemically fertilized and sprayed with pesticides, mechanically planted and harvested, this "tame" rice is not only very cheap to produce, California operators also receive federal subsidies for not planting the white rice paddies to keep the prices up for white rice. So the paddy operators in northern Minnesota cannot compete.

Most northern Minnesota tribes have made some experiments in tame paddy rice farming, although this saddens the traditional people. Cross-pollination of tame and wild rice has resulted in new strains infesting the rice bed lakes, where the traditional hand harvesting by canoe can still be carried on. The elders consider this a desecration of the gift. Because of the large price differential, the cash-crop small market has all but disappeared. If the harvesters are to make even a small amount of money for a whole family's efforts during the several weeks of the harvest, hand-harvested rice must be sold for higher prices.

Tribal spokespeople have suggested making ricing an Indian-controlled industry. This seems unlikely what with the involvement of giant international food corporations that buy up anything they can get their hands on. After pointing out that the traditional beds are threatened by dams, environmental pollution and a huge mining enterprise near the Mole Lake reservation, Vennum says: "For cultural reasons alone, the Ojibway people will probably never give up ricing willingly." Vennum's book is a sorrow song. It ends with words from Norma Smith of Mole Lake:

> We have a deep feeling of satisfaction and gratitude as we sack up the rice again toward evening.... I often wonder what my children will do when the rice is gone forever. What will take its place when this last tradition is gone?

—*Paula Giese*

Von Ahnen, Katherine, *Charlie Young Bear*, illustrated by Paulette Livers Lambert. Roberts Rinehart/Council for Indian Education (1994). 42 pages, b/w illustrations; grades 3-4; Mesquakie

Von Ahnen, in collaboration with Joan Young Bear Azure (Mesquakie), recounts a story about a nine-year-old child and his family who lived on the Mesquakie reservation in Tama, Iowa, in 1955. As this story unfolds, the Mesquakie are about to receive a cash treaty settlement from the U.S. government, for lands taken from their ancestors.

Charlie and his family are materially poor. They have needs that typify some of those the Mesquakie had in common at the time, many of which could be met with the settlement. Charlie's mother needs a new stove; his father needs tools to fix up the family home. Charlie wants a new red-and-silver bicycle, one he can use to perform errands, but most of all, one he can ride to school and have the other children admire.

The story opens with Charlie going to the woods to make an "offering" to the Great Spirit for his bicycle. Every day, Charlie prays silently for that bike. While children are taught by precept to pray for wisdom, generosity, courage, strength, being kids, they will sometimes pray for material things. But not like this:

> His first offering was his one and only aggie marble.... Along with the marble was his best piece of bubble gum, slightly used; a good length of string; several yellow feathers he had found in the woods; two perfectly shaped green leaves; an odd key; and three good fishing worms which had crawled away in the night.

Charlie also tries to convince his grandfather, who sits on the tribal council, of the importance of his desire. His little speech sounds more like an "Indian" orator from a B western movie than a little boy:

> "I am proud to be Mesquakie," Charlie said, placing his right hand upon his heart. "I do not mind that I do not have clothes as good as the children who live in town, nor do I turn away when they call me names.... Is there not a time when a small Mesquakie dream could come true? Have I in some way offended the Great Spirit or the spirits of my ancestors? Am I not worthy.... Never will a thing be of greater importance to me than having this bicycle."

His grandfather, who talks like this too, says that a portion of the money will be put into a trust fund to benefit the youngsters at a later date, and then, lapsing into Indian-speak, pontificates:

> "My grandson...how am I to say if you are worthy? A man's worth is not to be measured by another. Only the Great Spirit can make such judgments."

So Charlie goes off to nag the Great Spirit again, this time bringing along a newspaper ad with a picture so the Great Spirit doesn't make a mistake and give him the wrong bike.

Well, something works, because the tribal council reconsiders and gets all the kids brand-new bikes.

This fictionalized story based on actual events allegedly

attempts to present the value of community among the Mesquakie. While it is implied that the collective good of the people takes precedence over satisfying one's individual desires, this message is diminished. And the focus on Charlie's non-traditional spiritual practices for his own benefit overshadows the importance of this value. The fact that all the children receive new bicycles has the potential to convince children that if they wish hard enough, all their material desires will be realized. Nothing could be further from the truth. Not recommended.—*Naomi Caldwell*

Von Ahnen, Katherine, *Heart of Naosaqua*, illustrated by Paulette Livers Lambert. Roberts Rinehart/Council for Indian Education (1996). 114 pages, b/w illustrations; grades 4-6; Mesquakie

This coming-of-age-story-with-an-Indian-theme takes place in 1823, as a twelve-year-old Mesquakie girl "faces change, loss, young love, and the true meaning of friendship and courage" as her dispossessed people move west.

The point seems to be to acquaint the reader with Mesquakie culture by way of Naosaqua, her Nokomess (grandmother), her father Red Arrow, and her friends, Little Fawn and White Cloud. Some of the characters have Mesquakie names, and others have English ones.

When Naosaqua finds out that her people are leaving, she is very upset. ("There are more tears in my heart... than there is water in this stream.") The people move, Naosaqua continues to fret, the people almost starve, a cousin tribe saves them, Naosaqua falls in love ("Naosaqua gazed deeply into Gray Beaver's eyes.... Her heart beat steadily, like a small Mesquakie drum"), and all is well.

As is usual with novels of this genre, U.S. depredations are minimized, cultural misinformation abounds. The prose is replete with pseudo-cultural jargon—"We were very careful. We did not offend the Spirit of the River."—and stupefyingly terrible writing:

> The land produced much food, and the rivers and the forests abound (sic) with wildlife rich with furs and pelts.

This too:

> I see no happiness ahead.... I see no village in the moons to come where my wickiup will be a place of warm contentment. Once my heart was certain in the ways of our people, and my moccasins were set in the path I knew to be good. Now I travel in the moccasins of another and know not the path I follow or where it will lead.

Many animal metaphors ("Her heart fluttered like a bird within her breast"). Men are "braves" or "warriors." Women are ineffectual. Truly awful.—*Beverly Slapin*

Waboose, Jan Bourdeau (Ojibwe):
Morning on the Lake, illustrated by Karen Reczuch. Kids Can (1997). Unpaginated, color illustrations; grades 3-5; Ojibwe
SkySisters, illustrated by Brian Deines. Kids Can (2000). Unpaginated, color illustrations; grades 3-5; Ojibwe
Where Only the Elders Go—Moon Lake Loon Lake, illustrated by Halina Below. Penumbra (1994). Unpaginated, color illustrations; grades 1-3; Ojibwe

I was looking for a book for my nephew's eighth birthday when I spotted the front cover illustration of *Morning on the Lake*. The young boy on the cover looks just like my nephew, and as I read the story, I was reminded of my own growing up experiences learning about and believing in my potential from my grandmother. The story begins at sunrise and ends after dark, a long day filled with many special experiences for an Ojibwe mishomis (grandfather) and his noshen (grandson). The day's activities are not staged nor do they feel contrived, yet the grandfather takes advantage of opportunities for his grandson's learning and self-confidence building at every turn.

The last scene of the story made my heart skip a beat as a childhood memory of my own, so similar to that portrayed in the story, unfolded alongside the storyline. It is evening as Grandfather walks quietly and confidently into the deep woods with his grandson following as best as he can. But the darkness of the woods is an uncomfortable environment for the grandson who is not able to see his grandfather clearly. Pausing, the grandson realizes he is being watched by a pack of wolves. Though the child is not aware, Grandfather is close enough at hand not to let anything happen, yet far enough to allow his grandson his own experience in the situation. The grandson has an extraordinary and safe experience with the wolves and the grandfather folds him into his arms after the wolves leave and gives him the comfort and respect he deserves. My own growing up experience included countless similar situations where I had opportunities to learn on my own with the confidence that support was just around the corner if I was ever in real danger.

I read this story to my sister-in-law's fourth-grade class the last day of school before summer break, and you could have heard a pin drop as they listened to the story and enjoyed the beautiful illustrations by Karen Reczuch. It was hard to stop their enthusiastic discussion about the book and their own experiences when it was time to go home. This is a treasure for anyone who loves stories about meaningful relationships between the generations.

—*Pam Martell*

SkySisters is a beautiful companion to Waboose's *Morning on the Lake*. After putting on their warmest clothing, two youngsters—Alex (*Nishiime*, Younger Sister), and Allie (*Nimise*, Older Sister)—go out into the moonlight and walk across the frozen north country to Coyote Hill. Tonight they will see the midnight dancing and shimmering of the Sky-Spirits, which some people call the Northern Lights. While the sisters eat snow from their mittens, suck on glistening icicles, and meet a rabbit and deer close up and a coyote in the distance—whose call they joyfully answer—the exuberant Alex is learning from her sister how to be patient and quiet. At the top of the hill, they spin until they fall down dizzy in the snow. And then they see what they came for:

> High above us are the Sky-Spirits, dressed in my favorite green and Nimise's blue. We watch them sway and flicker in the four directions. Streamers of pink and purple swirl and flow across the sky. Twisting and turning, the Sky-Spirits join together. Around and around they spin. Faster and faster. Their shimmering parkas and scarves lift with the wind as they dance in the northern sky. They wave down to us. And we wave back. Over and over.

Waboose's words combined with Brian Deines's luminous illustrations will have young readers delighting in the chill of a northern night, the warmth and affection of a close-knit family, and the radiance of a child's wonder.
—*Beverly Slapin*

Where Only the Elders Go—Moon Lake Loon Lake is Waboose's first title, and it is very different from the others. The cover illustration has many layers of wonder. We see the head and face of an elder who has passed on, and he has a look of contentment. He is lying on the ground, his white hair spread out, mixing with the roots of the trees around him. There is a loon, and a full moon, and stars. This is a peaceful place.

This is as much a poem as it is a story, or maybe there is no difference. A child hears the call of a loon, and it brings him memories of his mishomis, his grandfather, who has gone to "a peaceful, restful place where only the Elders go, Moon Lake Loon Lake." In a story of long

ago, an elder remembers his life as he prepares to move on, just "as the Loon leaves her offspring when they have learned all that she can give." As he looks up, he hears the call of a loon, and he is ready. He "lies down, and closes his eyes. He lets his spirit go, peacefully. Where only the Elders go, Moon Lake Loon Lake." And the boy again hears the call of a loon.

Halina Below's vibrant watercolor art, in mostly blues and grays, complement the quietness of the story.

—*Beverly Slapin*

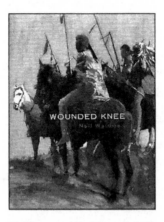

Waldman, Neil, *Wounded Knee*, illustrated by the author. Atheneum (2001). 54 pages, color illustrations; grades 4-6; Lakota

On December 28, 1890, the remnants of Big Foot's band were camped not far from Wounded Knee Creek. They had been on their way to join Red Cloud at Pine Ridge when they were intercepted by the Seventh Cavalry, Custer's division. It was forty degrees below zero of a South Dakota winter, the people were starving and they had no proper dress for this weather. The band at this point consisted mostly of women, children and older people. They had been herded by the soldiers into a ravine and were completely surrounded by military and armaments. Their leader, Big Foot, was dying of pneumonia. No people could have been less capable of defending themselves, never mind being a threat. They expected or were perhaps hopeful of continuing their journey on the next day.

The next morning, when the cavalry opened fire and the people realized what was happening, they grabbed up the children and babies and fled in terror. Only a few escaped and the rest—some 300 women and babies and old men—were mowed down. The men of Custer's division were out for blood and revenge, and on December 29, 1890, they got it. Black Elk, who witnessed the massacre as a young man, later said that

I did not know then how much was ended. When I look back now from this high hill of my old age, I can still see the butchered women and children lying heaped and scattered all along the crooked gulch as plain as when I saw them with eyes still young. And I can see that something else died there in the bloody mud, and was buried in the blizzard. A people's dream died there. It was a beautiful dream.

And I, to whom so great a vision was given in my youth,—you see me now a pitiful old man who has done nothing, for the nation's hoop is broken and scattered. There is no center any longer, and the sacred tree is dead.

Yet the tragedy that became known as the Wounded Knee Massacre is consistently portrayed in children's books and texts as a battle arising from a series of unfortunate cultural misunderstandings.

Neil Waldman's treatment is no different. In Chapter 1, which is called "Massacre," Waldman says,

> Thus ended the last battle between two proud and warring peoples. It was the inevitable conclusion of the clash between two disparate nations, the end of the culture of nomadic hunters who had roamed the great plains of North America for centuries.

Wounded Knee has been praised as "sympathetic" and "balanced" and "nonjudgmental," yet the question of just how a depiction of a massacre can be balanced has not been asked. Indeed, to present a "balanced" picture of a tragedy that is still being mourned more than 110 years later is not possible. On the scale of justice, some things are heavier than others, and genocide is one of them.

While Indian peoples were struggling to maintain land, culture, and community, the whites were trying to take it all away. And they did, by murder, by germ warfare, by wholesale kidnapping of children. How can anyone with integrity give a "balanced" account of that?

Several other things that Waldman has done here warrant discussion.

That hundreds of white people, including settlers, were killed in the Santee rebellion in Minnesota in 1862 is not disputed. This is Waldman's version (italics ours):

> The Santee planned to strike only the soldiers and their forts. But when they had ridden out into the settlements, years of *pent-up frustration* over their treatment on the reservation over-came them, and the Santee *reverted to their traditional methods of warfare*. Galloping through the countryside in small bands, they burned farms and houses, killed all the people they could find, scalped them and

mutilated their bodies. When the violence ended, nearly 500 settlers were dead. Another 500 lost their homes.

In truth, the military decision to go to war against the whites was not an easy one. It was deliberated in council for a long time. After a small group of young men killed a settler family, it was argued that no Santee was safe from the whites, and that a preemptive strike would be more effective than a defensive battle. Little Crow argued against warring with the whites at this time, because the whites had a stronger military presence. But in the end, he reluctantly agreed.

While groups of undisciplined young men picked off the settlers and burned their farms, Little Crow led the Santees in war against the army. A month later, as Little Crow had predicted in council, they were defeated.

When it was over, the cavalry rounded up some 600 prisoners of war, and in individual military trials that lasted from five to fifteen minutes each, found 303 of them guilty and sentenced them to death. Of these, Abraham Lincoln ordered thirty-eight executed, and on December 26, 1862, holding hands and singing their death songs, they climbed the scaffold and were hanged.

This was a bloody war, with many killed on both sides. It resulted in mass trials, and the largest mass execution in U.S. history, neither of which Waldman mentions. Instead, he simply and simplistically portrays the Indians as "reverting to their traditional methods of warfare," galloping off to slaughter helpless settlers.

Throughout Chapter 1, Waldman paraphrases *Black Elk Speaks* without attribution. For instance, Black Elk's "I painted my face all red, and in my hair I put one eagle feather for the One Above. It did not take me long to get ready, for I could still hear the shooting over there" becomes Waldman's "He hurriedly painted his face red. He wove an eagle feather into his hair."

And in the few places where he actually quotes Black Elk, he does so ineffectually. For instance, Black Elk says:

> Men and women and children were heaped and scattered all over the flat at the bottom of the little hill where the soldiers had their wagon-guns, and westward up the dry gulch all the way to the high ridge, the dead women and children and babies were scattered. When I saw this I wished that I had died too, but I was not sorry for the women and children. It was better for them to be happy in the other world, and I wanted to be there too.

Waldman's version:

Later that day, Black Elk walked out along the bloodstained banks of Wounded Knee Creek. He came upon the lifeless bodies of more than one hundred and forty men, women, and children. "When I saw this I wished I had died too," Black Elk later lamented.

Throughout, Waldman peppers his text with unattributed dramatic scenarios, such as this:

As the earth was littered with their belongings, the braves glanced nervously at one another, sensing that a bloody confrontation loomed just ahead.

While appearing to be sympathetic, Waldman's choice of words—"braves" and "warriors" instead of "men," "chants" instead of "prayers," "nomadic hunters" instead of "people"—distances the non-Indian child reader from the real people Waldman writes about. Here is an example (italics ours):

While *these proud people* were diminished and humiliated on the reservations, the leaders in Washington encouraged the destruction of the bison, the *ancient food source* of the Lakota as well as the other Plains tribes. They realized that once these beasts were gone, the Indians would no longer be able to live as *nomadic hunters*. It was their plan that all the Indians should eventually be forced onto farms, *where they would no longer pose a threat to white society*. And so the bison were systematically slaughtered. In the end, the great herds, which had once numbered in the millions, were brought to near extinction, and the families of the *nomadic hunters* began to starve.

This kind of writing encourages the non-Indian child reader to think in limited ways about Indian people: They were a threat to white society, so something had to be done. They became anachronistic in their own land and couldn't keep up with civilization.

While writing like this encourages a sort-of sympathy, it discourages real empathy. Rather, it gives the non-Indian child reader a reason to feel that some of what happened is too bad, but it also keeps the reader from identifying with the Indian people.

We cannot imagine what could have motivated Waldman to write this book, other than to showcase his art. But Waldman's impressionistic black-and-white and color acrylic paintings—mostly copied from the photographs of Edward S. Curtis and his contemporaries from the Smithsonian and Library of Congress collections—are nothing new and further distance the young reader from the real lives of real people. Young readers—both Indian and non-Indian—will do better reading Black *Elk Speaks* and Amy Erlich's adaptation of Dee Brown's *Bury My Heart at Wounded Knee*.

And be it noted: Twenty-eight members of the Seventh Cavalry received the Congressional Medal of Honor for their work in the "last great battle of the Indian Wars."

—*Beverly Slapin* and *Doris Seale*

(Thank-you to Jean Paine Mendoza.)

Wallis, Velma (Gwich'in), *Two Old Women: An Alaska Legend of Betrayal, Courage and Survival,* **illustrations by Jim Grant. Epicenter (1993). 145 pages, line drawings; grades 5-up (younger for read-aloud); Gwich'in**

One of the commonly held beliefs about Native peoples is that those who lived long enough to become old were no longer considered "useful," were not cared for, and in times of trouble, were routinely abandoned.

In truth, it would sometimes happen that, in the starvation times, or when there was great danger, those who might slow the People down would have to be left behind. Sometimes old ones, seeing how they might be a danger for all, would ask to be thrown away. *Two Old Women* is the story of one such time in the history of the Gwich'in people, passed down to Velma Wallis through her mother. It tells how Ch'idzigyaak and Sa' were left behind—not of their own choice, how they found the will in themselves to survive, and what the People learned from what they had done.

The words of *Two Old Women* sit on the page more like story than "literature," with the immediacy and solidity of reality.

Sa' marveled at the power the land held over people like herself, over the animals, and even over the trees. They all depended on the land, and if its rules were not obeyed, quick and unjudgemental death could fall...

This is history, and a teaching story, as Wallis herself makes clear in the introduction:

This story told me that there is no limit to one's ability—certainly not age—to accomplish in life what one must. Within each individual...lives an astounding potential of greatness. Yet it is rare that these hidden gifts are brought to life unless by the chance of fate.

This is a good and honest book.—*Doris Seale*

Walters, Eric, *War of the Eagles.* **Orca (1998). 224 pages; grades 7-up; Tsimshian/Haida**

This is primarily the story of Jed, a young Haida-Tsimshian boy, and his best friend Tadashi, a Japanese Canadian. Both of their communities are struggling against racism during World War II. In the plot, this takes the form of bullying, name-calling, opposition to interracial romance, and bar fights. After the bombing of Pearl Harbor, tensions heighten further. When Tadashi's family is among those removed from their home, Jed first defends it from looters and then—after finding out about the planned confiscation of personal items and homes—rescues some of Tadashi's family's possessions. Meanwhile on the local base, an injured eagle is nursed back to health, in large part by Jed, and finally freed.

Jed's grandmother can read his spirit: "I could feel your spirit's all wrong the instant you put your hand on the door." Her voice is crafted to sound mystical, other. Jed's grandfather, she claims, is now the eagle. And the eagle metaphor itself, which has become a cliché in Native-themed coming-of-age novels, is a bit inconsistent here—representing grandfather, Jed's identity, *and* the "caged" Japanese Canadians.

The dialogue poses other questions as well. Tadashi says, "Yellow skin, slanty dark eyes, dark hair. To some people I can't ever be a Canadian." The latter statement is an expression of frustration, and it's clear that the perspective of the first is being attributed to those same "some people." However, it's not clear why Tadashi would summarize their perspective in their terms like this. Later, Jed says, "You don't think I'm good enough because I'm a half breed?"

It would take a lot of carefully crafted set up for young readers to understand what might lead characters to speak this way about themselves. Jed does struggle with identity issues, thinking of himself more as the child of the English-Canadian father who never appears in the book, than his mother, who does. But Jed has no conflict with her or his people on his mother's side of the family. It seems as though internalized, socialized self-hate is a theme (and it could be a powerful one). But here, with the family and community structures presented in the novel, it's unclear why these particular boys speak this way.

In addition, both boys alternate between lecturing about their cultures and being baffled by them. For example, Tadashi says, "I want you to understand this isn't me or my family but some of the older, real Japanese." And Jed explains,

> "The Tsimshian, the old time Tsimshian, like my grandmother, live their whole lives right where the forest meets the sea. They never venture too far into the forest or too far out on the ocean. They believe both are inhabited by spirit creatures which take on the form of animals. These creatures are mostly good and playful, but if provoked or shown

disrespect, they can be malicious or deadly. Of course, I don't believe in that stuff."

We see a lot of this stopping to lecture the reader in children's literature, but even more so in cross-cultural stories. (This is different than telling a story within the story or a first-person character venting or thinking aloud.) From a character perspective, it's often inconsistent. Here, we have two boys growing up together in neighboring communities. Try to imagine a child telling his best friend, for illustration's sake, "Older Presbyterians live in the suburbs, but young ones shop downtown." Lecturing is also often erroneous, if only by over-generalizing, and unnecessary. If any more information is needed, really adds something, or clears up a misconception, it can be framed in an author's note. Unless a child is for some reason raised outside of a particular environment, it does not seem "other." Naturally, different generations have different perspectives and life experiences, but that doesn't make their members any less individuals.

This is an interesting historical period, and the plot does raise some questions. Why, for example, is Tadashi's family the target of government suspicion when relatively recent white immigrants are not? And there is a need for characters from different underrepresented communities to be reflected in children's literature.

However, in a story that attempts to bring to life a moment in history, the characters must live and breathe so that young readers can identify with them as human beings and, therefore, feel an emotional investment in not only the tale but also the greater historical context. This does not happen here.—*Cynthia L. Smith*

Wargin, Kathy-jo, *The Legend of Sleeping Bear*, illustrated by Gijsbert van Frankenhuyzen. Sleeping Bear Press (1998). Unpaginated, color illustrations; grades 1-3; Ojibwe

A mother bear and her cubs escape a forest fire in Wisconsin and attempt to swim across Lake Michigan to the northwestern part of Michigan's lower peninsula. Only the mother bear completes the swim, and she waits on a hill for her cubs. She waits forever and becomes the Sleeping Bear Dunes of the Leelanau Peninsula. The cubs are, in time, raised out of the waters of the lake and become the Manitou Islands.

There's no attribution for this story, other than that the author "believes" it was first told by the Ojibwe of Michigan.

Our traditional stories about landmarks are usually pretty short. Usually they talk about how the landmarks came to be and sometimes there's a lesson in them. They serve as cultural maps that connect the people with the land and her other inhabitants.

But in Wargin's story, there is no such connection with the land, there is none of the "aliveness" of our stories. "Long, long ago," Wargin begins, and children are treated to an illustration of a white guy chopping down a tree. Pictures of more settlers follow: "It was a time before pioneers planted colorful gardens of pumpkins, potatoes, and corn." (Since these are all indigenous crops, one would think that something said to be an Ojibwe story would show *Indian* people planting, harvesting "colorful gardens of pumpkins, potatoes, and corn.")

This story is belabored and dull, in the dumbed-down way that some authors seem to think children enjoy. Mother Bear's fur is "blacker than the darkest night," her eyes are "large and round," her cubs are "soft and playful," and their den is "small and cozy." But even worse than the way in which this story is told is the characterization of Mother Bear.

Bears are very strong, powerful animals; they're very smart, too. They are leaders and teachers; in many of our traditional stories, they provide great knowledge to people who respect them and understand their language. I have a really hard time imagining a bear teaching people to make silly sacrifices for their kids.

And the sickeningly sweet rhyming couplets in which Mother Bear talks—

> My children, do you promise
> That you'll swim with all your might?
> If we are to reach the other side,
> We must swim throughout the night!
> My children, are you coming?
> You are strong, and you are clever!
> My children, can you hear me?
> I will wait for you forever.

—is an insult to the bear and the language she would speak to her cubs.

It is clear that the author does not understand Ojibwe

stories, and just reading her introduction is enough to discredit this book. Here, she states,

> Most legends are based in fiction, which means that they're not necessarily true. However, the real magic of a legend exists in the fact that it is a story passed on from generation to generation.

Our traditional stories are not based in "fiction"—they're based on fact and spirituality and relationship to the land. Our stories are passed on from generation to generation, but this is not their magic. Their "magic" is the wisdom and knowledge that are passed on through the stories.

It offends me that this book is called a legend when it clearly is not. I don't know what the purpose of this book is.—*Barbara Potter*

Wargin, Kathy-jo, illustrated by Gijsbert van Frankenhuyzen. Sleeping Bear Press. Unpaginated, color illustrations; grades 1-3; Ojibwe:
The Legend of Lady's Slipper (2001)
The Legend of Leelanau (2003)
The Legend of the Loon (2000)
The Legend of Mackinac Island (1999)
The Legend of Sleeping Bear (1998)

The coastlines of the western Great Lakes, Huron, Michigan, and Superior are greater in distance than the coast of California. It is only natural that we, the Anishinaabeg, the indigenous people of the region, would have specific landmarks along those coastlines. It is only natural that we would fabricate stories about those landmarks in response to curious children. About three quarters of the way up the east coast of Lake Michigan north from the great swamp, Chicagonh, at its southernmost extremes, is big hill known variously as "a crouching bear," "bear lying down," and sometimes as "a sleeping bear." It's common to grow up hearing more than one story about a landmark. Most of them tend to have pragmatic messages about coping and surviving. This one roughly marked the halfway point in a long stretch of coastline without protective bays, before part of it collapsed overnight into the waters of Lake Michigan.

Eventually, a state park called Sleeping Bear Dunes was created and later transformed into a national park. The public land drew subdivision development of old homesteads in the form of summer homes and increasingly large permanent communities. The story about the bear who fled a forest fire on the opposite shore of the lake became the version most enjoyed by the non-Indian population. It tends to be romantic rather than pragmatic. Sleeping bear figurines, jewelry, posters, t-shirts, artwork, books and stories of any kind are sure sellers in this tourism-based community.

When Kathy-jo Wargin did her first book in her series of faux/borrowed/retold/abysmally interpreted northern Great Lakes Indian tales, *The Legend of the Sleeping Bear*, I gagged. But, hey, it's one of those Indian stories that's been so used and abused by non-Indians for so long that we kind of don't want it anymore. We tiptoe around it, and when someone tries to hand us a ten-foot pole and asks us to justify it, we respond with, "Haven't you got a twelve footer?" So, it's one of *those* stories, one of those white people's Indian stories. Ah, but Wargin didn't stop there. There was a whole collection of Indian stories put together and mistranslated by Henry Rowe Schoolcraft more than 150 years ago, just waiting to be dredged up and marketed, out of the context of the horrid era of extermination in which stories were collected and "interpreted." There was a whole niche to be filled, a niche for mushy, live-up-to-white-stereotypes-about-the-docile-Indians-who-willingly-give-everything-to-superior-white-author/interpreters, stories for white schoolteachers to fool themselves into thinking they're really doing justice by minority books. Yeah, like we need more of those.

I am tired of being the embodiment of your stereotypes about Indians, I am tired of living the consequences of your tired, antiquated, downright Elizabethan ideas that we are lesser but ignorant open targets for cultural appropriation, land appropriation, civil rights appropriation, your get the Indians out of the way because I need a summer cottage justification, your get the Indians with better credentials out of the way because I need a good paying job justification, your get the Indians out of the way because I need a subject to write about and interpret for whites like me justification.

Shame on Kathy-jo Wargin for abusing damaging stereotypes about Indians like me to find herself a money-making niche in the publishing for children industry, for purporting to retell, translate, interpret in an out-of-date manner for a non-Indian audience my culture, my history, my family's past. Shame on the bookstore and museum gift shop managers who tout them as representatives of Great Lakes/northern woodland culturama. Shame on the public school librarians who continue to buy them, read them, and use them to dehumanize and shame the Native American children who live in and near their school districts, who fail to educate themselves about better alternatives, and who continue to mistrust Native American authors—most of whom are better educated than they are. Shame on the legislators of the State of Michigan for making *The Legend of Sleeping Bear* the official state children's book, for officially sanctioning a revival of Little-Black-Samboism, for taking the attitude of anything goes when it comes to exploitation of Indians by whites and let the casinos take care of the Indians.

Can't we just sweep that whole mid-19th Century set of inappropriate expectations and values out the door and move on to the 21st Century, one in which college-educated Native American artists and illustrators tell our own stories in a way that lets you know *why* they are valuable, *why* they have survived, *why* they are good stories? I know that deep down inside it feels like non-Indians do a better job of telling Indian stories to non-Indians. The only problem is, you're not getting the real thing—and it *does* make a difference—in Indians' lives. And in yours, too.

There are not enough hours in a day, days in a week, weeks in a year for me to undo the damage that this series of books has done to contemporary Native American children. Wargin's language uses stilted, silly terms, such as "the Spirit Wood" and "Mother Bear." Her poetry, used for the speech of the "fairies" and animals, mimics the mid-19th Century poetry that Schoolcraft wrote to an expectant mid-19th Century audience. In *The Legend of Mackinac Island* (another enclave of summer homes adjacent to public land), Wargin has replaced our leading character in a flood story, Manaboozhou, a much-loved ancestor and teacher of ours, with a big painted turtle, who tells a group of other animals:

> May sunshine drip like honey-gold,
> and sweetness fill the air
> May diamonds fall upon the lake,
> and always glimmer there.
>
> I leave you with an island home,
> my sweet and treasured friends,
> forever there upon my back
> where splendor never ends.

Syrupy lyrics and major cultural faux pas aside, the format of Wargin's version of this story resembles one I've been selling on audiotape for more than a decade. It is only part of a larger story, one that is hysterically funny and full of sensible messages for adolescent children. It is a story that takes a lifetime to learn. Were we to insert Wargin's story of Turtle Island into our oral history, it would make no sense whatsoever. All of joyous double entendres would be completely lost.

While the Ojibwe language is very onomatopoetic, and 19th-Century ethnologists were intrigued by its strong sense of lyric and prose, Schoolcraft didn't come close to accurate translation. He was creating his own product with these poems, not recording in a scientific fashion. His approach to Native people, stories, and cultures in general needs to be put into the context of his era, which was one of eliminating Native cultures and people to the greatest extent possible to make way for the removal of great tracts of virgin forest and for the extraction of mineral wealth that would eventually exceed that of the great California Gold Rush. Wargin's character, Leelanau, is a white child's expectations of an Indian maiden—sweet, lovely, docile—certainly not someone who would stand up for her own rights or those of her children, not someone who would expect equal work for equal pay, not someone who would fight for the use of the land through previously unenforced treaty rights, and definitely not someone who would complain about cultural appropriation and misuse of traditional Native stories by a non-Native. No, *that* Leelanau character is not someone I could successfully emulate—I wouldn't want my daughter to either. Unfortunately, we run into a lot of resistance when we don't live up to those stereotypes.

Nothing could be more offensive to me than the cover of Wargin's *The Legend of Leelanau*—the ugly Indian face on the fairy dragonfly body, Tinkerbell with a bad profile. Centuries of Ojibwe cultural competence, demonstrated by loving parents through honing of the concept of the Little People into useful daily teaching and survival tools have been transmuted by author and illustrator into two-dimensional lawn jockeys. This is a marketed understatement of the beauty and interconnectedness of our traditional characters and their accompanying lightheartedness and humor as they apply to our everyday lives and decision-making—right up to the present—as our culture *does* persist, and we are perfectly capable of writing and telling about it ourselves, without the overlaying of historic, economic-based demeaning stereotyping. This is the crucifixion of Christ transformed into a big, plastic Easter bunny selling corn syrup-based products, only gone a step further—into Uncle Tom mockery. Yet one more non-Indian who has grown up playing Indian in the north woods has gone out and read Schoolcraft's collection of Native-based stories from the northern Great Lakes and has decided to cash in, no matter how damaging Schoolcraft's mid-19th Century approach and attitude, no matter how incongruent and far off the mark Schoolcraft's language and interpretations were from the real thing, no matter how available real Native Americans are, or how capable we are of telling these stories without Schoolcraft's and Wargin's life histories of misconceptions, cultural segregation, and cultural debasement being overlaid upon them. Wargin's books are just another piece in the puzzle that keeps the cultural misunderstanding and racism of Schoolcraft's era alive and well to the present in communities north of Chicago and Detroit.

The fairies. I've got to talk about the fairies. We don't have fairies. Oops! That's right. We don't have fairies. Schoolcraft had fairies. Schoolcraft grew up in a European-American culture that had fairies. He imposed those fairies upon Ojibwe characters that he couldn't, *didn't want to* understand. Wargin and her illustrator grew up with those fairies, too. Apparently neither can imagine the people and the north woods they so admire without those European fairies overlaid upon them, making them into the safe cottage-country groomed forests of their own childhoods, places where real Native Americans cannot fit unless they are cute and docile, naked and trailing firefly-like sparkles. Yes, I said *naked*. My seven-year-old son, whom I tried to protect from these volumes of clichés, got hold of *The Legend of Leelanau*: "Eeew, Mom, those Indian dragonflies are *naked*!" It's an age-appropriate response. Imagine his humiliation if that had been in his classroom.

Hey, when are you guys gonna quit showing Indians naked and with little scraps of leather over our loins? George Washington got naked, too. So how come you don't show *him* that way ninety percent of the time? Am I being oversensitive? No. Imagine if almost every book that purported to represent who your child is to her peers showed the cultural representatives as primitive, naked, somehow lesser. Italian American fairies naked with big noses, Polish American fairies naked with big noses—get my drift?

Young Leelanau is told by her parents (who are apparently dressed up to pose for a neo-classically trained illustrator or an in-studio Edward Curtis photo) to stay away from the fairies, because "They will be sure to cast a spell and carry you way for good!" That whole spell-casting thing is a European phenomenon. It was the Europeans who tended to believe in witches during the period of early contact, not the Indians—especially the sort of Europeans who were picked for their ability to convert people to Christianity or to haul a big bundle of furs, not the kind who were likely to be able to record the mathematical and scientific language of a competent people. If Wargin and van Frankenhuyzen want to create a fun fantasy collection of stories, that's fine—but that's not what they're doing here. They're purporting to honestly represent my people's history and culture.

Leelanau is not an Ojibwe name, although the adolescent girl she represents exists in our stories by various names. We don't have an "L" sound in our language, and it's always been assumed that the word was borrowed from one of the tribes on the western fringes of our lands that we had increased contact with after the fur trade disrupted traditional boundaries. It's one of those words nobody can accurately lay claim to, but it was used by Schoolcraft to name the Michigan county where the Sleeping Bear Dunes National Lakeshore is located, and it's become a marketable commodity.

Wargin's Indians are stereotypical, not real. In *The Legend of the Lady's Slipper* they live in "a village of peace" and live "a beautiful and simple way of life." The sappy sweet story and illustrations emphasize the young girl character's sacrifice, but it is a sacrifice without measured contemplation or justification. There is just nothing to sink your teeth into in these stories, just a sense of sweet, unrealistic forested purity in which Indians are somehow supposed to conveniently fit. It is pertinent that a fifth book, produced chronologically in the middle of this series, *The Legend of the Loon*, is supposed to be Scandinavian in origin, yet the format and illustration are indistinguishable from that used in the Indian stories. The language of the European-American story doesn't use the canned, jagged dialect of Wargin's "Native American" stories though. She dives right back into ignorant pseudo-dumb-Indian-speak when she begins reinterpreting Indian culture again. Intentional or not, this is racism, and it continues to hurt me and my family.

These books are non-Indian cottage-country childhood summer vacation style literature in which children make "braids with forest grasses, weaving them round to make sturdy nests for mother birds." They have absolutely nothing to do with traditional or contemporary Wood-land Indian culture and oral tradition. I'm glad that Wargin and her illustrator have found such pleasure in the north woods. However, I am not glad for the fact that people's love of the non-urban north, and the new development of technology that have allowed them to recolonize it in the form of suburbia have made the very land itself and the jobs needed to survive upon it contentious—because Wargin and Frankenhuyzen's works have done an excellent job of preserving an inappropriate status quo when it comes to stereotypes about the Native people of the Great Lakes.

Every day, my children and I have to walk out our front doors and confront those stereotypes and the real socioeconomic damage they still impose upon us in the real job market, and the real department stores where we are followed around by security guards in the northern communities of the Great Lakes. We are not simple, cute, naked, primitive quasi-human imaginary creatures that should just move out of the way for you to enjoy the jobs, the resources and the places you desire. We are real, blood and flesh, the kind that deserves respect in the classroom, respect in the field of children's literature, and the corresponding respect in the marketplace and the rest of our interaction that can only grow out of accurate and quality representation. Don't use defective tools to teach

children defective stereotypes that there are not enough hours in a day, days in a week, weeks in a year, to unteach.
—*Lois Beardslee*

Waterton, Betty, *A Salmon for Simon*, illustrated by Ann Blades. Douglas & McIntyre (1990). Unpaginated, color illustrations; preschool-grade 2

A little boy named Simon, who looks like he's about four or five years old, wants to catch a salmon, whom he calls "sukai." He goes fishing by himself, and fishes and fishes and nothing happens. Then an eagle "accidentally" drops a salmon at his feet. The salmon is still alive. "It must be the most beautiful fish in the world," thinks Simon, and feeling sorry for it, releases it. As the sun goes down, the salmon "gave a great leap into the air" and Simon goes home.

> And Simon thought, as he opened the door, that maybe he would go fishing again tomorrow, after all. But not for a salmon.

Given the culture, if Simon came from a traditional family it's pretty unlikely he would have tossed the salmon back. He probably would have seen it as an unexpected but very opportune gift, said thank you to the eagle and gone on home to get some help to bring the salmon back. His mom would have thanked him for the gift, cooked it up and very happily eaten it along with everybody else around because a salmon is a big fish. Probably afterwards, they would have returned the bones to the water so that the salmon could be reborn again and continue to feed the people.

This could have been a story about a young child's realization of the beauty of the compact between the human people and the animal people. Instead, written and illustrated by non-Native Canadians, it's just another "multicultural" story of a brown boy with white values.

—*Beverly Slapin*

Webster, M.L., *On the Trail Made of Dawn: Native American Creation Stories*. Linnet Books (2001). 70 pages; grades 3-7

The stunning cover painting is a reprint of work by Roy Thomas, an Ojibwe artist with decades of stories and knowledge of his culture inside him. There are images within images, layers upon layers. At the top, Sun, lifegiver, shines on the people and frames the canoe in which they are standing. At the bottom, Water, life-giver, frames Turtle, who holds up the canoe, Earth. The four people in the canoe are black, yellow, red and white—the four colors, the four directions, the four seasons, the four boys of Winona, a few of the important fours. On the canoe are animals who have particular importance because of their personalities and association with certain stories. Some will look at this luminous painting and be reminded of the stories it holds. Others will look at it and know that there is more here than they can understand. Still others—and I suspect the author is one of them—will look at it and see a "nice little Indian picture."

After the obligatory, oversimplified background material about the tribes and the introductory poem—almost always from another tribe—each so-called "creation" story is about three pages long. These truncated stories remind me of the children's game of "telephone," where a whispered phrase changes as each child hears it, and by the time the last child says the phrase out loud, it has become garbled. But this is more serious than a child's game.

Here, the author reinterpreted events that take a lifetime to comprehend—and whittled them into her own misconstrued shorthand. Like many non-Native retellers, she apparently found written elements of tribal stories that seemed to fit her own formula, manufactured an external context, invented stilted dialogue, and homogenized the whole mess. She even lifted the title from the very beautiful, very long, Diné creation story.

Without the cultural context that makes them viable, these mere snippets of complete thoughts, decontextualized actions without nuance, become simple and childlike "retellings." And once the actions and characters become simple and childlike in the stories, the young reader who is outside the culture then is led to assume that the people themselves are simple. There is no complex belief system; there is only superstition. There is no humanity, dignity, integrity, responsibility; there is only instinct.

The back jacket describes this book as "an outgrowth of the many summers (M.L. Webster) spent on a Chippewa reservation in northern Minnesota, where she first heard creation stories told by tribal elders." I'd like to think that the author didn't realize she was stealing something sacred; maybe if she had realized it she might not have done it.—*Beverly Slapin*

(Thank-you to Lois Beardslee.)

Weier, John, *Those Tiny Bits of Beans*, **illustrated by David Beyer (Cree/Métis). Pemmican (1995). Unpaginated, color illustrations; grades 3-4 (younger for read-aloud); Métis**

"Oncle Henri and Tante Madeline worked hard together, in the bush and in the garden, in the cabin near the river and in the village of St. Jean Baptiste." Oncle Henri didn't have many bad habits, but Tante Madeline was just a little upset with his table manners—Oncle Henri didn't have any. He gulped down his food. So when a giant wedding feast happens, Tante Madeline devises a way to let Oncle Henri know when he's eating too fast. This does not work out exactly as they had planned, because there's a big black-and-white dog sleeping under the table...

Beyer's simply rendered stylized artwork is bold and vibrantly colored, and his characters are like those relatives you would see at really big family gatherings, including the dog but maybe not the horse and wagon. Children will enjoy watching Oncle Henri cutting those beans into ever tinier bits.—*Beverly Slapin*

Whaley, Rick, and Walter Bresette (Ojibwe), *Walleye Warriors: An Effective Alliance Against Racism and for the Earth.* **New Society (1994). 272 pages, b/w photos, line drawings; high school-up; Ojibwe**

Bresette is a Wisconsin Red Cliff Reservation Ojibwe, and Whaley is one of the main organizers of what grew to be a large non-Indian support network for the treaty-based land and environmental issues whose struggles over the years are recounted here. This book is of enormous importance from many different angles. If college students are introduced to nothing else about Indian peoples but this, they will have a good grounding in historical, cultural, environmental and economic realities of Native Nations today—and something else as well.

This book recounts how a grassroots-level alliance between Native people and non-Indian supporters has successfully worked in non-violent ways to fight racism, and more importantly, to fight the covert interest and support of those racists (against Native land rights) by large corporations who are or plan to undertake major mining efforts on or near Native lands. Though this book covers a struggle that is particular to the upper Midwest Great Lakes region, and focuses on several Wisconsin Ojibwe communities there, it is a model with applications to Native Nations all over the U.S. and Canada, where similar overt racism and covert economic and governmental backing threaten Native lands and rights.

What is most significant about this book is that it recounts a history that is in opposition both to Native people dumping on whites, and white wannabes who mosey around ripping off bits and pieces of what they regard as Native spirituality. Here the alliance supported specific Native rights, accepted Native leadership to define the support group's tasks and became an effective political force. Without the support the Wisconsin struggle would be less well known than it is. Without the support there would have undoubtedly been more violence and deaths.

(One of the racist slogans was "Spear a Pregnant Squaw, Save 2 Walleyes.") As it is, two known deaths were most likely murders of white supporters, rather than killings of Indians. The struggle is not over. A 1992 injunction brought against the racists who mob the fish areas to "protest the Indians" has led to the state's saying they couldn't enforce nonviolence against "potential riots" by the racists against the Native fishing families.

Everything comes together in this book. Real working multiracial alliances, cross-cultural friendships built out of sharing common struggles, the importance of the cultural values, teachings, and ceremonies in strengthening everyone to endure, and the activism. This is Indian culture at work here; these are Indian values, survival motivates it, beauty and spiritual support against the gigantic, powerful, rich, power-controlling opponents are all that keeps this struggle going. It's about building real working alliances. So get this book, keep it, read it carefully. Think about it. Learn from it.—*Paula Giese*

Wheeler, Bernelda (Cree/Ojibwe), illustrated by Herman Bekkering. Portage & Main (1986, 1995). Unpaginated, b/w illustrations; preschool-grade 2:
Where Did You Get Your Moccasins?
I Can't Have Bannock But the Beaver Has a Dam

It's circle time, and in answer to his classmates' questions about his moccasins, a child describes in detail how his *kookum*, his grandmother, made them: "By washing and scraping and pulling and smoking a deer hide, my Kookum made the leather. And from the leather she made my moccasins for me." Each page builds on the previous one, and children will like the unexpected ending. There are some things you just buy from the store.

In Wheeler's companion story, Mom says she can't make bannock because the oven can't get hot because there's no electricity because the power lines are down because a big tree fell on them because a beaver took down the tree because she needed the branches to build a dam. Dad's gone to put the power line back up so eventually

the oven will get hot—and the beaver will still have her dam. A recipe for bannock follows the story, so children and their parents or teachers can read a story and have a snack.

In *Moccasins*, Bekkering's expressive and detailed pencil-and-charcoal drawings portray real kids in an urban classroom. In *Bannock*, his pictures are bolder and less detailed, and work well with the story.

—*Beverly Slapin*

Wheeler, Jordan (Ojibwe/Cree), *Brothers in Arms*. Pemmican (1989). 223 pages; high school-up; Cree

Here, Wheeler offers readers three complex and multi-layered contemporary short stories—each primarily focused on two characters who are brothers. The writing is often sharp and sometimes poetic—guaranteed to hold the attention of reluctant teen readers. It is perhaps most notable in terms of literary quality for the skilled interweaving of back-story to provide character motivation and construct setting.

"Hearse in Snow" opens with the death of Billy and Walt's father, who died walking while drunk in a snowy night. He had begun drinking during the war and became increasingly dependent on alcohol following the death of his wife. The father character, though appearing only briefly in dreams, is relatively well developed, but the focus is on the brothers and to a lesser extent their sister Brenda. It is she who emphasizes the need for the brothers to come together, for them all to rediscover one another as a family in this time of grief. And it is she who suggests they drive a hearse carrying their father's body back to the reserve—"to catch up on each other's lives," she says. Trapped in the car during a storm, the brothers work together to survive, connect, and face their memories.

"Red Waves" is the story of Wayne, a script-writing journalist, and his older brother John, a drifter involved in a group that has been blowing up buildings symbolic of oppression. Both care about their people and the wrongs imposed on them, but because of their individual life experiences have come to different perspectives on moving forward and fighting back. They talk about the American Indian Movement. John laments its demise, but Wayne recognizes it was essential to move away from the protests and into the government's own game to secure better rights for Native people.

Meanwhile Wayne tracks the story of the bombings, trying to determine if the source is a group of Native people, while the costs and benefits of such a revelation are debated. Wheeler does a good job of conveying the idea that different Indians have different ideas about the best paths ahead and how to handle the expectations and reactions of both whites and the Canadian government.

As the story progresses, it's revealed that as a teen John was with his and Wayne's mother hitchhiking. Along the way, a cop tried to rape and then killed her. The incident was covered up and in fact John had never been sure whether she'd died or had run off. Years later, that cop has become the Minister of Indian and Northern Affairs that had been directing John's group in an effort to "turn public sympathy against Native people." These revelations and the subsequent standoff make for a compelling read.

"Exposure" is a particularly timely story about AIDS and its effect on two brothers as well as their Native community. Kris and Martin have survived much together—the death of their brother Ralph to typhoid, their father's alcoholism, and the horrors of residential school. This last is depicted with tremendous emotional clarity:

> There was always crying at night, among the younger ones especially, huddled alone in the dark, crying for moms, for the warmth of kookum, to be anywhere else but this ugly building where a supreme god didn't want them to speak Cree or remain Indian, and so hired a priest and a pack of nuns to frighten, oppress and defeat them. They were children   in prison, in concentration camps where the church strived to alter their minds and their lives forever.

And now Martin has contracted AIDS and returned to the reserve to die. Kris does all he can for his brother as they face paranoia and discrimination from within and outside their family and community as well as the challenge of breaking the news to their emotionally fragile mother. But ultimately it's the story of wanting to die with dignity, of love between brothers, and of the need to come home.

> They laughed until Martin started coughing, a hoarse, painful cough that made Kris cringe. "Kris," Martin said when the coughing subsided, "make sure they bury me on the reserve." For a moment, Kris wanted to crack a joke to lighten the mood, but decided against it. "I mean it, I want to be buried on the reserve," Martin insisted. "I'll make sure," Kris said.

—*Cynthia L. Smith*

Wheeler, M.J., *First Came the Indians*, **illustrated by James Houston. Atheneum (1983). Unpaginated, line drawings; grades 2-up**

First Came the Indians is an attempt to describe the foods, clothing, shelters, social structures, and belief systems of five indigenous Nations and a confederacy—in a twenty-seven-page picture book for second-graders.

> A long time ago only Indians lived in *our* country. They did not call themselves Indians. They called themselves by many different names. Before they came, only animals lived here. The Indians came from Asia, following the animals they hunted. They were able to cross into America, for at that time the seas were lower than they are now, and there was more dry land. They traveled on, following the animals, until they had moved into all parts of *our* country. (italics mine)

This woman has an amazing facility for sticking a really lot of wrong concepts into one paragraph. Let's attempt to deconstruct this one. "...only Indians lived in our country." Since Wheeler refers to indigenous peoples as "they," it is safe to assume that it is not her intent to be talking to Indian second-graders here, so the "our" in "our country" can only mean non-Indians. So. "...only animals lived here." In taking the concept of Manifest Destiny to a new low, she is saying that, even before there were any humans here, this was the territory already belonging to a people yet to arrive—and she doesn't mean Indians. Okay, next. "The Indians" (who didn't call themselves that) "came from Asia" and "were able to cross into America (which hadn't been named that yet)...until they had moved into all parts of our country." So, in one page, she describes the Bering Strait theory as fact, espouses the concept of Manifest Destiny, and throws in the name of a country not yet "discovered."

Wheeler goes on to talk a little about the Creek people. Corn. Fruit. Nuts. Hunting. Living in the forest. Then she gets to the Iroquois. "This is how you say it—IH-ruh-kwoy." Longhouses. Corn. Beans. Squash. Three Sisters. Deer. Hunting. An original rendition of traditional healing ceremony. Then, on to the Ojibwa: "This is how you say it—o-JIB-wa." Didn't scold children. Birch trees. Maple trees. Wigwams. Next, the Sioux: "This is how you say it—sue." Buffalo. Nothing wasted. Tipis. Next, the Makah: "This is how you say it—muh-KAH." Big houses. Strong boats. Whale-hunting. Then comes this:

> [B]rave men washed every day in cold sea water and rubbed themselves with sand. They did this to make their bodies strong and to win the help of the spirits. Each one hoped that this would make him strong enough to kill a whale and to become a great man among his people.

Also to get clean.

In the obligatory section called "Indians Now," Wheeler neatly ties up the story, carefully omitting all the unpleasant little details, like massacres, disease, starvation, missionaries, residential schools, reservations:

> Indians were the first Americans. Along with the plants and animals, they lived at peace with the land. Then the settlers came in boats, over the ocean. The Indians helped the first settlers learn to live in their new country. The settlers were new to the land. They found it strange and wild. They cut down the trees and killed the animals. The buffalo died. The deer hid far back in the forests. The settlers made farms, roads, towns, and cities. There was no place for the Indians to live in their old ways.

"Now the Indians live much like the rest of us," she continues,

> It is not the same as their old way of life. That is gone forever....Indians have been a part of our country from the beginning. And Indians still have much to teach us about how to live in peace with the land to which we all belong.

The illustrations by James Houston, whom the jacket describes as a "recognized authority on North American Indians," and "the man who discovered Inuit art" (what a surprise that must have been to the Inuit artists) are a perfect complement to the text. This is how you say it—KON-duh-SEN-ding.—*Beverly Slapin*

White, Ellen/Kwulasulwut (Coast Salish), Theytus; grades 2-5:
Kwulasulwut: Stories from the Coast Salish, illustrated by David Neel (Kwagiutl), (1981); 76 pages, color illustrations
Kwulasulwut II: More Stories from the Coast Salish, illustrated by Bill Cohen (Okanagan), (1997); 79 pages, color illustrations

Ellen White, whose Salish name is Kwulasulwut, is an Elder in Residence at Malaspina University College in the First Nations Arts Program. She has told her stories to children and adults, from nursery school to university. That she is a gifted teller in the Coast Salish tradition comes through in stories that are alive with metaphor and detail, and that are sometimes also very funny.

In her first collection, White shares with us five traditional and contemporary stories—"The Stolen Sun," "Hulitun', the Magic Hunter," "Grandma Goes Fishing," "Raven and Raccoon," and "Father Barbeques"—which Kwagiutl artist David Neel's fresh and colorful stylistic paintings anchor in the territory. White provides intriguing twists to her stories. Seagull rather than Raven steals the

sun, and Raven with the help of Sea Urchin steals it back. The boys have to teach Grandma to fish, which is exactly opposite of our expectations of First Nations elders as teachers. The insight that the Magic Hunter gains melts his heart and he restores the village to its rightful order. Raven and Raccoon learn that cooperation gets them both farther faster. And finally, Father tries to barbeque a cod and finds out that sometimes, children know best.

White's second volume features four stories—"Smuy, the Little Deer," "The Mink and the Raccoon Family," "Deer, Raven and the Red Snow," and "Journey to the Moon"—that feature introspection and peer teaching. Okanagan artist Bill Cohen's illustrations are vibrant with color and expression, and bring White's words to life.

The little Deer, with the guidance of his grandfather, embraces the spiritual development of his vision quest. The Mink and Raccoon families discover that they live in the same territory but have very different habits and preferences for food and consequently must learn to respect one another. In an intricate ruse and counter-ruse, Raven steals salmon from Deer, Deer steals it back, and then boldly offers it to Raven when the farce has been played out. Finally, a young man journeys to the moon where, with the assistance of Spider Lady and a little mouse, he tries to retrieve his love whose out-of-body experience has taken her there. These four stories touch on cosmic themes with a certain clarity and humanity inherent in our traditional teaching stories.

Both volumes are highly recommended.
—*Marlene R. Atleo/ʔeh ʔeh naa tuu kwiss*

Whitethorne, Baje (Diné), *Sunpainters: Eclipse of the Navajo Sun*, **illustrated by the author. Salina Bookshelf (1994, 2004). 32 pages, color illustrations; grades 3-up; Diné (Navajo)**

A wonderful story, recounted by well-known Diné artist Baje Whitethorne about a solar eclipse he witnessed on the Diné reservation at age seven—and a story his grandpa told him then of the Little People—the earth-painters, who renew the life of the sun, earth, and all objects, when the sun has died, as it does occasionally.

At the end of the book is a very brief explanation—which would have been clearer for kids with a couple of simple diagrams of the moon's shadow on earth, and greatly improved by eliminating the rather condescending shallow remarks on tribal beliefs about eclipses.

The story itself is enlivened by certain remembered realities. Kii Leonard, the little boy, is hungry when the eclipse starts, at about dinnertime. He almost forgets this when Pipa, his grandpa, says:

> "It is dark outside, but don't look at the sun. Notice the deep purples and reds all around the mountainside." Kii Leonard saw a strange gloom all around him. Everywhere he looked, the deep purple and red darkness was there.

Pipa then tells Kii Leonard the story of the *Na'ach'aabii*, the Little People who repaint the sun when it dies—and all the colors of the earth. But Grandpa also tells Kii Leonard he must not eat, drink, sleep or even lie down during the darkness of the eclipse, until it is over and the sun has come back to life. Grandpa goes far away into the darkness to pray. Kii Leonard first tries to see the Little People painting the life and color back. But after catching a glimpse of some blue cornbread and a bucket of water he can think of nothing else—until the sun is reborn and the earth's colors repainted. He runs outside and gives thanks to the four directions from which the Little Painters had come and to which they've returned, then he draws the Navajo sun before he eats!

This beautiful and interesting book is good reading for elementary classes where studying the seasons and the earth's orbit can also lead to a discussion of eclipses.

—*Paula Giese*

Wilson, Darryl Babe (Pit River), *The Morning the Sun Went Down.* **Heyday (1998). 178 pages; high school-up; Pit River**

Darryl Wilson was in the second grade the morning the sun went down. That was the morning that his mother and baby brother, stopped on the highway because their car had run out of gas, were killed by a speeding lumber truck. That was the morning of his father's descent into the hell called alcoholism, and the morning that,

> [A]t seven years old, my life withered and turned a silent gray, like an old-time photograph of Indians in feathers and Buffalo Bill in buckskin. A photograph curled up at the edges, suncracked and moisture-warped. I had to escape. So, as the Elders of my tribe advised, 'Just dream,' I dreamed...

The Morning the Sun Went Down is Wilson's autobiography and the history of a people. It's about material poverty and richness of spirit, about taming rattlesnakes and daring to dream, about the nightmares of white foster homes and residential schools, and about the human responsibility for life upon Earth. It is a gift, put down in honesty and beauty.—*Beverly Slapin*

Wilson, Gilbert L., *Buffalo Bird Woman's Garden: Agriculture of the Hidatsa Indians.* **Minnesota Historical Society (1917, 1987). 129 pages, b/w photos, line drawings; high school-up; Hidatsa**

Wilson was an anthropologist, an unusual one who was open to friendly involvement with Indian people, interested in learning from elder women, and willing to watch, listen, learn, and present the results in the words of the people, not distorted by theory. For 1915—when anthropology was busily trying to become a science—this was unthinkably revolutionary. This little book is his University of Minnesota Ph.D. thesis. Unlike most such, it is absorbing reading. Representing years in the early 1900s spent with the Hidatsa people now living at Fort Berthold, North Dakota, and a particularly close relationship to the old lady he identified as Buffalo Bird Woman, and in other works as *Waheenee* and *Owl Woman*, this reads like a combination gardener's and cook's how-to, as the old lady speaks for herself. Tools and structures used in the planting, cultivation, harvest, processing, storage and cooking are shown in small, clear drawings.

The women had developed seven major varieties of corn, mainstay of the plains Native farmers' lives, and practiced careful seed selection. They also raised sunflowers, beans and squash. Buffalo Bird Woman tells about every aspect of the planting, processing, storage and cooking—and also sings a few teasing songs sung by women field-watchers to passing youths and other cross-cousins:

> You young man of the Dog Society, you said to me
> "When I go East on a war party, you will hear news of me, how brave I am!"
> I have heard news of you. When the fight was on, You ran and hid!
> Behold, you have joined the Dog Society.
> Therefore I call you just plain Dog!

Here's a recipe she gives for "Four vegetables mixed" for a family of five:

> I put a clay pot on the fire. Into the pot I threw one double-handful of beans. This was a fixed quantity, I put in that whether the family was large or small, for a larger quantity of beans was apt to make gas in the stomach. When we dried squash in the fall, we strung the slices upon twisted grass each seven Indian fathoms long. From one of these strings I cut

a piece as long as from my elbow to the tip of my thumb. I tied the two ends together in a ring and dropped this into the pot. When the squash slices were well cooked, I drew them from the pot by the string, and put it into a wooden bowl where I chopped and mashed it with a horn spoon and returned the cooked mess to the pot, throwing away the string. To the mess I now added five double-handfuls of mixed meal made of pounded, parched sunflower seed and pounded, parched corn. The whole was boiled a few minutes more and was ready for serving. A little alkali salt might be used, but was not usual. Meat was not boiled with this mess, as sunflower seed gave sufficient oil for fat.

The very detailed knowledge Buffalo Bird Woman relates is dazzling. Lengths of vegetable drying strings and corn-cob braids were calibrated to be a load the average woman could easily carry, to relate to the size of cache pits, and to be easily broken strings for a family-size cookpot. She describes the construction and lining of the cache pits, with drawings—only one certain type of grass could be used, others molded or didn't protect well enough against groundwater. Hundreds, perhaps thousands of years of successful agricultural adaptation are related in the woman's easy-to-read, colloquial narrative.

This book is the most detailed of any ever known to be collected for such practices, because Wilson met a woman who knew all the details and persuaded her family to make models and drawings of the many large structures and tools in use before the way of life was destroyed by forced move from the bottomlands village to the Fort Berthold reservation in North Dakota, after the passage of the Dawes Allotment Act, and the building of the Garrison Dam, which flooded the rich bottomlands.

Buffalo Bird Woman's Garden might sound boring to those whose idea of history is battles, leaders, speeches, governments. New-Agers looking for a spiritual mother lode will find none here, just the practicality of women's work in daily survival. I find this the real and material basis of spirituality: feeding the people, life of the land. I couldn't put this book down; it completely fascinated me. I got a better picture of real, day-to-day traditional community life here than from just about anything else I've read. It's more like a how-to book than an anthropology book. I think Native young people in high school will like it, especially young women.—*Paula Giese*

Witalec, Janet, ed., *Native North American Literature*. Gale Research (1994). 706 pages; high school-up

This huge literature reference work has two sections. The first is comprised of biographical-historical essays mostly about Native orators, most of them political leaders.

Songs and other parts of the oral tradition are represented by reprinted articles or introductory essays to collections by well-known scholars. The second half deals with mostly 20th-Century Native writers from the U.S. and Canada. It includes biographical data, critiques excerpted from books and literary reviews, a list of more sources and interviews with many of the writers. Thirty-five modern writers are included, among them Jeanette Armstrong, Lame Deer, Joseph Bruchac, Michael Dorris, Louise Erdrich, Linda Hogan, Basil H. Johnston, Markoosie, Scott Momaday, Leslie Marmon Silko. Even more important are key figures from the 19th and early 20th Centuries: William Apess, E. Pauline Johnson, Ella Deloria, Simon Pokagon, Alexander Posey.

Each author is represented by a brief biographical section, a listing of major publications and sometimes a short overview essay by the editors; followed by a reprinting of well-chosen essays or reviews of the author's works, often from hard-to-find publications.

The 20th-Century writers were chosen to provide a range of cultural, historical, political, spiritual and artistic perspectives. This is not a reference work of biographies that tend to focus on a few facts about an author's life, but a unique compilation of perspectives on each author's work. It is an essential college or university library item and it's a perfect companion to *Smoke Rising*, which contains excerpts from the writings of almost all the authors whose works are discussed in the reference.—*Paula Giese*

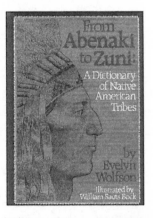

Wolfson, Evelyn, *From Abenaki to Zuni: A Dictionary of Native American Tribes*, illustrations by William Sauts Bock (Lenni Lenape). Walker (1988). 215 pages, b/w illustrations; grades 3-7

From Abenaki to Zuni has been denoted a "noteworthy children's trade book in the field of multicultural social studies." It has sold well since its publication, is still available in libraries and continues to be used in classrooms.

Wolfson's choice of Nations to include seems pretty random.

The author confines herself to "tribes" within the lower 48, and does not include the Inuit, Aleut, Athabascan peoples of Alaska or the peoples of Hawai'i. Gabrielenos, Karuk, Otoe, Kickapoo, Tonkawa, Caddo, Catawba, San Juan Pueblo, yes; Apache, Menominee, Pima, Paiute, Dakota, Taos Pueblo, Laguna Pueblo, San Ildefonso Pueblo, Ottawa, Puyallup, Salish-Kootenai, Makah, Wisconsin Ojibwe, no.

Aside from the impossibility of dealing with Native issues in any depth, the text, whether from ignorance or by intent, is biased against the very peoples about whom Wolfson has chosen to write. The treatment of land base and national sovereignty issues and history is confusing and misleading. Land base is essential to the survival, as Indian peoples, of all existing surviving Nations today. It is the nexus of legal rights of sovereignty and self-government—Nationhood—that differentiates Native people from all other "minorities." Cultural survival requires a land base; traditional religions and value structures of necessity require contact with the natural world. Those traditions and values are rooted in the land.

This reference book for non-Indian children consistently dehumanizes Native peoples, presenting them as having been originally (before white uplift) naked, primitive, simple, weird, pagan, heathen savages, violent and dangerous. Excesses of the historic past against these sub-humans are presented as excusable, though perhaps regrettable. From "A to Z," it distorts, destroys, omits truths; and spreads confusion. It excuses infamous massacres and lies about their size or scope. Its treatment of the varied Native religions is uniformly offensive but purposeful.

Termination is the 1950s-70s attack on Native National land bases, National sovereignty and hence survival. There are many signs it is surfacing again, with different words and actions ("modernizing old treaties," for instance). Termination is an end to Nationhood for Native Nations. How does *Abenaki to Zuni* treat this issue?

Menominees don't exist in "A-Z." This means that Ada Deer, past head of the Bureau of Indian Affairs, comes from a non-existent Nation. But it also means that the long Menominee struggle against termination, which Ada Deer was a leader of thirty years ago, is left out. Even in a couple of summary pages about the Menominee, termination could have been illuminated, because the Menominees were the tribe who rolled it back. Termination makes only one sly little appearance, for the other tribe that was fully terminated as the start of terminating all:

> The Klamath and their neighbors the Modoc, traded horses for slaves along the Columbia River. White settlers in wagon trains destroyed many of their wild foods, scared away their game, and left them sick with strange diseases.

Survivors signed a treaty in 1864 ceding most of their land in exchange for a small reservation. Later, they sold the reservation land and divided the money among tribal members.

In fact, they did not "sell" the reservation land. Their timber was immediately attractive to large corporate interests so they were subjected to more pressure and lacked the leadership of the Menominees' long political struggle against the forced termination. So their land was taken.

The only definition of "treaty," frequently mentioned in the text, is also to be found in the glossary:

> A formal agreement between two or more nations, relating to peace or an alliance. From 1835 to 1856, the U.S. signed 52 treaties with Native Americans to acquire 174 million acres of land—and broke every one of them.

Actually 372, not fifty-two, treaties were signed by Congress— all of which have been and continue to be ignored by the U.S. government. The fact that treaties are not signed "with Native Americans" (individuals) but between Nations, carries many legal implications. In addition to the U.S. treaties, treaties between other Nations are relevant to Indian rights.

The Dawes Act is mentioned only in the glossary:

> The Allotment Act (Dawes Act) was designed to reduce the size of reservation land given to Indians west of the Mississippi River. It gave tribe members parcels of their reservation land and the government the right to sell the remaining land to white settlers.

The Dawes Act destroyed Nations and National sovereignty; legal rights were simply rejected by it. In addition to taking various Nationally held communal lands within then-existing reservation boundaries, it allotted the rest of the land to Indians as individuals, as real estate parcels, which could be (and were) readily taken from the allotees by trickery, forced sales, tax forfeitures, or even plain need of a desperately poor Indian family to sell their little parcel for some money for immediate survival.

The whitewash (no pun intended) of massacres of Native peoples is blatant, either ignoring very famous events and people, or treating them in such a distorted way that they are unrecognizable. Sand Creek, and its follow-up, Washita, are infamous massacres, the first leading to a formal reprimand and removal from command of the officer in charge; the second, the beginning of George Armstrong Custer's military reputation.

Wilson's reference to Sand Creek (Washita isn't mentioned), under "Cheyenne," is as follows:

The Gold Rush brought miners and white settlers into their territory, but the Cheyenne refused to sell. United States troops went to war over the land and when Chief Black Kettle and two hundred of his people finally surrendered under a flag of truce, frightened troops massacred them all. This angered the Cheyenne and their friends, the Arapaho, who banded together to attack white settlements. The raiding and fighting lasted ten years and is known as the Sioux Wars.

Sand Creek, the first massacre of Black Kettle's band, occurred in November of 1864, when Col. John Chivington (Rev. Chivington, he was a Denver Methodist minister), who had raised a regiment of volunteers to inflict punishment on the Plains Indians, came upon Black Kettle's sleeping camp. Under a previous agreement, Black Kettle had "registered" his band as peaceables, and told the authorities at Fort Lyon where they would be camped for the winter, about forty miles from the fort. Chivington notified the Ft. Lyon garrison of his plans and was told to leave Black Kettle's band alone. But Chivington was on the Plains for a final solution to the Indian problem: "Kill them all, big and small, nits make lice" had been his recruiting slogan, and "take no prisoners" was his policy. Black Kettle's band weren't "good" Indians, whatever the local Army command said, because they were alive.

Black Kettle's camp was surrounded by Chivington's army and shelled by emplaced canons. They did try raising both surrender and American flags, to no avail. Black Kettle and about one hundred people got away, the rest—most of the band's women, children, elders—were slaughtered with great brutality. Troops cut off the breasts and genitalia of Indian women for souvenirs. They killed many little children deliberately, not something done in heat of battle, but an aftermath of butchery. A government investigation later actually reprimanded Chivington and removed him from command.

Washita, the second massacre, was the followup. In 1868, a young cavalry officer, new to command and looking to build his military reputation, came upon the remnants of Black Kettle's band encamped for the winter at the Washita River. Lt. Col. George Armstrong Custer deployed his men during the night, attacking the surrounded, sleeping camp at dawn, killing Black Kettle and almost all the other men who had survived Sand Creek. Custer achieved a promotion for this effort.

"Frightened troops massacred Black Kettle's Cheyennes" is a nasty gloss of a nasty pair of well-documented historical events. These crimes are common knowledge; Sand Creek figures in every book about the 19th-Century Plains wars, and Washita is usually mentioned too. Wolfson's wording is no naive error caused by insufficient research

of a bit of historical esoterica. These events are so well documented that they are impossible to miss.

The battle at the Greasy Grass (Little Bighorn), Custer's Last Stand is a famous Indian victory. In *Abenaki to Zuni*, it is not mentioned at all. There is no mention of Custer, as earlier there's no mention of his career-start at the Washita. Sitting Bull, Crazy Horse—no mention. This is as good a place as any to say that almost no names, either Indian or European, and almost no dated specific events in the alleged tribe-by-tribe purported histories appear in this supposed work of reference. There is no mention at all of the people called "Sioux" other than this glossary item under "Teton":

> The Teton are one of three major subgroups of the Sioux Indians. The other two are Yankton and Santee.... They fought for almost half a century to keep their lands and signed several treaties which were never honored. In 1868 Red Cloud, a chief of the Oglala band of the Teton, accepted reservation land in western South Dakota and moved there with his people. The nearby Black Hills were sacred to the Teton, who went there to worship. When gold was discovered in the hills, the Teton were forbidden to go into the hills to worship. Later their reservation was divided into five smaller reservations to make room for other homeless Indians.

Let it be noted that generally, the western division liked and likes to be called "Lakota." The other two major divisions are Dakota and Nakota. Within these major divisions are others. All together they are Oceti Sakowin—the Seven Council Fires. The Santee are Dakota, the Yankton are Nakota.

The Fort Laramie Treaty of 1868 resulted from a succession of military victories, led by Red Cloud and other patriots. This treaty, negotiated from a position of military strength, draws a border for extensive national lands that included all of the Black Hills and the Powder River country in Wyoming and Montana, encompassing most of the Dakotas and the northern half of Nebraska.

The Black Hills are not "nearby," they are entirely inside the 1868 Treaty reservation boundary and yes, they are one of the most sacred places on Earth. Alhough there were sacred sites and ceremonies, the Black Hills were also a fruitful hunting ground for animals other than buffalo. They provided sheltered winter campgrounds out of the fierce winds and storms of the open plains. The idea that the "Tetons" tripped in and out to "worship" as if going to church on Sunday is absurd. When an expedition led by Custer discovered gold in 1870, the U.S. refused to enforce the treaty, which would have kept their own citizens—the rush of miners—out.

The large, treaty-determined Lakota national land was broken up in several late 19th-Century phases. The idea that the big Nation was broken up and diminished to "make room for other homeless Indians" is nonsense.

The Ghost Dance and the following massacre at Wounded Knee was the end of any effective power for the Plains peoples. Wolfson says this:

> In the late 1800s the Teton began to hold a celebration called the Ghost Dance with the hope that these celebrations would, through supernatural means, bring an end to white settlers, who were taking Indian land and destroying the environment. Descendants of the Teton live on several small reservations in South Dakota.

That's it. There is a bit more about the Ghost Dance and Wounded Knee in the glossary, as a definition of "Ghost Dance."

> Ghost Dancing ended in 1890 at Wounded Knee, South Dakota, because the United States Army did not understand why the tribes had assembled, and killed most of the dancers.

To say that something borne out of a people's despair and desperation was a "celebration" is indecent. To say that Ghost Dancing "ended," to say that the army "killed most of them" is a slimy way of getting around the massacre of 300-plus unarmed men, women and children. To say that they were killed because the army "did not understand" is as shocking as it would be to say that Hitler killed quite a few Jews because he "did not understand" them.

Surrounded by the Seventh Cavalry—Custer's old command— still thirsting for revenge, the people didn't stand a chance. While the nearby soldiers celebrated their "victory," the wounded were left to freeze to the ground—on December 29, in the Dakotas, where the winter temperature can routinely drop to 30 below or worse. There is absolutely no excuse for this. There are immediate first-hand accounts of what it was like at Wounded Knee by the people who were first to go in there and saw.

There are similar treatments of earlier notorious incidents. Cherokees will be outraged to learn that supposedly only 1,600 of them were death-marched on the Trail of Tears, which "cost the lives of almost five hundred of them along the way." Actually, the number of Cherokees forcibly removed from their developed homelands was in the tens of thousands. Here's what one standard expert (Grant Foreman) said in his major multi-volume history, done in the 1930s:

> No report was made of the number of Cherokees who died as the result of the removal.... The Government did not wish to preserve any infor-

mation touching the fearful cost to the helpless Indians.... From fragmentary official figures, it appears that more than 1,600 just of those who removed under the direction of John Ross died on the journey. It is known that the rate of mortality was higher among the previously removed parties.... Hundreds died in the stockades, and the concentration camps, before the forced marches. Hundreds of others died soon after arrival in the new Indian Territory from sickness, exposure, and starvation. Only a very small percentage of the old, the infirm, or the very young survived. At least 4,000 Cherokee died in the removals....

Other estimates put the figures much higher.

Wolfson cannot plead innocence. The Trail of Tears is not some historically esoteric, little-known event, hard to find out about. It is a matter of public record. You can't find the false information; you have to make it up.

> In spite of their pain and hardship, the survivors prospered in the new land. They became one of the Five Civilized Tribes, which included...

The "Five Civilized Tribes" were called that long before removal when they were on their own land. In the process of adapting to a new way of life that offered comforts and enjoyments many liked, these people had developed and farmed the land, building houses, printing presses, schools, community halls, government centers, roads, and boat landings.

All this nicely developed land didn't require the sort of effort and financial investment that clearing a forest or even breaking farms out of prairie wilderness would have. So the white people took it. To suggest the Cherokee, Choctaw, Chickasaw, Creek, and Seminole only became "civilized" after their removals is supposed to justify the "pain and hardship" and death.

Each *Abenaki to Zuni* entry has a little paragraph-description of the supposed "religion" of a people.

> The Gabrielino believe that crow, raven, owl and eagle are sacred creatures, and they use eagle feathers when performing religious rituals because a dying chief once told them he would return in the form of an eagle.

> The Winnebago worship many gods, including Earthmaker, who created Sun, Moon and Water, each a spirit god.

> The Onondaga believe in Ha-Wah-Ne-U, Creator of the World. Each new year they hold a four-day celebration called the Midwinter Ceremony, when they thank the spirits for the bountiful harvest.

The Klamath believe in shamans, who obtain special powers by fasting, praying and seeking visions from animal spirits, especially birds.

The Creek worship the sun and believe that the Great Spirit gives them the black drink, which is reserved for important celebrations. Each year they express their thanks for a bountiful harvest by dancing, feasting and praying at the Green Corn Festival.

The Kiowa believe the Sun is the chief god and that owls and other nocturnal birds own the souls of the dead.

The chief god of the Assiniboin is named Wakan Tanka.

The Omaha believe in Wakan Tanka, an invisible force that controls all living events.

The Osage believe that Wakan Tanka, the Great Force, maintains order in the sky, and that Grandfather, the Sun, taught them to make bows of osage wood.

The Oto believe that Wakan Tanka, their most important spirit, is in charge of the entire spiritual world."

The Ponca worship Wakan Tanka, who is their Great Spirit.

The deity called Wakan Tanka is regarded as a supreme force to the Teton, who employ shamans and priests to interpret their dreams and visions and to conduct rituals and herbal cures for diseases. A celebration called the Sun Dance is held each summer during which the Teton fast, feast, dance and practice self-torture.

Wakan Tanka is a term in the Lakota language for a theological concept, generally translated as "Great Mystery" though there is no exact English equivalent. Other Nations have different terms (in their own languages) and theologically different concepts. Wolfson appears to have come across the Lakota term somewhere and assumed that it is a generic Plains term for "God." "*Manitou*" (an Algonkian-linguistic word meaning spirit) gets around similarly in the woods, he's everybody's "chief god."

Self-torture is an extremely offensive way to describe the Sun Dance and other self-sacrifice customs. "Self-torture" turns up any time the Sun Dance is mentioned and in several other tribal religious descriptions. The concept of self-sacrifice (in any Native rites) for some greater good should not be incomprehensible to white Christian children. Self-sacrifice is noble, awesome, admirable. "Self-torture" forwards the primitive, superstitious, irrational, savage, aspects laid onto all Indian peoples.

There are entries for many tribes whose men are characterized as "often" or "usually" wearing no clothes. The women of these naked men are invariably characterized as wearing aprons or little skirts; their breasts are bare. Here are some of the "naked savages": Bella Coola, Chumash, Gabrieleno, Haida, Karuk, Kwakiutl, Maidu, Miwuk, Nuu-chah-nulth, Quinault, Tlingit, Tsimshian, Wintu, Yokut. It will be observed that some of these "naked savages" lived in pretty chilly climates. In such cases, they are said to throw on some kind of crude cloak if it really gets cold. The majority of the other *Abenaki to Zuni* tribes wore "buckskin (or fiber or bark) breech cloths," and the women just skirts (naked breasts again, snicker snicker).

Everything positive of any importance from any Nation is absent. There is no mention of the Six Nations (Iroquois League) conceptual contributions to world order and the domestic formation of the U.S., the idea of a multi-part governmental confederacy of equals. Agricultural, artistic, philosophic, and modern literary achievements—gifts to the world—are not mentioned for any Nation.

There are a number of smaller misstatements. It is hard to decide whether they come from carelessness or whether they are deliberate. According to Wolfson:

"Acorn flour contained a poisonous substance called tannin," which had to be leached. Tannin isn't poisonous, only bitter. It's the main component of tea. Acorns were and are an important source of fat (oil), not only flour meal for many Nations.

Snowshoes have "large, round frames." Actually there are many shapes suited to different kinds of snow and travel conditions.

Pemmican is a "nutritious mixture of pounded, dried meat mixed with berries and nuts." Fat was "poured over the top to make it last many months" like a seal or lid. Such a method would result in spoilage and in a mix lacking in nutritional value. Meat, berries and nuts were pounded up and mixed with fat, a preservative and nutrient both.

A travois is "an unwheeled sledlike cart"—an odd description for the useful drag formed by two poles lashed at a point and initially dragged on the ground by dogs and later by horses.

Assiniboine supposedly live or once lived in "Northern Minnesota" but after a lot died of smallpox "were forced to cede their lands and move to a reservation in western Montana." Though the Assiniboine may have passed through Minnesota in some unrecorded past, they lived in northern Montana and Canada throughout known history. Their only U.S. cession treaty is a piece of land in Eastern Montana (1851) in the Bighorn watershed.

Each *Abenaki to Zuni* entry has a useless little map supposedly of the tribe's location, either precontact or presently; generalized "culture regions" show neither original ranges nor present locations for anyone.

Each tribal name is given a definition, but the names used are white names, often distortions of names given a tribe by its enemies. The "meanings" are thus meaningless. Most tribes had (and are trying to reclaim) their own names (none of which is even mentioned). These almost always mean some variant of "us, we, the people."

Quite a few professors are "thanked for their help." Only one identifiable Indian scholar, Vine Deloria, Jr., gets thanked. We cannot imagine that he would have endorsed any part of this thing.

Jeffrey P. Brain, Ph.D., is a functionary at the Peabody Museum of Archaeology and Ethnology of Harvard University, prestigious names both. He is thanked for "reading and critiquing the entire manuscript." Prof. Brain also writes a foreword, stating that this book "skillfully guides the reader through the diversity of Indian peoples and their cultures. I heartily recommend this handy reference for those just beginning to explore the world of the Indian."

Someone with Brain's background could hardly have missed the errors and racist distortions we have dealt with here at such length. Because of the limitations of the book's author, Brain had the responsibility to inform the educational publisher that this mess was not publishable. No amount of editing could have saved it—it's not a question of a few or a few hundred errors.

Brain's words would have been a sort of imprimatur. If publishers, reviewers, librarians or teachers using this reference had any misgivings about its content, endorsement by a representative of a prestigious scholarly institution would have quieted them.

Perhaps we should apologize for the length of this review. However, in sum it is impossible not to conclude that *Abenaki to Zuni* was written with malice aforethought. It is true that there is still enormous ignorance in this country about the lives and histories of the Native populations. It is true that there are many places in this country where we are still thoroughly hated—just visit any of the border towns. The single most significant thing for non-Indian children (and adults) to understand about Indians is the importance of our remaining land base to our peoples' survival and the nature of past threats—that reappear in different guises—to that survival. If a new generation of non-Indians actually learns about this our younger generation may perhaps have some political allies, some helpers whose sympathies are informed, not dangerously ignorant.

Wolfson's book seems deliberately designed to contravene

that possibility; to encourage young white Americans to believe that they are in fact the chosen of the Earth, and to justify what has been done to us in the name of our superstitious ignorance and our savagery; in the name of Divine Right and Manifest Destiny.

—*Paula Giese* and *Doris Seale*

Wood, Douglas, *Northwoods Cradle Song: From a Menominee Lullaby*, illustrated by Lisa Desimini. Simon & Schuster (1996). Unpaginated, color illustrations; preschool-grade 1; Menominee

Douglas Wood "discovered" this lullaby in an adaptation of an adaptation of what once might have been a Menominee cradle song. He then adapted it and "expanded the words and set them to music, and I have since performed the song as part of my EarthSongs collection." The only aspect that is related to the Menominee is the phrase "Ne pa Ko," which, according to Wood, means "sleepy head" (rhymes with "bed"). Actually "sleepy one" would be a more accurate translation from the Menominee.

Here is how it goes:

> Ne pa Ko, my sleepy head,
> Golden bees have gone to bed,
> Silver, grey-green dragonflies
> Close their great and burning eyes.

Besides the fact that dragonflies do not have eyelids and therefore cannot close their eyes, this is about as far removed from a Menominee cradle song as one can get. I am also bothered by the constant reference to a baby as "little warrior."

The illustrations fit the poem. They're dark and ugly and there's nothing Menominee about them. There are tipi-like structures, the pine trees are all in a row, the mother's dressed in southwest-style clothing "in order," according to the illustrator's note, "to give the story a more universal feel." Do cultural stereotypes provide a universal feel? Not recommended.—*Barbara Potter*

Wood, Nancy, *Thunderwoman: A Mythic Novel of the Pueblos*. Dutton (1999). 286 pages, b/w illustrations; high school-up

Nancy Wood is the author of many works that depend on Native histories and cultures for their existence. According to the ecstatic jacket copy, she has written her current novel with

> a truth and urgency that penetrate the soul...[it is] a brilliantly compelling allegory within which to

tell four hundred years of Southwestern history…. Unfolding simultaneously on the planes of myth, legend and history; filled with pathos, nobility… this haunting epic is a mirror of human nature.

The book was also praised by *Publishers Weekly* and given a pointer review in *Kirkus*, where it was recommended for young people.

In fact, *Thunderwoman* is a bizarre, and—certainly for the young reader—unintelligible mishmash of 500 years of history and Wood's own—might one say, unique?—use of elements of "Pueblo" culture and spiritual practices for her own purposes.

Kobili—read Kokopelli—an ancient shaman, is awaiting, impatiently, the rebirth of his beloved Thunderwoman, while doom, in the shape of the conquistadores, is moving up from the south. Lizard-Goes-Forth was "the first to know something was wrong" because when he woke up one morning, he was turning into a deer. That would give you a clue, I guess. Thunderwoman, who appears as a newborn infant; Sayah; Raven; Coyote; Macaw; Snake Sister and Grandmother Spiders (sic) and many other figures from Native stories, populate a work that seems to strive for a magical realism that is sadly lacking from this extremely strange ripoff. Here and there, one is re-minded of Leslie Silko's *Almanac of the Dead*, a far better book. In fact, why not read that instead? Not recommended.
—*Doris Seale*

Yamane, Linda (Rumsien Ohlone), illustrated by the teller. Oyate. Unpaginated, b/w illustrations; all grades; Ohlone
The Snake that Lived in the Santa Cruz Mountains and Other Ohlone Stories, (1998).
When the World Ended, How Hummingbird Got Fire, How People Were Made, (1995).

When the World Ended is remarkable in its genesis. Linda Yamane is an artist and basketmaker who has been working on retrieving the language of her people from near oblivion. These stories come out of the who-knows-

how-many hours spent working with the recordings and notes of ethnographer and linguist John P. Harrington.

"When the World Ended" is a flood story, and it is Eagle who saves the world. "How Hummingbird Got Fire" is brief, hardly a breath of a story, and it is exactly as long as it needs to be. After the flood, Eagle and Crow had to bring back the people, so they wouldn't be alone. The last story tells how they did that. Although it is only a part of something much longer, "How People Were Made" is one of the most tender and loving creation stories I have ever heard.

The stories are beautiful and fragile in their simplicity. In "The Story Behind the Stories," Yamane says:

> These stories as presented here are certainly dif-ferent than they were two hundred or five hundred years ago. They are two languages removed from the original—the remnants, I suppose, of cultural devastation. But they're still with us—and I believe the essence has remained intact. They are here for us to live with and learn from. They are still here.

A long time ago there was a snake that would come up out of the ocean into the Santa Cruz Mountains and eat up all the people. When it got up there and saw the people, "it would give a loud whistle and down it would come… quick as the devil…" The title story in *The Snake that Lived in the Santa Cruz Mountains* is the first of seven in Yamane's second gathering of Ohlone tales.

There's a whale who coughed up the first white man (he was brown when he went down) and a rain story that has the feel of something that really happened. "How Shelp Made the Acorn Soup," tells in Spanish and English how an old woman uses her witchcraft to fill her basket with an endless supply of acorn soup.

In "Trura—the Thunders," there is both a comment on the way people should treat each other and the story of how thunder came to be. "The Two Bears" is a Zen story if I ever heard one. Don't be surprised if you get to the end and turn the page to see where the rest is, then think about it.

In the beginning of the *Snake* book, Yamane tells "the Story Before the Stories." One especially nice thing about this title is that it has information about some of the elder storytellers, and old photographs as well.

These are also beautiful books physically. The stories are printed on thick, sand-colored paper, with Yamane's striking and elegant black-and-white drawings. In *When the World Ended*, there is only one touch of color: Hummingbird's brilliant red throat. The illustrations in *The Snake that Lived in the Santa Cruz Mountains* are less detailed, but they are just as evocative.

It would be hard for anyone who has never had their language taken away from them to understand just how important Yamane's work is. It seems like a miracle that any of the Ohlone languages has survived in any form. Yamane has spent many years researching the languages and stories of her people. I hope she'll be able to continue doing this for long time to come. Her work is a gift to all of us; balm for heart and soul.—*Doris Seale*

Yerxa, Leo (Ojibwe), *Last Leaf First Snowflake to Fall,* **illustrated by the author. Douglas & McIntyre (1993), Orchard Books (1994). Unpaginated, color illustrations; all grades; Ojibwe**

Leo Yerxa's delicate paintings in subdued colors convey the quiet mysteries of this change of season in the northern lakeland woods. They tell of the snow's first beginning— a whisper of wind between the sparkles of stars—in a time before time. A young person makes a hole in a windowpane frost forest, then goes out with a friend into a crisp, leaf-crunching autumn morning. They hike and canoe to a campsite, eating and playing on the way, and camp the night with their canoe sheltering them from the first snowfall of the changed season, awakening to find yesterday's blanket of leaves now blanketed in snow.

The story is carried by large pictures, often laid out in double-page spreads. The two people, who could be children, parent and child, or First Man and Woman, are usually seen in from above. In a picture of the snowy night, we see only circles of warmth, their campfire, in a snow-spattered moonlit scene that covers two full, facing pages. We see the beaver pond from above, and a couple of beavers carrying a few last branches to the underwater raft of branches they will feed from after freeze-up. This two-page layout is margined—but the corners all have bunches of colored leaves, extending, cut out into the white space.

Yerxa's pictures are representational but they are almost patterned abstracts, too. He collages large pieces of torn, textured paper and paints over them, incorporating the textures and torn edges as hills, underwater rocks, uneven leaf-blanketed forest floor, heaps of new-fallen snow, and the coats (embellished with painted beadwork embroidery strips) that blend the two Indian people almost into those scenes. In one marvelous use of the torn-paper technique near the beginning, water, forest shore, the rising sun and its reflection and the people are all underlain with textured paper, painted over with clear, sharp images of the final morning of the autumn forest.

The text is spare, and except for the poem at the beginning, it's all in the pictures, to be seen, "read," and talked about some fall or winter's evening. People who know the woods will be able to see much more in these scenes than those who don't, but by attentive looking, which these calm, meditative yet cheerful pictures encourage, you can learn to feel the spirit of the woods and waters at this quiet time, even if you've always lived in a crowded city environment.—*Paula Giese*

Young, Ed, *Moon Mother: A Native American Creation Tale,* **illustrated by the author. HarperCollins (1993). Unpaginated, color illustrations; grades 1-3**

Moon Mother is an odd adaptation of an adaptation of a Native American creation story, from a story called "How Animals and People were Made and How the Moon Was Placed in the Sky" by Charles Erskine Scott Wood, published in a 1901 collection called *A Book of Tales: Being Some Myths of the North American Indians.* Young's re-telling is said to be "authentic," but is not attributed to any specific Indian people. It seems to be a collection of parts of different creation stories—including the Christian Bible— and is confusing to read. Some of the illustrations are also strange, particularly the image of a human fetus (or maybe newborn) falling from the sky with its umbilical cord trailing skywards. Weird! Gives me the creeps! —*Barbara Potter*

Zitkala-Sa/Gertrude Bonin (Yankton), *American Indian Stories,* **introduction by Susan Rose Dominguez. University of Nebraska (1921, 1985, 2003). 195 pages; grades 5-up; Dakota**

A collection of childhood stories, traditional stories and an essay, many of which were written in the very early 1900s, *American Indian Stories* is one of the first books to be written by a Native woman without the "aid" of a white editor, interpreter or ethnographer. Controversial in her lifetime, Zitkala-Sa devoted her life—in what was essentially a foreign tongue—to seeking justice for her people. While she writes of the everyday humiliations that encompassed the Indian residential school experience, she also writes of resistance and rebellion:

One day I was called in from play for some misconduct. I had disregarded a rule which seemed to me very needlessly binding. I was sent into the kitchen to mash the turnips for dinner. It was noon, and steaming dishes were hastily carried into the dining-room. I hated turnips, and their odor which came from the brown jar was offensive to me. With fire in my heart, I took the wooden tool that the paleface woman held out to me. I stood upon a step, and, grasping the handle with both hands, I bent in hot rage over the turnips. I worked my vengeance upon them. All were so busily occupied that no one noticed me. I saw that the turnips were in a pulp, and that further beating could not improve them; but the order was "Mash these turnips," and mash them I would! I renewed my energy; and as I sent the masher into the bottom of the jar, I felt a satisfying sensation that the weight of my body had gone into it. Just here a paleface woman came up to my table. As she looked into the jar, she shoved my hands roughly aside. I stood fearless and angry. She placed her red hands upon the rim of the jar. Then she gave one lift and stride away from the table. But lo! the pulpy contents fell through the crumbled bottom to the floor! She spared me no scolding phrases that I had earned. I did not heed them. I felt triumphant in my revenge, though deep within me I was a wee bit sorry to have broken the jar. As I sat eating my dinner, and saw that no turnips were served, I whooped in my heart for having once asserted the rebellion within me.

These are stories from Red Bird's own life, in Red Bird's own words. Written with passion and determination in language that young readers will connect with, *American Indian Stories* is a gift to everyone, but most especially, it's a giving back to Indian youngsters.—*Beverly Slapin*

THE WINONA DILEMMA

When she first started dating Epingishmook, her mother was a little bit worried. He professed to be the West Wind, and indeed, he kept unusual hours. He came and went at whim, and seemed to be an unreliable sort. All sorts of rumors about their relationship have circulated over the years, and through the generations, and since Winona is no longer here to defend herself, I can't help but wonder about the sources of the various tales and rumors that abound.

Each contributor to her oral history, it seems, has brought his or her slant to the story over the years. There are those who say that the father of Winona's children was an untrustworthy sort, that he was a typical male, leaving the mother to raise the children alone. This may reflect the personal experiences of the teller, as there are others who say that it was an honor for Winona to have been selected as a wife by someone as powerful as the West Wind. After all, he had an entire continent to tend to, lakes and beaches to sweep, rainstorms to deliver, greedy fishermen to scare off of the lakes, fish spawn and toads' eggs to scatter, milkweed and all sorts of seeds to distribute. He had something of a time schedule to follow, when he could, bringing in the heaviest of storms and gales in the late fall and winter, resting for days at a time, during the lazy days of summer. He took only brief pauses at dawn and dusk... when he could, when there were not pressing issues to pursue... He was a busy man... a mysterious man... what we call a manidou, a spirit. Only a powerful, honorable woman could assume the responsibility of raising the four boys of a spirit being. Half spirit and half human, they were a handful for the woman! All boy, all powerful... Surely she did her best in raising them. Yes, it is all in the outlook of the storyteller.

It is said that Winona and Epingishmook had four boys, each raised in a different generation. Again, there are those who say she let this spirit man use her for far too many years. There are those who don't venture to explain the time reference; they simply say that things were different in the old times; that there were giants and that time meant nothing. There are others who think that it means that this loving, caring couple, ancestors to so many of us, lived long enough to see four generations. They became great grandparents. This was not so unusual, back when people married so much younger... when was that... earlier in this century?

Perspective. Storytellers tell their own stories. They don't mean to. They let their life experiences and ideas slip in, between the bits and pieces of history that have come to them. There are so many versions among us, of this first woman, this mother of Manaboozhou, Nanabush, our goofy, loving, mixed up teacher and hero. They are all valid. They are all real. They are all traditional. None of us knows them all by heart. We take the parts that we need and understand. These are the stories that we share with our children. In a sense, that makes us all a little bit like Winona and Epingishmook. We are the creators of the Anishnabe generations who come after us. I like that responsibility.

Personally, I lean toward the kinder, more understanding version of Winona and the West Wind, but I understand the need for harsher versions as well. Sometimes harshness does not come merely from bitterness. Frightening stories and tales of misadventures or deadly relationships are preventive in nature. There are ways to encourage our children and loved ones to avoid our errors and the mistakes we've observed: cultural shorthand, a form of beseeching others not to learn the hard way. To me, this implies that the West Wind is, indeed, a harsh character— and for good reason. Relationships can be as harsh as weather systems. The West Wind is powerful, is unreliable, is deadly... and, well, ya gotta love 'im for it. Nobody else is big enough to do the job, except maybe a storyteller.
—*Lois Beardslee*

NO WORD FOR GOODBYE

Sokoya, I said, looking through
    the net of wrinkles into
    wise black pools
    of her eyes.

What do you say in Athabascan
    when you leave each other?
    What is the word
    for goodbye?
A shade of feeling rippled
    the wind-tanned skin.
    Ah, nothing, she said,
    watching the river flash.
She looked at me close.
    We just say, Tlaa. That means,
    See you.
    We never leave each other.
    When does your mouth
    say goodbye to your heart?
She touched me light
    as a bluebell.
    You forget when you leave us;
    you're so small then.
    We don't use that word.
We always think you're coming back,
    but if you don't,
    we'll see you someplace else.
    You understand.
    There is no word for goodbye.

—*Mary TallMountain* (Koyukon)

Sokoya: aunt (mother's sister)
Tlaa: see you

ABOUT THE CONTRIBUTORS

Marlene R. Atleo/?eh ?eh naa tuu kwiss (*Nuu-chah-nulth*), is of the Ahousaht First Nation, Nuu-chah-nulth, West Coast of Vancouver Island. She is the wife and mother of chiefs of the Atliutakumlth, the lineage of Ahousaht whalers. Marlene is the grandmother of six, a keeper of names and cultural storyworker in the tradition of Umeek, the first whaler. She is also an assistant professor of adult education at the University of Manitoba.

Linda Baldwin (*Brotherton/Oneida*) holds a doctorate in educational leadership and change, and has taught for over twenty-five years at the elementary, middle school, and high school level. A board member of Oyate, Linda is presently an educational consultant. She and her two daughters, who are Diné, have lived and worked on the Diné reservation for over ten years.

Lois Beardslee (*Ojibwe/Lacandon*) is the author of *Lies to Live By* and *Rachel's Children* and has been a teacher and writer for more than twenty-five years. An artist whose paintings are in public and private collections worldwide, Lois also practices many traditional art forms, including birch bark biting, quillwork, and sweetgrass basketry.

Maria Beardslee (*Ojibwe/Lacandon*) is a Thompson Fellow in civil engineering at Michigan Technological University. She wrote "Maria's Mother's Story" after being assigned in freshman English to write about "a conflict that one would confront in everyday life." Although Maria argued that being Indian *is* conflict, the teacher rejected it because it didn't "show enough conflict." Maria received a "97" after this story was accepted for publication.

Joseph Bruchac (*Abenaki*) is a poet, writer, storyteller, and mentor to up-and-coming Native writers. The author of more than one hundred books, Joe and his wife of forty years, Carol, are the founders of The Greenfield Review Press and live in the same house Joe was raised in by his grandparents. Their two grown sons, James and Jesse, are active storytellers who work closely with their parents in drawing attention to contemporary Native writing and the survival and significance of Abenaki and other Native traditions.

Naomi Caldwell (*Ramapough*) is a librarian, educator and activist, and holds a doctorate in library science. A member and former president of the American Indian Library Association, Naomi works to ensure that Native people have access to accurate information and are honestly portrayed in children's literature. Naomi lectures at the university level, conducts workshops for teachers and students, and is a board member of Oyate. She lives with her son, Willy, in Barrington, Rhode Island.

Ella Rose Callow (*Cherokee*) is the mother of thirteen-month-old Isabella Rose Callow; a practicing family law attorney in Napa, California; and education coordinator of an after-school program in El Sobrante that serves refugee and Indian children, where she teaches reading and literacy.

April Carmelo (*Wintu/Maidu/Juaneño*) is the mother of three beautiful children and director of the Title VII Indian Education Program in Redding, California. She is famous for her ability to multitask.

Robin Carneen (*Swinomish*), whose biggest passion is her work as a national freelance radio journalist for Independent Native News, is living on ancestral grounds in Skagit County, Washington. She also works in tribal communities helping with repatriation of museum objects, teaching beadwork to Native college students and old people, and participating in the month-long annual journey in cedar canoes in the open water.

Peter Cole (*Inshuckch/N'Quatqua*) is an assistant professor in environmental studies at York University in Toronto. His doctoral dissertation relied on First Nations knowings rather than Euro-theorists. The Elsa he wrote about in "Elsa Remembers" is a Métis from a settlement in north central Alberta who doesn't like writing down stories herself.

Radley Davis (*Illmawi Band, Pit River*) is a teacher and activist, committed to working with the children in his community and to the preservation of indigenous cultures. He wrote "Welcome Home, Our Relative" in response to a San Francisco Chronicle editorial cartoon about "Ishi's brain." Radley and his wife, Irma Amaro Davis, have nine children, including two adopted and a new foster baby. They live in Shasta Lake City, California.

Robette Dias (*Karuk*) is co-executive director of Crossroads Ministry, a national non-profit, faith-based anti-racism training organization headquartered in Chicago. Robette, who is a board member of Oyate, lives with her children, Lino and Chiara, in Sonoma, California.

Judy Dow (*Abenaki*) is a basketmaker and educator who teaches ethnobotany at the grade school and college level and serves on the board of directors of Oyate and the American Indian Scouting Association. Judy is the recipient of the 2004 Governor's Award for Outstanding Vermont Educator, and lives with her family in Essex Junction, Vermont.

Judy Zalazar Drummond (*Pala/Chicana*) is a long-time Bay Area educator and community activist who now trains teachers at the University of San Francisco and is the education director at the Jericho Project.

Carolyn Dunn (*Cherokee/Muscogee/Seminole/Choctaw*) is the author of *Outfoxing Coyote* and the forth-coming *Echo Location*, and is the coeditor of *Through The Eye of the Deer* and *Hozho: Walking In Beauty*. She is a wife, mother, teacher, poet, playwright, journalist, singer and songwriter whose work has appeared in print and on air, currently on KPFK-FM in Los Angeles, where she lives with her family.

Marcia Fenn (*Uchucklesaht*), **Karen Frank** (Ahousaht), **Trudy Frank** (Ahousaht), **Coral Johnson** (Huu-ay-aht), **Nora Lucas** (Hesquiaht), **Patricia Mack** (Ahousaht), **Connie McPhee** (Ditidaht), **Patricia North** (Toquaht), **Della Patrick** (Ucluelet), **Tracey Robinson** (Tse-Shaht), **Marlene Watts** (Hupacasaht) and **Pam Watts** (Hupacasaht) were Nu-chah-nuulth community health workers who came together to write a book review for Oyate as part of a class taught by **Marlene R. Atleo** (Ahousaht).

L. Frank (*Tongva/Ajachmem*) is an artist, decolonizationist and all-around very funny person. She says, "My art is cultural maintenance. I am the art janitor. Koo-koo-ka-choo."

Cora Garcia (*Lumbee*) is a freshman at Merritt College in Oakland, California, and a former board member of Oyate. She wrote "Cora's Story" when she was in the fifth grade.

Paula Giese (*Ojibwe*) was an innovative educator, AIM activist, gadfly, and all-around phenomenon. *A Broken Flute* would have been much less without her writing, her curmudgeonly prodding, and constant, no, endless support. She has been looking over our shoulders all this time. She will be greatly missed.

Lakota Harden (*Minnecoujou/Yankton Lakota and Ho-Chunk*) is a grandma, activist, community organizer, facilitator and poet. Currently the project coordinator of mercury health education for the International Indian Treaty Council, Lakota also conducts trainings nationwide on unlearning racism, sexism and other social oppressions.

Raven Hoaglen (*Maidu/Konkow/Wailaki/Mono/Nomlaki*) is a student at Consumnes River Community College, a cook for Meals on Wheels and works as a tax preparer for H&R Block during tax season. She spends a lot of time with her nieces and nephews and likes to play pool. She wrote "Raven's Story" when she was in the seventh grade. Raven lives with her family in Elk Grove, California.

S. Sethlyn Honeycutt (*Cherokee/Choctaw/Blackfoot*) is a preschool teacher, traditional dancer and storyteller, and is working towards her Masters Degree in counseling. Seth is lead singer on Yona Sdigida, the family drum, and sits on Feather River, an all-woman drum.

Lenore Keeshig-Tobias (*Ojibwe*) was founding chair of the Racial Minority Writers' Committee and founding member of the Committee to Re-establish the Trickster, organized to reclaim the Native voice in literature. Lenore, with her daughter, Polly, received a Living the Dream Award for *Bird Talk*, a children's book about the racism experienced by a first-grader. Lenore, who is an advisory board member of Oyate, has three grown daughters, a young daughter and son, and four grandchildren. She lives in Wiarton, Ontario, with her younger children and her partner, David McLaren.

Janet King (*Lumbee*) works for the Family and Child Guidance Clinic at the Native American Health Center in Oakland, California, where she conducts cultural competency trainings so social service agencies can have a better understanding of Native issues. As a parent educator and activist, Janet is an advocate for culturally authentic children's literature and truth in history in school textbooks, and is the vice president of Oyate.

Michael Lacapa (*Apache/Hopi/Tewa*), was a teacher, artist, author, illustrator, storyteller and really nice guy, who used to dream of just painting all day long. For a little while, that dream was accomplished. Michael is survived by his wife, Kathy, and their three children, who live in Taylor, Arizona.

Barbara Landis is the Carlisle Indian School Biographer for the Cumberland County Historical Society in Carlisle, Pennsylvania. Her Carlisle Indian School web pages are dedicated to getting the names of the Indian School students to their respective Nations. She lives in Carlisle with her husband and their dog, Low Gear.

Mayana Lea (*Cherokee*) is a community activist and third-year student at the University of California at Santa Cruz, where she is majoring in Sociology. Throughout high school, Mayana conducted student-led workshops for teachers about student-teacher relationships, and remains committed to participating in the struggle for social justice. She wrote "Mayana's Story" when she was in the fifth grade.

Linda Lilly (*Diné/Laguna*) is an advocate for children's rights and a single mother of three. A counselor and case manager for the Family and Child Guidance Clinic at the Native American Health Center in Oakland, California, Linda was honored as the Distinguished Parent of the Year for 2003 by the California Conference On American Indian Education.

Pam Martell (*Ojibwe*) is Crane Clan and a citizen of the Turtle Mountain Band of Chippewa Indians of North Dakota, and is a doctoral candidate in teacher education. Formerly the state coordinator of the Native American programs unit of the Michigan Department of Education, Pam is a higher education consultant with the King-Chavez-Parks Initiative of the Michigan Department of Labor and Economic Growth.

Elizabeth (Betita) Martinez (*Chicana*) has been an anti-racist activist for more than forty years and has published six books on social justice struggles in the Americas of which the best known is *500 Años del Pueblo Chicano/500 Years of Chicano History in Pictures*. She is an adjunct professor in the California State University system and is director of the Institute for MultiRacial Justice, a resource center to help build alliances between communities of color.

Janet McAdams (*Creek*) has taught literature and creative writing at the University of Alabama, the American School of El Salvador, and the University of Oklahoma, and is presently the Robert P. Hubbard Professor of Poetry at Kenyon College in Kenyon, Ohio. Janet, whose book of poetry, *The Island of Lost Luggage*, won the Diane Decorah Award for Poetry in 1999 from the Native Writers Circle of the Americas and the American Book Award in 2001, is completing a novel and a second book of poems.

Dennis McAuliffe, Jr. (*Osage*) is the Native American Journalist in Residence at the University of Montana in Missoula. He directs "reznet," an online newspaper written by Native college students around the country, and helped create and teaches at the Freedom Forum's American Indian Journalism Institute at the University of South Dakota each summer. Dennis's book, *Bloodland*, won the 1995 Oklahoma Book Award for Non-Fiction.

Jean Paine Mendoza is a parent, a grandparent, and a doctoral student in early childhood education at the University of Illinois. She has been teaching children for more than twenty years, and is committed to seeing that Native peoples are represented honestly.

Adrianne Micco (*Seminole*) facilitated Indian Education programs for twelve years, and is currently a classroom instructional assistant working with emotionally disturbed young people. Adrianne has two grown sons and three grandchildren, and lives in Fairfield, California. She likes to swim and dance, and sleeps when she can.

Deborah Miranda (*Ohlone-Costanoan Esselen/Chumash*) is an assistant professor of English at Washington and Lee University in Lexington, Virginia, where she teaches Creative Writing, Native American Literatures, and Women's Studies. Her first book of poetry, *Indian Cartography*, won the Diane Decorah First Book Award from the Native Writers' Circle of the Americas. Deborah is grateful to share her life with her two children, Miranda and Danny, and partner Margo Solod, poet, cook, and hunter/gatherer.

Lisa Mitten (*Mohawk*) is a former president of the American Indian Library Association, and is currently a book review editor for *Choice Magazine*, a review journal for academic libraries. She has been a librarian for twenty-one years, and lives in New Britain, Connecticut.

MariJo Moore (*Cherokee*) is a storyweaver, poet, artist and editor who, in her copious spare time, conducts poetry workshops for children in the community and runs Renegade Planet Publishing. She lives in Candler, North Carolina.

Jim Northrup (*Anishinaabe*) is a grampa, poet, writer and mentor whose stories and poems have appeared in several anthologies and literary magazines. A survivor of both a federal Indian residential school and a Christian boarding school, Jim is the author of *Walking the Rez Road* and *The Rez Road Follies*, and writes a syndicated column called "Fond du Lac Follies." Jim lives with his wife, Patricia and their family on the Fond du Lac reservation in northern Minnesota.

Marco Palma (*Xicano*), born in Guatemala, works as an mild-mannered Internet programmer by day and as a technology consultant to progressive non-profit and community organizing groups by night. He currently resides in Los Angeles, California.

Carol Pancho-Ash (*Tohono O'odham*) has been teaching for twenty-four years in the Oakland public school system. She is currently teaching second-graders, in whom she instills the joy of reading, especially about their own diverse cultures. Carol is a mother of two college students and returns home to her Tohono O'odham reservation at least once a year to visit with her relatives. She lives with her husband in Oakland, California.

Barbara Potter (*Potawatomi*) is a parent, storyteller and teacher. Formerly on the teaching staff and board of directors of the American Indian Public Charter School in Oakland, Barbara was a founding member of the San Joaquin River Intertribal Heritage Educational Corporation in Auberry, California. Barbara, who works with Oyate, consults with her children, Ryan and Rachel, in the writing of book reviews, and lives with her family in Oakland, California.

Sachiko Reed is currently finishing her master's degree in the College of Ethnic Studies at San Francisco State University. An Asian American of mixed heritage, Sachiko's research interests include deconstructing American Indian biases in literature to examining racial hierarchy and white privilege within multiethnic families and larger society. Sachiko wrote the reviews here as an undergraduate intern with Oyate.

Debbie Reese (*Nambé Pueblo*) is a teacher and teacher educator whose research centers on the ways that Native Americans are presented in children's books.

Liz Reese (*Nambé Pueblo*) is a high school student who writes and gives lectures about her experiences with Native American imagery in children's books. She is an avid Shakespeare buff and an accomplished swimmer. Liz wrote "Liz's Story" when she was in the fourth grade.

LaVera Rose (*Lakota*) is a mother and grandmother, an archivist at the South Dakota State Historical Society, and author of *Grandchildren of the Lakota* and *Meet the Lakota People/Oyate Kin*.

Gayle Ross (*Cherokee*) is a direct descendant of John Ross, principal chief of the Cherokee during the Trail of Tears. Her grandmother told stories and it is from this tradition that Gayle's storytelling springs. Gayle is the award-winning author of five children's books, and for the past twenty-five years, she has performed throughout the U.S., Canada and Europe.

Johnny Rustywire (*Diné*) is from Toadlena-Two Gray Hills, New Mexico. He attended Indian boarding schools in Arizona, New Mexico and Colorado; and considers himself an "amateur" writer whose stories on the Internet have a life of their own. John lives with his wife, who is Ute, and six children on the Ute Reservation.

Crystal Salas-Patten (*Mescalero Apache/Lakota, Puerto Rican, Hawai'ian and Mexican*) is a mom and a grandma who keeps herself young by chasing around the kids she works with as the traditional arts program coordinator at the Youth Services Department of the Native American Health Center in Oakland, California. She was born and raised in Oakland, and resides there with her husband and children.

Doris Seale (*Santee/Cree*) is co-founder and president of the board of Oyate, an educator and activist, and long-time children's librarian. The recipient of the American Library Association's 2001 Equality Award for her life's work, Doris has contributed to several anthologies of writings by Native women, and *The Multicolored Mirror: Cultural Substance in Literature for Children and Young Adults*. She is co-editor of *Through Indian Eyes*, and author of two books of poetry. Doris lives in Burlington, Vermont.

Beverly Slapin is co-founder and executive director of Oyate, co-editor of *Through Indian Eyes* and co-author of *How to Tell the Difference: A Guide to Evaluating Children's Books for Anti-Indian Bias*. Beverly, whose passion for justice is tempered by a good sense of the ridiculous, is author of the *Basic Skills Caucasian Americans Workbook* and *10 Little Whitepeople*. She lives in Berkeley, California.

Cynthia L. Smith (*Muscogee*) is a reviewer of books for children and teenagers, and the author of literary trade fiction. She lives in Texas.

Monica Spencer (*Diné/Laguna, Filipino and Hawai'ian*) works as a part-time waitress in Hawai'i, where she attends community college. She wrote "Monica's Story" when she was in the third grade in Oakland, California.

Nisha Supahan (*Karuk*) is completing her bachelor's degree in photojournalism and Native American studies at Southern Oregon University. She lives in Southern Oregon with her husband and stepson. Her plans are to pursue photography and be very, very happy. When she was eleven years old, Nisha's review of *Let's Be Indians!* won first place in the Indian Education Writing Contest for the Klamath-Trinity Joint Unified School District.

Drew Hayden Taylor (*Ojibwe*) is an award-winning dramatist who writes for stage and screen and contributes essays, commentaries, and social and cultural observations to major Canadian newspapers and magazines.

Dovie Thomason (*Lakota/Kiowa-Apache*) has traveled throughout North America and abroad for more than twenty years, sharing her heritage through traditional and original stories. As a former teacher and university professor and a very active mother and grandmother, Dovie is hopeful that her stories will help spare Indian children today and in the future from the shame of stereotypes still evident in poor texts and curricula.

Jane Waite is a single mother of three, whose critical evaluative work with Oyate has roots in her deep commitment to the empowerment of her own children, the community's children, and the children of the world. Jane lives in the hills outside of Eugene, Oregon with her family, which includes a dog, two cats and a goldfish.

Elizabeth Villiana Jeffredo Warden (*Payomkawish [Luiseño]/Southern Channel Islander/Creek*) is an enrolled member of the Temecula (Pechanga) Band of Luiseños. The incident she related occurred at a preschool she attended. Throughout elementary school, Elizabeth continued to confront ill-mannered and inaccurate information about Native Americans. Now a strong and beautiful first-year high school student in whose creative heart humor, family, friends and athletics share a prominent place, she committed this story to tape when she was in the second grade.

Linda Yamane (*Rumsien Ohlone*) has been active in revitalizing Rumsien language, songs, stories, basketry, dance and watercraft. Linda lives in the Monterey, California, area where she works as a graphic artist and spends as much time as possible outdoors with the plants and land she loves.

INDEX

Authors/Editors

Artists/Illustrators/Photographers

Poets

Reviewers

Storytellers/Essayists

Subjects

28870621R10294

Made in the USA
San Bernardino, CA
09 January 2016